Cambridge studies in medieval life and thought

CHARITY AND COMMUNITY IN
MEDIEVAL CAMBRIDGE

Cambridge Studies in Medieval Life and Thought
Fourth Series

General Editor: J. C. HOLT Professor of Medieval History and
Master of Fitzwilliam College, University of Cambridge

Advisory Editors: C. N. L. BROOKE
Dixie Professor of Ecclesiastical History and
Fellow of Gonville and Caius College,
University of Cambridge

D. E. LUSCOMBE
Professor of Medieval History, University of Sheffield

The series Cambridge Studies in Medieval Life and Thought was inaugurated by G. G. Coulton in 1920. Professor J. C. Holt now acts as General Editor of a Fourth Series, with Professor C. N. L. Brooke and Professor D. E. Luscombe as Advisory Editors. The series aims to bring together outstanding work by medieval scholars over a wide range of human endeavour extending from political economy to the history of ideas.

Titles in the series

CHARITY AND COMMUNITY IN MEDIEVAL CAMBRIDGE

MIRI RUBIN

Research Fellow of Girton College, Cambridge

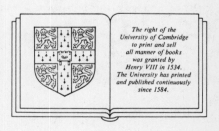

The right of the
University of Cambridge
to print and sell
all manner of books
was granted by
Henry VIII in 1534.
The University has printed
and published continuously
since 1584.

CAMBRIDGE UNIVERSITY PRESS

CAMBRIDGE

LONDON   NEW YORK   NEW ROCHELLE

MELBOURNE   SYDNEY

Published by the Press Syndicate of the University of Cambridge
The Pitt Building, Trumpington Street, Cambridge CB2 1RP
32 East 57th Street, New York, NY 10022, USA
10 Stamford Road, Oakleigh, Melbourne 3166, Australia

First published 1987

Printed in Great Britain by the University Press, Cambridge

British Library cataloguing in publication data

Rubin, Miri
Charity and community in medieval Cambridge. –
(Cambridge studies in medieval life and thought.
Fourth series)
1. Charities – England – Cambridge (Cambridgeshire) – History
1. Title
361.7′632′0942659   HV250.C3/

Library of Congress cataloguing in publication data

Rubin, Miri, 1956–
Charity and community in medieval Cambridge.
(Cambridge studies in medieval life and thought; 4th series, 4)
Bibliography
Includes index.
1. Charities – England – Cambridge (Cambridgeshire) – History.
2. Hospitals, Medieval – England – Cambridge (Cambridgeshire) – History.
3. England – Social conditions – Medieval period, 1066–1485.
1. Title. 11. Series: Cambridge studies in medieval life and thought;
4th series, vol. 4.
HV250.C33R83 1987 362.1′1′094265 86–9698

ISBN 0 521 32392 4

For P.T.

CONTENTS

Contents

TABLES

ACKNOWLEDGEMENTS

It is always a pleasure to give well-deserved thanks, and many institutions, teachers, colleagues and friends have earned my gratitude throughout the years.

In the years of my doctoral research at Cambridge I received financial aid from the British Council, from the Rothschild Avi-Hayishuv Foundation, from Girton College (the Doris Woodall Research Studentship) and from the University of Cambridge (the Crosse Studentship). As a research fellow at Girton I have enjoyed comfort and encouragement while finishing this book.

The colleges of Cambridge were a pleasant setting for my study of their medieval past. I am grateful to the Masters and Fellows of Clare College, Corpus Christi College, Jesus College, King's College, Peterhouse, Queens' College, St John's College and Trinity College and also to the Warden and Fellows of Merton College, Oxford, who allowed me to explore their archives. Those entrusted with the archival treasures of Cambridge helped me enormously: Dr Roger Lovatt of Peterhouse guided me through the muniments of his college and shared with me his erudition. The archivist of Corpus Christi and of Gonville and Caius Colleges, Mrs Catherine Hall, spent many hours introducing me to the muniments and to the streets and fields of medieval Cambridge. I especially wish to thank Mr Malcolm Underwood, archivist of St John's College, who devoted much time over the years to dealing with a barrage of inquiries and who was always so assiduous and able in responding to them.

In Cambridge and Jerusalem many helped me during the years of research and writing. Dr Sandra Raban clarified some of the mysterious ways in which religious houses acquired property in the Middle Ages. Dr Edward Miller and Dr Z. Razi read and extensively commented on the contents of chapter 2. Dr Roger Lovatt shared his knowledge of the world of medieval universities with me, and saved me from many errors by reading chapter 7. Dr Dorothy Owen guided me through the first grapplings with medieval English ecclesiastical records and

Acknowledgements

palaeography and generously answered a multitude of questions on the many areas of her expertise. With Professor Shulamit Shahar I discussed and pondered many aspects of our shared interest in medieval society, but above all I benefited from the encouragement and friendship which she and my teachers in Israel always offered. Through many conversations and patient reading of the draft of this book Dr Jon Parry helped improve both the substance and the presentation of my ideas.

My gratitude to the examiners of the doctoral dissertation Dr Marjorie Chibnall and Professor Barrie Dobson is immense. They pointed out valuable issues arising from my study and offered constructive remarks, and helped me conceive of it as an offering to a wider audience. In preparing this book for this series Professor J. C. Holt and Professor David Luscombe carefully read and expertly commented on points which needed further work. My interest in the Middle Ages was inspired long ago by my first teacher, Dr Ron Barkai, and his lively vision of that world. Finally, only those acquainted with Professor Christopher Brooke can appreciate my good fortune in having been supervised by him and the great debt I owe him: for his unfailing interest, his charitable criticism and his kind friendship.

Cambridge   M. R.
August, 1985

ABBREVIATIONS

Bonenfant, *Hôpitaux et bienfaisance publiques*	P. Bonenfant, *Hôpitaux et bienfaisance publiques dans les anciens Pays-Bas des origines à la fin du XVIIIe siècle*, Annales de la société belge de l'histoire des hôpitaux. Special volume 3, Brussels, 1965.
CCCA	Corpus Christi College Archives
CUL	Cambridge University Library
Ecc. Cant.	Ecclesia Cantebrigie
EDR	Ely Diocesan Records
EETS	Early English Text Society
HSJC	Hospital of St John the Evangelist, Cambridge
Mollat, *Etudes*	*Etudes sur l'histoire de la pauvreté*, 2 vols., ed. M. Mollat, Paris, 1974.
NRO	Norwich Record Office
PL	*Patrologiae cursus completus...series latina*, 221 vols., ed. J. P. Migne, Paris, 1844–64
PRO	Public Record Office
RS	Rolls Series
SJCA	St John's College Archives
VCH	Victoria History of the Counties of England (see *A history of the county of...*)
(1241 × 9)	Dated between 1241 and 1249

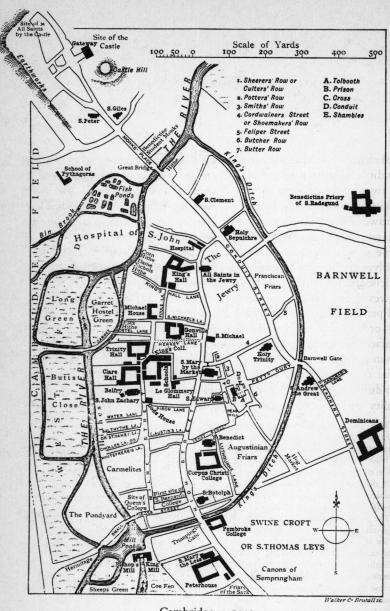

Cambridge, *c.* 1445

From T. H. Atkinson and J. W. Clark, *Cambridge described and illustrated: being a short history of the town and university* (London, 1897), p. 504.

Chapter 1

INTRODUCTION

That charity was a central preoccupation for medieval men and women is indisputable. In England alone some 220 hospitals were founded in the twelfth century and some 310 in the thirteenth.[1] The donors who endowed and maintained them were granting gifts, allocating property, bestowing food, money, clothes and spiritual care upon strangers, apparently denying themselves some comfort for the sake of others. Some would say that selfless denial is the crux of charity, in that it involves giving with no expectation of reward; and medieval preachers criticised those who 'sold' their alms in return for social acclaim.[2] However, gift-giving was also part of the symbolic articulation of social and personal relations, and is at any time an act of self-expression, of the presentation of one's innermost values.[3] Charity cannot be satisfactorily understood as a purely altruistic act since gift-giving is so rich in rewards to the giver. Gifts play an important role in maintaining social cohesion, peace and order; they are major tools for forging friendships and alliances.[4] With most social acts, gift-giving shares the quality of reciprocity and exchange,[5] while, on a personal level, it

---

[1] This is the minimal estimate counting only houses for which direct evidence of existence and of the period of foundation has survived. It is based on the list of hospitals compiled in D. Knowles and R. N. Hadcock, *Medieval religious houses: England and Wales* (London, edn of 1971), pp. 250–324.

[2] On the element of altruism in human behaviour see D. Collard, *Altruism and economy. A study in non-selfish economics* (Oxford, 1978), pp. 4–5. For an example of a view of charity as a unilateral act see O. Checkland, *Philanthropy in Victorian Scotland: social welfare and the voluntary principle* (Edinburgh, 1980), pp. 1–2 and *passim*.

[3] The psychological content of gift-giving has been studied in B. Schwartz, 'The social psychology of the gift', *Americal journal of sociology* 73 (1967–8), pp. 1–11; pp. 2–3.

[4] See the classic study on the nature of gifts, M. Mauss, *The gift: forms and functions of exchange in archaic societies*, trans. I. Cunnison (London, 1966), pp. 17–18; M. D. Sahlins, 'On the sociology of primitive exchange', in *The relevance of models for social anthropology*, ed. M. Banton (London, 1965), pp. 139–236; pp. 139–43, 174–9. For a close study of a society maintaining a gift economy and the social implications of it see C. A. Gregory, *Gifts and commodities* (Cambridge, 1982).

[5] C. Lévi-Strauss, 'The principle of reciprocity', in *Sociological theory: A book of readings*, ed. L. A. Coser and B. Rosenberg (New York, 1957), pp. 84–94.

I

portrays one's identity.[6] Gift-exchange maintains a society in a constant state of debt,[7] criss-crossed by a network of obligations and expectations of yet unfulfilled reciprocal gestures which bind it closely.[8] Charity as a form of gift-giving is similarly an act rich in meaning.

The study of charity is related to the current interest in the investigation of all groups of medieval society, an interest which has brought to the forefront of research not only the mass of peasants and craftsmen, but also marginal groups such as the poor.[9] Inasmuch as charity bound the poor and the rich together, its study can lead to a better appreciation of the nature of poverty and social relations. This is an indirect approach, through documentation emanating primarily from institutions founded by, or wills composed by the more comfortable members of society, merely one side of the charitable encounter. The danger of paternalism is inherent in any such attempt to capture an entity through an 'oblique' approach, but can be reduced by awareness of the biases embedded in our sources as well as in our method of studying them.[10]

Besides the wish to understand poverty and its relief, this study has

6 M. P. Banton, *Roles. An introduction to the study of social relations* (London, 1965), p. 2. For a beautiful expression of this idea, from Emerson's essay on gifts: R. W. Emerson, 'Gifts', in *Emerson's essays* (Philadelphia, Pa., 1936), p. 358: 'The only gift is a portion of thyself...Therefore the poet brings his poem; the shepherd his lamb; the farmer corn;...the girl a handkerchief of her own sewing. This is right and pleasing, for it restores society in so far to its primary basis, when a man's biography is conveyed in a gift.'

7 Mauss, *The gift*, p. 11 and Schwartz, 'The social psychology', pp. 5–6. On gift-giving in the early Middle Ages and its economic impact see P. Grierson, 'Commerce in the Dark Ages: a critique of the evidence', *Studies in economic anthropology*, ed. G. Dalton (Washington, D.C., 1971), pp. 74–83; esp. 77–8 [originally published in *Transactions of the Royal Historical Society* 5th ser. 9 (1959), pp. 123–40]. Mauss, *The gift*, p. 11; if unreciprocated it can wound one's pride, pp. 41, 63. Exaggerated gifts can function as signs of aggression, when one of the partners is denied, *a priori*, the ability to reciprocate adequately, *ibid.*, p. 127. For an expression of the inherent exchange nature of the charitable encounter see an example of gratitude by beggars in a Mexican village, G. M. Foster 'The dyadic contract: a model for the social structure of a Mexican peasant village', in *Peasant Society. A reader*, ed. J. M. Potter, M. N. Diaz and G. M. Foster (Boston, Mass., 1967), pp. 213–30.

8 It also raises the interesting question of whether medieval charity was part of a 'restricted' system of exchange, occurring solely between individuals, or a 'generalised' one, comprising a complex and multilateral network of transactions. On these terms and the social theories which gave rise to them see P. Ekeh, *Social exchange theory* (London, 1974), pp. 37–60.

9 See for example the essays collected in J. Le Goff, *Pour un autre moyen âge. Temps, travail et culture en Occident* (Paris, 1977), and the view expressed in the preface, pp. 7–15.

10 P. Burke, 'Oblique approaches to the history of popular culture', in *Approaches to popular culture*, ed. C. W. E. Bigsby (London, 1976), pp. 69–84.

been inspired by a preoccupation with the effect of religious ideas on works and practice. The study of charity is a case in which the effect of normative religious teaching and its internalisation can be examined. The activity spurred by the resounding teaching on charity can be a measure not only of the nature and forms of understanding and interpretation of religious and social ideas, but of the ability exhibited by the laity to integrate changing circumstances of life with prevalent moral and religious norms.

Viewing a society as a whole is a pursuit adopted from anthropological method, which has taught us to respect every facet of life and to seek rigorous explanation of the relations between apparently separate areas of human activity, producing what has come to be known as 'total history'. The modern dialogue between historians and anthropologists has shown both how to rid ourselves of some of the dangers of anachronistic judgement by attempting to evaluate those terms of analysis relevant in a different culture. It is through the application of values alien to the period that mixed assessments of medieval charity have arisen. Even Michel Mollat was tempted to voice them, and hastened to qualify his description of acts of charity: 'Charitable they are, but of what type of charity? The egocentric charity of a person who purchases his salvation with alms, or caring compassion? Perhaps one ought not and indeed cannot try to discover. All is in all, and all is intertwined'.[11]

Early research on charity was inspired by Michel Mollat in his seminar on Poverty in the Middle Ages at the Sorbonne in the 1960s. His students produced seminal studies on the image of poverty, on voluntary poverty and on poor relief examining an array of legal, theological, literary, and artistic sources. They soon recognised the importance of charitable institutions as a mirror of the life of the poor and as an expression of prevailing views on social and religious obligations. Thus, in the last two decades local and regional studies of charitable activity, mainly by French and Belgian historians, have broadened our view of the contacts between rich and poor through the forms of relief.[12] A lesson which can be drawn from these early

---

[11] 'Charitables, elles le sont, mais de quelle charité? La charité égocentrique de celui qui marchande son salut avec l'aumône, ou la miséricorde aimante? Peut-être ne faut-il pas et ne peut-on pas chercher? Tout est en tout, et tout s'entremêle', M. Mollat, 'En guise de préface: les problèmes de la pauvreté', in Mollat, *Etudes* 1, pp. 11–30; p. 30.

[12] Some of Michel Mollat's methodological guidelines have been expressed in M. Mollat, 'La notion de la pauvreté au moyen-âge. Position de problèmes', *Revue d'histoire de l'église de France* 52 (1966), pp. 5–23 as well as Mollat, 'En guise de préface', pp. 11–30.

works, and which underlies this study, is that charitable activities must be seen against the background of prevailing understanding of property, community, salvation – the mentality subsumed in every act of members of a particular society.[13] The attempt to unravel the practice of charity must be related both to the economic and physical environment, but also to the ideas and perceptions through which it was conceived.

Medieval men and women were exposed to an eloquent message of charity which they blended into their quest for spiritual salvation and social acceptance and harmony.[14] J. Rosenthal, who has studied charitable giving by the English aristocracy in the fourteenth and fifteenth centuries, has argued that their benevolence was largely wasted

His pupils have been producing seminal papers on poverty and charity many of which have been collected in Mollat, *Etudes*. Monographs on charity in Continental towns such as Bonenfant, *Hôpitaux et bienfaisance publiques*, J. H. Mundy, 'Charity and social work in Toulouse 1100–1250', *Traditio* 22 (1966), pp. 203–87; N. Gonthier, *Lyon et ses pauvres au moyen-âge (1350–1500)* (Lyon, 1978); J. Caille, *Hôpitaux et charité publique à Narbonne au moyen-âge* (Toulouse, 1978); A. Rubio Vella, *Probreza, enfermedad e y assistencia hospitaliaria en la Valencia del siglo XIV* (Valencia, 1984) have followed. The growing interest in charity guided the conveners of the 1978 session of the Fanjeaux Conferences 'Assistance et charité', the proceedings of which appeared in *Cahiers de Fanjeaux*, 13 (1978) as well as the 1979 and 1980 colloquia of the European University Institute on 'Poverty and urban development in Europe, 15th–19th centuries' and on 'Reaction of the poor to poverty'. The better documented *ancien régime* has produced studies of poverty and its contemporary treatment such as J.-P. Gutton, *La société et les pauvres: l'exemple de la généralité de Lyon, 1534–1789* (Paris, 1971); *idem, L'état et la mendicité dans la première moitié du XVIIIe siècle. Auvergne, Beaujolais, Forez, Lyonnais* (Saint-Etienne, 1973) and C. C. Fairchilds, *Poverty and charity in Aix-en-Provence 1640–1789* (Baltimore, Md, 1976). Many studies of particular rural and urban institutions of charity in the Low Countries have been undertaken by the contributors to the *Annales de la société belge de l'histoire des hôpitaux* founded by Paul Bonenfant in 1963. Yet his complaint 'malgré ces intérêts si multiples l'histoire des hôpitaux n'a pas, jusqu'à présent, donné lieu à des ouvrages de synthèse' (Bonenfant, *Hôpitaux et bienfaisance publiques*, p. 5) still held when this study was started.

13 For a similar structure of a study of charity which, like the present one, stresses the connection between the ideological and the economic circumstances of charity see L. Martz, *Poverty and welfare in Habsburg Spain. The example of Toledo* (Cambridge, 1983). On the problem of context in historical research and on the perils of normative judgements see H. Geertz, 'An anthropology of religion and magic. 1', *Journal of interdisciplinary history* 6 (1975–6), pp. 71–89; N. Z. Davis, 'Some tasks and themes in the study of popular religion', in *The pursuit of holiness in late medieval and Renaissance religion*, ed. C. Trinkaus and H. Oberman (Leiden, 1974), pp. 307–36, at pp. 307–12. Also E. P. Thompson, 'Anthropology and the discipline of historical context', *Midland history* 1 (1972), pp. 41–55.

14 For the relevance of current religious sensitivities for understanding of charity see G. Constable's view: 'Philanthropy cannot be studied apart from the doctrines of expiation and penance', G. Constable, 'Wealth and philanthropy in late medieval England. Review of J. Rosenthal, *The purchase of paradise*', *Journal of interdisciplinary history* 4 (1973–4), pp. 597–602, at p. 599.

owing to the nobility's failure to harness it to the furtherance of its political and social status.[15] In condemning their adherence to traditional forms of charity, Professor Rosenthal imputes to the aristocracy a predisposition towards change which is questionable. The analysis also underestimates the prominence of intercession not only as a form of display, but as an element of late medieval spirituality. Prayers for the soul were of undeniable importance and their pursuit was uppermost in the minds of benefactors as much for the rich display which they offered as for their spiritual efficacy.[16] In addition, the maintenance of a whole network of intercession in itself increased the sphere and the scope of influence of those able to supply generous doles, build magnificent chantries and maintain a host of chantry-chaplains.[17]

Another approach to the measurement and analysis of charity was tested in W. K. Jordan's studies of Tudor and early Stuart philanthropy. Through the use of a large number of wills (35,000) he examined changes in charitable activity and intent.[18] This mammoth statistical study produced a hierarchy of charitable undertakings according to their frequency and attempted to evaluate the degree of charitable disposition throughout the period by the aggregate charitable expenditure and by forms and recipients of charity.[19] The professed aim of

---

[15] J. Rosenthal, *The purchase of paradise: gift giving and the aristocracy, 1307–1485* (London, 1972), esp. pp. 130–2.

[16] For a more integrated view of the nobility's gift-giving see K. B. McFarlane, *The nobility of later medieval England* (Oxford, 1973), pp. 95–6, who believes that the nobility had reached a coherent balance between 'soul and flesh'.

[17] To judge its effect charitable expenditure should be seen against the background of their whole expenditure. The limitation to one class and to a single activity robbed this study of charity of its full social context. For a short and close study of charitable benefactions of one class of one county, the gentry of Yorkshire, see M. G. A. Vale, *Piety, charity and literacy among the Yorkshire gentry, 1370–1480* (York, 1976).

[18] W. K. Jordan, *Philanthropy in England, 1480–1660* (London, 1959); *idem*, *The charities of London, 1480–1660* (London, 1960); *idem*, *The charities of rural England 1480–1660* (London, 1961).

[19] See the reviews: L. Stone, in *History* 44 (1959), pp. 257–60; p. 260 as well as G. R. Elton, in *Historical journal* 3 (1960), pp. 89–92; p. 91 and R. Ashton, in *History* 46 (1961), pp. 136–9 and D. C. Coleman, in *Economic history review* second ser. 13 (1960–1), pp. 113–15; esp. pp. 113–14, and on Jordan's useful approach to poverty, p. 115. For a general discussion of Jordan's main findings see J. J. Scarisbrick, *The Reformation and the English people* (Oxford, 1984), p. 187, n. 38.

The ways in which Professor Jordan handled his data have been subjected to serious criticism, yet useful ideas and possible approaches to charity were raised, and some were taken up in the ensuing debate. An adjustment of Jordan's data by a price index showed no increase in charitable giving between 1480 and 1660, W. G. Bittle and R. T. Lane, 'Inflation and philanthropy in England: a reassessment of W. K. Jordan's data', *Economic history review* second ser. 29 (1976), pp. 203–10, at pp. 207–9; and a decline in *per capita* giving may very well be the truer picture, D. C. Coleman, 'Philanthropy

placing charity in its social, political and religious contexts was to reach a truer understanding of its nature. Unfortunately, this recognition was not fully embraced in the interpretation of his findings. The view of the London merchants as pious and honourable and increasingly charitable is simplistic and does not do justice to the sophisticated way in which they manipulated their giving for the furtherance of social and economic goals.[20]

These two interesting approaches to charity show that we are usually much better informed about the identity of the giver, the founder, donor or testator, than we are of the recipients. Who were the poor, the other half of the exchange, and how can we hope to encounter them? It was widely held in the Middle Ages, as it is by many modern economists, that poverty is to be measured relatively, in comparison with the comfort and security of others.[21] From this relative vantage point, poverty is seen as the want of something which can be reasonably expected, and medieval writers accepted the expectations usually associated with a person's status and possessed by his social peers as a reasonable measure. Understanding this view yields useful insights into the underlying logic of definitions of poverty adopted in particular medieval contexts.[22] In Carolingian and Anglo-Saxon society the majority of people existed on the edge of subsistence and lived in closely-knit rural communities in which every man was protected by his lord and his kin. In such a society the small freeholders of land who could support themselves and their families, but who were not protected by a lord and were not ensconced within a community of equally situated neighbours, were deemed to be the poor.[23] It was they

---

deflated: a comment', *Economic history review* second ser. 31 (1978), pp. 118–23; esp. p. 119.

[20] On the way in which this simple view obscures rather than enlightens our understanding of the merchant class mentality see Elton, 'Review', p. 90.

[21] For the relative approach see M. Rein, 'Problems in the definition and measurement of poverty', in *The concept of poverty*, ed. P. Townsend (London, 1970), pp. 46–63; p. 46 and C. A. Valentine, *Culture and poverty. Critique and counter-proposals* (Chicago and London, 1969), p. 126. For a discussion of the development of a relative view of poverty expressed in the notion of *pauperes verecundi* see G. Ricci, 'La naissance du pauvre honteux: entre l'histoire des idées et l'histoire sociale', *Annales* 38 (1983), pp. 158–77.

[22] For a discussion of the subjective elements incorporated in any definition of poverty see P. Mathias, 'Adam's burden: diagnoses of poverty in post-medieval Europe and the Third World now', *Tijdschrift voor geschiedenis* 89 (1976), pp. 149–60; pp. 149–51.

[23] K. Bosl, '"Potens" und "Pauper". Begriffsgeschichtliche Studien zur gesellschaftlichen Differenzierung im frühen Mittelalters und zum "Pauperismus" des Hochmittelalters', in *Alteuropa und die moderne Gesellschaft. Festschrift für Otto Brunner* (Göttingen, 1963), pp. 60–87; *passim* and esp. pp. 61–70. R. Le Jan-Hennebicque, '"Pauperes" et "paupertas" dans l'occident carolingien aux IXe et Xe siècles', *Revue du Nord* 50 (1968),

who were labelled *pauperes*, in their precarious personal security, rather than the landless or serfs, who were physically poorer but who were not obliged to compete, either economically or politically, as free men.[24]

Following this understanding of contemporary views of relative need, it is clear that the medieval definition of poverty was bound to change in response to the changing characteristics of rural and urban indigence, and it should also transcend views which emanate predominantly from a particular class. Drawing the relative view to its logical conclusion we must think of well-being in terms of possession of or lack of capabilities to function: 'Voluntary or involuntary poverty can be defined as a permanent or temporary situation of weakness, dependence and meekness, characterised by deprivation of minimal means (differing by period and by society) necessary for personal security and dignity, for intellectual capability...and for social relations'.[25] Thus, Michel Mollat, in a definition similar to the one which Amartya Sen, the student of Third World poverty, has suggested.[26] To Sen, well-being is not mere physical functioning, rather it is the capability to function *effectively* and to maintain some control over one's environment, the ability to take part in social life, to move

---

pp. 169–87 and J.-C. Dufermont, 'Les pauvres, d'après les sources anglo-saxonnes du VIIe au XIe siècles', *Revue du Nord* 50 (1968), pp. 189–201. For a similar use of the terms in the early Byzantine world see E. Patlagean, *Pauvreté économique et pauvreté sociale à Byzance, 4e–7e siècles* (Paris, 1977), pp. 25–35.

[24] Still, serfs were objectively poorer than the *pauperes*! Carolingian capitularies and ecclesiastical legislation demanded that bishops protect *pauperes* in legal procedures and alleviate the burden of frequent attendance in court sessions, clearly a reference to free proprietors, see J. Devisse, '"Pauperes" et "paupertas" dans le monde carolingien: ce qu'en dit Hincmar de Reims', *Revue du Nord* 48 (1966), pp. 273–87; pp. 274–7. This understanding of poverty is summarised by B. Geremek: 'Le pauvre, ce n'est pas seulement l'individu dépourvu de moyens d'existence, c'est *aussi* l'individu le plus faible dans un groupe ou dans une société', B. Geremek, 'Le renfermement des pauvres en Italie (XIVe–XVIIe siècle): remarques préliminaires', in *Mélanges en l'honneur de Fernand Braudel. Histoire économique du monde méditerranéen 1450–1650* I (Toulouse, 1973), pp. 205–17; p. 205.

[25] 'La pauvreté, volontaire ou involontaire, peut être définie ainsi: une situation permanente ou temporaire, de faiblesse, de dépendance et d'humilité, caractérisée par la privation du minimum de moyens, variables selon les époques et les sociétés, nécessaires à la sécurité et à la dignité personnelle, la capacité intellectuelle,...les relations sociales', M. Mollat, 'Pauvres et assistés au moyen-âge', in *A pobreza e a assistência aos pobres na Península Ibérica durante a Idade Média* I (Lisbon, 1973), pp. 11–27; p. 12; repeated in Mollat, 'En guise de préface', p. 12. For an attempt to classify the medieval poor see N. Gonthier, 'Les hôpitaux et les pauvres à la fin du moyen-âge: l'exemple de Lyon', *Le moyen-âge* 84 (1978), pp. 279–308; pp. 300–6.

[26] As expressed in the Boutwood Lectures delivered at Cambridge on 2 and 3 November 1983 on the subject 'Liberty, Utility and Freedom' and in the Tanner Lectures 'The standard of living' delivered in Cambridge on 11–12 March, 1985.

and improve one's fortune. At its fullest, well-being is tantamount to positive freedom.[27] In some periods freedom and welfare are undermined primarily by lack of security, in others by sheer physical indigence. At any time the privation of such basic capabilities creates a dependence of the poor on what society takes to be its 'altruism', its charitable prerogative, and ultimately on those who are to undertake it.

The poor became more noticeable as towns grew in the late eleventh and twelfth centuries and reached the limits of their medieval expansion by the end of the thirteenth century. The localised nature of the ever-present existence at subsistence level in earlier centuries, rendered it almost invisible, but now it was giving way to a more complex social and economic reality, through changes which will be surveyed in chapter 2.[28] Towns attracted migrants from an ever-more populous countryside to create a large supply of labour which subsequently produced falling wages and urban indigence. Jacques of Vitry, that keen observer of early thirteenth-century social and religious life, described the poor urban layman as: 'He who by working with his two hands acquires his meagre daily bread and has nothing left over after dining'.[29] Thomas Aquinas gives a similar definition of the poor: 'Workers who hire out their labour are poor, they seek their daily bread by their exertion'.[30] This urban labourer working in unfavourable conditions and earning too little to sustain a family, did not fall into the categories of poverty honoured by the Church, which were largely based on the realities of a rural economy and society. The prosperous townsman with funds to spare was able not only to live comfortably but to make choices, to take initiatives, even to spend some of his money on others. These freedoms were denied the poor, and were more than a mere physical

---

[27] He does allow for the effect of climate, custom, sex and region in determining a particular person's welfare.

[28] For some stimulating remarks on this change see C. Violante, 'Riflessioni sulla povertà nel secolo XI', in *Studi sul medioevo cristiano offerti a Raffaello Morghen* II (Rome, 1974), pp. 1061–81; esp. pp. 1062–3, 1070–9. Violante connects the earlier urbanisation of Italy with the first stirrings of discussions of voluntary poverty there, *ibid.*, p. 1080.

[29] 'qui, propriis manibus laborando, victum tenuem omni die sibi acquirebat, nec ei plusquam cenaret quicquam remanebat', Jacques of Vitry, *The exempla or illustrative stories from the 'sermones vulgares' of Jacques de Vitry*, ed. T. F. Crane (London, 1890), p. 27. This is an 'absolute' view of poverty shared by B. S. Rowntree, *Poverty: a study in town life* (London, 1910), p. 86: 'Poverty is an income insufficient to obtain the minimal necessaries for maintenance of merely physical efficiency' and L. Génicot, 'Sur le nombre des pauvres dans les campagnes médiévales', *Revue historique* 522 (1977), pp. 273–88; p. 273.

[30] 'Mercenarii qui locant opera sua, pauperes sunt, de laboribus suis victum quaerentibus quotidianum', *Summa theologiae* II–II q. 105 a. 2 ad. 6.

state. The problem of social imagery and its relation to reality has been eloquently raised by Georges Duby and discussed further by Jacques Le Goff. Le Goff argues persuasively that in twelfth- and thirteenth-century society, and mainly the urban milieu, new schemes of social, moral and political classifications came to replace conservative dualities — *potens–pauper*, *laicus–clericus* and *paradisum–infernum*.[31] People came to think in the sophisticated terminology of a more differentiated and varied society,[32] and in parallel intellectual inquiry reached into new social, religious and political spheres.[33] The discussions of charity were slower in adopting the more complex view; in exhortation towards almsgiving the pair *dives et pauper* remained, unwittingly expressing the ever-growing gap separating those able and those unable to support themselves.[34] By the thirteenth century, even this moral and economic opposition was questioned and qualified, but it served in the *exempla* of thirteenth-century mendicant preaching, which was the main tool of instruction and of dissemination of the charitable imperative.[35]

St Francis represented most powerfully the view that the poor were to be cherished and valued, recognising both the wretched misery of poverty and its power to purify and raise the human spirit.[36] The

---

[31] J. Le Goff, *La naissance du purgatoire* (Paris, 1981), pp. 304–10. This observation lies at the basis of his analysis of the emergence of *purgatorium*, the 'middle place', in the late twelfth century.

[32] They also diversified old and static social classifications; see Bosl, '"Potens" und "pauper"', pp. 70, 87.

[33] A complex picture of the social body emerges from the variety of audiences to which the writers of *sermones ad status* such as Humbert of Romans and Jacques of Vitry addressed themselves, J. Le Goff, 'Le vocabulaire des catégories sociales chez St. François d'Assise et ses biographes du XIIIe siècle', in *Ordres et classes. Colloque d'histoire sociale de St. Cloud, 24–25 Mai 1967* (Paris, 1973), pp. 93–123; p. 106 and in the same volume P. Michaud-Quantin, 'Le vocabulaire des catégories sociales chez les canonistes et les moralistes du XIIIe siècle', pp. 73–86, at pp. 83–5.

[34] Mendicant preaching utilised the power of simple and stark opposing terms in their preaching, like the basic *bonum–malum*, see L. E. Boyle, 'Three English pastoral *summae* and a "Magister Galienus"', *Studia gratiana* 11, *Collectanea Stephan Kuttner* 1 (Bologna, 1967), pp. 133–44; pp. 135, 136–7. On the dichotomy *dives–pauper* in the minds of canonists see Michaud-Quantin, 'Le vocabulaire des catégories sociales', pp. 80–1, and for the later Middle Ages see M. Moisa, 'Fourteenth-century preachers' views of the poor: class or status group?', in *Culture, ideology and politics. Essays for E. Hobsbawm* ed. R. Samuel and G. S. Jones (London, 1983), p. 160–75; p. 164.

[35] Mollat, 'En guise de préface', pp. 14–15.

[36] D. Flood, 'Poverty in the Middle Ages', *Collectanea franciscana* 43 (1973), pp. 409–15. See also V. Turner, *Dramas, fields and metaphors: symbolic action in human society* (Ithaca, N.Y., and London, 1974), pp. 234–5. Poverty could also be a destabilising force when preached to the masses of poor as a reason for rebellion. On the connection between religious heresies and the idea of voluntary poverty see T. Manteuffel, *Naissance d'une hérésie: les adeptes de la pauvreté volontaire au moyen-âge*, trans. A. Posner (Paris, 1970), *passim*; esp. pp. 101–2. See also C. Thouzellier, 'Hérésie et pauvreté à la fin du XIIe et au début du XIIIe siècle', in Mollat, *Etudes* I, pp. 371–88.

intensification of religious instruction in the twelfth and thirteenth centuries, expressed in forms and conveying a message which will be discussed in chapter 3, underlay the accelerated charitable activity witnessed in this period.[37] The rights of the poor to receive charity were undisputed by canonists and preachers, although few recognised them as positive rights and differing scales of merit coexisted in their writings and sermons.[38] Traditional teaching on charity also imposed an obligation on the poor: they were to guard themselves from envy and sloth and be humble, to be worthy of their task as intercessors for the benefactor's soul. It is the ability of both parties to fulfil their respective parts in an exchange which fed and sustained the act. Men and women were faced not only with the need to accommodate their personal inclinations and resources to charitable expectations, but also to fit their observations of real poverty around them, with the teachings of the Church and the needs of their community. In periods of change and reevaluation of social relations, the image of the poor reciprocating partners, as well as the ability to apportion funds to almsgiving was reassessed. When potential givers failed to trust the merit and disposition of the poor as social and charitable partners, a sort of moral dissonance would set in making them reluctant to initiate what was becoming a rather insecure transaction. At the same time irritation with their own lapses from the charitable norm would be generated.

A solution to this embarrassment could be found in a reformulation of duties, the creation of alternative forms for the exhibition of piety, and the development of a social theory which would rationalise their unwillingness to alleviate the real poverty around them. By reasoning that the poor were sinful, unruly, lazy and generally undeserving, by dispossessing the poor from the title *pauperes Christi*, an understanding could be effected which liberated those better off from responsibility for relief. An additional consequence would be the creation of some alternative charitable forms, which were pious phrases but which

---

[37] On social sanction and cooperation in society see Banton, *Roles*, p. 2; T. B. Veblen, *The theory of the leisure class*, intr. J. K. Galbraith (edn of Boston, Mass., 1973), p. 217; B. Pullan, *Rich and poor in Renaissance Venice. The social institutions of a catholic state, to 1620* (Oxford, 1971), p. 317.

[38] On the diverse views of poverty in the late Middle Ages see C.-M. de La Roncière, 'Pauvres et pauvreté à Florence au XIVe siècle', in Mollat, *Etudes* II, pp. 661–745. On the development of the concept of natural rights and its influence on attitudes towards property see R. Tuck, *Natural rights theories. Their origin and development* (Cambridge, 1979), which suggests a meaningful breakthrough in the fourteenth century, while an early date and more intricate development are suggested in B. Tierney, 'Tuck on rights: some medieval problems', *History of political thought* 4 (1983), pp. 429–41.

effectively benefited a group more acceptable to potential givers.[39] It will be interesting to see how the charitable exchange weathers the stormy changes of late medieval economic and social life. The earlier charitable solutions within urban hospitals will be examined in chapters 4–6, and the later forms, most of which existed outside institutions of charity, will be studied in chapter 7.

Most intense charitable activity was manifested in the period when the concepts of purgatory, of the efficacy of prayers for the dead and of the spiritual utility of good works, were being defined, discussed and more widely taught. In the society which absorbed these terms, the charitable exchange was deemed a profitable undertaking and *dives* and *pauper* were frequently represented in art, literature and theology, engaged in the fulfilment of their roles.[40] This formal ascription of moral value and a social role to the poor would combine with the shared family, work and survival experiences to reinforce a 'culture of poverty'.[41] Their sense of identity was reinforced, wrought and maintained, by the shared experience of urban mendicancy or rural indigence, from frequent meeting in the rounds of distribution, doles and funerary attendance as well as by the external views which other groups projected onto them.[42] The changing economic and social world of the later Middle Ages entailed reexamination which generated change in these same roles and in relations between classes, as mentalities were touched and refashioned.[43]

In towns money changed hands rapidly, journeymen sought employ-

---

[39] On the value set on poverty in the thirteenth century see Mollat, 'La notion de la pauvreté au moyen-âge', p. 10.

[40] M.-L. Thérel, '"Caritas" et "paupertas" dans l'iconographie médiévale inspirée de la psychomachie', in Mollat, *Etudes* I, pp. 295–317. On the rise of these categories see M. Mollat, 'Hospitalité et assistance au début du XIIIᵉ siècle', *Actes du symposium 'Poverty in the Middle Ages'*, ed. D. Flood (Paderborn, 1975), pp. 37–51; p. 37.

[41] Valentine, *Culture and poverty*, pp. 15–21. See the observations in O. Lewis, *The children of Sanchez* (Harmondsworth, 1961), pp. xxiv–xxviii. On some social and psychological attributes of poverty see D. Matza, 'The disreputable poor', in *Class, status and power: social status in comparative perspective*, ed. R. Bendix and S. M. Lipset (London, 1967), pp. 289–302.

[42] On the attribution of characteristics to the poor by other classes see R. Houston, 'Vagrants and society in early modern England', *Cambridge anthropology* 6 (1980), pp. 18–32. For a discussion of views of poverty and its solutions among late eighteenth- and nineteenth-century reformers see J. R. Poynter, *Society and pauperism. English ideas on poor relief, 1795–1834* (Toronto, 1969), pp. ix–xxvi.

[43] On the changing evaluation of categories of poverty as expressed within *Piers Plowman* see D. Aers, '*Piers Plowman* and problems in the perception of poverty: a culture in transition', *Leeds studies in English* new ser. 14 (1983), pp. 5–25. On the role of the poor see G. Simmel, *On individuality and social forms*, ed. D. N. Levine (Chicago and London, 1971), p. 178.

ment, villagers sold and bought and mingled with townsfolk, merchants passed through sometimes carrying new ideas as well as cloth in their panniers, friars preached and the poor assembled and begged.[44] Towns witnessed intensive economic activity and a greater variety of social situations; in them existed deeper and more evident indigence, on the one hand, and more frequent and vehement exhortation towards charity, on the other.[45] Throughout their period of growth towns attracted men and women from their surroundings, but the scope of livelihood which towns could offer to newcomers altered dramatically throughout the period under study. By the end of the thirteenth century there were few jobs, mostly low-paid, which caused a new and more noticeable kind of distress; the weak, the unemployed and unemployable, women and dependents, were removed from family and community help.[46] Some of the needy exhibited the signs of poverty which friars encouraged their urban audiences to alleviate. They occasionally exerted pressures on civil authorities, and regularly burdened parish relief and touched a human compassion rendered more sensitive by frequent and effective teaching. The urban milieu and the spiritual challenges which it raised were the ground on which new means for salvation were created but in their limited and crowded spaces, anxieties could erode the spirit of cooperation and altruism.[47] In periods of prosperity charity loomed large in them, and as in all areas of town life the parallel activities of high and low, of the great men

[44] For some studies of charity in an urban context see Pullan, *Rich and poor in Renaissance Venice*; W. J. Marx, *The development of charity in medieval Louvain* (New York, 1936) and see above n. 12. For a study of urban poor relief in the early modern era, A. L. Beier, 'The social problems of an Elizabethan country town: Warwick, 1580–90', in *Country towns in pre-industrial England*, ed. P. Clark (Leicester, 1981), pp. 46–85.

[45] In Cambridge preaching must have been especially frequent due to the existence of large groups of friars of the four mendicant orders, T. H. Aston, G. D. Duncan and T. A. R. Evans, 'The medieval alumni of the University of Cambridge', *Past and present* 86 (1980), pp. 9–86, at pp. 18–19. On the relation between the values of mendicant and urban life see J. Le Goff, 'Ordres mendiants et urbanisation dans la France médiévale', *Annales* 25 (1970), pp. 924–46 and B. H. Rosenwein and L. K. Little, 'Social meaning in the monastic and mendicant spiritualities', *Past and present* 63 (1974), pp. 4–32; pp. 20–32; for a more cautious view of this relation see D. L. d'Avray, *The preaching of the friars. Sermons diffused from Paris before 1300* (Oxford, 1985), pp. 216–39.

[46] Génicot, 'Sur le nombre des pauvres', p. 274. Georges Duby sees distress as an almost exclusively urban phenomenon, 'Les pauvres des campagnes dans l'occident médiéval jusqu'au XIIIᵉ siècle', *Revue d'histoire de l'église de France* 52 (1966), pp. 25–32; pp. 29–30; Mollat, 'La notion de la pauvreté', pp. 13–14 and *idem*, 'Hospitalité et assistance', p. 45. Charity is related with population growth in H. Hasquin, 'Note sur les origines de l'hôpital Notre Dame à Courtrai (1209–1211)', *Annales de la société belge d'histoire des hôpitaux* 9 (1971), pp. 3–10; p. 8, related to population growth.

[47] On the influence of money on medieval attitudes see A. Murray, *Reason and society in the Middle Ages* (Oxford, 1978), pp. 59–61, 77–83.

of commerce and the smaller craftsmen, coexisted to create a comparative dimension for study.[48]

Of such communities Cambridge is a pregnant example. The existence of the medieval university and the colleges in this medium-sized market town has allowed the survival of abundant sources related to the town's religious institutions. The archives of the Hospital of St John are kept as part of the muniments of St John's College, and this foundation of the main charitable institution of Cambridge, *c.* 1200, on the crest of a wave of hospital foundations, provides a convenient starting point. Its refoundation as a college in 1509–11 augurs the arrival of new times and ideas, in a century which saw momentous political, social and religious change that fundamentally altered the picture of poverty and relief.[49] The study of Cambridge also enables us to compare academic and non-academic charity, and to see whether patronage from the hands of kings, noblemen and prelates heightened the charitable awareness of the burgess community. Throughout the book an attempt will be made to relate the story of one town to what is known of the charitable dilemmas experienced and solutions devised by other medieval towns, bearing in mind the peculiarities of Cambridge, but also shared structural problems and attitudes which render such comparisons valuable.

[48] On the social composition of smaller medieval towns see R. H. Hilton, 'Lords, burgesses and hucksters', *Past and present* 97 (1982), pp. 3–15 and *idem*, 'Small town society in England before the Black Death', *Past and present* 105 (1984), pp. 53–78; J. Le Goff, *Marchands et banquiers du moyen-âge* (Paris, 1956), pp. 42, 47. Some prefer to study charity through the activities of one class, but this limits the relevance of any findings to the working of the class studied, see Rosenthal, *The purchase of paradise*.

[49] The activities connected with the transformation of the hospital into a college are extremely revealing and interesting. However, Lady Margaret Beaufort and John Fisher were exalted personages alien to the context of urban charity in Cambridge. In this work I have chosen to refer to the hospital's end only as an epilogue.

Chapter 2

THE ECONOMIC BACKGROUND: SUPPLY AND DEMAND FOR CHARITY

THE ROLE OF ECONOMIC CONSIDERATIONS IN CHARITABLE ACTIVITY

Charitable activity has a fascinating hold on the minds of economists and sociologists:[1] it is the enigma of altruistic behaviour, the need to be able to account for activity which is apparently unselfish, and hence not arising from purely economic considerations.[2] As the giving of charity transcends strictly utilitarian aims, a purely economic view of charity must be abandoned; yet a view according to which economic considerations are not relevant is also misleading. A considered study of charity must encompass both the economic and the moral factors prevailing, since 'forms and functions of giving embody moral, social, psychological, religious, legal and aesthetic ideas'.[3] Thus, a true appreciation of the meaning of charity can be achieved only through studying both economic and non-economic considerations in its determination.

In purely economic terms one can make a distinction between what may be called the demand for charity by the poor and its supply by the rich and by charitable institutions. Both the demand and the supply are influenced by economic factors: changes in a society's prosperity and in the distribution of wealth affect the facility with which funds can be allocated for the help of strangers. Concurrently, they also affect the number of people experiencing the need to receive charitable relief. In this chapter I will trace separately the influence of economic

[1] An example of the view of a social and economic reciprocal relationship: 'it must provide rewards...which compare favourably with those in other competing relationships or activities available to individuals.', J. Thibaut and H. H. Kelly, *The social psychology of groups* (New York, 1959), p. 49.

[2] This has been studied from the point of view of a theoretical economist believing in the inherent human altruistic motivation in Collard, *Altruism and economy*. Michel Mollat agrees that the provision of relief is not an immediate response to need, Mollat, 'En guise de préface', pp. 11–30.

[3] R. M. Titmuss, *The gift relationship* (London, 1970), p. 81.

circumstances on the well-being of givers and of potential recipients using what is known of the general economic history of the period, and as far as possible of the circumstances of Cambridge. The extent to which a change in supply (givers) would automatically follow a change in demand for charity (of recipients, due to, say, a famine, or change in long-term economic trends) will in itself largely depend on non-economic factors such as religion and prevailing values.[4] In sum, economic factors will determine the ability to give and the need to receive, but will not guarantee charitable disposition nor prescribe the forms in which relief will be dispensed, considerations largely governed by non-economic, religious and cultural values.[5] In this survey I have followed the fluctuations in the economic factors bearing in mind particularly those which would have led to changes in urban poverty and in the composition of the group of poor, and which would have affected the prosperity of towns. The concluding section explicitly draws out the implications of these changes for charitable activity.

GENERAL ECONOMIC AND DEMOGRAPHIC TRENDS, 1200–1500

The period under study, 1200 to 1500, is one in which England knew the most striking social and economic changes. It saw the furthest limits of agrarian expansion, the growth of towns, the reclamation of waste, forest and fen; as both the cause and the effect of these factors it experienced a general rise in population. This period also saw the worst years of famine, the most morbid visitations of plague, abandonment of lands, depopulation of towns and manors and freeing of villeins.[6] A great deal of study has been devoted to improving our understanding of this period. Most historians agree that demographic change determined the trend in prices, wages, settlement and agricultural exploitation.[7] It is widely accepted that a period of expansion caused

[4] This interplay is the foundation of the discussion in chapter 3, but in this chapter has been largely ignored.
[5] On the importance of non-economic factors in entitlement to relief from hunger and famines see A. K. Sen, *Poverty and famines. An essay on entitlement and deprivation* (Oxford, 1981).
[6] For excellent general surveys of the economic and social history of the period see E. Miller and J. Hatcher, *Medieval England. Rural society and economic change, 1086–1348* (London, 1978); and J. Hatcher, *Plague, population and the English economy 1348–1530* (London, 1977). For developments in rural society see R. H. Hilton, *The decline of serfdom in medieval England* (London, 1969).
[7] See the seminal article of M. M. Postan, the Pirenne of late medieval history, 'Some economic evidence of declining population in the later Middle Ages', *Economic history review* second ser. 2 (1949–50), pp. 221–46.

growing demand for land and food which lasted from about 1150 to the late thirteenth century.[8] Many will also agree that some time in the first half of the fourteenth century the demographic trend reversed itself, the 'nemesis' of the period of intensive exploitation set in, and a decrease of the population which could no longer be sustained by existing produce began, signalling a new trend in prices, wages, land settlement and agricultural activity.[9] Thus, though the timing is disputed, the fact of decline is not.[10] In late thirteenth- and early fourteenth-century England the Malthusian reaction to the overextension of cultivation and to the fall in yields per acre was well under way.[11] The population decrease was further exacerbated by such events as the famine years of 1315–17,[12] the great mortality of 1348–9 and the

[8] H. E. Hallam, 'Some thirteenth-century censuses', *Economic history review* second ser. 10 (1957–8), pp. 340–61; *idem*, 'Population density in medieval fenland', *Economic history review* second ser. 14 (1961–2), pp. 71–81. G. Bois places the end of growth in the decade 1250–60, *Crise du féodalisme* (Paris, 1976), pp. 240–1.

[9] B. F. Harvey suggested that the reversal occurred only because of and after the Black Death in 'The population trend in England between 1300 and 1348', *Transactions of the Royal Historical Society* fifth ser. 16 (1966), pp. 23–42. Admittedly, the body of evidence on which the case for an early fourteenth-century population decline is not large, but the trend appears consistently in those limited studies that have been undertaken, and which have been cited above. An important contribution to the study of the rural population trend in the early fourteenth century is L. R. Poos's doctoral dissertation, 'Population and resources in two fourteenth-century Essex communities: Great Waltham and High Easter, 1327–1389', (Ph.D. dissertation, Cambridge, 1983) the evidence for population decline is plotted in tables 3.1–3.3 (between pp. 75–6), and is summarised on pp. 287–9. On the state of the discussion see Z. Razi, *Life, marriage and death in a medieval parish. Economy, society and demography in Halesowen, 1270–1400* (Cambridge, 1980), pp. 27–8; also S. Reynolds, *An introduction to the history of English medieval towns* (Oxford, 1977), p. 141. An even later and more limited dating of the change in wages and prices is proposed by A. R. Bridbury, 'The black death', *Economic history review* second ser. 26 (1973), pp. 577–92. For a general book on the chronology of the Black Death and its consequences for the whole of Europe see P. Ziegler, *The Black Death* (London, 1969).

[10] For a dissenting interpretation of population growth in developing countries today, which sees it as a sign of expansion of resources, P. T. Bauer, *Dissent on development* (London, 1971), pp. 123–4.

[11] For a theoretical model explaining growth and development of the labour market and subsequent decline without recourse to exogenous factors see R. H. Day, 'Instability in the transition from manorialism: a classical analysis', *Explorations in economic history* 19 (1982), pp. 321–38. In his analysis of economic change R. Brenner rejects the Malthusian effects as part of a feasible explanation, R. Brenner, 'Agrarian class structure and economic development in pre-industrial Europe', *Past and present* 70 (1976), pp. 30–75; however, his criticism is rebutted in an explanation of the Ricardian principles which underlie most current explanations, J. Hatcher and M. M. Postan, 'Agrarian class structure and economic development in pre-industrial Europe. Population and class relations in feudal society', *Past and present* 78 (1978), pp. 24–37.

[12] I. Kershaw sees the point of break in these years, 'The great famine and agrarian crisis in England 1315–1322', *Past and present* 59 (1973), pp. 3–50; pp. 4, 6; the crisis is recognised for its decisive value by most historians; see Bois, *Crise du féodalisme*, pp.

recurring outbursts of plague.[13] Although there are widely differing assessments of the extent of plague mortality,[14] there can be no doubt that it deepened dramatically the trend towards population contraction. Widely differing observations on the rate of recuperation and population replacement in the post-plague years exist, but it is accepted that the recovering society suffered periodic recurrences of the epidemic (of lesser virulence) throughout the fourteenth and even in the fifteenth century, mainly in 1361–2 and 1371, coupled with many bad harvests in crucial years, to aggravate the general high mortality of a world in which plague had become endemic.[15] By 1400 the decline of population may have been arrested and quick recovery was possible in the North and in rural areas, all of which saw relatively few recurrences of epidemics.[16] Yet there is no question of a full recovery of the already falling population numbers of the pre-plague years until the end of the fifteenth century.[17]

How did these general demographic trends affect the standard of

246–9. For information on the climatic conditions in these crucial years see J. Z. Titow, 'Evidence of weather in the account rolls of the bishopric of Winchester 1209–1350', *Economic history review* second ser. 12 (1959–60), pp. 360–407.

[13] Harvey, 'The population trend in England', *passim*. On the combination of endogenous and exogenous factors in the fourteenth-century crisis see Hatcher, *Plague, population and the English economy*, pp. 69–73.

[14] See C. Morris's review of Shrewsbury's book [J. F. D. Shrewsbury, *A history of the bubonic plague in England* (Cambridge, 1970)] 'The plague in Britain', *Historical journal* 14 (1971), pp. 205–15.

[15] Hatcher, *Plague, population and the English economy*, pp. 25–6. The subsequent plagues were of more regional character and tended to rage mainly in towns, J. M. W. Bean, 'Plague, population and economic decline in England in the later Middle Ages', *Economic history review* second ser. 15 (1962–3), pp. 423–37; pp. 432, 436. Where plague recurred it dominated patterns of mortality and diminished the prospects for recovery, P. Slack, 'Mortality crises and epidemic disease in England', *Health, medicine and mortality in the sixteenth century*, ed. C. Webster (Cambridge, 1979), pp. 9–59; p. 19; the less ravaged countryside (Razi has calculated a mortality rate of 6% for Halesowen in the plague of 1361, *Life, marriage and death*, p. 117), did inject new life into the towns by maintaining a level of demand and of surplus marketed to them. This would have diminished the debilitating effects in employment and in production which would follow each recurring plague, effects discussed, *ibid.*, p. 59.

[16] From the returns of royal subsidies between 1334 and the sixteenth century it appears that the wealth ranking of both Yorkshire and Lancashire relatively declined, R. S. Schofield, 'The geographical distribution of wealth in England, 1334–1649', *Economic history review* second ser. 18 (1965), pp. 483–510; p. 506.

[17] M. M. Postan, 'The fifteenth century', *Economic history review* 9 (1938–9), pp. 160–7. For a summary of the situation of towns in the late Middle Ages, see C. Phythian-Adams, 'Urban decay in later medieval England', in *Towns in societies. Essays in economic history and historical sociology*, ed. P. Abrams and E. A. Wrigley (Cambridge, 1978), pp. 159–85. A. R. Bridbury sees the fifteenth century as a period of growth in the non-agricultural sector, A. R. Bridbury, *Economic growth in England in the later Middle Ages* (London, 1962).

living, poverty and wealth? Looking at the countryside of thirteenth-century England, and particularly that of East Anglia, one encounters a constant growth in population attested through a multitude of indicators: rise of land prices and land rents, rise of entry fines, growth in the number of tenants on manors, growth in the area of arable land, fragmentation of holdings.[18] The late twelfth and thirteenth century growth of the area of land under plough, the process of reclamation and colonisation, allowed food production to rise and to yield a better and wider variety of crops. The rise in the demand for food rendered 'high-farming' more profitable than ever, drawing capital, closer administration and interest from landlords wishing to ensure their income,[19] but also to expand their demesne and thus, their profits. Production and distribution were controlled increasingly by the landlords' officials, customary dues more effectively extracted.[20] This intensive growth was arrested when good lands became scarce and diminishing returns set in, making it impossible to sustain adequately a still-growing population by continued expansion of the cultivated area or by more intensive production.[21] Prices steadily rose in the thirteenth century, a trend established by its second decade,[22] further aggravated by monetary factors.[23] A customary tenant family would have felt the squeeze of higher rents, fragmented holdings, higher prices and falling yields.[24] However, all were not uniformly affected.

[18] For a discussion of these phenomena and their effectiveness as indicators of population growth see Harvey, 'The population trend in England', pp. 23–6. See again Hallam, 'Population density in medieval fenland', pp. 76, 79 and J. Z. Titow, 'Some evidence of the thirteenth century population increase', *Economic history review*, second ser. 14 (1961–62), pp. 218–24.

[19] E. Miller, 'England in the twelfth and thirteenth centuries: an economic contrast?', *Economic history review* second ser. 24 (1971), pp. 1–14; p. 11.

[20] *ibid.*, p. 12; Hilton, *The decline of serfdom*, pp. 21–4.

[21] E. Miller, 'The English economy in the thirteenth century. Implications of recent research', *Past and present* second ser. 28 (1964), pp. 21–40; pp. 30–1.

[22] Miller and Hatcher, *Medieval England*, pp. 64–9; D. L. Farmer, 'Some price fluctuations in Angevin England', *Economic history review* second ser. 9 (1956–7), pp. 34–43; *idem*, 'Some grain price movements in thirteenth century England', *Economic history review* second ser. 10 (1957–8), pp. 207–20; the rise affected all types of grain, *ibid.*, p. 218.

[23] A bullion glut in the thirteenth century contributed to the price trend induced by population growth, P. D. A. Harvey, 'The English inflation of 1180–1220', *Past and present* 61 (1973), pp. 3–30. For a monetary explanation of the rise in prices in the early fourteenth century see N. J. Mayhew, 'Numismatic evidence and falling prices in the fourteenth century', *Economic history review* second ser. 27 (1974), pp. 1–15.

[24] Evidence for impoverishment and increasing shortage of cash among tenants which must be cautiously accepted is presented in A. N. May, 'An index of thirteenth century impoverishment? Manor court fines', *Economic history review* second ser. 26 (1973), pp. 389–402; table on p. 393; more fines were being waived in response to a claim of *quia pauper*, p. 398.

Customary rents were fixed, but rents on scraps of land added to customary holdings paid flexible and rising rents. Dues and fines were also given to some fluctuation at the lords' will, and contributed to the increase of seigneurial incomes. Faced with the obligation to sell a large part of their produce in order to pay customary dues and to buy manufactured goods and essential dietary components, little was left to a smallholding family for subsistence, let alone for investment or improvement.[25] Thus, the number of agricultural wage-labourers was ever growing.[26] With fewer new lands to be taken up by the landless, holdings were further fragmented so that by 1279 41% of the villeins of Cambridgeshire and 68% of freeholders held less than a quarter-virgate (around $7\frac{1}{2}$ acres) when the minimum for subsistence must have been a half-virgate holding,[27] and a process of pauperisation of the rural population, especially that of customary smallholders, was in operation,[28] and rendered them highly vulnerable to fluctuations in weather conditions, harvest yields and prices.[29] Freeholders who had

[25] R. H. Hilton, 'Rents and capital formation in feudal society', in *The English peasantry in the later Middle Ages* (Oxford, 1975), pp. 174–214; pp. 198–200, 213.

[26] Miller, 'England in the twelfth and thirteenth centuries', p. 12. The high prices of foodstuffs bore profits for landlords and substantial holders, while a customary smallholding family had too little control over its yield to be able to enjoy it fully, Hilton, *The decline of serfdom*, pp. 24, 30–1.

[27] E. A. Kosminsky, *Studies in the agrarian history of England in the thirteenth century*, trans. R. Kisch (Oxford, 1956), pp. 216, 221–3 (including tables), see also Hallam, 'Thirteenth-century censuses', p. 342–4; on the fragmentation of holdings even of the Lincolnshire freeholders see *idem*, *Settlement and society. A study in the agrarian history of south Lincolnshire* (Cambridge, 1965), pp. 197–222. For calculations of subsistence needs in relation to size of holding see J. Z. Titow, *English rural society, 1220–1350*, London, 1969, pp. 78–82. On fragmentation of holdings and high activity in the peasant land market see D. G. Watts, 'A model for the early fourteenth century', *Economic history review* second ser. 20 (1967), pp. 543–7; pp. 543–4.

[28] For conclusive evidence within one manor see Razi, *Life, marriage and death*, pp. 28–32, Titow, 'Some evidence of the thirteenth century population increase', pp. 222–3. On the percentage of smallholders in the rural community see Poos, 'Population and resources in two fourteenth-century Essex communities', p. 93. On labour services owed by customary tenants in Leicestershire in the early fourteenth century see C. Howell, *Land, family and inheritance in transition: Kibworth Harcourt, 1280–1700* (Cambridge, 1983), pp. 22–4.

[29] For an example of the prevalence of starvation when harvests failed see the evidence of Berkshire rectors protesting against impositions in 1240: 'tum quia nonnunquam fames in regione ingruit, messe deficiente, tum quia tanta est multitudo pauperum et adventantium quorum mori partem vidimus pro defecto alimentorum', *Councils and synods* II part 1, ed. F. M. Powicke and C. R. Cheney (Oxford, 1964), p. 289. On the level of nutrition among smallholders see C. C. Dyer, 'English diet in the later Middle Ages', in *Social relations and ideas. Essays in honour of R. H. Hilton*, ed. T. H. Aston, P. R. Coss, C. Dyer and J. Thirsk (Cambridge, 1983), pp. 191–216; esp. pp. 203–5. An impression of the frequency of widespread crop failure and hunger in the Middle Ages can be gleaned from the evidence for Germany collected in

land over and above what was needed for their families' sustenance, however, were in a position to profit from the rising prices of produce (wool and foodstuffs).[30] In Fenland areas sources of income were more varied; dues and customary labours were also reflective of the needs of a Fenland economy.[31] Peasants could supplement their diet and income by fishing, harvesting hay crops in meadows and salt production, depending on the extent of freedom allowed by landlords.[32] East Anglia possessed a higher proportion of free tenants than other regions; their tenures were created in the period of robust expansion and reclamation in the twelfth and thirteenth centuries and they enjoyed more of the fruits of their produce and the rising prices which were paid for it, than other tenants did.

This interpretation of the evidence does not overlook the fact that the income of a peasant family was not confined to revenues from its holding. Agricultural wages supplemented many a family's income, while home industry and crafts were taken up during the winter months of slack agricultural routine.[33] However, the inadequacy of most smallholdings to supply subsistence gave rise to an almost unlimited supply of labour in agriculture and subsequently in the towns. If in the twelfth and in the early thirteenth centuries towns attracted men who could offer skills, services and some resources, later thirteenth-century migrants to the towns were mostly the rural poor seeking employment or, when that was not readily obtainable, charity.[34] This abundance of labour-power kept wages near subsistence level there, as well. At the most difficult stage of the crisis, when prices were highest, a multitude of rural and urban poor was experiencing a fall in nominal

F. Curschmann, *Hungersnöte im Mittelalter. Ein Beitrag zur deutschen Wirtschaftsgeschichte des 8. bis 13. Jahrhunderts* (Leipzig, 1900).

[30] East Anglia was rich in freeholders compared to other parts of England; in 1279 up to 40% of tenants were freeholders, Hilton, *The decline of serfdom*, pp. 18–19, but the majority were smallholders with below-subsistence holdings, H. E. Hallam, *Rural England 1086–1348* (Brighton, 1981), p. 62. For evidence of such fragmentation on the continent see G. Sivery, 'Herchier, un village du Hainaut (1267–1314)', *Revue du Nord* 52 (1970), pp. 309–24; p. 314 and Génicot, 'Sur le nombre des pauvres', p. 278.

[31] Customary labour included such activities as fishing and water carriage.

[32] H. C. Darby, *Medieval Cambridgeshire* (Cambridge, 1977), pp. 3–8, 28–32.

[33] M. M. Postan, *The famulus; the estate labourer in the twelfth and thirteenth centuries*, Economic history review supplement 2 (Cambridge, 1954).

[34] Miller, 'The English economy in the thirteenth century', p. 35; D. Herlihy, 'Population, plague and social change in rural Pistoia, 1201–1430', *Economic history review* second ser. 18 (1965), pp. 225–44; p. 226. In the market town of Evesham in 1322 50% of the burgesses carried place-name surnames indicating rural origin, R. H. Hilton, 'The small town and urbanisation – Evesham in the Middle Ages', *Midland history* 7 (1982), pp. 1–8, at pp. 3–4.

wages; the lowest real wages were earned in this period.[35] To these people hunger was a recurring experience.[36] Civic and ecclesiastical authorities were forced to deal with the problem, or at least to acknowledge its existence.[37] Yet one must acknowledge that only a part of the rural needy migrated, since even at the time of the worst indigence social, customary and family ties would have inhibited such mobility.[38]

The varying effects of the economic trends on different sectors of the population must be recognised. While the smallholders felt the pressure of rents, land prices, food prices and low wages most acutely, landlords and substantial holders derived advantage from the booming market and the high demand for all types of cereal. But even if the latter contributed to a steady demand for manufactured goods and services many of which were supplied by town labourers,[39] this would have led to an increase in demand for skilled, rather than for semi- or unskilled workers. As the rise of food prices affected the whole population, the sustained or even growing level of consumption by the prosperous could not fully counteract the ever growing availability of manpower created by the need for money wages. Thus, even if towns were continuing to expand until the end of the thirteenth century, they still accommodated a large pool of underemployed people,[40] the number of which might have started to fall by the second decade of the fourteenth century.

When the population trend changed it brought about major

[35] Bois reckons the early fourteenth century to have been the weakest stage of real wages in Normandy, Bois, *Crise du féodalisme*, p. 244.

[36] See the story of the theft of half a bushel of peas from a chaplain's barn by two girls in a year of great dearth, and the Jury's decision against action taken by the chaplain in revenge, *The assizes held at Cambridge, AD 1260*, ed. W. M. Palmer (Linton, 1930), p. 4.

[37] For an early example of action taken in a famine year, 1204, when great mortality prevailed, see the exhortation to bishops to encourage parish relief, 'ad subveniendum pro posse suo pauperibus parochianis suis et egenis ne fame pereant diligenter moneantur' in C. R. Cheney, 'Levies on the English clergy for the poor and for the King, 1203', *English historical review* 96 (1981), pp. 577–84, at pp. 580, 583.

[38] See for example the effect of some inheritance laws on motivation for movement B. Dodwell, 'Holdings and inheritance in medieval East Anglia', *Economic history review* second ser. 20 (1967), pp. 53–66; pp. 59–60. On some forms of customary provision for unproductive or weak members of peasant society see F. M. Page, 'The customary poor-law of three Cambridgeshire manors', *Cambridge historical journal* 3 (1929–31), pp. 125–33.

[39] Some perhaps by rural craftsmen or even from overseas.

[40] Underemployment and seasonal employment were constant realities for a large portion of medieval society. For useful definitions of categories of employment see A. K. Sen, *Employment, technology and development* (Oxford, 1975), *passim*; esp. pp. 3–10, 31–40.

repercussions. With greater availability of land, fewer people migrated to towns, which allowed wages there to rise. With fewer mouths to feed, poor lands could be turned into pasture or deserted,[41] while better lands impoverished by overcultivation could be left fallow to regain their vitality. Production per head rose, if only because there were more factors of production per head, while a downturn in the long-term trend of food prices set in, processes which were gradual and whose rate was affected by local factors.[42] Furthermore, there were attempts to arrest or counter the trends, through wage restriction and limitation of freedom of movement of manpower, and to maintain seigneurial rights which had not been exercised fully by more rigorous administration of manors.[43] Freedom of movement was also restricted by the exclusive claims of urban gilds and employers, but on the whole, population decline improved the standard of living of most people who tilled the land or who offered their labour. If setbacks such as the famines of 1315–22 caused prices to rise to fantastic heights, they also increased mortality, a fact which improved the lot of survivors.

This analysis is similarly applicable to the aftermath of the Black Death. Be it the bubonic plague, brought by infected rodents reaching England in August 1348 carrying the epidemic which had originated in the Asian steppes, or, as has been recently suggested, an anthrax epidemic,[44] the mortality was devastating. This is true even if we take the low estimate of 30% of the population dying.[45] Much more land was suddenly in need of cultivators, who were found among the ranks

---

[41] Cf. K. J. Allison, 'The lost villages of Norfolk', *Norfolk archaeology* 31 (1955–7), pp. 116–62.

[42] For indices of prices and wages see table 2.1.

[43] Hilton, *The decline of serfdom*, pp. 36–8. On the working of the Statute of Labourers see B. Putnam, *The enforcement of the Statute of Labourers during the first decade after the Black Death 1349–1359* (New York, 1908). On means of enforcement in Cambridgeshire see A. Way, 'Notices of the King's seals for passes given to labourers and servants', *Cambridge Antiquarian Society. Proceedings and communications* 1 (1851–9), pp. 280–6; for an analysis of the enforcement of the Statute see L. R. Poos, 'The social context of Statute of Labourers enforcement', *Law and history review* 1 (1983), pp. 27–72.

[44] G. Twigg believes that the pattern of the plague's progress in England, suits an anthrax epidemic better than the bubonic plague, G. Twigg, *The black death: a biological reappraisal* (London, 1984), pp. 54–89; esp. pp. 213–22.

[45] For a discussion of sources available for the assessment of mortality see Hatcher, *Plague, population and the English economy*, pp. 21–5. In Halesowen parish more than 40% of the population died in the Black Death, Razi, *Life, marriage and death*, pp. 101–7; in the Crowland Cambridgeshire manors peasant mortality has been estimated as 56%, F. M. Page, *The estates of Crowland abbey* (Cambridge, 1934), pp. 120–5. Mortality in towns was higher than in the countryside, R. S. Gottfried, *Epidemic disease in fifteenth century England* (New Brunswick, N.J., 1978), pp. 138–42. On mortality among the masters of the Hospital of St John, Cambridge, see below pp. 173–4.

of smallholders still searching for ways to enlarge their holdings.[46] The 1350s and 1360s knew some very bad harvests and visitations of the plague, which exacerbated the trend of high wages and, until the 1370s, of high prices.[47] An additional reason for improvement of the standard of living of survivors in a society suffering from recurrent plague and famine is that those first to succumb to the ravages of hunger and disease were most probably its poorer and more badly nourished members.[48] A further population check evolved since plague survivors developed physical immunity: thus the young were more vulnerable to recurring waves, while the aging and less fertile section of the population remained comparatively unharmed.[49] On the other hand, sons and daughters of peasant families could now marry at a younger age, since they could more easily acquire a home and a source of livelihood.[50]

The general fall in population and the alleviation of the struggle for subsistence was not a smooth and simple process. Periods of high mortality cause dislocation and temporary suspension of work routines.[51] Food scarcity due to lack of harvesters, untended fields and the collapse of communications rendered the process of recovery more difficult. A period of realignment and rectification of gaps in production and manufacturing was necessary, and several years might pass before

[46] In Halesowen all the land vacated due to the Black Death was taken up soon after 1349, Razi, *Life, marriage and death*, pp. 110–13; this in a time when buildings were still being abandoned, M. Mate, 'Agrarian economy after the Black Death: the manors of Canterbury cathedral priory 1348–91', *Economic history review* second ser. 37 (1984), pp. 341–54; pp. 341–2.

[47] *Ibid.*, pp. 347–51.

[48] On the connection between malnutrition and Black Death mortality see B. H. Slicher van Bath, *The agrarian history of western Europe*, trans. O. Ordish (London, 1963), p. 84; J. N. Biraben, 'Les pauvres et la peste', in Mollat, *Etudes* II, pp. 505–18; pp. 511–12; as well as E. Carpentier, *Une ville devant la peste: Orvieto et la peste noire de 1348* (Paris, 1962), pp. 153, 220; R. Baehrel, 'La haine de classe en temps d'épidémie', *Annales* 7 (1952), pp. 351–60; p. 352; also J. C. Russell, 'Effects of pestilence and plague 1315–1385', *Comparative studies in society and history* 8 (1965–6), pp. 464–73; p. 470. There is, however, no proof of direct influence of malnutrition on susceptibility to infection, rather the assumption that a generally deteriorated physical state would have lowered the body's resistance and the ability to cope with the sickness once contracted. For a broad general survey of the effects of the plague arising from recent research, see E. Carpentier, 'Autour de la peste noire: famines et épidémies dans l'histoire du XIVe siècle', *Annales* 17 (1962), pp. 1062–92.

[49] F. R. H. Du Boulay, *An age of ambition: English society in the late Middle Ages* (London, 1970), pp. 33–4. For a counter-argument based on modern plague data see Bean, 'Plague, population and economic decline', pp. 431–2.

[50] Razi, *Life, marriage and death*, pp. 135–8.

[51] On the effect of high mortality and wage behaviour see some discussion in H. Neveux, 'La mortalité des pauvres à Cambrai (1377–1473)', *Annales de démographie historique* (1968), pp. 73–97; p. 95.

a peasant could reap the full benefit of the new market forces.[52] In parallel, the adjustment of customary dues, rents and fines would spread over a number of years even in a situation where no group tried to arrest these natural developments. Even once land was plentiful, time was needed before a landless man, the potential tenant, could muster sufficient capital for entry and for investment. A shortage of capital undoubtedly denied some people the potential benefits of enlarged holdings, and it is hard to assess the degree to which the early fourteenth-century amelioration yielded sufficient comfort to allow robust expansion on the morrow of the plague. Attempts were made by landlords to cope with the momentous economic and demographic changes by negotiating short-term low-rent provisional tenancies in response to the sudden abundance of empty lands after the plague.[53] The existence of rent strikes in the fourteenth century reflects the attempts of landlords to counter the falling rents and the stronger bargaining power of their tenants.[54] Only in the 1370s was the full impact of the changes felt with the dismantling of demesnes and the farming of these quality lands for long terms.[55]

Opportunities in the countryside increased and sons of peasant families had favourable chances of acquiring holdings and continuing the traditional way of life.[56] However, not every villein could look for a drastic improvement, since lands tended to go to those who were already substantial owners and influential members of the village community.[57] But an enlargement of the average size of holdings did

[52] C. Howell sees the full expression of the effects of the post-plague economy in the 1420s; by then the favourable and purgative influence of population decline had been absorbed and the endemic plague was shattering a newly created stability, Howell, *Land, family and inheritance*, p. 47.

[53] See an example from the Aldborough section of the 1426–7 accounts of the Bailiwick of Knaresborough: 'de antiqua relaxatione redditus...facta...durantibus istis mediocribus annis quousque seculum emendetur'. In the case of the township of Clifton the *relaxatio* was made in 1384–5, PRO.DL29.465.7607 (this example has been given to me by E. Miller). In Kibworth Harcourt entry fines dropped immediately but Merton College resisted reduction in rents, Howell, *Land, family and inheritance*, p. 50.

[54] C. C. Dyer, 'A redistribution of incomes in fifteenth-century England?', *Past and present* 39 (1968), pp. 11–33; pp. 22–31. In the struggle against the landlords the tenants of Kibworth Harcourt were victorious, Howell, *Land, family and inheritance*, pp. 43–4, 51.

[55] *Ibid.*, p. 13; F. R. H. Du Boulay, 'Who were farming the English demesnes at the end of the Middle Ages?', *Economic history review* second ser. 17 (1964–5), pp. 443–55; pp. 443, 445; Bridbury, 'The black death', pp. 581, 584; Mate, 'Agrarian economy', pp. 352–4.

[56] On the return to land see A. R. Bridbury, 'English provincial towns in the later Middle Ages', *Economic history review* second ser. 34 (1981), pp. 1–24, at p. 4.

[57] Razi, *Life, marriage and death*, pp. 147–50. On internal ranking and conflicts of interest within peasant society see Poos, 'The social context of Statute of Labourers', *passim*.

occur, and conditions of tenure became more favourable. By the mid-fifteenth century whole demesnes were farmed out for long terms.[58] With a larger supply of land as a constant feature of the rural economy, rents fell and customary burdens virtually disappeared.[59] Greater freedom of movement between holdings, rationalisation of holdings and exchange emerged within and between villein communities.[60] On the whole, it seems that people remained on or returned to the land although many were attracted to those towns experiencing growth.[61] In spite of the eventual decline in seigneurial revenues and the diminishing of the purchasing power of the upper classes,[62] the general improvement of the standard of living of the majority of villeins and labourers and the growth in the number of substantial tenants[63] assured continuous demand for goods produced in towns, even if this demand was contracted in comparison with the thirteenth century.[64] A larger share of the profits of agricultural production were in the hands of farmers and labourers who were likely to spend the proceeds on the sort of goods which absorbed the energies of greater numbers of 'industrial' workers, giving a stimulus not to

[58] On the manors of the Canterbury See large-scale farming of the demesne was under way by 1400 and the whole demesne was farmed out by 1450, Du Boulay, 'Who were farming the English demesnes?', pp. 445–6. Admittedly, this process was by no means a straightforward one: owners of large estates oscillated between the two systems of management before, in most cases, deciding to farm out, as in the Canterbury estates in M. Mate, 'The farming out of manors: a new look at the evidence from Canterbury cathedral priory', *Journal of medieval history* 9 (1983), pp. 331–43; pp. 337–42. On farming out in the 1350s see Razi, *Life, marriage and death*, pp. 110–11.

[59] Postan, 'The fifteenth century', pp. 161–2; Hilton, *The decline of serfdom*, p. 32. Labourers were unwilling to waste their time on customary services and landlords were obliged to hire ploughmen and shepherds at market wages, N. Kenyon, 'Labour conditions in Essex in the reign of Richard II', *Economic history review* 4 (1934), pp. 429–51; pp. 431–2.

[60] *The decline of serfdom*, pp. 34–5.

[61] Such as York. Cf. J. N. Bartlett, 'The expansion and decline of York in the later Middle Ages', *Economic history review* second ser. 12 (1959–60), pp. 17–33.

[62] On the fall in revenues in the fifteenth century see J.-P. Genet, 'Economie et société rurale en Angleterre au xve siècle d'après les comptes de l'hôpital d'Ewelme', *Annales* 27 (1972), pp. 1449–71; pp. 1457–60. Although revenues fell as a whole, developments in estate management and efficiency could compensate for some of the losses as shown by A. J. Pollard, 'Estate management in the later Middle Ages: the Talbots and Whitchurch, 1383–1525', *Economic history review* second ser. 25 (1972), pp. 553–66; pp. 553–4.

[63] Hilton, 'Rent and capital formation in feudal society', p. 201. Substantial tenants tended to hold their land by a variety of titles: leasehold, copyhold, freehold etc., while traditional attributes of villeinage were becoming obsolete.

[64] Hatcher, *Plague, population and the English economy*, pp. 33–4. On the resilience of markets in the post-plague years see A. F. Butcher, 'Rent and the urban economy: Oxford and Canterbury in the later Middle Ages', *Southern history* 1 (1979), pp. 11–43; 42–3.

Table 2.1 *Indices of average national prices of wheat and of a carpenter's wages, 1301–1450*

Years	(1) Wheat-price index	(2) Phelps Brown index	(3) Nominal-wage index	(4) Real-wage index	(5) Wheat real-wage index
1301–1310	100.0	100.0	100.0	100.0	100.0
1311–1320	138.6	136.6	120.9	88.5	87.2
1321–1330	119.3	122.8	120.2	97.8	100.8
1331–1340	91.2	102.8	112.8	109.7	123.7
1341–1350	84.2	94.8	105.0	110.8	124.7
1351–1360	122.8	129.9	139.0	107.0	113.2
1361–1370	140.4	144.2	152.1	105.5	108.3
1371–1380	117.5	121.2	153.2	126.3	130.4
1381–1390	91.2	106.2	156.0	146.9	171.1
1391–1400	96.5	106.8	146.5	137.2	151.8
1401–1410	112.3	111.3	164.2	147.5	146.2
1411–1420	101.8	108.8	160.0	147.0	157.2
1421–1430	96.5	105.7	160.3	151.7	166.1
1431–1440	128.1	113.6	168.4	148.2	131.5
1441–1450	86.0	95.5	183.7	192.4	213.6

Sources:
Column (1) Ten year averages of wheat prices in s, from Hatcher, *Plague, Population and the English Economy*, p. 51, expressed as an index.
Column (2) Ten year averages were calculated from the data in Phelps Brown and Hopkins, 'Seven Centuries of the Prices of Consumables', pp. 311–12.
Column (3) = Ten year averages, from Hatcher, *ibid.*, p. 49.
Column (4) = Column (3)/Column (2)
Column (5) = Column (3)/Column (1)

the specialised highly skilled producer, but rather to the low-skilled mass-market.[65] It has also been argued that the post-plague mentality created a more consumer-oriented attitude in surviving generations.[66]

[65] This may explain some of the findings of A. R. Bridbury in connection with the buoyant industrial sector.
[66] H. A. Miskimin, 'Monetary movements and market structure: forces for contraction in fourteenth- and fifteenth-century England', *Journal of economic history* 24 (1964), pp. 470–90; pp. 486–90; F. E. Baldwin, *Sumptuary legislation and personal regulation in England* (Baltimore, Md, 1926), pp. 46–87. On post-plague mentality see the classic study of Italy, M. Meiss, *Painting in Florence and Siena after the Black Death* (Princeton, N.J., 1951), esp. pp. 70–93. At the same time it diminished investment and the spirit

Fourteenth-century price and wage data reflect the population trend and the changes in the standard of living. As seen in table 2.1, between 1301 and 1320 an extraordinary rise in prices occurred, largely due to monetary factors; but this rise contributed to the long-term trend since it added pressure for higher wages and it increased mortality.[67] After the peak of 1301–1320 prices on the whole fell and wages rose.[68]; the third quarter of the century apart, the price of a basket representative of consumption was falling.[69] The wage data for agricultural and skilled labourers show a rise in real wages in the early fourteenth century, after the decade of famines (1311–20), with fluctuations in the decade of the Black Death.[70] At the same time the price of wheat, though unstable in a century of frequent harvest failures, showed a general tendency for decline. The real wages of a carpenter expressed as the ratio of wages to wheat prices were higher compared with their initial level throughout the fourteenth century (see table 2.1.). The rise in real wages allowed an improvement in the standard of living of wage-earners. This must have contributed to the common view of labourers as living well and demanding excessive pay.[71]

In towns landless men could find high wages in spite of recurring

of entrepreneurship, as shown in a study of the mentality of Italian merchants in post-plague years, B. Z. Kedar, *Merchants in crisis. Genoese and Venetian men of affairs and the fourteenth-century depression* (New Haven, Conn., 1976).

[67] M. Mate, 'High prices in early fourteenth-century England: causes and consequences', *Economic history review* second ser. 28 (1975), pp. 1–16. On the monetary factor in the assessment of evidence for population decline see J. Schreiner, 'Wages and prices in England in the later Middle Ages', *Scandinavian economic history review* 2 (1954), pp. 61–73. See table 2.1.

[68] Mate, 'High prices', pp. 14–15.

[69] For the behaviour of prices and wages in this crucial period see E. H. Phelps Brown and S. V. Hopkins, 'Seven centuries of the prices of consumables, compared with builders' wage-rates', *Economica* 23 (1956), pp. 296–314. D. L. Farmer suggests an alternative basket of consumables to the one used in the Phelps Brown index, D. L. Farmer, 'Crop yields, prices and wages in medieval England', *Studies in medieval and Renaissance history* new ser. 6 (1983), pp. 115–55; pp. 123–7.

[70] The data collected by Lord Beveridge are conveniently presented in Hatcher, *Plague, population and the English economy*, p. 49.

[71] As in the vision of Piers the Plowman (version B *c.* 1377):

Laborers þat have no land to lyue on but hire handes
Deyned noȝt to dyne a day nyȝt olde wortes
May no peny ale hem paie, ne no pece of bacun,
But if it be fressh flessh ouþer fissh (y) fryed
And þat *chaud* and *plus chaud* for chillyinge of hir mawe.
But he be heiȝliche hyred ellis wole he chide;
(That) he was werkman wroȝt (warie) þe time

Piers the plowman: the B version, ed. G. Kane and E. T. Donaldson (London, 1975), Passus VI, lines 307–13, p. 367. On changes in the diet of peasants and agricultural labourers see Dyer, 'English diet', pp. 210, 213–16.

attempts to curb their rise;[72] however in rural areas plots of land remained the predominant source of livelihood. It is likely that in aggregate, there was a marked decrease in migration to towns by the beginning of the fourteenth century. The chronology of late thirteenth- and early fourteenth-century migration is not clear. Some towns restricted the inflow of labourers while others experienced difficulties in attracting immigrants of potential burgess status.[73] Most evidence connected with middle-sized towns in the late Middle Ages reflects depopulation, decline in enterprise and contraction of markets and exchange. This falls in with our knowledge of decline in rents and the appearance of waste or vacant holdings in the rentals of urban prop- erty owners.[74] The accumulation of arrears and decayed rents appears frequently in the rentals and accounts of corporate property holders such as Oseney, Oxford.[75] Even if some accounts recorded decayed rents and lost revenues in the hope of retrieving them in the future,[76] one cannot escape the impression of falling property values and high incidence of urban vacancies.[77] In such circumstances individual and middling non-corporate property owners would have been the first to feel the fall in demand and the burden of maintenance of vacant plots.[78] Corporate bodies, the holdings of which grew dramatically after the Black Death, could step in and consolidate holdings which townsmen no longer found a lucrative source of income.[79] Such holdings were constantly passing into their hands either

---

[72] See the behaviour of labourers' wages in Paris under the labour legislation of the fourteenth century, B. Geremek, *Le salariat dans l'artisanat parisien aux XIIIe-XVe siècles*, trans. A. Posner and C. Klapisch-Zuber (Paris and La Haye, 1968), p. 23.

[73] The royal settlement of Kingston-on-Hull was not attracting a sufficient number of people who could set themselves up in business, see *Selected rentals and accounts of medieval Hull, 1293-1528*, ed. R. Horrox (Leeds, 1981), pp. 5-8.

[74] Butcher, 'Rent and the urban economy', pp. 25-8, 42.

[75] A fall in rents and a rise in the frequency of vacancies appears in the Oxford rentals from around 1317 as studied by Butcher, *ibid.*, p. 24.

[76] Postan, 'The fifteenth century', p. 564. Some such hopes were proved to be justified, as in the case of the God's House, Southampton, *The cartulary of God's House, Southampton*, ed. J. M. Kaye (Southampton, 1976), p. lxix-lxx.

[77] This impression is supported by frequent contemporary statements in chronicles and ordinances as shown by R. B. Dobson, 'Urban decline in late medieval England', *Transactions of the Royal Historical Society* 5th ser. 27 (1977), pp. 1-22; p. 3. However, after a period of adjustment there seems to have been some recovery and a stabilisation of rents in the years after the Black Death, Butcher, 'Rent and the urban economy', pp. 30, 42.

[78] *Ibid.*, p. 43.

[79] Indeed, in the fifteenth century, the distribution of town properties was more polarised and tended to be in the hands of large religious houses and few large property owners, Hilton, 'Rent and capital formation', pp. 211-12.

by testamentary bequests to perpetual corporations (such as the town or religious houses),[80] or in exchange for large sums of money needed by burgesses for investment. By 1400, it seems, most urban properties were owned by religious houses,[81] hospitals becoming important proprietors.[82] The late fourteenth- and fifteenth-century countryside still needed the markets and services of towns. However, in this society, producers and consumers alike were less numerous even if they were for the most part more prosperous.[83] Thus, a period of realignment and contraction set in, in which the size of markets, towns, inhabited areas and parishes were adjusted to the new demands. This trend was countered in some areas by the development of industries, such as mining or textiles, or by playing a part in international trade.[84]

While towns were attracting labourers by high wages, men of consequence, owners of urban property, turned to the countryside where good land was available on long leases. This interest of substantial townsmen comes as no surprise; as they could no longer collect very high rents from town properties, they tried to obtain a foothold in the countryside free from seigneurial dominance.[85] But the question is one of balance; in the earlier period these men still maintained a great business and political interest in the towns, while their landed existence was more a way of acquiring prestige and providing a healthier environment for their families.[86] Even if higher numbers of admissions to the citizen body of some towns can be proved, this is by no means

[80] R. S. Gottfried, *Bury St. Edmunds and the urban crisis, 1290–1539* (Princeton, N.J., 1982), p. 186. Perpetual institutions have longer time horizons than individuals and could see ahead into a period of rising land prices.

[81] Hilton, 'Rents and capital formation', p. 211; Dobson, 'Urban decline in late medieval England', p. 18.

[82] Gottfried, *Bury St. Edmunds*, pp. 195–6.

[83] Miller, 'The English economy in the thirteenth century', p. 36.

[84] Some ports were resilient and show signs of prosperity and growth, Reynolds, *Introduction to the history of English medieval towns*, pp. 150–4; though others declined, like Hull and Boston. On the role of local industry in mitigating economic decline see J. Hatcher, 'A diversified economy: later medieval Cornwall', *Economic history review* second ser. 22 (1969), pp. 208–27; p. 226.

[85] Investment in land by very prosperous townsmen was not a new phenomenon. Late thirteenth- and fourteenth-century rich townsmen of Cambridge bought lands in the villages and even moved their households to the country for part of the year. See the case of Roger Harlston, *The west fields of Cambridge: terrarium Cantabrigiense*, ed. C. P. Hall and J. Ravensdale (Cambridge, 1976), p. 64.

[86] This wish persisted in the fifteenth century, S. Thrupp, *The merchant class of medieval London, 1300–1500* (Chicago, 1948), pp. 226–7. See also the purchasing activities of the burgesses of Bury St Edmunds, Gottfried, *Bury St. Edmunds*, pp. 138–42. For similar evidence in twelfth- and thirteenth-century York see E. Miller, *VCH. Yorkshire*, pp. 45–7. For an interpretation which sees the merchant class thriving in the fifteenth century see Bridbury, 'English provincial towns', p. 19.

a sign that the general urban population trend is one of growth. As R. B. Dobson has observed, the rising number of new citizens reflects a growing number of men who could afford the entrance fees to this status, rather than a general increase in population.[87] This expresses a transformation in the citizenry of late medieval towns and the distribution of power and wealth within it. More modest men, simple craftsmen, could join in through the prosperity of their earnings from manufacture,[88] but these were not men of capital or owners of large portions of town property who might have invested in and advanced the urban prospects.[89]

The new availability of land and the freer terms of tenure together with the eventual fall in the price of grain, initially reduced the aggregate incomes of landlords and allowed peasants to enlarge their holdings and their profits. The disintegration of demesnes meant that larger portions of landlords' incomes were in the form of cash, rather than a combination of service, rent and produce.[90] Changes in manorial management and in forms of exploitation of the soil followed the decline in prices of agricultural produce. When arable land was converted to pasture removal of farmers was easier, since many of the binding customary obligations had not entered the various fourteenth- and fifteenth-century agreements of land leasing.[91] New holdings were less secure than customary ones, and customary obligations had been greatly eroded over a century, to render a population more vulnerable to changes in landlords' prerogatives.[92] Shouldering more independent responsibilities coupled with the larger and freer tenures, pressures

---

[87] R. B. Dobson, 'Admissions to the freedom of the city of York in the later Middle Ages', *Economic history review* second ser. 26 (1973), pp. 16–21. The new trend in admissions has been discussed in Bridbury, *Economic growth*, pp. 58–9 and *idem*, 'English provincial towns', p. 12.

[88] In French and German towns this was strenuously opposed by the town patriciates, P. Dollinger, 'L'évolution politique des corporations strassbourgeoises à la fin du moyen-âge', in *Pages d'histoire. France et Allemagne médiévales. Alsace*, Paris, 1977, pp. 229–37; p. 232.

[89] Dobson, 'Urban decline in late medieval England', p. 13. On the decline in business enterprise and investment see Kedar, *Merchants in crisis*, pp. 85–90, 118–25. It is doubtful whether men under the level of master-craftsman could acquire the freedom of a town.

[90] F. R. H. Du Boulay, 'A rentier economy in the later Middle Ages: the archbishopric of Canterbury', *Economic history review* second ser. 16 (1963–4), pp. 427–38; p. 432. The portion of cash in revenues was rising until 1450, p. 437.

[91] Hilton, *The decline of serfdom*, p. 44. On the evolution of freer forms of tenure in the fourteenth and fifteenth centuries see Howell, *Family, land and inheritance*, pp. 51, 57; also Genet, 'Economie et société rurale', pp. 1461–2.

[92] For the discussion of the effect of this development in the sixteenth century see B. Geremek, 'La popolazione marginale tra il medioevo e l'era moderna', *Studi storici* 9 (1968), pp. 623–40; pp. 625–6.

created by the need for capital and of occasional insolvency would have caused some tenants to surrender their holdings, or to take up pasture-farming, favoured by landlords in the fifteenth century.[93] Conversely, greater freedom encouraged mobility and attempts to succeed in towns as artisans and small merchants. The records of a town such as Romney (Kent) show very active migration and immigration mainly to and from the immediate neighbourhood in the fifteenth century.[94] Migrants were by no means destitute, some came to town with money and with the desire to remain in contact with both town and countryside.

Employers identified workers as the source of their own economic plight. It was true that the decline in population left employers with only a diminished control over the working environment in town and country, which led to a lower level of profits. The decline in revenues was caused by higher wages and of lower customary payments and duties; the culprits were peasants and labourers whose standard of living had noticeably risen. These were now able to choose the length and the terms of their employment, and they could not easily be forced into tasks and contracts which were disadvantageous.[95] A vigorous image of the labourer as disrupter of social order, and as greedy and harmful to the general weal developed in this period when his services were most desperately needed.[96] However, this image did not only affect the relations between employers and labourers, it coloured a wider range of social relations and aspirations, since those traditionally of the labouring classes were associated with unproductivity, idleness, lawlessness, immorality and greed. From the Statute of Labourers of 1349 onwards unemployed healthy folk were presented as lazy and criminous: 'many able beggars, as long as they can live of alms-begging, refuse to work and laze in idleness and sins...thefts and deceit'.[97] Workers were accused of failing to fill an adequate working day or a full contract; instead they worked as much as necessary to keep body and soul together, shirking their social and religious obligations: 'and

---

[93] R. H. Hilton, 'A study in the pre-history of English enclosure in the fifteenth century', *Studi in onore di Armando Sapori* 1, ed. G. Sapori (Milan, 1957), pp. 673–85; p. 680 [repr. in *The English peasantry in the later Middle Ages* (Oxford, 1975)].

[94] A. F. Butcher, 'The origins of Romney freemen, 1433–1523', *Economic history review* second ser. 27 (1974), pp. 16–27; pp. 24–5.

[95] Kenyon, 'Labour conditions', pp. 429–31.

[96] B. Geremek, 'Criminalité, vagabondage, paupérisme: la marginalité à l'aube des temps modernes', *Revue d'histoire moderne et contemporaine* 21 (1974), pp. 337–75.

[97] 'multi validi mendicantes, quandiu possent ex mendicantis elemosinis vivere, laborare renuunt, vacando ociis et peccatis...latrociniis et aliis fiduciis', Putnam, *The enforcement of the Statute of Labourers*, p. 11*.

they say that due to the high daily wages which they are accustomed to receive they work only two days a week '.[98] Even in this period when the lot of labourers was improving, those who lived a precarious existence on the verge of subsistence, the *paupérisables* – workers and their families, dependants, and those unsuitably skilled – were affected by the shift in attitude on the part of those who were employers, and who were the traditional givers of charity.[99] Now the poor were not to be helped but to be hunted down and put back to work, or into prison[100] since they had no place within society and did not merit enjoyment of its benefits.[101] They did not only cause a shortage of labour but defied social morality:

for they lyue in no loue, ne no lawe holden;
Ne weddeth none wymmen. þat they with deleth,
Bringeth forth bastardus, beggares of kynde.[102]

French royal labour legislation was as recurrent as the English and far more violent.[103] Similar legislation was enacted in the Italian cities; Venice prohibited begging in the late fourteenth century and Genoa expelled beggars in the fifteenth century.[104] The fifteenth century saw the foundation of municipal hospitals in Italian towns whose main aim was the enclosure of poor unproductive folk in a framework of punitive correction.[105] Spanish royal legislation forced arrested idlers to work for periods without payment.[106]

Labour legislation attempted to alleviate the acute shortage of working hands and to increase the employers' control over terms of employment. Most cases tried by the Justices of Labourers dealt with

[98] 'et dient que pour le grant pris des journées qu'il ont accoutumés de prendre, que il ne ouvriront la sepmaine que deux jours', Geremek, 'La renfermement', p. 231.

[99] W. P. Blockmans and W. Prevenier, 'Poverty in Flanders and Brabant from the fourteenth to the mid-sixteenth century: sources and problems', *Acta historiae neerlandicae* (1977), pp. 20–57; p. 23.

[100] *Memorials of London and London life*, ed. H. T. Riley (London, 1868), p. 390 (1375).

[101] When Piers the Plowman obtained a Pardon for humanity it was clear that: 'Beggeres [and] bidderes. beþ nogt in e bulle', *Piers the plowman: the B version*, Passus VII, line 65, p. 373.

[102] *Piers the plowman: an edition of the C text*, ed. D. Pearsall (London, 1978), Passus IX, lines 167–8, p. 187. For a similar accusation in a French royal ordinance of 1354 see Geremek, 'La renfermement', p. 231. For a full discussion of attitudes to poverty in this period, see below chapter 3.

[103] *Ibid.*, pp. 230–6.

[104] On measures of repression by towns see D. M. Nicholas, 'Crime and punishment in fourteenth century Ghent', *Revue belge de philologie et d'histoire* 48 (1979), pp. 289–334, 1141–76; p. 307; J.-C. Schmitt, *Mort d'une hérésie* (Paris, 1978), pp. 188–9, 191–2.

[105] Geremek, 'Renfermement des pauvres', pp. 205–17; pp. 207–17; see also *idem*, 'Criminalité', p. 372. [106] *Ibid.*, p. 347.

manual labourers and with premature departure from employment.[107] Annual commissions of Justices were nominated in each county, chosen from wealthy burgesses and gentry.[108] In the countryside it was not only the great landlords who inspired and enforced the legislation but rather the new class of substantial tenants. These men enjoyed strong positions within the village and township communities; they were men who had greatly profited from the disintegration of demesnes after the Black Death and had stepped into the newly available land as well as positions of administration and policing.[109] They lived within the tenant community and were advantageously placed both to track down recalcitrant labourers and to enforce the power of the statute on them.[110] Landowners' fears were aggravated as the ordinances failed to restore an abundant supply of labour, and their anxieties were eloquently transformed into petitions to parliament which subsequently evolved into legislation.[111] If charity depends on the existence of spare funds which can be put to communal use and conspicuous consumption, then the late medieval society felt less equipped to do so. At the same time, the numbers of unemployed or underemployed were falling, in a world which had developed an acute shortage of labour. However, the period of change and disruption following a period of acute pauperisation of some groups in towns and countryside had seriously affected attitudes and relations between potential givers and recipients. So much so that even a diminished demand for charity was less likely to be met by townsfolk and landlords, those active relievers of the thirteenth century. The changes in the factors of the charitable equation will now be examined in the capabilities and activities of Cambridge folk.

ECONOMIC AND SOCIAL CHANGE IN MEDIEVAL CAMBRIDGE

Medieval Cambridgeshire was an area of comparatively dense and old settlement, where the pressure of population growth was acutely felt

---

[107] Putnam, *The enforcement of the Statute of Labourers*, p. 175.

[108] See nomination of Justices for Cambridge in *Calendar of patent rolls 1348–50*, p. 526 (1350); *Calendar of patent rolls 1350–54*, p. 509 (1353); *Calendar of patent rolls 1354–58*, p. 424 (1356), p. 554 (1357); *Calendar of patent rolls 1358–61*, p. 151 (1358).

[109] On this group see Razi, *Life, marriage and death*.

[110] Poos, 'The social context of Statute of Labourers', pp. 30–5.

[111] For the Statute of Cambridge (1388) and the background for its promulgation see J. A. Tuck, 'The Cambridge parliament, 1388', *English historical review* 84 (1969), pp. 225–43; pp. 228–37.

in the twelfth and thirteenth centuries.[112] As its settlement and the process of reclamation began earlier than in many regions it had a comparatively high proportion of freeholders within its tenant population. Heavy customary obligations burdened the villeins, while the fragmentation of holdings was acute.[113] A higher demand for manufactures and services as well as for food was another consequence of the growth of population, which raised the incomes of lords and substantial tenants alike. Thus, a greater level of exchange prevailed in the economy, markets thrived in small towns and even in villages. For a while, the extensive cultivation and high yields of the Cambridgeshire uplands producing wheat, barley, rye and meslin held good profits in store for those exporting grains to the London region.[114] On a lower level, less specialised rural markets filled the needs of agricultural labourers and of peasant households for manufactured goods.[115] In Cambridgeshire, rural markets such as those of Linton, Whittlesford, Burwell, Swavesey, Wilbraham, Eltisley and Caxton abounded.[116] Thus, it is not surprising to find great resilience in these markets during the thirteenth century despite the fall in production per head. Landlords were reaping high profits from their extended demesnes and from rents; substantial tenants were benefiting from the rising prices of their produce and, more crucially, a greater part of peasant produce was sold to obtain the coin needed for the payment of higher dues.

Cambridge was one of the most important centres for marketing

[112] Cambridgeshire was one of the most densely populated counties, Miller and Hatcher, *Medieval England*, p. 144.

[113] *Ibid.*, pp. 122–3, 145. On the Cambridgeshire estates of Crowland abbey almost half of tenant-holdings were under 5 acres, Page, *The estates of Crowland abbey*, pp. 84–7.

[114] N. S. B. Gras, *The evolution of the English corn market from the twelfth to the eighteenth century* (New York, edn of 1967), pp. 42–55. On the response to the economic pressures of the thirteenth and fourteenth centuries in the field of agricultural management and planning see B. M. S. Campbell, 'Agricultural progress in medieval England: some evidence from eastern Norfolk', *Economic history review* second ser. 36 (1983), pp. 26–46.

[115] On the development of markets see R. H. Britnell, 'The proliferation of markets in England 1200–1349', *Economic history review* second ser. 34 (1981), pp. 209–21, the peak period of market foundation was in 1250–75, p. 210.

[116] Miller and Hatcher, *Medieval England*, p. 76. On the basis of tax returns Cambridgeshire could be described as a middling–prosperous county throughout the later Middle Ages: Schofield, 'The geographical distribution of wealth in England, 1334–1649', p. 506. Table 1 in J. F. Hadwin, 'The medieval lay subsidies and economic history', *Economic history review* second ser. 36 (1983), pp. 200–17; p. 215, reinforces this observation by showing that the extent of fall in the valuation of Cambridgeshire for lay subsidies was close to the general county average. On Linton see J. H. Clapham, 'A thirteenth-century market town: Linton, Cambridgeshire', *Cambridge historical journal* 4 (1932–4), pp. 194–202.

of agricultural surplus in East Anglia.[117] Corn was shipped down the river, and thence to London, as part of the busy trade between London and the ports of northern East Anglia.[118] Built on a convenient bend in the river, with its royal castle, the town served its hinterland and beyond. Its fair at Stourbridge was founded in the twelfth century and later developed into a centre of international renown.[119] Though its academic standing drew the interest of scholars, Cambridge remained primarily a medium-sized market town.

The University entered Cambridge life soon after 1200 and influenced its fortunes in various ways. The influx of students seeking lodging, food, clothes, books and services brought with it a great demand for almost every commodity that the townsmen could offer. It is difficult to assess the number of scholars residing in Cambridge in the Middle Ages. It has been recently suggested that in the second half of the fourteenth century there were up to 700 students, and that by the late fifteenth century the number approached 1300.[120] Burgesses stood to gain from the greater turnover in their businesses, from letting accommodation, from feeding, clothing and serving a population which was a source of imported consumption from other regions of England.[121] The University soon received privileges and greatly restricted the scope of profit by limiting prices of grain, ale and lodging,[122] and clamped down on the takings of other traders through

---

[117] Besides Bury and Norwich, E. Miller, *The abbey and bishopric of Ely* (Cambridge, 1951), pp. 84–5. On Cambridge as an economic and administrative centre see H. M. Cam, *Liberties and communities in medieval England. Collected studies* (Cambridge, 1933, repr. 1963), p. 19. The first charter instituting a *gilda mercatoria* was granted by King John in 1201, *The charters of the borough of Cambridge (Henry I–1685)*, ed. and trans. F. W. Maitland and M. Bateson (Cambridge, 1901), pp. 4–6.

[118] On the water traffic between King's Lynn, Cambridge and London see *The making of King's Lynn. A documentary survey*, ed. D. M. Owen (London, 1984), pp. 49–50.

[119] This is surely true by the sixteenth century, *Charters of the borough of Cambridge*, p. 97. The fair which was originally granted to the lepers of St Mary Magdalene's hospital at Stourbridge was held by the town by the early fourteenth century. On the fair's history see *VCH. Cambridgeshire* III, pp. 92–4. The fair was originally granted by King John to the leper community at Stourbridge, see below pp. 112,117.

[120] Aston, Duncan and Evans, 'The medieval alumni of the university of Cambridge', pp. 13, 14–19. This number includes the religious, a considerable part of the student population.

[121] For the distribution of Cambridge students by geographic origin see *ibid.*, pp. 28–34, esp. pp. 29–30; in the fourteenth and fifteenth century more than half of the student body originated from the dioceses around Cambridge: Ely, Norwich and London. On funding and patronage of students see *ibid.*, pp. 40–51.

[122] From 1231 the supervision of prices of accommodation and foodstuffs in Cambridge was entrusted to a committee of two burgesses and two regent masters, *Calendar of close rolls 1227–31*, pp. 586–7. The well-known *taxatio* of 1246 is the oldest surviving

its jurisdiction over marketing, pricing and distribution.[123] The presence of the scholars, though, must have always played an important role in the town's economy well into the fifteenth century, by fostering additional consumption. Until the mid-fifteenth century a majority of Cambridge scholars still lodged in University Halls and rented accommodation, and were direct consumers in the Cambridge market.[124] Even with the advent of the academic colleges, no serious change in the economic influence of the body of scholars on the town took place, as the endowed colleges did not usually draw on their estates for the provision of foodstuffs.[125] Being fairly large-scale consumers they could procure more advantageous terms, buy in bulk, and purchase at great fairs and markets leaving a lower margin of profit to traders and middlemen. Colleges were few throughout most of the period under study; in the late fifteenth century a great wave of building connected with the foundation of three new colleges transformed depopulated tenements and provided employment for many craftsmen.[126]

The fortunes of modest towns like Cambridge were especially closely linked to their hinterland.[127] As we have seen above, twelfth- and thirteenth-century reclamation and growth allowed the development of a class of freeholders, especially in newly assarted land, with fewer burdens and a greater freedom to sell, exchange and market its produce, holding or labour. A middling class of holders was thus created, people who constituted a lower-privileged group in the feudal

document: M. B. Hackett, *The original statutes of Cambridge university. The text and its history* (Cambridge, 1970), pp. 55–6 (n.2), 86.

[123] A privilege divided the responsibility and the profits from such control between the chancellor and the sheriff, CUL. University archives, Luard *8, *51. University control grew after the Peasants' Revolt of 1381.

[124] A. B. Cobban, 'Origins: Robert Wodelarke and St. Catharine's', in *St. Catharine's college, Cambridge, 1473–1973*, ed. E. E. Rich (Leeds, 1973), pp. 1–32; pp. 27–8; also W. A. Pantin, 'The halls and schools of medieval Oxford: an attempt at reconstruction', in *Oxford studies presented to Daniel Callus* (Oxford, 1964), pp. 31–100; pp. 31, 34 and T. H. Aston and R. Faith, 'The endowments of the university and colleges *circa* 1348', in *The history of the University of Oxford* I, ed. J. I. Catto (Oxford, 1984), pp. 265–309; pp. 286–7.

[125] Cf. T. H. Aston, 'The external administration and resources of Merton college to *circa* 1348', in *The history of the University of Oxford* I, ed. J. I. Catto (Oxford, 1984), pp. 311–68; pp. 359–64. Like most big landlords colleges moved to farming out by the fifteenth century, and thus reduced the likelihood of reliance even on the very limited supplies which were provided by their manors, R. L. Storey, 'The foundation and the medieval college 1379–1530', in *New College Oxford, 1379–1979*, ed. J. Buxton and P. Williams (Oxford, 1979), pp. 3–43; p. 10.

[126] This is pointed out in Dobson, 'Urban decline', p. 14.

[127] On the degrees of urbanisation coexisting in the thirteenth century see Hilton, 'Small town society in England before the Black Death', pp. 56–7.

setting, and who provided the rank of demesne officials with the shift of many estates to demesne farming *c.* 1200.[128] Pressures on the feudal nobility also induced subinfeudation and the devolution of property downwards.[129] These middling knights and substantial tenants were involved not only in the exploitation of their own lands but also in the disposal of surplus produce, and often of that of their lords' manors. Thus, they had interests both in the rural community and in the growing towns through their double interest in agricultural production and feudal manorial administration on the one hand, and in distribution and trade, on the other.[130] The records of the 1177 amercement and some thirteenth-century town tallages reflect the sources of burgess recruitment to Cambridge.[131] Most surnames in the list of burgesses of 1177 were toponyms of origin: de Len, de Ponte, de Cantebrige, de Welle, de Froisselake, de Cestertone, de Dittone, de Exninga, de Swaveshed;[132] some were names of the lower feudal families of the county: Ruffus, le Brun, de Bradeleya.[133] The returns for tallages imposed on the burgesses of Cambridge in 1211 and in 1219 allow an interesting acquaintance with active burgesses.[134] In these years occupational names were much more common than in the previous list: *mercator*, *piscator*, *tanator*, fitter, gaunter, tailor, *faber*, comber.[135]

---

[128] A whole cadre of bailiffs, officials, reeves with dealings on the estates and in market towns emerged; see Miller, 'England in the twelfth and thirteenth centuries', p. 10.

[129] Miller and Hatcher, *Medieval England*, pp. 170–1; S. Raban, *The estates of Thorney and Crowland: a study in medieval monastic land tenure* (Cambridge, 1977), pp. 33–5.

[130] On this 'double origin' of the patriciate of thirteenth-century towns see A. B. Hibbert, 'The origins of the medieval town patriciate', *Past and present* 3 (1953), pp. 15–27. Also R. H. Hilton, 'Some problems of urban real property in the Middle Ages', in *Socialism, capitalism and economic growth*, ed. C. H. Feinstein (Cambridge, 1967), pp. 326–37; p. 326.

[131] *Pipe roll 23 Henry II* (London, 1905), pp. 183–5.

[132] On the significance of the *de* prefix to surnames as a sign of recent arrivals to the town see J. A. Raftis, 'Geographical mobility in lay subsidy rolls', *Mediaeval studies* 38 (1976), pp. 385–403; p. 386.

[133] The use of surnames as evidence in studies of population growth and mobility is fraught with dangers. In the thirteenth century people were still often known by more than one name: a place-name surname, an occupational name and/or a patronym, and a name could refer to a man's father as well as to himself. Such dangers have been kept in mind throughout the study of the Cambridge evidence. For other cautious remarks related to the study of surnames see P. McClure, 'Patterns of migration in the late Middle Ages: the evidence of English place-name surnames', *Economic history review* second ser. 32 (1979), pp. 167–82; pp. 168–73.

[134] *Pipe Roll 13 John* (London, 1953), pp. 100–3; *Pipe roll 3 Henry III* (London, 1976), pp. 68–70.

[135] As M. M. Postan has observed, many thirteenth-century occupational names were related to victualling and cloth and clothes manufacturing, M. M. Postan, *The medieval economy and society* (Harmondsworth, 1975), p. 202; for a similar occupational distribution in a small town see Hilton, 'Small town society in England', pp. 60–2.

The tallages report the portions paid by individual burgesses towards the whole contribution and can provide us with a view of the distribution of wealth within the group as presented with the other tallages in table 2.4.[136] As we see there, some 20% of the burgesses (24 men in 1211) held almost half of the wealth in Cambridge. The distribution is not highly polarised in the middle sections of burgess society, but greater differences must have existed, as in the thirteenth century some men held large landed estates in the Cambridge fields and in the surrounding villages, adding to their wealth and prestige. One can say, then, that among thirteenth-century Cambridge burgesses there were a handful of rich and influential members, but that on the whole the distribution of wealth, and thus of power, was graded. It allowed the coexistence of 'great', 'middling' and 'small' men.[137]

A growing body of men with interests both in town and country, together with a group of artisans and traders based in the town providing and distributing the manufactured goods, formed the patriciate of thirteenth-century towns.[138] The striking feature is that of continuity and connection with the rural environment rather than of greatly differing orientation and interests. These, undoubtedly, developed through time, yet it is a telling fact that some of the people of highest standing in early thirteenth-century Cambridge were not highly taxable in moveables or in town properties. Their names, nonetheless, appear on hundreds of deeds, and their influential standing was undisputed.[139] As Maitland noted, great men like Baldwin Blancgernon and the mayor Harvey Dunning did not enter the highest tax brackets.[140] This discrepancy between their apparent and actual wealth is reflected in the fact that both men were obliged to mortgage lands to the Jews and sell properties to religious houses in order to maintain themselves.[141] This group of leading burgesses with a foothold in the town and another in the surrounding manors, is the backbone of religious patronage in small and large towns all over thirteenth-century Europe. Capital and human resources were drawn

---

[136] See below p. 45.
[137] Cf. on the social composition of Halesowen, Hilton, 'Small town society in England', pp. 67–9, 73–7; on the *continuum* of degrees of wealth and lack of polarisation in thirteenth-century towns see also Hilton, 'Rents and capital formation', pp. 208–11.
[138] On the formation of the patriciate and on the sources of power among the burgesses of Bury, see Gottfried, *Bury St. Edmunds*, pp. 132–3.
[139] As in most witness-lists of thirteenth-century charters of donation to the Hospital of St John, Cambridge and to St Radegund's Priory, Cambridge.
[140] F. W. Maitland, *Township and borough* (Cambridge, 1898), p. 168.
[141] See below pp. 218–9.

into the towns which became the new homes of men involved in trade, artisanry and industry.[142]

As the century unfolded, more and more impoverished people were attracted to the town with the contraction of opportunities in the countryside. The town would have drawn the majority of its migrants from settlements within a distance of 10 miles.[143] As in other medieval towns, in addition to the leading citizens, who by the mid-thirteenth century included many town-born men who had no rural links, and to middling burgesses involved in small trade and artisanry, there must have been a growing multitude of unskilled labourers, underemployed or unemployed, servants, poor widows, sick and unemployable folk whose lot deteriorated throughout the century.[144] Within this group of unproductive people whose survival depended on external help a distinction can be drawn between local poor and passing or newly arrived poor.[145] The latter enjoyed only weak social links within the community and could expect little benefit from the established forms of charity which were largely directed at parish poor, neighbours and fellow-artisans.[146] Their lack of connections and of burgess standing would have rendered the finding of secure employment very difficult; it would also have denied them access to the favourable terms of leases for accommodation.[147]

In 1278 workers employed for repairs of the castle earned the wages shown in table 2.2. These wages were paid for a five-day week,[148] and when two feast days fell in one week one day's pay was reduced from the weekly wage.[149] It is true that workers could find some casual

---

[142] Hibbert, 'The origins of the medieval town patriciate', p. 25. Well-to-do craftsmen and property owners were the core of mid-thirteenth century burgess communities, such as Cambridge, see *The west fields of Cambridge*, p. 64.

[143] McClure, 'Patterns of migration in the late Middle Ages', pp. 175, 177.

[144] Miller, 'The English economy in the thirteenth century', p. 35. For evidence of pressure of immigrants on the borough and for the entry of 'undesirable' elements see Hilton 'Small town society in England', pp. 63–5, 73–4.

[145] For this distinction, observed for the late Middle Ages, see Geremek, 'La popolazione marginale tra il medioevo e l'era moderna', p. 624.

[146] See below pp. 237–45, 267–9.

[147] Much urban property was held from religious houses, most of which was leased to burgesses and rented to labourers and artisans on a short-term insecure basis, *The cartulary of God's House, Southampton*, p. lxvi.

[148] These seem to be highly representative wages; see D. Knoop and G. P. Jones, *The mediaeval mason* (Manchester, third edn., 1967), p. 110 for wages of London builders in the same period.

[149] Knoop and Jones, *The mediaeval mason*, pp. 106–7. For wage material see *Accounts of the fabric of Exeter cathedral, 1279–1326 1*, ed. A. M. Erskine (Torquay, 1981), pp. 175–211. The wages on the whole are quite stable, though this is not surprising as terms for such a large project must have been negotiated in advance. Additionally, life-cycle

Table 2.2 *Wages earned by workers on repairs of Cambridge castle, 1278 for a working week (in d)*

Occupation	Wage per working day	Average earning per day
Master mason	6.0	4.3
Mason labourer	3.6	2.6
Tiler	4.8	3.4
Tiler's man	2.4	1.7
Stonecutter	3.6	2.6
Bricklayer	1.7	1.2
Whitewasher	3.2	2.3
Whitewasher's boy	2.0	1.4

Source: W. M. Palmer, 'Cambridge castle building accounts', *Cambridge antiquarian society. Proceedings and communications* 26 (1923/4), pp. 66–89; pp. 71–2, and own calculations.

employment on their free day, and some probably did, which would raise the earnings per day. There must also have been a second source of income in many families, from women's and children's labour. On the other hand, in the winter working days were shorter and wages lower just when expenditure on food, clothes and heating was at its zenith.[150] In these years 1d per day was considered the very lowest sum for the maintenance of a poor man, as given in directives for distribution at funerals (a day's wages) and in calculations of expenses for the support of poor in charitable houses.[151] If a labourer who had some dependants earned the sums that semi-skilled workers did in

effects would influence the careers and wages of individuals. John Lolleworth, a mason, was hired over a long period, and his earnings in the first week of Michaelmas term: were

1299–1300	1s 10d *ibid.*, p. 175.
1301–2	1s 10d *ibid.*, p. 178.
1306–7	1s 11d *ibid.*, p. 182.
1308–9	2s *ibid.*, p. 185.
1312–13	2s *ibid.*, p. 191.

Florentine gardeners and masons worked 260–5 days a year in the early fourteenth century. For information on their wages see de La Roncière, 'Pauvres et pauvreté à Florence', pp. 673–85.

[150] This was the wage-behaviour in Paris as well, Geremek, *Le salariat dans l'artisanat parisien*, p. 92.

[151] The daily expense for the maintenance of Oxford converts by the Domus Conversorum in London in 1242 was 1½d, C. Roth, *The Jews of medieval Oxford* (Oxford, 1951), p. 148; 1d was given to each poor person attending the funeral of Bishop Gravesend in London in 1303, *Account of the executors of Richard bishop of London, 1303 and of the executors of Thomas bishop of Exeter, 1310*, ed. W. H. Hale and H. T. Ellacombe (London, 1874), p. 100; see also *ibid.*, p. 23 for similar distributions in 1310. See also the monastic

Cambridge in 1278 it is easy to see how very difficult it must have been even with supplementary earning of a spouse (women generally earned lower wages than men). Even the combined income of a bricklayer, earning 1.2d per day, and his wife, would only have amounted to no more than some 2d per day, on which the family would have found it most difficult to manage.[152] In any case employment was by no means assured, and the medieval labour market was constantly shifting according to season and weather.[153] As has been noted above, skilled craftsmen suffered less from the excess labour supply, since this supply consisted of a greater portion of unskilled and semi-skilled working hands than of master craftsmen.

With an improvement in the conditions of life experienced by peasants in the fourteenth century, changes in the fortunes of urban labourers set in. Poor lands were abandoned and more good land was available to allow for the growth of average peasant holdings. By 1341 lands had been abandoned in 36 of 139 Cambridgeshire parishes.[154] It is reasonable to assume that all other circumstances being equal, peasants would, on the whole, prefer to take up holdings and earn more in the country rather than migrate to the town to earn a comparable living even if they had the skills to do so.[155] All these factors combined would have relieved the pressure on towns in the beginning of the century and would have contributed to the further intensification in the need for working hands.

The fourteenth-century tax returns for the borough of Cambridge can be used to discern the changing fortunes of some of its burgesses. Lists exist for the subsidies of 1314–15 (fifteenths), 1327 (twentieths) and 1341 (ninths).[156] In 1304 a tallage was imposed on the burgesses in

distribution of a penny per pauper by the monks of Worcester priory on Maundy Thursday, *Liber elemosinarii: the almoner's book of the priory of Worcester*, ed. J. H. Bloom (Oxford, 1911), pp. 5–6.

[152] Miller and Hatcher, *Medieval England*, pp. 58–9. The average size of rural households in this period has been calculated as 4.5–5.2, J. Krause, 'The medieval household: large or small?', *Economic history review* second ser. 9 (1956–7), pp. 420–32; p. 432. In Italy urban households were on average some 20% larger than rural ones, D. Herlihy and C. Klapisch-Zuber, *The Tuscans and their families: a study of the Florentine Catasto of 1427*, New Haven, Conn., 1984.

[153] Knoop and Jones, *The mediaeval mason*, pp. 104–5, 110–11.

[154] A. R. H. Baker, 'Evidence in the "Nonarum inquisitiones" of contracting arable lands in England during the early fourteenth century', *Economic history review* second ser. 19 (1966), pp. 518–32; 525 (description of Cambridgeshire in *Nonarum inquisitiones*, pp. 201–18).

[155] Postan, 'Some economic evidence', p. 230. Town wages, even in the post-plague years, were never much higher than agricultural ones.

[156] *1314*: PRO.E179.81/5, transcribed in *Cambridge gild records, 1298–1389*, ed. M. Bateson (Cambridge, 1903), pp. 151–7; *1327* transcribed by J. J. Muskett in *East anglian new*

royal towns but the factor levied on wealth is not known,[157] a progressive element may have existed in the assessment for it.[158] One cannot use the 1304 returns for calculation of mean wealth but they will be partially presented with the other findings, although not entered into the analysis.[159] Medieval tax returns are full of pitfalls for those seeking economic valuations since they did not record the whole population and the size of the untaxed population is unknown.[160] Within the taxed group the tax returns did not reflect the relative standing of individuals fully, as it was levied on moveable property only; the wealth of those rich in real estate would be under-represented. In comparing the subsidy returns for different years one assumes that the extent of evasion and of false reporting of income and mistaken calculations by the *taxatores* is more or less constant.[161] Since the system of collection of subsidies did not greatly change until 1334, and the subsidy of 1341 in Cambridge was collected in the old way, this assumption seems possibly to be justified. However, the findings, if significant, represent a trend, and will not supply us with definitive measurements.

The tax returns have been manipulated so as to provide the full value of moveables corresponding to the tax assessment returned.[162] Since we are dealing with a quarter of a century which might have seen

ser. 12 (1907–8), pp. 88–90, 106–8; *1341* PRO.E179.81/18 in *Nonarum inquisitiones*, pp. 416–18. However, J. F. Hadwin suggests that the very reason for preservation of lists of contributions by burgesses might have been the necessity to check them on grounds of inadequacy of the returns, Hadwin, 'The medieval lay subsidies', pp. 202–3.

[157] From comparison to other subsidy returns it seems to have been around 10%.

[158] See table 2.4 where the tallage is compared with other years. A far larger tax rate seems to have been exacted from the richest burgesses.

[159] Many thanks are due to Mr David Gleave who offered advice and help in connection with the Cambridge economy and particularly on the subject of lay subsidies. He has made available for my use his tabulation of the returns for the tallage of 1304. Mr Gleave's transcript of the returns accompanied by an introduction and notes are forthcoming in a volume of the Cambridge Antiquarian Records Society.

[160] On personal taxation in the late Middle Ages see J. F. Willard, *Parliamentary taxes on personal property 1290 to 1334: a study in medieval English financial administration* (Cambridge, Mass., 1934), *passim*. The value of minimal taxable wealth was usually decided by parliament, *ibid.*, pp. 87–8.

[161] There is evidence to suggest that the higher the tax rate the higher the degree of evasion. By this argument the degree of evasion would have been highest in 1341 followed by 1314 and 1327, *ibid.*, pp. 343–4. For objections to this working assumption see Hadwin, 'The medieval lay subsidies', pp. 200, 210–11.

[162] This was done by multiplying by the factors corresponding to the fraction of wealth levied (1314 – fifteenth, 1327 – twentieth, 1341 – ninth). Henceforth 'wealth' will be used to mean the moveable wealth valued for the subsidies. In addition, the wealth of religious houses: Barnwell priory, St Radegund's priory and the Hospital of St John have been excluded from all calculation due to their extraordinary size and their existence outside the circle of burgesses.

Table 2.3 *Characteristics of tax returns in Cambridge, 1314, 1327 and 1341*

Years	1314	1327	1341
Tax rate	1/15	1/20	1/9
Number of payers	466	273	422
Wealth threshold[a]	10s 0d	12s 1d	4s 6d
Wealth threshold adjusted by 1310–14 index	10s 0d	10s 9d	5s 8½d
Mean wealth	£1 17s 11d	£1 12s 5d	17s 1d
Mean wealth adjusted by 1310–14 index[a]	£1 17s 11d	£1 9s 2d	£1 1s 8d

[a] Adjusted by the average price index for 1310–14, 1327: 112.1; 1341: 78.9, calculated from the Phelps Brown data.

dramatic changes in prices, and which knew several years of famine, it seemed necessary to adjust the mean values of wealth by a price index and to study these figures both in current and in real values.[163] As we see in table 2.3 the indications are that between 1314 and 1341 a decline in the burgesses' moveable wealth occurred. The category 'moveable wealth' covered only a part of townsmen's belongings; some owned land in the fields around Cambridge and in villages surrounding it, but on the whole in the early fourteenth century, most burgesses would have held savings in stores of foodstuffs, raw materials, cash, house utensils, clothes and artefacts, all of which were taxable in the subsidies studied here.[164] The lowest taxed assessment in 1314 was 10s and in 1327 12/1, but in terms of 1314 prices (adjusted by 1310–14 price index) the wealth threshold of 1327 is 10s 9d. The total number of people assessed dropped by 58.6% between 1314 and 1327 from 466 to 273 when the real threshold of payment was similar. The mean wealth of the later group of burgesses is lower than that of 1314 indicating that the wealth of individuals within the group on the whole was closer to the threshold in 1327, and thus was more equally distributed than in 1314. This can be partly explained by the particular circumstances of the preceding years 1315–22, a period of acute famine and food

[163] In order to do so I have used the year indices calculated in Phelps Brown and Hopkins, 'Seven centuries of the prices of consumables', p. 311. It seems preferable to apply an average index for the five years preceding the given figure since in the case of 1327 adjustments by single year indices corrupt the data through the very high prices prevailing in famine. Nonetheless, single year indices and 10-year average indices have been used and yield fairly similar findings to those which are presented in table 2.3.

[164] On categories of assessment and exemption see Willard, *Parliamentary taxes on personal property*, pp. 73–81, 85–6.

shortage. Prices soared, and even the more prosperous burgesses were forced to spend part of their resources including their accumulated goods, depleting the value of their savings, as represented in the wealth values of 1327.[165] In 1341 a much lower threshold than that of 1314 yielded a similar number to that of the taxable population of the earlier subsidy. Only 90.6% of the number of assessed of 1314 (422 as opposed to 466) passed a threshold of wealth lower by 44.2%.[166] The mean valuation declined between 1314 and 1341 from £1 17s 11d to 17s 1d or, in real terms, from £1 17s 11d to £1 1s 8d.[167]

J. F. Willard has warned against the use of the subsidy lists for demographic computations.[168] Nevertheless some cautious calculations may help us establish a minimal size of early fourteenth-century population. Taking the returns for 1314, containing the largest number of burgesses – 466, one reaches some 2,100 members of burgess households by using the factor of 4.5 persons per household,[169] or 1,650 when using 3.5. Assuming that burgesses accounted for 75% of townsmen we reach the number 2,800 for the whole town population, and adding a tentative estimate of 700 scholars,[170] the population of Cambridge cannot be conceived as lower than 3,500 in the beginning of the fourteenth century.[171]

How did the decline in mean wealth of Cambridge burgesses affect the distribution of wealth within the group?[172] A way of assessing the

[165] On this famine see Kershaw, 'The great famine and agrarian crisis in England, 1315–1322', *passim.*

[166] The number that would have been above the 1314 threshold in 1341 is only 205 (in current prices) and 155 (in real prices).

[167] The total assessment declined in Cambridgeshire between 1314–15 and 1334 by some 27%, Hadwin, 'The medieval lay subsidies', p. 215 (the average decline for all counties was 23.7%). Valuations for all counties declined steadily between 1275 and 1334, but this is seen largely as a result of improving methods of evasion. Still, in conjunction with the evidence of a falling mean personal wealth this evidence may be taken to go some way in expressing a general decline in economic power of active burgesses. Cambridgeshire was usually slightly above average in these assessments, Hadwin, 'The medieval lay subsidies', table on p. 217.

[168] Willard, *Parliamentary taxes*, pp. 174–82; esp. pp. 181–2.

[169] Krause, 'The medieval household: large or small?', p. 432.

[170] Aston, Duncan and Evans, 'The medieval alumni of Cambridge', p. 13.

[171] If we take the number returned for the ninth of 1341 (422) to cover a wider section of the town population due to its lower tax threshold (although this is counteracted by the fact that the burgesses were, on the whole, poorer) and see it as representing 90% of burgess population, we reach an estimate of around 2,100 townfolk which, combined with scholars, yields *c.* 2,800 inhabitants around the mid-century.

[172] Plotting Lorenz curves as a measure of the distribution of wealth within the group of burgesses contributing to tolls and taxes produced almost totally overlapping curves which were not very revealing of change. On the basis of this comparison the only thing that can be said is that within the group of richer burgesses, even when there

Table 2.4 *Shares of total valuation held by various sections of taxed population of Cambridge (in %)*

Population shares	1211	1219	1304[a]	1314	1327	1341
Bottom 5%	1.7	1.3	0.7	1.3	2.0	1.3
Bottom 10%	3.4	2.9	1.4	2.5	4.1	2.5
Bottom 20%	6.9	6.2	2.9	5.8	8.2	5.1
Bottom 40%	15.8	15.5	7.6	13.8	16.8	14.3
Top 40%	71.5	71.2	84.7	73.1	70.9	74.5
Top 20%	49.6	47.4	67.4	52.6	51.4	53.4
Top 10%	31.6	28.8	48.5	35.4	35.4	35.8
Top 5%	12.3	16.6	38.7	22.9	23.2	20.3
Top five people	16.7	17.7	19.7	6.7	10.9	6.5
Number	119	92	400	466	273	422
Gini coefficient	0.436	0.431		0.464	0.430	0.480

[a] The portion of total wealth represented by the assessments of the tallage of 1304 is unknown.

degree of inequality in a given distribution pattern is the calculation of shares of wealth held by sections of the town. Table 2.4 presents the portion of wealth held by various sections of the taxed population. It is striking how stable the pattern of distribution remains over a period of 130 years[173] and even the figures for 1327 do not upset the picture. In towns one would expect to find interdependence between the well-being of people in the different productive strata of society. Thus, although there is a fall in wealth on the whole, it occurs without deeply changing the pattern of distribution and the element of inequality. This also clarifies the way in which a few men could rise to great power in a town where some five people held almost a fifth of the wealth, as in thirteenth-century Cambridge. In a more populated town with many individual owners of property a wider spreading of power would have been likely.

was decline in the level of wealth there was no drastic polarisation. On Lorenz curves see A. B. Atkinson, *The economics of inequality* (Oxford, 1975), pp. 15–16; A. K. Sen, *On economic inequality* (Oxford, 1973), pp. 29–31; on the Gini coefficient see Atkinson, *ibid.*, p. 45, and Sen, *ibid.*

[173] Given the similarity of the distributions and the problems of such tax data it would seem best to see the patterns for each of the two centuries as independent observations of the same reality, and to approach our results with greater confidence.

Table 2.5 *Movements in the placing of Cambridge burgesses in the hierarchy of assessment, 1314–27 and 1327–41*

Ranks in: 1314	1327 0–5	6–10	11–20	21–30	31–60	61–100	101+	Total
0–5	1	.	.	.	.	.	.	1
6–10	1	.	1	.	.	.	1	3
11–20	.	.	1	.	1	.	.	2
21–30	2	1	1	.	.	.	.	4
31–60	.	1	1	1	2	3	5	13
61–100	.	1	1	1	3	.	3	9
100+	.	1	2	1	3	2	36	45
Total	4	4	7	3	9	5	45	77

77 = 14 declined, 23 rose and 40 remained in place.

Ranks in: 1327	1341 0–5	6–10	11–20	21–30	31–60	61–100	101+	Total
0–5	1	.	1	.	1	.	.	3
6–10	2	.	.	.	1	.	.	3
11–20	.	.	2	.	2	1	.	5
21–30	.	.	.	.	1	.	3	4
31–60	.	.	2	.	2	1	4	9
61–100	.	.	1	.	3	2	9	15
100+	.	.	2	1	7	2	27	39
Total	3	.	8	1	17	6	43	78

78 = 24 declined, 20 rose and 34 remained in place.

It is interesting to note that although the overall distribution of wealth was stable in the years studied and the degree of inequality constant, great mobility within the group of richer burgesses is evident. Some participants could be identified in more than one subsidy list, and their fortunes traced. Table 2.5 describes the mobility of those identified burgesses, concentrating on the upper 100 people, as the differences of valuation in that section are much higher than in others. Plotted as they are, the diagonal line registers those burgesses who remained within the same group of wealth, the top triangle those who moved to lower brackets and the bottom triangle those who improved

Table 2.6 *Changes in the moveable wealth of people recurring in the tax returns*

	1314–27			1327–41		
	All	'Rich'[a]	'Poor'	All	'Rich'[b]	'Poor'
Number	77	17	60	78	19	59
Percentage of sample recording a fall:						
(i) Current prices	64.9	76.5	61.7	62.8	73.6	59.3
(ii) Constant prices	62.3	76.5	68.3	57.7	63.2	55.9
Average[c] percentage change in wealth:						
(i) Current prices	−19.7	−41.6	−12.1	−38.9	−52.4	−33.0
(ii) Constant prices	−28.4	−47.9	−21.6	−12.5	−32.4	−4.9

[a] 'Rich' in the case of 1314–27 has been taken to mean those whose assessment in 1314 exceeded £4.
[b] 'Rich' in the case of 1327–41 has been taken to mean those whose assessment in 1327 exceeded £2 10s.
[c] Geometric mean.

their economic lot. The rows show where they end up while the columns show where they started.[174] It is fascinating to view the mobility which existed within a group of burgesses, which retained approximately the same internal order of wealth overall. Comparing the two it appears that the extent of movement in years 1327 to 1341 is larger than in the earlier span. Turning to the change in wealth of this group of identified individuals, the findings summarised in table 2.6 reinforce the impression of decline in the burgesses' fortunes. As we can see, the majority record a fall; the richest tend to fall fastest.[175]

How do these findings affect our knowledge of the economic changes in the lives of medieval Cambridge townsfolk? The period which is most difficult to assess and whose fortunes have been most disputed is the first half of the fourteenth century, the period covered by the subsidy returns and the ninth of 1341. It can only be established

[174] Thus, in the first line of the second table we see that three of the top five people in 1327 could be traced in 1341, one of whom stayed in the top five, one moved down to the 11–20 group and one declined to the 31–60 group.
[175] The changes in the placing can also be seen as a result of greater evasion with the growth of the influence of richest men. On the other hand, these numbers are an underestimate of the average decline in fortune since those who fell to lower than the taxable threshold would not be recorded or entered into our calculations.

that the mean wealth of taxable burgesses declined between 1314 and 1341. It is also true that in spite of the general decline, the pattern of distribution and the shares of wealth held by sections of burgess society remained remarkably similar, maintaining the social distances which followed the differences in wealth. However, on the whole, it seems that burgesses had smaller nest-eggs, that savings were declining. These findings reflect the well-being of taxed burgesses; beside them lived a section which did not reach the tax threshold: labourers, widows, apprentices, as well as poor and old folk, many of whom were productive self-maintaining individuals.[176] One may ask whether the welfare of these untaxed townsfolk can be deduced from the findings about their well-to-do neighbours: is it not possible that the group of employers and proprietors, represented largely by the taxed burgesses, suffered a diminution of wealth mainly due to the fact that their employees were earning more and their tenants could bargain for lower rents?[177] It appears that fortunes created and sustained in a period of cheap labour and lucrative urban properties (that is, most of the thirteenth century) was suffering from change in those same factors that allowed their creation.[178]

This is not to say that Cambridge changed dramatically in the fourteenth century, though a certain trend is discernible which is also reflected in Cambridge rentals, such as those of the Hospital of St John.[179] In most town parishes some degree of contraction set in around the mid-century, which meant that HSJC was losing some income from some of its tenements: in the parish of All Saints it lost two of its six tenements, and in St Botolph's, three of seven. However, remaining rents retained their level. In St Benet's, St Andrew's and St Mary's parishes the number of tenements was stable, though rents were slightly adjusted. The changes occurred some time between the rental of 1350 and that of 1356, and can be connected with the depopulation

---

[176] For an attempt to assess the size of this group, which might have reached some 30% of some English towns see Willard, *Parliamentary taxes on personal property*, pp. 174–7.

[177] In Cambridge the market must have been partially sustained by the demand of the body of scholars, even if this group was much depleted in the late fourteenth century.

[178] Since chattels largely represented accumulated savings, a fall in their value reflects a real fall in income compared to price changes, meaning that their expenditure was greater than their income. This is especially true in our case, since the fall in land prices would have discouraged investment of moveable wealth in land in this period.

[179] Since it was a small house with property mostly in Cambridge and in very close villages, it must have been responsive to local change. The fourteenth-century rentals cover the years *c.* 1343, *c.* 1349, *c.* 1350, 1351, 1356, 1361, 1366, 1369, 1371, SJCA. Rental Rolls 2.2.1–2.2.6, and Cartulary of HSJC, fols. 8–10, 24, 80. These rentals will be studied closely in pp. 226–32 in connection with the management of the estate of the Hospital of St John.

immediately after the Black Death. The later rentals, of 1361, 1366, 1369 and 1371, show a sustained level of slightly lower rents compared to 1350–6. Most changes occur in parishes away from the town centre.

It seems that the pressing demand for town properties was lightened, but that well-placed housing was appreciated and maintained its value (albeit in a period of a real fall in prices). This would mean that property owners were collecting less in rents, and that tenants could choose with greater freedom and move into better dwellings.[180] However, an individual proprietor would have been less able, perhaps, to maintain levels of rent than was the hospital, which could exercise some monopolistic powers owing to the size of its urban estate.

CONCLUSION: IMPLICATIONS RELATED TO CHARITY

The study of some of the economic evidence for medieval Cambridge coincides fairly well with the general trends in the English economy. By the early thirteenth century a thriving urban community had established itself in Cambridge profiting from the provision of services and from marketing of agricultural surpluses over a wide region. Some prominent men had made their mark based on their connections within the landed nobility and bolstered by their economic superiority. Yet the community of burgesses was not deeply polarised; in it existed a continuum of status and wealth even after a decline in fortunes had set in. A connection between the decline in affluence and in the sense of economic and social security on the one hand, and a rise in the well-being of the labourers and the underemployed in Cambridge on the other, has been tentatively suggested.[181]

The supply and demand for charitable resources seems thus to have been affected in two main ways. The thirteenth-century growth benefited landlords, townsmen, and through the production of a substantial marketable food surplus, those who held large parcels of land. Townsmen who prospered undertook responsibilities in the legal, social and religious spheres of town life, in a period which saw a great surge of patronage and of the foundation of charitable institutions in

[180] In the context of York see Dobson, 'Admissions to the freedom of the city of York', p. 8. The endowment of new and old colleges devoured large sections of the Cambridge town centre, *Rotuli parliamentorum (1278–1503)* v, p. 623 and vi, pp. 40, 114.

[181] Some analogous evidence of the lightening of the burden on the lower classes can be found in the sharp decline in cases of petty indebtedness, usually associated with subsistence loans, tried in the comital court of Provence, R. Lavoie, 'Endettement et pauvreté en Provence d'après les listes de la justice comtale xive–xve siècles', *Provence historique* 23 (1973), p. 201–16; esp. p. 205.

every English town. When these leading men declined in fortune, their ability to allocate funds and to undertake obligations would have been much impaired. If the period of growth and expansion of investment in trade and small industry led to urban prosperity, the stream of poor peasants seeking urban employment had nonetheless an adverse influence on town life. Although migration created a supply of labour which was absorbed in the twelfth century and in the first half of the thirteenth, it continued well after the supply of employment had met the demand.[182] Once this level was met new arrivals helped to bring wages down, and were often forced to join the ranks of beggars or poor folk dependent on charity. When the demographic trend reversed itself some time between 1300 and 1330, a gradual diminution of labour supply occurred, which was exacerbated by the Black Death, and which caused a rise in wages together with a contraction in the economy on the whole. Towns still supplied goods and services for peasants, substantial tenants and landlords, and for the urban labourers who were most probably better off. The lower rents paid by tenants as well as the higher wages paid to labourers affected the well-being of rural and urban employers; thus the demand for relief, in the form of needs of poor and hungry folk, would have diminished at the same time as the prosperity of potential givers was falling.

These transformations suggest a fundamental change in the power structure of urban and rural society, a shift in the bargaining power of social groups and altered mutual expectations. Although the Statute of Labourers was probably only very patchily enforced and was more often a weapon for fighting competing employers than a direct sanction against employees, its preoccupations reflect the interests and anxieties of large landowners and urban entrepreneurs. The Justices of Labourers nominated for Cambridgeshire between 1349 and 1359 were burgesses of high status or members of middling feudal families. Men like John of Brigham, William Horwood (twice mayor) and Robert of Thorpe shared economic and social interests, expressed in their common membership in the most prestigious fraternity of fourteenth-

[182] The limited investment of profits in development of industrial infrastructure in towns limited employment opportunities, see Miller, 'The English economy in the thirteenth century', p. 35; Hilton, 'Rents and capital formation', *passim* and M. M. Postan, 'Investment in medieval agriculture'. *Journal of economic history* 27 (1967), pp. 576–87. Thus, the possible beneficial effects of a large supply of labour on the economy were not realised; on such effects see W. A. Lewis, 'Economic development with unlimited supplies of labour', *The Manchester school of economic and social studies* 22 (1954), pp. 139–91.

century Cambridge, the gild of Corpus Christi.[183] John Cheney, Thomas Deschalers, John de Frivill and Constantine Mortimer were members of old Cambridge families and represented the interests and views of rural landlords. The Peasants' Revolt of 1381 and its urban repercussions can be understood as an outburst against injustices inherent in the fact that the same social system was maintained in a world which had known deep economic change.[184] But this underlying cause for unrest, the tension between reality and traditional relations, did not mean that the townsfolk of Cambridge wished to see an end to the existing order. Those who rebelled were not the abject poor, but small craftsmen and labourers wishing to free themselves from the yoke imposed by town patriciates and corporations.[185] They complained about the enclosure of a common, they spent their energies against justices, the chancellor, a university bedel.[186] The new economic reality improved labour conditions for wage-earners, freed them from fear and caused them to voice demands, albeit violently, but it did not change the basic order. When labourers earned sufficient sums, they wished to join the burgess community and conformed to its rules.[187]

Yet the sequence of growth and overexpansion, then pauperisation and its ultimate alleviation, left its mark on relationships between social groups in towns and villages. These changes affected charitable disposition beyond the change in the levels of its supply and demand: in the period of migration from countryside to town of the thirteenth century, were the ties of family and community not weakened? Furthermore, in a period when seigneurial and peasant interests were so deeply opposed, was the spirit of responsibility towards tenants and cooperation within the manorial system not eroded? Could not recurrent complaints about sheaf-stealing, on default of repayment of

---

[183] On their offices see *Cambridge gild records*, pp. 32–6, 40, 134. Even one of the rural justices, Richard of Kelleshull, knight, was a member of this gild.

[184] This change was opposed by town oligarchies and landlords and agricultural employers, who felt threatened by its consequences, R. H. Hilton, 'Idéologie et ordre sociale dans l'Angleterre médiévale', *L'Arc* 72 (1978), pp. 32–7; and Aers, '*Piers plowman* and problems in the perception of poverty', pp. 5–25.

[185] Blockmans and Prevenier, 'Poverty in Flanders and Brabant', p. 57. Mathias, 'Adam's burden', p. 150.

[186] For the chronology of events in Cambridge see R. B. Dobson, *The peasants' revolt of 1381* (London, second edn, 1983), pp. 41–2, 240 as well as R. H. Hilton, *Bond men made free: medieval peasant movements and the English rising of 1381* (London, 1973), pp. 141, 203–6. For a contemporary account of the events in Cambridge see *Rotuli parliamentorum* III, p. 108.

[187] In towns experiencing buoyancy many wished to gain the freedom of the city, as in York, Dobson, 'Urban decline', pp. 17–20.

loans, betray a reality of diminishing adherence on the part of the more comfortable members of the rural community to those customary forms of mutual help which kept much of rural poverty from turning into destitution and misery?[188]

In a more harmonious setting in which the respective powers of peasants and landlords were more balanced, there may have existed a greater willingness to invest, to help at times of need, to distribute grain and lend money; in the polarised setting of the thirteenth-century countryside, the charitable instinct may have been greatly injured, leaving a late medieval society which was more comfortable but which had lost some of its power to evoke cooperation and mutual help.[189] In towns, where labourers had seen their wages diminishing as prices of foodstuffs soared, the feeling of antagonism must have been as sharp. From the town labourers' ranks came the poor in need of relief, dependent on the charity of those same men who had suffered a fall in revenues and who nursed a grudge against those who were not fulfilling their productive labouring role. When the change set in, employers opposed it bitterly and attempted to retain the *status quo* of subsistence wages, which contributed to such events as 1381. Potential givers felt that the weaker towndwellers had strayed from their proper status and from their useful function in society, bringing about disorder and insecurity, which turned into fear and indignation.[190] It would have been an extraordinary feat of abstraction and self-control which would have produced a more subtle understanding of poverty. Thus legislation as well as secular and religious literature reflected a painful identification between poverty and idleness, between begging and a dangerous and lawless existence.[191]

The loss of economic security among the group of merchants, master craftsmen, proprietors – the burgesses of Cambridge – turned them towards activities which would ensure their income and status and towards more individualistic ways of securing spiritual salvation. The benefits of participation in public office, investment in town economy, undertaking of charitable activities, these duties and privileges which

---

[188] The area of rural relief has been very little studied. On cooperation among tenants of a royal manor in the late Middle Ages in providing it, see M. K. McIntosh, *Autonomy and community: the royal manor of Havering 1200–1500* (Cambridge, 1986), pp. 235–40.

[189] This would have surely been true in a community such as Halesowen where landlord–tenants relations had all but exploded in a rebellion in the 1280s. For the story of this community see Z. Razi, 'The struggle between the abbots of Halesowen and their tenants', in *Social relations and ideas*, eds. T. H. Aston, P. R. Coss, C. Dyer and J. Thirsk (Cambridge, 1983), pp. 154–64.

[190] Hilton, 'Idéologie et ordre sociale', pp. 33–4.

[191] Schmitt, *Mort d'une hérésie*, pp. 193–4.

lay at the basis of town life in the thirteenth century, were being reviewed. Seeing the spirit of charity as strengthened and reinforced by norms of cooperation and altruistic customary obligations, a decline in overt charitable acts could contribute greatly to its weakening. If burgesses had less to spare and harboured ill-feeling towards the group of people who might fall into distress, one can see how the 'spirit of charity', inasmuch as it is an independent entity, was likely to decline.

Chapter 3

THE IDEA OF CHARITY BETWEEN THE TWELFTH AND FIFTEENTH CENTURIES

FORMAL VIEWS OF CHARITABLE OBLIGATIONS

The influence of ideas formulated in the schools on popular religion

One of the most obvious questions about medieval religious culture is the degree to which ordinary folk shared the ideas expressed in academic theological writings. The problem exists not only in the extent of the dissemination of such ideas, but also in the terms applied and the interpretations given in the process of absorption. Most of our evidence for the contents and scope of religious concepts, such as that of charity, is drawn from material written by the learned and not by the poor or their patrons. But in order to recognise the multitude of ways in which ideas progressed and evolved, we must also examine the common man's views which were part of a wide popular culture.[1] Any attempt to assess the ideas of artisans and peasants will be totally distorted if we treat the written cultural creations as accepted and disseminated ubiquitously, successfully and literally.[2] However, two

---

[1] Davis, 'Some tasks and themes', pp. 307–36. On the importance of the study of processes of popularisation for the understanding of popular spirituality see P. Vilan's remarks in A. Vauchez, 'Une enquête sur les "spiritualités populaires"'. Premier bulletin', *Revue d'histoire de la spiritualité* 49 (1973), pp. 493–504; p. 504: 'une étude indirecte, partant des "popularisations" des grandes spiritualités, des efforts pour les adapter à des milieux différents de leur support de départ, des milieux moins culturés,...l'on pourrait faire l'hypothèse qu'il s'agit en fait de la perception par les porteurs...de se trouver en face de systèmes différents auxquels il doivent s'adapter'. For preliminary discussion of the definition of popular culture see Z. Barbu, 'Popular culture. A sociological approach', in *Approaches to popular culture*, ed. C. W. E. Bigsby (London, 1976), pp. 39–64.

[2] When dealing with the absorption of sermons by the laity one must consider the English tradition of anti-clerical, and subsequently anti-mendicant, satire, J. Mann, *Chaucer and medieval estates satire* (Cambridge, 1973), pp. 37–54. See also P. R. Szittya, 'The antifraternal tradition in Middle English literature', *Speculum* 52 (1977), pp. 287–313. A recurrent satirical representation of preachers was related to the story of the fox preaching to the geese from *Reynard the fox*, often displayed on misericords. For examples see G. L. Remnant and M. D. Anderson, *A catalogue of misericords in Great Britain* (Oxford, 1969), pp. xxxiv–xxxv and plates 10a, 24a, 35c. For a discussion of satirical representations of the fox as priest or friar see K. Varty, *Reynard the fox* (Leicester, 1967), pp. 51–7 and plates 24, 35, 61, 63, 64, 69, 70.

main factors render our quest for a popular idea of charity potentially more fruitful: first, medieval preachers and teachers, being aware of the heterogeneity of their audience and of the problems inherent in the popularisation, simplified and injected life into ideas meant for presentation to the public at large, even at the expense of what they saw as intellectual rigour. Secondly, popular literature, proverbs, humour and verse were wrought into the tools of instruction.[3] Secure in our appreciation of the problems we can attempt a cautious evaluation of charity in its many interpretations by different groups and in different periods.

An enlightening example of contemporary awareness of such dilemmas has been analysed by A. Bernstein in a study of the theology of William of Auvergne.[4] William, a thirteenth-century theologian, dealt with a question which had never been satisfactorily resolved: are the fires and pains suffered in purgatory physical and material, or mere abstract metaphors?[5] Because of its central place in exhortation to penitence, the doctrine of purgatory was frequently discussed in the twelfth and thirteenth centuries and had an immediate impact on the contents of preaching. If the pains of purgatory were to be considered in abstract and immaterial terms, laymen might not grasp the enormity of the horror. William wished to reconcile the intellectual challenge of the conflicting literal and non-literal interpretations of punishment after death, but he also wished for a doctrine which would act as a powerful deterrent to wrong-doing and heresy. In response to popular dissent such as Catharism, the theologian was obliged to abandon the refined distinctions of scholarship and to provide a vigorous answer which would allay the anxieties of confused laymen and counter the arguments of heretics.[6] William developed an esoteric view of purgatory combining a subtle psychological abstraction of the purgatorial suffering gleaned from Arabic philosophy with the traditional view of hell and purgatory as dens of fearsome torments;[7] but he was aware that one

---

[3] For an example of such a process see R. W. Scribner, *For the sake of simple folk. Popular propaganda for the German Reformation* (Cambridge, 1981). However, one must bear in mind the differences between popular and popularised culture; some of which are discussed in Barbu, 'Popular culture', pp. 41–3.

[4] A. E. Bernstein, 'Esoteric theology: William of Auvergne on the fires of hell and purgatory', *Speculum* 57 (1982), pp. 509–31.

[5] *Ibid.*, pp. 510–15. See also A. E. Bernstein, 'Theology between heresy and folklore: William of Auvergne on punishment after death', *Studies in medieval and Renaissance history* 5 new ser. (1982), pp. 5–44, at pp. 5–6.

[6] For examples in William's writings of 'argument' against Cathar views denying the existence of purgatory and the need for intercession see *ibid.*, pp. 7–22, 42–3.

[7] *Idem*, 'Esoteric theology', pp. 529–30.

level of interpretation suited the Schools and his fellow theologians, and another the masses in the marketplace.[8] As a theologian and a pastor – he was bishop of Paris 1228–49 – William understood that successful instruction needed not only a simplified message, but one that would act most effectively on the mind of a simple believer. Another brilliant theologian and preacher, Stephen Langton, believed that different audiences required different styles of preaching: some would understand the pure truths only when presented in rude and vulgar language.[9]

The theology of charity was discussed and developed in the intellectual centres of Christendom, where the twelfth and thirteenth centuries saw a lively formulation of the norms and values of Christian society over a wide range of ideas and practices. The Christian view of the world strove to incorporate the diversified society and the many types of existence maintained by Christians within one ethical framework. The formulations and compromises of theologians and canonists were taught and read by those who were to become bishops, archdeacons, abbots and preaching friars. Bishops preached to lower clergy, who in turn instructed parishioners, while friars concentrated their efforts in towns and on major thoroughfares.[10] Canonical developments were contained in conciliar decrees and implemented through provincial councils and diocesan synods, which guided and supervised the teaching and dissemination of Christian law and doctrine.

Other channels for the diffusion of ideas and the provision of guidance were developing in the work of canonists, popes and reforming bishops. From the twelfth century, collections of material to assist the clergy were being composed both in Latin and in the vernacular,[11] collections which provided a simplified yet orthodox view of Christian morality and its application in daily life. Great theologians and canonists undertook the task of compilation and arrangement of the doctrine into schemes that would be both sound and useful. Prominent among such guides, the *Summae confessorum*

---

[8] *Ibid.*, p. 510: 'credulitas ipsius [inferni] utilis est valde et errores circa ipsum noxij, et impedientes correctiones hominum a vitiis suis, et perversitate morum suorum'. For a slightly different interpretation of William's purgatorial doctrine see J. Le Goff, *La Naissance du purgatoire*, pp. 325–30.

[9] B. Smalley, *The study of the bible in the Middle Ages* (Oxford, third edn, 1983), pp. 253–4.

[10] On the diffusion of ideas from the university of Paris through the preaching of the friars see d'Avray, *The preaching of the friars*, pp. 132–63, 180–203.

[11] On instruction books for clergymen see Boyle, 'Three English pastoral *summae*', pp. 135–44.

helped parish priests in their task of meting out penance and guidance.[12] The penitential encounter was appreciated for its potential didactic value; both Robert of Flamborough (d. 1224) and Thomas of Chobham (fl. 1230) expressed this recognition in their penitential guidebooks for the clergy. Robert's work was constructed in the form of a dialogue between a penitent and his confessor, in which a whole range of dogmatic and moral discussion ensued, and an understanding of true penance was achieved through a reciprocal process of questioning.[13] Such instruction deepened understanding of the framework and implications of sin and enabled the clergy to widen the scope of the confessional experience.[14] The conservative methods of teaching, which hinged on the grouping of sins, virtues and works of mercy, were incorporated into the guidebooks for instruction of priests and, subsequently, of believers.[15] New theological concepts reached the didactic sphere through the coming of the friars and with them of a new learned style of preaching.

General conciliar decrees on religious instruction were energetically applied to the English diocese.[16] Parish priests were to be the vehicles for deeper education of the laity, but synodal rulings assumed the existence of only a low level of clerical education. The simile most often employed to describe this sorry state is that of the blind leading the blind; Bartholomew of Exeter uses it in his penitential when discussing *scientia sacerdotum*.[17] In the introduction to his early fifteenth-century instruction book for parish priests, John Mirc explained the need for such a treatise in similar terms:

[12] These developed in the twelfth and mainly the thirteenth centuries in response to the decree of Lateran IV (1215) demanding yearly confession from all believers. See A. Morey, *Bartholomew of Exeter, bishop and canonist. A study in the twelfth century* (Cambridge, 1937), which includes the text of Bartholomew's penitential. Cf. T. N. Tentler, 'The summa for confessors as an instrument of social control', in *The pursuit of holiness*, ed. Trinkaus and Oberman, pp. 103–26 and L. E. Boyle, 'The *summa* for confessors as a genre and its religious intent', in *The pursuit of holiness*, pp. 126–30.

[13] On this genre see C. Vogel, *Les 'Libri paenitentiales'* (Turnhout, 1978). Robert of Flamborough, *Liber poenitentialis*, ed. J. J. F. Firth (Toronto, 1971).

[14] Penitentials became doctrinal guides: P. Michaud-Quantin, *Sommes de casuistique et manuels de confession du moyen-âge (XII–XVI siècles)* (Paris, 1962), pp. 21–3

[15] See the treatment of almsgiving by Bartholomew of Exeter in his twelfth-century penitential, c. 12 'De elemosina', Morey, *Bartholomew of Exeter*, p. 184.

[16] C. R. Cheney, *English synodalia of the thirteenth century* (Oxford, 1941, repr. 1968), pp. 1–50.

[17] He quotes Augustine from the *Decretum*: 'Augustinus: Que ipsis sacerdotibus necessaria sunt ad discendum...Ex quibus omnibus si unum defuerit, sacerdotis nomen uix in eo constabit, quia ualde periculose sint mine evangelice, quibus dicitur: si cecus ceco ducatum prebeat, ambo in foveam cadunt' (D.38 c.5), Morey, *Bartholomew of Exeter*, c. 23, p. 192.

God seyth hym self, as wryten we fynde,
That whenne þe blynde ledeth þe blynde,
Into þe dych þey fallen boo,
For þey ne sen whareby to go[18]

Priests were seen to be in need of assistance and training before they could transmit the truths formulated in the Schools.[19]

From Paris, Bologna and Rome, the centres of academic study and of Church government, the vital developments in ecclesiastical law spread to every corner of Christendom. It is clear that the processes of dissemination of the Christian message involved changes and modification wrought by parish priests and friars alike. Theologians as well as canonists reacted to the needs and circumstances of their age, but greater proximity to and more frequent encounter with a lay audience exerted pressure towards simplicity, precipitating an intellectual exchange between the popular and the learned traditions of Christian society.[20]

Theological and canonistic formulations on poverty, property and charity

Every Christian writer, preacher, priest and layman would agree that charity was the love of God expressed on earth through love for one's neighbour and for oneself.[21] It was the greatest of virtues[22] without which faith alone was imperfect.[23] Stephen Langton saw charity and faith intertwined, leading to the development of the symbolism of charity as a tree bearing fruit.[24] Love of one's neighbour required *opera*, both spiritual and corporal, the character and scope of which occupied

[18] John Mirc, *Instructions for parish priests by John Mirc*, ed. E. Peacock and rev. F. J. Furnivall (London, 1868, rev. 1902), lines 1–4, p. 1.

[19] Applied through episcopal examination and supervision. See the case of John of Lavenham, parish priest of Wicken, who was too ignorant to offer the cure of souls and had promised to take up a course of study at an English university. He confessed failure to fulfil this obligation to the bishop who absolved him on the condition that he fulfil it immediately, CUL.EDR.Register Montacute, fol. 7r (4 April 1339) and fol. 10v (25 July 1340).

[20] On this relationship see A. J. Gurevich, 'Popular and scholarly medieval cultural traditions: notes in the margin of Jacques Le Goff's book', *Journal of medieval history* 9 (1983), pp. 71–90.

[21] But these always remain as forms of love for God: 'Caritas quippe est amor Dei atque proximi, amplectens Deum super omnia, proximum autem super cetera', F. Courtney, *Cardinal Robert Pullen. An English theologian of the twelfth century* (Rome, 1954) p. 197.

[22] Alan of Lille crowned it as the queen of virtues, J. Longère, *Oeuvres oratoires des maîtres parisiens du XII siècle* I, (Paris, 1975), p. 326, 346–7 and *ibid.*, II, p. 257, n. 8.

[23] Courtney, *Cardinal Robert Pullen*, pp. 200–1.

[24] Longère, *Oeuvres oratoires* I, pp. 333, 348–9, On the imagery of charity as a tree see B. H. Smith Jr., *Traditional imagery of charity in 'Piers Plowman'* (The Hague and Paris, 1966), pp. 58–73.

theologians and canonists. The obstacles on the charitable path, such as private property, ambition, family allegiances were discussed in an attempt to define the channels and boundaries of charitable sharing.

Justification of the existence of private property, enjoyed abundantly by some, and sadly needed by others, was an intellectual and pastoral task which became all the more urgent with the advent of the friars.[25] Gratian's *Decretum* presented the traditional view of the Fathers of the Church which saw all property as belonging to all men by natural law.[26] This view lingered and even Ockham in the fourteenth century still upheld this view and explained the possibility of holding private property as a result of the Fall from grace.[27] However, those who held property by divine wish were not seen to be privileged but rather as having a special responsibility towards the poor. Ambrose was quoted in the *Decretum* to confirm the view that a rich man was not free to dispose of his goods at will, but that he should employ his superfluous goods in the help of others.[28] This view accepted the existence of rich and poor but placed the former under an incessant obligation to help the latter. Many thinkers enlarged on the dangers inherent in the possession of earthly goods. The twelfth-century Parisian theologian Peter Comestor (fl. *c.* 1168–78) saw riches as a great danger to piety, a view shared by Alan of Lille (*c.* 1130–1203).[29] In the twelfth century most theologians agreed that a poor man was spiritually less vulnerable than a rich man and Alan believed that Christ dwelt in the poor alone: 'Where does Christ dwell? only in Christ's poor'.[30] The discussion developed in the course of the century and in the following one, towards a clearer definition of the duties of the holders of property. Having accepted that earthly goods were inferior to spiritual ones[31] and that their distribution was uneven, theologians and canon lawyers proceeded to refine the definitions of the scope and frequency of charitable giving required from a Christian. If superfluous goods were

[25] For a basic discussion of views on property see R. W. and A. J. Carlyle, *The history of mediaeval political thought in the West* (Edinburgh, 1903–36), 1:4, 12; II i:5; II ii:6.

[26] *Decretum* D.8 C.1: 'Iure divino omnia sunt communia omnibus iure vero constitutionis hoc meum illus alterius est'; cap.13: '..unde quis possidet, quos possidet?..Pauperes et divites Deus ex uno limo fecit, et pauperes et divites una terra supportat'.

[27] J. Viner, *Religious thought and economic society*, ed. J. Melitz and D. Winch (Durham, N.C., 1978), p. 69.

[28] *Decretum* D.47 c.8.

[29] J. Longère, 'Pauvreté et richesse chez quelques prédicateurs durant la seconde moitié du XIIe siècle', in Mollat, *Etudes* I, pp. 255–73, p. 266. On Peter Comestor see also Longère, *Oeuvres oratoires*, pp. 20–1; on Alan of Lille, *ibid.*, pp. 25–7.

[30] 'Ubi hospitabitur Christus? In solis Christi pauperibus', Alan of Lille, *Textes inédits*, ed. M.-T. d'Alverny (Paris, 1965), p. 283.

[31] Viner, *Religious thought*, p. 61.

to be given away, what was considered to be the test of a man's basic needs? What was the nature and scope of one's obligation towards the poor? Who were the deserving poor?

The traditional model of social relations was expressed by Augustine and reapplied by the canonists: 'justice exists in the relief of misery'.[32] Cardinal Robert Pullen (d. 1146) saw charity as the sole source of virtue.[33] The Parisian master Raoul Ardent (d. *c.* 1200), described almsgiving as an act of restitution and justice, not of mercy.[34] Iohannes Teutonicus, the glossator of the *Decretum* (writting *c.* 1215–17), saw charity given from one's superfluous goods as merely an act of justice, but praised giving which entailed self-denial as an act of mercy. Thomas Aquinas recognised the social hierarchy and the different needs of different people. His was not an appeal for 'heroic charity', the definition of superfluity depended on one's social station.[35] Returning to Ambrose, thirteenth-century canonists insisted that possession of property was not wrong, rather that the accumulation of excess riches beyond reasonable need was criminal: 'who is as unjust and avaricious as the man who hoards the food of many people which is of no use to him? Therefore it is no smaller crime to take from him who has than to deny the needy what you can give them in abundance'.[36] This acceptance of the social commitments of each individual was well established in the thirteenth century. In the next century, Henry of Bohic counted the needs of one's dependants as 'bare necessities'; most canonists saw the maintenance of one's social obligations and expectations as a reasonable wish.[37] In addition, Henry thought that property was to be shared at a time of need.[38] The idea of stewardship placed one constantly under the obligation of parting with superfluous goods for the use of those in need, which developed into a fascinating controversy

[32] 'Justicia est in subveniendo miseris', B. Tierney, *The medieval poor law: a sketch of canonical theory and its application in England* (Berkeley and Los Angeles, 1959), p. 35.

[33] 'Sola caritas ea virtus est quae virum bonum creat', Courtney, *Cardinal Robert Pullen*, p. 107, n. 2.

[34] An interesting use of the term *restitutio* usually employed in the context of unlawful gains; Longère, 'Pauvreté et richesse chez quelques prédicateurs', p. 260. On Raoul Ardent see Longère, *Oeuvres oratoires* I, pp. 30–1.

[35] Aquinas, *Summa theologiae* II–II q.32.a.6. *ad objectiones*. See S. Thrupp, 'Social control in the medieval town', in *Society and history: essays by Sylvia Thrupp*, ed. R. Grew and N. Steneck (Ann Arbor, Mich., 1977), pp. 9–24; p. 18. Viner, *Religious thought*, p. 74.

[36] Commenting on 'Quis enim tam iniustus tam avarus quam qui multorum alimenta suum non usum, sed habundantiam et delicias facit? Neque enim minus est criminis habenti tollere, quam, cum possis et habundas, indigentibus denegare', *Decretum* D.47 c.8.

[37] Tierney, *Medieval poor law*, p. 36 and *Glossa ordinaria ad* C.12.q.1.c.11.

[38] *Glossa ordinaria ad* D.1 c.7.

in the thirteenth century.[39] Aquinas believed that the surplus should be continually distributed and pressure be brought to bear on those reluctant to do so.[40] Another consequence of the wish to preserve order and decorum in the practice of charity was the view expressed in the fifteenth century by St Bernardino, who doubted the wisdom of almsgiving by certain groups, mainly people who were wards, or who owed obedience to others. Thus, he questioned the duty of giving by nuns and monks, legal wards, wives, minors and servants.[41]

The nature of ownership and the duties entailed are encapsulated in the active debate which began in the twelfth century by the examination of the circumstances of theft due to poverty, a debate which subsequently developed into a discussion of the rights of the poor. The greater emphasis on individual motive and intention, introduced to all areas of inquiry by theologians such as Abelard and later Peter the Chanter, opened the way to such questions as whether dire need could justify theft, and whether when stealing for sustenance a man was less culpable than otherwise.[42] From such ideas stemmed the notion that a poor person stealing for sustenance was not guilty of theft.[43] Alan of Lille believed that the sinner's circumstances were all important and must be taken into account in judging the crime: 'and the person's status must be considered...a poor man has a more impelling urge to steal than a rich man, and it follows that a rich man sins more gravely if he steals, than a poor man';[44] Aquinas justified theft only in cases of the greatest urgency.[45] Many believed that 'in urgente necessitate omnia

---

[39] G. Couvreur, *Les pauvres ont-ils des droits? Recherches sur le vol en cas d'extrême nécessité depuis le concorde de Gratien (1140) jusqu'à Guillaume d'Auxerre (d. 1231)* (Rome, 1961).

[40] Aquinas, *Summa theologiae* II–II q.32.a.5.ad 2 & ad 4. See also *ibid.*, q.66 a.7: 'Et ideo res quas aliqui superabundanter habent, ex naturali jure debentur pauperum sustentationi'.

[41] In his discussion 'Quis potest facere eleemonsynam', c.15 of 'De eleemosyna', Bernardino of Siena, *Opera omnia*, VIII, ed. College of St Bonaventure (Quaracchi, Florence, 1956), p. 71. This view denied the ability to discriminate and give from true intention when the goods were not fully those belonging to the giver in his own right or by his own exertion.

[42] Couvreur, *Les pauvres ont-ils des droits?*, pp. 30–80. This view is not only a theological development connected with the understanding of intention but is also rooted in the maxim inherited from Roman law which appears in pseudo-Isidore 'necessitas non habet legem', *ibid.*, pp. 66–7.

[43] *Glossa ordinaria ad* C.12.q.2.c.11; Bernard of Parma, *Glossa ordinaria ad* X.5.18.3 in *Decretales d.Gregorii papae IX* (Turin, 1621).

[44] 'Considerandus etiam est personae status;...majorem causam impulsivam ad furtum habet pauper quam dives, unde magis peccat dives si furetur, quam pauper', Alan of Lille, *Liber poenitentialis*, ed. J. Longère (Louvain and Lille, 1965), lib.I, C.XV, pp. 30–1.

[45] Aquinas, *Summa theologiae* II–II, q.66 a.7 *responsio ad* 1. In cases of great need both receiving and taking property belonging to another is not deemed to be theft, *responsio*

61

communicanda sunt' ('in urgent need all things are to be used in common'), but definitions of urgent need were widely divergent and canonists were reluctant to open the gates to definitions which could be socially harmful and disruptive.[46] In the thirteenth century the debate progressed from a discussion of intent to an assessment of the positive right of poor folk to demand their basic needs. Iohannes Teutonicus saw the poor as having a positive right to the property held by rich men and believed that the *denunciatio apostolica*, the act of public denunciation and demand of excommunication, could be enacted by a poor man against a rich one.[47] Peter the Chanter and his school maintained that a secular ruler should enforce the rich people's duties to relieve the poor.[48] These were minority views, the logical conclusion of the line of thought pursued by most canonists and theologians who upheld the maxim of community of property in times of need.

The acknowledgement of the positive right of the poor to expect charity is reflected in the parallel imperative on propertied people to act charitably. Robert of Flamborough's penitential enjoined punishment on those who did not offer hospitality: 'and whoever does not receive guests in his home, as God has ordained, nor give alms, if he makes no amends by bread and water for an equivalent period, let him do penance'.[49] It is interesting to note that the rigorous view of the social responsibility of the 'haves' towards the 'have nots' appeared in the tenth-century English Blickling Homilies. There, the age was lamented since in it men did not give tithes sufficiently and thus were deemed to be murderers of the poor.[50] This view still prevails in the fifteenth-century collection of English councils, Lyndwood's *Provinciale*: 'Those who do not relieve the needy kill spiritually, as do those who

---

ad 2: 'uti re aliena occulte accepta in casu necessitatis extremae non habet rationem furti' and *responsio ad* 3: 'potest aliquis occulte rem alienam accipere ut subveniat proximo sic indigenti'.

[46] One solution was to permit theft to only those bare necessities needed for survival, *The Summa Parisiensis of the Decretum Gratiani*, ed. T. P. McLaughlin (Toronto, 1952), p. 42.

[47] *Glossa ordinaria ad* D.47.c.8.

[48] Couvreur, *Les pauvres ont-ils des droits?*, pp. 193–4, 202–3.

[49] 'Quicumque hospites non recipit in domo sua, sicut Dominus precipit...nec eleemosynam fecerit, tanto tempore in pane et aqua si non emendet, poeniteat', Robert of Flamborough, *Liber poenitentialis*, c.357, p. 278.

[50] *The Blickling homilies of the tenth century*, part III, ed. R. Morris (London, 1880), p. 53: 'swa feala earmra manna swa on þaes rican neaweste & þaes welegan sweltaþ, & he him nele syllan his teoþung-sceatta dael, þonne biþ he ealra þara manna deaþes sceldig & myrþra beforan þaes ecan Deman heahsetle'. For a view of those letting the poor die as murderers see *Decretum* D.86 c.21.

withhold [from the poor] or those who oppress and confuse the innocent'.[51]

Goods accumulated through the profit-making activities of townsmen could be put to good use.[52] Once subjective intention had become the test of true religion it also emerged as a factor to be considered in judging the merit of a charitable act.[53] Thus, property became a vehicle for the expression of true religion and could be used in a way that was spiritually profitable.[54] Stephen Langton saw in a man's relation with the poor the test of true religion.[55] Albert the Great and then Thomas Aquinas liberated the concept of private property by giving it the utility of a tool for the testing of conscience.[56] One could have a healthy attitude towards riches and use them justly and piously or one could harbour a sinful attachment to them, yet attainment of riches alone was not a sin or a moral blemish. This arises clearly from Aquinas' discussion of avarice: avarice ruled only those people who exceeded the measure of attachment to their property.[57]

The Fathers of the Church had maintained that church property was the patrimony of the poor.[58] Priests held ecclesiastical property only as part of their office and had no rights in it, beyond those which enabled them to use it for the benefit of their parishioners and the poor. The twelfth-century *Summa Parisiensis* is clear on the question of the absence of any claim to church property by anyone but the poor.[59] Similarly to rich laymen priests were stewards of the wealth of their offices, but their duties were more rigorous; church property was not

[51] 'Spiritualiter enim occidunt qui non reficiunt indigentes, similiter occidunt qui detrahunt vel qui innocentes opprimunt et confundunt' (compiled in the 1420s), William Lyndwood, *Provinciale seu constitutiones Angliae* (Oxford, 1679, repr., Farnborough, 1968), Lib I.tit.II.c.I, pp. 57–8.

[52] Only after proper payment of general and personal tithes was made. On the problems in tithe collection connected with urban commercial activities see A. G. Little, 'Personal tithes', *English historical review* 60 (1945), pp. 67–88.

[53] *Decretum. De poen.* D.3 c.19; *Glossa ordinaria. De poen.* D.3 c.19.

[54] Rosenwein and Little, 'Social meaning in the monastic and mendicant spiritualities', p. 30. [55] Longère, 'Pauvreté et richesse chez quelques prédicateurs', p. 258.

[56] But this is not a unanimous view. For example St Bonaventura preached total renunciation of private property, F. Tocco, *La quistione della povertà nel secolo XIV. Nuovi documenti* (Naples, 1910), pp. 6–7.

[57] 'avaritia importat immoderatam quamdam circa divitias dupliciter...', *Summa theologiae*, II–II, q.118,a.3.r.

[58] Ambrose and Jerome in *Decretum* C.12.q.1.c.28; C.12.q.2.c.70; C.16.q.1.c.68. Also Innocent IV's *In V libros decretalium commentaria ad* X.2.12.4 (Venice, 1570), p. 267.

[59] *The Summa Parisiensis*, c.xii.q.1.post c.25: '*Illi et post dispensatori ecclesie* relinquant, i.e. de rebus ecclesiae nihil percipiant sed dimittant eas conferendas pauperibus', pp. 157–8.

to be put to their own use, and they were only to live off a portion of its income.[60]

Besides being acts of justice, of restitution, of proper stewardship, almsgiving and charity were of great utility to those who practised them, being a part of the *operis satisfactio* in the process of penance along with fasts and prayers. Stephen Langton ascribed an even greater importance to charitable deeds: 'Fasting without alms is of no value; alms without fasting are more valuable than fasting without alms. Fasting with almsgiving is of double goodness; fasting without almsgiving is of no good. And abstaining from food is of no value unless you abstain from sins'.[61] Alms, fasts and prayers were acts of penance which followed true contrition and confession. In penitentials circulating in the late twelfth and thirteenth centuries a constant link was maintained between the description of the mode of confession combined with the signs of genuine contrition, and the means for subsequent penance. In his twelfth-century penitential for the instruction of parish priests Bartholomew of Exeter presented this view of the means of penance: 'For alms extinguish sins according to the saying: "water extinguishes the burning fire and alms extinguish sin"'.[62] Distribution to the poor was a virtuous act and a means for making amends for sin.[63] Perjurors motivated by avarice were directed by Robert of Flamborough to sell their goods and distribute the proceeds to the poor.[64] With the greater emphasis on confession and penance in the

[60] There is general agreement on this point by the twelfth century and until the late Middle Ages: Iohannes Andreae, *Glossa ordinaria ad Sext.* 3.9.2 (written in 1294–1303 and 1326) in *Constitutiones Clementis papae quinti cum una apparatu Iohannis Andree* (Nurnberg, 1486), and Panormitanus, *Abbatis panormitani omnia quae extant commentaria* (Venice, 1588), *ad* x.2.12.4 III, fol. 237. See also discussion of the duties of parish priests towards the poor, below pp. 237–45.

[61] 'Ieiunium sine elemosina non valet. Elemosina sine ieiunio plus valet quam ieiunium sine elemosina. Ieiunium cum elemosina duplex bonum est. Ieiunium sine elemosina nullum bonum est. Item nihil valet abstinere a cibis, nisi abstinere a peccatis', Longère, 'Pauvreté et richesse chez quelques prédicateurs', p. 262.

[62] Morey, *Bartholomew of Exeter*, c.8, p. 179. This the most common proverb on the efficacy of almsgiving and its occurrences range from Aelfric to late medieval writers. See *The homilies of Aelfric* II, ed. B. Thorpe (London, 1846), p. 106, lines 5–7: 'seo aelmysse ure synna lig adwaescte, swa swa hit awriten is "swa swa waeter adwaescd fyr, swa adwaescd seo aelmysse synna"'; as well as the Wycliffite Bible on Ecclesiastes III, 33, *The Book of Job, Psalms, Proverbs, Ecclesiastes, and the Song of Solomon according to the Wycliffite Version...1381, revised...1389*, ed. J. Forshall and F. Madden (Oxford, 1881): 'Watir quenchith fier brennynge, and almes ayenstondith synnes'.

[63] But always assuming that the act is motivated by true intent, otherwise it is merely an attempt to 'buy' charity: 'Non ergo se fallant qui per largas elemosynas fructus vel pecuniae se existimant impunitatem emere', *Glossa ordinaria. De Poen.* D.3 c.19.

[64] Robert of Flamborough, *Liber poenitentialis*, c.302, p. 247: 'omnes res suas vendat et pauperibus distribuat'. Almsgiving is part of many schemes of penance in this book.

thirteenth century, almsgiving developed as a ritual both spiritual and practical.[65]

The idea of purgatory and its penitential value received the concentrated attention of theologians in the twelfth century.[66] Although the concept of a 'middle' place of suffering after death existed throughout the early Middle Ages, it reached its full scholarly formulation only around 1170–90.[67] Thus, in the mid-twelfth century Master Robert Pullen wrote of the place where final penance will be made: 'Where are the penitent after death? in the purgatorial places. Where are they? I do not know yet'.[68] Yet the concept gained popularity and clarity of presentation in the subsequent decades. If purgatory was the place where truly confessed believers complete their penance during a limited period of suffering, meritorious acts could alleviate their torments by transferring to them grace accumulated on earth.[69] The whole scheme of prayers for the dead was an attempt to alleviate purgatorial sufferings through acts of the living since the dead could effect no good works.[70] The links between the dead in purgatory and the living were strong, loyalty and love could be expressed through intercession in favour of a dead soul.[71] In his *Summa aurea*, William of Auxerre (d. 1231) compared the souls in purgatory to pieces of wood

---

The fornicating laywoman 'omnia dereliquat et res suas pauperibus tribuat et conversa in monasterio Deo usque ad mortem serviat', *ibid.*, c.280, p. 234.

[65] The connection between penance and charity is expressed in the development of some Italian charitable confraternities into flagellant societies concentrating on penitential mortification of the flesh, J. Henderson, 'The flagellant movement and flagellant confraternities in central Italy, 1260–1400', *Studies in Church history* 15 (1978), pp. 147–60; pp. 148, 155.

[66] Le Goff, *La naissance du purgatoire*, *passim*; esp. pp. 181–241.

[67] *Ibid.*, p. 25; R. Southern suggests that by the early twelfth century the idea had been full*ʸ* developed as an alternative, offering salvation to the mass of believers, R. Southern 'Between heaven and hell. Review of J. Le Goff, *La naissance du purgatoire*', *Times literary supplement* 18 June 1982, pp. 651–2. On the continuity of this theme in the early Middle Ages see the following review articles: Gurevich, 'Popular and scholarly medieval cultural traditions', p. 80 and A. H. Bredero, 'Le moyen-âge et le purgatoire', *Revue d'histoire ecclésiastique* 78 (1983), pp. 429–54; pp. 443–6. See also the review by P. Ariès, 'Le purgatoire et la cosmologie de l'au-delà. Note critique', *Annales* 38 (1983), pp. 151–7; esp. p. 153.

[68] 'Ubi sunt penitentes post mortem? in purgatoriis. Ubi sunt ea? Nondum scio', Courtney, *Cardinal Robert Pullen*, pp. 275–6, n. 48.

[69] This concept and services for the dead existed in the monastic milieu and in popular lore before the twelfth century, Gurevich, 'Popular and scholarly medieval cultural traditions', p. 73.

[70] Longère, *Oeuvres oratoires* 1, p. 36.

[71] *Ibid.*, pp. 436–42. This is developed further by St Thomas Aquinas by introducing the idea of unifying charity, which allows one person's prayers to intercede for another, see R. Ombres, 'The doctrine of purgatory according to St. Thomas Aquinas', *Downside review* 99 (1981), pp. 279–87; pp. 284–6.

which burnt at a different rate depending on the degree of humidity stored in them, humidity meaning suffrages.[72] This doctrine grew into a fundamental belief of the late medieval world and weight was added to it by the growing preoccupation with death. Theologians and preachers stressed the importance of the belief in purgatory and saw great danger to souls who did not fear it.[73] The fifteenth-century guide for parish priests, the *Speculum sacerdotale*, explains the feast of All Souls as the 'commemoracion of alle true peple':

And why say I of true peple that ben dede? For I mene of alle hem that haue i-made confession of here synnes and haue no3t doo no parte of here penaunce inioynyd or ellis that hath begon here penaunce and haue no3t fully fulfillyd it, and or they my3te do it here, they were passid hens and are dwellynge in peynes til the tyme that they be fully purgyd...[74]

Heaven was for the perfect souls and hell for the 'utterly evel' but most people would suffer in purgatory after death.[75]

Not all alms were efficacious in the quest for spiritual attainment through disposal of goods. The fruits of usurious or unlawful activities could not be accepted as charity.[76] The Fathers of the Church condemned usurious gain unequivocally and eleventh- and twelfth-century theologians and canonists were obliged to take up this subject owing to the growth in monetary activities.[77] They returned to the authority of the Fathers and cited the prohibition on usurious lending, reasoning from it that gain was theft and therefore entailed restitution.[78]

[72] 'Ligna equaliter sicca in eodem igne equaliter comburuntur, sed equaliter mali sunt ligna equaliter desiccata ab humore gratie, ergo in eodem igne, scilicet in igne gehenne, equaliter puniuntur...Non enim est necesse quod ligna equaliter sicca equaliter comburentur in eodem igne. Si enim irrigetur et madefiat, reliquum non, non equaliter cumburuntur. Eodem modo in inferno cum suffragia ecclesie sint quasi quedam irrigationes, si pro altero equaliter malorum suffragia fiant, pro reliquo non, non est necesse equaliter eos puniri', *Summa aurea in quattuor libris sententiarum* (Paris, 1500, repr. Frankfurt, 1964), fol. 303va, also quoted in Bernstein, 'Esoteric theology', p. 524, n. 65.

[73] Longère, *Oeuvres oratoires* I, pp. 14–20, 32–3. On the concepts of hell and purgatory as tools for social control see Bernstein, 'Theology between heresy and folklore', pp. 28–31.

[74] *Speculum sacerdotale*, ed. E. H. Weatherly (London, 1936), c.61, p. 224. This is an early fifteenth-century handbook with guidelines for sermons and instruction on church liturgy and customs, *ibid.*, pp. xxi–xxiv, xxvi.

[75] 'and there be som in the mene be-twyx there two wayes and for hem is siche commendacion and prayers to be made', *ibid.*, c.62, p. 234.

[76] Discussion in *Summa theologiae*, II–II, q.32.a.7.

[77] For the theological discussion of usury see J. T. Noonan Jr, *The scholastic analysis of usury* (Cambridge, Mass., 1957), *passim*; B. Nelson, *The idea of usury: from tribal brotherhood to universal otherhood* (Chicago & London, 2nd edn, 1969), pp. 6–24.

[78] Noonan, *The Scholastic analysis of usury*, pp. 15–17.

Clergymen were forbidden to lend in usury by Pope Leo I in the fifth century, a prohibition imposed on all Christians by canon 13 of Lateran II (1139).[79] From this line of thought arose the ruling against charitable giving from the fruits of usury, first formulated by Ivo of Chartres.[80] Henceforth councils and canonists proceeded to extend the prohibition so as to include transactions in which usurious gain was disguised.[81] The twelfth-century *Summa Parisiensis* judged that 'verily, because alms cannot be given from usurious (gains)...And if in fact alms are given from unlawful gains, then it will not benefit you but rather the person whose money it had been'.[82] In no way could unlawful gains be used for the acquisition of merit through charitable deeds, and this was clearly stated in canon 25 of Lateran III.[83] Thus, a usurer could not benefit from charitable activity, nor could his heirs enjoy the goods amassed by him.[84] Unlawful gains were to be restored to the usurer's victims; in cases when they could not be found they were to be given to the poor or to a religious house.[85] In the discussion of the absence of efficacy in alms offered from illegal gains the importance of intent rather than of practical performance was confirmed expressing a growing awareness of intent and conscience in religious activity.[86] At

[79] *Ibid.*, pp. 15–18; J. T. I. Gilchrist, *The church and economic activity in the Middle Ages* (London, 1969), p. 63; *Conciliorum oecumenicorum decreta*, ed. G. Alberigo *et al.* (Bologna, third edn, 1973), p. 200.

[80] For an example of the teaching against giving of sinful gains see Alan of Lille, 'Summa de arte praedicatoria', *PL* 210, col.175, c.33: '*Quid* insinuatur quod de proprio debeat fieri eleemosyna, non de alieno. Non enim de furto vel de rapina'.

[81] Noonan, *The scholastic analysis of usury*, pp. 19–20. On the theological discussions *ibid.*, pp. 41–81. Two schools of thought developed among theologians and canonists, differing in the degree to which they accepted the validity of the profit economy, R. de Roover, *La pensée économique des scolastiques. Doctrines et méthodes* (Montreal, 1970), pp. 20–1.

[82] 'et verum est, quia de usurio non potest fieri eleemosyna...Si ergo de facto fiat eleemosyna de male acquisito, non tibi sed ei forte cujus erit pecunia proderit', *The Summa Parisiensis, ad* c.14 q.5, p. 171.

[83] *Conciliorum oecumenicorum decreta*, p. 223. On the nature of illicit earnings see St Bernardino's distinctions, *Opera omnia* VIII, c.15, pp. 80–2, who divided them into three types: 'ilicita substantia potest tripliciter nominari: iniqua,...iniusta,...turpis', *ibid.*, pp. 80–1.

[84] On the duties of usurers' sons to make restitution see *Les statuts de Paris et le synodal de l'Ouest*, ed. O. Pontal (Paris, 1971), c.113, p. 218.

[85] Robert of Flamborough, *Summa de matrimonio et de usuris*, ed. J. F. Schulte (Giessen, 1868), c.5, p. xxvii: 'solvat lucrum pretium illis, a quibus receptae sunt usurae, si sciuntur; si non, pauperibus detur, vel dentur possessiones illae alicui domui religiosae'. However, the true victims took precedence over the poor, see Teutonicus' commentary on Lateran IV, c.69: 'Si autem dominus inveniretur a quo istud extortum est, illi potius esset reddendum quam dandum pauperibus', *Constitutiones concilii*, p. 268.

[86] Knights were advised that their generous benefactions were only a form of necessary restitution, *Les statuts de Paris*, c.113, p. 218: 'consuletur militibus qui largiores

the end of its discussion of the categories of the poor, the *Summa elegantius* (*c.* 1169) reminds its reader that 'God will reward you not according to the quality of life of those you receive [in alms], but by your own will and mercy'.[87]

What were the signs of poverty? One simple scholastic answer says: 'poverty is discerned by its effects: it can be seen by the quality of place, because one lives in a hospital; or by weakness of body, because one is sick, and cannot feed oneself'.[88] The canonical debate on the identity of the deserving poor has been discussed in detail by Brian Tierney who has identified the lines of thought which prevailed in the twelfth and thirteenth centuries.[89] If theologians saw the poor as living the life of Christ, ordinary people who encountered poverty and begging all around them were inclined to be less charitable. Even in theological terms the poor possessed neither *dignitas* nor *auctoritas*.[90] Ugly poverty hovered over most medieval men and women; revulsion towards and rejection of the poor must have been a common attitude, sufficiently so to cause the thirteenth century glossator Iohannes Andreae to insist: 'Paupertas non est de genere malorum'.[91] In practice finer distinctions of degrees of poverty were needed not only for pious faithful but for the administrators of parochial relief and for almoners of religious institutions.[92]

The basic text in the *Decretum* relating to discrimination in almsgiving came from St John Chrysostom who was taken to recommend indiscriminate giving: 'In hospitality there ought not to be discrimination between people, but we must act hospitably without difference to any one however we can'.[93] Many agreed with Chrysostom that

spontaneas elemosynas faciunt, ut...videretur quod dampnificatis daretur et resacretur'.

[87] 'Non ex vita eorum quos recipis tibi redditurus est Deus, set ex voluntate et misericordia tua', *Summa 'elegantius in iure divino' seu coloniensis*, ed. G. Fransen (Vatican, 1969), c.54, p. 67.

[88] 'Paupertas probatur ab effectu. Item probatur ex loci qualitate, quia moratur in hospitali; tam probatur ex corporis debilitate, quia est infirmus, et non potest quaerere sibi victum', Baldus, as in R. C. Trexler, 'The bishop's portion: generic pious legacies in the late Middle Ages in Italy', *Traditio* 28 (1972), pp. 397–450; p. 435.

[89] B. Tierney, 'The decretists and the "deserving poor"', *Comparative studies in society and history* 1 (1958–9), pp. 360–73.

[90] *Decretum* c.2 q.1, x.20.32, x.1.6.22. Michaud-Quantin, *Etudes sur le vocabulaire philosophique du moyen-âge* (Rome, 1970), p. 175. Thus, they were not fit to hold public office, nor to plead or testify in court, *idem*, 'Le vocabulaire des catégories sociales', pp. 80–81.

[91] *Glossa ordinaria ad Sext.* c.1.q.3.c.11; also Teutonicus 'paupertas non est de numero malorum' *Glossa ordinaria* c.2 q.1 c.14.   [92] See below pp. 245–59.

[93] 'In hospitalitate autem non est habendus delectus personarum, sed indifferenter quibuscumque sufficimus hospitales nos exhibere debemus', *Decretum* D.42 *dictum post* c.1.

no discrimination should be made between needy recipients[94] but most canonists felt that when charitable offerings could not meet the demand some meaningful scale of merit should be applied. Ambrose recommended special consideration of the age and fortunes of the recipient, while Augustine prohibited the giving of alms to people in unlawful professions.[95] The latter held that it was better to take bread away from a hungry man than to provide food which would allow him to pursue sinful activities. The *Glossa ordinaria*, the basic commentary on the *Decretum* throughout the late Middle Ages, surveyed all current views and settled for a scale of merit based on the recipient's virtue as well as his closeness to the giver; thus a heretical father was less deserving than a virtuous stranger.[96] When quoting the Augustinian prohibition on alleviation of criminals it cautioned against one who can work and earn his bread and chooses not to, but rather 'plays all day long with dies and cubes'.[97] When discussing parochial poor relief, Teutonicus stated that: 'the Church need not provide for those who can work. One must take into account wholeness of body and strength of constitution when alms are dispensed'.[98] A distinction which became more common in later centuries, the ability to work, was only a sideline to the many discussions of deserving poverty in the thirteenth century.[99]

Canonists were obliged to cope with the existence of these two approaches which favoured differing degrees of discrimination in almsgiving, and to provide guidelines. In the twelfth-century *Summa decretorum* Rufinus developed the scale of preferences suggested by Ambrose, using the term *caritas ordinata* to justify the application of an 'ordered' discrimination.[100] The order was described in the form of

94 Tierney, *Medieval poor law*, pp. 59–60.

95 *Decretum* D.86 cc.7–9, 14–18.

96 *Glossa ordinaria ad* D.86 c.14 and *ad* D.30 c.1 expressing the widespread twelfth-century interpretation.

97 'Set hic intelligitur in eo casu cum quis potest laborare et suo labore sibi victum querere et non vult, set tota die ludit, in alea vel taxilis', *Glossa ordinaria ad* C.5.q.5.c.2.

98 'Et qui potest laborare, non debet ecclesia providere. Integritas membrorum enim et robur membrorum in conferenda elemosyna est attendenda', *Glossa ordinaria ad* D.82 ante c.1.

99 On views of work in the Central Middle Ages see K. Bosl, 'Armut, Arbeit, Emanzipation. Zu den Hintergrunden der geistigen und literarischen Bewegung vom 11.–13. Jahrhundert', in *Beiträge zur Wirtschafts- und Sozialgeschichte des Mittelalters. Festschrift für Herbert Helbig*, ed. K. Schulz (Cologne, 1976), pp. 128–46; and for the later Middle Ages based on *Piers plowman* see Aers, '*Piers plowman* and problems in the perception of poverty', pp. 5–25.

100 Rufinus, *Die summa decretorum der Magister Rufinus*, ed. H. Singer (Paderborn, 1902), p. 100, Dist. 42: 'Caritas debet esse ordinata, ut post Deum parentes, deinde filii, post domestici ad ultimum extranei diligantur'.

concentric circles emanating from the individual to his children, household, friends, neighbours and so on.[101] When a giver was confronted with two cases of equal proximity, he was to apply another scale which tested the recipient's virtue. This approach considered the petitioner's moral quality, the giver's resources, the reason for request and the amount needed. The twelfth-century glossator, Stephen of Tournai, suggested a useful classification, distinguishing between alms and hospitality; discrimination was to be used in almsgiving while indoor hospitality should be given to any one who needed it.[102]

Rufinus' compromise was widely accepted in Italy and later in France. His view was put succinctly in the *Summa elegantius*: 'In almsgiving there should be distinction between people. You had better give to your own than to strangers, to the sick rather than to the healthy, to ashamed rather than to aggressive beggars, to the have-not rather than to him who has, and amongst the needy, first to the just and then to the unjust. That is ordered charity'.[103] An Anglo-norman *summa* originating probably from Oxford *c*. 1186 followed the *Summa elegantius* in the view that only in the case of known petitioners could one discriminate, not with strangers. It also maintained that a man who was able to work was to be corrected, rather than sustained.[104] Like Stephen of Tournai, the author of this English *summa* differentiated between hospitality and almsgiving, since it was difficult for a wayfarer seeking shelter to prove his identity.

Most discussions of the 'deserving poor' dealt with situations where limited funds were available and decisions on the identity of those most meriting help were to be taken.[105] As we have seen, the view inspired by Augustine recommended denial of alms to those who could work or who led evil lives.[106] Another view sought to help all needy by a scale of preference in which kinship and friendship were major factors, with the reservation that those who would immediately proceed to crime and sin should not be helped.[107] The poor were not to be offered

[101] This is the scale applied by Aquinas, *Summa theologiae*, II–II, q.26; also by St Bernardino who supplied an 'ordo' of grounds for discrimination between the poor on the basis of need, proximity, sanctity, virtue, friendship, Christianity and shame (in poverty), *Opera omnia* VIII, 'De eleemosyna' c.13, pp. 86–7.

[102] Tierney, 'The "deserving poor"', pp. 364–5.

[103] 'In elemosina autem delectus personarum habendus ut potius suis quam alienis, infirmis quam sanis, mendicare erubescenti quam effronti, egenti quam habenti, et inter egentes iusto prius quam iniusto des. Hec est caritas ordinata', *Summa elegantius*, c.54, p. 67.

[104] Tierney, 'The "deserving poor"', p. 367.   [105] *Ibid.*, p. 368.

[106] Cf. Rufinus, *Summa decretorum*, p. 100: 'Per haec omnia claret quia non omni ad nos venienti debemus indifferenter nos exhibere largificos'.

[107] In his reference to begging William of St Amour maintained that only the sick, old and unemployable should be allowed to beg, never the healthy, C. Thouzellier, 'La

rich and fine foods which would not agree with their constitution and which might excite their senses.[108] Thomas Aquinas clearly believed that alms ought not to provide an easy life for the recipient,[109] and should be given only to those who had no other source of livelihood.[110]

With the growth of fear of the poor as agents of change and disruption in the later Middle Ages, attitudes towards religious poverty were bound to be affected. In the late thirteenth and fourteenth centuries doubts within the mendicant orders on the nature of poverty led to a wide-ranging debate on the poverty of Christ and the Apostles and its relation to human perfection.[111] The mendicants taught that by pursuing a life of poverty they were imitating the life of Jesus, a demand which the Church never exacted from its ordained. The alternative of mendicancy imperilled the hierarchy of the Church, but also endangered the souls in its care. Bishops and secular theologians guarded the view that there was little in common between Christ's poverty and the recommended religious life of believers. Even Aquinas saw virtue not necessarily in the renunciation of all goods but in the absence of attachment to them.[112] Pope John XXII finally condemned the view that Jesus and the Apostles 'had not the right of using, giving, selling or exchanging the goods which they held'.[113] Moreover, not all Christians were encouraged to renounce the world nor were all poor seen as meritorious.[114] But if voluntary poverty was

place de *De Periculis* de Guillaume de Saint Amour dans les polémiques universitaires du XIIIe siècle'. *Revue historique* 156 (1927), pp. 67–83; p. 73. Tierney, *Medieval poor law*, p. 58; example *Summa Parisiensis ad* D.86. *dictum post* c.6, p. 67.

[108] Tierney, 'The "deserving poor"', p. 366.

[109] *Summa theologiae* II–II, q.32.a.1, a.2 & *ad*. 3.

[110] *Ibid.*, q.32.a.5 *ad.4*.

[111] R. Manselli, 'Da Dante à Coluccio Salutati. Discussions sur la pauvreté à Florence au XIVe siècle', Mollat, *Etudes* II, pp. 637–59; p. 645. For the main claims against mendicant absolute poverty see those expressed by William of St Amour, Thouzellier, 'La place de *De Periculis*', *passim* as well as M. M. Dufeuil, *Guillaume de St. Amour et la polémique universitaire parisienne, 1250–1259* (Paris 1972); esp. pp. 1–82. On the disputes within the Franciscan order see G. Leff, *Heresy in the Middle Ages* I (Manchester and New York, 1967), pp. 51–166. See also A. Vauchez, 'La pauvreté volontaire au moyen âge', *Annales* 25 (1970), pp. 1566–73; pp. 1571–2.

[112] *Summa theologiae* II–II q.18; Tocca, *La quistione della povertà*, p. 9. For other views against the proponents of total poverty see Manteuffel, *Naissance d'une hérésie*, pp. 86–8. For some fourteenth-century treatises arising from the debate see John Peckam, *Fratris Iohannis Peckam tractatus tres de paupertate*, ed. C. L. Kingford, A. G. Little and F. Tocco (Aberdeen, 1910).

[113] M. D. Lambert, *Franciscan poverty: the doctrine of the absolute poverty of Christ and the apostles in the Franciscan order, 1210–1323* (London, 1961), p. 236. The decisive bull was *Cum inter nonnullos* of 1323. For a survey of papal legislation on this matter, see *ibid.*, pp. 225–42.

[114] For the expression of this view in the workings of the papal inquisition see J. Paul, 'Narbonne et la querelle de la pauvreté', *Narbonne. Archéologie et histoire* I,

not of the quality of the poverty of Christ, what was its merit? Once divested of the mystique of holiness, poverty could seem rude and cruel. Yet in some circles the adherence to the ideal of absolute poverty and the imitation of Christ were regarded as indivisible.[115]

The acceptance of poverty as a beneficial aspect of a life of religious perfection was scrutinised in the late thirteenth and fourteenth centuries in the great debate on poverty: the challenge of the friars' external poverty threatened to usurp the autonomy of the established pastoral Church and the virtue of monastic life. This danger called for a reexamination of the social and spiritual benefits of poverty which were rephrased in more restricted terms. Those who insisted on the absolute necessity of total poverty, like the Spiritual Franciscans, came in the end to be seen as heretics and remained on the fringe of religious existence. As hostile attitudes towards labourers, and subsequently towards those deemed to be shirkers – the able-bodied beggars – hardened, the polemic on religious poverty was increasingly couched in terms current in labour legislation. Thus, poverty was divorced from its association with voluntary denunciation of goods, which was occasionally seen as a departure from the established ecclesiastical and doctrinal norms; it came to be seen as a form of begging, of living off the hard-won earnings of others.[116] In the late Middle Ages those pursuing religious poverty, like the beguines and beghards in the Rhineland, were denounced, not as somewhat heretical adherents to the idea of absolute poverty, but as people refusing labour and shirking their social duties.[117] In a society which was highly sensitive to fulfilment of social and economic roles, these extraordinary groups were noticeable as a social anomaly. It was only a matter of time before their voluntary poverty and their ragged, unendowed existence were compared to and identified with vagrants and beggars.[118]

An interesting off-shoot of these clear scales of relative merit is the case of the *pauperes verecundi*, the shame-faced poor, people who had fallen from comfort to poverty. The consideration of the particular misery of a person who had fallen from power and riches appears in the writings of the Fathers of the Church, especially treated by

---

(Narbonne, 1973), pp. 157–62. On changes in the views of real poverty see F. Graus, 'Au bas moyen-âge: pauvres des villes et pauvres des campagnes', *Annales* 16 (1961), pp. 1053–65; p. 1056.

[115] Manselli, 'Da Dante', p. 653.   [116] See above pp. 31–3.

[117] J.-C. Schmitt, *Mort d'une hérésie*, p. 137: 'hérésie c'est effacée au profit d'un autre grief, nouveau venu dans la polémique: le mendiant valide'. On the image of beguines and beghards in fifteenth-century polemic as vagabonds see *ibid.*, pp. 174–5.

[118] *Ibid.*, pp. 153–61.

Ambrose and Augustine. Yet the theme remained largely dormant until the thirteenth century.[119] G. Ricci has traced the history of thinking about the shame-faced poor from the early Christian writers to the renewed discussions of thirteenth-century theologians and canonists.[120] Concern developed because the *pauperes verecundi* suffered not only privation and physical need, but also shame and dislocation. Once gained, this insight was ripe for reintroduction into discussion when scales of poverty were being reassessed. A new awareness not only of poverty but also of subjectivity encouraged an appreciation of the difference between habitual poverty and the state of the *déclassé*. Even the champion of work, William of St Amour, in his diatribe against mendicancy, recognised cases in which people could be justified in living off charity: scholars, children, those weak by nature and those weak by habit.[121] Thirteenth-century theologians were also disturbed by the aspect of social disruption embodied in the condition of the shame-faced poor. When writers revived interest in this category of poverty they noted the aggravating circumstances of such poverty, which ran contrary to social order and obligations.[122] In the later Middle Ages, these fallen poor were seen as a case especially deserving, when many other poor folk were being chastised as wilful and undeserving.[123]

As happened in other fields of intellectual inquiry into social and religious problems, the twelfth-century view of poverty was based on the Fathers of the Church, while the next century witnessed a more developed debate. In the later Middle Ages qualification and correction continued as social reality and scholastic refinement demanded. A parallel development has been observed in English vernacular homiletic writings of the eleventh and twelfth centuries. From a preoccupation with the establishment of social hierarchy and order there is a shift to finer distinctions and subtler demands from believers. Sermons of the late twelfth and the thirteenth centuries campaigned less against violence; in a society which had achieved some degree of political, legal and social organisation, they exhorted the rich and powerful to be

---

[119] Most appearances in *exempla* and hagiographical material appear after 1250, Ricci, 'La naissance du pauvre honteux', p. 168.

[120] Ricci, 'La naissance du pauvre honteux', pp. 160–2.

[121] *Ibid.*, pp. 163–4. Aquinas also believed that the old, sick and those fallen from their status were justly deserving of charity, *Summa theologiae* II–II q.86 *post* c.6 and cc.14, 16–17. See Tierney, *Medieval poor law*, pp. 54–8

[122] Where an aggravating factor in the condition of the poor is, undoubtedly, shame, *Summa theologiae* II–II q.32 a.10.

[123] Ricci, 'La naissance du pauvre honteux', p. 173.

charitable and to show pure intent in their help to the weaker members of society.[124]

The basic maxim underlying charitable giving was that earthly goods existed for the subsistence of all men as ruled by the law of charitable sharing. The onus of distribution was on the one who had been provided with goods, and when this duty was not carried out it warranted a certain degree of social pressure – according to some writers, actual violence – in the enforcement of the obligation. The poor were instruments towards perfection and salvation in the hands of ordinary members of society, landlords, householders, businessmen, artisans and peasants. Between the 'haves' and 'have-nots' there was scope for mutually beneficial material and spiritual exchange. A conservative message which did not make rigorous demands and which was couched in ambiguities and flexible interpretations allowed the faithful to interpret their duties within a system that accepted inequality yet sought to modify its effects by the extension of charitable bonds.[125]

THE IDEA OF CHARITY IN POPULAR SERMONS AND RELIGIOUS INSTRUCTION

The development of the system of religious instruction

How were the ideas formulated in the schools of Christendom brought to the attention and comprehension of Christians? Not every *clericus* was allowed to teach and give spiritual guidance. In twelfth-century Europe those who lawfully delivered sermons were the bishops, parish priests, secular canons, deacons, archdeacons and Doctors of Theology.[126] Preaching was regarded as so important an office that the right to preach was closely guarded. Within a diocese preaching was under the control of bishops through a system of licensing.[127] From the thirteenth century the world of religious instruction changed with the undertaking of a

---

[124] K. Greenfield, 'Changing emphases in English vernacular homiletic literature, 960–1225', *Journal of medieval history* 7 (1981), pp. 283–97; 294–5.

[125] On the gap between teachings and popular views see Geremek, 'Criminalité', pp. 346–51.

[126] H. G. Pfander, *The popular sermon of the medieval friar in England* (New York, 1937), p. 1; G. R. Owst, *Preaching in medieval England* (Cambridge, 1926), pp. 1–6. A fourteenth-century guide for preachers by Robert of Basevorn defined the right to preach as held by: 'Praedicator ex officio est: papa, cardinales, episcopi, et curam habentes animarum, et hoc ex ordinaria jurisdictione; et ex commissione religiosi, secundum privilegia eis indulta', T.-M. Charland, *Artes praedicandi* (Paris and Ottawa, 1936), p. 238. For a general survey of medieval preaching see J. Longère, *La prédication médiévale* (Paris, 1983).

[127] *Councils and synods* II part I, Canterbury statutes I (1213 × 4), c.51, pp. 33–4.

part of this mission by the mendicant orders.[128] The admission of the
new orders into the group of licensed teachers was a consequence of
the greater need for evangelisation and education which manifested
itself in a society encountering serious internal change and dissent.
Parish priests, burdened with the tasks of pastoral care, were not free
to propagate a popular religious awakening and to lead the campaign
against heresy. The friars, free from temporal connections and duties,
were more suited to fulfil the task.

Sermons were usually delivered on Sundays and feast days, the
occasions on which laymen were most likely to enter a church.[129] In
a short study of the religious practices of the poor in thirteenth-century
France, based on the testimony of Humbert of Romans, A. Murray
concludes that church attendance was very low indeed among artisans,
servants, day-labourers and the poor.[130] If few attended church
regularly this hampered attempts at wide-ranging religious instruction;
consequently, the friars went out to the streets and market-places and
sought out their audiences.

The impulse towards reform, culminating in the decrees of Lateran
IV, attempted to widen the basis of laymen's knowledge. Annual
confession and communion were demanded and great emphasis was
laid on the encounter between laymen and priests at confession.[131] On
this occasion priests were to examine their parishioners on their
knowledge of the Pater Noster, the Ave Maria and the Creed. Several
clauses stressed the need to explain the teachings in the vernacular,
'ydiomate',[132] Children (*pueri*) were to be instructed by the parish
priests since parents quite often neglected their duties or were
themselves ignorant.[133] The statutes of Durham II (1241 × 9) added the
baptismal formula and some psalms to the minimal knowledge

128 On the Franciscan view of the task see C. N. L. Brooke, 'The missionary at home:
the Church in the towns 1000–1250', *Studies in Church history* 6 (1970), pp. 59–83; pp.
59–62, 83.

129 On the occasions on which a famous preacher such as Stephen Langton delivered
sermons see P. B. Roberts, *Stephanus de lingua tonante. Studies in the sermons of Stephen
Langton* (Toronto, 1968), pp. 62–3.

130 'Raro veniunt in ecclesiam', A. Murray, 'Religion among the poor in thirteenth-century
France: the testimony of Humbert de Romans', *Traditio* 30 (1974), pp. 285–324, pp.
298–9; 301. An *exemplum* praises the pious matron who encouraged her maid to go
and hear a sermon in church, Jacques of Vitry, *The exempla*, no. 224, p. 93.

131 *Conciliorum oecumenicorum decreta*, c.21, p. 245.

132 *Councils and synods* II part I, Salisbury I, (1217 × 9), c.3, p. 61; Winchester statutes I
(1224), c.5, p. 134, demanded instruction of the missing knowledge *in materna lingua*
as do the statutes of Worcester III (1229), c.8, p. 172.

133 *Ibid.*, Exeter statutes I (1225 × 37), c.2, p. 228; Durham statutes II (1241 × 9), c.2, p.
424; Winchester statutes III (1262 × 5), c.59, p. 713.

demanded of laymen.[134] The deepening of knowledge and of religious sentiment could not occur without a massive campaign of instruction and education carried out by priests and friars. Already in Lateran III some provision was made for teaching in cathedrals, aimed at improving the theological knowledge of local clergy.[135] In Lateran IV it was decreed that every diocese should have a resident theologian[136] and bishops were to employ preaching assistants to complete the teaching task.[137] But only in the *Cum ex eo*, promulgated by Pope Boniface VIII in 1298, was an effective arrangement proposed not only for the training of cathedral canons but to attract young and able men to parish priesthood.[138] The bull allowed the incumbent of a parish to be absent during a course of university study. The demand that he be ordained within the period of study indicates that the people it wished to attract were men in lower orders who otherwise might not have shouldered the cure of souls. The duties of such parish priests were expanded throughout the thirteenth century as instruction improved;[139] priests were to be examined before admission to a living with cure of souls.[140] Yet legislating assemblies continued to lament the still rampant ignorance: 'because many ignorant and illiterate people usurp the pastoral office to the danger of souls'.[141]

Archdeacons were entrusted with the dissemination of local synodal decisions and of articles of the faith to parish clergy[142] and priests were to have suitable liturgical books and records of synodal decrees.[143] From the mid-thirteenth century it was required that priests know the list of the Ten Commandments, the seven deadly sins and the seven

---

[134] *Ibid.*, c.2, p. 423; also enacted in Ely diocesan statutes (1239 × 56), c.5, p. 517.

[135] Canon 18, *Conciliorum oecumenicorum decreta*, p. 220.

[136] Canon 11, *ibid.*, p. 240.

[137] As in canon 10 of Lateran IV, *ibid.*, pp. 239–40.

[138] On the *Cum ex eo* see L. E. Boyle, 'The constitution "Cum ex eo" of Boniface VIII: education of parochial clergy', *Mediaeval studies* 24 (1962), pp. 263–302; on its aims see esp. pp. 274–83.

[139] On the influence of Lateran IV in French pastoral life with special reference to the Midi see R. Foreville, 'Les statuts synodaux et le renouveau pastoral du xiiie siècle dans le Midi de la France', *Cahiers de Fanjeaux* 6 (1971), pp. 119–50; pp. 119–26.

[140] *Councils and synods* II part 1, Worcester statutes III (1240), c.97, p. 320; Ely statutes (1239 × 56), c.2, p. 517; Wells statutes (1258), c.43, p. 609.

[141] 'Quia multi inscii et illiterati pastoris officium in periculum animarum usurpant, precipimus quia...', *ibid.*, Wells statutes (1258), c.43, p. 609.

[142] *Ibid.*, Salisbury statutes I (1217 × 9), c.3, p. 61; Durham statutes II (1241 × 9), c.4, p. 424.

[143] As demanded by the north-western French constitutions of *c.* 1203, *Les statuts de Paris*, c.50, p. 70; see also *ibid.*, pp. lxviii–lxxvii. Peter of Poitiers praised the diocese of Paris in which parish priests were obliged to possess collections of synodal statutes, *Summa de confessione. Compilatio praesens*, ed. J. Longère (Turnhout, 1980), c.38, pp. 43, 45–6.

sacraments.[144] Archbishop Peckham's canons of Lambeth of 1281 summarised a whole century's developments. These obliged priests to preach at least four times a year in the vernacular, to teach the Creed, the Commandments, the works of mercy; to expound the lists of virtues and vices and to explain the meaning of the sacraments.[145]

An early fourteenth-century compilation for use by parish priests, the *Summa summarum*, combined contemporary theology and canonists' decrees as well as the contents of a *Summa confessorum*, to create an encyclopedic reference book for the parish priest.[146] This was a simplified yet sound and updated compilation which was meant to fill gaps in pastoral knowledge. The author of this and of other pastoral instruction books, William of Pagula (*c.* 1320), expressed his aim in the preface:

And since the cure of souls is the art of arts, science of sciences, as the souls of men are more precious than any other things and bodies...We decree that it is indeed ignoble for priests called to this mission to be almost ignorant of its cause, just as it is repugnant for a lawyer to lack the knowledge of the law in which he is versed... And so that henceforth no one can be accused of ignorance of canon law, I have composed this *summa* to be as brief and concise as the little learning given me by God has allowed me...And I have done this for ignorant folk and those who know nothing of canon law...I have made this *summa* for the benefit and use of poor clerics, so that having books thus collected into a compendium they should be able to find all the things they may require.[147]

---

[144] *Councils and Synods* II part 1, Lincoln statutes (1239), c.1, p. 268: 'Quia igitur sine decalogi observatione salus animarum non constitit...firmiter iniungentes ut unusquisque pastor animarum et quilibet sacerdos parochialis sciat decalogum, id est decem mandata legis mosaice, eademque populo...predicet et exponat. Sciat quoque que sunt septem criminalia...sciat insuper saltem simpliciter septem ecclesiastica sacramenta..'; also Worcester statutes III (1240), c.34, p. 304; Norwich statutes, c.1, p. 345; Winchester statutes II (1247), c.1, p. 403. On legislation concerning preaching see Cheney, *English synodalia of the thirteenth century*, pp. 96–109.

[145] *Councils and synods* II part 2, Lambeth statutes (1281), c.9, pp. 900–5; Owst, *Preaching*, pp. 281–2.

[146] L. E. Boyle, 'The "Summa summarum" and some other English works of canon law', in *Proceedings of the second international congress of medieval canon Law*, ed. S. Kuttner and J. J. Ryan (Vatican, 1965), pp. 415–56; p. 423.

[147] 'Et quia regimen animarum est ars arcium, sciencia scienciarum, cum anime hominum sint preciores omnibus aliis rebus et corporibus...Precipimus, valde ignominiosum est clericis ad hoc regimen vocatis causam ipsius regiminis penitus ignorare, sicut turpis est advocato ignorare ius in quo versatur'; 'Ne quis igitur de cetero ignorancia iuris canonici valeat honeste accusari, hanc summam composui quam breviter et levius potui secundum modicam scienciam mihi a Deo ministratam...Et hoc feci pro rudibus et penitus ignorantibus ius canonicum...Hanc eciam summam feci ad profectum et utilitatem pauperum clericorum ut si forte copiam librorum habuerint hic collecta sub compendio multa de hiis inveniant que requirunt', Boyle, 'The "Summa summarum"', pp. 440, 442.

In this literary genre of instruction books for the clergy programmes of sermons were provided. Scholars and bishops consciously attempted to bring theological formulations to the knowledge and comprehension of parish priests.[148] These compilations drew from earlier homiletic and exegetical writings to create a sound and useful guidebook for preaching clergy; an effort heavily supported at the diocesan level. In England, bishops responded to the general need and to the demands of Lateran IV by compiling guidebooks locally.[149] One such was the treatise of Bishop Alexander Stavensby on Sunday sermons offered to his diocesan clergy in the statutes of Coventry (1224 × 37).[150] Bishop Peter Quivil's *Summula* dealt with confessional practices and discussed the Ten Commandments and the seven deadly sins.[151] The *Instituta* of Bishop Roger Weseham of Coventry served to guide his diocesan clergy on confessional practices.[152] Alphabetical indexes, concordances, new tools for the quick location of instruction material developed in the service of parish clergy and preaching friars.[153] A multitude of tools prepared by scholars, bishops and friars became the weapons of the great mission of teaching in which the friars themselves came to play a vital role.

The friars devoted the fullest attention to religious instruction and to the conquest of souls.[154] By their mere existence the mendicants presented an alternative to secular urban society which was antithetical

---

148 William of Montibus is an example of such activities, see H. MacKinnon, 'William de Montibus: a medieval teacher', in *Essays in medieval history presented to Bertie Wilkinson*, eds. T. A. Sandquist and M. R. Powicke (Toronto, 1969), pp. 32–45; *passim*; 'He was an early and forceful participant in a movement that was to transmit new ideas in a popular way', p. 45. It is through him and other bishops, archdeacons and diocesan officials with higher education that the university of Paris directly influenced the contents and scope of instruction to clergy, and subsequently to laity; on his connection with Peter the Chanter, *ibid.*, p. 33.

149 D. W. Robertson Jr, 'Frequency of preaching in thirteenth–century England', *Speculum* 24 (1949), pp. 376–88; Cheney, *English synodalia*, pp. 1–50. By 1265 every English diocese had contributed to the synodal effort, *ibid.*, p. 36. For France see Foreville, 'Les statuts synodaux', pp. 123–4.

150 *Councils and synods* II part 1, pp. 214–20 (an exposition on the seven deadly sins), pp. 220–6 (an exposition on penance); Cheney, *English synodalia*, pp. 40–3.

151 It also analysed the implications of the circumstances of a sin upon the penance imposed, providing a practical aid to the priest-confessor, *Councils and synods* II part 2, Exeter statutes II (1287?), pp. 1060–77.

152 Cheney, *English synodalia*, p. 150.

153 R. H. Rouse and M. A. Rouse, *Preachers, florilegia and sermons: studies on the Manipulus florum of Thomas of Ireland* (Toronto, 1979), pp. 3–4, 6; Roberts, *Stephanus de lingua tonante*, pp. 44–5.

154 On the friars' preaching see Pfander, *The popular sermon*, *passim*; and pp. 2–6. They did, of course, follow in a tradition of preaching by secular clergy; on the importance of preaching in the twelfth century see Longère, *Oeuvres oratoires* I, pp. 37–41.

yet not antagonistic. They sought to show the way towards correction, but did not preach a total renunciation of this world; their lives were intended to be a constant reminder of faith and charity and the love of God far superior to material life. In an instruction book for young Dominicans Humbert of Romans insisted that preachers should accept no more than the food needed for their sustenance and a place to rest, and even this only in humble households,[155] for the benefit of their souls and to set an example for layfolk. Friars left their mark on the world of instruction and of religious thought and were able, through participation in the intellectual activities of the Schools, to assimilate the latest developments in theology and to transform them into tools of their mission.[156] The mendicants also offered a framework in which laymen could actively participate and share the merit accumulated by the friars. A rule for a third order of layfolk was formulated in connection with the Franciscan order as early as 1221,[157] and confraternities developed in the mendicant orders throughout Europe.[158] In the fourteenth century a clear reaction against the privileges of the mendicant orders is evident with the curtailment of their freedom within the parish framework. Nonetheless their modes of presentation and instruction remained in use well into the fifteenth century with the continual circulation of *artes praedicandi*, collections of *exempla* and the copying of mendicant works.[159]

Sermon writers and compilers of materials for religious instruction in the twelfth and thirteenth centuries could draw from many earlier sources. England was especially rich, possessing a homiletic tradition in Old English, including the works of such great writers as Aelfric and Wulfstan. These homilies conveyed a whole Christian moral system and a model of behaviour for a society still in the throes of political and religious instability.[160] However, traditional writings could no longer answer problems of a growing and diversified society. Those sins most frequently mentioned in thirteenth-century sermons were no

[155] In 'De eruditione praedicantium', in *Treatises on Preaching*, ed. W. M. Conlon (London, 1955), c.40, pp. 138–41.

[156] Rosenwein and Little, 'Social meaning in the monastic and mendicant spiritualities', p. 31. For a Dominican treatise written with this end in mind see Boyle, 'Three English pastoral *summae*', pp. 135–9.

[157] J. R. H. Moorman, *A history of the Franciscan order* (Oxford, 1968), pp. 216–18.

[158] For Florence see R. F. E. Weissman, *Ritual brotherhood in Renaissance Florence* (New York, 1982), pp. 43–6.

[159] On the form, contents and function of mendicant preaching in the thirteenth century see d'Avray, *The preaching of the friars*.

[160] Greenfield, 'Changing emphases in English vernacular homiletic literature 960–1225', esp. pp. 283–4.

longer murder and rapine but avarice, gluttony and sloth; the advent of the friars served to intensify the treatment of these questions.

The most popular form of sermon used by the friars was the thematic sermon which had already flourished in the late twelfth century. This incorporated the scholastic system by which a theme, be it a verse of scripture or a line of prayer, was minutely analysed and used as a basis for discourse.[161] The main topics were divided and analysed, grouped and delivered in a convenient and comprehensible way. Verse sermons were developed from existing homilies; similarly to prose sermons, they were interspersed with Latin which marked the structure and drew attention to important distinctions. The theme and protheme were dissected into *distinctiones* which brought into relief the main points to be learned and remembered. The use of *distinctiones* is a scholastic device employed 'as a springboard' for the dissemination of an underlying truth.[162] By the thirteenth century the preachers were well versed in the form of theme, protheme, division, amplification and exemplification. Sources for sermons were being glossed, indexed, compiled and collected under subject headings to make them more readily accessible to preachers, be they parish priests or friars.[163]

A sermon would begin with a reading from the lesson of a particular feast, and continued to comment on and discuss its theme with the help of examples from everyday life. Here *exempla* originating in patristic writings, legends and lives of saints were used.[164] Verse sermons, which were very popular in the English tradition, dictated a closer adherence to the preexisting format, while a prose sermon left more place for flexibility and for *extempore* responsiveness to the preacher's audience. Collections of *exempla* were a mine of edifying yet amusing and easily comprehensible subject-matter on every question of Christian belief, and English collectors feature prominently amongst 46 known compilers of *exempla* between 1200 and 1500.[165] The *exempla* were not only a

---

[161] On the thematic sermon see Roberts, *Stephanus de lingua tonante*, pp. 77–8.

[162] R. H. Rouse and M. A. Rouse, '*Statim invenire*: schools, preachers and new attitudes to the page', in *Renaissance and renewal in the twelfth century*, ed. R. Benson and G. Constable (Oxford, 1983), pp. 201–25; p. 217.

[163] Rouse and Rouse, *Preachers, florilegia and sermons*, pp. 1–92.

[164] On the use of *exempla* and *similitudines* see Roberts, *Stephanus de lingua tonante*, pp. 89–94; also Alan of Lille, 'Summa de arte praedicatoria', *PL* 210, c.114c and Longère, *Oeuvres oratoires* I, pp. 58–63. For a wide discussion of *exempla* as a source for historical study see C. Bremond, J. Le Goff and J.-C. Schmitt, *L'"exemplum"* (Turnhout, 1982). Between 1200–1500 there were 46 such compilations on which see J.-C. Schmitt, 'Recueils franciscains d'*exempla* et perfectionnement des techniques intellectuelles du xiiie au xve siècle', *Bibliothèque de l'Ecole des Chartes* 135 (1977), pp. 5–22.

[165] Schmitt, 'Recueils franciscains d'*exempla*', pp. 19–20; for general survey see J. A. Mosher, *The exemplum in the early religious and didactic literature of England* (New York,

literary device in the hands of the friars and a means for effecting comic relief, but also a channel for interpretation through which religious and moral ideas were put into terms with which the laity was conversant. A thirteenth-century English preacher of the old, pre-mendicant school recognised their value: 'as Gregory said that examples sting so much more than words, I shall open my mouth with parables and similitudes and exempla which are eagerly heard and which are retained in memory more firmly than words, I say, and which once having been understood, make the wise wiser'.[166]

Sermons also used traditional representations of vices and virtues (in groups of six or seven) in Latin and in the vernacular. Cycles of sins that had been inherited from the classical world and adapted by early Christian writers reached England mainly through the writings of Gregory the Great, and combined with local traditions.[167] In English writings one often finds the group of eight sins and twelve abuses of this world – a Celtic theme put to use in a Christian context.[168] The presentation of virtues as fighting against vices and of good deeds undoing evil ones was a popular iconographic scheme in medieval

1911), pp. 75–83. For such a collection of *exempla* for English Franciscan preachers see *Liber exemplorum ad usum praedicantium*, ed. A. G. Little (Aberdeen, 1908); the *Speculum laicorum* (*c.* 1284), ed. J. T. Welter (Paris, 1914); the *Gesta romanorum* (*c.* 1300) was the widest collection of Franciscan *exempla: A Middle English Version of the Gesta Romanorum*, ed. K. I. Sandred (Uppsala, 1971); for a Dominican collection from the Cambridge friary: S. L. Forte, 'A Cambridge Dominican collector of exempla in the thirteenth century', *Archivum fratrum praedicatorum* 28 (1958), pp. 115–48; *Catalogue of romances in the department of manuscripts in the British Museum* III, 3 vols., ed. H. L. D. Ward and J. A. Herbert (London, 1883–1910), pp. 477–503; a French collection: *La tabular exemplorum secundum ordinem alphabeti*, ed. J. T. Welter (Paris, 1926). A vast collection of sermon material upon every topic analysed and presented in an elaborate scholastic structure can be found in the collection by the English Dominican John Bromyard (d. 1390), *Summa praedicantium* (Antwerp, 1614).

166 Odo of Cheriton in Mosher, *The exemplum*, p. 13. Alan of Lille recommended such use: 'In fine vero, debet uti exemplis, ad probandum quod intendit, quis familiaris est doctrina exemplaris', 'Summa de arte praedicatoria', *PL* 210, col. 114.

167 M. W. Bloomfield, *The seven deadly sins: an introduction to the history of a religious concept* (East Lansing, Mich., 1952), p. 66. The Egyptian ascetics developed the Gnostic idea of a struggle within the individual, while writers such as Evagrius of Pontus and Cassian drew up lists of sins and virtues which proceeded to dominate medieval writings *ibid.*, pp. 40–5, 56–78. Prudentius developed the drama of the *psychomachia* which was redeveloped in Romanesque art in which the opposing personifications of vices and virtues were frequent themes in church sculpture. A scheme of six sins was used in the influential twelfth century 'Summa de arte praedicatoria', of Alan of Lille, *PL* 210, cols. 119–33.

168 Bloomfield, *The seven deadly sins*, pp. 107–9, 123. For an example see *Old English homilies and homiletic treatises of the twelfth and thirteenth centuries*, ed. R. Morris (London, 1867), p. 107. On the vices and virtues as a topic of theological and homiletic discourse in the twelfth century see Longère, *Oeuvres oratoires* I, pp. 277–355.

sculpture.[169] In such representations *caritas* vanquishes the sin of *avaritia*, a struggle frequently depicted in thirteenth-century English minor arts.[170]

Numerical schemes of the works of mercy were formulated by the end of the twelfth century.[171] Lists of the works of spiritual and corporal mercy were to appear in such universal instruction books as the *Speculum christiani*,[172] for fourteenth-century literate laymen and their families, who were able to read and learn without the mediation of clergy, as well as in a vernacular catechism for laymen of that period.[173] With these tools in hand preachers proceeded to attack the ills of this world; the friars surpassed all other preachers in the refinement of their instruments of teaching and in their effective approach. Latin mendicant writings came to influence and dominate the late medieval world of preaching.[174]

The message of charity conveyed in popular instruction

One of the important intellectual developments of the thirteenth century was the greater expression of social awareness in religious writings. The emergence of sermons *ad status* is the reflection of a sophisticated view of society recognising its various groups and their differing functions and orientations.[175] The place in society occupied by a believer dictated the choice of words and figures which a preacher could make in his attempt to persuade and convert him, and to that extent it influenced the choice of means for his salvation.[176] The greatest

---

169 Thérel, '"Caritas" et "paupertas"', pp. 300–3.

170 R. B. Green, 'Virtues and vices in the chapter house vestibule in Salisbury', *Journal of the Warburg and Courtauld Institutes* 31 (1968), pp. 148–58; 154.

171 M.-H. Vicaire, 'La place des oeuvres de miséricorde dans la pastorale en Pays d'Oc', *Cahiers de Fanjeaux* 13 (1978), pp. 21–44; pp. 26–7.

172 *Speculum christiani: a Middle English religious treatise of the fourteenth century*, ed. G. Holmstedt (London, 1933), pp. 41–7.

173 *The lay folks' catechism or the English and Latin versions of archbishop Thoresby's instruction for the people*, ed. T. F. Simmons and H. E. Nolloth (London, 1901), pp. 74–6.

174 Schmitt, 'Recueils franciscains', *passim*.

175 Rouse and Rouse, *Preachers, florilegia and sermons*, p. 65. D. L. d'Avray and M. Tausche, 'Marriage sermons in *ad status* collections of the central Middle Ages', *Archives d'histoire doctrinale et littéraire du moyen-âge* 47 (1980), pp. 71–119; pp. 72–5. Also Longère, *Oeuvres oratoires* I, pp. 368–71. On the social categories current in the works of contemporary canonists and theologians see Michaud-Quantin, 'Le vocabulaire des catégories sociales chez les canonistes et les moralistes du XIIIᵉ siècle', pp. 73–92. We are reminded, however, not to overestimate the importance of *ad status* preaching as only few collections of such sermons seem to have existed, d'Avray, *The preaching of the friars*, pp. 127–8.

176 D. L. d'Avray, 'Sermons to the upper bourgeoisie by a thirteenth century Franciscan', *Studies in Church history* 16 (1979), pp. 187–99; 189.

of all thirteenth-century preachers, Humbert of Romans, wrote sermons for every social and religious group: Augustinian canons, servitors in hospitals, servitors in leper houses, students, the poor, poor in hospitals, poor women in towns.[177] Guibert of Tournai wrote for rich merchants and Jacques of Vitry (d. 1240) addressed the members of each and every type of religious community and of the urban ruling classes.[178] The poor were directly approached as a *status* less frequently than rich burgesses. A splendid example of the demands of the poor as a group appears in the section *ad pauperes* in the mid-twelfth-century *sermo generalis* of Honorius Augustodunensis: 'the poor carry the burden of poverty patiently...let them know that in alms they receive the sins of men and also that they can reciprocate by offering prayer in return'.[179] Earlier in the sermon the rich had been reminded 'And I warn you, the rich, that God wanted the rich to be fathers to the poor'.[180]

Since their activity centred in the towns, on roads, in fairs – centres of mercantile and artisan activity – the friars developed themes and approaches suitable for their audience.[181] While illustrating the logic of almsgiving a Franciscan example explained: 'As a toll is exacted from him who transports goods...thus alms and hospitality are exacted from the rich. But if the carrier of goods fails to pay the toll, he will be made to pay it and additionally incur a fine'.[182] When a preacher spoke in an urban milieu where money changed hands frequently and where riches could be amassed, the preoccupation with the sin of avarice loomed large. L. K. Little has demonstrated the rise in prominence of avarice in twelfth- and thirteenth-century lists of cardinal sins, in which

---

[177] Humbert of Romans, *Beati Umberti sermones* (Venice, 1603), part I, sermons 8, 40, 41, 62, 86, 92 and 99. d'Avray, 'Sermons to the upper bourgeoisie', pp. 188–9.

[178] *Ibid.*, p. 189; *Jacobi de Vitriaco sermones in epistolas et evangelia dominicalia totius anni* (Antwerp, 1575).

[179] 'Pauperes autem paupertatis onus patienter ferant...Sciant se peccata hominum in elemosinis accipere, et ideo pro eis satagant orationem reddere', Honorius Augusto-dunensis, 'Speculum ecclesiae', *PL* 172, col. 864.

[180] 'Nunc moneo vos, divites, quod divites Dominus voluit esse pauperum patres', *ibid.*

[181] Rosenwein and Little, 'Social meaning in the monastic and mendicant spiritualities', pp. 20–32. On some of the social categories of early Franciscan writings see Le Goff, 'Le vocabulaire de catégories sociales', pp. 93–123. The friars' activities were not, of course, limited to the urban milieu, d'Avray, *The preaching of the friars*, pp. 29–43.

[182] 'qui portat merces, exigitur pedagium...sic a divite elemosina et hospitalitas. Quod si portans merces non solverit pedagium, non solum pedagium non amittit capitale verum eciam penam incurrit', *La tabula*, ed Welter, p. 24. For the meaning of *pedagium* (a transport toll) see *Councils and synods* 1 part 2, p. 826, n. 1. For an assessment of the friars' use of urban terminology see d'Avray, *The preaching of the friars*, pp. 216–39.

it occurred most frequently as the gravest sin.[183] Avarice lay at every man's doorstep; especially susceptible were those who had frequent dealings with credit and loans – in Gratian's words: 'Homo mercator nunquam aut vix potest Deo placere' ('a merchant can never or very rarely be pleasing to God'). All the *exempla* under the heading 'De avaricia' of the English Franciscan *Liber exemplorum* (compiled between 1270 and 1279), dealt with men who collected riches but hardened their hearts to the poor. Yet the prevalent view in these stories did not reject earthly goods which could be put to good use by good men. Possessions may have hindered a bad man but were a source of charity in the hands of a virtuous one.[184] Thus, goods were only as good as the person who put them to use. This is a traditional view which grew in dominance in the thirteenth century: property could be of great spiritual value.[185]

Almsgiving was seen as an act that any man could practice as a custodian of wealth, but a rich man lived under a specially strong obligation to do so. Views of the rich and poor and their roles became more complex as preachers encountered these same people in their audiences. Rich men were judged by the scale of their charity and poor men were admonished not to allow envy and covetousness to enter their hearts. Men of humble means could act charitably, if not by the giving of money then by the toil of their hands. Jacques of Vitry described these possibilities:

but artisan craftsmen must be helpers to the poor through their crafts, each one according to his ability, thus a shoemaker should sometimes repair the shoes of the poor for free, for God's sake;...masons and carpenters – by making houses and providing shelter for the poor and by mending the roofs of the houses of poor neighbours.[186]

---

[183] L. K. Little, 'Pride goes before avarice: social change and the vices in Latin Christendom', *American historical review* 76 (1971), pp. 16–59. On the prominence of the subject of avarice in medieval literature see A. Murray, *Reason and society in the Middle Ages*, pp. 77–8.

[184] d'Avray, 'Sermons to the upper bourgeoisie', p. 196.

[185] As in a twelfth-century Middle English homily: 'efne þaes ding beod gode, ȝif þu heom wel notest; Gif þet þu ufel bist, ne miht þu heom wel notiȝen. Beod for þi gold & seoluer yfele yfelum, & gode godum', *Twelfth century homilies*, ed. A. O. Belfour (London, 1909, repr. 1963), p. 134.

[186] '..sed et pauperibus de arte sua subvenientes debent artifices mechanici, unusquisque secundum propriam facultatem, ut sutores aliquando gratis et pro Deo reparent pauperum sottolares,...cementarii autem et carpentarii aliquando in edificiis faciendis pauperibus cooperentur et tecta domorum pauperum vicinorum recooperiant', Longère, 'Pauvreté et richesse', p. 272. This idea falls in with the view that when a man is too poor to give alms to the needy, he can always show kindness and sympathy: ' and ȝif þou þou haue no good bodeliche, ȝitt ȝeue a good will...for God crownes with-in þe a good will where at he fyundeþ withowte-forthe no catell', *Middle English sermons*, ed. W. O. Ross (London, 1940), p. 42.

Spouses could act charitably together and offer hospitality in their conjugal home.[187] When a Sussex peasant blessed by a divine vision was approached by an old man, St Julian in disguise, he first offered the hospitality of his neighbours but eventually offered his own, when he was told that his wife had already given shelter to two poor women.[188] All people, even the humble, needed the possibility of charity since 'Al swa þet water acwenched et fur, swa þa elmesse acwenched þa sunne'.[189] The conservative view prevailed which valued the existence of poor people as an opportunity for the practice of soul-saving charity.[190] An opposing view saw the poor man as being twice accursed by his poverty, since it left him not only without food but without means for saving his soul.[191] An original view of the rationale for almsgiving appears in the fifteenth-century *Summa praedicantium*; to the question 'Why does God not provide for His poor?' four answers are given: 'first, that he has provided sufficiently for all poor in giving to the rich...second, so that the rich could show their charity...third, to increase the merit of the poor...fourth, for the benefit of the rich'.[192]

---

[187] As put by Raoul Ardent in 'Homilia de tempore VII', *PL* 155, col. 1328.

[188] *Visio Thurkilli*, ed. P. G. Schmidt (Leipzig, 1978), p. 5: 'Coniunx tua duas pauperculas mulieres in hospitio tuo iam recepit'. This vision was recorded *c.* 1206 at Stisted abbey by Ralph of Coggeshall, the writer and historian, who was evidently well acquainted with the circumstances of life and the mores of the peasantry. This story may describe the piety of one Thurkill, as suggested by the editor (p. vii), yet surely represents the standards that were presented to these rustic folk by their priests. Spouses could encourage each other to charity, but might also hinder it; in a fifteenth-century document for spiritual instruction husbands are encouraged to share their spiritual activities with their wives, W. A. Pantin, 'Instructions for a devout literate layman', in *Medieval learning and literature. Essays presented to Richard William Hunt*, ed. J. J. G. Alexander and M. T. Gibson (Oxford, 1976), pp. 398–422 at p. 421. Jacques of Vitry tells of a wife who hoarded 'absque pauperum compassione' all that her husband had given her for distributions to the poor, Jacques of Vitry, *The exempla*, no. 182, p. 77.

[189] *Old English homilies and homiletic treatises*, pp. 37, 39.

[190] R. Manselli, 'Evangelismo e povertà', in *Povertà e ricchezza nella spiritualità dei secoli XI e XII* (Todi, 1969), pp. 11–41; p. 35. For this traditional view see the eighth-century 'Vita Sancti Eligii episcopi Noviomensis' II, 15, *PL* 87, c.533: 'potuit nempe Deus omnes homines divites facere, sed pauperes ideo in hoc mundo voluit quomodo divites peccata sua redimerent'.

[191] J. Batany, 'Le vocabulaire des catégories sociales chez quelques moralistes français vers 1200'., *Ordres et classes. Colloque d'histoire sociale St. Cloud 24–25 mai 1967* (Paris, 1973), pp. 59–72; p. 66. Aquinas answered this current view by invoking the poor man's reward in the kingdom of heaven, *Scriptum in quatuor libros sententiarum P. Lombardi*, XLV 9.2 a.4 q.1. For some evidence from a later period of attempts made by poor folk to procure intercession for themselves see W. Monter, *Ritual, myth and magic in early modern Europe* (Brighton, 1983), p. 14.

[192] John Bromyard, *Summa praedicantium*, pp. 243–4.

Of all good deeds almsgiving was said to be the very best. A twelfth-century English sermon for St Laurence's feast taught:

> Fele kinne weldede ben.
> ac þe holie apostel muneȝed here to on of hem.
> þat is almes-delen.
> and seid þat me hit shal giuen hauenlese men.[193]

A twelfth-century poem for moral instruction saw alms as a shield to protect man from the evils of this world

> Mid ealm[i]hties godes luue ute we us bi-werien
> wid þes wrecches worldes luue þat he ne mawe us derien
> Mid fasten and almesse and ibede we us wid sunne.[194]

Charity was superior to the other virtues.[195] Every deed of charity is counted towards the final reckoning and even a single act of charity could admit a man to heaven.[196] The twelfth century was the period in which the individual Christian conscience gained prominence as a measure of virtue. Acts were to be judged by the intent of the doer more than by their final effect.[197] Thus, almsgiving in the prime of life was thought to be superior to charity ordained at the deathbed or in a will. A Dominican *exemplum* of the thirteenth century compares these forms of almsgiving to having one candle in front giving light and guidance rather than two candles behind, providing no help.[198] Jacques of Vitry wrote of a man who failed to distribute his goods during his lifetime but left them to the poor in his will. When he fell ill four kinds of almsgiving appeared to him in a vision: of gold, silver, lead and clay corresponding to almsgiving in youth, in old age, in sickness and after death.[199] In 1377, Bishop Thomas Brinton recounted this vision and presented the general rule: 'almsgiving is more worthy and virtuous when it is done in health and during one's lifetime'.[200]

---

[193] *Old English homilies of the twelfth century*, ed. R. Morris, EETS 53, London, 1873, p. 157.

[194] *Old English homilies and homiletic treatises*, lines 333–5, p. 179.

[195] *Piers the plowman: the B version*, Passus XII, lines 30–31: 'Feiþ hope and charite, and alle ben goode, And saven men sondry tymes, ac non so soone as charite'.

[196] *Catalogue of romances* III, eds. Ward and Herbert, no. 9, p. 328.

[197] M.-D. Chenu, *L'éveil de la conscience dans la civilisation médiévale* (Montreal, 1969), *passim* and p. 20.   [198] *Catalogue of romances* III, eds. Ward and Herbert, no. 92, p. 489.

[199] *Die Exempla aus den sermones feriales et communes des Jakob von Vitry*, ed. J. Greven (Heidelberg, 1914), no. 58, p. 38. For this idea *c.* 1350 see also: 'To do penaunce is hit is ful late when the deth is at the gate', in the *Proprium sanctorum*, ed. C. Horstmann in *Archiv* 81 (1888), pp. 83–114, 299–321; p. 302, lines 335–6.

[200] 'Elemosina est magis meritoria et virtuosa si fiat in sanitate et in vita', Thomas Brinton, *The sermons of Thomas Brinton, bishop of Rochester (1373–1389)*, ed. M. A. Devlin (London, 1954), sermon 44, p. 194.

Yet a popular *exemplum* tells of a rich man who threw a loaf of bread at a poor man in anger and was saved by the merit of this act of giving.[201]

Giving to those who may repay or benefit the giver was considered to be the 'sale' of alms. A twelfth-century Lent sermon criticised those who do good deeds for the sake of social benefit and for the approval of their neighbours and friends: 'Hie giuen here tigede noht for to hauen heuene blisse. ac for hauen here þe hereword of eorðliche richeise. Hie giuen here elmesse noht for godes luue ac for neheboreden. oðer for kinraden. oðer onur to hauen. oðer ne mai elles for shame. oðer for þonc to hauen...'.[202] Although a rich man could do good deeds, suspicion of the corrupting powers of money lingered in even the most urban-oriented sermons. Rich folk were reminded again and again that they could not achieve perfection without charity.[203] In the early fifteenth-century *Dives et pauper*, a work well grounded in prevailing mores and thought, the belief in the corrupting power of the arch-sin of avarice is clear:

DIVES: Qhy clepyȝt Crist rychesse a deuelshene of wyckydnesse?
PAUPER: For coueytyse of rychesse makyt folk to seruyn þe deuel and brynggyt hem to synne and shrewydenesse.[204]

The world of the central Middle Ages was experiencing growth and commercial expansion; profit-makers were more numerous and men with fortunes more conspicuous. As it represented a spiritual challenge, the image of the pious merchant developed together with the duty and hope presented by charitable activity. The rich man was no longer doomed to be unrighteous since he could act in a variety of charitable ways with pure intent as a perfect steward of God-created riches.[205]

---

[201] *Liber exemplorum*, ed. Little, pp. 74–5.
[202] *Old English homilies of the twelfth century*, p. 83. For a similar idea see Thomas Brinton, *The sermons of Thomas Brinton*, p. 157.
[203] This view appears in the vision of Piers Plowman, of the late fourteenth century:
    For þouȝ ye be trewe of youre tonge and treweliche wynne,
    And as chaste as a child þat in chirche wepeþ,
    But if ye louen leelly and lene þe pouere
    [Of] swich good as god sent goodliche parteþ
    Piers Plowman: the B version, Passus I, lines 179–83, p. 252.
[204] *Dives et pauper* 1, ed. P. H. Barnum (London, 1976), p. 54, lines 14–16.
[205] An alternative existence as rich and virtuous was offered in thirteenth century teaching, d'Avray, *The preaching of the friars*, pp. 213–15. On the fate of the rich see the following question in *Dives et pauper*:
        DIVES: I assente. I was aferd þat God hadde nought louydde ryche men.
        PAUPER: Abraham, Ysaac and Iacob...And many thousand moo weryn

Demands were made of the giver of alms to prepare spiritually for this act of penitence and faith, following thorough introspection. In the chapter dealing with the deeds of mercy in the fourteenth-century *Book of vices and virtues*, almsgiving was said to be the most spiritually significant deed.[206] In its practice three things were to be noted: the source of the funds, the quality of the recipient and the manner of giving. For the intent to be pure and the effect beneficial, four matters were to be considered: the giver's gladness, his promptness, the means at his disposal and the modesty with which he acted.[207] The giver was urged not to despise the poor and to give spontaneously.[208] Here we witness the transmission of theological ideas of a high order to the world of literate laity. In a late fourteenth-century sermon the preeminence of intention is explained: 'Of your goods you must give alms. And if you have no earthly goods, give good will, doing what Saint Augustin has requested: "if you can give, give; if you cannot, be kindly; God crowns the will within where he finds no ability"'.[209] The forceful preacher Thomas Brinton, Bishop of Rochester, emphasised the importance of the attitude in which one gave charity: 'And I preach this against them and against the ingratitude of those rich people who, even if they do give the poor some trifle, first exasperate them and scorn them so much that it would have been better for the poor to lack the alms rather than obtain them through such abuse'.[210]

While theologians and canonists distinguished the categories and degrees of usurious activity, the preachers brought the message home in a less scholastic and more vivid way.[211] Usurers were a popular subject in mendicant preaching which most vehemently attacked those sins characteristic of the mercantile urban *milieu*.[212] However, some

> wol ryche and now been wol hye in blisse.
> For thoe ryche meen been nought lackyd in holy
> wrygt for here rychesse but for here wyckyd coueytise
> and mysuse of rychesse

Dives et pauper I, p. 57.

206 *The book of vices and virtues*, ed. W. N. Francis (London, 1942), this is an English translation, originating in the Midlands *c*. 1375, of a thirteenth-century book for lay education written by the Dominican Lorens d'Orleans, the 'Somme le Roi'.

207 *Ibid.*, pp. 212–16.

208 *Ibid.*, pp. 216–20.

209 *Middle English sermons*, ed. W. O. Ross (London, 1940), p. 42.

210 *The sermons of Thomas Brinton*, sermon 44, p. 196.

211 Stephen Langton embarked on preaching campaigns against usury in the towns of France; Roberts, *Stephanus de lingua tonante*, p. 19 and J. W. Baldwin, *Masters, princes and merchants. The social views of Peter the Chanter and his circle* I (Princeton, N.J., 1970), p. 297, yet this was not a major theme in his preaching, *ibid.*, p. 30 and n. 145.

212 On the new views of mercantile life developed in this period see Gilchrist, *The church and economic activity*, pp. 53–8.

justification of the notion of compensation for the risk in moneylending was developing in the Schools and in mendicant preaching.[213] The usurer often appeared in *exempla* on his deathbed either repenting and making restitution and charitable bequests, or as persevering in his sin and wishing to take his riches to the tomb.[214] In a collection of *exempla* compiled by a Cambridge Dominican who preached in East Anglia in the mid-thirteenth century many stories feature usurers.[215] They describe the tomb of a usurer being opened for the expulsion of his body from the cemetery, and the horrific sights witnessed there: toads with coins in their mouths (nos. 240, 266) or a toad in a usurer's girdle holding 30 marks in coins (no. 271). In the *Book of vices and virtues*, usury is discussed in the section on the sin of avarice. Usury, theft and rapine were branches of avarice, and there were seven types of usury, overt and covert.[216] A usurer could do no effective charitable deed for the health of his soul, condemned to eternal fires, unless he had made full restitution.[217] A usurer's offering of oats to a church turned into writing serpents (no. 242). Similarly a fifteenth-century homiletic treatise tells of a usurer's charitable bequest for the erection of a church: during the consecration ceremony the church was occupied by the devil who claimed that it was his own since it was built with his gains. The message of this story is clearly presented at the end: 'þerfore, restoryth euyl ȝetyn good to þe ownerys & noȝt robbe hem to make þer-wyth cherchys'.[218] Usurers were even rejected by their families, as when a usurer's son obstructed a priest praying for his late father's soul.[219]

When alms were given generously and with true intent they were the surest approach to the paths of salvation. This is an exchange clearly set out from the earliest Christian writings – good deeds on earth will open the paths to the heavenly kingdom. The twelfth and thirteenth

[213] Rosenwein and Little, 'Social meaning in the monastic and mendicant spiritualities', p. 30.

[214] See the *exempla* of Jacques of Vitry in *The exempla*, nos. 106, 167, 172, 173, 178, 179, pp. 49, 71–2, 72, 73, 73–4, 75–6, 76.

[215] Forte, 'A Cambridge Dominican collector of exempla', pp. 117–48, a list of all examples in this collection in *Catalogue of romances* III, eds. Ward and Herbert, nos. 240, 241, 242, 265, 266, 271.

[216] *The book of vices and virtues*, pp. 30–6. The psychological intent is stressed: 'For it is (not) onliche almesse to geve, but it is grete almesse to lene wiþoute usure and wiþ-oute evele entencion, but pureliche for God', *ibid.*, p. 205.

[217] This story recurs well into the fifteenth century, see *An alphabet of tales* II, ed. M. M. Banks (London, 1904), no. 785, p. 523.

[218] *Jacob's well. An English treatise on the cleansing of man's conscience*, ed. A. Brandeis (London, 1900), p. 203.

[219] 'Nolite orare pro anima patris mei, qui usurarius fuit et usura restituere noluit', Jacques of Vitry, *The exempla*, no. 216, p. 91.

centuries saw the greatest development of the 'arithmetic' of the soul[220] and the undertaking of charitable activity was frequently described as a wise investment which would yield fruit.[221] The most common simile employed in this context is that of the biblical sower who sows in tears and reaps in joy a manifold harvest:

Weldede is icleoped sed. for twam þingen. An is det alrihtes swa alse me sawed sed on ane time and gadered þet frut on oder time. al swa mon ded nude his dede in þisse liue, and on dere eche weorlde he scal hafon der of his mede. Det oder is. Alswa of ane sede cumed feole folde weste. Alswa of ane edeliche dede mon scal afon eft feole felde mede and muchele.[222]

The concept of fructifying a small investment, of making a seed yield crops, must have appealed to the minds of peasants and merchants alike; yet some may have deemed the profits inadequately tangible. A popular *exemplum* describes the empty jars in the pantry of a charitable couple being miraculously replenished with food which they proceeded to offer to the poor. The fruitless vineyard of a charitable man bore abundant fruit after he had sold his wife's cloak to provide two Dominican friars with hospitality.[223] These were exchanges, an acquisition of benefits in the most lucrative way. Even more outstanding rewards were granted to charitable givers through miraculous intervention: the amputated leg of a giver was restored,[224] a vision appeared to the sons of a charitable man after his death, informing them that their father was being rewarded one-hundred-fold.[225]

Exempla dwelt largely on the fate of the rich man who realised his avaricious folly at a time of sickness or on his deathbed. Such a man had clearly miscalculated his deeds and faced the consequences as described in a Franciscan *exemplum* which concludes in Latin and then in its English translation: 'melius erat ei certe quod nunquam denarium vidissit, melius erat quod nunquam fuisset natus, quia eternaliter dampnatus est. Anglice dicitur: hym were bettre þat he ne were ne neuer

220 On this development see J. Chiffoleau, *La comptabilité de l'au-delà. Les hommes, la mort et la religion dans la région d'Avignon à la fin du moyen-âge (vers 1320–vers 1480)* (Rome, 1980).

221 Charity is often likened to a tree bearing fruit in exegetical as well as vernacular literature, Smith, *Traditional imagery of charity*, pp. 56–73.

222 *Old English homilies and homiletic treatises*, p. 135.

223 Forte, 'A Dominican collector of exempla', no. 124, p. 131; also *Catalogue of romances* III, eds. Ward and Herbert, no. 139, pp. 132–3. A rich man's goods distributed to the poor during his lifetime were returned to him one-hundred-fold after his death. Jacques of Vitry, *The exempla*, no. 96, p. 45.

224 *An alphabet of tales*, no. 81, p. 64.

225 *Ibid.*, no. 32, pp. 22–4.

boren for liif and soule he his forloren'.[226] A fifteenth-century lyric describes a rich man's sad 'Farewell to the world':

and as he was on death-bed he was asked by friends what could give him greatest consolation; the rich man said that the many and plentiful things in front of him could not console him and he said to those standing there, in English: 'cursed be the time when I was born! I have lost heavenly bliss forever and go to the place of eternal sorrow and cares'.[227]

Riches could be used in many beneficial ways, but prosperity was not a sign of moral superiority and acceptance by God.[228] Alan of Lille saw riches as a source of constant anxiety which bred avaricious thoughts.[229] Most writers agreed that a poor man was less susceptible to avarice and ambition and some saw poverty as a state of simple virtue. Jacques of Vitry tells of a king who passed by a humble basement dwelling and saw a dirty and ragged poor man and his poor wife standing and chanting together. The astonished king said to his soldier 'It is indeed amazing that neither I nor you, who are so showered by delicacies and glory, have ever known such pleasure in our lives'.[230] Humbert of Romans warned of the danger that avaricious thoughts and wishes might be passed from the rich to the poor.[231] An *exemplum* from the Cambridge collection tells of a poor man who lived happily until the day when he found ten marks[232] and that a pauper elected to be king never knew another day of contentment.[233]

Yet not all poor were resigned to their state and simple folk must have often wondered whether these were the poor in whom Jesus dwelt. As vernacular and popular instruction developed there was a need to accommodate the dissonance between the willingness to give and the indignation felt by believers towards slothful and sinful poor. Like the legal discussions on the identity of the 'deserving poor' the *exempla* distinguish between the good and the bad poor. Jacques of Vitry tells of a *humilis pauper* and a *pauper superbus*. The first begged for some

---

[226] *Liber exemplorum*, ed. Little, p. 45.

[227] 'Hic scribitur de divite...et cum esset in extremis querebatur ab amicis quid posset eum magis consolari, quibus dixit divicie qui cum essent coram eo multa et ineffabilia nec possunt eum consolari et dixit astantibus in loco anglice... "y-cursyd be þe tyme þat ych was bore! y have lore for-ever hevun blys, and go now þeras ever sorow and car ys"', *Religious lyrics of the fifteenth century*, ed. C. Brown (Oxford, 1939), p. 253.

[228] For a discussion of this point see Raoul Ardent, 'Homilia LIX', *PL* 155, col. 1882bc.

[229] 'De arte praedicatoria', *PL* 210, col. 115bc.

[230] 'Valde mirabile est quod nunquam mihi et tibi ita placuit vita nostra, que tantis deliciis et tanta refulget gloria...', Jacques of Vitry, *The exempla*, no. 78, pp. 35–6.

[231] Murray, 'Religion among the poor', p. 307.

[232] *Catalogue of romances* III, eds. Ward and Herbert, no. 236, p. 497.

[233] *Ibid.*, no. 269, p. 500.

grain and offered his glove as a receptacle while the other passed through the town with a bag: 'and since he could find only few who would give to him, it so happened that the humble pauper with the glove gained more than the proud one with his bag'.[234] Humbert of Romans, who preached to laity and instructed fellow Dominicans, found the poor often hard and bitter and lacking in resignation: 'there is a type of poor who blaspheme and swear maliciously at God for having made them poor'.[235] *Accidia*, rather than *caritas*, was often rampant among the poor, leading them to a sinful life, to fraud and theft.[236]

Books of religious instruction exhorted people to work, as idleness rendered man spiritually vulnerable: 'For whan a man is ydele and the devyl fyndeth hym ydel, he him setteth a-swith to worke'.[237] However, scales of merit and instructions to almsgivers rarely insisted on examination of the cause of need, besides the cases of moral turpitude discussed above. Greater attention to the person of the poor beggar is clearly manifest in fourteenth- and fifteenth-century writings, doubting the veracity of beggars' claims for subsistence. Denunciation of false beggars appears frequently in vernacular literature.[238] Even more telling is the view of lower orders of society as steeped in useless and frivolous activities: 'ydel pleyes and japes, carolinges, makynges of fool, countynaunces, to yeve giftes to iogelours...in wrastlynge, in other dedes of strength doynge'.[239] In a sermon explaining the existence of poverty in God's world Bishop Brinton differentiated between voluntary and involuntary poverty. Voluntary poverty was the 'sweetest' way of serving God and a sure path to heaven. Involuntary poverty was to be helped, it enabled the rich to prove their love of God, but the poor were not necessarily good.[240] They were often sinful

---

234 'et quia paucos invenit qui darent ei, accidit quod magis lucratus est pauper humilis cum cyrotheca quam pauper superbus cum sacco', Jacques of Vitry, *The exempla*, no. 77, p. 35.

235 'est quidem status pauperum qui modo blasphemant Deum perversa iurando eo quod fecit eos pauperes', Murray, 'Religion among the poor', p. 308.

236 *Ibid.*, pp. 311–2.

237 *The book of vices and virtues*, p. 27, lines 6–8. On lay literacy see J. H. Moran, *Education and learning in the city of York, 1300–1560* (York, 1979).

238 See R. St Jacques, 'Les mendiants dans l'épopée anglaise au XIVe siècle', in *Aspects de la marginalité au moyen-âge* (Montreal, 1975), pp. 24–33. See also G. Shepherd, 'Poverty in *Piers Plowman*', in *Social relations and ideas*, pp. 169–89 and Aers, '*Piers plowman*', pp. 5–25.

239 British Library. Harl 45, fol. 58. See also *Jacob's well. An English treatise on the cleansing of man's conscience*, ed. A. Brandeis (London, 1900), pp. 295–6.

240 Thomas Brinton, *The sermons of Thomas Brinton*, sermon 44, p. 195: 'Primam paupertatem sustinent pauperes involuntarii qui libenter si possent divitias optinerent'.

and criminous,[241] many would have preferred to be rich. François Villon held that wretchedness was necessarily corrupting.[242] The fifteenth-century *Jacob's well* spoke of 'paupertas spiritus' and of the difference between external and internal poverty: 'for manye poure & nedy man is rychere in herte, in will, and desyre þan sum ryche ma. For sum beggere desyreth in wyl to have more rychesse gif ne migte have it, & wolde have more worschypp and makyth more of hymself & heyere in herte beryth him þan sum ryche man'.[243] In *Dives et pauper* the reason for poor men's bitterness is explained: 'And þey þat been pore aʒens here wyl, summe han pacience, summe han noo pacience, and þey because of myschef lyghtly fallyn in synne'.[244]

A recurrent theme connected with the exhortation towards alms-giving on all occasions identified the poor with Christ Himself. Several *exempla* describe the case of a man giving innocently to a poor man and later discovering that he had helped Christ.[245] A monk carrying a leper to his monastery's door heard a voice saying 'You carried me on earth and I shall carry you in heaven', after which the leper disappeared from upon his back.[246] The fourteenth-century *Lay folks' catechism* enumerated the works of mercy and related each of them to an act done by Christ for humanity, thus presenting works of mercy as a return for His sacrifices:

Furst men schuld wilfully fede pore hungry men and þrusty
Forin þat þey fede Iesu Crist he hym self sayþ in þe gospel
And also Iesu Crist gyfys budy and sowle lyf and catel to us for þis ende
And fedes us wyþ his flesch and his blod in þe sacrament of þe awter.[247]

The attraction of beholding Christ in the pauper was an incentive for almsgiving; even when Christ was not present in the flesh He existed in the spirit in the sufferings of His poor.

---

[241] *Ibid.*, 'aliquando per impacienciam accusent Deum de iniquitate, proximum de tenacitate, apti sunt ad murmura, ocia, mendacia, atque furta'.

[242]   Necessité fait gens méprendre
        Et faim saillir le loup du bois
    Oeuvres de François Villon, ed. J. Dufournet and A. Mary (Paris, 1970), 'Le testament XXI', p. 24, lines 7–8.

[243] *Jacob's well*, ed. Brandeis, c.50, p. 308.   [244] *Dives et pauper* 1, p. 58, lines 27–9.

[245] Jacques of Vitry, *The exempla*, no. 95, p. 45.

[246] 'Tu me portasti in terris, ego te portabo in celis' (cf. Matt. 25, 34–6), *La tabula*, ed. Welter, p. 77. Another such case in *Liber exemplorum*, ed. Little, no. 124, pp. 72–4, nos. 130–1, p. 78; *Beati Umberti sermones*, p. 42: 'erat enim Christus quem receperat in specie leprosi ad probandum misericordiam eius'. For the story of a pious woman who tended a leper, and on one occasion, while washing his feet, saw the cross wounds on them, see *Catalogue of romances* III, eds. Ward and Herbert, no. 119, p. 489. See also Jacques of Vitry, *The exempla*, no. 94, p. 69.

[247] *Lay folks' catechism*, lines. 1100–1103, p. 72.

If Christ was present in the community of the poor, He was even more attached to the most miserable poor, the sick and the leprous. Among his sermons *ad status* Humbert of Romans dedicated one to the brethren and sisters serving in hospitals. Those who chose to serve God through the service of His wretched poor, could not have chosen a more pleasing and meritorious path. He commended their work as the height of charitable deeds: 'Of all works of mercy those exercised for the poor and sick are finest'.[248] Yet most recommendations for charitable acts were not so very demanding, and most believers were expected to give alms as their situation allowed and to help provide cover and food to the needy, but not to forsake their own kin and neighbour. Only exceptionally devout people dedicated their lives to service in hospitals and demands from ordinary believers were less rigorous and attractively flexible.[249]

In a framework of theological inquiry canonists and theologians, and subsequently preaching priests and friars were able to propose a viable and attractive scheme of charitable activity which offered those following it means for religious fulfilment through a limited allocation of superfluous goods. The poor were ascribed a role in a charitable exchange inspired by a predisposition towards giving and based on a particular understanding of the means of salvation. In the later Middle Ages, when potential givers endowed with superfluous funds were probably fewer, the charitable giving which they undertook was curtailed. Combining the growing urge towards personal religious activity and the need to act more discriminately in allocating fewer superfluous funds, townsfolk created religious gilds and fraternities, bodies in which they exercised more control and where religious activity was more personal. They granted charitable help and procured intercession, along the lines of the traditional purgatorial, charitable and penitential teachings, but their scope was limited to peers and colleagues. They sifted out from the ambiguities of popularised religious teaching those interpretations which allowed criticism of their environment and chastisement of members which they deemed to be undeserving. Outside the context of intercession the plight of the needy and suffering was seldom examined.[250]

The process of evangelisation and education undertaken by the friars

---

[248] Humbert of Romans, *Beati Umberti sermones*, p. 40.

[249] For a description of the devotion and spirituality of communities serving in hospitals and leper houses see *The 'Historia occidentalis' of Jacques de Vitry: a critical edition*, ed. J. F. Hinnebusch (Freiburg, 1972), pp. 146–7.

[250] But rather universally abhorred. See the description of poverty in the Middle English translation of the *Roman de la rose* from *c.* 1375:

encouraged a preexisting trend towards self-help in religious quests.[251] In the changing world of the fourteenth and fifteenth centuries ideas on society and religion were being reassessed; the result of generations of instruction was a more knowledgeable laity, keen on determining some of its religious fortunes.[252] An aspect of the revision of religious ideas is expressed in the growth of dissenting anti-clerical doctrines.[253] In England these views were expressed by thinkers such as Wyclif and by the Lollards.[254] One of the themes of contention raised by the Lollards was the treatment of the poor and the charitable activity of the Church.[255] The Lollards renounced conservative forms of piety such as pilgrimage and the cult of relics, since holiness could be found everywhere in Christ's poor,[256] and preached true charity and religion through good works and charity to one's fellow. The institutionalised channels of relief were denounced; the system of relief which evolved through the workings of two centuries of canonistic and theological teaching was deemed to be an aberration of true piety. Intercession was challenged as a form of false piety favouring the rich and as an obstacle

> And alderlast of everychone
> Was paynted Povert al alone
> That not a peny had in holde,
> Although she her clothes solde
> ....
> For poure thyng, where so it be
> Is shamefaste, and dispysed aye.
> Acursed may wel be that daye
> That poore man conceyved is.

The Romaunt of the Rose and Le Roman de la Rose: a parallel-text edition, ed. R. Sutherland (Oxford, 1967), p. 10, lines 449–452, 466–9.

[251] On the types of literature for personal spiritual guidance circulating in late medieval England see P. S. Jolliffe, *A check-list of Middle English prose writings of spiritual guidance* (Toronto, 1974), pp. 37–56. See also an early fifteenth-century document of instruction for a literate layman, W. A. Pantin, 'Instructions for a devout literate layman', in *Medieval learning and literature*, ed. J. J. G. Alexander and M. T. Gibson (Oxford, 1976), pp. 420–2.

[252] The instructions conveyed to the devout layman stressed internal and personal improvement shared with the family rather than participation with others, *ibid.*

[253] Such views spread through the continent from the eleventh and twelfth centuries, in the teachings of both reform groups and heresies, Manteuffel, *Naissance d'une hérésie*; Thouzellier, 'Hérésie et pauvreté', pp. 371–88.

[254] G. Leff, *Heresy in the Middle Ages. The relation of heterodoxy to dissent c. 1250–c. 1450* II (Manchester and New York, 1967), pp. 494–558.

[255] On these views see J. A. F. Thomson, *The later Lollards, 1414–1520* (Oxford, 1965).

[256] 'quod peregrinaciones nullo modo deberent fieri ad Thomam Cantuariensem nec ad aliqua alia loca sive ymagines, sed ad ymagines Christi que sunt pauperes, quibus erogande sunt pecunie quas populus expendit et consumit in aliis imaginibus et peregrinacionibus', *Heresy trials in the diocese of Norwich, 1428–1431*, ed. N. P. Tanner (London, 1977), p. 71.

to poor relief: 'We mythtily afferme . . . þat special preyeris for dede men soulis mad in oure chirche preferryng on be name more þen anothir, þis is þe false ground of almesse dede, on þe qwiche alle almes houses of Ingelond ben wikkedly igrounded . . . for preyere meritorie and of value shoulde ben a werk proceding of hey charite, and perfythe charite accepte no persons, quia diligis proximum tuum etc. . . . '.[257] Membership in fraternities was derided on similar grounds, since their main *raison d'être* was procuring intercession.[258]

Tithes and obligations were seen by Lollards as offerings to the corrupt clergy, not as sources for charitable relief: 'lefully withdrawne and withholde tythes and offeringes from prestes and curates and geve hem to the pore peeple, and that is more plesyng to God'.[259] Parishioners owing personal tithes on the profits of commercial enterprises were encouraged to deal them straight to those truly deserving, the poor, rather than to the clergy.[260]

By the fifteenth century plans for alleviation of poverty formulated in Lollard circles relied on the availability of funds from the disendowment of the clergy and religious houses.[261] Around 1410 such plans were even voiced at the highest level, as a bill was presented to parliament offering a blueprint for disendowment of the clergy and the consequent beneficial uses which should be made with the revenues: the creation of lay baronies, the foundation of new universities and a massive provision of almshouses to provide the lawful needs of the sick, poor and lame.[262] The lower strata of urban society who most often appear as defendants in Lollard trials, the tailors, weavers and dyers who often needed the help of parish relief, were expressing a similar view, that a man should arrange his spiritual life without ecclesiastical mediation. Priests were accused by the Lollards and their followers of establishing feast days for the collection of oblations.[263] These views

---

[257] In a Lollard treatise written by 1396, *Selections from English Wycliffite writings*, ed. A. Hudson, Cambridge, 1978, p. 26. For a similar view attributed to a Lollard in a provincial examination see *The metropolitan visitations of William Courtenay archbishop of Canterbury 1381–1396*, ed. J. H. Dahmus (Urbana, Ill., 1950), p. 164.

[258] *Selections from English Wycliffite writings*, pp. 27–8.   [259] *Ibid.*, p. 141.

[260] Little, 'Personal tithes', *passim*. This view was denounced in Oxford in 1425: *Statuta antiqua universitatis Oxoniensis*, ed. S. Gibson (Oxford, 1931), p. 229.

[261] R. B. Dobson in introduction to *The church, politics and patronage in the fifteenth century*, ed. B. Dobson (Gloucester, 1984), p. 13.

[262] On the concept of disendowment and the 1410 plan see the fascinating article M. E. Aston, '"Caim's castles": poverty, politics and disendowment', in *The church, politics and patronage*, ed. Dobson, pp. 45–81; pp. 52–7.

[263] Dobson, 'Introduction', *The church, politics and patronage*, p. 16. This bears evidence that feasts, pilgrimages and masses were occasions on which most believers felt obliged to give alms.

were popularised through preaching by the Augustinian and Franciscan friars. They appealed not only to those weaker members of society who resented the rich and powerful church, but also to those townsfolk interested in exercising more control over their religious lives.[264]

A multitude of urban poor depended on parish distributions and sporadic hand-outs in cases of sickness, old age, unemployment or a large family. If the system failed to meet these needs, if legislation abused workers and criticised their activities, and if sympathy was not as forthcoming as in earlier times, the urban poor were ripe for the calling of the Lollard preachers, vulgarisers of Wyclif's teachings, who were often the lower clergy, poor themselves.[265] The cases tried in the diocese of Norwich[266] were usually against humble people who did not fit in with the traditional views of the meritorious poor, but who nonetheless constituted the bulk of the needy.[267] Their views challenged ecclesiastical hierarchy and the social order since they wished for a Church which was poor and which turned to the poor.[268] Mainstream orthodoxy relied on intercession and institutional devotion, and the criticism of the 'have-nots' gave rise to this marginal antinomian view. It was a militant anti-clerical piety, a spirituality which awkwardly surfaced in theological works. It had much in common with the trends in lay piety which remained within the established ecclesiastical framework: the belief by the laity in self-help, the attempt to accommodate social and religious ideas and the increasingly sparing and controlled employment of the clergy. Most believers were led by their reassessment of religion to diminished charitability, while the Lollards saw in it the essence of Christian society.

Thus, the men and women of Cambridge were the subjects of instruction and preaching in which prevalent themes recurred, but which also harboured serious ambiguities.[269] We have seen how theological concepts penetrated popular preaching through the mediation of literature which instructed parish priests. Yet in the process of popularisation ideas succumbed to the needs and circumstances of

---

[264] Thrupp, *The merchant class*, p. 185.

[265] Leff, *Heresy in the Middle Ages* II, pp. 573–8.

[266] On the occurrence of Lollardy in the diocese of Ely in the mid-fifteenth century see R. M. Haines, 'The practice and problems of a fifteenth century English bishop: the episcopate of William Gray', *Mediaeval studies* 34 (1972), pp. 435–61; pp. 457–9.

[267] For some prevalent views of the poor see below pp. 264–9 and de La Roncière, 'Pauvres et pauvreté à Florence', pp. 685–706.

[268] M. E. Aston, 'Lollardy and sedition, 1381–1431', *Past and present* 17 (1960), pp. 1–44. This view was current among the Spiritual Franciscans, Manselli, 'Da Dante', p. 641.

[269] For such an evaluation of the attitude towards poverty see Gutton, *La société et les pauvres*, pp. 215–18.

contemporary audiences. Although it appears that the faithful were influenced by penitential and coercive teachings, they could never totally disregard their own interpretation of their environment. People were able to accommodate conflicting evaluations in their minds; they might give charity in church, yet scoff at a beggar in the streets. The degree of flexibility in standards of conduct preached in sermons is a result of the need and ability of pastors to respond to prevailing mores and to the pressures of human frailty and economic exigency. Vernacular literature reveals the harsher evaluations of poverty and some very uncharitable practices towards labourers and beggars. Whatever the depth of instruction, responsiveness to a meassage of charity was determined by the understanding which men and women possessed of their own well being. Burgesses made personal evaluations as to the best way in which to accommodate a moral imperative with their understanding of the general weal, and of the identity of those deserving compassionate help. A long process of disenchantment both with the poor and with workers, who in the fourteenth and fifteenth centuries were better off and more socially mobile, led to a decline in the trust in poverty's virtue. Servants and poor young men were now seen as the most dangerous members of society; their gatherings attracted the legislative and punitive attention of the settled members of urban and rural communities.[270] The forms of charitable activity responded to these changes in circumstances of life and in social relations.

[270] McIntosh, *Autonomy and community*, pp. 238–9.

Chapter 4

THE CHARITABLE HOUSES OF MEDIEVAL CAMBRIDGE AND ITS SURROUNDINGS

The charitable institutions of Cambridgeshire comprised the urban hospitals and leper houses of Cambridge, Ely and Wisbech, and the rural charitable houses at Stow (now Longstow), Fordham, Anglesey, in the fields of Royston and in Newton.[1] The largest and best documented is the Hospital of St John the Evangelist in Cambridge, but a survey of other hospitals in the county, which is largely identifiable with the diocese of Ely, sets this charitable institution in sharper focus. It also allows us to examine the degree of integration between urban and rural provision for the poor, and the degree of episcopal involvement in charitable activities within the diocese.

IN THE TOWN OF CAMBRIDGE

The Hospital of St John the Evangelist (HSJC)

Hospitals were founded in widely differing circumstances, but for most hospitals very little knowledge about their earliest years remains. Some time after its foundation, with the accession of an active bishop, with the grant of a sizeable donation or with the provision of a rule, a hospital emerged from the shadows. Our knowledge of the circumstances of the foundation of HSJC depends on the insecure evidence of an inquisition held some 70 years later.[2] It is of great interest to speculate whether the hospital was founded by the community of Cambridge

---

[1] Both the Order of St John of Jerusalem at Chippenham and the Templars at Denny founded hospitals for members of their orders in Cambridgeshire, but since these were internal provisions for the orders, they will not be discussed here. For some general guidelines on writing a hospital's history, see L. Le Grand, 'Comment composer l'histoire d'un établissement hospitalier. Sources et méthode', *Revue d'histoire de l'église de France* 16 (1930), pp. 161–239. For a criticism of hospital histories taking a 'tunnel vision', see J. R. Guy, 'Of the writing of hospital histories there is no end', *Bulletin of the history of medicine* 59 (1985), pp. 415–20, esp. p. 416.

[2] For an attempt to trace the hospital's early history see N. H. A. Newman, 'The foundation of the hospital of St. John the Evangelist', *Eagle* 48 (1934), pp. 20–33, where the foundation is placed *c.* 1195, some years before the episcopal grant of a chapel and cemetery.

burgesses, by the bishop of Ely or by a pious individual townsman, even though we will not be able to say for certain where the truth lies.

The first mention of HSJC is in the roll of letters patent for 6 John, where an entry of mid-October (1204) states: 'The house and brethren of the hospital of St John Apostle and Evangelist of Cambridge have letters patent of the lórd King for simple protection'.[3] By 1207 it had become the subject of a patronage dispute: a plea and inquisition were presented before the king's council concerning the patronage of the church of St Peter without Trumpington Gate. The jurors alleged that it had been presented to the HSJC by one Henry, son of Segar, who had it from his father who had inherited it from a relative, Langinus, parson of St Peter's church.[4] Indeed, Peterhouse possesses the deed by which Henry granted the church to the hospital 'for the use of the poor to be sustained in that house'.[5] Since by the jurors' testimony Henry's family had held the church for some 80 years, it was his right to dispose of it as he saw fit after receiving it from his father. If the church had been proved to be patronless, it would have been placed in the king's gift, as lord of the borough. The hospital is also mentioned in the Pipe Rolls of 1210, 1212 and 1214 as the king's tenant for a part of the Mortimer fee in Newnham.[6]

The church of St Peter was also mentioned in the earliest letter of confirmation of the grant of Bishop Eustace, who had authorised its appropriation to the hospital.[7] In 1235 another inquisition was held, by the Official of the bishop of Ely; the jurors reaffirmed that the *ius presentandi* had been in the hospital's hands for some 30 years since Henry, son of Segar had passed it to the house, followed by Bishop Eustace's collation of an incumbent to the rectory.[8]

More evidence of the hospital's endowment is to be found in the records of an inquisition held in 1274.[9] Twelve jurors testified that the

---

[3] 'Domus et fratres Hospitalis sancti Iohannis Apostoli et Evangeliste de Cantebrigia habent litteras domini Regis patentes de simplici protectione', *Rotuli litterarum patentium (1201–1216)*, Record Commission (London, 1835), p. 47a.

[4] *Curia regis rolls* v, p. 39.

[5] 'in usum pauperum in eodem domo sustinendorum' (the document is from the reign of King John). Peterhouse muniments. Ecc. Cant. A2.

[6] For which it was paying 39s 4d. in annual rent; *Pipe roll 12 John*, p. 112; *Pipe roll 14 John*, p. 77; *Pipe roll 16 John*, p. 71.

[7] The confirmation is by Bishop John of Fountains in SJCA.D98.42.

[8] The jurors also mentioned the inquest of 1207, Peterhouse muniments. Ecc. Cant. A4.

[9] *Abbreviatio placitorum*, Record Commission (London, 1811), p. 263. This inquiry took place in connection with the plea brought by the queen-mother against the bishop of Ely for the right of presentation to the mastership of HSJC, see *Calendar of close rolls 1272–1279*, p. 131.

site of the hospital had once been a poor and vacant plot belonging to the commonalty of Cambridge. Henry Eldcorn, a burgess of Cambridge, erected a humble cottage there for the hospitality of poor people. He later asked Eustace, Bishop of Ely for permission to add an oratory and a cemetery, which would be built by the town. The bishop conferred the church of Horningsea and with the town's consent remained its patron. The plea touched upon the question of presentation to the mastership of the hospital which was being disputed by the queen mother and the bishop.

The jurors' testimony suggests a plausible story which falls in with our knowledge of the law and the practice of hospital foundation. However, five years later, in the process of the wide survey of 1279, a different account was unfolded. On this occasion the jurors attested that a burgess had made a gift of the site to the town for the purpose of building a hospital for the care of poor and sick people. The right of presentation belonged to the borough community which held the town at farm from the king, a right unjustly alienated by Hugh Northwold, Bishop of Ely.[10] Hugh and his successors had nominated masters to the hospital by their own will, usurping the town's, and consequently the king's, privilege. This claim had been presented by the borough to Henry III and Edward I, to their justices and escheators, but to no avail. This injustice had prevailed for 30 years – said the jurors.

Whichever version is nearer to the truth, they tell similar tales. A burgess of Cambridge, with the cooperation of the town, erected a humble dwelling in which poor and sick people were to be relieved. He had either owned the land or had been given it by the town, in order to build on it at his own expense.[11] Through this collaboration the town became the patron of the new house, and no episcopal intervention had occurred before it was sought, according to one version, or imposed, according to the other. The first view, in a modified form, seems more acceptable as it agrees with our knowledge of the canonical procedure governing the foundation of hospitals. The hospitals could not have had an oratory without episcopal licence, necessitating the involvement of the bishop of Ely. Indeed the rights

---

[10] *Rotuli hundredorum tempore Henrici III et Edwardi I* II, Record Commission (London, 1812–18), p. 359. Similar complaints were made by the burgesses of Norwich and Nottingham *ibid.* I, p. 530; II, p. 2.

[11] Waste land was seen as belonging to the king, and encroachment on it was a crime, but boroughs did dispose of waste with and without licences. F. Pollock and F. W. Maitland, *The history of English law before the time of Edward I* I (Cambridge, second edn, 1895), pp. 653–5.

of chapel and burial were granted in the time of Bishop Eustace and the rectory of Horningsea was appropriated to the house.[12] It is doubtful whether the town agreed to accept the bishop and his successors as patrons so very peacefully. Here there may be some truth in the second version: it was often the custom to name as patron of religious and charitable institutions not the person who had actually founded the place, but the one who gave it its most substantial and lasting endowment, or who provided its site.[13] Such was the case of the Hospital of St John the Baptist, Oxford which was in existence by 1180 × 90 and which claimed Henry III as its patron. Henry III's grant in 1231 of the garden outside East Gate as a site for the erection of a new building had earned him this status.[14]

In Cambridge, Bishop Eustace looms large in the early history of the hospital. He gave the appropriated rectory of Horningsea to it (reserving a vicarage of 100s per annum) to help support the poor inmates.[15] In a confirmation charter by Bishop John of Fountains (1220–5) reviewing all of Bishop Eustace's grants, the church of St Peter is mentioned as wholly appropriated to the house, provided that one of the brethren acted as vicar; the living of St Peter's could never have been wholly appropriated without episcopal consent. Bishop Eustace also granted two annual boat loads of reeds and other combustibles from the episcopal marshes. These provisions constituted a great part of the hospital's endowment, together with the chapel rights and burial site which were vital for its functioning. Since the bishop was so active in its endowment and organisation one can understand how he came to be considered as its special benefactor and patron. Later generations of Cambridge townsmen may not have appreciated his contribution, as to them the hospital was the town's concern, a foundation existing for the physical and spiritual welfare of the burgesses and poor townsmen. As expressed towards the end of the thirteenth century, the bone of contention was the bishop's assumption of the patronage of the hospital in return for the provision of the house's most basic needs as a charitable house. Yet it was immediately following this episcopal recognition of the hospital as an ecclesiastical entity that the townsmen provided it

[12] In an agreement with the nunnery of St Radegund of 1208 × 15, SJCA.D98.41 and D98.49.

[13] For the effect of the change of site on patronage of monasteries see S. M. Wood, *English monasteries and their patrons in the thirteenth century* (London, 1955), pp. 27–8.

[14] His continued benevolence to the house further supplied it with timber and other building materials together with various tenements in Oxford, *A cartulary of the hospital of St John the Baptist* III, ed. H. E. Salter (Oxford, 1920), pp. iv, xiv–xviii.

[15] SJCA.D26.20.

with abundant sources of income through a multitude of donations.[16]

Which was seen to be the proper process of hospital foundation in the Middle Ages? A hospital, a house of relief for the poor, sick and aged, could be founded by anyone, just as any man could open his door to a needy person.[17] The *glossa ordinaria* to the *Clementines* states that 'a hospital can be built without episcopal licence, any person can allocate his whole house or a part of it to hospitality of the poor'.[18] Hospitals were founded by individuals, sometimes in fulfilment of a vow, or by a corporation[19] or along main routes of pilgrimage and commerce.[20] But whenever a hospital was meant to offer spiritual care, that is, whenever a chapel or an oratory was added to the establishment,

---

[16] For a similar development in a hospital of late twelfth century burgess foundation which passed into episcopal patronage by 1255 × 85, *The cartulary of God's House, Southampton* I, p. xli.

[17] The earliest reference appears in the gloss of Cardinal Hostiensis (*c.* 1200–1271), Hostiensis, *In primum...sextum decretalium librum commentaria* (Venice, 1581): c.de xenodochiis x, III, 36, 3: 'Hospitale quilibet domo sua potest sine aliqua authoritate facere'.

[18] 'hospitalis domus potest edificari sine licentia episcopi, quilibet domum suam vel partem domus suae ad hospitalitatem pauperum disponere posset'. Hospitals were fully discussed by canonists only from the beginning of the fourteenth century: Iohannes Andreae, *Glossa ordinaria* in *Constitutiones Clementis papae quinti* II, col. 297 in c. Quia Contigit Clem., III, 11, 2.

[19] For a foundation by an individual, see the example of Adam Rypp of Whittlesey, a builder of a hospital at Whittlesford who received two indulgences from Bishop Fordham for aid towards his sustenance and for the construction of his hospital, CUL. EDR. Register Fordham, fol. 176v, 181v (1391 and 1394). Another individual of more exalted circumstances fulfilled a vow in the *Roman de Gaufrey*, L. Gautier, *La chevalerie* (Paris, 1884), p. 83:

> Et Grifon reclama le roi celestial
> Et si promet a Dieu, le pere esperital
> Que s'il peut echapper de cet estour mortal
> Que pour l'amour de lui fera un hopital
> Ou il bergera tout pauvre communal.

In 1226 a widow from Brussels turned her house into a hospital, *Cartulaire de l'hôpital St. Jean de Bruxelles*, ed. P. Bonenfant (Brussels, 1953), p. 32; by a town, St John's hospital in Huntingdon. F. Gerald Vesey, 'St. John's hospital, Huntingdon', *Transactions of the Cambridgeshire and Huntingdonshire Archaeological Society* I (1900–3), p. 122; by a gild, in Lincoln in 1204–5, *Calendar of inquisitions post mortem* I, p. 204; by a fraternity: the Holy Cross hospital in Stratford, *The register of the gild of the Holy Cross, the Blessed Mary and St. John the Baptist of Stratford-upon-Avon*, ed. J. Harvey Bloom, London, 1907, pp. v–vi as well as A. Ramière de Fortanier, 'Hospitalité et charité à Fanjeaux et dans sa région: les confréries de Notre-Dame', *Cahiers de Fanjeaux* 13 (1978), pp. 147–67; p. 152; also Y. Dossat, 'Les confréries du Corpus Christi dans le monde rural pendant la première moitié du XIVe siècle', *Cahiers de Fanjeaux* 11 (1976), pp. 357–85; pp. 371–2.

[20] On hospitals along the road to Compostella see R. de La Coste-Messelière and G. Jugnot, 'L'acceuil des pèlerins à Toulouse', *Cahiers de Fanjeaux* 15 (1980), pp. 117–35.

episcopal licence was required.[21] Thus, there were two kinds of hospitals, those providing physical relief, which might be established anywhere by anyone, and those in which mass was celebrated, confession heard and burial and some parochial rights enjoyed. The first type was called by the canonists *hospitale simplex* or *locus privatus* and the other *locus religiosus*.[22] Houses of the latter type were founded by ecclesiastical licence and existed under episcopal supervision. Religious foundation could occur by the authority of a pope, a bishop, a chapter, but most often it was a diocesan affair; papal confirmation often followed upon episcopal licensing.[23] HSJC must have begun as a *hospitale simplex* founded on land of the community, but from the time of the episcopate of Eustace there was clear episcopal intervention and the bestowal of ecclesiastical standing.[24]

A hospital's status as a religious institution placed it within the ecclesiastical sphere. Like other thirteenth-century hospitals HSJC was visited by the officials of the bishop of Ely and by those of the metropolitan see.[25] Later medieval canonists decreed that this religious standing provided many privileges: 'hospitals enjoy the same privilege as churches'[26] or 'hospitals come under the title, and enjoy the immunity and privileges, of churches'[27]; that is, burial rights, exemption from tithes, exemption from lay exactions, asylum, inalienability of endowment.[28] The exercise of these rights was a cause of many disputes between hospitals and parish priests.[29] The conflict would have

---

[21] John of Turrecremata (1388–1468) summarised this point in the early fifteenth century: 'Hospitalia bene licet aedificare sine licentia episcopi, sed ecclesia vel oratoria non', John of Turrecremata, *Repertorium Iohannis de Turrecremata super toto Decreto* III (Lyons, 1519), p. 150.

[22] Iohannes Andreae, *Glossa ordinaria*, c.de monachis 18, 25, 12: 'Tamen simplex hospitale potest construi sine licentia episcopi'.

[23] See letter of Gregory IX to HSJC, SJCA.D4.1, lines 197–202.

[24] As in the case of St John's hospital, Huntingdon, Gerald Vesey, 'St. John's hospital, Huntingdon', p. 123.

[25] SJCA.D26.72; CUL. Microfilm Ms. 1837, Register Whittlesey, fol. 153. See such relations between the bishop and the hospital founded by a group of burgesses in R. Van der Made, *Le Grand Hôpital de Huy. Organisation et fonctionnement, 1263–1795* (Louvain, 1960), pp. 16–7.

[26] 'hospitalia gaudent eodem privilegio quo gaudent ecclesie', Fernandus Vasquius, *Controversarium libri tres* (Venice, 1595), no. 33, p. 201.

[27] 'hospitalia veniunt appellatione ecclesiarum et…immunitate guadent et…privilegiis', Panormitanus, *Commentaria*, c.ad haec, x, III, 36, 4.

[28] On the right of asylum as assimilated to hospital chapels see P. Timbal Duclaux de Martin, *Le droit d'asile* (Paris, 1939), pp. 200–1, 234–5. John Noble, accused of theft, fled to the Hospital of St John, Leicester in 1297 before abjuring the realm, *Records of the borough of Leicester, 1103–1603* I, ed. M. Bateson (London, 1899), p. 359.

[29] J. R. H. Moorman, *Church life in England in the thirteenth century* (Cambridge, 1945), p. 15.

been especially acute in an English town like Cambridge with a multitude of small parish churches competing for sufficient income, patronage and even the attendance of believers.[30] The proximity of many churches and chapels gave rise to friction and the addition of a new house infringed on the benefits of the older foundations. Some hospitals were denied the right of bell-ringing lest the peals attract parishioners from their parish churches.[31] The HSJC was situated in the parish of All Saints (which came to be known as All Saints in Jewry or *iuxta hospitale*), a parish appropriated to St Radegund's nunnery. Bishop Eustace arranged an agreement between the hospital and the nunnery (1208 × 1215) by which the master of the hospital swore before the bishop's official that no parishioner of All Saints would receive sacraments or would be allowed to give oblations to the hospital in a way that would harm the nunnery's interests. The prioress and convent conceded the right of free burial and chantry to the new institution and HSJC was allowed to choose the burial site; in return a compensation of 3s per annum was to be paid by three Cambridge burgesses – Harvey Dunning the mayor, Robert Seman and Maurice, son of Aubrey, each paying 1s.[32] In 1257 the burial and bell-ringing rights were renewed in the presence of the prior of St Osyth's priory in Chichester and recorded in a confirmation charter by the prior of Barnwell, following a payment of one mark by the hospital.[33]

Especially with the rise in the importance of visitation of the sick,

---

[30] On the churches of Cambridge see C. N. L. Brooke, 'The churches of medieval Cambridge', in *History, society and the churches: essays in honour of Owen Chadwick*, ed. D. Beales and G. Best (Cambridge, 1985), pp. 49–76. A good example of the friction is the judgement of the papal judge delegate of 1234, between the Hospital of St John the Baptist, King's Lynn, and the Prior and Convent of Norwich concerning the status of the hospital in the parish of St Margaret. It was resolved that the hospital could not offer the sacraments to its inmates, not bury its dead, and that a collection box could no longer hang in its chapel, *The making of King's Lynn*, pp. 105–6.

[31] The Hospital of St John, King's Lynn, was allowed only one bell to call its inmates and brethren to its chapel, *ibid.*, p. 106. Cf. J. Imbert, *Les hôpitaux en droit canonique* (Paris, 1947), p. 87.

[32] SJCA.D98.41. A similar agreement was reached between Barnwell priory and the Carmelites who moved into St John Zachary's parish in 1291. The friars were to pay 14s per annum, and they were restricted in receiving parishioners in their chapel. Again, a townsman shouldered the expenses: John Porthors, mayor of Cambridge in the 1280s and 1290s, paid 13s 4d of the sum, *Liber memorandum ecclesie de Bernewelle*, ed. J. W. Clark (Cambridge, 1907), pp. 201–11.

[33] SJCA.D15.105. For a typical agreement of this kind drawn in 1271 between the Holy Spirit Hospital and the baptismal church of Munich see *Die Urkunden des Heiliggeistspitals in München, 1250–1500*, ed. H. Vogel (Munich, 1960), no. 4, pp. 8–9. The hospital was allowed to bury its dead, brethren, servitors and inmates, and to maintain services in its chapel, fully independently from the city's main church. Here, the privilege was granted by the burgesses' request.

reception of the *viaticum* and the sacrament of extreme unction, chapels and graveyards were seen to be essential for hospitals which sheltered the sick and dying.[34] A hospital with burial rights was allowed to bury its members, its sick and its servants. It could also bury other folk who had so requested and had committed this wish to writing. In case of such burial a *portio canonica* was paid to the parish church to which the dead man had belonged[35] but was not paid in the case of additional legacies left to the hospital.[36] In our case, the convent seems to have been compensated in advance for all losses, as no further arrangement for the division of income is mentioned in the agreement.[37]

Founders of hospitals usually followed some conventions when choosing a site for their house. Sites of leper houses were usually located beyond town boundaries, often near springs and rivers.[38] The underlying view is reflected in the tenor of the thirteenth-century French legislation: 'For it would be dangerous to keep the leprous with the healthy, since the healthy could become leprous; therefore leper houses are built outside towns'.[39] The lepers of Nottingham lived outside the ditch, those of Hereford were outside Eign Gate; St Giles' hospital in London lay so far in the countryside as to be called 'in the fields'. The leper hospital in Cambridge, founded before 1169, was situated some two miles away from the centre of town beyond the

---

[34] For evidence of awareness of the problem see the papal provision of 1172 for the French almonry at Epinal: 'Infirmi de Sparnaco sepe pro defectu capellani gravia incurrant pericula, et sine viatici participacione decedunt', *PL* 200, col. 830. On the development of the pastoral obligations to the sick and dying see J. Avril, 'La pastorale des malades et des mourants aux xiie et xiiie siècles', in *Death in the Middle Ages*, ed. H. Braet and W. Verbeke (Louvain, 1983), pp. 88–106.

[35] Imbert, *Les hôpitaux*, pp. 92–3.

[36] John of Lapus de Castellione, *Tractatus hospitalitatis* (Lyons, 1549), XIV, fol. 166v.: 'Si testator dixit expresse, hoc relinquo hospitali non pro sepultura, sed alia causa justa, de tali causa nihil recipiet parochialis ecclesia'. For an interesting case of the appropriation of burial rights to a charitable order see R. B. Pugh, 'The Knights Hospitallers of England as undertakers', *Speculum* 56 (1981), pp. 566–74. The hospitallers possessed the right to bury any person commended to their community, a great infringement of parish rights, *ibid.*, pp. 571–4; they also buried executed criminals, pp. 566–7, 572–4. Hanged criminals were buried in the cemetery of St John's Hospital, Leicester in 1308. *The records of the borough of Leicester* I, p. 373.

[37] For an interesting resolution of a dispute between a hospital and a parish in 1430 see *The register of the gild of the Holy Cross*, p. ix.

[38] On leper communities near rivers see the example of L. Hannecart, 'Les établissements de bienfaisance à Chièvres au xiie siècle', *Annales de la société belge d'histoire des hôpitaux* I (1963), pp. 20–8; p. 24 and outside walls, p. 26.

[39] 'Car perilleuse chose seroit de converser meseaus aveques sains pour ce que li sain en pueent devenir mesel, et pour ce furent les maladeries fetes hors des viles', Philip of Beaumanoir, *Coutumes de Clermont en Beauvaisis* II, ed. A. Salmon (Paris, 1970), p. 329, c. 1623.

Barnwell precinct.[40] Hospitals for the old and sick were also kept away from the centres of economic and political activity, preferably outside the town walls, but often within suburban precincts.[41] In twelfth-century Nottingham the hospitals of St John the Baptist and St Sepulchre were outside the ditch and the leper houses lay even further away. In Bristol all six hospitals lay outside the gates, except St Mark's which was founded as part of St Augustine's priory. The fourteenth-century hospital of Sts Anthony and Eligius in Cambridge was built outside Trumpington Gate.[42]

HSJC was situated in a residential area not far from the centre of town, an unlikely choice for a hospital site. The jurors of the inquest of 1274 swore that the hospital was built on a site which was 'a very poor and empty place belonging to the community of the town of Cambridge'.[43] In 1279 the area housed few dwellings and was the least populated parish but one, St Radegund's, which was composed of the convent precinct and was largely rural.[44] The site was a stretch of marshy land, liable to flooding, which extended along the east bank of the Cam and which, in the twelfth century, was crossed by lanes giving access from the town centre to the river as well as some hythes. The area was artificially raised and densely built upon only after the foundation of the new colleges in the fourteenth and fifteenth centuries.[45] Since the community of Cambridge held the town at farm including, in practice, vacant and waste lands, it could allot part of this waste for a charitable purpose.[46] Thus, the hospital was inside the town,

[40] See below pp. 114–15. For admirable maps and topographic notes on medieval English towns see [*The atlas of*] *historic towns*, 2 vols., ed. M. D. Lobel (London, 1969–75).

[41] D. Keene, 'Suburban growth', in *The plans and topography of medieval towns*, ed. M. W. Barley (London, 1976), pp. 71–82; p. 81.

[42] All hospitals in Bury St Edmunds were situated outside the gates, away from inhabited areas, often along main routes. See map in Gottfried, *Bury St. Edmunds*, pp. 16–7. Venetian hospitals were thought to be polluting the air, and in the fourteenth century new hospitals were built on the Murano island, which came to lodge some 1,000 inmates by the end of the century, R. C. Mueller, 'The procurators of San Marco in the thirteenth and fourteenth centuries: a study of the office as a financial and trust institution', *Studi veneziani* 13 (1971), pp. 105–220; pp. 210–11.

[43] 'locus pauperrimus et vacuus de communitate ville Cant'', *Abbreviatio placitorum*, p. 263.

[44] There were 10 houses, 1 vacant space, 3 shops and 4 barns in the parish of All Saints, *Rotuli hundredorum* II, pp. 358–90; the small number of houses in the parish may be due to the registration of Jewish properties as part of the queen mother's dower rather than as part of the town, see also Maitland, *Township and borough*, pp. 101, 143–58.

[45] J. W. Clark and A. Gray, *Old plans of Cambridge, 1574 to 1798* (Cambridge, 1921), p. xv. On Cambridge topography see P. V. Addyman and M. Biddle, 'Medieval Cambridge: recent finds and excavations', *Cambridge Antiquarian Society. Proceedings and communications* 58 (1965), pp. 74–137.

[46] Pollock and Maitland, *A history of English law* I, pp. 153–5.

but its site had not yet been drawn into urban life. The loss of this site did not impinge on rent incomes, and its poor nature fitted the prevalent view of the isolation required for a house of poor and sick people.[47]

The site of HSJC had two additional interesting characteristics. Most English Jewries were situated either near market-places or near castles, for protection.[48] In Cambridge the Jewry was situated between these two points, in the cispontine parishes of All Saints and Holy Sepulchre which came to be known as 'in Jewry'.[49] HSJC lay across the High Street from the Jewry, while some tenements in All Saints' parish which were granted to the hospital had been formerly held by Jews.[50] Similarly, the hospital of St John the Baptist, Oxford, moved to a new site in 1231 in an area previously allotted to the Jews for use as a burial ground.[51] Upon their arrival in Oxford the Dominicans installed themselves in the midst of the Jewry,[52] while when the Franciscans settled in Cambridge they were given half of the house of Benjamin the Jew which had served as a gaol.[53]

One may assume that the placing of religious and charitable houses in the midst of or beside the Jewish quarter was conceived as an assertion of Christian faith. In the words of C. N. L. Brooke they were 'a symbol and monument of Christian welfare in the heart of Jewry'.[54] Placing a charitable institution close to the Jewish quarter may have been a subtle juxtaposition of *ecclesia* and *synagoga* in the minds of medieval people, since care for the poor and sick was the expression of the Christian truth.[55] Alice, a converted Jewess from Oxford, was installed

[47] This view dictated the choice of sites for charitable foundations well into the fifteenth century. In the later part of that century William Brown, a wealthy merchant, founded his almshouse in Stamford on what had been 'loco vocatur cleymont qui locus antea fuit vilissimum sterqulineum'; as described in the hospital's account book of 1495, Bodl. Rawlinson B.352, fol. 1.

[48] Roth, *The Jews of medieval Oxford*, p. 83.

[49] Earlier historians believed the Jewry to be near the Guildhall where the house of Benjamin the Jew, part of which served as a synagogue, was found, H. P. Stokes, *Studies in Anglo-Jewish history* (Edinburgh, 1913), pp. 113–14 and Brooke, 'The churches of medieval Cambridge', p. 73.

[50] SJCA.D20.25.

[51] Roth, *The Jews of medieval Oxford*, pp. 108–9. See above p. 102.

[52] W. A. Hinnebusch, 'The pre-Reformation sites of the Oxford Blackfriars', *Oxoniensia* 3 (1938), pp. 57–82; 58–60.

[53] However, not in the Jewry, J. R. H. Moorman, *The Grey Friars in Cambridge* (Cambridge, 1952), pp. 6–8; they were subsequently given a larger site in the parish of All Saints, which also contained part of the Jewry.

[54] Brooke, 'The churches of medieval Cambridge', p. 60.

[55] The provision of charitable loans was another step in the battle against Jewish moneylenders. As we will see HSJC was involved in the credit market of Cambridge, below pp. 217–26.

in the Hospital of St John, Oxford by royal command, and was to be sustained by the charitable house.[56] Endowments of religious and charitable houses were often created through the accumulation of lands from the forfeited lands market, as religious houses could redeem the lost lands at lower than market prices. Walter of Merton's foundation was founded on the site painstakingly accumulated through purchases of lands pledged to Jewish moneylenders and lost to them through failure of repayment. The Hospital of St John the Baptist in Oxford received from the king many Jewish tenements which had been escheated.[57] By helping Christians to redeem their pledges religious houses were freeing them from the Jewish moneylenders through acts of mercy. Thus, the location of HSJC so close to the moneylending centre of Cambridge posed a religious and economic challenge.

The hospital was also situated near the budding academic quarter of Cambridge, the parish of St Michael which came to house most fourteenth-century colleges. In the thirteenth century it was the parish of the old burgess elite and of the new university officials. Its houses were owned by old families like the Tuylets, the Crochmans, the Wombes and it attracted such men as the Chancellors Andrew of Giselham (1283) and Stephen of Haslingfield (1300–3, 1307) as well as the Masters Boudon and Botecourt. The archdeacon of Ely and the prior of Anglesey owned houses in the parish for their own use and for accommodation of officials and guests.[58] St Michael's and St Peter without Trumpington Gate were the most sought-after parishes in town; they were outside the hubbub of the centre, yet conveniently situated for business, worship and civic activity. The hospital, being the creation of the town patriciate, was conveniently situated for its chapel to be at the disposal of its benefactors and its life – under their scrutiny. Its proximity to what was to become the academic quarter also allowed for its subsequent absorption into the university sphere once its relationship with the town had deteriorated. The chancellor conferred on it, *c.* 1470, some of the privileges which the neighbouring academic charitable houses, the colleges, enjoyed.[59]

Pope Gregory IX confirmed the hospital's ecclesiastical rights in a letter of 1228.[60] This is a short letter of grace placing the hospital under

[56] Roth, *The Jews of medieval Oxford*, p. 25.
[57] *Ibid.*, pp. 108–9.
[58] H. P. Stokes, *Outside the Trumpington Gates before Peterhouse was founded* (Cambridge, 1908), p. 2.   [59] SJCA. Cartulary of HSJC, fol. 47v.
[60] SJCA.D4.I lines 197–202. Hospitals and their founders attempted to secure papal confirmation soon after foundation: St Giles' Hospital, Norwich which was founded in 1246 received its papal letter in 1255, *Calendar of papal letters* I, p. 312.

papal protection and warning those who may infringe upon its rights. In 1250 Innocent IV granted a letter confirming in great detail the hospital's possessions and rights.[61] Innocent IV was the first to mention the hospital as living under an Augustinian rule[62]; and he reviewed the house's holdings by parishes and listed its ecclesiastical rights: free burial for members and testators, prohibition of erection of new chapels in the parish without the hospital's consent,[63] and the right to hold services during an interdict. In order to encourage interest in the hospital, and to ensure its prosperity through the receipt of alms, an early papal indulgence was granted by the Cardinal of Sta Sabina in 1246–7 offering remittance of 40 days of penance to those aiding the hospital and its poor.[64]

The urban hospital founded by burgesses in the early thirteenth century was clearly influenced by the changing fortunes of the town. The house underwent some change when, in the course of the reign of Henry III, scholars were admitted to it. The precise status of these scholars is far from clear but we know that in 1280 HSJC was the formal residence of the scholars of the bishop of Ely.[65] Some privileges from Henry III's reign describe benefits granted to the hospital as being 'for the maintenance of poor scholars and other sick people of the hospital'.[66] The scholars were removed in 1283 together with part of the endowment which had been granted to the hospital for their support and were placed in the new academic house, Peterhouse,[67] but not before the connection between academic and non-academic charity

---

[61] *Ibid.*, lines 173–197.

[62] In the hospital's rule there is reference to an 'ordo', 'secundum regulam predicatam et ordinis constitucionem', SJCA.D4.1 (clause 15); see below p. 301. The house was clearly titled so in 1426: 'custos domus sive hospitalis Sancti Iohannis Ewangeliste Cantebr' ordinis Sancti Augustini', SJCA. Cartulary of HSJC, fol. 80v.

[63] *Ibid.*, lines 165–6: 'Prohibemus insuper ut infra fines parochie vestre nullus sine asensu diocesani Episcopi et vestro capellam seu oratorium de novo construere audeat'.

[64] SJCA.D98.43. St Giles' Hospital in Norwich received episcopal indulgences in 1279 and 1294. They were granted for the benefit of those who prayed for the hospital's benefactors, for visitors on the feast of St Giles and on the anniversary of the dedication of the altar, NRO.24/a/9. For indulgences granted early in a hospital's life in aid of its financial establishment, cf. St Katherine's hospital, Bamberg: K. Guth, 'Spitäler in Bamberg und Nürnberg als bürgerliche Sozialeinrichtungen der mittelalterlichen Stadt', *Jahrbuch für fränkische Landesforschung* 38 (1978), pp. 39–49; p. 41.

[65] *Documents relating to the University and Colleges of Cambridge* II (London, 1852), pp. 1–4; see below pp. 271–3.

[66] 'ad sustentationem pauperum scholarium et aliorum infirmorum hospitalis eiusdem', CUL. University archives. Luard*51, a confirmation dating from 1378.

[67] On the separation see Peterhouse Muniments. Collegium A3 and SJCA.D98.3 as well as the royal *inspeximus* of 1285, Peterhouse muniments. Cista comm. C. For a roll containing fourteenth century copies of pertinent charters see SJCA.D98.44.

had impressed itself on the mind of the community. A few years before the refoundation of the hospital as a college it was granted an exemption from the payment of subsidies on account of its contact with the university, dating back to its relationship with Peterhouse.[68]

HSJC came into being through the convergence of the piety of townsmen and the organisational system of the Church. The town provided the physical basis for the house's existence while the bishop turned it into a full ecclesiastical institution which was able to fulfil the spiritual expectations of townsmen. A portion of Cambridge, in economic and religious resources, was carved out for the new house. The hospital's functions and orientations were altered during the centuries of its existence: from a general house of mercy it developed into an institution with pronounced chantry functions and by the late thirteenth century with expanded liturgical celebrations. In the fourteenth century it was receiving corrodarians and by the mid-fifteenth century it was sufficiently similar in function to the colleges to be accorded the privileges of the University and colleges. Yet it remained a house of charity throughout the period of its existence and the changes in its activities must be understood in connection with the changing meaning of charity. We shall see that this process of change occurred in many of the charitable institutions in and around Cambridge.

The leper hospital of St Mary Magdalene at Stourbridge

A beautiful Norman chapel on the outskirts of Cambridge (2 miles east of the town centre on today's Newmarket Road) is the only substantial physical remains of the hospitals of medieval Cambridge. The chapel was part of the leper hospital which was the earliest town hospital. The first evidence for its existence can be found in the Pipe Rolls for the years 16–18 Henry II (1169–72). The sheriff's returns for Cambridge-shire contain accounts of sums paid as alms to various religious institutions. In 1169–70 the sheriff reported 'And to the hospital of the sick of Barnwell 20s for this year. And to the same 13s 4d for last year'.[69] In 1199 a writ of *novel disseisin* was granted to the hospital,[70] and in

---

[68] SJCA.D3.72 (29 May 1500). The hospital was granted membership in the University *c.* 1470, SJCA. Cartulary of HSJC, fol. 42v.

[69] *Pipe roll 16 Henry II*, p. 96. In 1171 and 1172 as well 20s were reported as alms paid to the hospital, *Pipe Roll 17 Henry II*, p. 116; *Pipe Roll 18 Henry II*, p. 116. In 1171–2, 8s 8d were paid 'Infirme de Ponte de Bernwell' – a recluse female leper? On royal alms to the hospital of St John of Ely see below p. 129.

[70] As part of its case against Walter of Branford, *Pipe roll 1 John*, p. 161.

1227 a mandate was directed to the custodian of the See of Ely to continue the allocation of episcopal alms of 20s per annum which 'the lepers of St Mary Magdalene of Stourbridge used to receive in the times of the bishops of Ely as their ordained alms'.[71] It appears that the bishop now paid to the lepers a sum equal to the former royal alms, annually. The hospital was addressed by its formal dedication, and its toponym Stourbridge appeared already in 1199.[72]

The early history of Stourbridge hospital was recorded in the great inquiry of 1279. The jurors testified that both the advowson and patronage of the leper hospital had belonged originally to the burgesses of Cambridge who held the town at fee-farm from the king. It was alleged that Hugh Northwold, Bishop of Ely (1229–54) seized the right of presentation from the burgesses unjustly and presented to the hospital various chaplains, to the detriment of the men of Cambridge. In spite of pleas to the escheators and to the itinerant justices nothing was amended.[73] This is borne out by the record of the assizes held at Cambridge in 1260, at which the question of the advowson of St Mary's church was discussed. As a side issue it was mentioned that HSJC and Stourbridge chapel had once been in the king's gift and that Hugh, Bishop of Ely, removed and replaced the latter's last chaplain.[74] The jurors also knew of the right for a three-day fair at Stourbridge due to the largesse of King John,[75] allowing us to trace royal patronage of the hospital from Henry II to John. During the latter reign the patronage was understood to be part of the fee-farm of the whole town granted in 1207.[76] At some point during the reign of Henry III, and coinciding with Hugh Northwold's episcopate, a change of status must

[71] 'leprosi Beate Marie Magdalene de Steresbregg' temporibus episcoporum Eliensium percipere consueverunt singulis annis de elemosina sua constituta', *Calendar of close rolls 1256–1259*, p. 170 (9 December 1257). This was at the time between the consecration of Bishop Balsham (14 October 1257) and the return of the temporalities of the See (15 January 1258).

[72] It appears as 'Stiebrig' in 1199, *Pipe Roll 1 John*, p. 161. The etymology of this place-name is 'steer's (ox) bridge', which was later spelt 'Stourbridge' by mistaken popular identification as 'bridge on the Stour'. See P. H. Reaney, ed., *The place-names of Cambridgeshire and the Isle of Ely* (Cambridge, 1943), p. 43. For a photograph of the restored interior see W. H. Godfrey, *The English almshouse* (London, 1955), p. 1.1.

[73] *Rotuli hundredorum* II, p. 359b: 'de dictis burgensibus iniuste per dictum dominum Hugonem de Norwold et per eius successores qui ad eorum voluntatem dederunt dictum osspitalem capellanis ibidem commorantibus in exheredacione domini Regis et predictorum burgensium'.

[74] *The assizes held at Cambridge, A.D. 1260*, ed. W. M. Palmer (Linton, 1930).

[75] 'leprosis in dicto hospitali commorantibus ad eorum sustentacionem concessit', *Rotuli hundredorum* II, p. 360a.

[76] *The charters of the borough of Cambridge*, ed. F. W. Maitland and M. Bateson (Cambridge, 1901), pp. 7–9.

have taken place. The bishop, perhaps in an attempt to bring ecclesiastical foundations under proper control, took over the *ius presentandi*.[77] Such claims were repeated elsewhere in the Hundred Rolls as well as in the case of HSJC: 'They say that the advowson and gift of the hospital of St John the Evangelist of Cambridge and of the leper hospital of Stourbridge used to belong by right to the burgesses of Cambridge who held the said town of Cambridge at fee-farm from the lord king'.[78]

The precise circumstance of the foundation of the Stourbridge hospital remain unknown. Its royal connection may indicate royal patronage; indeed royal foundation of leper hospitals was a common phenomenon in twelfth-century England.[79] Piety and responsibility towards these miserable folk combined biblical associations and the care of leprosy and inspired royal interest. Out of 42 hospitals in direct royal patronage, of which we have sufficient knowledge, 20 were leper houses.[80] Most were founded in the twelfth century; the century which saw the foundation of more leper houses than any other. Between 1150 and 1250 we know of the creation of more than 130 leper hospitals, between 1250 and 1350 of over 70, but after 1350 only 12 new foundations are known.[81] Mary Magdalene was the most popular patron saint for leper houses.[82] Later the wave diminished considerably

---

[77] The jurors said that this had occurred 30 years earlier, that is *c.* 1250, *Rotuli hundredorum* II, p. 359b.

[78] 'Dicunt quod advocacionem et donacionem Hospitalis Sancti Iohannis Evangeliste de Cantebrigia et Hospitalis leprosorum de Steresbrig' de jure solebat pertinere ad burgenses Cantebrigie qui tenent dictam villam Cantebrigi' ad feodi firmam de domino Rege', *ibid.* However, a leper house which wished to exercise chapel rights and have the *cura animarum* of its inmates was required to procure an episcopal licence and enter under episcopal control, N. Huyghebaert, 'L'origine ecclésiastique des léproseries en Flandre et dans le Nord de la France', *Revue d'histoire ecclésiastique* 58 (1963), pp. 848–57; pp. 854–5.

[79] However leprosy existed in England as early as the Romano-British period. On archaeological remains in cemeteries see R. Reader, 'New evidence for the antiquity of leprosy in early Britain', *Journal of archaeological science* 1 (1974), pp. 205–7.

[80] E. J. Kealey, 'Anglo-Norman policy and public welfare', *Albion* 10 (1978), pp. 341–51, esp. pp. 348–50.

[81] This count is based on the details of patronage tabulated in R. M. Clay, *The medieval hospitals of England* (London 1909), appendix B. For the chronology is the Low Countries, cf. Bonenfant, *Hôpitaux et bienfaisance publiques*, p. 16. For a typical leper hospital of this period see D. M. Meade, 'The hospital of St. Giles at Kepier near Durham, 1112–1545', *Transactions of the architectural and archaeological society of Durham and Northumberland*, new ser. 1 (1968), pp. 45–58.

[82] V. Saxer, *Le culte de Marie Madeleine en Occident des origines à la fin du moyen-âge*, 2 vols., Auxerre and Paris, 1959, pp. 84, 123–7, 196. The hospitals of St Mary Magdalene in Ely and at King's Lynn (*c.* 1145) were of mid-twelfth century foundation. Of the 59 known leper houses dedicated to Mary Magdalene, 43 were founded between

and very few new leper houses were founded, while many existing houses were absorbed into others, transformed or died out.[83] These centuries were the most active for all types of hospital foundations.[84]

When communities of lepers were created under episcopal supervision they tended to follow the statutes which were often based on the Augustinian rule. These communities would consist of brethren and sisters serving a group of lepers. Lepers could never be fully professed religious, but they often assumed penitential discipline, were separated by sex, donned a habit and observed some canonical routine.[85] Many small leper communities living off alms must have existed without reaching our knowledge,[86] being transient unendowed units which left no mark in surviving documents. Many such communities must have died out within a short period from their creation and some have left their trace only in toponyms which remained long after the lepers had departed.

By the third quarter of the twelfth century Stourbridge hospital was certainly in existence. The Norman chapel suggests a mid-twelfth-century foundation date.[87] As it was one of few religious foundations in and around Cambridge it must have received donations from townsmen from the moment of its foundation.[88] Its distance from the centre of settlement falls in with the general tendency for building

---

1100–1300, 23 in the twelfth century, a calculation based on Knowles and Hadcock, *Medieval religious houses*, pp. 250–324, and contain only houses for which the foundation dates are known.

[83] The theory relating leprosy and tuberculosis has been expounded by Dr. K. Manchester of the University of Bradford at the conference 'Medieval Hospitals', University of Oxford, Extra Mural Board, December 13–15, 1985. L. De Maitre suggests that improved understanding of the disease by physicians may have contributed to its disappearance, L. De Maitre, 'The description and diagnosis of leprosy by fourteenth-century physicians', *Bulletin of the history of medicine* 59 (1985), pp. 327–44, at pp. 343–4. For another attempt at explanation see J. Tisseuil, 'La régression de la lèpre ne fut-elle pas aussi fonction de l'evolution économique du xive siècle?', *Bulletin de la Société française de pathologie exotique* 68 (1975), pp. 352–5.

[84] D. M. Owen, *Church and society in medieval Lincolnshire* (Lincoln, 1971), p. 55.

[85] J. Avril, 'Le iiie concile du Latran et les communautés des lépreux', *Revue Mabillon* 60 (1981), pp. 21–76; pp. 65–66.

[86] For some royal letters of protection permitting the community of lepers of St Giles, Huntingdon, to seek alms for its sustenance see *Calendar of patent rolls 1327–30*, p. 259 and *Calendar of patent rolls 1334–38*, p. 433.

[87] For this suggested date of the chapel I am indebted to Mr H. Richmond, Dr. R. Brooke and Prof. C. N. L. Brooke. C. H. Jones suggested an early twelfth-century date for the chapel: C. H. Jones, 'The chapel of St. Mary Magdalene at Stourbridge, Cambridge', *Cambridge Antiquarian Society. Proceedings and communications* 28 (1925–6), pp. 126–50, esp. p. 140.

[88] The others being Barnwell priory, founded in 1092 and St Radegund's nunnery, founded before 1138.

hospitals, above all leper houses.[89] There is no way of assessing the size of the hospital, but 'apostolic' communities of twelve lepers with a master were common.[90] Generally speaking, there appear to have been two phases in the development of leper hospitals. Our house falls in the earlier period, 1100–1250, in which leper communities organised themselves as autonomous, quasi-regular units.[91] This arose as a response to the frequency of leprosy and to the growing demands for separation of lepers. Legislation aimed at separation of lepers demanded that those afflicted be separated 'due to contagion of the said sickness and the deformity of body which it causes'.[92]

Stourbridge hospital was built at a time when provision for leprosy was at its height in medieval Europe. Throughout the twelfth century ecclesiastical legislation formulated some clear demands on lepers while providing them with protection. A draft canon prepared for the Council of Westminster of 1175 stated the basic rules: 'leprosi inter sanos amodo non conversentur' ('lepers should never circulate among the healthy').[93] In 1200 another council at Westminster reiterated largely verbatim the decree of Lateran III (1179) as to the needs of lepers separated from society.[94] Under the heading *Ut leprosi cimiterium et proprium habeant capellanum* it was decreed that wherever a congregation of lepers lived, it should have a church, a cemetery and a priest.[95] Their

---

[89] As discussed above pp. 107–8. On sites of leper houses see C. Petouraud, 'Les léproseries lyonnaises au moyen-âge et pendant la Renaissance', *Cahiers d'histoire* 7 (1962), pp. 425–64, esp. pp. 432–3.

[90] For an example see the hospital of Mary Magdalene in Lyons, Gonthier, 'Les hôpitaux et les pauvres à la fin du moyen-âge', pp. 287–8.

[91] Robert of Flamborough refers to leper communities among other regular groups: 'ad etiam templarios, hospitalarios, leprosos qui sunt de congregationibus (de vagabondis enim non loquor)', *Liber poenitentialis*, c. 148, p. 150.

[92] 'propter contagionem morbi predicti et propter corporis deformacionem', Petouraud, 'Les léproseries', pp. 436–9; W. de Keyzer, 'Une léproserie en mutation. La bonne maison St. Ladre de Mons aux XIIIᵉ siècles', *Annales de la société belge de l'histoire des hôpitaux* 14 (1976), pp. 5–25, esp. pp. 7–8, 16, 24–5; C. Probst, 'Das hospitalwesen in hohen und späten Mittelalter unde die geistliche und gesellschaftliche Stellung des Kranken', *Sudhoffs, Archiv* 50 (1966), pp. 246–58, esp. pp. 246–7. On separation ceremonies see Imbert, *Les hôpitaux*, pp. 72–3.

[93] *Councils and synods*, I part 2, c. 36, p. 981; See M. G. Cheney, 'The council of Westminster 1175: new light on an old source', *Studies in Church history* 11 (1975), pp. 61–8; p. 67, where the author explains that the proposal above was one of nine that did not become canons of the council after papal consultation. The issue was not whether lepers should live with whole people, but concerned complex problems such as their marital status.

[94] *Councils and synods* I part 2, c. 13, p. 1068. Compare with c. 23 of the Lateran council, *Conciliorum oecumenicorum decreta*, pp. 222–3.

[95] Huyghebaert, 'L'origine ecclésiastique des léproseries', pp. 855–6. See the thirteenth-century law in Philip of Beaumanoir, *Coutumes de Clermont* II, pp. 326–9, cc. 1217–1623.

religious orientation often placed them under diocesan jurisdiction or patronage and motivated the provision of a rule,[96] or placed them as dependants of another religious house.[97] The lepers were to be free of tithes on the produce of their gardens and on feed for their animals.[98] The leper represented not only physical danger but evoked the deepest fear of moral contamination and served as a reminder of retribution for sinful lives.[99] Thus a sense of revulsion and fear drove communities to create distant asylums for their lepers.[100] In the later phase, after 1250, leper houses were founded by or in connection with secular authorities which regulated admission and undertook the seeking out of suspected leprosy cases.[101]

A leper from Cambridge or its surrounding area would seek entry into such a community, at least from the stage when his affliction could no longer be hidden. Such a man or woman would join a leper community with some of his belongings to begin a new life among similarly unfortunate people.[102] He would belong to a self-regulating community demanding obedience and offering cooperation and mutual help. Lepers would beg for alms together, eat together and meet in the chapel for divine service. The community at Stourbridge must have lived in a similar way until the mid-thirteenth century, by which time

---

[96] *Ibid.*, p. 328, c. 1620.

[97] An example of such a relationship, unfortunately a *mésalliance*, see R. Mortimer, 'The prior of Butley and the lepers of West Somerton', *Bulletin of the Institute of Historical Research* 53 (1980), pp. 99–103.

[98] S. Rubin, *Medieval English medicine* (Newton Abbot, 1974), pp. 152–3.

[99] For a discussion of the use of leprosy as a term denoting sin in the twelfth-century theological debates see Longère, *Oeuvres oratoires* I, pp. 266–7, 316, 422 (and n. 117, II, p. 326).

[100] The preamble to an ordinance of expulsion of lepers from London describes their lascivious ways and the transmission of the disease through intercourse with healthy women, *Memorials of London*, ed. Riley, p. 384 (1375). On such attitudes and their expression in contemporary literature see P. Remy, 'La lèpre, thème littéraire au moyen-âge. Commentaire d'un passage du roman provençal de Jaufré, *Le moyen-âge* 42 (1946), pp. 195–242 and D. Rocher, 'Exclusion, auto-exclusion et readmission du lepreux dans *Le pauvre Henri*', *Exclus et systèmes d'exclusion dans la littérature et la civilisation médiévales* (Aix-en-Provence, 1978), pp. 91–103; esp. pp. 94–97, 102–3. On the psychological influence of seclusion on its victims see Z. Gussow and G. S. Tracy, 'Status, ideology and adaptation to stigmatized illness: a study of leprosy', in *Culture, disease and healing: studies in medical anthropology*, ed. D. Landy (New York, 1977), pp. 394–402.

[101] This was seen as a duty of towns to their citizens: a similar development took place in twelfth century Flanders, Huyghebaert, 'L'origine ecclésiastique des léproseries', pp. 855–6. See below pp. 119–26, on the fourteenth-century hospital of St Anthony and St Eligius, as well as *Memorials of London*, pp. 510–11.

[102] Some ensured their entry by earlier donations, S. C. Mesmin, 'The leper hospital of St. Gilles de Pont-Audemer' (Ph.D., Reading, 1978) I, p. 58. Inmates were expected by some leper hospitals to provide their own bedding and eating utensils, *ibid.*, p. 49.

it had been dissolved and its chapel had gained the status of a free chapel in the patronage of the bishops of Ely.

Some information relating to the hospital's financial resources has survived in the Hundred Rolls; it held 24½ acres in Cambridge fields, land accumulated from various benefactions.[103] The pattern of donation to medieval charitable institutions was such that the formation of the endowment and the acquisition of most grants occurred within the first years of the house's existence, corresponding with a generation of founders, their relatives and friends.[104] The lands described in the survey of 1279 were, most probably, acquired in the twelfth century. Already in 1199 the master of Stourbridge was involved in a plea to the royal court in connection with some lands in Comberton.[105] Besides lands, there was the income from the letting of stalls during the fair (13–15 September). Stourbridge fair was a major international commercial event which remained an important market of the East of England even in the late Middle Ages.[106] In addition, there were alms to be collected on the highway and produce from gardens and livestock kept by the inmates. However, after its transformation into a chapel, this endowment passed on to the new incumbents.[107]

If it were true that leprosy was extinct by the mid–thirteenth century, the change in the hospital's function could be explained. However, this would seem much too early a date for total extinction of the disease since some 90 years later a new leper hospital was founded in Cambridge.[108] The townsmen's cry against the loss of Stourbridge may

[103] Less than a quarter of the size of HSJC's holdings in the Cambridge fields in 1279, *Rotuli hundredorum* II, p. 359b: '..quas habent de dono plurimorum qui dederunt dictas terras ad dictum hospitale ad sustinendum ibidem leprosos in perpetua elemosina'.

[104] See below pp. 202–12 on the formation of HSJC's endowment.

[105] Unmentioned in the Hundred Rolls, *Rotuli hundredorum* I, p. 329. In 1219 the brethren of Stourbridge hospital were mentioned in a plea, as tenants of some land in Bourn, *Calendar of the plea rolls of the Exchequer of the Jews* I, ed. J. M. Rigg (London, 1905), p. 13.

[106] *VCH. Cambridgeshire* II, pp. 87–8. Grant of income from fairs was a common form of endowment of leper hospitals, P. M. G. Russell, *A history of the Exeter hospitals 1170–1948* (Exeter, 1976) and Mesmin, 'The leper hospital of St. Gilles de Pont-Audemer' I, p. 70.

[107] In 1412 the warden of the free chapel recovered from the bailiffs of Cambridge stallage payments from booths pitched in the chapel yard during the fair. CUL. EDR. Register Fordham, fols. 228r–229v. However, this relates to stallage for stalls on the chapel's land, not to income from the fair's proceeds. From the second half of the thirteenth century the University and the town became more involved in the fair and it may be that the chapel's exclusive rights were revoked when it ceased to be a charitable institution.

[108] In the capital, where travellers might have reintroduced the sickness from abroad, frequent action was taken to ensure the separation of lepers from the rest of society:

indicate a still extant need for a leper asylum.[109] The Official of the bishop of Ely demanded the presentation of accounts of the administration of the chapel from the warden (*custos*) in 1390, a vestige of episcopal control over the once-charitable house.[110]

Throughout the fourteenth and fifteenth centuries, whenever the survival of episcopal registers allows, we learn of the dates and circumstances of the collation of wardens to the free chapel. Between the years 1376 and 1412, and 1453 and 1477, 11 collations occurred and three exchanges with holders of other livings.[111] Only one incumbent was titled priest at the time of his collation (Robert Flatte, 1402), and another was a notary public (Roger Malmesbury, 1456). The living appears to have been attractive as it was exchanged once for a rectory in county Durham (*Waldeneuton*), and twice for attractive chaplaincies: All Saints and St Mary, York and St Radegund's chapel in St Paul's Cathedral. In 1477 the chapel was held by Richard Robinson who later that year became the archdeacon of Ely; the living was assessed at £5 for the subsidy of 1463 and at 10 guineas in 1536.[112] Since it held no obligations towards a parish this was equivalent to a much larger income for a living with cure of souls.[113]

Thus, a twelfth-century leper hospital under royal patronage passed into the patronage of the burgesses of Cambridge in 1207, but ceased to receive lepers soon after the mid-thirteenth century. The hospital was transformed into a free chapel, a sort of chantry, a living to be held by men whom the bishop favoured.[114]

---

see a royal mandate for the expulsion of lepers (1341), *Memorials of London*, pp. 230–1, and supervision of leper houses by town officials, *ibid.*, pp. 510–11.

[109] The warden and the chapel no longer fulfilled any charitable function. For an example of a similar transformation of a hospital see A. F. Butcher, 'The hospital of St. Stephen and St. Thomas, New Romney – the documentary evidence', *Archaeologia Cantiana* 96 (1980), pp. 17–26; esp. pp. 20–1, 25.

[110] CUL. EDR. Consistory court Arundel, fol. 139r. In 1390 an indulgence was granted to those visiting and helping the chapel, CUL. EDR. Register Fordham, fol. 12v.

[111] Collations: CUL. EDR. Register Arundel, 21r, 52v (1376, 1385), Register Fordham, fols. 20r, 53r, 77v–78r, 83v, 104 (1389, 1391, 1396, 1402, 1403, 1407); Register Bourchier, fol. 37v (1453); Register Gray, fols. 96r, 96v (1477, 1477). Exchanges: CUL. EDR. Register Arundel, fol. 52 (1385); Register Fordham, fols. 29v–30r, 99r (1392, 1407).

[112] CUL. EDR. Register Gray, fol. 96v; CUL. EDR. Register Gray, fol. 115r; CUL. EDR. Register Goodrich, fol. 134v.

[113] For estimates of the needs of parish chaplains: P. Heath, *The English parish clergy on the eve of the Reformation* (London, 1969), pp. 22–4. On the financial obligations of parish priests see below pp. 237–41.

[114] For an example of the transformation of a charitable house into a sinecure after the disappearance of its *raison d'être* see the case of the *Domus conversorum* in London, *VCH. London* I, pp. 551–4.

The Hospital of Sts Anthony and Eligius

About 1361 a new hospital was founded in Cambridge, the leper hospital of Sts Anthony and Eligius, situated on the east side of Trumpington street some 50 yards to the north of its intersection with today's Lensfield Road.[115] In 1392 the new hospital was helped by an episcopal indulgence granted to those frequenting and aiding the leper house and its staff.[116] In Lyne's map of Cambridge of 1574, touching the south edge named 'meridies', one can see the words 'spyttle ende' and a row of houses abutting on Trumpington Street. The hospital gave its name to the southern-most part of town, the 'spyttle end'.[117]

At first sight, the creation of a leper house in the second half of the fourteenth century is surprising. Leprosy was dying out in England when this new leper house was founded. After 1300 cases of leprosy were rarer, and many hospitals found difficulty in filling the quotas laid down in their statutes. The disease was moving northwards, to Scotland, Denmark, Sweden and Norway and remaining there until the nineteenth century.[118] Cambridge was a town more prone to infection than others as it drew many of its passing residents merchants and scholars, from a wide geographic range in England and the Continent.[119] In other parts of East Anglia, where ties with the Continent and northern Europe were lively, provision for lepers is made well into the fifteenth century: in a will dated 1481 from Havering, Essex, £8 6s 6d were left for poor lepers, albeit of other regions.[120]

In this period of evident decline in leprosy the Hospital of Sts Eligius and Anthony was founded as a *hospitium lazarorum* according to a

---

[115] This corresponds with numbers 6–7 on Trumpington street now owned by Corpus Christi College. These houses are situated on the site of the almshouses which succeeded the medieval hospital and were torn down in 1852. For a map of medieval Cambridge see [*The atlas of*] *historic towns* II, Cambridge, map 6.
[116] CUL. EDR. Register Fordham, fol. 179.
[117] Lyne's map in J. Caius, *De antiquitate Cantabrigiensis academiae libri duo* (London, second edn, 1574).
[118] P. Richards, *The medieval leper and his northern heirs* (Cambridge, Mass., 1977), pp. 3–4.
[119] However, from the examination of the figures for the student population of Cambridge it appears that very few northern students frequented it: 'Very few scholars indeed came from the Low Countries, Eastern Europe and Scandinavia', Aston, Duncan and Evans, 'The medieval alumni of the university of Cambridge', p. 35.
[120] McIntosh, *Autonomy and community*, p. 239, n. 72. Cases of leprosy still existed and lacked proper treatment, see *Calendar close rolls 1327–30*, p. 155. That leprosy was still thought to exist is evident from bequests of fifteenth century testaments: 'Item lego cuilibet domui leprosorum prope portas civitatis Norwic' VIs VIIId', (1947), *Register of Henry Chichele, archbishop of Canterbury, 1414–1443* II, 4 vols., ed. E. F. Jacob (Oxford, 1937), p. 143; 'Item lego leprosis ad singulas portas civitatis Norwic xIId' (1416), *ibid.* III, ed. E. F. Jacob with H. C. Johnson (Oxford, 1945), p. 418

sixteenth-century tradition and the name 'leper' or 'lazar' was connected with it from its foundation. The indulgence of 1392 was given to the domus *leprosorum*,[121] and in a document of 1526 it was titled 'House of lepers'.[122] This would mean that it did, perhaps not exclusively, serve a population suffering from some skin disorder. With the extinction of leprosy in most parts of Europe by the late Middle Ages, houses which had begun as asylums for those who had to be separated from society, retained their stigma and were transformed to accommodate those who were currently seen as marginals. Names of such houses remained and rites of admission were performed even when they housed vagabonds, the new dangerous group, rather than lepers.[123]

With the new awareness on the part of municipal authorities of their responsibility to maintain order and protect their citizens from undesirable members of society, separation and maintenance of lunatics, vagabonds and beggars was undertaken in the later Middle Ages.[124] It is, therefore, revealing to find in the Cambridge Treasurers' accounts of 1584 an entry reporting the purchase of 'a paire of sheets for ye madd woman in ye spittle house'.[125] This is late evidence but it shows that although in the sixteenth century the house was still called a leper house it admitted mad women as well. The function of the late medieval almshouse was to relieve society of its unacceptable members through provision of asylum, houses of seclusion.

In 1569, when writing a history of the foundation of Corpus Christi College, J. Josselin described the most prominent benefactors of the College. While extolling the deeds of Henry Tangmere he recounted: 'and he recently caused the hermitage of St Anne and a leper hospital to be built out of his own funds, and bequeathed them to the college'.[126] Henry Tangmere was a Cambridge burgess during the

---

[121] CUL. EDR. Register Fordham, fol. 179.

[122] *Cambridge borough documents* I, ed. W. M. Palmer (Cambridge, 1931), p. 55.

[123] For the description of survival of separation rites see M. Foucault, *Folie et déraison: histoire de la folie à l'âge classique* (Paris, 1961), p. 7. On perceptions of marginality see J. Le Goff, 'Les marginaux dans l'occident médiéval', in *Les marginaux et les exclus dans l'histoire* (Paris, 1979), pp. 19–28. On the treatment of lunacy see G. Rosen, *Madness in society: chapters in the historical sociology of mental illness* (London, 1968), ch. IV, pp. 139–50.

[124] For legislation concerning the duty of separation and maintenance of lepers by town authorities see Philip of Beaumanoir, *Coutumes de Clermont*, pp. 326–9, cc. 1617–1623.

[125] *Annals of (the borough of) Cambridge* II, ed. C. H. Cooper (Cambridge, 1843), p. 401. p. 401.

[126] 'fecitque hermitagium nuper sancte Anne et hospitium lazarorum ibidem suis sumptibus expressis edificari, eademque collegio legavit', J. Josselin, *Historiale collegii corporis christi*, ed. J. W. Clark (Cambridge, 1880), p. 12. Repeated in R. Masters, *The history of the college of Corpus Christi, Cambridge* (Cambridge, 1753; repr. London, 1898), p. 21.

years of the foundation of the College, 1351–2.[127] He was a prominent figure, and appeared high on the lists of witnesses in donation charters to the town and to the gild.[128] In a donation of a messuage to the gild of St Mary in 1349 Henry appears at the top of the witness list,[129] which may indicate that he was a member of the older gild of St Mary before the union. Corpus Christi College archives contain various deeds by which lands and tenements were conveyed to Henry Tangmere or let at farm to him.[130] His business transactions were intimately connected with the process of endowment of the new college both by the transfer of gild possessions to it and by the legacies left by him.

Henry Tangmere's will is no longer fully extant. From it we could have learnt more about the foundation of the hospital and of his plans for it after his death. However, a part of a small work-book containing reckonings of his executors has survived, and in it there is a copy of those provisions in the will made to the college or entrusted to the college for execution.[131] The 31 clauses reveal Henry's plans for enfeoffing the college with a large part of his real property before his death.[132] These clauses ordered the college to keep most of the property *ad opus collegii* and to enjoy the terms of some outstanding leases. They also made various bequests to churches (St Benet's and St Edward's), to his wife, to the religious houses of Denney and Waterbeach, gifts which were transmitted to the beneficiaries by the college which had been granted many of these properties. We do not know the exact arrangements for execution which would have appeared in the will, but the formula 'Item quod Magister Thomas de Eltesle et alij feoffati...feoffent' ('that Master Thomas of Eltisley and the other enfeoffed...should enfeoff') recurs in our document. Utensils, beds and plates were given to family and friends, and some bequests were to revert to the college after the death of their beneficiaries. The welfare and custody of his son Henry was entrusted to the hands of the college, which was to sustain, clothe and educate the boy for seven years. The college was the chief beneficiary, executor and trustee of Henry's will; according to the accounts it received some fifteen shops, six

[127] See above and cf. *Cambridge gild records 1298–1389*, p. 45 (1352–3).
[128] CCCA. xv, 118 (1348); xxxi, 40 (1349).
[129] CCCA. x, 3a.
[130] CCCA. xxxi, 42 (1352); 47 (1353); 66 (1361).
[131] CCCA. xxxi, 70. The dates in the book are in year 35 Edward III. At the beginning of the copy of the will the date is given in XXV Edward III. This seems to me to be an error, since, if true, it would mean that the will, leaving so much to the college was written before its actual foundation. There must have been an omission of one 'X' in the date.
[132] CCCA. xxxi, 61, 62 (1357).

messuages, more than 150 acres of arable, meadow, rents, granges and silver bullion. The demands that Henry made of the college in return were 'to intercede and celebrate...so that one of the chaplains of the college...will celebrate daily for the souls of Henry of Tangmere, of Amphelisa his wife, and of John and Amelina, Henry's father and mother'.[133]

No mention was made in our partial version of the will of the Hospital of Sts Anthony and Eligius or of the Hermitage of St Anne, but the college received some tenements on Trumpington Street very near the site of the hospital.[134] One of the holdings was a messuage with shops abutting on Swinecroft, which by its description would fit very closely to the site of the hospital.[135]

The tradition enshrined in Josselin's history would in fact provide a satisfactory explanation for some elements in Henry Tangmere's disposition towards the college; and we may probably accept that he did indeed found a hospital and that it was connected to the college. He did so in a part of town in which he had wide proprietary interests, and which became a basis for his charitable undertakings. Another insight into the mind of this founder may be gained by consideration of the choice of the hospital's patrons. Sts Anthony and Eligius were not a very popular choice; the former may be St Anthony the desert Father (251–356), which would have been a conservative choice. Another possibility is the Franciscan friar Anthony of Padua (1195–1231) who preached against usury and avarice, and became the patron saint of the poor, the travellers and of pregnant women, but was not very popular in England.[136] St Eligius (588–660) was a Merovingian saint, royal goldsmith to Kings Chlotar II and Dagobert and the inspirer of many precious medieval religious artefacts in gold and enamel.[137] Eligius became the patron saint of the medieval *aurifaber* who was often also a moneylender. As bishop of Noyon he was also known for his great generosity in bestowing upon the poor the riches

---

133 'ad rogandum et celebrandum...ita quod quilibet capellanus dicti collegii...cotidie celebret pro animabus Henrici de Tangmere, Amphelise uxoris eius Iohannis et Ameline patris et matris dicti Henrici', CCCA. XXXI, 70, p. 13.

134 CCCA. XXXI, 70, p. 13. A licence to this effect was granted to John Barnwell, chaplain and hermit at St Anne's, for his maintenance and for the repair of the road between Cambridge and Trumpington, CUL. EDR. Register Fordham, fol. 191v.

135 CCCA. XXXI, 70, p. 13. See again [*The atlas of*] *historic towns* II, Cambridge maps 3 and 6.

136 *The Oxford dictionary of saints*, ed. D. H. Farmer (Oxford, 1978) and *A dictionary of saints*, ed. D. Attwater (Harmondsworth, 1965).

137 *Dictionnaire d'archéologie chrétienne et de liturgie* IV, ed. A. Vacant and E. Mangenot (Paris, 1921), cols. 2674–2687.

he had accumulated in royal service.[138] Henry Tangmere had a special involvement with each of these saints. In the book of his executors one finds many entries relating to collection of debts – Henry was a moneylender.[139] Anthony of the Desert was chosen as patron of a house which was to be a penance for a life of monetary, perhaps even usurious, activity. The bullion distributed to various people in his will might indicate involvement with the precious-metal trade, which could explain how St Eligius had found a place in Henry's mind.[140]

To what class of hospital does this house belong? It was clearly a house of lay foundation, without episcopal patronage or regular personnel. One may accept Josselin's version that it was originally under the patronage of Corpus Christi College since the college held most of the Tangmere estate.

The involvement of laymen and the municipal patronage that was spread over the hospital is part of a tendency of late medieval towns to supervise and control relief.[141] In the fourteenth and fifteenth centuries older charitable houses of religious foundation sometimes entered into some degree of municipal control.[142] The foundation of small hospitals by pious rich merchants, commending them into the

---

[138] By the thirteenth century he was reputed as a healer of bad legs and tumours, F. Barlow, 'The king's evil', *English historical review* 95 (1980), pp. 3–27; p. 11. Eligius was a popular patron of the charitable foundations of goldsmiths, see van der Made, *Le Grand Hôpital de Huy*, pp. 18–19.

[139] CCCA. XXXI, 70, pp. 3–4, 'ex mutuo' entries explain the nature of the payments.

[140] Another dedication to Sts Anthony and Eligius is to be found in a leper house in Hoddesdon founded *c.* 1390 in honour of St Clement which by 1470 had changed its title and issued a seal on which the two saints are shown, St Anthony with a book and a cross and a pig at his feet. This might support the attribution of the Cambridge hospital to the earlier saint, since the coupling of Anthony of the Desert and Eligius (here holding a hammer and pincers) seems to have existed in contemporary minds; see P. Nelson, 'Some British medieval seal-matrices', *Archaeological journal* 93 (1936), pp. 13–44, at p. 42 no. 91.

[141] In the Low Countries twelfth- and thirteenth-century hospitals often evolved under municipal tutelage, J. Godard, 'La maladrerie de St. Ladre et la condition des lépreux à Amiens au moyen-âge', *Bulletin de la société des antiquaires de la Picardie* 35 (1933–4), pp. 173–291; pp. 285, 290; in Liège the house of 'communs pauvres' was a lay twelfth-century foundation to which a chapel was added in the fourteenth century, R. Hankart, 'L'hôpital Saint-Michel dit des communs pauvres-en-île à Liège. Histoire des origines (XIIe–XVe siècles)', *Bulletin de l'institut archéologique liégeois* 90 (1978), pp. 157–95; pp. 161–3.

[142] See J. Rowe, 'The medieval hospitals of Bury St. Edmunds', *Medical history* 2 (1958), pp. 253–63, esp. p. 260 – St Saviour's hospital of monastic foundation, entered into municipal control in the fourteenth century; the city of London maintained two purveyors of leper houses, *Memorials of London*, pp. 510–11 (1389). Also Bonenfant, *Hôpitaux et bienfaisance publiques*, pp. 25, 33–4, 38, and R. Bolzinger, E. Gilbrin and F. Larrang, 'L'hôpital St. Nicholas de Metz avant la Révolution. Sa fondation laïque, ses singulières prérogatives financières', *Histoire des sciences médicales* 13 (1979), pp. 369–77.

hands of a secular or a mixed management, rather than to the hands of an order, is characteristic of fourteenth-century European towns and fifteenth-century English ones.[143] In some such houses lay fraternities were created for the provision of nursing care.[144] An indulgence of 1392 was awarded to the helpers of 'the house of lepers or hospital of saints Anthony and Eligius in Cambridge...and the brothers and sisters of that house' which may indicate that a number of layfolk tended to their care.[145] John Harreys, who was mayor of Cambridge in 1394–6 and 1404 and Member of Parliament in 1385–6, left in his will sums for the fabric of Great St Mary's church, but also 6s 8d for the 'lazar hous toward Trumpiton gate'[146] and the humbler John Smith of Cambridge left 3s 4d to the 'spetilhouses' in 1498.[147] The town was clearly in charge of the hospital at the beginning of the sixteenth century. In 1526 an agreement was drawn up between the mayor and bailiffs of Cambridge on the one hand and Robert and Margaret Brunn, on the other.[148] This arrangement leased the house of lepers at the south of the town, known as the 'spetylhouse', with gardens and all its appurtenances to the couple

---

[143] See for example William Brown's hospital, Stamford, P. A. Newton, 'William Brown's hospital at Stamford', *Antiquaries journal* 46 (1966), 283–6. Hospital of St John the Baptist, by testamentary foundation of a rich Alicantese merchant: R. Martinez de San Pedro, *Historia de los hospitales en Alicante* (Alicante, 1974), pp. 32–3. For France: P. Amargier, 'La situation hospitalière à Marseille', *Cahiers de Fanjeaux* 15 (1978), pp. 239–60; esp. p. 253. For an even earlier thirteenth-century foundation created by a layman and administered by the town officials well into the fifteenth century see B. Loriaud, 'Les pauvres malades et le personnel de l'aumônerie Auffredi à La Rochelle vers 1470', *Revue de la société d'archéologie et d'histoire de la Charente Maritime* 25 (1973–4), pp. 137–42. See also G. Maréchal, *De sociale en politieke gebundenheid van het Brugse hospitalwezen in de Middeleeuwen* (Heule, 1978).

[144] Such a brotherhood existed *c.* 1414 at St Giles, Cripplegate, London: *VCH. London* I, p. 585, and in Stratford, *The register of the gild of the Holy Cross*, p. vi and elsewhere: S. F. Roberts, 'Les consulats du Rouergue et l'assistance urbaine au XIIIe et au début du XIVe siècles', *Cahiers de Fanjeaux* 13 (1978), pp. 131–46, esp. p. 139. Also, G. C. Meersseman, *Ordo fraternitatis: confraterne e pietà dei laici nel medioevo* I (Rome, 1977), pp. 136–49.

[145] 'domus leprosorum sive hospitalis sanctorum Anthonij et Eligij in Cantebrigi'...et fratrum et sororum eiusdem domus' CUL. EDR. Register Fordham, fol. 179 – (21 October 1392).

[146] *Cambridge borough documents* I, p. 1.

[147] SJCA. D32. 234. He also left £3 6s 8d for the 'makyng of a crosse betwixt the spetylhous and trumppynton forthe '('spetyl house' is used only to describe St Anthony and Eligius' hospital).

[148] British Library. Add. Ms. 5842, pp. 237–8. Also in *Cambridge borough documents* I, pp. 55–6. See the example of a lay hospital, Roland Blacader's hospital, Glasgow, administered by a married couple, J. Durkan, 'Care of the poor: pre-Reformation hospitals', in *Essays on the Scottish Reformation 1513–1625*, ed. D. McRoberts (Glasgow, 1962), pp. 116–28; p. 122. On the provisions in Lyons see Gutton, *La société et les pauvres*, p. 222.

for life. They were to manage the house, receive leprous men and women and collect alms for their maintenance.

An inventory was attached to the indenture in which the Brunns were shown to be responsible for the state of the goods under the pain of 10 marks. This is a clear example of town control and of lay management of a small urban charitable institution. The inventory is extremely interesting; it contains very few items of daily use, and as cooking utensils and beddings it counted only 'a grette brass pot', 'a pewter platter', 'a paynted coffer', 'oon flexen shete', 'an old grene coverlytt', 'a grene coverlett'.[149] These would not have sufficed for the normal maintenance of a shelter. It appears that either only the very costly items were entered, or that the Brunns were to supply cushions, blankets, sheets, plates from the income that they would draw on the basis of the current indenture.[150] The inventory is, however, very full in listing religious vessels, books and ornaments. Four altar-cloths, five alabaster images, cruets, a holy water container, two sprinklers for holy water, a missal, a chalice, two pairs of vestments, four images, an altar-frontal and five bells.

This impressive list brings us to the question of religious life in such a community. In his will of 1500 William Wood of Cambridge bequeathed 'to the chapell of Seynt Antony at the Spittill 8d'.[151] Even in the hand of secular administration relief was never divorced from its spiritual setting. The lay founders expected prayers in return for their bounty, the inmates needed a place for worship and lepers required a separate chapel and burial grounds. The ornaments clearly indicate that a chapel existed and that there was perhaps more than one altar. The hospital fell within the boundaries of St Benet's parish, whose vicar provided spiritual services to the hermitage of St Anne nearby;[152] he or a parish chaplain may have performed the same service for the

---

149 Hospital inventories often contain kitchen utensils of all kinds and bedding. See as an example H. Neveux, 'Un établissement d'assistance en milieu rural au XIVe siècle. L'hôtel-dieu de Villers-Bocage', *Annales de Normandie* 27 (1977), pp. 3–17; pp. 12–16. In some leper hospitals inmates provided their own sheets, blankets and utensils, Mesmim, 'The leper hospital of St. Gilles de Pont-Audemer' I, p. 49. When thieves broke into the hospital of St Mary Magdalene, King's Lynn, in 1453 they took away the most valuable possessions, which were vestments and liturgical objects, as contained in an inventory of the stolen goods, *The making of King's Lynn*, pp. 429–30.

150 Wardens often supplied the utensils used by members of leper houses, as ordered by the statutes of the Enköping hospital (1367 × 88), Richards, *The medieval leper*, c.4, p. 138.

151 SJCA. D23. 235.

152 CUL. EDR. Register Gray, fols. 33v–34r – a licence for celebrating offices in the hermitage granted on 18 July 1458.

hospital.[153] An entry in the Cambridge Treasurers' accounts for 1561–2 mentions the payment of 1d rent by the churchwardens of St Benet's for a piece of ground at Spittlehouse end, which had been made into a churchyard.[154] This may have been a burial ground provided by the parish church for the hospital within its boundaries.

Some of the items in the inventory were said to have been gifts to the hospital. Such was 'oon flexen shete of the gift of Maister Keali' or 'a fronte on an auter, steyned with an ymage of our Lady, Saynt Anthony and Seynt Loye of the gift of John Grene', 'an image of our Ladye of Timber new paynted'[155]. The hospital was one of those places in late medieval Cambridge to which gifts could be given in exchange for prayers. Wherever there were poor recipients of charitable relief, potential spiritual gain was to be had. In the hospital of Sts Anthony and Eligius no order established itself, but it housed poor lepers, vagrants, mentally deranged 'wild' men and women, who would not be admitted to institutions such as HSJC at the opposite end of town. But the house was enmeshed in the net of spiritual activities of burgesses and in the provision of shelter and asylum to those members whose problems affected the town as a whole, and whose alleviation could be a source of social display and spiritual benefit.[156]

---

[153] In the lay hospital at La Rochelle 10 priests and an organist were employed during the fifteenth century for the provision of spiritual services in this non-ecclesiastical house, Loriaud, 'Les pauvres malades', pp. 141–2.

[154] *Cambridge borough documents* I, p. 90.

[155] *Ibid.*, p. 56.

[156] After the Reformation its religious character, in its old form, would have disappeared. In 1558 and in 1591 the hospital was granted testamentary bequests of money for distribution to its poor. They were also included among the Cambridge poor and received 8d and 12d respectively, *Annals of Cambridge* II, pp. 143, 510. The hospital remained the main asylum for the sick and poor in Cambridge. It recurs in the accounts of the churchwardens of Great St Mary's in 1597 and in 1620, *Churchwardens' accounts of Great St. Mary's, Cambridge, 1504–1635*, ed. J. E. Foster (Cambridge, 1905), pp. 265, 362. One finds late entries in the town's accounts, relating to the hospital-almshouse.

In 1584:
Item to Mr Foxton for fraise for ij gownes given at ye
    spittle house – 13s 10d
Item to Mr Maior for a paire of sheets for ye Madd
    woman in ye spitle house – 4s
In 1612:
Item laid out in expense for the spittle-houses – £7 11s
In 1657–8:
Item to John Love for a baskitt and lattice for the Spitlehouse
    – 2s 4d

Annals of Cambridge II, p. 401; III, pp. 53, 469, In 1686 bishop Turner of Ely reported that the house was a poor one, an unendowed almshouse with a master at its head, who begged for his sustenance and for that of the inmates.

The almshouses in late medieval Cambridge

The second half of the fifteenth century saw the creation of four almshouses by Cambridge townsfolk, houses which reflect a new departure in the provision of shelter and the correction of the poor. Urban as well as rural communities attempted to meet the growing needs of the transient poor on the roads of migration, as well as local indigence, with new solutions. The parish emerges as the framework which was deemed to be most useful and effective for the execution of works of charity. In towns this represented a neighbourhood and in the countryside, the whole village community. In 1450 the leading men of Romford, Essex, founded an almshouse with pronounced disciplinary objectives; its inmates were to be kept within doors between 9 p.m. and 6 a.m.[157] Most almshouses provided for the local known poor; and in the university town of Cambridge, colleges came to play a prominent role as perpetual supervisors of almshouses, responsibilities usually entrusted to town corporations or gilds.

In 1463, Reginald Ely, a citizen of Cambridge, left in his will lands in Barton and Comberton to be used for the maintenance of three poor people, preferably from the parish of St Clement. Gonville Hall was cited as executor and by 1475 had created the almshouse, in what is now Trinity Lane. Reginald Ely was a successful mason, connected with the building of King's College, and was sufficiently involved in university life to appreciate the executory services of a college, and to be able to secure them.[158]

Another townsman, Andrew Dockett, the queen's agent and first president of Queens' College, ordered the foundation of a similar house in his will of 1484. He requested the maintenance of exequies with distributions and the transformation of an existing alsmhouse for three poor young women into a house for poor people praying for his soul.[159]

In 1473, Margaret Fawkner, the widow of Roger Fawkner, founded a house for poor men and women in the parish of St Mary. She enfeoffed Henry Clyff, a chaplain, who subsequently enfeoffed John

157 See McIntosh, *Autonomy and community*, p. 239. The religious element is expressed in the will of the founder of the Reede hospital at Havering, Essex in 1481; the inmates were to be five local poor 'of good governance and fallen into poverty', p. 240.

158 J. Venn *et al.* (eds.), *Biographical history of Gonville and Caius College* III (Cambridge, 1901), pp. 261–2. The site was finally sold to Trinity College.

159 The will was proved in 1485 and is printed in W. G. Searle, [*The history of the*] *Queens' college*, [*Cambridge 1446–1662*] (Cambridge, 1867–71), pp. 56–8. The site was bought from Corpus Christi College in 1461 and was located in what is today Silver Street (then Smallbridges).

Hogkyns, a Fellow of King's College, with the endowed tenements.[160] In 1504, John Hogkyns granted the tenements and the charitable obligation to the College who managed it until the site was taken over by the University, ultimately to form part of the grass quadrangle in front of the Old Schools.[161]

In 1479 some land near St Mary's church which belonged to the town corporation was given to Thomas Jakenett and Thomas Ebbon, citizens of Cambridge, for the creation of an almshouse for four poor men and women.[162] The inmates were to be chosen by the churchwardens of St Mary's parish and by some trustee-feoffees.[163] These almshouses were established to the south of the church and were maintained and repaired by its churchwardens and would probably have comprised separate cells surrounding a courtyard, in an architectural form which came to dominate fifteenth-century hospitals and almshouses.[164] Almsfolk appear occasionally in the sixteenth- and seventeenth-century accounts and they sometimes took part in the cleaning of the church.[165] The founder's obit was observed yearly by the parish until 1542.[166]

Little more can be said about these humble foundations. We can, however, appreciate the motives which urged on their founders: the quest for intercession and the treatment of an urban problem in a controlled and effective manner. The parish emerges as a highly favoured framework for devotional and charitable organisation by

[160] A copy of the 1473 transfer to John Hogkyns exists in King's College muniments, 136/1. Thanks are due to Mr. A. Owen for his help in making the documents available to me.

[161] King's College muniments, 136/2. For the map of the site see R. Willis and J. W. Clark, *An architectural history of the University of Cambridge and the colleges of Cambridge and Eton* II (Cambridge, 1886), p. 240.

[162] Similar almshouses were founded by the brothers Walter and John Daniel, prominent burgesses of Norwich in the first half of the fifteenth century, N. P. Tanner, *The church in late medieval Norwich 1370–1532* (Toronto, 1984), p. 133.

[163] Cambridge corporation archives, deeds 30/4(1). The almshouse was mentioned in 1490 in a charter of St Radegund's Priory: 'inter...et domum Elimosinarium nuper Thome Jakenet ex parte occidentale', *The priory of St Radegund*, ed. A. Gray, Cambridge, 1898, p. 118.

[164] *Churchwardens' accounts of Great St Mary's*, 1518, p. 26; 1545, p. 107. A solar at the top of the almshouse provided 8s per annum and was leased to various bailiffs and auditors of the parish, *ibid.*, pp. 25, 55, 58, 62, 69 (and others). For examples of this 'small cell' model in England see the plans of Ewelme hospital and the fifteenth-century buildings of St Cross, Winchester, Godfrey, *The English almshouse*, figs. 28–9, pp. 44, 46.

[165] *Churchwardens' accounts of Great St. Mary's*, 1597, p. 265; 1608–9, p.308; 1632–3, p. 455.

[166] Expenses for Thomas Jakenett's obit were recorded by the churchwardens until 1547. See for example the following entries: *ibid.*, 1513, p. 21; 1518, pp. 35–6; 1522, p. 46, 1523, pp. 51, 53. Thomas Jakenett's obit was also observed by the town throughout the 1490s and 1500s, see below p. 263. The almshouse is mentioned in the Treasurers' account rolls of 1561–2 when the churchwardens were paying rent for the site, *Cambridge borough documents* I, p. 85.

believers in the fifteenth century. This tendency to favour the parish will be further examined below in connection with funerary distributions.

The Hospital of St John the Baptist, Ely

The Hospitals of St John the Baptist and of St Mary Magdalene at Ely were united in 1225 to form a house similar in many ways to HSJC. A hospital in Ely is mentioned as early as 1162 in the returns of the sheriff of Cambridgeshire to the Exchequer[167] and in 1163–4 an entry mentions the bishop's hospice which may have pre-dated the hospital, a shelter for pilgrims to the shrine of St Etheldreda.[168] From 1169–70 on the hospital was mentioned as the recipient of greater sums paid from the proceeds of the episcopal estates under the heading *de elemosinis constitutis* ('of customary alms').[169] In 1225 the tithes of the parish of Littleport were appropriated to the hospital of St Mary Magdalene in Ely.[170] However, another hospital, dedicated to St John the Baptist, coexisted. It was the recipient of an early thirteenth-century grant by John of Beverand comprising five acres and one rood of arable together with half an acre of meadow in the fields of Ely: 'To God and the hospital of the Blessed John the Baptist outside the town of Ely for the maintenance of a chaplain there for living and dead benefactors of the said hospital'.[171] Thus, at least from the mid-twelfth century, there was a hospital in Ely and in the next century there were two houses; the dedication of one to Mary Magdalene suggests that it was a leper hospital.[172] As we have seen in the case of Stourbridge

[167] *Pipe Roll 8 Henry II*, p. 48 (1161/2): 'Et fratribus hospitalis 10s'.
[168] *Pipe Roll 10 Henry II*, p. 16 (1163/4): 'Et Episcopo Eliensi 5s. in quitantia hospicii sui'. The churches of Melbourn and Swaffham were appropriated to the Prior and Convent of Ely in 1225 to allow the provision of hospitality and of poor relief in connection, no doubt, with the pilgrimage which the Cathedral and its relics attracted. A confirmation of this charter appears in CUL. EDR. Register Arundel, fol. 63v: 'pro sustentacione hospitum et pauperum domus'.
[169] *Pipe Roll 16 Henry II*, p. 96 (1169–70): 'hospitali de Ely £8.8s. per maneria Episcopatus et eidem 18s 5d hoc anno in decima anguillarum de Well''; also in *Pipe Roll 17 Henry II*, p. 115 (1170–1) and *Pipe Roll 18 Henry II*, p. 116 (1171–2).
[170] This is attested at a later date in a certificate of bishop Gray concerning the rights of the hospital in the parish, CUL. EDR. Register Gray, fol. 115. On appropriation of parishes to hospitals see below pp. 192–3.
[171] 'deo et hospitali beati Iohannis Baptiste extra villam de Ely ad sustentamentum capellani ibidem pro vivis et defunctis benefactoribus prefati hospitalis', Clare College muniments. The charter is written in an early thirteenth-century hand, and is now without its seal.
[172] For occurrence of this dedication at this period see above pp. 113–14.

leper house, royal patronage of leper hospitals was widespread in the twelfth century, and a common way of endowing them was to allocate part of the farm of a county to the use of such houses. Yet, by the mid-thirteenth century it was seen to be necessary to unite the houses in Ely. It may be that by the mid-thirteenth century the need for a separate leper house had declined.[173] Bishop Northwold provided instructions for the conduct of the united community of Ely.[174] The early rule was incorporated in the notification of union by the bishop:

We will that it comes to your notice…concerning the state of the two hospitals in the town of Ely, namely the hospital of St John and the hospital of St Mary Magdalene, because we know one of them to be in excess, and thus have ordained that the same hospital of St John will be united to the same hospital of St Mary Magdalene and enlarge it with all its possessions and rights.[175]

The thirteenth-century rule is similar in tone to that granted by Bishop Northwold to HSJC.[176] Thirteen brethren were to live a communal life, taking meals together and sleeping in one dormitory. A large part of the rule concerns the establishment of a disciplinary link between the hospital and the sacrist of Ely. Institutional links and dependencies between monasteries and hospitals were common and often existed in cases when the charitable house originated from a monastic almonry or infirmary.[177] The master heard confessions and corrected the members' behaviour. Candidates for admission were presented by the master and the community and were inducted by the sacrist after due inquiry.[178] Unlike his colleague in HSJC the master at Ely had little

---

[173] It is around this time that the leper hospital at Stourbridge near Cambridge changed its function to that of a free chantry, above pp. 116–18.

[174] This rule was copied into the register of Bishop Fordham who in 1403 confirmed it together with a later rule, CUL. EDR. Register Fordham, fols. 218–219.

[175] 'Ad noticiam vestram volumus pervenire…super statu duorum hospitalium existencium in villa de Ely scilicet sancti Iohannis et sancte Marie Magdalene quia alterum ipsorum superhabundere cognovimus, taliter ordinasse quod dictum hospitale sancti Iohannis predicto hospitali sancte Marie Magdalene uniatur et cum omnibus suis pertinenciis et iuribus eidem acrescat', CUL. EDR. Register Fordham, fol. 219. In the mid-fourteenth century the hospital was still titled '..hospitalis sancti Iohannis Baptiste et sancte Marie de Ely…', CUL. EDR. Register Lisle, fol. 36r. (1350) and recurs in the beginning of the fifteenth century, CUL. EDR. Register Fordham, fol. 109v (1421).

[176] SJCA.D4.1, see below appendix 1, pp. 300–1.

[177] See the hospitals of Bury St Edmunds, Gottfried, *Bury St. Edmunds*, pp. 192–213, as well as Peterborough abbey's links with St Thomas's and St Leonard's hospitals, *The book of William Morton almoner of Peterborough monastery 1448–1467*, ed. W. T. Mellows and P. I. King with intr. by C. N. L. Brooke (Oxford, 1954), p. xxx.

[178] CUL. EDR. Register Montacute, fol. 19v mentions an inquiry led by the sacrist. For other examples of induction of a presented candidate see Register Lisle, fol. 23v and

authority over the house's property, since conveyance and acquisition of property rested in the hands of the sacrist.

As in HSJC the community consisted of both lay brethren and chaplains, but little is known of the lay member's life; they must have been charged with manual chores, treatment of the sick and administration. Admissions of clerics to the hospital are attested in the episcopal registers of the fourteenth and fifteenth centuries, but only in one case is the admission of lay brethren mentioned.[179] The surviving bishops' registers begin with Simon Montacute (1337–45), with some *lacunae* in the fourteenth century, and continue more fully from Bishop Fordham's episcopate (1388–1425). By looking at a limited number of years at a time, we may study the admission rate of brethren to the house. Between 1340 and 1352, for example, 12 new brothers were admitted. This rate is of almost one brother a year, but it covers the years of high mortality and high admission rates during and after the plague; between July 1349 and spring 1350 five new brethren and two lay brethren were admitted.[180] Between the years 1377 and 1394, only seven new members were admitted.[181] A rare glance at the number of brethren is provided by the list for the Clerical Poll Tax of 1379 in which the hospital was recorded as having a master and five brethren.[182] In this list, four of the five brethren had been members of the house for over 25 years and the master had received first orders 39 years earlier![183] Of the 12 brethren admitted between 1340 and 1352, seven were priests, two clerics and three cases are unknown. In the late fourteenth century the course of advancement in major orders was quicker; two cases in which brethren entered as acolytes and became priests within a year are recorded.[184] Henry of Wisbech entered as acolyte and became a deacon within four months and John Ingolf entered in January 1394 as a subdeacon and became a priest before the end of

---

fol. 36r and fol. 40v (1351): 'Et recepta obediencia canonica ab eo dominus episcopus scripsit sacriste ecclesie cathedralis Eliensis et ipsum Iohanem...induceret'.

[179] In 1350 John Cok and John of Wisbech were admitted. CUL. EDR. Register Lisle, fol. 36r.

[180] CUL. EDR. Register Lisle, fols. 23v, 36r.

[181] CUL. EDR. Register Arundel. fols. 21v, 28r, 44r, Register Fordham, fols. 4r, 10v, 180r, 181r.

[182] PRO. E179. 23/1 (Clerical subsidy).

[183] CUL. EDR. Register Montacute, fol. 10v – 25 November 1340 date of manumission of John Cardinal and the bestowal of first tonsure; Register Fordham fol. 176 – 14 February 1391 date of admission of the next master due to John Cardinal's resignation.

[184] CUL. EDR. Register Fordham, fols. 180r, 234v – Robert Stretham 21 December 1392–20 September 1393; fols. 194r, 242v – John Patrik 11 March 1402–31 March 1403. For below, Register Arundel, fol. 121, Register Fordham, fols. 121, 235.

the year. It appears that most clerical brethren were already in major orders at the time of their admission, and that those who were not, entered them within a short while of their admission, being of suitable age, estate and character. The hospital also granted titles for ordinands as so many other small religious houses did in the late Middle Ages.[185] In the fifteenth century dozens of clerics were ordained through a connection with the hospital; these connections were extremely tenuous and in no case ended in the admission of a titulary to the hospital.[186]

The masters of the Hospital of St John, Ely, were presented by the brethren of the house and collated by the bishop. They stood at the head of the community and led its liturgical life, but enjoyed limited administrative and executive power. Bishop Orford's rule of 1303 prohibited any special delicacies to be served to the master; he was expected to dine with the brethren but had a separate chamber.[187] In an *inspeximus* by Bishop Hothum of 1333 some ordinances for the election of master were laid down. These passed the right to elect a master to the bishop in cases when no suitable man could be found within the hospital.[188] Throughout the fourteenth century there seems to have been a steady succession of masters, most of whom were originally brethren of the hospital. One master's career can be followed for several years: John Cardinal was admitted to the hospital in 1350,[189] by 1379 he had become master,[190] and in 1391 retired to a corrodarian's existence in the house. He was provided with daily rations of food and drink, clothes, lighting materials and with rooms for himself and his servant.[191]

The priestly element in the life of the brethren of the Ely hospital serves to illustrate the liturgical aspect of the medieval hospital. Like most thirteenth-century hospitals the house had a chapel which here was invested in the sacrist.[192] Its relations with the parish were regulated by episcopal ordinances which prohibited the receipt of parishioners'

---

[185] Cf. R. K. Rose, 'Priests and patrons in the fourteenth century diocese of Carlisle', *Studies in Church history* 16 (1979), pp. 207–18; p. 211. See below p. 164.

[186] There were 24 ordinands with the title of hospital of St John, Ely ordained in the years 1410–1421, 1445, 1462 & 1492–1500.

[187] Confirmed by Bishop Fordham in 1408 and copied on that occasion in CUL. EDR. Register Fordham, fols. 218–219. In the hospital of St Giles, Norwich, the master and brethren-chaplain were to sleep in a common chamber, NRO. Case 24/b/1.

[188] *Calendar of patent rolls 1330–1334*, p. 411. Bishop Hothum granted similar ordinances to HSJC and ordered that when a suitable candidate for the mastership could not be found, a brother from the hospital of St John, Ely, might be presented, below p. 169.

[189] CUL. EDR. Register Lisle, fol. 36r.

[190] PRO. E179. 23/1 (Clerical subsidy).

[191] CUL. EDR. Register Fordham, fol. 177.

[192] CUL. EDR. Register Fordham, fol. 219.

offerings on great feasts, limited its burial rights to brethren and inmates, and forbade the receipt of testamentary bequests from the parishioners.[193] However, the house's function as a religious centre could not be obscured and in the early thirteenth century grants of land were made to support a chaplain celebrating for the welfare of the founder's soul. Bishop Orford (1302–10) ordered daily commemorations of the house's benefactors.[194] In an agreement of 1323 Mary of Bassingbourn laid down the terms for anniversary celebrations;[195] she granted a messuage in Ely (near one of the hospital's own tenements) in return for an annual distribution for her soul and for those of her two late husbands. Thus, the hospital doled out farthing loaves to 144 poor people on her anniversary.

Little is known of the Hospital of St Mary Magdalene and St John the Baptist since the medieval charters which had been transferred to Clare College after the Dissolution perished in the fire in the College Treasury in 1571.[196] The hospital enjoyed an annual income allocated by the Crown to one of the original hospitals, most probably to St Mary Magdalene, as royal patronage of leper houses was very common. These payments (£8 8s in the twelfth century) were given from the income of the episcopal manors of Ely, held in chief from the king. That they were paid well into the fourteenth century is attested by two royal letters ordering the keepers of the temporalities of the See to fulfil the obligation.[197] Further information on the extent of donations can be gleaned from the Mortmain licences acquired by the hospital throughout the fourteenth century.[198] It received a general licence in 1319 for grants up to an income of 10 marks per annum and another in 1385 for up to £10,[199] as well as three particular licences in 1327, 1358 and 1392 allowing the alienation of incomes not exceeding the sum of £5 2s 8½d per annum.[200] Unlike HSJC, the hospital was not cautious in its acquisitions under Mortmain, and in 1376 lands were seized by the escheator since the hospital had exceeded the limit.[201] As

---

[193] *Ibid.* As we have seen above the settlement of parochial rights was an important stage in the establishment of the hospital, see above pp. 104–6.

[194] CUL. EDR. Register Fordham, fol. 218.

[195] Clare College muniments.

[196] Willis and Clark, *An architectural history* I, p. 79.

[197] *Calendar of close rolls 1337–1339*, p. 75 (1337) and *Calendar of close rolls 1354–1360*, p. 359 (1357), by which time the payment was £11 14s 1d.

[198] See the acquisitions of HSJC under Mortmain, below pp. 212–17.

[199] *Calendar of patent rolls 1317–1321*, p. 319; *Calendar of patent rolls 1381–1385*, pp. 298–9.

[200] *Calendar of patent rolls 1327–1330*, p. 144; *Calendar of patent rolls 1358–1361*, p. 15; *Calendar of patent rolls 1391–1394*, p. 144.

[201] *Calendar of patent rolls 1374–1377*, p. 277.

the sacrist of Ely managed the house's endowment this was a failing on the part of the priory.[202]

Grants to the hospital were made mainly in Ely (messuages in the town, arable and marsh land) and Downham with some in Littleport, Elm and Dodyngton. Another source of income were the tithes of the parish of Littleport, a parish which had been appropriated to the Hospital of St Mary Magdalene by the bishop of Ely, which passed to the united hospital in 1225. The Valuation of Norwich of 1254 assessed the living at 15 marks, as did the archdeacon of Ely in his visitation *c.* 1278 who also reported the existence of a vicarage.[203] Tithe collection was often a source of litigation between the incumbents and parishioners as well as between the incumbents and communal rectors such as hospitals.[204] The Hospital of St John, Ely and the vicars of Littleport were locked in legal cases throughout the fourteenth and fifteenth centuries.[205] In 1384 an agreement was drawn up,[206] and in 1464 a full history of the appropriation and the hospital's rights was entered into Bishop Gray's register.[207]

In 1339 Bishop Montacute exempted the house from the payment of procurations[208] and the Clerical Poll Tax of 1379 assessed the hospital's annual income as being under £20.[209] This is quite a small income for a house of five chaplains and some lay brethren, a house similar in size to HSJC. In 1405 it must have suffered considerable loss by a fire which destroyed some of the properties in Littleport. The diminution of revenues which followed moved Bishop Fordham to grant an indulgence to benefactors of the hospital.[210] By the mid-fifteenth century the hospital's situation was seen to be so grave as to

---

[202] Indeed, the Priory of Ely incurred large fines for Mortmain infringements on its own estates, S. Raban, *Mortmain legislation and the English church, 1279–1500* (Cambridge, 1982), p. 95.

[203] *The valuation of Norwich*, ed. W. E. Lunt (Oxford, 1926), p. 216. *Vetus liber archidiaconi Eliensis*, ed. C. L. Feltoe and E. H. Minns (Cambridge, 1917), p. 140.

[204] Parishioners were occasionally summoned to court for tithe evasions, CUL. EDR. Consistory court Arundel, fol. 132v (1379).

[205] An agreement of 1301 concerning the division of hay tithes of *Presthous Fen* was still disputed when it was entered into the Bishop Goodrich's register in 1540, CUL. EDR. Register Goodrich, fol. 133r.

[206] CUL. EDR. Register Arundel, fol. 50 (1384).

[207] CUL. EDR. Register Gray, fol. 116r. This must be connected with the reopening of the case.

[208] HSJC, the academic colleges at Cambridge and some monasteries in the diocese were likewise exempted, CUL. EDR. Register Montacute, fol. 48.

[209] PRO. E179. 23/1 (Clerical subsidy).

[210] CUL. EDR. Register Fordham, fol. 200r. – 19 May 1405, he also left the hospital £5 in his will in 1425: *The register of Henry Chichele* II, p. 327.

justify the removal of management of its affairs from the hands of the master and brethren to those of an external administrator.[211] This was a decisive step, though the bishop did not mention the involvement of the priory and its sacrist in the hospital's management.

The effect of the hospital's dependence on the bishop is manifested in various ways.[212] Admission and presentation were closely supervised by the bishop and sacrist, while the latter managed the hospital's financial affairs. The bishop must have regarded the house as part of his household in some ways: corrodarians in the hospital of St John, Ely, were related to him.[213] In 1295 Bishop William of Louth granted a corrody to Maud, the widow of William Tavell, who was to live in the house and receive sustenance and pittances as one of the brethren.[214] Thus, the bishop of Ely, as a very close and powerful patron, exerted his rights frequently and extensively.

Some small houses of relief existed in the rural surroundings of Cambridge, houses which provided for vagrant poor who were not cared for by relatives, or for lepers who were separated from society. Very few documentary or architectural remains have survived; but this form of charitable organisation was as widespread as it was transient.

Stow hospital or chapel

We read of the foundation of a charitable house in the section of the Hundred Rolls referring to 'Stowe'. Walter, vicar of Stow, had once acquired $7\frac{1}{2}$ acres 1 rood of land, part of a sergeantry in Stow held by one Aubrey. Two acres of this land were dedicated to the building

---

[211] 'Cum domus sive hospitale sancti Iohannis Baptiste et sancte Marie Magdalene per regulares et religiosas personas regi et gubernari solitur per negligenciam, incuriam ac malam administracionem magistrorum eiusdem ad maximam pervenerit inopiam, ruinam et miseriam...sagacitatem tuam et probitatem considerantes per quas speramus et confidimus huiusmodi inopiam ruinam ac miseriam domus sive hospitalis predicti posse relevari dictam domum sive hospitale tibi conferimus ac te magistrum et administratorem tam in spiritualibus quam in temporalibus eiusdem tibi in domino committentes...', CUL. EDR. Register Bourchier, fol. 40r, in letter to bishop of Dunkeld, who was entrusted with the mastership. For an example of the appointment of a new master by the hospital's patron at a time of financial difficulties see the royal nomination of a new custodian in the hospital of St John the Baptist, Oxford, *Calendar of patent rolls 1292–1301*, p. 168.

[212] M. E. Aston, *Thomas Arundel: a study of church life in the reign of Richard II* (Oxford, 1967), p. 86, n. 1.

[213] For examples of the use of hospitals by their episcopal and monastic patrons see R. B. Dobson, *Durham priory 1400–1450* (Cambridge, 1973), pp. 60, 168.

[214] Clare College Muniments.

of an alsmhouse.[215] We are also told that he had instituted an order of young women who wore russet garments,[216] in this house which was titled 'the hospital of St Mary of Stow' and its members 'the sisters of the chapel of Stow'.[217] The sisters held one messuage and 24 acres 3 roods of arable.[218] The earliest dated mention of the house was in the Book of Fees where in 1250 the sergeantry of Aubrey of Stow was recorded and its tenants listed.[219] The latest mention is in 1338, when royal letters patent exempted it from the subsidy granted to the king from ecclesiastical holdings.[220]

The house at Stow must have been a small hospital providing shelter and relief to the extent that its tiny endowment allowed. The young women in it lived as a religious community with a habit and a chapel of their own. A master is mentioned in 1274 when action was taken against one of the sisters' tenants.[221] The vicar of Stow may have initiated the house as part of his pastoral duty to supply hospitality to the poor as is suggested by his connection with it at the time of the foundation.[222] A semi-regular group of women lived in it and ministered to the poor – such undertaking of charitable devotion by widows or young unmarried women being a phenomenon well known in the thirteenth century.[223]

The house existed for at least 100 years. Perhaps the Black Death swept away the small community, which lived in constant contact with sick people, and was thus susceptible to infection. Had they survived it, the decline in the value of land later in the fourteenth century would have rendered their endowment insufficient for the maintenance of hospitality. Little is known about the house, but there are many

---

[215] 'Et idem Walterus fundavit super predictas ij acras quandam domum elemos' ad hospitandum pauperes in honore Beate Marie Virginis', *Rotuli hundredorum* II, p. 538a.

[216] *Ibid.*: 'et constituit ibidem unum ordinem puellarum que vestuntur de russet'. The sisters and brethren serving in the Holy Cross hospital, Stratford, also wore a russet habit, *The register of the gild of the Holy Cross*, p. vi.

[217] 'Sorores capelle de Stowe', *Rotuli hundredorum* I, p. 54a and II, pp. 536b, 537a.

[218] Ten acres held in free alms from Aylmar of Stowe, a messuage and 14 acres of John Caxton, 3 roods of Martin Le Freman.

[219] *Liber feodorum. The Book of Fees commonly called Testa de Nevill*, part II (London, 1923), pp. 1181, 1233.

[220] *Calendar of patent rolls 1338–1340*, p. 19 (16 February 1338).

[221] *Rotuli hundredorum* II, p. 536b and *VCH. Cambridgeshire* II, p. 310. Stephen son of Baldwin held land of John of Caxton, part of which was held by the sisters from the latter.

[222] On the subject of parish hospitality see below pp. 237–45.

[223] E. W. McDonnell, *Beguines and beghards in medieval culture* (New Brunswick, N.J., 1954), *passim*, esp. p. 82. For examples of communities of lay women in Norwich in the fourteenth century see Tanner, *The church in late medieval Norwich*, pp. 64–6.

examples of similar small houses in the countryside of medieval England.[224]

The almshouse at Fordham Priory

The Gilbertine priory at Fordham was founded before 1227 by Henry, dean of Fordham, and was endowed by Hugh Malebisse, lord of the fee of Fordham and Wykes. In 1279 it was reported as holding a watermill and fourteen acres of arable, some lands given in alms by later benefactors, besides its basic endowment of a messuage which included 125 acres and the advowson of Burwell church. In addition, there were 60 acres of arable and 5 acres of meadow given by the family of Walter, son of Robert, for the following use: 'of which the prior of Fordham holds of the same Walter a messuage and 60 of those acres...and 5 acres of meadow from the gift of the same Walter's ancestors for the perpetual maintenance of 13 poor in food and clothing in Fordham hospital'.[225]

The priory must have had a section or almonry in which relief was provided, which would explain the use of the term *hospitale* in connection with it. As a religious house in a rural setting the priory was considered suitable for the fulfilment of a charitable role.[226] The canons were expected to feed some poor and to distribute clothes, but this did not mean the creation of a permanent dependent group of poor within the community. They were custodians of a charitable benefaction, and like many small rural religious houses of the period intimately combined their spiritual routines with the provision of intercessory services entailing some limited charitable acts.

Anglesey Hospital

Some hospitals founded in the late twelfth century developed subsequently into full religious houses which attracted more patronage.[227] An urban house of charity transformed into a religious house might retain some of its charitable duties since a corporation representing

---

[224] Cf. Owen, *Church and society*, p. 55–6.

[225] 'unde Prior de Fordham tenet de eodem Waltero j. mesuagium et lx. acras terre de predictis...cum v. acris prati ex dono antecessorum dicti Walteri xiij pauperum in perpetuum sustinendorum victum et vestitum in hospit' de Fordham', *Rotuli Hundredorum* II, p. 502a.

[226] This is a common occurrence in the very early thirteenth century. Some twelve hospitals became priories, ten of which changed before 1230; Knowles and Hadcock, *Medieval religious houses*, for this data.

[227] Owen, *Church and society*, pp. 56–7.

communal interests could demand the implementation of the original obligations. But when a house was in private patronage and in a rural setting it may have easily been transformed from a house providing poor relief to a community of voluntary *pauperes Christi*.

The rural hospital at Anglesey underwent such a transformation. Founded some time in the second half of the twelfth century,[228] the hospital attracted donations in which it is styled 'the hospital of St Mary of Anglesey' and its property was meant to be 'in the use of the poor sick'.[229] In these documents the house is addressed as 'ecclesie et fratribus de Anglesey' which may already have been the priory combined with the brothers of the hospital.[230] The head of the community was addressed as *rector* and received grants and farmed out the hospital's land much as did HSJC's masters.[231] An early thirteenth-century grant to the 'canons and brethren' suggests that the hospital was in an intermediate stage of this change.[232] By 1220 Anglesey priory had become an important Augustinian priory retaining no special charitable obligations.

A similar transformation happened at Creake priory and at Hempton priory in Norfolk in 1200 and 1206 respectively.[233] The Hospital of St Mary of Anglesey was another short lived charitable house which did not disappear due to the ravages of time, but due to its transformation into a form of religious community more attractive to contemporary benefactors.

Wisbech Hospital

Sometime in the first half of the thirteenth century the commonalty of Wisbech set aside five cottages and five acres of arable for the support of a house for the poor.[234] There is no further mention of the house

[228] 'Hospitale de Angleshei' is mentioned in a twelfth century list of religious houses owing dues to the papacy, which was copied in a letter of pope Martin IV in 1281, *Calendar of papal letters* I, p. 476.

[229] PRO. Ancient deeds E326 3794, E40 14464, 14469. It also purchased lands in Fulbourn paying a *gersumma* to the vendor, PRO. Ancient deeds. E326 3052, 3652.

[230] And in PRO. Ancient deeds E326 3733, 3791, 3796.

[231] PRO. Ancient deeds E40 7671, see below pp. 169–71.

[232] J. C. Dickinson, *The origins of the Austin canons and their introduction into England* (London, 1950), p. 147, though these may be the priory's lay brethren.

[233] Knowles and Hadcock, *Medieval religious houses*, pp. 295, 276.

[234] As attested in the entry of the Escheator's Roll of 1352: 'in dicta villa de Wysbech...hospitale in eadem villa quod quid hospitale dudum per comunitatem eiusdem ville fundatus fuit et ordinatus pro sustentaione infirmorum', PRO. E136. 8/24. The first half of the thirteenth century is a reasonable date since the foundation of small hospitals in towns became very popular in these years of widespread enfranchisement

until 1343 when it was styled 'hospitale sancti Iohannis Baptiste' in a letter of collation to the wardenship.[235] In the years 1335–53 there were eight collations to the office; three due to resignation, one following an exchange and three (two in the fatal year 1349–50) seem to have followed the incumbent's death. Though the hospital was in episcopal patronage, it had been founded by the community of Wisbech for its own people.[236] The collated warden is reminded that the goods of the house must be 'faithfully transferred to the use of the poor of the parish of Wisbech town'.[237] The warden was responsible for the support of the poor, for the house's fabric and for all expenditure on which he gave accounts annually to the bishop.[238] In 1352 the hospital was already held by the king due to its 'state of devastation'.[239] There was a collation to the mastership in 1353, an office which was clearly becoming a sinecure. In 1375 the house's properties were granted to a groom of the royal kitchen for life, and were regranted in 1377 with the right of inheritance.[240]

The foundation by the town is an interesting phenomenon, as it is around this time that the site intended for HSJC was assigned by the burgesses of Cambridge. The town clearly saw the foundation of asylums for the poor as a duty pertaining to their obligations towards the welfare of the citizenry. It also commonly occurred that a charitable house entered episcopal patronage, since it could not enjoy ecclesiastical rights, have a chapel or a cemetery, without episcopal authorisation and supervision.[241] The decay and dissolution of the hospital in the early 1350s may safely be ascribed to the effect of the Black Death. As there was no permanent religious community in the house, and sick and poor people were highly susceptible to the plague, such a community of sick people may have perished leaving the charitable establishment vacant. A vacancy of this kind was often taken up by the king in free towns and was integrated into the royal network of patronage.

and of development of town patriciates. The foundation also clearly antedated the Statute of Mortmain.
[235] CUL. EDR. Register Montacute, fol. 28v.
[236] CUL. EDR. Register Lisle, fol. 26r: 'patronatus dicti episcopi'.
[237] 'in usus pauperum parochie eiusdem ville de Wysbech fideliter convertantur', CUL. EDR. Register Montacute, fol. 28 (1343).
[238] *Ibid.*
[239] PRO. E136. 8/24.
[240] *Calendar of patent rolls 1374–1377*, pp. 175, 430.
[241] See above pp. 99–106.

The Hospital of St Nicholas, Royston

The leper hospital of St Nicholas in the fields near Royston was founded *c.* 1200 by the pious lady Amphelisa with the cooperation of her husband and the help of her sister Amabel.[242] The hospital was endowed with 2 acres and 1 rood in Kneesworth fields,[243] granted to the Blessed Virgin, St Nicholas, All Saints and the blessed poor of the hospital. A rush of donations followed this prompting: some 20 donors for whom evidence has survived granted small parcels in the fields of Melbourn, Bassingbourn and Kneesworth amounting to some 25 acres. The transcripts of the charters indicate an almost totally rural endowment, besides the chapel and the warden's house. It is reasonable to assume that this picture is close to the full extent of the hospital's possessions since, according to a fourteenth-century inquisition, it held a house and 30 acres of land. The hospital soon entered royal protection under King John in 1213,[244] who also granted a two-day fair on the feast of the Translation of St Nicholas and its morrow (9–10 May).[245]

The hospital is described as a leper house in some of the charters of donation,[246] and its community was described as 'firm and infirm brothers',[247] while sometimes sisters are mentioned.[248] The house had

---

[242] Since Amphelisa's husband who confirmed her donation died in 1206 and Amabel's husband, who confirmed her grant died in 1203, a date *c.* 1200 seems reasonable. The hospital was in the fields of Royston, a fact which placed it within the diocese of Ely and the county of Cambridge.

[243] W. M. Palmer, *John Layer (1586–1640) of Shepreth, Cambridgeshire: a seventeenth century local historian*, (Cambridge, 1935), no. 48, p. 50; her sister Amabel's granted is mentioned in *ibid.*, no. 33, p. 48. Most evidence about the hospital has reached us in the form of transcripts made by John Layer in 1635 from extracts made by his friend John Welbore of Foxton, who had derived them from the hospital's cartulary and who had also extracted documents from the cartulary of the hospital of St John and St James in Royston. Layer's notes (Oxford. Bodl. Rawlinson B.278) are the single source of information on the hospital's foundation and its early history.

[244] *Rotuli litterarum patentium* I, p. 96: 'suscepimus in defensione et protectione domus et fratres Sancti Nicholai de Cruce Roes'.

[245] *Rotuli chartarum in Turri Londinensi asservati, 1199–1216*, Record Commission (London, 1837), p. 189b (2 January 1213): 'unam feriam singulis annis in festo Translationis Sancti Nicholai per duos dies duraturam'. As in the case of Stourbridge hospital (above p. 112), a grant of fair rights was a popular way of enlarging the sources of incomes of a charitable house. The fair was extended to the day after the feast by Henry III, *Calendar of charter rolls 1226–1257*, p. 218 (17 March 1236).

[246] Palmer, *John Layer*, nos. 29, 39, 42, 47, pp. 48–50.

[247] *Ibid.*, nos. 16, 22, 34, 38, pp. 46–8.

[248] *Ibid.*, nos. 46, 50, pp. 49, 50. This combination of healthy and leprous brethren and sisters is often found in leper houses, as the religious vocation overshadowed the fear of contagion. See the example of the Norman leper hospital of St Gilles de Pont-Audemer, S. C. Mesmin, 'The leper Hospital of St. Gilles de Pont-Audemer' I, pp. 109–113.

a chapel which was inspected by the Officials of the bishop of Ely on diocesan visitations.[249]

A foundation, *c.* 1200, a dedication to St Nicholas and a rush of donations from a mixed group of substantial peasants and local knights were normal characteristics of an English rural leper hospital. The future fortunes of the house were also quite characteristic: during the first half of the fourteenth century the hospital became depopulated and developed into a sinecure, a chapel which maintained only its liturgical obligations to the patrons. By 1359 the king's escheator had seized the house's land; however, following an inquisition by royal mandate it was established that the seizure had been unjust.[250] The escheator argued that the house was an ancient royal foundation for the housing of lepers, and since it was no longer frequented by them, the lands were to return to the king.[251] The warden, John of Norwich, was there to answer that the founder had been Ralph, son of Ralph, son of Fulk (great grandson of the foundress), and that many men had added to the endowment. He also claimed that the patronage had descended by inheritance directly to Agnes, the widow of John d'Argenten who held it as part of the manor of Wendey from the Earl of Richmond.[252] Its liturgical obligations to the patrons included three weekly services in the chapel of the Hospital of Sts John and James, Royston, which had previously been conducted in St Nicholas' when lepers still resided there, and the maintenance of a lamp in Wendey church.[253] The warden's testimony shows the extent to which the house's character had changed throughout the late thirteenth and the early fourteenth centuries. It no longer received lepers, and its income was concentrated in the hands of a warden who supplied intercessory services for patrons and for past benefactors. With a decline in the number of lepers, such adjustments would have been a reasonable development;[254] in addition, after the Black Death, rent income from so small an endowment would have

---

[249] It was found to have *c.* 1278 'j.missale, j.vestimentum cum pertinenciis, j.calix argenteus, crismatorium, j.portiforium', *Vetus liber archidiaconi Eliensis*, p. 110.

[250] *Calendar of inquisitions miscellaneous* III, no. 322, p. 111 (18 November 1358).

[251] *Calendar of close rolls 1354–1360*, p. 587 (6 July 1359).

[252] The advowson of the hospital together with two acres in Melbourn were sold by Ralph, son of Ralph, son of Fulk to Richard d'Argenten, Palmer, *John Layer*, no. 3, p. 44.

[253] For a similar attempt to escheat a depopulated hospital see the case of Wisbech, above p. 139.

[254] Leper hospitals either disappeared or changed their function. See for example St Petronilla's hospital in Bury St Edmunds which was a community for poor leper women in the thirteenth century and had become a house for poor men and women in the fourteenth century, Rowe, 'The medieval hospitals', p. 258. Also above pp. 119–20.

fallen drastically. In 1371 the warden of the hospital invested 20s to obtain a confirmation of the right to hold the fair.[255] In 1467 it was the subject of a dispute between the prior of Royston and the master of the Hospital of St James over the right to celebrate mass in the chapel; no more is heard of this.[256]

Fulfilling this limited function the chapel existed well into the fifteenth century. A late fourteenth-century visitation described the possessions of its chapel; besides liturgical books and vessels which it had owned in the thirteenth-century visitation report, it now boasted of 7 bronze crosses, 15 banners, 4 bells and an incense boat.[257] Such objects would suggest the existence of a local cult centred in the chapel or the activities of a confraternity connected with it, as in the case of Newton College, to which we now turn.

College Hospital at Newton

The college or chantry at Newton is an interesting example of the revival of a popular place of worship by the creation of a charitable institution. Newton-on-the-sea, by the Wash, lay exposed to invasions of the coastline and to flooding. The parish had lost much of its inhabited area at the end of the thirteenth century owing to flooding, and a chapel stood abandoned there. The place was known for miraculous celestial lights, *coruscaciones luminum*, which appeared occasionally and haunted local tradition long after the chapel had become inactive. When Sir John Colvylle, constable of Wisbech castle, sought a place for the foundation of a college and bedeshouse he chose the old site at Newton. He rebuilt the chapel and constructed new buildings for the accommodation of the priest, chaplains, clerics and poor, who inhabited the house from around 1403.[258] Sir John had in mind a foundation in the form of a secular college functioning as a private chantry, to which a group of poor would be attached. In a privilege of Pope Innocent VII of 1405, reviewing a letter of Boniface IX, it was laid down that the chapel be served by priests and 12 bedesmen (or more). The college was placed under the protection of Sts Peter and Paul and was free to receive oblations, under the jurisdiction of the parish of Newton.[259] This situation was altered in

[253] *Calendar of patent rolls 1370–1374*, p. 123 (8 July 1371).
[256] Palmer, *John Layer*, no. 55, p. 51.
[257] *Vetus liber archidiaconi eliensis*, p. 111.
[258] *Calendar of papal letters* VI, pp. 24–5 (6 May 1405) and p. 290 (15 October 1411).
[259] *Ibid.*, pp. 24–5. The parish church was situated about one mile away from the chapel and was in the gift of the bishops of Ely.

142

1411 when [anti-]Pope John XXIII appropriated the parish to the chantry, so that upon the next presentation the living was to pass into the hands of the master, chaplains and clerks of the college, and one of their number was to serve the parish.[260]

The foundation at Newton was a secular college engaged in prayers and charity for the benefit of the founder and his friends. The house revived an old local cult and became a centre of devotion, to the detriment of the parish church which was eventually appropriated to it. Thus, by 1411 the college was a chantry, an almshouse and the communal rector of Newton. The earlier form of a house of clerics and 12 bedesmen was modified in 1454 in a set of minute statutes granted by Bishop Bourchier.[261] There was to be a priest at the head of the house, nominated by the bishop of Ely and answerable to him in all matters. As laid down by the statutes of 1454, the chantry was under episcopal supervision and its wardens were presented by the bishops of Ely, as various entries in the episcopal registers show.[262] By his side were three chaplains for the performance of continual prayers, one of whom served as the parish chaplain. Three clerics who could sing and read well assisted in the services, one of whom was the holy water cleric (*aquabaiulus*) of the parish.[263] In addition, three poor men were to live there with one poor woman who executed the bedeshouse chores.[264]

The stipends of the chaplains and the clerics were quite generous but sums were deducted for their upkeep at the master's table.[265] An extensive liturgical routine was ordered in the statutes with special prayers for the king and his consort, John Colvylle and his wife, and Bishops Fordham (1388–1425) and Morgan (1426–35) of Ely, with provisions for Bishop Bourchier after his death.[266] All members of the college owed obedience to the master; the chaplains were obliged to take an oath upon entry and to promise observance of the statutes.[267]

---

[260] *Ibid.*, p. 219. On life in collegiate churches see A. Hamilton Thompson, 'The collegiate churches of the bishopric of Durham', *Durham University journal* 36 (1944), pp. 33–42.

[261] CUL. EDR. Register Bourchier, fols. 50r–52r.

[262] CUL. EDR. Register Bourchier, fol. 7v (1452); Register Alcock, p. 108 (1495).

[263] Heath, *The English parish clergy*, p. 19.

[264] CUL. EDR. Register Bourchier, fol. 50r: 'et unam mulierem satis validam ad ea facienda que inferius exprimentur'.

[265] Thus a chaplain received £5 0s 0d minus 53s 4d leaving £2 6s 8d. Clerks received 40s minus 30s leaving 10s 4d, CUL. EDR. Register Bourchier, fol. 50.

[266] These were the bishops during the years of the foundation and endowment of the chantry.

[267] CUL. EDR. Register Bourchier, fol. 51v: 'Quod fidelis erit dicte cantarie sive collegio capelle beate Marie...et statuta nostra...observabit'.

It is interesting to observe the role played by the four poor people. They lived in what was known as the 'bedeshous' and although their duties were not as elaborately described as the chaplains', it is clear they were bound by obedience to the master, and that they were expected to live together in the college and adhere to its rules. This was achieved by the annual reading of the statutes, within the Octaves of the Annunciation: 'and if the need arise he will expound or have expounded in English for their full comprehension in such a way that not one of them could pretend to be ignorant of these ordinances or statutes'.[268] Reading of statutes was a common occasion in religious communities demanding obedience and restricting personal liberties.[269] Every Friday, six pence were given to each poor person for the purchase of foodstuffs, food perhaps from the master's pantry, which was cooked by the poor char-woman. Clothes were distributed once a year in the form of 6 ells of white 'blankette' material for the making of four robes with hoods; shoes were provided twice a year. The poor woman washed the clothes, prepared the meals, and spread the beds for those who could not tend themselves. She was a general factotum in the bedeshouse: 'and she will serve them in other necessary honest female occupations'.[270] The small community inherited the goods of its dead members, which were allocated for various uses by the master, observing the rule that 'all the goods of every poor...will stay in the said house called Bedeshous'.[271]

In addition to offering posts for eight clergymen, the college at Newton provided relief for four people and distributions of food and coins on the founder's anniversaries.[272] In 1467 Bishop Gray granted an indulgence to those contributing to the repair of the chapel and to the support of its chaplains and poor.[273]

[268] 'et in quantum necessitas postulaverit in anglicis ad eorum plenum intellectum declarabit seu faciet declarari sub tali forma quod nullus eorum in dictis ordinacionibus sive statutis ignoranciam pretendere posset'. Here Bishop Bourchier made allowances for the non-clerical members of the college by including recitation of the statutes in the vernacular, CUL. EDR. Register Bourchier, fol. 52r.

[269] See below pp. 180–1 on HSJC.

[270] 'ac in alijs officijs mulierum necessarijs et honestis eisdem ministrare', CUL. EDR. Register Bourchier, fol. 50v. Women were deemed more suitable for the task of treating inmates of charitable houses, as in St Giles' hospital, Norwich, NRO. 24/b/1.

[271] 'omnia bona cuiuscumque pauperis...remaneant in dicto domo vocato Bedeshous', *ibid.*

[272] As in the similar foundation, Wimpole chantry, where distributions were made on the founders' exequies, 6s 8d were divided amongst the clerks and poor, CUL. EDR. Register Gray, fols. 121v–122r.

[273] CUL. EDR. Register Gray, fol. 67r. The indulgence mentions 12 poor or sick people, but a growth in the number of poor is unusual in medieval charitable houses.

The college seems to have managed its finances well. The *Valor ecclesiasticus* assessed it at £18 14s 8½d per annum, an evaluation which agrees with the Mortmain licences granted to Sir John Colvylle.[274] In 1408 he granted lands and rents to the value of £5 10s and in 1446 to that of £6 16s 11d, a total of £12 6s 11d in the mid-fifteenth century.[275] In 1291 Newton church was valued at £40. The parish had since been heavily flooded and lost much of its tithe value, but even with a third of this income the college would have balanced its books. There were also revenues from alms, gifts in kind and cash from members of the parish, of the fraternity and from occasional pilgrims. The stipends amounted to a yearly sum of £26 23s 8d.

Besides its function as chantry and bedeshouse, Newton chapel became a centre of local devotion.[276] A confraternity was attached to the chantry as early as 1403, when its members gained a papal indulgence.[277] Letters of fraternity to benefactors were issued by the college throughout the fifteenth century. Such letters were a common form by which religious houses bestowed spiritual favours upon those who had shown them pecuniary ones.[278] Seven such letters survive from the fifteenth century and from the beginning of the sixteenth. This indicates that there was continual interest in the house by members of the confraternity from its foundation until close to the Dissolution. In 1511 the custodian, Dr William Thornburgh, granted the benefit of all indulgences accumulated by the house to a new member of the confraternity.[279]

A similar institution was founded in 1440 beside Tattershall Castle in Lincolnshire by Ralph, Lord Cromwell, in memory of his wife. This intercessory foundation consisted of a warden, 7 chantry priests, 6 secular clerks, 6 choristers and a bedeshouse for 13 poor men and 13 poor women.[280] In it charity and intercession were combined on a grand scale, featuring elements which existed in the Newton College as well. In the former charity was related to education while the chantry

---

[274] In 1535 *Valor ecclesiasticus* III, p. 500.

[275] *Calendar of patent rolls (1405–1408)*, p. 388; *Calendar of patent rolls (1441–6)*, p. 403.

[276] It could boast of a stained glass window with the image of the Virgin, CUL. EDR. Register West, fols 77v–78r which was mentioned in the will of the master William Thornburgh in 1525.

[277] *Calendar of papal letters* v, p. 565.

[278] Clark-Maxwell, 'Some letters of confraternity', *Archaeologia* 75 (1926), pp. 19–60 and 'Some further letters of fraternity', *Archaeologia* 79 (1929), pp. 179–216.

[279] He reviewed such grants made by popes Boniface IX, Nicholas V and Innocent V. CUL. University archives. Luard 150.

[280] As described in E. F. Jacob, 'Founders and foundations in the later Middle Ages', *Bulletin of the Institute of Historical Research* 35 (1962), pp. 29–46; pp. 42–4.

provided schooling for the choristers as well as for sons of Tattershall tenants.[281] As in Newton, the founder believed that best kind of intercession would be effected by the converging contributions of priests and grateful poor folk.

Newton was a charitable institution typical of its time: in a rural setting, a private chantry was founded in which clerics were engaged in an elaborate liturgical routine combined with pastoral care. Poor folk were supported and were expected to live within the college, and by their mere existence to contribute to the founder's pious act. This was not a hospital primarily for the needy, rather it was a chantry with a group of poor as a liturgical appendage of great value provided for the founder's soul.[282] No great schemes for healing body and soul were proposed, nor views of regular community life; the chaplains did not minister to the sick, and the bedesmen were not cared for tenderly, but paid their weekly wages. A clear functional division, precise hierarchy and a general practical disposition are found in the documents related to the college.[283] It was a form of expression of piety by which a direct path to salvation through human planning was realised. The mediation of an order, a monastic house or a regular body was not invoked. Sir John Colvylle hired the people best equipped for the execution of his end: the provision of perpetual and efficacious intercession for his soul and for the souls of his friends and benefactors.

SUMMARY OF THE DEVELOPMENT OF INSTITUTIONS OF CHARITY

This survey of 300 years of charitable foundation in town and countryside has embraced several different forms in which relief was organised. Towns saw the foundation of new institutions in the twelfth and thirteenth centuries, but no new religious foundations after the end of the thirteenth century.[284] Later foundations were usually secular

---

[281] This combination of the education and maintenance of young choristers resembles the chantry functions of the colleges in Cambridge and Oxford which often sustained poor boys who were to be instructed and who served in the college chapel, see below pp. 277–8. On a fifteenth-century educational charity outside the universities see *Early Yorkshire schools* II, ed. A. F. Leach, 1903, pp. 109–30, statutes of the Grammar School founded by archbishop Rotherham. On education in the late Middle Ages see J. H. Moran, *Education and learning in the city of York*.

[282] On direct benefactions to the poor as intercessors in the fourteenth century see F. Leclère, 'Recherches sur la charité des bourgeois envers les pauvres au XIVe siècle à Douai', *Revue du Nord* 48 (1966), pp. 139–54; pp. 151, 154.

[283] K. Wood-Legh, *Perpetual chantries in Britain* (Cambridge, 1965), *passim* and pp. 306–7.

[284] As in Bruges, Maréchal, *De sociale en politieke gebundenheid*, p. 310.

hospitals, almshouses and chantries. Yet, in all houses, of all different types, the alleviation of need was combined with the establishment of an intercessory routine maintained by the mixed efforts of professional clerics and grateful poor.

In the early thirteenth century the form of communal life deemed to be most suitable for the hospital staff was one which combined some of the rigours of regular life with the care of poor. A collegiate existence which imposed some of its routine and restrictions on the inmates was chosen in all religious institutions. Through the enforcement of the hospital's rule and the maintenance of religious services the houses entered episcopal jurisdiction; even the few maidens at Stow assumed a habit, to create and sustain the image of a religious community.

By the fourteenth century, hospitals and almshouses were conceived as existing in the secular sphere under the supervision of secular bodies such as the town or a college. To this type of institution, administered by laymen in a religious environment, one may add the late fifteenth-century parish almshouses which offered shelter and some work. At the same time, poor relief was integrated into a rigorously planned system of intercession, a development on the earlier theme, so that when elaborate chantries were founded for perpetual personal intercession, the poor were assured of a place. Charitable houses were created in various forms; these differing forms expressed the variety of aims which motivated the founders, and the changing orientation which steered the institutions through the centuries of their existence. Another side of the diversity of charitable activity lies in the multiple functions which a charitable house could maintain within the community which nurtured it.

Chapter 5

LIFE IN A MEDIEVAL HOSPITAL: THE HOSPITAL OF ST JOHN, CAMBRIDGE

Throughout the survey of charitable foundations in medieval Cambridgeshire a diverse picture of forms and activities has emerged. Their complex and flexible character can be appreciated further from the structure and orientation of their institutional lives and services. Therefore, we turn now to the urban hospital of Cambridge for a study in depth of one such institution bearing in mind that its character reflected changes in society's attitudes towards and expectations of a house of mercy.

HOSPITALS AND THE ATTITUDES TOWARDS PHYSICAL HEALING

Pauper et infirmus is the commonplace description of those intended to benefit from charitable giving. Some sick people were necessarily poor, not only through their loss of working capacity, but, as in the case of lepers, through being prohibited from holding property.[1] Some types of sickness were seen as punishment for sin, and imposed on the sick a double stigma.[2] Yet it is usually in vain that one searches for medical orientation in the activities of institutions devised for the relief of the sick and poor. Although medicine was studied in medieval universities,[3] on a practical level healing was not seen primarily as a purely physical transformation; if sickness was caused by sin, it was to be remedied

---

[1] Henry of Bracton, *De legibus et consuetudinibus Angliae* IV, ed. G. E. Woodbine and trans. S. E. Thorne (Cambridge, Mass., 1977), p. 308; Philip of Beaumanoir, *Coutumes de Clermont* II, pp. 326–7, c. 1617.

[2] On sickness and stigma see H. E. Siegrist, 'The special position of the sick', in *Culture, disease and healing: studies in medical anthropology*, ed. D. Landy (New York, 1977), pp. 389–94; esp. pp. 389–92. For a discussion of leprosy as a moral stigma rather than an actual danger to health see Richards, *The medieval leper*, pp. 48–9.

[3] V. L. Bullough, 'Medical study at mediaeval Oxford', *Speculum* 36 (1961), pp. 600–12; *idem*, 'The mediaeval medical school at Cambridge', *Mediaeval studies* 24 (1962), pp. 161–8; P. Kibre, 'Arts and medicine in the universities of the later Middle Ages', in *Les universités à la fin du moyen-âge*, ed. J. Paquet and J. Ijsewijn (Louvain, 1978), pp. 213–27.

by conquering sin.[4] A wide range of measures was taken to induce spiritual healing,[5] traditional practices were employed and expected to work transformations in the patient's psyche.[6] The formal dichotomy of medicine/healing is manifested in twelfth- and thirteenth-century synodal legislation which reiterated the need for spiritual balm to counteract the sinful state which causes physical ailment,[7] a view clearly stated in the *Decretum*, 'contraria sunt divine conditioni precepta medicine' ('the principles of medicine are contrary to divine command').[8] Believers were urged to seek spiritual rather than corporal doctors at the time of illness.[9] Lateran IV decreed that sickness was a reflection of sin, and that a physician of souls should be the one to offer remedy;[10] this canon reverberated throughout thirteenth-century diocesan legislation.[11]

[4] On the connection between spiritual and physical sickness in medieval mentality see R. I. Moore, 'Heresy as a disease', in *The concept of heresy*, ed. W. Lourdaux and D. Verhelst (Louvain, 1976), pp. 1–11.

[5] R. C. Finucane, *Miracles and pilgrims. Popular beliefs in medieval England* (London, 1977), pp. 68–9.

[6] S. Rubin, *Medieval English medicine* (Newton Abbot, 1974), pp. 111–12.

[7] *Conciliorum oecumenicorum decreta*, c.21, p. 245.

[8] However, twelfth-century doctors were often members of episcopal households, as some physicians of the bishops of Ely, E. J. Kealey, *Medieval medicus: a social history of Anglo-norman medicine* (Baltimore, Md., 1981), pp. 125, 134. The simile physician of souls for a priest was current in the thirteenth century, in the words of the French synods 'Sacerdos autem sit cautus et discretus, ut more periti medici superinfundant vinum et oleum vulneribus sauciati, diligenter inquirens et peccatoris circumstancias et peccati', *Les Statuts de Paris*, c. 76, pp. 190, 192.

[9] For a discussion of the evolution of the pastoral duties of parish priests to the sick and dying see, Avril, 'Le pastorale des malades et mourants aux XIIe et XIIIe siècles', pp. 88–106.

[10] *Conciliorum oecumenicorum decreta*, c.22: 'Quod infirmi prius provideant animae quam corpori', pp. 245–6: 'cum infirmitas corporalis nonnunquam ex peccato proveniat... statuimus...medicis corporum, ut cum eos ad infirmos vocari contigerit, ipsos ante omnia moneant et inducant, quod medicos advocent animarum'. For some interesting commentaries on this canon see *Constitutiones concilii quarti Lateranensis una cum commentariis glossatorum*, ed. A. García y García (Vatican, 1981), pp. 316–17, 429, 469, 486–7. On this popular view of the effect of sins on the body in a later period see K. Thomas, *Religion and the decline of magic. Studies in popular beliefs in sixteenth- and seventeenth-century England* (London, 1971), pp. 106–7.

[11] For English synodal legislation see *Councils and synods* II part 1, Worcester I (1219), c.12, p. 57; Salisbury I (1217 × 19), c.98, p. 92; Worcester II (1229), c.11, p. 173; Salisbury II (1238 × 44), c.15, p. 371; Durham particulars (1241 × 9), c.58, p. 444; for France 1216 × 9 see the *Les statuts de Paris*, c.69, p. 184. The spiritual view of sickness and its healing is the reason for the prohibition of the use of Jewish doctors by sick Christians: *ibid.*, Exeter II, c.49, p. 1045. Surgeons and physicians were often condemned and those seeking their help were deemed to be foolish and misguided, Finucane, *Miracles and pilgrims*, pp. 65–7. See Vincentus Hispanus' view in his commentary on canon 22 of Lateran IV (*c.* 1217): 'Quia melius est mortem subire quam malo consentire', *Constitutiones concilii quarti Lateranensis*, p. 316.

From the twelfth century, an alternative view developed which saw the art of medicine as given by God for the benefit of man[12] sometimes reflected in the symbolism of Jesus as healer.[13] It is also echoed in the words of the introduction to the medical encyclopedia of Guy of Chauliac, the papal physician in Avignon writing in 1363, in its Middle English translation: 'þankyngis to almy3ti god þe 3euere boþe of euerlastyng lijf of soulis & helþe of bodies þat heeliþ alle oure grete soris bi grace þat he haþ 3ouen to al mankynde...þat grauntiþ us to undirstonde þe craft of medicyne'.[14] Clergymen studied medicine in the universities, though their numbers were very small, and they were by no means encouraged by the ecclesiastical establishment.[15] Once ordained, a clergyman was forbidden to participate in surgery involving incision;[16] the study of medicine was not recognised as sufficient grounds for a rector's absence from his parish.[17] In university towns the need for supervision and regulation of the practice of medicine was pressing, in Oxford only university graduates were granted licences to practise medicine.[18] Other cities came to see the supervision of medical care as an aspect of municipal responsibility.[19]

Most large secular hospitals maintained physicians as permanent members of their staff.[20] In contrast, the conservative view prevailed

[12] John of Salisbury, *Policraticus* I, ed. C. C. J. Webb (Oxford, 1909), p. 168: c.2.29: 'Quia medicina a Domino Deo est et vir sapiens non contemnet eam. Nemo siquidem magis necessarius est aut utilior medico, dummodo sit fidelis et prudens'.

[13] Longère, *Oeuvres oratoires* I, p. 170 and II, n. 11, p. 130, n. 21, p. 87.

[14] This is a fifteenth-century translation, Guy of Chauliac, *The Middle English version of the introduction to Guy de Chauliac's 'Chirurgia Magna'*, ed. B. Wallner (Lund, 1970), p. 3.

[15] On the medical material studied in the universities see C. H. Talbot, *Medicine in medieval England* (London, 1967), pp. 72–87.

[16] *Les statuts de Paris*, c.34, p. 160; and canon 18 of Lateran IV, *Conciliorum oecumenicorum decreta*, p. 244.

[17] On the prohibition of study of medicine imposd on various religious groups, and its gradual extension see, D. W. Amundsen, 'Medieval canon law on medical and surgical practice by the clergy', *Bulletin of the history of medicine* 52 (1978), pp. 22–44; pp. 34–8, though there never was a total prohibition, *ibid.*, p. 43.

[18] *Statuta antiqua universitatis Oxoniensis*, ed. S. Gibson (Oxford, 1931), pp. 40–2. According to these statutes dating from before 1350, scholars were instructed both in theoretical and practical medicine: 'legant unum librum de practica et alium de theoretica', *ibid.*, p. 42, and were to attend anatomy sessions.

[19] Italian towns were first to adopt this view, C. M. Cipolla, *Public health and the medical profession in the Renaissance* (Cambridge, 1976), pp. 6, 11–18.

[20] E. Wickersheimer, 'Médecins et chirurgiens dans les hôpitaux du moyen-âge', *Janus* 32 (1928), pp. 1–11; pp. 9–11. On this development see S. R. Ell, 'The two medicines: some ecclesiastical concepts of disease and the physician in the high Middle Ages', *Janus* 68 (1981), pp. 15–25; pp. 18–19. On the development of the medical gild see C. Rawcliffe, 'Medicine and medical practice in later medieval London', *Guildhall studies in London history* 5 (1981), pp. 13–25. For examples of charitable bequests directed

in the majority of ecclesiastical hospitals under episcopal control, such as HSJC. Here sickness was still connected with sin, and healing with prayer and penance. In some houses a middle way was achieved: the rule of the Hospitaller Order provided for a physician's care when needed.[21] In the Hôtel-Dieu of Paris, doctors were introduced at the beginning of the thirteenth century.[22] In most hospitals, inmates' confessions were heard and they were given communion upon arrival, and an atmosphere of devotion and purity was maintained within the hospital walls. Another aspect of the belief in the physical efficacy of spiritual intervention caused hospitals to be examined by the quality of their spiritual treatment. The *Liber fundationis* of St Bartholomew's Hospital in London (founded 1123) is a book reporting miracles wrought by the Saint's relics.[23] Invoking saints and their relics was compatible with the process of healing;[24] a thirteenth-century charitable fund financed pilgrimages in pursuit of healing.[25] Another source of spiritual healing was believed to be found in the royal person, a popular view current in England and France by the twelfth century.[26]

This is not to say that medieval hospitals were totally unaware of the physical needs of their inmates.[27] Confession and attendance at

towards the maintenance of medical treatment for a hospital's inmates see Thrupp, *The merchant class*, p. 179.   [21] *Statuts*, c.12, p. 12.

[22] *Archives de l'hôtel-dieu de Paris (1157–1300)* I, ed. L. Brièle (Paris, 1894), p. 97. At St John's Hospital, Brussels, a doctor was called whenever the need arose and even when the sick person could not afford to pay him, *Cartulaire de l'hôpital St. Jean de Bruxelles*, c.25, p. 24.

[23] Translated into Middle English *c.* 1400 from the Latin book written *c.* 1180, *Liber fundationis: the book of the foundation of St Bartholomew's hospital in London*, ed. N. Moore (London, 1923). An example of this view is the case of a carpenter whose 'leggis were clevynge to the hynder parte of his thyes that he myghte nat goo' and who was, thus, deprived of his source of livelihood. His healing was brought about when 'Therfore, for that he was ferre from that chirche he yave shipmen for hyr hyyr, and by shippe he was browght to the chirche and put yn the hospitall of pore men. And ther a while of the almes of the same chirche y-sustenyd. And he began yn the meyn while by the vertu of the Apostle come ageyne...when othir membrys usyd ther naturall myghte', c.28, pp. 28–9. For a Spanish hospital founded in a healing centre see W. A. Christian, *Local religion in sixteenth-century Spain* (Princeton, N.J., 1981), p. 85.

[24] Individual saints were believed to relieve particular sicknesses, E. Patzelt, 'Pauvreté et maladies', in *Povertà et ricchezza nella spiritualità dei secoli XIe e XIIe* (Todi, 1969), pp. 163–87; p. 174; P. Bachoffner, 'Remèdes et soins aux malades dans les monastères alsaciens du moyen-âge (VIIIe au XIIe siècle)', *Revue d'histoire de la pharmacie* 22 (1975), pp. 329–39; Christian, *Local religion*, pp. 93–105.

[25] P. Heupgen, 'La Commune aumône de Mons du XIIIe au XIVe siècles', *Bulletin de la commission royale d'histoire de Belgique* 90 (1926), pp. 319–72; p. 327. On healing and pilgrimage see Finucane, *Miracles and pilgrims*; P.-A. Sigal, 'Maladie, pèlerinage et guérison au XIIe siècle', *Annales* 24 (1969), pp. 1522–39; p. 1534.

[26] Barlow, 'The king's evil', pp. 3–27.

[27] V. L. Bullough, 'A note on medical care in medieval English hospitals', *Bulletin of the history of medicine* 35 (1961), p. 74–7; Probst, 'Das Hospitalwesen im hohen und späten

canonical hours were recommended, yet clean beds and nourishing food were also offered. Most attempts at alleviation of physical suffering were concentrated on the provision of food, drink, clothing and cover.[28] In most cases these provisions would have allowed recuperation from casual ailments, and improvement in the condition of those who were merely cold and undernourished. Thus, it is not surprising to find in the kitchen accounts of HSJC for year 1343–4 no mention of purchases of any medications or special food.[29] The only mention of a physician in the hospital archives is that of *Robertus medicus* as a witness in a donation charter from before 1230. He may have been the same as Robert *le surgien*, a tenant in All Saints' parish *c.* 1200.[30] One Master Nigel of Thornton, *medicus* (died 1270 × 9), owned land in St Botolph's Parish and in Barnwell, and was active in university life.[31]

Although HSJC existed in the midst of a university town, and scholars often lodged in it or conducted business transactions with it, no evidence of practical medical contact can be found. There is more evidence from the fourteenth and fifteenth centuries that Cambridge University graduates practised in the town.[32] Most people would have been treated for minor ailments by barbers and surgeons.[33] In the accounts of 1485 the wages paid to a barber are recorded: 'and to our barber − 8od'.[34] No other mention is found which can be related to medical treatment, and at this late day in the hospital's history it may well be that the barber served the community of brethren. It is

Mittelalter', p. 250. On the influence of the plague on the hiring of doctors see Baehrel, 'La haine de classe en temps d'épidémie', p. 352.

[28] For a very general description of care in medieval hospitals see Talbot, *Medicine in medieval England*, pp. 173–8.

[29] SJCA. Cartulary of HSJC, fols. 89–90.

[30] SJCA. Cartulary of HSJC, fol. 4v; C. H. Talbot and E. A. Hammond, *The medical practitioners in medieval England. A biographical register* (London, 1965), p. 286; *Rotuli hundredorum* II, 390. Some land in Cambridge was sold to 'magister Hugo medicus' of Ely in 1314, SJCA.D25.136.

[31] Talbot and Hammond, *The medical practitioners in medieval England*, p. 230. There is no evidence of any connection between him and the University.

[32] See Thomas Reed, M.D., Fellow of Peterhouse who paid personal tithes for his consultations to the parish of Little St Mary, Cambridge, Little, 'Personal tithes', p. 83.

[33] Finucane, *Miracles and pilgrims*, pp. 59–62. Medical guide books such as *herbaria* and *lunaria* were used by surgeons and popular healers. See C. Weisser, 'Das Krankheitslunar aus medizinhistorischer Sicht', *Sudhoffs Archiv* 65 (1981), pp. 390–400. For a popular medical treatise which was in circulation between the thirteenth and fifteenth centuries see O. Redon, 'Un traitè médical du XIIIe siècle', *Bollettino senese di storia patria* 88 (1981), pp. 304–8.

[34] SJCA.D.106.9, fol. 5r. On books that a French surgeon may have had at his disposal see A. Saunier, 'Les connaissances médicales d'un barbier et chirurgien français en 1455', *Annales de l'université d'Abidjan. Histoire* 8 (1980), pp. 27–46; pp. 30–42.

important to remember that hospitals offered shelter, food, spiritual comfort and a disciplined environment. Some contemporaries would have considered these all that is needed for a man's recuperation and regeneration.

THE SOURCES OF HOSPITAL RULES AND THE RULE OF HSJC

The rule of the Hospital of St John the Evangelist, Cambridge has reached us as a part of a letter, dated 31 March 1344, from Bishop Simon Montacute.[35] This letter is a combined *inspeximus* of earlier episcopal and papal letters to the hospital and a list of ordinances provided by the bishop. Four items copied into the letter are of special importance for an attempt to reconstruct the pattern of life in the hospital: (1) the rule given by Bishop Hugh Northwold (1229–54) (lines 145–56); (2) an ordinance by Bishop John Hotham (1316–37) for the election of masters (lines 58–71); (3) an ordinance by Bishop Montacute (1337–45) for the administration of hospital property by the master and by other hospital officials (lines 156–74); and (4) a letter by Pope Innocent IV (1243–54) confirming HSJC's rule and its ecclesiastical privileges (lines 174–97). The rule, given by Bishop Hugh Northwold whom we have seen to be so instrumental in the establishment of the hospital's ecclesiastical standing, is incomplete:[36] it deals mainly with the internal life of the hospital, and does not provide some of the clauses which usually appear in hospital rules.[37]

Some help in filling the *lacunae* in our knowledge of the life of the HSJC can be found in the statutes for the Hospital of St John in Ely, given around 1240 at the union between the Hospitals of St Mary Magdalene and of St John the Baptist, by Bishop Northwold.[38] A later set was granted by Bishop Orford in 1303 and copied into an *inspeximus* by Bishop Fordham of 1408. The second set was based on the statutes provided in the thirteenth century by Bishop Balsham (1257–86) and Bishop Walpole (1299–1302). The Ely hospital was dependent upon the priory and was ruled by the sacrist; hence some differences from the rule of HSJC, but the ethos and principles of the internal life were strikingly similar and were expressed in many places in almost identical phrasing.

[35] SJCA.D4.1. See below Appendix 1, pp. 300–1.
[36] See above p. 101.
[37] This clearly appears by comparison with the very closely related rule of the hospital of St John, Ely, as in CUL. EDR. Register Fordham, fol. 219 given to the Ely hospital around 1225 × 40 by Bishop Northwold.   [38] *Ibid.*, fols. 218–19.

Hospital rules appear in great abundance from the last years of the twelfth century. The rules of French hospitals have been collected and studied and lines of transmission and regional influences have been established.[39]. Writing around 1226, the keen observer Jacques of Vitry described such houses under the heading 'On hospitals of the poor and leper houses': 'and there are other communities of men as well as of women, who have renounced the world and live a regular life in leper houses or hospitals of the poor...in all regions of the West. They live according to the rule of St Augustine'.[40] Indeed, hospitals often adopted and adapted the Augustinian rule as the guideline to their communal life.[41] These hospitals 'normally followed a rule of life which might differ little if at all from the demands of the Rule of St Augustine'.[42] In Cambridgeshire most hospitals lived by this rule: St John's at Cambridge, St John's at Ely, and Anglesey hospital which became a full Augustinian priory in 1212.[43]

The rule referred to by Jacques of Vitry was ultimately based on the letter attributed to St Augustine in which advice and instruction were given *ad servos dei*.[44] From the eleventh century, an expanded version of this rule regulated the life of many reformed communities of priests.[45] In England some hospitals were full members of the order such as Elsing Spital, London, St Mary's, Bishopsgate and Maiden Bradley, Wiltshire,[46] but most hospitals abiding by an Augustinian rule were not members of the Augustinian chapters. In the lists for the diocese of Ely for the thirteenth and fourteenth centuries only Barnwell

---

[39] *Statuts, passim.*

[40] 'Sunt insuper alie, tam virorum quam mulierum seculo renunciantium et regulariter in domibus leprosorum vel hospitalibus pauperum viventium..., in omnibus occidentis regionibus congregationes. Vivunt autem secundum Sancti Augustini regulam...', de Jacques of Vitry, *The 'Historia Occidentalis', Jacques de Vitry: a critical edition*, ed. J. F. Hinnebusch (Freiburg, 1972), c.29, pp. 146–7.

[41] On the significance of the adoption of the Augustinian rule by hospital communities see G. Schreiber, *Gemeinschaft des Mittelalters: Recht und Verfassung. Kult und Frömmigkeit* (Regensburg and Munster, 1948), pp. 39–40.

[42] Dickinson, *The origins of the Austin canons*, p. 146. In Germany new hospitals were commonly associated with a religious or hospitaller order, Probst, 'Das hospitalwesen', pp. 246–7.

[43] See above pp. 99–111, 129–35, 137–8.

[44] *PL* 32, cols. 1379–84, 1449–52; L. Verheijen, *La règle de Saint Augustin* I (Paris, 1967), pp. 417–37; Dickinson, *The origins of the Austin canons*, pp. 273–79. For such advice to a feminine community see in *PL* 33, cols. 958–65.

[45] C. Dereine, 'Vie commune, règle de St. Augustin et chanoines réguliers au XIe siècle', *Revue d'histoire ecclésiastique* 41 (1946), pp. 365–406. For a survey of the development of the rule throughout the Middle Ages see C. Giroud, *L'ordre des chanoines réguliers de Saint-Augustin et ses diverses formes de régime interne. Essai de synthèse historico-juridique* (Martigny, 1961), pp. 31–47.

[46] Dickinson, *The origins of the Austin canons*, p. 146.

and Anglesey priories appear as houses of the order.[47] Although no formal ties of dependence bound HSJC to Barnwell priory it is possible that customs from the great priory were transmitted to the hospital; we should pay special attention to the Observances of the priory as a possible source for some of the hospital's customs.[48]

The Augustinian rule provides advice for a religious community which may be living in contact with laymen.[49] It recommends moderation and mutual help in the face of the temptations of the *saeculum* where their pastoral and charitable duties were executed.[50] It did not provide an answer to all the needs of a religious community and specific customaries developed on the basis of the Augustinian precepts. An important branch of the Augustinian theme was the rule of the hospital of St John of Jerusalem. The order was provided with two rules in the twelfth century, one in 1125 × 53 and another in 1181, emphasising communal living, lack of private property, continence, observance of canonical hours, mutual correction and obedience.[51] The Hospitallers added to the Augustinian rule the dimension of charitable activity – the treatment of sick and poor people.[52] Their insistence on the obligations to 'Les seignors malades' resounds in a whole series of French hospital rules influenced by them, as well as in some English ones.[53] The Augustinian rule inspired those orders devoted to hospital

---

[47] *Chapters of the Augustinian canons*, ed. H. E. Salter (Oxford, 1920), Appendix. When the statutes of the 1371 chapter decreed that Augustinian scholars should hold their chapter meetings in nearby priories, the Cambridge men were directed to Barnwell priory, *ibid.*, p. 69.

[48] Hospitals were aware of their dependence on the Augustinian rule and in the statutes of St Giles' hospital, Norwich a clear instruction was given to refer to it in matters of religious practice: 'In ieiuniis et uberibus et refeccionibus modum illorum servabunt qui servant regulam beati Augustini, habitum tamen eorum non habebunt', NRO. 24/b/1.

[49] Cf. C. N. L. Brooke and G. Keir, *London 800–1216, the shaping of a city* (London, 1975), p. 325. For an attempt to distinguish canonical from monastic spirituality, see C. W. Bynum, 'The spirituality of regular canons in the twelfth century: a new approach', *Medievalia et humanistica* new ser. 4 (1973), pp. 3–25.

[50] This canonical way of life was highly regarded by twelfth-century thinkers, Longère, *Oeuvres oratoires* I, pp. 368–71.

[51] *Cartulaire général de l'ordre des Hospitaliers de S. Jean de Jérusalem*, I, ed. J. Delaville Le Roulx (Paris, 1894), pp. 62–8, 425–29; *Statuts*, pp. 7–15; E. J. King, *The rule, statutes and customs of the Hospitallers, 1099–1310* (London, 1934), pp. 20–8, 34–40.

[52] In Cambridgeshire there were the preceptories at Shingay and at Chippenham, the latter being the order's main infirmary in England, cf. Knowles and Hadcock, *Medieval religious houses*, pp. 325–49; *The Knights Hospitallers in England*, ed. L. B. Larking (London, 1857), pp. 75–80.

[53] *Statuts*, pp. v–xviii; J. Riley-Smith, *The knights of St. John in Jerusalem and Cyprus, c. 1050–1310* (London, 1967), pp. 46–8; T. S. Miller, 'The knights of St John and the hospitals of the Latin West', *Speculum* 53 (1978), pp. 709–33.

care such as the Order of the Holy Spirit, St Anthony of Vienne and those created in the Crusader state.[54] The order of the Holy Spirit originated in Provence and its rule was granted in 1198 × 1208; in it the attitude to the poor is described: 'they are to be received willingly and treated charitably'.[55] The composer of a rule for a late twelfth- or thirteenth-century hospital could thus draw from basic works outlining principles for the life of a secular religious community – the rule of St Augustine – and its many derivative rules for the use of colleges and priories, as well as from versions of rules governing twelfth-century hospitals.[56]

Hospital rules regulated the life of the various groups within: the servants, the permanent *familia* of the hospital, lay and priestly groups, as well as the sick and poor inmates of either or both sexes. The extent to which a rule was developed and elaborated undoubtedly depended on the circumstances of the hospital's foundation, on the wealth of its founder and on its size. Although rules differed in their attention to detail, they all insisted on communal living, lack of private property, kindness to the inmates, canonical observances, chastity and obedience – the Augustinian and Hospitaller principles.

No mention of the Augustinian connection is made in the rule of HSJC, but many of its clauses reveal the direct derivation. In addition, in his letter of confirmation, Pope Innocent IV ordered: 'we have decreed that the order of canons known to be instituted in that church according to God and the rule of St Augustine, should be observed there securely forever'.[57] A visitation of 1373 mentioned a lapse in the confessional practice of the brothers 'according to the ordinance of their rule'.[58] In 1426 a brother of the hospital was freed from his obedience to the rule of St Augustine so as to allow him to join a stricter religious community.[59]

---

[54] J. Richard, 'Hospitals and hospital congregations in the Latin kingdom during the first period of the Frankish conquest', in *Outremer*, ed. B. Z. Kedar, H. E. Mayer and R. C. Smail (Jerusalem, 1982), pp. 89–100.

[55] 'Libenter suscipiantur et caritative tractentur', *Liber regulae sancti spiritus*, ed. A. Francesco La Cava (Milan, 1947), c.43, p. 164.

[56] The Augustinian rule remained as a model for hospital life well into the late Middle Ages. Based on it were the statutes of St Bartholomew's hospital, Oxford, of 1367 and of the Gantois hospital in Lille founded in 1466, Chanoine Coppin, 'Les statuts de l'hospice gantois à Lille (1467)', *Revue du Nord* 29 (1947), pp. 26–42.

[57] 'statuimus ut ordo canonicus qui secundum deum et beati Augustini regulam in eadem ecclesia institutus esse dinoscitur perpetuis ibidem temporibus inviolabiliter observetur', SJCA.D4.1 lines 176–77.

[58] 'iuxta ordinacionem regule sue', CUL. EDR. Microfilm Ms. 1837, Register Whittlesey, fol. 153v.

[59] SJCA. Cartulary of HSJC, fol. 80v.

MEMBERS OF THE COMMUNITY OF HSJC

Inmates

The rule of HSJC states that the sick and weak should be admitted to its care except for pregnant women, lepers, wounded people, cripples and the insane (clause 13). Similar limitations are found in the rules of other hospitals, as they were designed to receive passing inmates who left when cured or dead. The rule's exclusion of *vulnerati* probably stems from the fact that it could not offer urgent medical attention, or cope with riots and their aftermath as barbers and surgeons could. Following the same reasoning, HSJC and most other hospitals did not receive the insane,[60] a term which seems to have been generally understood yet rather loosely defined;[61] they were often thought to bear diminished responsibility for their actions like children,[62] and to need similar protection from themselves.[63] Very few facilities for treatment of the insane existed in the Middle Ages; the rule of the Hospital of the Holy Spirit, Montpellier (1178×9) directed the community to seek the insane in the streets and to take them to the house.[64] Occasionally exorcism or pilgrimage to a holy shrine was recommended as a cure for mental illness.[65] In late medieval Cambridge the afflicted could perhaps find asylum in the Hospital of Sts Anthony and Eligius, but most remained the burden of their families and neighbours, often left to their own devices as long as they harmed no one; this freedom let them do harm to themselves, and coroners' rolls testify to a large number of self-inflicted injuries and accidents involving the insane.[66]

---

[60] Few facilities for these tormented people existed in the Middle Ages. In some hospitals separate quarters were allocated to them: *Archives de l'hôtel-dieu de Paris* I, p. 109. At St Mary of Bethlehem (Bedlam) hospital, London, there were six insane women in 1403, G. Rosen, *Madness in society*, p. 139. See B. Chaput, 'La condition juridique et sociale de l'aliéné mentale', in *Aspects de la marginalité au moyen-âge* (Montreal, 1975), pp. 38–47; pp. 42–3.

[61] For a very loose legal definition see Philip of Beaumanoir, *Coutumes de Clermont* II, p. 329, c.1624.

[62] See the case of Margaret d. of Robert who was arrested in Cambridge in 1332 for murder of her daughter and who was pardoned due to diminished responsibility in a state of madness: 'Margareta infirmitatis frenetice detenta...filiam suam... interfecit...nequam per maliciam...set tanquam causa infirmitatis...', *A Cambridgeshire gaol delivery roll 1332–1334*, ed. E. G. Kimball (Cambridge, 1978), pp. 36–7.

[63] Thomas Aquinas, *Summa theologiae* III q.68 a.11.

[64] Chaput, 'La condition juridique', pp. 42–3.

[65] Finucane, *Miracles and pilgrims*, pp. 107–10.

[66] Cases of self-inflicted injuries appear in court rolls. For cases of madmen killing themselves through accidents or during a fit see *The assizes held at Cambridge*, pp. 33, 124. A description of the peasant Thurkill who was thought to be mad after his

Life in a medieval hospital

Guided by similar considerations, and by some moral stricture against single pregnant women, the Hospital of St John, Oxford, excluded from its help those suffering from a series of debilitating and incurable states: 'lepers, paralytics, people suffering of dropsy, mad people, those suffering of falling sickness, ulcers or incurable diseases will not be admitted, nor will lewd pregnant women'.[67] The unfortunate afflicted whose state was beyond help and who went through life suffering lingering misfortunes were not to take the place of curable sick folk.[68] Another ground for exclusion, perhaps the moral one, barred wounded people, *vulnerati*, as well as pregnant single women, from entry to some hospitals. The former may have been excluded in order to discourage victims of brawls and personal violence from expecting treatment. Indeed, Coroners' rolls do not mention cases in which those wounded through violence were sent to hospitals for treatment. Single mothers were probably denied access since their lonely condition suggested pregnancy outside wedlock and family circle; but these strictures were not universal. In its statutes of 1197 × 1202 the hospital at Angers provided for poor pregnant women;[69] the mixed Order of the Holy Spirit was obliged by its rule 'to feed orphans and pregnant women'.[70] In the mixed community of St Paul's Hospital, Norwich, poor pregnant women were accepted: 'And also the ailing and the infirm and poor pregnant women will be received'.[71] Homeless pregnant women were also helped in St John's Hospital, Brussels, which was served by a mixed community: 'pregnant women close to labour who have nowhere to lay their head will be received'.[72] HSJC probably could not accommodate women in and

awakening from a vision illustrates the usual treatment: 'quod illi cernentes estimabant eum incurrisse amentiam et ligare eum decreverunt', *Visio Thurkilli*, ed. P. G. Schmidt (Leipzig, 1978), p. 8, lines 2–3. Leniency was usually exhibited in the punishment of crimes perpetrated by the insane, D. M. Nicholas, 'Crime and punishment in fourteenth century Ghent', pp. 289–334, 1141–76.

67 'Non admittant leprosos, paraliticos, ydropsicos, furiosos, morbo caduco laborantes, fistulas aut morbos incurabiles pacientes nec mulieres lascivas pregnantes', *Cartulary of the hospital of St. John* III, p. 3.

68 As explained by the statutes of the hospital of Troyes: 'Nullo modo recipiantur, nisi sint gravi infirmitate detenti, quia debilitas membrorum non est infirmitas in uno impotenti, et statim cum valuerint, recedant', *Statuts*, c.90, p. 115.

69 *Ibid.*, c.14, p. 25.

70 'orphanis nutriendis et feminis pregnantibus', *Liber regulae sancti spiritus*, c.41, p. 164.

71 'Preterea egrotantes et infirmi et parturientes pauperes...recipiantur', E. H. Carter, ed., 'The constitution of the hospital of St. Paul (Normanspital) in Norwich', *Norfolk archaeology* 25 (1935), pp. 342–52; p. 350. For an example of obstetric treatment in a hospital in Italy see *Acta Sanctorum Maii* v (edition of Paris and Rome, 1866), p. 103.

72 'Mulieres pregnantes, qui vicine sunt partui, nec habent ubi caput reclinent recipiantur', *Cartulaire de l'hôpital St.-Jean de Bruxelles*, c.26, p. 24; the house also received poor women's babies, c.27, p. 24.

after labour since it was a male religious community. Although there was an objection to treating women of immoral character in a male community, where circumstances allowed there was some willingness to help the poorer ones. Perhaps poor pregnant women were helped by the nuns of St Radegund, the only female religious community in Cambridge.

The inmates of HSJC were styled in grants to the hospital as *infirmi* or *pauperes*, while the community serving them were invariably named *fratres*. Communal religious life created the framework for charitable activity in the hospital. Those who were deemed eligible for hospital care became members upon admission and had to abide by its rule. Few clauses devoted to the life of inmates appear in hospital rules: of 18 clauses of the rule only three refer directly to the treatment of the sick in HSJC; and in that of St John's hospital, Oxford, only one of its 11 sections dealt with the lives of the inmates. The elaborate rule of St Laurence's Hospital in Canterbury, issued in 1294, contains no information on the care of inmates. This does not mean that treatment was neglected but that there was a common understanding of its scope and nature which did not require a regulating document.[73] It was the life of the religious community that needed supervision and which profited from written guidance. However, those Continental rules closely related to the Hospitaller principles show greater preoccupation with nursing tasks. An especially elaborate description of these obligations towards the inmates can be found in the statutes of the hospital of Angers.[74]

The rule of HSJC is silent as to the process of admission of inmates. The normal procedure in hospitals, as revealed in the rule of St John's Hospital in Oxford, and in French statutes of the period, was for the chaplain to administer the sacrament of communion to the new inmate following confession.[75] Jacques of Vitry tells us that mass was usually celebrated daily in hospitals in a place close to the inmates' beds allowing them to hear and participate.[76] Some of the brethren of HSJC

[73] Clauses relating to the inmates usually described their commons and the frequency of allocation of clothes.

[74] *Statuts*, pp. 21–33. The hospital was founded in 1175 by the sénéschal of Anjou, and received its rule from Bishop William of Chemille 1197 × 1202. As this was a hospital based closely on the Augustinian rule the study of it may help us in filling gaps in our knowledge of HSJC.

[75] *Cartulary of the hospital of St. John*, p. 3: 'precipimus quod infirmorum admittendorum confessionem audiat priusquam admittantur; *Statuts*, c.16, p. 11: 'ita recipietur: primum peccata sua presbitero confessus, religiose communicetur, et postea ad lectum deportetur'.

[76] Jacques of Vitry, *The 'Historia occidentalis'*, p. 147.

were *fratres capellani* who administered sacraments to the sick and maintained the liturgical routine of the house. As we have seen the hospital was a kind of parish for its inmates and servants, providing that spiritual care of the sick and poor which surpassed mere physical care in its importance. In the Observances of the Augustinian canons at Barnwell one finds a description of the physical and spiritual care which must be accorded to the sick and poor:

About the poor sick folk...the almoner must be kind, so as to provide them not only with food, drink and clothing, but also with spiritual goods, such as confession and communion and he must admonish them frequently about the soul's welfare.[77]

On admittance, after communion, the sick person was led to his bed among the other inmates,[78] and was to be treated with compassion and mercy.[79] These are echoes of the demands which appear in the Hospitaller rule under the title: 'coment les segneurs povres doivent estre recehuz et serviz', and in the hospital rules inspired by them.[80] Bearing these guidelines in mind, the following clause in the rule of HSJC falls into place: 'so that the sick brethren will have a house assigned to them where they can be served meat or whatever may please them'.[81]

Inmates usually took their meals separately from the brethren. The composition of the diet must have been dictated by contemporary medical lore; the rules of Ely and Cambridge refer to meat dishes provided to fortify the sick. The brethren were to have meat on three days a week – Sunday, Tuesday and Thursday.[82] The inmates seem to

---

[77] 'De infirmis pauperibus...debet elemosinarius esse sollicitus, ut eis provideat, non tantum de cibis, potibus, et vestimentis, set eciam de bonis spiritualibus, ut de confessione et communione et anime salute frequenter debet commonere', *Observances in use at the Augustinian priory of St. Giles and St. Andrew at Barnwell, Cambridgeshire*, ed. J. W. Clark (Cambridge, 1897), p. 174.

[78] At St Bartholomew's, Oxford, they were to recite 50 Pater Nosters and 50 Ave Marias thrice daily for the soul of the king and founder (1367), *Oriel College records*, ed. C. L. Shadwell and H. E. Salter (Oxford, 1926), p. 298.

[79] 'Quod omnis humanitas fratribus infirmis exhibeatur' (clause 8 of HSJC).

[80] *Statuts*, c.16, p. 11; and in the rule of the Order of the Holy Spirit, *Liber regulae Sancti Spiritus*, c.6, pp. 128–9, an oath to 'dominis nostris infirmis'. See also the fifteenth century hospital rule of the Gantois hospital, Lille, Coppin, 'Les statuts', c.1, p. 29 and the charter of foundation of the Grand Hôpital of Huy in 1263 for 'les poevres et foibles gens qui sont membres du Christ', Van der Made, *Le Grand Hôpital de Huy*, p. 16. On the view of the Poor as lords see Schreiber, *Gemeinschaft des Mittelalters*, pp. 32–3.

[81] 'Ita scilicet quod fratres infirmi habeant domum sibi assignatam ubi carnes quibus uti possunt et quas appetant sibi ministrentur' (clause 8). The second Hospitaller rule of 1181 enlarges on the subject of treatment and expects doctors to be at the disposal of the sick, *Statuts*, c.2, p. 12.

[82] CUL. EDR. Register Fordham, fol. 218v.

have eaten meat only on these days if we may judge by the hospital's kitchen accounts for 1343–4 which record purchases of meat only on two, three or four days a week. Since other perishables such as butter and fish were bought daily, one may assume that meat was not served as frequently at the hospital table. Neither did meat appear during Lent, except for one case when it may have been bought specially for an inmate.[83] There appear to have been distinctions between foods served to different members of the house.[84] In Thomas Tuylet's corrody of 1260 × 70, the daily foods mentioned were to be of the quality given to *fratres capellani* or *fratres presbiteri*.[85] The corrody included daily rations of bread, beer and a hot dish of meat or fish.[86] Correspondingly, the kitchen accounts of 1343–4 contain many entries for the purchase of eggs, milk and butter, fresh foods with high protein content.

The rule mentions the kindly attention which must be given to the inmates' comfort through supervision of their food and bedding (clause 14).[87] The Hospitaller rule actually states that the beds should be of commodious size and that clean sheets and blankets should be supplied.[88] Two donors to the hospital granted rents for the provision of beds and beddings. One of them, Harvey Dunning, mayor of Cambridge, granted some land in Chesterton in 1210 × 35: 'to maintain two beds in linen and woollen beddings for the use of the sick'.[89] The rule of the Order of the Holy Spirit devoted a whole chapter to the description of the inmates' clothes.[90] The inspiration may

[83] SJCA. Cartulary of HSJC, fols. 89–90, see fol. 90r (for 3 April 1344). In the rule of Dudston hospital (Gloucs.) the community was similarly allowed to eat meat on Sunday, Tuesday and Thursday, Kealey, *Medieval medicus*, p. 201. For the components of the diet at the Holy Spirit hospital in Marseille in 1409–10 see B. Benassar and J. Goy, 'Contribution à l'histoire de la consommation alimentaire du xive au xixe siècle', *Annales* 30 (1975), pp. 402–30; p. 410: mainly bread, meat, fish and cheese.

[84] The statutes of the hospital of Angers required that the sick eat before their servitors, and that their fare be as good as that of the brethren, *Statuts*, c.9, pp. 24–5.

[85] SJCA. Cartulary of HSJC, fol. 80v.

[86] The hospital at Enköpig near Uppsala supplied a variety of ales, meat and dairy produce and breads according to the season, Richards, *The medieval leper*, c.2, p. 137. The lay brethren and servitors would have had some inferior fare, which explains the clear definition by the corrodarian of his status as that of a chaplain.

[87] In Ely an identical demand was made of the sacrist who supervised the hospital for the see.

[88] *Statuts*, c.3, p. 13. At St Thomas's hospital, London, the inmates slept on piles of straw, E. M. McInnes, *St. Thomas's hospital* (London, 1963), p. 17.

[89] 'Ad sustendandum ii. lecta in opus infirmorum in pannis lineis et laneis imperpetuum', SJCA. Cartulary of HSJC, fol. 69v. In the acknowledgement of its obligation in return, master Anthony reviewed his duty to provide two beds (*grabata*) and coverlets, Merton College Charters, M1558. The other, Stephen of Hauxton, granted a rent for the purchase of beddings (sheets–*lintheamina*) for two beds in the hospital, SJCA.D20.55.

[90] They were to be changed every season and to be identical for all inmates: *Liber regulae sancti spiritus*, c.39, p. 163.

lie not only in the need to maintain special standards of hygiene in a hospital, but in the Augustinian rule which ordered cleanliness of body and of clothing. The statutes of St Laurence's hospital at Canterbury demanded monthly washing of clothes and fortnightly washing of heads, so as to avoid unpleasantness to the inmates, and in the HSJC accounts of 1505–10, wages for a laundress are regularly recorded.[91] Hospital inventories usually record a variety of sheets, covers, hangings, pillows and blankets.[92]

Fuel was provided by the grant of Bishop Eustace of two boat loads of reeds and other fuel materials from the episcopal marshes.[93] Some donors provided sources of income for the upkeep of lights in the inmates' quarters. Hugh of Barton gave a messuage in Newnham 'for the illumination of the infirm'.[94] A rent of 4s owed by the hospital was remitted in return for maintenance of lights for the sick.[95] The lights were for the patients' comfort and part of the vigil kept at night in some hospitals.[96]

The rule provides no more information about the lives of the HSJC inmates. Their numbers are not known, nor their identities, ailments or the treatment they received. In a letter of 1245 from Pope Innocent IV to HSJC, the endowment was confirmed for 'the relief of poor scholars and other miserable people'.[97] Like the hospital of St John, Oxford, it was stated that the house was meant to tend to sick poor scholars.[98] This may indicate that scholars were occasionally among the hospital inmates, as may be expected in a university town.[99]

---

91 Verheijen, *La règle de Saint Augustin* I, V–4, p. 431; CUL. Add. 6845 (rule of St Laurence's), fol. 6v. A rare glimpse into the sanitary arrangements of a medieval hospital is gained by Mr T. Tatton-Brown's recent discovery of the eleventh-century privy at St John's Hospital, Canterbury. The hospital at Sherburn employed two washer-women to clean the heads of the members on Saturdays, to clean their clothes twice a week and to clean their utensils daily, Richards, *The medieval leper*, c.12, p. 127. See also the rule of a fifteenth century hospital, Coppin, 'Les statuts', c.19, p. 37. For HSJC accounts, see SJCA.D106.10, fols. 5r, 12v, 20r, 25v, 31v, 39r.

92 Caille, *Hôpitaux et charité publique*, pp. 183–6.

93 SJCA.D3.61.

94 SJCA. Cartulary of HSJC, fol. 27v., (1265 × 74). Also SJCA.D25.182.

95 SJCA.D19.150.

96 *Statuts*, c. 10 (Angers), p. 25, c.35 (Montdidier), p. 40.

97 'Ad sublevationem pauperum scolarium et aliarum miserabilium personarum', SJCA. D4.1.

98 *Cartulary of the hospital of St John* III, p. 8, Innocent IV's letter of 23 March 1246: 'ad sustentationem pauperum scolarium et aliorum miserabilium'.

99 On the connection between the hospital and scholars see below pp. 272–4.

The brethren

We know much more about the life of the religious community which administered the hospital both from the rule and from related documents. The opening clause of the rule draws a distinction between *fratres clerici* and *fratres laici*, the clerical brothers were named *fratres capellani* or *fratres presbiteri*. These terms are used interchangeably, and the corrody of Thomas Tuylet provided him with one white loaf as a *presbiter* received together with one gallon of beer like a *capellanus*.[100] Both groups were to sleep and eat together if circumstances allowed (clause 2).[101] The difference between lay and clerical brethren was maintained inside the house though outside all brethren appeared in an identical single-coloured habit.[102] In the Hospital of St John, Oxford, the habit was of russet or brown cloth with capes bearing a double cross over the breast.[103] However, the differences in rank were sometimes noted within the community by differing habits:[104] in Angers the colour of habit was determined by the office held by each brother, either white, black or red.[105]

In the privilege of Pope Innocent IV it was permitted that clerics and laymen wishing to join the hospital were to do so after sufficient proof had been given of their true conversion, and following confession.[106] Some hospital rules demanded a period of probation, as St Julian's near St Albans, and the French hospitals of Montdidier and Amiens.[107] In the hospital of St Paul at Norwich new brethren and sisters swore allegiance to St Paul and to the hospital and promised to obey the master. They then relinquished their property to the community and proceeded to kiss the other members and to take their place among them.[108] When hospitals depended on other houses an oath to the mother-foundation was sometimes sworn. Thus, the

---

[100] SJCA. Cartulary of HSJC, fol. 8ov.
[101] Identical provisions existed in the Hospital at Ely, CUL. EDR. Register Fordham, fol. 218r.
[102] Cloth of a single colour, as the Augustinian rule demands: 'Non sit notabilis habitus vester, nec affectetis vestibus placere sed moribus', Verheijen, *La règle de Saint Augustin* I, IV–I, p. 423.
[103] *Cartulary of the hospital of St. John* III, p. 5.
[104] In the Hospital of the Holy Cross, Stratford, a slight difference existed between the lay confraternity members who served and the chaplains, *The register of the gild of the Holy Cross*, p. vi.
[105] One tunic was provided yearly, *Statuts*, c.31, p. 27.
[106] SJCA.D4.1 (lines 182–3).
[107] Richards, *The medieval leper*, c.4, p. 129 (new statutes of 1344); *Statuts*, c.3, p. 36; 'Si quis ingredi in domum voluerit per annum probabitur in habitu seculari'.
[108] Carter, 'The constitution of the hospital of St. Paul', p. 352.

brothers of St Bartholomew's, Oxford, swore to Oriel College: 'to the provost and scholars of the house of the Blessed Mary, Oxford'.[109] The Hospital of St John at Oxford demanded six months' probation before acceptance, after which the following oath was taken: 'I profess to God almighty and St John, the patron of this church, to live honestly and chastely according to the statutes of this house, and to serve the poor as befits this house; so help me God and all his holy gospels'.[110] A grant made to HSJC from before 1260 was connected with entry to the religious community of the hospital. John, son of Adelard, gave the hospital a messuage in All Saints' parish, but he is already named *frater* in the document. This may relate to the order of admittance whereby after spending a period in the hospital, a brother was expected to relinquish his earthly goods.[111] Once within the community the new member was bound to obey the master in all matters according to the rule (clause 15) and to confess his sins to him alone (clause 17). There may have been some episcopal supervision of the admission of brethren, especially in the later years of the hospital.[112] In 1470 Bishop Gray granted a licence to the master of HSJC allowing him to admit William Colyn as a brother and permitting his progression in Holy Orders.[113] Like all late medieval religious houses HSJC provided titles, the formal promise of income, to ordinands.[114] This curious relationship must have benefited the houses financially since they granted the titles abundantly, and it has been suggested that this was a service to the diocesan officials rendered by local houses which examined the candidate's personal eligibility for ordination as well as his claim to a sufficient income.[115]

109 *Oriel College records*, p. 297.
110 'Profiteor Deo omnipotenti et sancto Iohanni, huius ecclesie patrono, me honeste et caste vivere secundum statuta istius domus, et pauperibus deservire ut decet in hac domo; sic Deus me adiuvet et omnia sancta eius evangelia' *Cartulary of the hospital of St. John* III, p. 3, the oath on p. 7.
111 SJCA.D17.53. Another grant, by Geoffrey of Ely (1220 × 40) was of 1½ acres in Cambridge fields 'pro fraternitate eiusdem domus', but this may mean entry to the spiritual fraternity of prayers, a common practice of religious houses, SJCA. Cartulary of HSJC, fol. 16v.
112 On the admission ceremony in the hospital of the Holy Cross, Stratford, *The register of the gild of the Holy Cross*, p. vi.
113 This may be due to William Colyn originating from a different diocese and the need for episcopal examination of letters dimissory, CUL. EDR. Register Gray, fol. 79v.
114 H. S. Bennett, 'Medieval ordination lists in the English episcopal registers', in *Studies presented to Sir Hilary Jenkinson*, ed. J. Conway Davies (London, 1957), pp. 20–34; pp. 26–31.
115 R. N. Swanson has recently suggested this understanding of the titles for ordination in R. N. Swanson, 'Titles to orders in medieval English episcopal registers', in *Studies in medieval history presented to R. H. C. Davis*, ed. H. Mayr-Harting and R. I. Moore (London, 1985), pp. 233–45, for earlier descriptions and discussions see R. K. Rose,

The brethren lived a communal life in one chapel, one dormitory and one refectory, though in smaller and poorer establishments where sufficiently large rooms were lacking separation might have been necessary. The rule of HSJC allows for this, and the brethren were to separate into groups of lay brethren and clerics if the need arose. This was a useful division which fell in with the different schedules followed by the two groups. The chaplains lived by the rhythm of canonical hours, and the lay brethren by the needs of their patients and domestic chores. Non-clerical brothers at St Bartholomew's Hospital, Oxford, were to be chosen according to their working skills, as ordained by the rule of 1316: 'a healthy brother strong and skilled in wainage will be admitted...and a healthy brother strong and able to work and tend the curtilages and to make roofs for houses will be received'.[116] The ideal of communal life is upheld by all hospital rules notwithstanding the different functions allocated to different groups of brethren. In mixed communities separate quarters existed by sex.[117]

The rule provided annual allowances for clothing and for other miscellaneous needs (clause 5). The master's was 40s per annum, a chaplain's, 20s, and a lay brother's 13s 4d. In all payments and provisions the master was to receive a portion double that of a brother-chaplain, except for food and drink which should be provided as befitted his status.[118] Most hospitals made annual provisions for shoes and cloaks, less frequently for boots and capes. Upon entry, a brother of St Mary Magdalene's in King's Lynn was given new clothes and shoes of decent and humble design and colour.[119] The corrody of Thomas Tuylet is again helpful: he was to receive the bread, beer and hot dish as mentioned above, and the pittances as distributed among the

'Priests and patrons', pp. 207–18. Hospitals were especially given to granting titles, perhaps due to the precariousness of their financial situation in the late Middle Ages and their relative autonomy, E. F. Jacob, 'Thomas Brouns, bishop of Norwich 1436–45), in *Essays in British history presented to Sir Keith Feiling*, ed. H. R. Trevor-Roper (London and New York, 1964), pp. 61–83; pp. 75–6.

[116] 'unus frater sanus et potens ad laborandum ac sciens de Waynagio admittatur...frater sanus ad laborandum potens sciensque facere curtilagium et cooperire domos recipiatur', *Oriel College records*, no. 333, p. 285. The hospital had only one clerical member, the master.

[117] In St Julien, Cambrai, there were 'refroitoir, dortoir et autres officines avoir di frere par yaus, et les seurs par elles', *Statuts*, c.3, p. 54. For Angers, *ibid.* c.25, pp. 26–7.

[118] As in Ely, where food consumption by the master was limited: 'Magister domus quoquomodo deputatus non se recipiat in camera singulari ad (sic) uberiis et delicacius reficiendum nisi infirmitate detentus', CUL. EDR. Register Fordham, fol. 218r. A general difficulty lies in the fact that when describing the members of a hospital medieval writers used the word *fratres* interchangeably for the regular community and for the group of sick, and in leper houses often to describe the lepers.

[119] *The making of King's Lynn*, pp. 106–7.

brethren.[120] In the Hospital of St Paul, Norwich, ½d was given to the brethren thrice a year on Christmas, Easter and on the Feast of the Purification.[121] The rule of St John of Jerusalem expected the brethren to ask for no more than 'bread, water and clothing',[122] yet pittances were an important part of regular life, a distribution which alleviated the rigidity and austerity of routine, when a treat was offered in food, clothing, candles or a few pennies. Special foods were distributed on feast days: beer was served at St Julian's Hospital near St Albans on all feast days and a pig was slaughtered on the Feast of St Martin.[123] The mere break in the regular life-cycle would have induced people to return to their duties with greater relish, it promoted fellowship and love, and thus can be seen as charitable in spirit.

An important part of the Augustinian way of life was the chapter, the meeting in which the community checked and corrected its members and discussed its affairs. The rule gives clear instructions about these meetings. There were to be weekly gatherings for correction and deliberation at a time most suitable for the brethren (clause 16). Twice or thrice a year the statutes were to be read aloud so as to remind all brethren of their obligations (clause 17). The Hospital of St Laurence, Canterbury, held a weekly meeting at which culprits were punished, as did the Hospital of St John, Oxford and the hospitals of Montdidier, Amiens and Cambrai.[124] Jacques of Vitry mentions these occasions as some of the basic characteristics of hospital life.[125]

The Augustinian rule relied on mutual correction and on strict internal discipline.[126] It was each brother's responsibility to admonish his fellow brethren and if necessary, to report their failings to the chapter.[127] In St Mary Magdalene's Hospital in Exeter (founded

120 Thomas Tuylet was a cleric and would receive the sums as brethren-clerics did; the pittances were distributed on thirteen feasts: All Saints' Day, Christmas, St John the Evangelist's feast, Circumcision, Epiphany, Purification, Annunciation, Easter, Ascension, Pentecost, Nativity of St John the Baptist, Assumption and Nativity of St Mary, SJCA. Cartulary of HSJC, fol. 80v.

121 On the latter, the pittances were given in wax candles, Carter, 'The constitution of the hospital of St. Paul', p. 350.

122 In the first rule, *Statuts*, c.2, p. 8.

123 Richards, *The medieval leper*, c.12, pp. 133–4. Clothes and shoes were distributed on feast days at Enköping hospital, near Uppsala, *ibid.*, c.3, p. 138.

124 CUL. Add. Ms. 6845, c.5, fol. 6r; c.25, fol. 7v; *Cartulary of the hospital of St. John* III, p. 6. Dudston hospital (Gloucs.) met in chapter on all feast days, Kealey, *Medieval medicus*, p. 201; cf. *Statuts*, c.39, p. 55.

125 Jacques of Vitry, *The 'Historia occidentalis'*, p. 147.

126 In the monastic tradition: *La règle de St. Benoît* II, ed. A. de Vogüé (Paris, 1971–2), c.23, p. 542.

127 Verheijen, *La règle de Saint Augustin* I, IV–8, pp. 426–7.

1451–2) offences against fellow brethren by word, deed or violence, were punished by seclusion in the stocks and periods of feeding on bread and water.[128] In St Bartholomew's, Oxford, brethren were expelled for recurrent sins of the flesh or violent behaviour.[129] The ordinances of Bishop Montacute for HSJC demanded that all things ordained by the chapter be kept secret,[130] while the rules of Montdidier and Amiens imposed excommunication on those revealing secrets from the chapter meetings.[131] Evidently, these gatherings were the heart and living conscience of the hospital community, guarding its administrative efficiency and moral standards.

The master

The master of HSJC, styled *prior*, *magister* or *custos* in contemporary documents, was the spiritual and temporal head of the community. The master was to hear the brothers' confessions and prescribe penance (clause 17), and all owed him complete obedience. The rule provided the master with an annual allowance of 40s and his provisions were double those of the brother-chaplains. The master's standard of living depended on the house's prosperity; the master of HSJC led a relatively humble life, but in some hospitals the masters maintained stables and a livery of servants.[132]

Innocent IV's letter of confirmation ordained that upon the death of a master the successor should be elected unanimously or by the majority of brethren, in accordance with the Augustinian rule.[133] The rule itself did not discuss this point, but normally in Augustinian houses election took place in the chapter house immediately after the funeral of the late prior. A committee of brethren dealt with the selection and pronounced it to the community who duly accepted the candidate.[134]

The responsibility and status of masters differed from one hospital to another. The master of St John's Hospital in Ely was subordinate to the priory sacrist and swore fealty to him;[135] in the mixed

---

[128] Richards, *The medieval leper*, cc.5, 6, 7, p. 140.

[129] *Oriel College records*, p. 299.

[130] SJCA.D4.1, lines 169–170.

[131] *Statuts*, c.25, p. 39: 'Qui secreta capituli revelare presumpserit, se super hoc convictus fuerit, excommunicatur'. At Exeter a brother who disclosed secrets from the chapter was fed bread and water for twelve days, Richards, *The medieval leper*, c.8, p. 140.

[132] A page of the master of HSJC is mentioned in the account of the episcopal household of Ely in 1383 during the episcopate of bishop Arundel, CUL. EDR. Roll D.8.

[133] SJCA.D4.1, lines 189–190.

[134] *Observances*, ed. and trans. Clark, p. xxxvi.

[135] CUL. EDR. Register Fordham, fol. 218r.

community of St Laurence's, Canterbury, there was a prioress at the head of the female group, but she seems to have been subject to the master, though both were nominated by the abbot of St Augustine's.[136] In the Hospital of St Paul, Norwich, the master was one of the monks of the cathedral priory.[137] At Bury St Edmunds the hospitals were totally attached to the founding monastery and were administered by its obedientiaries.[138] St Thomas' Hospital, Stamford, depended on Peterborough Abbey which supervised the allocation of revenues and the liturgical routine. In a house such as this the master could not alienate property, although he could protect it by representing the house in legal cases.[139]

The masters of HSJC (see appendix 2) were men of humble status who usually held no other benefice or ecclesiastical office. Of the 27 masters of the hospital only 3 can be connected with any other office. Hugh of Stanford who occurs in 1271 may be the same as Hugh Stanford the commissioner general of the bishop of Ely in 1261.[140] Geoffrey of Alderheath occurs as master in 1273, but was also rural dean of Cambridge and the vicar of St Sepulchre in 1273, when he acted as master in a tithe case.[141] Adam, a master in 1318, was also rector of St Michael's church.[142] No fourteenth-century masters appear to have been scholars of the university; they tended to be resident and to serve the hospital for fairly long periods. An exception is William Killum (master, January 1401–June 1403), of York diocese, who was a BA by 1390 and who seems to have served as master while awaiting a better benefice.[143] The house offered a very small income which did not attract men of high status or distinction.

Whatever the external and administrative responsibilities of the master, he was always the spiritual head of the community. He guarded

---

136 CUL. Add. 6845, fol. 7v, cc. 25–6.
137 Carter, 'Constitution', p. 350. The religious community was made up of priory monks who served in the hospital.
138 J. Rowe, 'The medieval hospitals of Bury St. Edmunds', pp. 258, 261.
139 *Visitations of religious houses in the diocese of Lincoln* I, ed. A. Hamilton Thompson, Lincoln record society (1915), pp. 117–19.
140 PRO. Assize Roll 84, m. 14; *Calendar of patent rolls 1258–66*, p. 455 and *Calendar of patent rolls 1266–72*, pp. 13, 190. Also A. B. Emden, *A biographical register of the University of Cambridge to 1500* (Cambridge, 1963).
141 SJCA.D3.65; *Calendar of the plea rolls of the Exchequer of the Jews* II, ed. J. M. Rigg (London, 1910), p. 29.
142 *Register of Thomas of Cobham, bishop of Worcester 1317–1327*, ed. E. H. Pearce, Worcestershire historical society (1930), p. 13.
143 Emden, *A biographical register*. He appears in a petition to Rome on behalf of Cambridge scholars in 1390, A. H. Lloyd, 'Notes on Cambridge clerks petitioning for benefices 1370–1399', *Bulletin of the Institute of Historical Research* 20 (1943–5), pp. 75–96, 192–211; p. 195.

the adherence to the hospital's rule, corrected lapsed members, led the liturgical routine and heard the brothers' confessions.[144] However, most autonomous hospitals elected their masters and their choice was brought to the patron or diocesan for confirmation. Periods of vacancy were seen to be detrimental to a hospital's welfare and swift action upon a master's death was recommended.[145] In the letters of admission to mastership issued by the bishops of Ely, the candidate's age, status, clerical order, character and legitimate birth were noted. Proposed candidates were examined before their institution.[146] In 1332, William of Cosefeld, master of HSJC, resigned his office to the bishop of Ely and the brethren proceeded to elect his successor from their number. The bishop accepted their nomination, relying on the community's candidate to be of suitable status and character.[147] In 1349, after the death of master Alexander Ixning, the brethren offered Robert Sprouston, who was a *frater presbiter*, formerly the cellarer,[148] to Bishop Thomas of Lisle.[149] Bishop Hotham's ordinance decreed that when no suitable candidate could be found among the brethren the hospital was to choose one of the brethren of the hospital at Ely.[150] Only when this failed did the right of presentation pass to the bishop.

The masters represented the hospital in legal matters and they were often named in grants and leases of hospital property; they appeared in law-suits involving the hospital; in the fourteenth century they sometimes nominated a *procurator* to represent the house in cases heard

---

[144] One of the *comperta* of the visitation by the keeper of the temporalities of the See of Ely in 1373 was: 'quod fratres non confitentur frequenter suo magistro iuxta ordinacionem regule sue...', CUL. Microfilm Ms. 1837, Register Whittlesey, fol. 153v.

[145] In the case of vacancy in St Giles's hospital, Norwich, the ordinances, confirmed in 1272, instructed the following procedure: 'Defuncto magistro et eius corpore tradito sepulture...per duos fratres nunciabitur...', NRO. 24/b/5. The prior of Norwich and the archdeacons of Norwich and Norfolk were to proceed to examine the candidate proposed by the brethren within three weeks.

[146] In 1374 following a mandatory letter from the bishop the Official of Ely examined Henry Brown, brother of HSJC, and subsequently installed him as master, CUL. EDR. Consistory court, Arundel, fol. 7r (1374).

[147] SJCA.D4.1 lines 104–120. For the admission of the new master Alexander Ixning on 20 February 1333, SJCA.D98.34.

[148] His name appears at the head of the kitchen accounts for 1343–4, SJCA. Cartulary of HSJC, fol. 89r.

[149] CUL. EDR. Register Lisle, fol. 20v.

[150] SJCA.D4.1, lines 58–71. See *The register of Henry Chichele* IV, pp. 322, 330 ordinations of masters at the time of vacancy of the Norwich see. See also the visitation of the keeper of the spiritualities of the See of Ely, Thomas Wormenhale, to the religious houses of the diocese, including HSJC, in 1373, CUL. EDR. Microfilm Ms. 1837, fol. 153v.; Aston, *Thomas Arundel*, p. 46.

outside Cambridge.[151] In 1294, the master Guy together with a brother of the hospital were charged with entry into a field in Newnham and seizure of chattels. They were represented by an attorney who claimed that the master had entered to distrain since the rent of the fees had fallen in arrears.[152] In the single register of the consistory court of the bishops of Ely (March 1374–October 1381) the hospital was named in three cases of testamentary administration.[153] He was presented by the jury of the Town Leet in 1502 for failure to maintain the pavement in front of the hospital and for digging a latrine in St John's Lane.[154] The master also represented the house and its appropriated parish of Horningsea in diocesan convocations.[155]

Most rules did not supply sufficient guidelines for control of hospital administration. This subject drew the attention of canonists in the fourteenth century and new decretals were formulated, among them the *Quia contigit* of Pope Clement V, which regulated hospital administration.[156] In a period when few new hospitals were being founded and existing ones drew few new donations, greater control was needed to ensure the survival of these houses. Masters were requested to render accounts at regular audits and more vigorous episcopal supervision was recommended.[157] The main problem was

---

151 This custom became general during the mastership of Robert of Huntingdon (*c.* 1260–1270). The hospital had two seals throughout the period of its existence: one which served it in the thirteenth and early fourteenth centuries, and can be seen on the following documents: SJCA.D25.32; Peterhouse muniments. Collegium. A3; Peterhouse muniments. Collegii Situs. A19: SIGILL' OPITALIS S' IOHÂNIS DE CÂTE and features an eagle supporting a cross between his wings. The later seal is inscribed: IN PRINCIPIO ERAT VERBUM and SIGILL' OSPITALIS S' IOHAN'IS DE CA'TE, and examples can be seen in CCCA.XXXI, 95 and CCCA.XIV, 64, featuring an eagle.

152 PRO. Assize Roll 84. Action was brought by 'Simon de Lenn versus magistrum hospitalis de placito capiendi catallas', for having seized a gate and a hurdle from the plaintiff. The master claimed a right based on his predecessor Nicholas who had leased the property which had fallen into arrears of 12d rent and some boon work, *Cambridge borough documents* I, pp. 3, 7. In SJCA.D98.4, D98.32, D26.132 the brethren appointed Master Burton to act as proctor in the case heard in 1279 in Huntingdon concerning the appropriation of the living of Horningsea.

153 CUL. EDR. Consistory court, Arundel, fols. 24r, 54v, 86r. Inmates and corrodarians left parts of their belongings to the hospital.

154 Cambridge Corporation archives, X, 72.

155 CUL. EDR. Consistory court, Arundel, fol. 4v (1374).

156 *Corpus iuris canonici* II, ed. E. Friedberg (Leipzig, 1879), Clementinarum Liber III, cc. 1170–1. The reason for this revision was: 'xenodochiarum, leprosorum, eleemosinariarum seu hospitalium rectores, locorum ipsorum cura postposita, bona, res et iura ipsorum interdum ab occupatorum et usurpatorum manibus excutere negligunt', col 1171. This canon was invoked in 1423 as the basis for the enforcement of episcopal supervision of the property of Brackley hospital (Lincs.) during a vacancy, *Visitations of religious houses* I, p. 11.

157 Tierney, *Medieval poor law*, pp. 86–7.

abuse of hospital funds through negligence, incompetence and corruption by masters who 'sinfully deflect those incomes to their own uses'.[158] The bishops of Ely fell in with these recommendations. The ordinances of Bishop Hotham dealt mainly with the process of election of the HSJC's master. Those of Bishop Montacute provided means of control over financial dealings of the master and other hospital officials. Accounts were to be presented to the community twice a year and money was to be kept in a chest under two locks to which the master and a brother held the keys.[159] Most masters remained in office until their deaths; only three resigned, two of them after a very short period, probably to take up better benefices.[160] In the last years of the hospital's existence the bishop of Ely still showed concern regarding the fulfilment of the master's tasks. On the occasion of the admission of the last master, William Thomlyn, Bishop Alcock provided some injunctions. The master was reminded to conduct the divine services personally, to supervise the temporal and spiritual government of the house, to enforce the statutes and to live a chaste life.[161]

Corrodarians

Besides clerics, lay brethren and inmates, a group of layfolk was often to be found in hospitals such as HSJC. These were people who were allowed to live within a religious house, monastery or hospital, in return for a gift or an expected inheritance. Corrodies became a common form of retirement insurance which greatly strained monastic finances.[162]

---

[158] 'proventus eosdem in usus suos damnabiliter convertentes', *Corpus iuris canonici* II, Clementinarum liber III, II, c.1170.

[159] SJCA.D4.1 lines 163–169. In St Mary Magdalene's hospital in King's Lynn a chest containing the seal, books, alms, accounts, vestments and relics were locked with three keys one of which the master held and two others were kept by healthy members of the community, B. Mackerell, *The history and antiquities of the flourishing corporation of King's Lynn in the county of Norfolk* (London, 1738), pp. 245–6; also in *The making of King's Lynn*, no. 84, pp. 106–8.

[160] In the hospital of St John, Ely, Master John Cardinal retired in 1391, CUL. EDR. Register Fordham, fol. 177; in St Mark's, Bristol the retired master was given two rooms, a servant and a maintenance allowance, *Cartulary of St. Mark's hospital, Bristol*, ed. C. D. Ross (Bristol, 1959), p. xix; see also *Cartulary of God's House, Southampton*, p. xix. For a discussion of a monastic arrangement of this kind, and the problems arising from it see A. Hamilton Thompson, 'A corrody from Leicester abbey, AD 1393–4, with some notes on corrodies', *Transactions of the Leicestershire Archaeological Society* 14 (1925–6), pp. 114–34.

[161] CUL. EDR. Register Alcock, p. 121 (19 November 1498).

[162] On corrodarians in hospitals see R. B. Dobson, *Durham priory 1400–1450* (Cambridge, 1973), p. 169. On corrodarians in monasteries see I. Kershaw, *Bolton priory. The economy of a northern monastery 1286–1325* (Oxford, 1973), pp. 134–6 and in friaries

Corrodarians planned to spend their last days within a religious community, participating in its religious life, sharing its merit and enjoying the provision of all their physical needs.[163] The entrant or his patron often granted a sizeable donation in perpetuity in return for sustenance until his death.[164] The corrody of Thomas Tuylet has been discussed above;[165] being a cleric, he may have joined in the community's liturgical life.[166] Another agreement of *c.* 1260 × 70 was that reached with Michael of St Benedict of Huntingdon who granted 8 acres in Cambridge fields. In return he expected to receive food in the hospital at the brethren's table whenever and as long as he stayed with them. He was also allowed to wear his secular clothing and to go in and out of the hospital on his business at will.[167] Michael granted the land for the soul of his uncle Robert who was probably Robert of Huntingdon, master of the hospital *c.* 1260–70, which may explain the unusual terms of the agreement by which Michael became neither lay brother nor inmate nor permanent corrodarian, but rather a paying guest within the hospital. Those in royal favour were often sent as pensioners to religious houses with royal connections.[168] In 1317, Hugh of Babraham was sent to retire in HSJC.[169] Townsmen who were patrons or business associates of the hospitals were likely candidates for corrodies. In 1375, John Seggeville, a prominent Cambridge burgess who had acted as feoffee for HSJC on various occasions in the 1350s,[170] died while 'staying at the hospital of St John, Cambridge, as its corrodarian'.[171] John's servant, Robert, remained in the hospital after

A. G. Little, 'Corrodies at the Carmelite friary of Lynn', ed. E. Stone, *Journal of ecclesiastical history* 9 (1958), pp. 8–29.

[163] For a typical example from a monastic community see Juliana Canon's will and the bequest for Ickleton priory, CUL. EDR. Consistory court, Arundel, fol. 86r (1377).

[164] See the case of John of Pakenham who granted 26 marks to St Saviour's hospital in Bury St Edmunds, and received food, a chamber in the house, clothes and shoes for the rest of his life, E. Rowland Burdon, 'St. Saviour's hospital, Bury St. Edmunds', *Proceedings of the Suffolk Institute of Archaeology and Natural History* 19 (1927), pp. 255–85; p. 271.

[165] See also pp. 161, 165–6.

[166] The widow M. joined St Giles' Hospital, Norwich in 1309 as a sister in return for a grant of some tenements, NRO. 25/310. On categories of corrodarians in the bigger religious houses see R. H. Snape, *English monastic finances in the later Middle Ages* (Cambridge, 1926), pp. 19, 139–47; Kershaw, *Bolton priory*, pp. 134–6.

[167] SJCA.D32.11.

[168] Hamilton Thompson, 'A corrody from Leicester abbey', pp. 121–2.

[169] *Calendar of close rolls 1313–1318*, p. 564 (29 August 1317). The name might explain the choice of Cambridge, perhaps Hugh still had relations in that village near Cambridge.

[170] See below p. 215.

[171] 'Commorans infra hospitale Sancti Iohannis Cantebrigie et corrodiarius eiusdem'; his will was inspected by the Official of Ely on 19 December 1375, CUL. EDR. Consistory court, Arundel, fol. 31r.

his patron's death and died there in 1378, when the master was nominated as his executor.[172] In 1378 a woman, Christine of Luton, was described as 'corrodarian and lodger in the house' despite the fact that it was a male community.[173]

Size of the community

What, indeed, was the size of the community? The rule suggests that the community was a small one.[174] The hospital of St John, Oxford was meant to consist of three brethren-priests, six lay brethren and six lay sisters.[175] In 1340 it had a master, seven sisters and nine brethren, while its rule is more elaborate than that of HSJC.[176] But besides the assumption based on impressions from the rule, what can we know of the size of the hospital?

The first list of hospital brethren appears in a letter of Bishop Hotham of January 1321 in which he confirmed the removal of excommunication from the hospital.[177] The master and five brethren are named, and when this was reconfirmed in December 1321 the same master and five brethren appear. But in a letter of 1323 eight brethren were mentioned besides the master; this must have included lay brethren.[178] In 1332, when the master William of Cosefeld resigned his office, four brethren proposed a fifth to the vacancy.[179] Thus, in the fourteenth century there were usually a master and five brethren-chaplains and perhaps the same number of lay brothers.

As it was everywhere, 1349 was a very bad year for the HSJC. After the death of Alexander Ixning, the five remaining brethren chose one of their number, Robert Sprouston, as master. Within a month Sprouston was dead and the four brothers presented Roger Broom to the mastership. By the end of another month Broom died, and the bishop of Ely was called to confirm a new election by the two remaining brothers and one addition to their company.[180] With sick and poor

---

172 Robert was described as 'perhendinans et commorans infra domum Sancti Iohannis', *ibid.*, fol. 97r (14 August 1378).
173 'corrodiaria et perhendinans infra domum', *ibid.*, fol. 97r (29 July 1378).
174 The elaborate rule of Angers was given to a hospital of ten clerics, ten lay brethren and ten lay sisters, *Statuts*, c. 15, p. 25.
175 *Cartulary of the hospital of St. John* III, p. xvii.   176 *Ibid.*
177 Excommunication was imposed in connection with a tithe dispute with Peterhouse. It was removed by the bishop of Tusculum SJCA.D17.73. The members are: John of Colonia (master), Michael of Melbourn, William of Eversden, Robert Beche, Henry of Maddingley and Alexander Ixning. This dispute is discussed below pp. 196–8.
178 SJCA.D2.16.
179 SJCA.D4.1, lines 104–20.
180 The sad tale fills a whole side of a folio in CUL. EDR. Register Lisle, fol. 20v.

folk clamouring to receive help, infection risks in the hospital must have been high, and this may go some way to explain such mortality among its members.[181]

The Clerical Poll Tax of 1379 was a payment which was imposed on and exacted of every cleric, beneficed or living in a religious community, as well as from religious houses according to the size of their annual income.[182] In HSJC the tax collectors found a master and five brethren.[183] If the number of lay brothers − not noted in such a clerical tax − was at most the same as that of clerics then it would have been a community of 10–12 members.[184] In 1427 three brethren presented a candidate for institution and the same number elected John Dunham Jr to the mastership in 1458.[185] There were four brethren and a master at the presentation of 1474;[186] thus the community contracted only slightly in the fifteenth century.[187]

The hospital was a household which needed the services of domestic workers. On the dorse of a rental roll for 1343 there appears a list of payments of rents and stipends by the hospital.[188] This is the only evidence for general expenditure which has survived before the complete set of accounts for 1485.[189] Under the heading *stipendia famularum* one finds:

[181] In A. T. Luttrell, 'Los hospitalarios en Aragón y la Peste Negra', *Anuario de estudios medievales* 3 (1966), pp. 499–514, it is suggested that mortality during the Black Death among the brethren of the Order was much lower relative to the rest of the population since they received better medical attention, more hygienic conditions and better nutrition. These circumstances most probably did not apply to the small and rather poor hospital of Cambridge. On mortality of the poor inmates of a fifteenth century hospital see Neveux, 'La mortalité des pauvres', pp. 73–97.

[182] *Cambridgeshire subsidy rolls 1250–1695*, ed. W. M. Palmer (Norwich, 1912), pp. 143–64.

[183] *Ibid.*, p. 149.

[184] In St Giles' Norwich the rule provided for a master, four clerical brethren and four lay brethren, NRO. 24/b/1. It was common for monastic houses to have a number of lay brothers equal to that of the monks, D. Knowles, *The monastic orders in England* (Cambridge, second edn 1963), pp. 439–41. The apostolic number (12) was a choice favoured by founders of small religious houses. The hospital at Ely was supposed to sustain 13 (1 + 12) members, CUL. EDR. Register Fordham, fols. 218r, 219r, although it had a smaller endowment than HSJC, between £20 and £40, while HSJC was valued 'ultra £40'. The hospital at King's Lynn was founded in the twelfth century for twelve members and a master, *The making of King's Lynn*, pp. 106–7.

[185] CUL. EDR. Register Gray, fols. 29v–30v (22 February 1458).

[186] CUL. EDR. Register Gray, fol. 89v (28 December 1474). SJCA. Cartulary of HSJC, fol. 23v, 42v (1470).

[187] See below pp. 182–3.

[188] SJCA. Rental roll D2.2.3 dorse.

[189] SJCA.D106.9; Cartulary of HSJC, fols. 89–90. These kitchen accounts describe a period in which the hospital was, most probably, not housing many sick and poor. No additional knowledge on the number of inmates can be gleaned from them.

Item Andree cok	10s	0d
Item Willelmo clerico	6s	0d
Item Iohanni pastori	0s	6½d
Item Iohanni Malster	6s	0d
Item Iohanni Voneyer	1s	9½d[190]

Thus, the Hospital of St John paid £1 4s 2d to male servants who performed domestic chores. The wages are extremely low for some of the servants so they may have been living-in servants, or occasional workers. In 1485 the hospital community of the master, the chaplain of Horningsea and three brethren maintained a cook and his boy, a steward, a barber and an almsman.[191] Between 1505 and 1510, the hospital's last years, the house employed a cook, a steward, a launderer, the chaplain of Horningsea, the master and three brethren, an organ-player and maintained an almsman.[192] There were also two university masters in frequent residence and the Official of the bishop of Ely maintained rooms for use during his visits to Cambridge.[193]

There is no way by which one may assess the number of poor and sick who came to enjoy the hospital's relief. Occasionally there is mention of a great multitude of poor flowing to the hospital as in the grant by Roger Alemer *c.* 1249 'for the maintenance of the poor flowing there'.[194] But this may mean no more than that the hospital indeed functioned and received the poor.[195] Except for the short-lived Stourbridge leper hospital, which was in decay by 1250, and the later Hospital of Sts Anthony and Eligius, it was the only house in Cambridge or within 13 miles of it, the obvious place to which the Cambridge poor and sick, or the needy of its closest villages, would resort for help.[196] One Cambridge donor, Aze *ad oppodum* expected

---

[190] I have not been able to establish the meaning of the name or occupation of Voneyer (or Boneyer) in Middle English or in Old French dictionaries. In the fourteenth century Exeter College, Oxford, maintained a similar crew, A. F. Butcher, 'The economy of Exeter College, 1400–1500', *Oxoniensia* 44 (1979), pp. 38–54; p. 41.

[191] SJCA.D106.9, fol. 5r. The almsman's stipend was recorded as 'Iohanne Howlyn de domo elemosinario – 2s 6d' at four terms (in sum – 10s).

[192] SJCA.D106.10. This seems to have been the relic of the house's charitable obligation to the poor and sick.   [193] *Ibid.*

[194] 'Ad sustentationem pauperum ibidem confluentium', SJCA.D24.85.

[195] In an indulgence to those visiting the hospital chapel and offering alms of 1246–7 the bishop of Sta Sabina states that the house was poor on account of 'quod pauperibus et infirmis ad dictam hospitale confluentibus de propriis facultatibus nequeant eis necessaria ministrare', SJCA.D98.43, but this is a conventional description of religious houses needy of alms.

[196] Ely is 15 miles away. There were rural almshouses at Fordham (14 m) and at Stow (9 m). Anglesey hospital became a priory by 1220 × 5, see above pp. 135–8.

in return for his grant that one poor man be clothed and fed and kept in the hospital.[197] Harvey Dunning's grant was to supply for two beds and their linen.[198] One may assume that a dozen inmates would be a considerable undertaking for the community described above. In any medieval town the need for relief surely outstripped the succour offered by hospitals such as HSJC, even in the period when their charitable functions concentrated on the original task of relieving the poor and sick.

COMMUNAL LIFE

Within the hospital

Like other communities of Augustinian canons who provided the cure of souls, the brethren of HSJC lived in daily contact with lay society and its problems. Their rule attempted to shield them from these evil influences and to mitigate the danger posed by the world which they wished to serve. It is this awareness which inspired the adapters of St Augustine's rule for hospitals to insist that brethren never walk about towns alone but in pairs, and only in the pursuit of necessary business.[199] The rule of HSJC prohibited eating and drinking in town without licence (clause 11), while Ely's rule forbade visits to taverns and the playing of dice games.[200] The fear of contact with secular society lay at the bottom of these demands, and only brethren of suitable character were to fulfil the external ministries of the hospital (clause 12).

The brethren of HSJC were not allowed to hold property (clause 9); at St John, Oxford, no private property could be held, nor gifts received or handled.[201] All goods belonging to the sisters and brothers of St Laurence's, Canterbury passed to the ownership of the hospital. This insistence on lack of property is a basic characteristic of Augustinian rules and their derivatives. The Hospitaller rule demanded the triple oath of poverty, obedience and chastity.[202] If a brother was found to possess personal property, he would be made to fast for 40 days and be humiliated before the community.[203] If property was found after a brother's death, he was to be buried excommunicate. When this

---

[197] Around 1220 × 35, SJCA.D32.12.

[198] SJCA. Cartulary of HSJC, fol. 70r.

[199] Verheijen, *La règle de Saint Augustin* I, IV–2, p. 423.

[200] CUL. EDR. Register Fordham, fol. 218r. Prohibitions on eating and drinking in the town can be found in the rules of St John's Hospital, Oxford and St Laurence's, Canterbury, *Cartulary of the hospital of St. John* III, p. 5; CUL. Ms. Add. 6845, fol. 6r, c.7; as well as the hospital of Angers, *Statuts*, c.39, p. 29.

[201] *Cartulary of the hospital of St. John* III, p. 5.

[202] *Statuts*, c.1, p. 8. [203] *Ibid.*, c.13, p. 10.

happened in the hospital of Angers the culprit was buried outside the hospital's cemetery with no prayers or services.[204] Certainly the letter of some of the harsher measures was not applied, but the principle appears in HSJC's rule and is summarised in Jacques of Vitry's writing on hospital life: 'And they live according to the rule of St Augustine, without property and in common, in obedience to one head, and having taken the regular habit, they promise perpetual continence to the Lord'.[205]

A case heard by the Official of the bishop of Ely in 1380 reveals a divergence from the precepts which were meant to govern the life of this hospital community. William Potton, a *confrater* of HSJC who had professed to the rule of the hospital in the order of subdeacon, was discovered to have contracted marriage before his profession.[206] Agnes Knotte, a widow, brought charges against him in the consistory court claiming that marriage had been contracted between them clandestinely before his ordination. She demanded the annulment of William's profession which was made under false pretences.[207] Since William did not appear and Agnes' witnesses were found to be truthful, William was released from his religious obligations and was recognised as Agnes' lawful husband.

An important area of hospital activity was that of prayer and liturgical celebration. The rule of HSJC demanded that silence be maintained in chapel (clause 3), that all brethren–chaplains celebrate mass daily and that all brethren attend canonical hours, unless forced to be absent (clause 7). The whole community was to attend services together, unless they were busy at work or otherwise excused (clause 4).[208] The Hospital of St John, Oxford, demanded attendance at matins and at mass which were celebrated by the hospital's sacrist before the beginning of the day's business.[209] Jacques of Vitry observed that canonical hours could not always be attended as the brethren were often detained by chores and by the inmates' needs.[210] Some grants to HSJC mention its chapel. In 1279, Alan Det granted 2 acres 'for the

---

[204] *Ibid.*, c.22, p. 26.
[205] 'Vivunt autem secundum sancti Augustini regulam, absque proprio et in communi sub unius majoris obedientia; et, habitu regulari suscepto, perpetuam Domino promittunt continentiam', Jacques of Vitry, *The 'Historia occidentalis'*, p. 147.
[206] CUL. EDR. Consistory court Arundel, fol. 139.
[207] Aston, *Thomas Arundel*, p. 40.
[208] In the hospital of Angers, besides full daily offices, there was a daily meeting in the chapter house for the recitation of the *kalenda* in memory of benefactors and for the reading of the daily lesson, *Statuts*, cc. 1–2, p. 23.
[209] *Cartulary of the hospital of St. John* III, pp. 4–5.
[210] Jacques of Vitry, *The 'Historia occidentalis'*, p. 147.

maintenance of the light of St Mary in the said hospital's chapel where divine service is daily celebrated'.[211] In its chapel prayers were offered for the health of the souls of benefactors and dead brethren, exequies and anniversaries and chantry obligations were observed.[212] Some benefactors were buried in the hospital chapel; a brass which was moved from the old chapel to the modern one (now situated in the south wall of the organ chamber) can be related to Eudo de la Zouche, Chancellor of the University in 1380, 1382 and 1396–1400 who may have been a benefactor of the hospital, a protector or provider of University privileges.[213]

The old hospital chapel was later used by St John's College and existed until 1868 when it was demolished to make way for the new chapel.[214] The foundations of the old chapel can still be seen today on the north side of First Court. The chapel was well lit with windows suggesting Early English building and decoration;[215] in the second half of the thirteenth century it was redecorated and perhaps enlarged to accommodate the execution of its liturgical duties.[216] The existence of the chapel as the main hospital building was a characteristic of thirteenth-century hospitals such as St Mary's, Chichester, where one large hall, usually a chapel's nave, functioned as sick room with two

---

[211] 'ad sustentacionem luminis sancte Marie in capella predicti hospitalis ubi cotidie celebrentur divina', SJCA.D98.12. See also D24.7 and D24.8 for grants to sustain the chapel lights.

[212] An eighteenth-century copy of a list of benefactors exists in SJCA.D57.134. On prayers for benefactors see below pp. 184–92.

[213] See Emden, *A biographical register*; this influential man, who held tens of ecclesiastical livings in plurality, was buried in the hospital chapel in 1414, and can be identified by the family crest of La Zouche (see J. Woodward and G. Burnett, *A treatise on heraldry, British and foreign* (Edinburgh, 1892), plate XIX – Bezantes). However, there is no reason to believe that he was the master of the hospital, as assumed by the editors in *An inventory of the historical monuments in the city of Cambridge* II (London, 1959), pp. 190–1.

[214] Willis and Clark, *An architectural history* II, pp. 302–8 and a map on p. 240; C. C. Babington, *The history of the infirmary and chapel of the hospital and college of St. John the Evangelist at Cambridge* (Cambridge, 1874).

[215] For a sketch of the pattern which decorated the hospital hall's windows see M. Biddle, 'A thirteenth-century architectural sketch from the hospital of St. John the Evangelist, Cambridge', *Cambridge Antiquarian Society. Proceedings and communications* 54 (1960), pp. 99–108; pp. 100–1; drawing p. 102, reconstructed pattern, p. 105.

[216] A late thirteenth-century double *piscina* with intersecting blind arches very similar to the one found in Jesus College chapel (originally in the chapel of St Radegund's priory), has been preserved in the south wall of the chancel in the modern chapel, see N. Pevsner, *The buildings of England. Cambridgeshire* (Harmondsworth, second edn, 1970), p. 153. For some of the liturgical objects to be found in hospital chapels see the inventory of goods stolen from the hospital of St Mary Magdalene, King's Lynn, *The making of King's Lynn*, no. 476, pp. 429–30.

aisles of beds along the walls.[217] The inmates could lie in their beds while the chaplains celebrated in the chancel. To the north of the hospital's chapel (on the site of the modern chapel), there was another thirteenth–century building, the 'Labyrinth', a rectangular structure which was converted into students' quarters after the refoundation, and was torn down in 1863.[218] This was a multi–purpose hall in which brethren could have eaten, slept and conducted daily chores, in what was a well-lit chamber which subsequently accommodated three separate students' rooms. The chapel was often used by episcopal officials who held audiences there during their sessions in Cambridge throughout the fourteenth century,[219] but the hospital's buildings were not always kept in a proper state of repair. In 1341 Bishop Montacute allowed the master and brethren to celebrate divine office 'in some proper and decent place' in the hospital, outside the chapel.[220] One of the *comperta* of a provincial visitation in that year demanded the immediate repair of the hospital's buildings which were in a state of neglect.[221] Yet the hospital was considered to be a safe edifice; the proceeds of the royal subsidy of 1339–40 were deposited in HSJC for safe-keeping.[222]

Lay brethren were not expected to participate fully in the canonical hours and most hospitals made special provisions for them. At HSJC they were to recite the Pater Noster and the Ave Maria 20 times for matins, seven times for every canonical hour and once before and after their meals instead of grace (clause 18). In St Laurence's hospital, Canterbury, the lay brethren were expected to know the Pater Noster, Ave Maria and the Credo, and they recited 250 Pater Nosters (300 during Lent) and 50 Ave Marias daily.[223] At Barnwell priory the *conversi* said 13 Pater Nosters and 13 Ave Marias, a *gloria patri* and *sicut erat* for matins and vespers. For other canonical hours they said five

[217] For a plan of St Mary's, Chichester, see Godfrey, *The English almshouse*, fig. 3, p. 20 and for other examples, figs. 8–9, p. 25. See also C. Jones, 'The Hôtel-dieu of Beaune', *History today* 32 (1982), pp. 42–4, on p. 44.

[218] C. C. Babington, 'On some remains of the hospital of St. John the Evangelist at Cambridge', *Cambridge Antiquarian Society. Proceedings communications* 2 (1860–4), pp. 351–63; pp. 351–2; Willis and Clark, *An architectural history* II, pp. 296–302; Babington, *The history of the infirmary and chapel*, p. 6. On hospital architecture, see D. Leistikow, *Ten centuries of European hospital architecture* (Ingelheim, 1967) which includes many examples from England.

[219] Examples: CUL. EDR. Consistory court, Arundel, fol. 30v, 34v.

[220] 'in aliquo loco honesto et decente', CUL. EDR. Register Montacute, fol. 16r.

[221] CUL. Microfilm Ms. 1837, Register Whittlesey, fol. 153v.

[222] CUL. EDR. Register Montacute, fols. 51v–52r.

[223] CUL. Add. 6845, fol. 6r, c.1.

Pater Nosters and five Ave Marias, and the Credo was recited occasionally during the day.[224] Stronger inmates would have attended some of the hours; those who were bedridden could listen to mass when it was celebrated at the far side of the hospital building. In some of the houses of the Order of St John of Jerusalem a special prayer was led by one of the brethren for the benefit of the inmates who could not participate in the daily hours.[225] In the rule of the Hospital of St John, Oxford, the office of the sacrist, in charge of vestments, holy vessels, books and the proper practice of offices, is described.[226] Being a small community, HSJC had no such formal division of responsibilities in its rule.

The hospital possessed liturgical books as well as archival and scribal arrangements. The cartulary was drawn up in a fine thirteenth-century hand, and although it is not richly decorated it shows good workmanship and the use of good parchment. At the beginning of a sixteenth century terrier of St John's College one can see a page (43 cm × 21.5 cm) out of the hospital's book of ordinances.[227] This leaf contains three paragraphs (one of which is incomplete): a copy of Simon Montacute's ordinance of 1344; a statute concerning the exequies for dead brethren; a copy of the mutual agreement between HSJC and the Ely hospital for the celebration of masses for their members. The page is written in a fine fourteenth-century formal gothic hand and is decorated with blue and red initials. Such a book would have been kept in the chapel and its contents read aloud twice or thrice a year, and consulted more often. Parchment from the hospital's library seems to have found its way to the College archive, and the fragments of Augustine's *De civitate Dei*, and musical notes for the celebration of saints' days tucked into the binding of a sixteenth-century college terrier, bear witness to the hospital's liturgical and cultural activities.[228]

Many hospital rules mention reading aloud to the community during meals.[229] The statutes of St John's hospital, Brussels, were read to each

---

[224] The Augustinian canons at Barnwell had heavier liturgical duties than those of the hospital brethren-chaplains of HSJC, *Observances in use*, p. 24.

[225] K. V. Sinclair, 'The French prayer for the sick in the hospital of the Knights of St. John of Jerusalem in Acre', *Mediaeval studies* 40 (1978), pp. 484–8; p. 487, the text has been published in L. Le Grand, 'La prière des malades dans les hôpitaux de l'ordre de St.-Jean de Jérusalem', *Bibliothèque de l'Ecole des Chartes* 57 (1896), pp. 325–38.

[226] *Cartulary of the hospital of St John* III, p. 3.

[227] SJCA.D47.15.

[228] *De civitate Dei* lib. 17, c.5 in SJCA.D61.1–3.

[229] Verheijen, *La règle de Saint Augustin* I, III–2, p. 421. The rule of the hospital of St John, Ely, recommended study of scriptures, CUL. EDR. Register Fordham, fol. 218r; also *Statuts*, c.4, p. 23.

new member and explained in the vernacular,[230] as Jacques of Vitry observed that in hospitals 'they often make them recite readings from divine scripture while they feed their bodies'.[231] In some hospitals, edification was deepened by sermons preached to the *familia* and sometimes to the general public.[232]

Upon the death of one of the brethren the whole community attended his exequies and burial.[233] According to the statute in the leaf of the ordinance book, a chaplain would pray for the soul of the departed brother for a whole year after his death and such prayers were provided for *fratres capellani* and for *fratres laici*.[234] In an agreement between the HSJC and the Hospital of St John at Ely of 1343, it was arranged that whenever a *frater* or a *conversus* of either hospital died, each *frater capellanus* would celebrate three masses and each *conversus* would recite 30 Pater Nosters within 20 days of the notification of the death.[235] As in daily services the duties of lay brethren were different from those of the clerics, though the community prayed for its dead together: requiems and common prayer for the dead contributed to the community's cohesion. In St Mary Magdalene's at King's Lynn the dead brother or sister was dressed in the finest clothes and caps, candles were lit and beer was drunk by the surviving members of the community.[236] In the accounts of HSJC for 1485 some entries record expenditure on the funeral of Thomas Kyling: 3d were spent on ale, 12d on wax candles around the litter, and 2d on bread for distribution to the poor.[237] Inmates were buried in the hospital cemetery and a late mention of a tombstone erected for a poor man indicates that even when the hospital no longer housed sick people it was still seen as a suitable place for the burial of the poor.[238]

---

[230] *Cartulaire de l'hôpital St.-Jean de Bruxelles*, pp. 24–5.

[231] 'Lecciones etiam divinarum scripturarum plerumque, dum reficiuntur corpora, sibi faciunt recitare', Jacques of Vitry, *The 'Historia occidentalis'*, p. 147.

[232] An annual series of sermons was endowed in St Mary's hospital outside Cripplegate in the 1440s, Thrupp, *The merchant class*, p. 187.

[233] The burial site was probably across St John's street, near the churchyard of All Saints, an area shown in the Hammond plan of Cambridge of 1576. In a charter of 1249 describing the boundaries of a parcel of land in All Saints' parish the term 'novum cimiterium hospitalis' was employed, SJCA.D17.3. This may mean that the hospital expanded its burial ground granted by Bishop Eustace within 40 years of its ecclesiastical foundation.

[234] SJCA.D47.51, fol. 1r.   [235] SJCA.D3.64.

[236] Trentals were provided for the welfare of the departed soul, *The making of King's Lynn*, p. 107. At Sherburn hospital 300 Pater Nosters were said for 30 days in memory of a dead brother or sister, Richards, *The medieval leper*, c.19, p. 128.

[237] SJCA.D106.9, fol. 10r.

[238] SJCA.D106. 9 fol. 10r. On burial of poor folk in a French hospital see Neveux, 'La mortalité des pauvres', *passim*.

Relations with the university and scholars

Guests and corrodarians were expected to blend into the pattern of regular life of a religious house. However, the occurrence of paying guests in HSJC in the fourteenth and fifteenth centuries could not but have affected its character. Payments by guests amounted to £3 7s 9d out of a yearly total income of £66 0s 4½d in 1485. In that year, Masters Gegge and Pynchbek rented rooms in the hospital;[239] they and Master Guy paid commons for 17½, 8 and 8½ weeks in the hospital respectively.[240] The occurrence of such lodgers is connected with the house's entry into the University sphere, culminating in the assumption of University status *c.* 1470.[241] Like the colleges, the hospital was a house living under statutes which maintained a quasi-regular existence; it was founded by benefactors for the promotion of religion (through study or through charity) and was occupied with the commemoration of these founders. Its economic standing, as a separate corporation in the town, and the similarity in functions to the colleges, justified the grant of University privileges and autonomy for the furtherance and benefit of its endowment.[242]

The hospital was chosen as the abode of the scholars of the bishop of Ely in 1280.[243] A thirteenth-century privilege of the University of Cambridge benefiting the hospital, reveals the link with the University and student population at this early date. In 1292 Edward I renewed the privilege bestowed by his father allowing the chancellor and sheriff to try regrators and forestallers of foodstuffs; foods seized from these speculators were to be passed to the inmates and scholars of the Hospital of St John the Evangelist.[244] It may be that Henry III, wishing to bestow a favour on the community of scholars, favoured the hospital, which

---

[239] SJCA.D106.9, fol. 2v.

[240] SJCA.D106.9, fol. 4r, Master Guy and Master Gegge paid 1s 2d for a week's commons. The commons spent on the scholars of King's Hall in the years 1439–44 were: 1s 11d, 1s 5¾d, 1s 6d, 1s 4¼d, 1s 7¾d p.w. on average. A. B. Cobban, *The King's Hall within the University of Cambridge in the later Middle Ages* (Cambridge, 1969), facing p. 216.

[241] SJCA. Cartulary of HSJC, fol. 23v; there are also two partial copies of the privilege in fol. 42v, and fol. 80v. [242] They were removed in 1283; see below pp. 271–3.

[243] *Calendar of patent rolls 1292–1301*, p. 18. The Official of the bishop of Ely stayed in the hospital for a week in 1485, paying 10d for his stay. The existence of scholars in the hospital at an earlier date can be deduced from thirteenth-century privilege which was renewed on several occasions in the fourteenth: CUL. University archives *51 (1378): 'hospitali sancti Iohannis Cantebr' assignarentur et magistro hospitalis predicti ad sustentacionem pauperum scholarium et aliorum infirmorum hospitalis eiusdem' (also CUL. University archives *8(1293) and *14(1309) which are barely legible); *Calendar of patent rolls, 1307–1313*, p. 119 (1309); *Calendar of patent rolls, 1327–1330*, p. 60 (1327); *Calendar of patent rolls, 1377–1381*, p. 264 (1378).

in a town so densely populated with young clerics was bound to accommodate them at time of need.[245] It is most probable that University scholars took rooms in the hospital; in 1393 a papal pardon excused the hospital for various infringements of discipline and for non-payment of *salaria* of University masters.[246] This seems to indicate participation of the hospital in university privileges and enjoyment of services rendered by the University's officers. The hospital maintained links with university masters as tenants from the thirteenth century until the last years of its existence,[247] and with other colleges.[248]

Thus, the hospital housed a religious community, a group of passing sick and poor people, lay paying-guests and lay brethren and servitors who resided in the hospital fulfilling different tasks and roles. It proceeded from the care of the sick and poor and intercession for benefactors to a role increasingly confined to chantry services, and the maintenance of token almspeople and distributions. This change reflected the changes in the perception of charity and in the choices of contemporaries. In the particular case of Cambridge especially, the view of charity as possessing a strong liturgical and scholastic quality is not surprising. There were benefits to be gained from involvement in the University sphere, privileges and attraction of intercessory bequests. The hospital remained in the patronage of the bishop of Ely, who housed his officials there, and whose consistory court assembled therein. But in a town full of academic chantries, as the colleges can accurately be described, the charitable house of regular canons drifted more and more into the sphere of clerical, liturgical preoccupation, culminating in the refoundation as an academic college in 1509–11. The hospital related to the needs and exigencies of its surroundings; when its benefactors established it as a house of mercy it received the sick and poor, when they sought ordered intercession and elaborate funerals and exequies, these were developed within the hospital.[249] Thus, the history of the endowment and the changes of the hospital's functions within society can be sensitive indicators of changing ideas and expectations related to charitable giving.

[244] This was one of the many privileges granted to both Oxford and Cambridge: *Cartulary of the hospital of St. John* II, no. 936, pp. 408–9; 'prout huiusmodi victualia in villa Oxoniensi et extra taliter forisfacta hospitali sancti Iohannis extra portam orientalem... sunt assignata'; this is a confirmation by Edward III in 1378.

[245] Admittedly, the experiment had failed. See below pp. 271–3. [246] SJCA.D98.48.

[247] For example see SJCA.D106.9, fol. 2r, the leasing of St Clement's hospice to its warden.

[248] Mainly those in neighbouring parishes, see *ibid.*, for an example in the accounts of 1485.

[249] For examples of the flexibility and variety in the structure of small hospitals, see Guy, 'Of the writing of hospital histories', p. 415.

Chapter 6

THE RELIGIOUS AND ECONOMIC
FUNCTIONS OF THE HOSPITAL OF ST JOHN

As a charitable institution existing within a town, sustained by properties in it and by the patronage of burgesses, the hospital's fortunes were affected by the changes in the urban environment and the town's prosperity, its life-style and religious orientation and in attitudes towards charity entertained by townsfolk. Changes in the hospital's functions and services to society can thus betray shifts in the spiritual aspirations of the host community, and also help us reveal the objectives that houses like HSJC were expected to fufil.

CHANTRY SERVICES FOR BENEFACTORS

Religious houses induced and responded to patronage by offering a perpetual flow of prayer.[1] Theirs were the prayers of the ordained living a pure and rigorous life. Hospitals could additionally offer the grateful prayers of Christ's poor, and leper houses of those afflicted and humble. The expectation of spiritual reward did not diminish the penitential value of charitable acts. In a letter authorising collections of alms for hospitals Pope Innocent III explained this value:

Since, as the Apostle said, we shall all stand before Christ's tribunal, to receive as we had merited in life…we must anticipate the day of final harvest with works of mercy…And since the hospital's resources do not suffice for the brethren and poor flowing to it, we warn and exhort you all in the Lord, and enjoin for the remission of your sins, that you bestow some of the goods given to you by God to pious alms as charitable aid to them…so that you can arrive at eternal joy.[2]

---

[1] See above pp. 65–6 on the idea of purgatory and intercession; A. Hamilton Thompson, *The English clergy and their organisation in the later Middle Ages* (Oxford, 1947), p. 132: 'At the basis of all medieval pious foundations lies the idea of continual intercession for the living and the departed'.

[2] 'Quoniam, ut ait Apostolus, omnes stabimus ante tribunal Christi, recepturi prout in corpore gessimus…oportet nos diem messionis extremae misericordiae operibus praevenire,.. Cum igitur ad sustentationem fratrum et egenorum ad tale confluentium hospitale propriae non suppetant facultates, universitatem vestram

Charitable deeds were a form of earthly penance, as well as a means for mitigating purgatorial suffering. A flow of intercessory prayers between the quick and dead could also alleviate the sufferings of those languishing in purgatory.[3] Beginning in the twelfth century, charters of donation state this aim as 'pro salute anime mee et animarum antecessorum et successorum meorum' ('for the salvation of my soul and the souls of my ancestors and successors'), which became part of the legal formula not only of donation but of exchanges, sales and leases to religious houses.[4] A religious house was expected to reciprocate through the maintenance of a virtuous way of life and a fitting liturgy, and to dedicate a part of this routine to the commemoration of founders and donors. A more formal sharing of grace and spiritual benefits was created by spiritual confraternities, appearing from as early as the ninth and tenth centuries. These conferred a sort of 'brotherhood' upon the patrons and benefactors of religious houses, which spread the spiritual merit accumulated by the religious.[5] Similar links were formalised between hospitals and benefactors. In 1249, St Mary's Hospital in Chichester was given land in return for entry into the fraternity of its prayers.[6] In 1323, HSJC admitted to its community of prayers Bishop John Hotham of Ely who had undertaken some reforms of management in the hospital.[7]

A pious burgess of Cambridge could have chosen Barnwell priory, St Radegund's nunnery, various chapels, a leper hospital or HSJC as recipients of pious benefactions. From the second quarter of the thirteenth century the houses of mendicant orders, Franciscans, Dominicans, Carmelites – and not much later Crutched friars, Penitential friars and Austin friars – were added to the list of possible recipients.

monemus et exhortamur in Domino, atque in remissionem vobis iniungimus peccatorum, quatenus de bonis vobis a Deo collatis pias eleemosynas et gratas eis caritatis subsidia erogetis, ut…per haec bona et per alia..ad eterna possitis gaudia pervenire', *Corpus iuris canonici* II, x.5.38.14, incorporated in the Lateran IV canons, for which see *Conciliorum oecumenicorum decreta*, pp. 230–71.

[3] As phrased by Thomas Aquinas: 'Caritas, quae est vinculum uniens membra Ecclesiae, non solum ad vivos se extendit, sed etiam ad mortuos…; caritas enim vita corporis non finitur', *Scriptum in quatuor libros*, D.45 q.2 a.1 qu.2. J. Ntedika, *L'évocation de l'au-delà dans la prière pour les morts. Etudes de patristique et de liturgie latines* (Paris, 1971), pp. 114–25.

[4] For a discussion of these phrases in early charters of donation see *Early Yorkshire charters* IV, ed. C. T. Clay, Yorkshire Archaeological Society. Record ser. extra ser. 1 (1935), pp. xxvii–xxx.

[5] The earliest confraternity of this type dates from *c.* 810 in St Gall, E. Bishop, *Liturgica historica* (Oxford, 1918), pp. 346–69; Clark-Maxwell, 'Some letters of confraternity', *Archaeologia* 75 (1926), pp. 19–60 at p. 57.

[6] 'The cartulary of St. Mary's hospital, Chichester', ed. A. Ballard, *Sussex archaeological collections* 51 (1908), pp. 37–64; no. 24, pp. 48–9.   [7] Bodl. Charters Cambridge 31.

Hospitals were usually fairly new foundations in the late twelfth and early thirteenth centuries; they enjoyed greater favour and excited more interest than the old religious houses.[8] In them lived a community of religious with a group of inmates ensuring the existence of proper liturgical observances together with the merit of continuous works of mercy.[9] Thus in addition to a liturgical routine they could ensure that gift and bequests reached the poor.[10]

HSJC remembered all benefactors, but some were especially honoured. An eighteenth-century copy of a list of benefactors was entitled: 'These are the names of the founders and other benefactors of this house for the souls of whom the master and brethren have specially undertaken to pray'.[11] It comprises Eustace, bishop of Ely, Robert and Thomas Mortimer whose estate in Newnham was a part of the original endowment, and some thirteenth- and fourteenth-century burgess donors, as well as three knights from Cambridgeshire. Some male donors were enrolled with their wives. In the early fifteenth-century rule of the Hospital of St John, Ely, confirmed by Bishop Fordham in 1407, it was laid down that daily remembrances be made for the bishop, prior and convent of Ely and all benefactors of the hospital.[12] The hospital also interceded for its dead members and for the dead of related religious houses, primarily those of the hospital at Ely.[13]

Various arrangements were devised in the quest for intercessory prayer, from the foundation of a perpetual light at an altar to the institution of an annual obit, or a full perpetual chantry.[14] Hospitals functioned as intercessors and combined 'a disciplined programme of intercession with the relief of the poor'.[15] Some of these forms existed

---

[8] S. Raban, *The estates of Thorney and Crowland: a study in medieval monastic land tenure* (Cambridge, 1977), pp. 33–6; P. D. Johnson, *Prayer, patronage and power. The abbey of La Trinté, Vendôme, 1032–1187* (New York, 1981), p. 86.

[9] On the influence of intercessory obligations on a religious community see J. Dubois, 'Les moines et la société du moyen-âge', *Revue d'histoire de l'église de France* 60 (1974), pp. 5–37; pp. 29–33.

[10] R. C. Trexler, 'Death and testament in the episcopal constitutions of Florence (1327)', in *Renaissance studies in honor of Hans Baron*, ed. A. Molho and J. A. Tadeschi (Florence, 1971), pp. 29–74; pp. 52–3.

[11] 'Haec sunt nomina fundatorum et aliorum benefactorum huius domus pro quorum animabus magistri et confratres...specialiter orare tenentur', SJCA.D57.13.

[12] CUL. EDR. Register Fordham, fol. 218.

[13] On obits for dead brethren see SJCA.D3.64 and above p. 181. Barnwell priory and Colchester priory had similar reciprocal agreements, *Liber memorandum*, p. 219.

[14] A. Kreider, *English chantries: the road to dissolution* Cambridge, Mass. 1979), pp. 5–8; K. Wood-Legh, *Perpetual chantries in Britain* (Cambridge, 1965) is the basic general survey of English chantries.

[15] Kreider, *English chantries*, p. 64. Hospitals are seen as 'super chantries' by Rosenthal, *The purchase of paradise*, p. 69.

within HSJC, the earliest being the donation by Eustace, son of Harvey Dunning, around 1230 × 50, which was to provide for an observance of an obit to be celebrated in its chapel by one of the brethren: 'one of our own brethren-chaplains within the confines of our house at Cambridge'.[16] The bishop of Ely was chosen to supervise and implement the terms of the agreement by which, in 1290, Sir John Lovetoft of Horningsea ordered his exequies and those of his wife to be observed: 'and additionally the same master and brethren…are bound to celebrate annually the anniversary of lady Margaret my late wife…and to celebrate my anniversary after my death'.[17] Observances of obits were often coupled with the distribution of food or money to the poor. As we have seen, in 1323 Mary of Bassingbourn instituted at the Hospital of St John, Ely a yearly obit for herself and her two late husbands, combined with 144 poor.[18]

Another form of intercession was established by the more formal creation of a chantry in a church or chapel served by an incumbent with set personal duties.[19] Two such institutions were founded by Cambridge burgess benefactors of HSJC before the end of the thirteenth century. In both cases the patrons chose not the hospital's chapel but a parish church as the location of their chantry, perhaps because the hospital's chapel was too small for its many functions as well as for private altars.[20] In 1265 × 79 William Tuyllet and his wife

---

[16] 'unum capellanum fratrum nostrorum capellanorum infra limites domus nostre de Cantebrigia', SJCA.D.25.51. Eustace gave 25½ acres of land in Madingley 'ad sustentacionem unius capellani qui celebrabit divina imperpetuum pro anima mea et patris et matris mei et omnium antecessorum et successorum…'. A similar arrangement was devised in St John's hospital in Bath to which, about 1256, a chaplain granted much land, rents and a cash sum for the maintenance of another chaplain in the hospital, 'Deeds of St. John's hospital, Bath', ed. B. R. Kemp, *Somerset Record Society* 73 (1974), no. 37, pp. 29–30. Chantry services were provided by St Mary's hospital, Chichester as well, as early as 1241, see 'The cartulary of St. Mary's hospital, Chichester', ed. Ballard, nos. 36–8, pp. 52–4, for a chantry founded by a widow for her late husbands. An institution of a trental by a widow for her late husband was created at New Romney hospital, Kent, in 1278, A. F. Butcher, 'The hospital of St. Stephen and St. Thomas, New Romney – the documentary evidence', *Archaeologia Cantiana* 96 (1980), pp. 17–26; p. 20.

[17] 'Et insuper predicti magister et fratres…tenentur annuatim ad celebracionem anniversarie domine Margarete quondam uxoris mee defuncte,…Et post decessum meum ad celebracionem anniversarii mei', SJCA.D98.11.

[18] Clare College muniments, above, p. 133.

[19] For some ideas on the relations between chantry chaplains and parish priests in the later Middle Ages see C. Burgess, '"For the increase of divine service": chantries in the parish in late medieval Bristol', *Journal of ecclesiastical history* 36 (1985), pp. 46–65.

[20] For the size of HSJC's chapel see above pp. 178–9. For an example of involvement of hospital chaplains in external chantry duties see E. E. Williams, *The chantries of William Canynges in St. Mary Redcliffe, Bristol* (Bristol, 1950), pp. 15–16.

Avicia (who outlived him) established a chantry service of daily prayer by a brother of HSJC in St Mary's chapel in Holy Sepulchre's church, for which they granted 15 acres in Cambridge fields and two messuages in St Sepulchre parish.[21] John Shelford instituted a chantry in St Sepulchre; the properties which provided for the maintenance of a chaplain, a shop in St Clement's parish and land in the Cambridge fields, appear in the hospital's earliest rental.[22] On 4 December 1318, Thomas of Chobham, bishop of Worcester, dedicated three altars in the HSJC which were probably related to commemoration arrangements.[23]

The next chantry foundation was one in St Botolph's church for which a licence in Mortmain was granted in 1392.[24] Four Cambridge burgesses were allowed to alienate to the hospital 4 acres 3 roods of arable land, 6 acres of meadow in Cambridge, Coton and Chesterton in return for the maintenance of daily prayers by one of the hospital's brethren. In 1477, Pope Sixtus IV ordered the archdeacon of Ely to examine a petition by HSJC for the removal of the chantry from St Botolph's church to the hospital's chapel.[25] A similar change was authorised by the bishop of Lincoln in 1432, allowing St John's Hospital, Northampton, to replace a maintained chaplain by the services of a hospital brother.[26] By the fifteenth century hospitals were encountering increasing difficulties in maintaining their external intercessory commissions.[27]

Chantry foundations were especially numerous in the fourteenth century,[28] generating a great demand for chantry chaplains, a role

---

[21] SJCA.D3.65. SJCA D20.30. William's son Thomas entered the hospital as a corrodarian before 1279, SJCA. Cartulary of HSJC, fol. 80v.

[22] SJCA.D2.2.2–5; also in two arrears lists D2.3.1. for 1361–2 and D2.3.4 for 1371–2.

[23] *Register of Thomas Cobham*, p. 13.

[24] *Calendar of patent rolls, 1391–6*, p. 99. Copy of the agreement with HSJC in SJCA.D2.18.

[25] *Calendar of papal letters* XIII, 2, pp. 614–15.

[26] The reason given is 'terra et tenementa...ad onus antedictum supportandum non sufficiunt illo modo', *Visitations of religious houses* I, p. 95. In many Norwich chantries the original number of chantry chaplains was reduced in the late fourteenth and fifteenth centuries, Tanner, *The church in late medieval Norwich*, pp. 93–4.

[27] In 1485 the master was paid 12d for the celebration of the exequies of Henry Somer, a Cambridge burgess, SJCA.D106.9, fol. 5r. For the terms of some thirteenth-century chantries maintained by chaplains living as corrodarians in Barnwell priory see *Liber memorandorum*, p. 97.

[28] See the example of York, R. B. Dobson, 'The foundation of perpetual chantries by the citizens of medieval York', *Studies in Church history* 4 (1967), pp. 22–38; p. 28; For the same situation in Bristol see *Cartulary of St. Mark's hospital*, p. xviii. However, the number of chantries in St Paul's Cathedral had declined in the late fourteenth century, C. N. L. Brooke, 'The earliest times to 1485', in *A history of St. Paul's cathedral*, ed. W. R. Matthews and W. M. Atkins (London, 1957), pp. 1–99, 361–5; pp. 75–6,

which hospital brethren often fulfilled.[29] The greatest occurrence of licences in Mortmain for the foundation of chantries appears between 1300 and 1330, though these figures may exaggerate the rate of growth since our evidence increases dramatically in the period after the Statute of Mortmain's promulgation in 1279.[30] Hospitals were usually the choice of townsmen while ecclesiastical dignitaries, noblemen and knights founded collegiate chantries.[31] In York intercessory arrangements by townsmen existed, but at the beginning of the thirteenth century only 3 out of 38 chantries in the Minster were founded by them. They preferred to endow 39 chantries in 19 parish churches, the majority of which were founded in the late thirteenth and fourteenth centuries.[32] In Norwich the laity clearly preferred the foundation of chantries in the framework of their gilds, or individually in parish churches, hospitals and collegiate churches. Not one burgess foundation was made in Norwich Cathedral, which abounded with the chantries of bishops and of members of the nobility and of the gentry.[33] Later in the fourteenth century, the creation of chantries spread from the urban patriciate to humbler townsmen.[34] Chantries in parish churches and in institutions which were seen as burgess foundations expressed the

---

362. On urban chantries see also R. Hill, "'A chaunterie for soules": London chantries in the reign of Richard II', in *The reign of Richard II: essays in honour of May McKisack*, ed. F. R. H. Du Boulay and C. M. Barron (London, 1971), pp. 242–55.

[29] Kreider, *English chantries*, pp. 71–8. On the problems of recruitment of chantry priests see R. N. Swanson, 'Universities, graduates and benefices in later medieval England', *Past and present* 106 (1985), pp. 28–61; pp. 38–9. The demand for chantry priests must have been great, despite complaints and petitions for livings in the later fourteenth century; a cantarist's living was usually only the beginning of a clergyman's career while he was waiting for a living (or a retirement post). On the pressure for livings in the late Middle Ages see E. F. Jacob, 'Petitions for benefices from English universities during the Great Schism', *Transactions of the Royal Historical Society* 27 (1945), pp. 41–59; *idem*, 'On the promotion of English university clerks during the later Middle Ages', *Journal of ecclesiastical history* 1 (1950), pp. 172–86. See K. Guth, 'Spitäler in Bamberg und Nürnberg als bürgerliche Sozialeinrichtungen der mittelalterliche Stadt', *Jahrbuch für fränkische Landesforschung* 38 (1978), pp. 39–49; p. 44.

[30] Kreider, *English chantries*, pp. 72–6. In Cambridge there were fourteenth-century chantries in St Mary's church, *Calendar of patent rolls 1301–1307*, p. 466 (1306) and *Calendar of petent rolls 1334–1338*, p. 488 (1337); in St Clement's, a chantry for two chaplains, *Calendar of patent rolls 1321–1324*, p. 290 (1323). See the case of Bristol in E. E. Williams, *The chantries of William Canynges in St. Mary Redcliffe, Bristol* (Bristol, 1950), p. 18.

[31] For examples of merchants' chantry foundations in a hospital see *Cartulary of God's House*, p. xviii.

[32] Dobson, 'The foundation of perpetual chantries', pp. 23, 25–6, 33–4.

[33] Tanner, *The church in late medieval Norwich*, pp. 97–8; on the chronology of foundation see appendix 10, pp. 212–19.

[34] Who often arranged their intercession through the services of a gild or religious fraternity, Owen, *Church and society*, p. 95.

considered choice of townsmen and the range of their financial resources. In the Minster full of great names, theirs might be a humble foundation, whereas amongst their fellows a more meaningful self-display could be achieved while a greater involvement and supervision could be maintained by friends and relatives.[35] In Cambridgeshire too we find humble personal chantries in the rural parishes. Adam Cam's foundation was created *c.* 1300 in the church of All Saints in Long Stanton 'for the use of one chaplain celebrating forever'.[36]

The development of external chantry obligations could not but affect the internal structure of charitable houses. In 1400 an ordinance of Bishop Fordham's tried to regulate the compensation granted to brethren–chaplains of HSJC.[37] In order to preserve the proper execution of intercessory obligations in St Sepulchre and St Botolph's churches (Tuyllet and Morreys chantries) he ordered the division of 40s between the cantarists on top of the ordinary allowances to brethren–chaplains in the hospital.[38] In this period when £5 to £5 6s 8d was a good annual wage for chantry priests the hospital brethren in external chantries were doing well at £3 with no household expenses.[39]

Hospitals not only received commissions for intercession but were sometimes deliberately transformed into houses providing prayers.[40] The hospital of St Mary at Botham near York was refounded in 1330 to accommodate a master, two chaplains, six poor chaplains and a clerk.[41] The poor chaplains were recipients of charity who would pray effectively for the founder while the master and chaplains were first and foremost cantarists for the benefit of his soul. From yet another glance outside Cambridge, at the Kent Chantry Deeds collected for the 1536 Chantry Act, we find that out of 115 chantries 15 were in hospitals

---

[35] Cf. Cambridge, in the year of the foundation of the HSJC chantry in St Botolph's church (1392) a chantry was founded in St Clement's church by a group of burgesses *Calendar of patent rolls 1391–1396*, p. 139 (copy in Cambridge Corporation archive P27/28(8)); St Mary's hospital, Chichester attracted a chantry foundation for two chaplains from the gild of St Mary, *Calendar of patent rolls 1348–1350*, p. 12.

[36] For which he granted two messuages, Bodl. Gough Cambridge 20, p. 600.

[37] SJCA.D98.2: 'confratres...in dictis canteriis celebraturi...in recompensationem laborum de fructibus...dicti domus...quadraginta solidos annuatim...tantummodo dividendos ultra stipendium'.

[38] For a discussion of aspects of cantarists' life see Kreider, *English chantries*, pp. 19–33.

[39] C. Burgess, '"For the increase of divine service": Chantries in the parish in late medieval Bristol', *Journal of ecclesiastical history*, p. 50.

[40] St Giles' hospital, Norwich was practically a college of secular priests in the late Middle Ages, Tanner, *The church in late medieval Norwich*, pp. 132–3.

[41] *Early Yorkshire schools* 1, pp. 33–8.

at the eve of the Reformation.[42] Many donors expected in return merely a commemoration in the daily prayers of the brethren and poor, together with other benefactors.

HSJC existed in the midst of a university town with many academic colleges, which can be justly titled 'academic chantries', their *raison d'être* being the commemoration of the founder and benefactors.[43] The earliest chantry in Cambridge was founded by Bishop Kilkenny of Ely in 1257 for the maintenance of two chaplain-scholars of the University for celebration in his memory in St Mary's. The endowment of 200 marks was entrusted to Barnwell priory which was to pay the chaplains' annual stipends.[44] The colleges and the religious houses could offer similar intercessory services. Apart from Corpus Christi, the colleges attracted little patronage from townsmen.

All chantry founders were concerned to secure the continuation of services after their death, for a number of years or even in perpetuity. Rivalry between religious houses providing similar services was exploited to ensure proper future fulfilment of the chantry arrangement. The tenements given by Edith Chamber in 1497 for the foundation of an obit in Michaelhouse were to pass to HSJC in case of neglect.[45] Prominent townsmen entrusted the execution of their obits to the town.[46]

The choice of house in which one entrusted the welfare of one's soul reflected an evaluation of the function of the recipient and of the amount of funds available. We have seen that hospitals were called to supply individual chantry services, obits, special commemorations and membership in its spiritual community. These are prevalent forms of intercession in which even humble people could find an answer to their anxiety for the welfare of their souls. The considerations which

---

[42] Chantries in 15 of 32 hospitals, *Kent chantries*, ed. A. Hussey, Kent Archaeological Society. Records Branch Kent Records 12 (1936).

[43] Brooke, 'The churches of medieval Cambridge', pp. 49–76; pp. 61–4.

[44] The priory neglected its duties which gave rise to a dispute recorded in *Liber memorandum*, pp. 94–6.

[45] SJCA.D20.61.

[46] The fifteenth-century account rolls show the annual expenditure on the exequies of dead burgesses. The Treasurers' account rolls for various years in the second half of the fifteenth century show regular expenditure on obits of prominent burgesses. In years 1423–4/1427–8, 1431–2, 1433–4/1435–6 the obit of John Harrys was celebrated, Cambridge Corporation archives x, 70, 1–x 70, 10. In years 1483–4/1485–6 and 1488–9/1490–1 the town arranged the obits of John Harrys and Thomas Jakenett, Cambridge Corporation archives, x, 71, 1–x, 71, 6; and in years 1493–4 and 1498–9 the obits of John Harrys, Thomas Jakenett and John Erlich were observed and incurred the expenditure of £1 14 5. Cambridge Corporation archives x, 71, 7–x, 71, 8. Five

motivated foundation of obits and personal services were the same as attracted the multitude of donations to the hospital, though in the fourteenth and fifteenth centuries the forms of intercession became increasingly specified.[47] In Cambridge the HSJC attracted two or three chantry foundations by rich burgesses (or a group of burgesses), but more than that it attracted the seekers of obits, yearly distributions and the maintenance of lights.[48] It was increasingly a provider of commemorative services, at a period when the poor make no appearance in its annals.

APPROPRIATED PARISHES

A popular way of endowing a religious house was the appropriation of a parish church. Appropriation transferred the rights to tithes and other sources of income as well as parochial duties to a communal body of a religious house on condition that a steady and sufficient income for the fulfilment of pastoral duties be secured.[49] This practice raised the danger of abuse and loss by the parish, as a religious house was free to interpret its pastoral obligations within a rather loose framework of supervision.[50] From the twelfth century a flow of papal and episcopal legislation attempted to regulate the adequate provision of vicars and vicarages in appropriated parishes. Formulas were established to this effect and the normal division of tithes allocated two-thirds to the rector

obits were arranged by the Corporation in the first years of the sixteenth century when it spent £4 18 10 in 1499–50/1500–1, Cambridge Corporation archives, x, 71, 9–x, 71, 10.

[47] On the developing elaboration of funerary provisions see Chiffoleau, *La comptabilité de l'au-delà*, esp. pp. 429–35.

[48] Some donors granted income merely for the maintenance of a light in the hospital's chapel, SJCA.D98.12. Also St Mary's hospital, Chichester, 'The cartulary of St. Mary's hospital, Chichester', no. 50, p. 57; and at St John's, Bath, 'Deeds of St. John's hospital, Bath', no. 122, p. 63.

[49] On the legal meaning of advowsons see Pollock and Maitland, *The history of English law* II, pp. 136–40. For an extensive study of the institution of vicarages see R. A. R. Hartridge, *A history of vicarages in the Middle Ages* (Cambridge, 1930); corrected in C. R. Cheney, *From Becket to Langton: English church government 1170–1213* (Manchester, 1956), pp. 131–6.

[50] On attempts to control provisions for appropriated parishes see Innocent III's letter to the bishop of Ely, *Selected letters of Pope Innocent III concerning England (1198–1216)*, ed. C. R. Cheney and W. H. Semple (Nelson's Medieval Texts, 1953), p. 75 (19 December 1204). For a systematic study of the pastoral policies pursued by monasteries and houses of canons in northern France in the twelfth and thirteenth centuries see J. Avril, 'Recherches sur la politique paroissialle des établissements monastiques et canoniaux (xie-xiiie siècles)', *Revue Mabillon* 59 (1980), pp. 453–517; p. 466. Monks did not minister to their appropriated parishes, but were encouraged to take care that help was provided to the poor.

and a third to the vicar.[51] Active legislation to enforce this influenced the practice to such a degree that by the fourteenth century a vicarage was considered as a proper benefice. In cases of absentee priests the institution of sufficient vicarages provided pastoral care for the parish. But when a parish lost its rector as a result of appropriation to a religious house, compensation was not always fully secured from the recipient house's funds; patrons and benefactors were reluctant to burden their protégés, and consequently parishes suffered.[52] Where pastoral duties were fulfilled they involved the religious house, and HSJC as such, in diverse contacts with lay society which were not all related to their religious and charitable functions.

The parish of St Peter without Trumpington Gate

The church of St Peter (later named Little St Mary's) was one of the hospital's earliest possessions.[53] Henry, son of Segar of Cambridge granted the advowson to HSJC in the time of King John: 'for the use of the poor maintained in that house, for the salvation of King John and for the souls of King Henry and King Richard'.[54] The church was appropriated to the use of the hospital by Eustace, bishop of Ely, who granted 'the church of St Peter outside the Gate, Cambridge, to God and the poor hospital of St John of Cambridge and to its brethren *in usus proprios* for the maintenance of the poor'.[55] The title was disputed in 1207 by the chaplain of St Michael's church and three other Cambridge burgesses.[56] An inquiry was also held by the Official of the bishop of Ely in 1235 due to a claim of vacancy,[57] which concluded that the church was not vacant, and the Hundred Rolls additionally

---

[51] On the development of tithes and their uses see G. Constable, *Monastic tithes from their origins to the twelfth century* (Cambridge, 1964), pp. 9–19. In England it came to be established that the rector maintained the fabric of the chancel. See also below pp. 237–45.

[52] Most obligations to maintain sufficient vicarages instituted in parishes appropriated to Augustinian houses in England had been relaxed by the fifteenth century, Kershaw, *Bolton priory*, pp. 60–3.

[53] See above p. 100.

[54] 'ad usus pauperum in eodem domo sustentandorum pro salute Regis Iohannis et pro anima Regis Henrici et pro anima Regis Ricardi', Peterhouse muniments. Ecc. Cant. A.1. These deeds became part of the Peterhouse muniments when the church was granted to the newly founded College of the Scholars of the bishop of Ely after the separation from the Hospital of St John in 1283. On the Peterhouse muniments see R. Lovatt, 'The early archives of Peterhouse', *Peterhouse record* (1975–6), pp. 26–38.

[55] 'Deo et pauperi hospitali sancti Iohannis de Cantebrigia et fratribus eiusdem hospitalis ad sustentationem pauperum, ecclesiam sancti Petri extra portam de Cantebrigia in usus proprios', Peterhouse muniments. Ecc. Cant. A2 and A3 (copy).

[56] *Curia regis rolls* V, p. 39 (see also *Abbreviatio placitorum*, p. 98).

[57] Peterhouse muniments. Ecc. Cant. A4.

confirm the hospital's claim to the church. In the testimonies concerning Cambridge churches the jurors said that the hospital held the patronage and advowson of St Peter's church, but that it had done so for so long a time that memory failed to establish *quo warranto*, 'by what warrant'.[58]

The advowsons of most churches of Cambridge were in the hands of burgess families in the twelfth and early thirteenth centuries, and during this period they were passing to religious houses.[59] In the attempt to effect a substantial benefaction, the appropriation of the living was often added. For this, an episcopal licence, which insisted on the appointment of an adequate vicarage, was needed.[60] Thus, we find Sturmin presenting the church of All Saints to the nuns of St Radegund's in 1180 and Bishop Geoffrey Ridel instituting a perpetual vicar there who was to pay a portion of his income to the nuns.[61] St Clement's church was presented to St Radegund's almonry by Hugh, son of Absalon, a Cambridge burgess, *c.* 1215 × 18; Bishop John of Fountains (1220–5) reserved a vicarage there with a pension for the nuns payable from its proceeds.[62] By mid-century nine of the fourteen churches of Cambridge were appropriated to religious houses and by the end of the century its two free private chapels which had belonged to burgess families were held by the members of two religious orders, the Gilbertines and the Friars of Penitence. St Michael's parish was given to Michaelhouse in 1325 and completed the passage of parish churches into the hold of religious or collegiate houses. With the growth of diocesan control over patronage and the provision of vicars came a parallel rise in litigation over patronage. Lay patrons could no longer practice customary ecclesiastical privileges in parishes under their patronage or granted by them to religious houses. Upon the death of a vicar there was a rush towards the next presentation; thus, St Peter's church was claimed by some burgesses and clerics but to no avail. Their opponent, HSJC, was a recently founded charitable house, held in esteem by many burgesses and living under the protection and patronage of the bishop of Ely.

---

58 *Rotuli hundredorum* II, p. 393a.

59 For a survey of Cambridge churches see *VCH. Cambridgeshire* II, pp. 123–33; *Rotuli hundredorum* II, p. 3; Maitland, *Township and borough*, pp. 174–7. To cite a few, the Blancgernons held All Saints by the Castle and gave it to Barnwell in 1219; the Absalons held St John's and St Clement's; the Walds were patrons of St Michael's; William of Yarmouth gave Holy Trinity church to West Derham Abbey *c.* 1200.

60 Cheney, *From Becket to Langton*, p. 131.   61 *The priory of St. Radegund*, p. 25.

62 *Ibid.*, pp. 26–7. The case of St Radegund has been studied since it is chronologically and topographically close to HSJC. Barnwell priory was a subject of burgess patronage as well, see *Liber memorandorum*, pp. 38–46.

As rector of St Peter's the hospital received all the parish income: tithes, offerings, confession-pennies, rents from tenants on the glebe, occasional alms.[63] In the early thirteenth century (1217?) the living was assessed at $4\frac{1}{2}$ marks; according to the report of the archdeacon of Ely on a visitation *c.* 1278, the living was worth six marks (£4) and it paid 3s per annum in diocesan dues.[64] The church appears to have been well equipped with liturgical books and had three sets of vestments.[65] HSJC supplied a brother to celebrate offices although no clear stipulation was made in the actual confirmation charters of the bishops of Ely. In 1284, in what seems to us and evidently to some of the citizens of the day heavy-handed action, the bishop granted the parish to the new college of St Peter together with two hostels near the church where the scholars had been installed four years earlier.[66] The college provided for the cure of souls by maintaining a parish chaplain and the church became the college's chapel and functioned as the parish church until it collapsed around 1325.[67]

Whenever a hospital was founded within an existing parish, steps were taken for the protection of the parochial income and to preserve attendance at parish services. In St Peter's parish HSJC assumed the role of rector and protected itself against the entry of new ecclesiastical bodies. When Maurice Ruffus wished to build a chapel in honour of St Lucy in his courtyard, the hospital granted its permission but limited the chaplain's rights to receive offerings and to admit parishioners to the chapel.[68] In 1249 the master of HSJC granted leave to the newly arrived Carmelites to establish themselves in their holdings in Newnham and to worship in St Peter's church.[69] In 1265 the Friars of the Penitence of Jesus Christ were allowed to erect an altar in St Peter's. The bishop ordered two Officials to look into the possible damage to the parish,

---

[63] On the components of parish income see Moorman, *Church life in England in the thirteenth century,* pp. 110–37.

[64] *The valuation of Norwich,* pp. 538, 219; in 1291 the assessment was $10\frac{1}{2}$ marks (£7), *ibid.,* p. 538. *Vetus liber archidiaconi Eliensis,* p. 38.

[65] *Ibid.*

[66] The two hostels were a part of the church's patrimony, Stokes, *Outside the Trumpington Gates,* p. 72. On the site and the early buildings of Peterhouse see Willis and Clark, *An architectural history* I, pp. 2–4. In compensation for this loss of the parish and hostel the hospital received two hostels and a house in All Saints' parish, Peterhouse muniments. Collegii Situs. B2.

[67] The new church was dedicated to St Mary and reconsecrated on 3 November 1352, CUL. EDR. Register Lisle, fol. 65v.

[68] SJCA. Cartulary of HSJC, fol. 19r. For a similar arrangement between St Giles' hospital, Norwich and a burgess see NRO. 25/514.

[69] A full description of the agreement appears in Bishop Hugh's confirmation. Peterhouse muniments. Collegium. A1.

and subsequently granted a licence for settlement and for the erection of a private altar, reserving all the rights of the hospital.[70]

Upon the separation from the hospital, the scholars of the bishop of Ely were given the church of St Peter,[71] which meant that all incomes from the parish were to belong to the new house of scholars.[72] The first mention concerning a dispute on this transfer appears in a letter to the archbishop of Canterbury of May 1320, from his Official and the Dean of Arches. This reviewed a dispute heard by them in the Court of Arches arising between the master and scholars of St Peter and Guy Lespicer, mayor of Cambridge, concerning the tithes from the watermill in St Peter's parish.[73] The town collected the mills' incomes as part of the farm of the borough, but was obliged to pay the tithes owed from the mills to the parishes in which they were situated. Thus, the defendants were the townsmen who customarily continued to pay a part of the income to the hospital, and the hospital who had not relinquished these revenues.[74] The Official's decision was that the scholars were to receive the tithes amounting to £80 in arrears which the mayor and bailiffs of Cambridge together with the brethren of HSJC had collected and had failed to pay to the house of scholars for the last 30 years (c. 1284–1320). Additionally, the Official laid down the payment of £80 to cover expenses incurred by the master and scholars throughout the litigation. An appeal by the hospital was rejected and additional expenses were imposed on it in hearings which were conducted in the absence of the hospital's master and with no proctor acting on his behalf. Action directed by archiepiscopal mandate was taken by Richard of Ormesby, deputy of the archdeacon of Ely, and by the Chancellor of Cambridge, Richard of Badew, to

---

[70] Peterhouse muniments. Ecc. Cant. A5 and A6. HSJC granted a licence for the extension of their site, Peterhouse muniments. Collegii Situs. A19 (c. 1270).

[71] 'Et habeant illam ecclesiam cum duobus hospicijs predictis…iuxta ecclesiam Sancti Petri extra portam de Trumpytone', Peterhouse muniments. Collegium A3; SJCA.D98.3. The scholars were also granted the rectory of Thriplow which had been given to the hospital in 1280 for the scholars' sustenance, Peterhouse muniments.Thriplow.A1 and A2.

[72] 'decimas garbarum cum alteragiis quas fratres prenominati habere et colligere solebant et decimas utriusque molendini ad ecclesiam ipsam spectantes', SJCA.D98.3.

[73] Peterhouse muniments. Ecc. Cant. A8; A9. On the mills of Cambridge see H. P. Stokes, 'The old mills of Cambridge', *Cambridge Antiquarian Society. Proceedings and communications* 14 (1909–10), pp. 180–233; pp. 185–6. The tithes of two mills were given to the college at the separation from HSJC in 1284, those of King's mill and the Bishop's mill.

[74] See the charter of King John of 1207 confirming the mills as part of the *firma burgi* of Cambridge, *The charters of the borough of Cambridge*, pp. 6, 8: 'Habeant et teneant predictam villam cum omnibus pertinenciis suis…in pratis et pascuis, molendinis…'.

ensure payment by the mayor and HSJC. The names of the defendants involved are recorded in this document and include the mayor and bailiffs for the year, the master and the brethren of the hospital together with some former mayors from the earlier stage of the dispute.[75] In June the deputy of the archdeacon of Ely wrote to the archbishop notifying him that the mayor had been warned and that excommunication had been proclaimed in all churches of the diocese.[76] The hospital tried to remove the dispute to the king's court and petitioned for a writ owing, no doubt, to the fact that the town's mills belonged to the king. But the king wished the case to remain in the metropolitan court,[77] and in January 1321 the bishop of Ely received the absolution granted to the hospital by Berengar, cardinal bishop of Tusculum (Frascati) on the grounds that the master and brethren had not been able to appear in the metropolitan court on account of their poverty.[78] Thus by February 1321 the archbishop could announce that owing to the hospital's willingness to pay the arrears of tithes the brethren were to be absolved.[79]

However, the dispute did not end there. The hospital still claimed exemption from all tithe payments as part of its ecclesiastical privileges, and did not agree to pay the mills' tithes to the college. In 1338 Bishop Montacute commissioned the chancellor of the University, the rector of Hadenham and a canon lawyer to investigate the title of St Peter's church, as the hospital had been harassing the college.[80] Later that year the parties submitted to episcopal arbitration.[81] An agreement was reached in 1340 by which the hospital quitted all claims to any income pertaining to the college and the college agreed to pay the hospital a

---

[75] Peterhouse muniments. Ecc. Cant. A10. For 1319–20: mayor Eudo of Elpringham and bailiffs John Berefot, Richard Modebrok, Henry of Wimpole; the master John of Colonia and brethren John of Shalford and Alexander Ixning. Ten additional names were listed, mayors and bailiffs serving between 1306 and 1319.

[76] Peterhouse muniments. Ecc. Cant. A12 (4 June 1320).

[77] Peterhouse muniments. Ecc. Cant. A 1 or SJCA.D98.5 (14 December 1320). A fourteenth-century roll containing copies of charters related to the installation of the scholars in HSJC and their separation was, perhaps, prepared for use during these hearings, SJCA.D98.44.

[78] SJCA.D17.37; D14.177; D2.16. HSJC appealed to Rome in parallel with the hearings in the metropolitan court, a common procedure in England, F. D. Logan, *Excommunication and the secular arm in medieval England. A study in legal procedure from the thirteenth to the sixteenth century* (Toronto, 1968), p. 117. Excommunication must have been awkward for the hospital, bearing in mind the obligations it had for the provision of prayers and for parochial celebration.

[79] Peterhouse muniments. Ecc. Cant. A13.

[80] Peterhouse muniments. Collegium. A5.

[81] By HSJC in SJCA.D98.1 and D98.24; by Peterhouse in CUL. EDR. Register Montacute fol. 19r. In fol. 18v appointment and exchange of proctors is attested.

compensatory pension of 20s per annum.[82] An interesting point arising from the dispute is the degree of involvement of the town officials in the hospital's affairs.

St Peter's church, one of the earliest donations to the hospital granted to it by a burgess, passed on to another charitable institution after some 80 years. The hospital had come into contact, at times amicable and at times litigious, with other religious orders and burgesses through its relation with the parish; and it continued to hold property and interests in it even after the church was removed from its hands.

The parish of Horningsea

Horningsea church was appropriated to HSJC by Bishop Eustace in 1208 × 15 as part of his endowment of the episcopal–ecclesiastical foundation.[83] Its revenues were to be used for the support of the hospital's poor with the reservation of 100s per annum for the maintenance of a vicar.[84] In 1217 the living was valued at $27\frac{1}{2}$ marks and in 1254 at $25\frac{1}{2}$ marks.[85] Taking the sum of 25 marks (£16 12s 8d) as representing the thirteenth-century value, the hospital was collecting £11 12s 8d from the parish, from which it paid 5s 10d in diocesan dues, leaving £11 6s 10d net income.[86] In 1267, Bishop Hugh Balsham allowed the consolidation of the vicarage of Horningsea on account of the hospital's poverty due to war and fire.[87] A vicar was to be provided from among the hospital's brethren–chaplains who would celebrate mass and tend to the cure of souls. The church seems to have been fairly well kept, as the archdeacon's visitation of around 1278 found it sufficiently endowed with vestments, books and vessels.[88]

The consolidation of the vicarage of Horningsea engaged the hospital in litigation. During a metropolitan visitation in the 1270s Master Raynald of Lynn petitioned the archbishop for institution to what he claimed to be the vacant vicarage of Horningsea. On the basis of this evidence Master Raynald became the vicar and the church was taxed as a perpetual vicarage. The hospital appealed to Rome whence a letter of justice ordered the prior of St Mary's, Huntingdon, to hear the case. The priory sacrist held some eight sessions in which the parties'

[82] SJCA.D3.66, D3.68 and D20.59.
[83] SJCA.D26.20. See above pp. 99–103 about the process of foundation.
[84] SJCA.D26.9 and a copy in D26.83.
[85] *The valuation of Norwich*, p. 138. According to the report of the archdeacon of Ely *c.* 1278 the church was valued at 25 marks, *Vetus liber archidiaconi Eliensis*, p. 40.
[86] *The valuation of Norwich*, pp. 44–5.
[87] SJCA.D26.9; D26.38.   [88] *Vetus liber archidiaconi Eliensis*, p. 40.

proctors presented documents proving their claims.[89] The sentence favoured the hospital's proven claim that following the dissolution of the vicarage by Bishop Balsham[90] the parish had been wholly appropriated to it for the support of its poor and sick inmates.[91]

Another case for arbitration arose in connection with services due to the lords of Eye manor.[92] In 1299 the king's court sat in Cambridge in the case of Simon of Bradenham and his wife against William, master of HSJC. The couple claimed the customary right in land in Eye manor which formed part of the parish glebe.[93] With it the plaintiffs claimed three weekly celebrations of mass and a celebration on the Feast of St Andrew in St Andrew's chapel on the manor.[94] A compromise was reached by which the hospital would perpetually supply the services of a chaplain to celebrate mass on Rogation Tuesday and on the Feast of St Andrew.

Tithe disputes plagued Horningsea parish as they did so many other medieval communities. In 1293, the hospital was summoned to answer the claims of the rector of Ditton regarding the collection of tithes.[95] This dispute continued throughout the fourteenth and fifteenth centuries with frequent new agreements and arbitrations.[96] The tithes of Eye manor, 8 acres of which were in the parish church's patrimony, were divided between the hospital and Denney abbey. In an agreement of 1377 × 79 the hospital was given the crop tithes and the abbey held the rest with an annual allowance of 3s 4d to Horningsea church.[97]

Once it was established that a vicar need no longer be appointed, a brother of the hospital was entrusted with the duty of parish chaplain. He was to celebrate mass, administer sacraments, visit the sick and help the poor; unless he actually resided in the parish, these duties could not be regularly fulfilled. There can be no doubt that in some

---

[89] The record of these proceedings appears in the *inspeximus* of bishop Montacute of 1344 from which so much of our knowledge about the hospital is gleaned, SJCA.D4.1.

[90] For a late fifteenth-century confirmation of the appropriation, see SJCA.D37.142.

[91] A bull of Nicholas IV (31 January 1289) to the prior of Barnwell ordered the execution of the sentence, SJCA.D98.14.

[92] SJCA. Cartulary of HSJC, fol. 37v.

[93] This amounted to 8 acres out of 48 acres as mentioned in the Hundred Rolls, but no customary rights were known to be attached in 1279; *Rotuli hundredorum* II, p. 442a.

[94] A letter of Bishop William of Louth of 1293 surviving in the hospital's archive summoned Sir Simon to answer for the erection of this private chapel, SJCA.D26.8. Such a customary service may have been given to the lords of the manor as patrons of the parish church before the appropriation through an informal customary arrangement with the incumbent.

[95] Summons by the archdeacon of Ely, SJCA.D26.65.

[96] See roll of evidence SJCA.D26.131–4, 136. The master acted as proctor in these cases see SJCA.D98.4; D98.32.　　　　　　　　[97] SJCA.D26.128.

appropriated churches poor relief slipped between the vicar and the absent rector to the detriment of the parish poor.

During the years when a vicarage existed in Horningsea its incumbent was paid £5 per annum.[98] Vicars' portions were often as high as a third of the parish's income (here it falls slightly short of the third of £16 11s 8d), to which the vicar's use of the glebe-lands must be added. From this accumulated income the vicar was supposed to allocate sufficient surplus funds for poor relief. In the Hundred Rolls the hospital was said to hold 48 acres as church glebe in Horningsea, land which was leased to seven tenants.[99] In the account roll of HSJC for 1283 (partly copied into the cartulary) one reads at the end of the revenues' section: 'Horningsea: from John the chaplain for altarage 26s 8d', which is completed by an entry giving the names and sums paid by the tenants holding parts of the church's glebe amounting to £1 7s 1d, two capons and six hens.[100] These payments of altarage and rents came on top of the tithes of the parish assessed in 1254 at $25\frac{1}{2}$ marks (£17). In the late fifteenth century the hospital's steward was collecting about £18 a year from the living, a quarter of the house's income.[101] In the testimonies heard in connection with the vicarage dispute, the hospital stated that it had duly served Horningsea which had been given it as a gift.[102] However, from the entry *de capellano* in the 1283 roll we may gather that a parish chaplain was paid and shouldered some of the hospital's duties there, though the hospital still supplied some of the services directly. In 1346–7 the master, Alexander Ixning, was granted a licence by Bishop Lisle to hear confessions of the parishioners of Horningsea in some houses and not in the church as usual.[103]

An episcopal licence of 1405 reveals the reality of appropriation of parochial temporalities: 'he has granted to the master and brethren of the house of St John the Evangelist of Cambridge a licence to let at farm the parish church of Horningsea...for five years'.[104] There is no other licence of this kind, but the practice was widespread; farming out the collection of tithes was done under episcopal licence as it

---

98 This sum answers the requirements of the Oxford Council of 1222, Hartridge, *The history of vicarages*, pp. 39–42.
99 *Rotuli hundredorum* II 442a, b.
100 SJCA. Rental roll 2.2.1 and SJCA. Cartulary of HSJC, fol. 24r.
101 SJCA.D31.16.
102 SJCA.D4.1.
103 CUL. EDR. Register Lisle, fol. 9v.
104 'Concessit magistro et confratribus domus sancti Iohannis Evangeliste Cantebr' licentiam dimittendi ecclesiam parochialem de Hornyseye ad firmam...per quinquennium', CUL. EDR. Register Fordham, fol. 201r.

involved the transfer of church property, though this practice must have taken place often without licensing.[105] This is the only example in the surviving episcopal registers of Ely, but farming of a parish's income for a limited period and a fixed part of the income was the common way of managing and collecting ecclesiastical revenues.[106] In 1463 a brother of the hospital was counted as the parish chaplain of Horningsea with a salary of 100s, which meant that a brother was entrusted with the 'benefice' of the parish in a manner similar to the office of cantarist held by other brethren.[107] In 1468 a list of procurations due to the See recorded John Dunham, master of HSJC, as the parish priest of Horningsea.[108] In the earliest full set of accounts of the hospital for 1485, Stephen Wiche, a *confrater*, received 100s yearly at four terms, as chaplain of Horningsea.[109] Between 1505 and 1510 an annual sum of £4 16s was paid to the chaplain of Horningsea, although payments from the living were already in arrears.[110] It appears that at this late date the brother entrusted with the parish duties resided there in the rectory.[111] The accounts were rendered in the name of the master, who appears to have visited Horningsea quite often, or at least to have incurred expenses on its behalf. There are six entries in the 1485 accounts described as 'for my expenses in Horningsea' totalling 2s 2d. This is isolated evidence from a very late date and may not, therefore, reflect the situation of earlier times. With the shift of emphasis away from the hospital's charitable and pastoral obligations it is understandable that the vicarage developed into a living for a hospital brother.

To sum up, it appears that the hospital's relations with the appropriated parish passed through several phases. Between 1210 and 1267 it was appropriated to HSJC with the reservation of a vicarage (100s per annum) and with a vicar charged with pastoral and charitable duties. From 1267 the vicarage ceased to exist and a hospital brother was to fulfil all obligations. The hospital came to entrust some regular duties to the hands of a parish chaplain who was paid 10s per annum. Some time in the late fourteenth or the fifteenth century, a brother of the hospital, although he was not formally instituted, came to hold

---

[105] See a typical agreement concerning the parsonage of Costessey which was farmed out in 1509 by the Hospital of St Giles, Norwich, NRO. 25/253.

[106] See the farming of Thurlton rectory by the Hospital of St Giles, Norwich in 1507, NRO. 24/b/53.

[107] CUL. EDR. Register Gray, fol. 115v.

[108] *ibid.*, fol. 193.

[109] SJCA.D106.9, fol. 10r.

[110] SJCA.D106.10, fols. 5r, 12v, 20r, 25v, 31v, 39r. Entries reporting the income from Horningsea are followed by notes of *non solvit*, fols. 10v, 23v.

[111] As shown by an entry 'cuidam mulieri in rectoria de Horn' – 1d', *ibid.*

the living as a vicar for 100s per annum from which he would have sustained all duties such as hospitality and poor relief. The hospital developed close connections with the parishioners in the role of rector, landowner and business partner. Many of the parishioners received loans from the hospital. Thus, HSJC was involved not only in provision for the health of the souls, but also for the physical welfare of the people of Horningsea.[112]

THE DEVELOPMENT OF THE ENDOWMENT OF HSJC

The pattern of donations and purchases in the thirteenth century

The foundation of a religious house in the Middle Ages was usually a combination of two parallel processes: the endowment with temporal goods and the creation and regulation of a religious community and of a liturgical routine. An individual founder usually supplied a substantial part of the endowment and stirred the interest of other benefactors. Episcopal supervision of the foundation was intended to ensure that the endowment was sufficient for the needs of the newly created community.[113]

The story of the Hospital of St John in Cambridge, as we described it in chapter 4, was not one of direct personal foundation and endowment. The ground on which the hospital was founded belonged to the town and Henry Eldcorn had a humble building erected on it.[114] The episcopal foundation provided for a cemetery, bells, and chapel rights and confirmed the appropriation of St Peter's church (1208 × 15), and must have been a sign of the beginning of systematic donation.[115]

The archives of St John's College contain material illuminating an institutional history going back almost 800 years and they are kept with exemplary care.[116] The cartulary was compiled about 1260 × 70 and

112 On the provision of loans to members of Horningsea parish see below, pp. 223–4.
113 As an example see the foundation of God's House, Southampton, *The cartulary of God's House, Southampton* I, pp. xv–xxx, lxi–lxii. Also the Hospital of St John the Baptist in Bath, 'Deeds of St. John's hospital, Bath', pp. 7–8. For the activities of a great Norman patron for the promotion of the popularity of his foundation see Mesmin, 'The leper hospital of St. Gilles de Pont-Audemer' I, pp. 90–3.
114 See above pp. 100–1.
115 Bishop Eustace himself provided some help from the episcopal demesne in the form of the right of collection of fuel from the episcopal marshes near Ely as well as two boats for its transport, SJCA.D3.61, D98.42. These were confirmed by Bishop John, his successor (1220 × 5). For similar initial donations by bishops see the case of the hospital of St John the Baptist, Bath, 'Deeds of St. John's hospital, Bath', nos. 3, 5, 6, pp.15–17.
116 On the nature of hospital archives and their possible use for the study of poverty see H. van der Wee, 'Les archives hospitalières et l'étude de la pauvreté aux Pays-Bas du

into it 339 contemporary documents were copied, most of which also survive in their originals.[117] The cartulary also contains copies of eight later documents from the fourteenth and fifteenth centuries. Among its 90 folios there are 3 interspersed leaves of accounts, and the final 10 leaves are rentals and kitchen accounts of the thirteenth and fourteenth centuries.[118] The charters include some twelfth-century title deeds (earlier than the foundation of the hospital) and cover the whole period of the house's existence down to its refoundation as a college in the first decade of the sixteenth century.

Needless to say, not all deeds in the medieval section of the archives relating to the hospital were direct grants to it. Of 347 deeds in the cartulary only 117 were such grants. It is a normal feature of medieval cartularies and charter collections to contain many earlier background deeds sustaining the claim to each property.[119] In some cases conveyances apparently connected to no known benefaction must have been the background deeds of donations which have not survived in charters; in many cases they can be reconstructed with the help of marginal notes and endorsements.

The main source for our knowledge of the hospital's economic fortunes lies in the charters of donation to HSJC. These appear from the very first years of the hospital's existence and are phrased in a uniform thirteenth-century charter wording.[120] They usually state the

xve au xviiie siècle', *Revue du Nord* 48 (1966), pp. 5–16; the HSJC archive contains only some of the types of hospital documents surveyed.

[117] For some very useful observations on the making of cartularies see D. A. Walker, 'The organisation of material in medieval cartularies', in *Study of medieval records: essays in honour of Kathleen Major*, ed. D. Bullough and R. Storey (Oxford, 1971), pp. 132–50.

[118] The custom of cartulary compilation was most common in monastic houses and had become a normal part of estate administration by the thirteenth century. Cf. M. T. Clanchy, *From memory to written record: England 1066–1307* (London, 1979), pp. 79–80. For hospital cartularies see the entries in G. R. C. Davis, *Medieval cartularies of Great Britain: a short catalogue* (London, 1958).

[119] Some seven to eight documents in average were kept with every grant to St John's hospital in Bath, 'Deeds of St. John's hospital, Bath', p. 12; similarly in *The cartulary of St. Mark's hospital*, p. xxx. This is true even in the case of fifteenth-century foundations, see A. Rogers, 'The use of deeds for medieval urban history', in *The medieval town in Britain*, ed. P. Riden (Cardiff, 1980), pp. 1–14; pp. 4–6.

[120] Example:

Notum sit omnibus tam presentibus quam futuris quod ego Iohanna filia Anketill' dedi et concessi et hac presenti carta mea confirmavi Deo et beate Marie et hospitali sancti Iohannis Evangeliste de Cantebrigia et fratribus etc. pro salute anime mee et animarum patris mei et matris mee et antecessorum et successorum meorum in puram et perpetuam elemosinam redditum quinque solidorum et vi. denariorum de tenemento quod Simon Niger tenuit de me in parochia Omnium Sanctorum, quod scilicet tenementum iacet inter tenementum Cristiane uxoris Radulfi Prodfut

name of the donor who grants his gift to God, St Mary, the saints and the hospital as recipients, describe the property minutely by its boundaries and location, state the dues and rents attached, and record a warranty clause, the price paid (*gersumma*), a sealing clause and the list of witnesses.[121]

Dating clauses in gift charters do not become common until the end of the thirteenth century.[122] Nevertheless, the approximate period of undated charters can be deduced by the occurrence of prominent burgesses and officials as donors, witnesses, or neighbours.[123] In the absence of precise dates it appeared useful to divide the donations into periods corresponding to 'generations' of donors.

Besides grants which created the hospital's endowment, an important part of its management is revealed through charters of alienation. The hospital received grants of lands in fee, rents and quit-rents; the rents ranged from 1d to 1 mark and flowed constantly to the hospital on two or four customary terms of payment. Some lands given to the hospital remained in the hands of their former sub-tenants and produced rent payments,[124] but tenancy of urban property was highly

et terram predicte domus, cum homagio, releviis et cum omnibus aliis rebus que mihi vel heredibus meis possint contingere sine aliqua retenemento. Recipient autem inde predicta domus et fratres ibidem Deo servientes a predicto Symone et heredibus suis annuatim predictum redditum quinque solidorum et vi. denariorum ad duos terminos, scilicet ad hokeday ii. solidos et ix. denarios et ad festum sancti Michaelis ii. solidos et ix. denarios, libere et quiete et honorifice. Reddent vero predicta domus et predicti fratres Godefrido filio Gwarini et heredibus suis annuatim dimidiam libram piperis ad pascha scilicet pro omnibus serviciis. Et ut hec mea donatio rata maneat et stabilis sigillo meo apposito presens scriptum/(fol. 2v) roboravi et pro me et heredibus meis predictum redditum cum pertinenciis predicte domui in perpetuum quietumclamavi. Et ad maiorem securitatem cartam meam quam de Warino fratre meo habui predicte domui integre reddidi. Et ego et heredes mei warrantizabimus predictum redditum cum pertinenciis predicte domui et fratribus ibidem Deo servientibus contra omnes homines et feminas. Et sciendum est quod Ricardus tunc prior predicte domus dedit mihi caritative quatuor marcas argenti ad suscipiendum iter meum Ierusalem. Hiis testibus Bartholomeo decano, Petro capellano de sancto Petro, Galfrido capellano, magistro Gilberto, Baldwino filio Baldwini Blancgernum, Herveo filio Eustacii, Roberto Seman, Rogero Perleban, Mauricio Ruffo et aliis. SJCA. Cartulary of HSJC, fol. 2. See Clanchy, *From memory*, pp. 64–5.

[121] For the analysis of medieval conveyances and their components see *Calendar of Antrobus deeds before 1625*, ed. R. B. Pugh, Wiltshire Archaeological and Natural History Society, records branch 3 (1947), pp. xxxii–lv.

[122] Dating of private charters appears often in the reign of Edward I but it was not until Edward II's time that this was a regular practice. On diplomatic developments in this period see Clanchy, *From memory*, chapter 1. On the occurrence of dating see *Carte nativorum: a Peterborough abbey cartulary of the fourteenth century*, ed. C. N. L. Brooke and M. M. Postan (Oxford, 1960), p. xviii.

[123] In some cases donations were sealed by a dated fine.

[124] The current rate of rent for arable was 1d per acre in the thirteenth century, Maitland, *Township and borough*, p. 160.

prized throughout the thirteenth century and often led the hospital to sell its rights to a certain rent for a lump sum, retaining a quit-rent in most cases. This was common practice in the twelfth and early thirteenth centuries when nominal rents were retained by vendors while the sale price was expressed, at least approximately, in the *gersumma*;[125] transactions which supplied the hospital with ready cash and with a constant flow of low rents. At the same time the hospital was granting land in fee-farm and creating perpetual sub-tenure in return for fixed rents. From the mid-thirteenth century the form of lease for life became more common and was dominant in later centuries.[126] Thus, a wide range of documents attests the variety of transactions undertaken by the hospital in the management of its property.[127] In the fourteenth and fifteenth centuries the alienations and leases are styled in a clearer fashion and allow a better understanding of the actual exchanges which they were meant to attest.[128]

Donations to the hospital, both in free alms and in fee-farm, often entailed various customary obligations attached to the property. By the thirteenth century most customary dues in towns had been commuted into money payments,[129] though this occurred at different stages in different towns depending on their rate of urban growth. We find rents of half pounds of cumin, pairs of gloves, capons, ducks and shoes in charters well into the thirteenth century, serving as a sign of recognition of the landlord's seisin by the tenant.[130] Lords of urban fees often waived the right to the customary annual rose or weight of pepper by quit-claim, in phrases reminiscent of a donation. We also find the hospital paying for the quittance of small dues and rents by individuals holding such rights in connection with property which had passed into the hospital's hands. A common practice of this kind is the purchase of the widow's 'third', her dower rights in her late husband's donation, which was the only way by common law to eliminate her claim as widow.[131] Some widows waived their rights and

---

[125] W. Urry, *Canterbury under the Angevin kings* (London, 1967), p. 134.

[126] *The cartulary of God's House, Southampton*, p. lxv.

[127] Dating alienations and leases is easier since the charters usually state the name of the grantor or lessor, who was in these cases the master of the hospital.

[128] See below pp. 212–36.   [129] Urry, *Canterbury*, p. 27.

[130] See *The cartulary of God's House, Southampton*, p. lxii and Urry, *Canterbury*, p. 142. Some Cambridge tenements owed 'high gabel rent' to the king, a relic of the feudal burgage dues, and the hospital owed it on several town properties, see Maitland, *Township and borough*, pp. 70, 180–1. For lists of 'high gabel' rents paid in the thirteenth century, amounting to 6s 4¾d *per annum* see SJCA. Cartulary of HSJC, fols. 42v, 80v. For fifteenth-century contributions made by the hospital see Cambridge Corporation archive XVIII 8 (1483) and X 92 (1491), paying 8s 2d.

[131] Pollock and Maitland, *A history of English law* II, p. 409.

thus became donors themselves, foregoing rights which in some cases can be shown to have been very substantial and lucrative.

Most donations to the hospital were made 'Deo et beate Marie et hospitali sancti Iohannis Evangeliste de Cantebrigia'. The only difference in form between a free donation and a sale lies in the statement of *gersumma* or consideration – and even in a sale a pious motive is usually recorded. Very often 'what purports to be a pious gift will...turns out to be a sale or exchange'.[132] These sales must be seen as investments in urban property on the part of the hospital, but one must bear in mind that neither the vendor nor the buyer were simple business partners.[133]

The donor was rewarded by prayers for the benefit of his soul and for the souls of relatives and other Christians, a return which was as real as it may seem intangible.[134] In some cases it was clearly stated that the donor had entered into confraternity with the house, thus becoming a member of the spiritual community and partaking of its accumulated merit.[135] In some donations rents were paid by the hospital to the donors, while in others a full price was exacted, establishing it as a real sale. The rate of donation altered dramatically during this period: 235 in the thirteenth century, 16 from the fourteenth and 12 from the fifteenth, and as we will see below their forms changed in response to new legislation and changing economic circumstances.

Table 6.1 shows the locations of thirteenth-century donations and the origin of their donors. HSJC was granted 235 separate properties by 181 donors.[136] Of the properties granted, 138 were by townsmen and townswomen of Cambridge and 94 by residents of the surrounding villages. More than half of the properties given by townsmen were located in Cambridge and if the properties in the Cambridge fields are considered then some 70% of the donations of townsfolk were

132 C. N. L. Brooke, 'Princes and kings as patrons of monasteries, Normandy and England', in *Il monachesimo e la riforma ecclesiastica 1049–1122* (Milan, 1971), p. 127.

133 Urry, *Canterbury*, pp. 134–5: 'dare in elemosynam' was clearly not a charitable phrase by the thirteenth century. French merchants used it as a synonym for 'sale'; they saw the donation to a religious house as an exchange, J. M. Bienvenu, 'Pauvreté, misères et charité en Anjou aux xie et xiie siècles', *Le moyen-âge* 72 (1966), pp. 389–424; p. 420.

134 On the multiple purpose of donations see C. A. F. Meekings and ed. R. F. Hunnisett, 'The early years of Netley abbey', *Journal of ecclesiastical history* 30 (1979), pp. 1–37; p. 20.

135 Example: St Mary's hospital, Chichester, 'Cartulary of St. Mary's hospital, Chichester', no. 24, pp. 48–9.

136 Some donors conveyed more than one property, but most people made a single donation to the house.

Table 6.1 *Distribution of donations to HSJC by origin of donor and by location 1200–1300*

Donors	Townsfolk		Villagers		Unknown
Location	no.	%	no.	%	no.
Cambridge	69	50.0			2
Cambridge fields	25	18.1	2	2.1	
Villages	41	29.7	91	96.8	1
Unknown	3	2.2	1	1.1	
Total	138	100.0	94	100.0	3

contained within the town limits.[137] Most properties were situated in the most lucrative central parishes of St Mary, St Edward and All Saints, the hospital's own parish, and the focus of religious, administrative, social and economic activity.[138] The remaining properties were in the villages, mainly those within a close circle surrounding Cambridge: Newnham, Grantchester, Barton, Trumpington. Almost all villagers gave properties in their own villages and only two properties in the Cambridge fields were granted by village-donors. Of the 235 grants, 137 were granted in free alms, a form of conveyance which preserved no obligations owing to the donor.[139] Thus, 58.3 % of the hospital's endowment reached it unencumbered and the house could immediately convert these properties to profitable holdings by sale or lease. Of the grants in free alms, 55 were properties situated in the town, 80 in the villages, and the location of three cannot be discerned. The dichotomy of town and village donations is not as clear-cut as might be expected; Cambridge was surrounded by fields and almost merged with the rural communities of Chesterton, Grantchester and Newnham. Population movement was active and fluid; townsmen carried top-onyms from Cambridgeshire villages, and sons of town artisans appear as village dwellers. Townsmen owned arable and meadow land mainly in the Cambridge fields but also in the immediately surrounding villages.[140] The group of donors was a mixed one, comprising

[137] For a similar distribution see *Cartulary of God's House, Southampton*, p. lxi.

[138] Most donations to St Mark's hospital were in the town, *Cartulary of St Mark's hospital*, p. xxxii.

[139] Occasionally, these donations still entailed a service to the king, connected with the original burgage tenure.

[140] See *The west fields of Cambridge*. On ownership by townsmen see Cam, *Liberties and communities in medieval England*, pp. 19–26; Maitland, *Township and borough*, pp. 150–1. The same trend of ownership in fields round a town can be found in Lincoln,

Table 6.2 *Earliest and latest chronology of distribution of donations in the thirteenth century*

	Earliest		Latest	
	donations	% of whole	donations	% of whole
I *Division into periods of 50 years*				
Up to 50	211	89.8	186	79.1
1251–1300	24	10.2	49	20.8
II *Division into periods of 30 years*				
1210–40	195	83.0	153	65.1
1241–70	31	13.2	61	26.0
1271–1300	9	3.8	21	8.9

burgesses, modest knights and substantial peasants.[141] Within the town the abundance of small gifts of rents reminds us that not only the leading citizens of Cambridge were involved in the endowment of the hospital, but also a multitude of artisans and petty traders. The latter joined the pattern of religious patronage of a foundation created and primarily sustained by their more prosperous and powerful neighbours.[142]

The chronology of the endowment in the thirteenth century reveals a trend characteristic of modest religious houses: largely a rentier approach to a scattered endowment in town or in countryside.[143] The dating of this material is extremely difficult and must be done within wide parameters. Yet, notwithstanding the uncertainties, it is possible to assign two approximate dates to each charter, earliest and latest, and to derive two distributions, one where the earliest possible date has been assumed, the other, where the latest date has been taken (table 6.2).[144] Thus, a clear trend can be discerned: the rate of donation was steadily falling.[145] A hospital was founded in wood and stone, its community was immediately supplied with means of sustenance and its future

J. W. F. Hill, *Medieval Lincoln* (Cambridge, 1948, repr. 1965), pp. 392–5 and in Canterbury, Urry, *Canterbury*, p. 177.

[141] For a similar pattern see *Cartulary of St. Mark's hospital*, p. xxx as well as the accounts of Bolton priory, *Bolton priory rentals and ministers' accounts, 1473–1539*, ed. I. Kershaw, Yorkshire Archaeological Society, record ser. 132 (1970), p. x.

[142] On the social composition of thirteenth-century small towns see the observations made in Hilton, 'Lords, burgesses and hucksters', pp. 3–15 and *idem*, 'Small town society in England before the Black Death', pp. 53–78.

[143] See *Bolton priory rentals*, p. xi.   [144] See above p. 204.

[145] The same trend is found in donations to St Mark's Hospital, Bristol, *Cartulary of St. Mark's hospital*, pp. xxvii, xxxiv.

inmates with the promise of care. Townsmen favoured the house and as they did so they enjoyed the reward of donation to a newly endowed community, fruits which were of social and religious value. After a generation or two the excitement of sharing in a new foundation must have declined as new men wished to donate to new foundations.[146] As the hospital grew in means, the need for further help subsided and with it the charitable activity to provide new sources of livelihood. Yet benefactions were not greatly motivated by the objective needs of religious houses, otherwise fewer hospitals would have fallen into decay during the Middle Ages. However, one may assume that the members of a small urban community like Cambridge would have been aware of the extent of economic resources which their town's only hospital had at its disposal. The donors had made the hospital into a property owner amongst them, living in the public eye. This may mean that later gifts were given in kind, perhaps to the chapel, such as offerings of wax, vestments, prayer books, candles; especially in a period by which the endowment was seen to be sufficient.[147] In parallel to the decline in the need for additional endowment, interest in a new religious house would naturally wane after some years of existence.

In 57 cases the donations were coupled with quittances of rights in the property. These rights often arose from obligations between kin and from feudal customary dues.[148] Of 63 quit-claims most were waived by wives and lords of the donors.[149] Wives quitted their future claim to their deceased husband's property as widow's share: of 12 cases in which wives quitted their rights 9 were compensated by the hospital.[150] Out of 63 quit-claims, 22 were purchased by the hospital, costing a total of £13 15s 10d. Of the 57 properties involved, 33 were

---

[146] The privileged aristocracy much preferred to found new houses or to endow those recently founded, Rosenthal, *The purchase of paradise*, p. 52. This dynamic of medieval religious foundations is clearly stated in a Venetian decree of 1359 in which the Council implored citizens not to endow new hospitals but to help maintain the existing ones from whom donations had been deflected in favour of new ventures, Mueller, 'The procurators of San Marco', p. 209.

[147] On donations to the chapel for the maintenance of lights, see above p. 162. See the inventory of the Hospital of St Mary Magdalene, King's Lynn, *The making of King's Lynn*, no. 476, pp. 429–30. Many of the legacies left to hospital by the Avignon testators included blankets, mattresses and sheets, Chiffoleau, *La comptabilité de l'au-delà*, p. 316. Most such gifts would not, of course, be recorded in charters. On donation of moveables as a replacement for diminishing gifts of land in a period of high land value see Raban, *Mortmain legislation*, pp. 139–41.

[148] In some cases rights in the holding were quitted by more than one person.

[149] Amongst the known quitters: wife – 12, lord – 11, son – 7, brother – 3, mother – 2, father – 1, grandfather – 1.

[150] On the process of redemption of widows' portions see *Cartulary of St. Mark's hospital*, pp. xxx–xxxi.

rural and 24 were urban, which may indicate a greater tendency to observe customary rights of siblings within the rural community.

In 47 cases one can trace a donation from its acquisition to its alienation or its putting to farm. In 30 of these cases the properties were sold for a lump sum of *gersumma* with an annual rent retained. Of these transactions, which will be called sales, 21 were in the town and its fields and 8 were outside Cambridge. Most exchanges were made in the central parishes of St Mary, St Michael, St Edward and St Botolph. Of these 30 sales, 13 had been given as gifts in free alms and were directly converted into cash and a source of steady income without any investment or expense. The hospital invested £3 6s 8d in the purchase of four of the sold properties and once alienated had gained £47 13s 4d in cash and £8 18s 4d per annum in rents. Of the 47 cases in which the alienation is known only one is the sale of a fee-rent from an urban property.[151] The hospital usually continued to collect these rents which were granted to it at the terms previously negotiated between the landlord and the tenant, with warranty on the part of the donor.

HSJC did not exploit its estates directly so that even in the thirteenth century, when the price of foodstuff was at a peak, the hospital would have collected a fairly stable nominal income from rents paid by long-term tenants.[152] As we have seen, town tenements or strips in the fields were quickly alienated during a period of high market prices, to produce a source of cash and steady rent income enjoyable while leaving HSJC unencumbered by extensive duties as proprietor. One wonders what considerations dictated the decision whether to sell or to lease: most probably the needs of the prospective buyer prevailed, whether he could pay a large sum at once and maintain the payment of a small nominal rent or preferred the obligation of high yearly payments in expectation of future profit.[153] Thus, a tenement in St Mary's parish was alienated for 4s 6d of yearly rent and a sum of 10 marks, while one shop in that parish was alienated at 1 mark rent per annum and a mere half-mark in *gersumma*.[154] In this period when the hospital frequently participated in the land market sums of ready cash, the sale-prices, could have been reinvested in the purchase of lucrative

---

[151] SJCA.D24.5: 12d of rent from a parcel of land in Newnham – 225 sq. ft.

[152] This is the case with the hospitals of Bury St Edmunds as well, Gottfried, *Bury St. Edmunds*, p. 196.

[153] Urry, *Canterbury*, p. 135. On possible ways of conveying land in conditions of cash strain see P. R. Hyams, 'The origins of a peasant land market in England', *Economic history review* second ser. 23 (1970), pp. 18–31; p. 30.

[154] SJCA. Cartulary of HSJC, fols. 21v, 13r. On the whole thirteenth-century rentals tend to be free of regular rent lapses, as in the accounts of Bolton priory, *Bolton priory rentals*, p. xiv.

urban rents.[155] Fully reported in surviving documents are 29 such sales, a majority of which involved urban properties. The hospital seems rarely to have interfered with the cultivation of its rural estate and was satisfied to leave the rural properties as they were given, since they were usually small and dispersed. But town properties were in great demand in the second half of the thirteenth century and were subject to fewer constraints than rural customary holdings. The hospital could subdivide properties and thus improve and enlarge the potential income: a messuage in the market, the gift of Bartholomew, son of Orgar, was leased in two separate portions to a father and his daughter.[156] Matilda Benedicta granted a messuage in St Michael's parish which was leased to two tenants.[157] The hospital also received fragmented holdings: halves of messuages, of shops and of houses. This is a well-known feature of the thirteenth-century urban land market. By the mid-thirteenth century holdings were much smaller than the original tenures, which would have fitted two–three lots into an acre.[158]

The hospital did not rely solely on the spontaneous gifts of donors. The early rush of donations to a new religious house was given without a guiding pattern to render the properties as profitable and convenient for exploitation as possible. It tried to combine the piecemeal gifts with well-planned purchases and exchanges for the improvement of its estate.[159] The positive disposition towards a new charitable house was, undoubtedly, a power acting in the house's favour. Since the hospital was granted land in villages situated up to 15 miles away from Cambridge, stretching over many fields within this area, an attempt at concentration was made in order to facilitate the collection of rents. Thus, a single holding in Caldecote was exchanged for land in Toft where the hospital held several other properties.[160] The hospital also exchanged strips within a single field, to create a more homogeneous

---

[155] It will be important to remember that this source of extra-budgetary income existed in the first half of the thirteenth century, when the hospital's activity in the credit market is examined below pp. 217–26.

[156] SJCA. Cartulary of HSJC, fol. 20v.

[157] SJCA. Cartulary of HSJC, fol. 10.

[158] R. H. Hilton, 'Some problems of urban real property in the Middle Ages', in *Socialism, capitalism and economic growth*, ed. C. H. Feinstein (Cambridge, 1967), pp. 326–37; pp. 328, 331 and Postan, *The medieval economy and society*, p. 201; Urry, *Canterbury*, pp. 149–50.

[159] On attitudes towards land acquisition and investment see Hilton, 'Rents and capital formation', pp. 178–81. For such a policy see *Bolton priory rentals*, p. xi and on the land purchasing policies of small religious houses in the thirteenth century, Kershaw, *Bolton priory*, pp. 113–17.

[160] SJCA. Cartulary of HSJC, fols. 45r, 51r. In Caldecote, 7 acres and 1 rood were exchanged for the same area in Toft.

holding. In 1246 × 9, it traded 2 acres for 2½ acres granted by John, son of Walter, in the Grantchester field, in three strips two of which abutted on hospital land.[161] Even within one parish advantageous exchanges could be made. Thus, the hospital acquired land attached to the cemetery of All Saints' parish on which the hospital's tenements abutted.[162]

By the end of the thirteenth century the hospital had accumulated most of its estate. It was now settled firmly within the town as landlord, religious intercessor, rector of a parish, neighbour and potential business associate. The house maintained relations with various townsmen, religious houses and the needy. In its hey-day the hospital was favoured by townsman and peasant alike; as the shape of its dispersed endowment testifies, it had a wide appeal within the area of Cambridge and its close surroundings.[163]

The endowment of HSJC in the fourteenth and fifteenth centuries

The hospital accumulated most of its holdings in town and country during the thirteenth century, mainly during the first 50 years of its existence. The general trend of donation to religious houses in the late twelfth and thirteenth centuries was towards grants to new orders, hospitals, leper houses and secular colleges. On the whole donations were becoming smaller, fewer and were originating from people of less wealth throughout this period.[164] Thus, a new house could expect a rush of donations, in the beginning, which would establish its basic endowment, but which would diminish rapidly after two or three generations. More enduring ties were those established through participation in the foundation of a house or through the bestowal of a substantial benefaction. Townsmen and villagers shared the act of patronage with their families in groups of father and son or siblings who made simultaneous grants, often dictated by a joint stake in a family property. However, even in such cases, benefaction to one house did not continue over a period of more than two generations. Thus, the fourteenth and fifteenth centuries saw the hospital holding a steady

---

[161] SJCA. Cartulary of HSJC, fol. 36.

[162] SJCA.D17.197. On the process of concentration and rationalisation of field holdings see T. Rowley, 'Medieval field systems', in *The English medieval countryside*, ed. L. Cantor (London, 1982), pp. 25–55; p. 38.

[163] Substantial peasants were closely related to the urban markets, but also to urban religious activity. For some observations on the cultural influence of town on countryside see Banton, *Roles*, p. 51.

[164] Raban, *Mortmain legislation*, pp. 130–2.

estate in lands, rents and tithes, while potential benefactors were largely uninterested. After some 90 years of existence the hospital came to be seen as an established part of the town and new forms of patronage were attracting pious bequests.

The fall in donation coincided with the new restrictions imposed by the Statute of Mortmain. The Statute changed the forms of land acquisition and a superficial examination would deem the period sadly deficient in pious gifts. S. Raban suggests that in this period donors moved to donations of moveables, to objects of ornamental value and cash offerings, which were usually not recorded and whose financial impact can hardly be assessed.[165] We have seen that the fall in donations to the hospital began before 1279 and is apparent already in the pattern of donation around the mid-thirteenth century.[166]

The Statute of Mortmain of 1279 initially forbade all alienation of property to religious houses. After a period of comparative stagnation in pious bequests, a *modus vivendi* emerged to make benefaction and acquisition possible under the new law. By 1292 it was established that following an *inquisitio ad quod damnum* a licence for alienation could be obtained for a particular benefaction.[167] From 1299 licences for alienation in return for fines paid to the hanaper were widely granted.[168] By the beginning of the fourteenth century religious houses came to acquire general licences for future acquisition of properties up to a certain annual income, which was a sort of insurance that future applications for particular licences would be more readily available and less costly.[169] It was somewhat doubtful whether hospitals entered the scope of Mortmain legislation, but HSJC complied with the formal demands made by it. Between 1290 and 1347 one finds only a single charter of donation to the hospital granting a small parcel of land in Newnham.[170] In 1347, following the customary *inquisitio*, a licence was acquired to allow the alienation of three messuages, arable land and meadows in the parishes of All Saints and St Edward in Cambridge, as well as land in Babraham, Grantchester, Horningsea, and in Clavering and Langley in Essex.[171] The licence was granted on 12 July 1347 and a rush of transactions immediately followed. Groups of two

---

[165] *Ibid.*, pp. 140—1.

[166] After 1270 only 9 donations to HSJC occur, see above p. 208. For a similar trend see *Cartulary of St. Mark's hospital*, p. xxxiv.

[167] Raban, *Mortmain legislation*, pp. 39—40. [168] *Ibid.*, pp. 23—4.

[169] *Ibid.*, pp. 44—6; HSJC acquired such a licence for alienation of properties up to a yearly income of 100s in 1336, *Calendar of patent rolls 1334—1338*, p. 229.

[170] SJCA.D24.192.

[171] *Calendar of patent rolls 1345—1348*, p. 352; HSJC's copy in SJCA.D39.36.

or three, most often a clergyman and one or two burgesses, gave the hospital various properties in these locations. Most often one of the grantors in each group was a clergyman and another a prominent burgess.[172] Within three weeks the hospital was granted the messuages, crofts and tenements in Cambridge and its surrounding villages and the conveyances to the full entitlement allowed by the licence, accompanied by a multitude of title deeds attesting the grantors' sequence of purchases.

This is clearly a case of transfer from the hands of feoffees to use to the true beneficiary. One of the ways of evading the restrictions of the Statute of Mortmain was found soon after its enactment in the enfeoffment of an agent with properties which a religious house could no longer acquire. Enfeoffment to use generally: 'allowed an owner to circumvent...limitation by divesting himself of the legal estate in his property in favour of one, or more generally, a group of feoffees who could fulfil his wishes for him'.[173] In the medieval context this meant that ecclesiastical bodies arranged for nominees by appointment to be enfeoffed with a donation or a purchase which they wished to acquire, thus making the agents legal owners. The distinction between *usus* and *dominium* which was developed in the thirteenth century in connection with holdings of the mendicants served well to broaden the concept of rights while detaching partial rights from the concept of full ownership.[174] The conflicting view of usufruct as a basic proprietary right rendered the theoretical separation difficult, but the debate created the terms which could subsequently be applied under the Statute of Mortmain. It made it possible for a house to enjoy a property without being legally seised of it. In these situations although the religious house in question was not seised of the property the implicit understanding granted it the benefits of tenure, an understanding that it subsequently developed into a defensible right. The arrangement relied heavily on the honesty of the feoffees and on internal checks within the group of agents. Most often clergymen were chosen to act as nominees as they at least were liable for ecclesiastical legal action in the case of mismanagement. HSJC usually chose respectable townsmen and local chaplains and priests: John the Ironmonger appears in three transactions in 1347 and William of Eversden, a chaplain, appeared in three

---

[172] Examples: SJCA.D17.38 – Richard Glavett, chaplain and John Ironmonger, burgess of Cambridge; SJCA.D26.70 – John Borewell and William of Eversden, chaplains.

[173] E. W. Ives, 'The genesis of the Statute of Uses', *English historical review* 82 (1967), pp. 673–97; pp. 673–4.

[174] Lambert, *Franciscan poverty*, esp. pp. 68–102, 133–4.

conveyances and in the licence. These men had actually acquired and accumulated the lands for the hospital and held them in seisin during the period that elapsed until the receipt of the royal licence. Once this had been granted the fiction was dissolved and the real status of the properties was asserted. The properties in question had been acquired over the years preceding that in which the actual transfer to the hospital took place.[175]

The acquisition of new properties in the first half of the fourteenth century was a planned and deliberate act on the part of the hospital, as they fitted well with existing estates and interests of the house. Some were in Horningsea parish, the appropriated parish in which the hospital held the glebe land, and others were often in the parish of All Saints, the hospital's immediate environment; lands in Babraham were added onto an already sizeable arable estate. In a period when spontaneous donation was in decline, the hospital was obliged to buy new holdings to develop, enlarge and improve the existing estate. In addition to the enfeoffment of agents, a long-term lease was another form of tenure in expectation of a licence.[176] This may explain the lease of a piece of land and meadow in Grantchester in 1338 for 14 years, which became a grant under the licence of 1347.[177]

The next licence for alienation was granted in 1362[178] to two nominees, Robert of Wimpole, rector of Kirtlyng and John of Seggeville, a burgess of Cambridge. It covered the acquisition of 4 messuages, 11 cottages, 15 acres of arable and 1 acre of meadow in Cambridge fields, tenements and marshes in Toft, Bourn and Trumpington, and the alienees paid £101 for it on behalf of the hospital.[179] However, between 1347 and 1362 we find two donations that fall under no existing licence: half a messuage in St Andrew's parish left by John Cowryks in his will of 1359 and Robert Tulke's donation of a messuage in St Sepulchre parish.[180] Evidently the hospital reckoned it an unnecessary expense to apply for a licence in the case of such small holdings. It was up to the royal officials to detect the infringements and minor encroachments on the law could easily remain undetected if they harmed no one in particular.[181] Ironically, the estate acquired

---

[175] The hospice in All Saints' parish granted by Robert the Mason and John Ironmonger had been bought in 1340, SJCA.D17.109, the grant is in charter D17.117.

[176] Raban, *Mortmain legislation*, pp. 107–114.

[177] SJCA.D24.131,which appears to be the only personal donation in this period.

[178] *Calendar of patent rolls 1361–1364*, pp. 259–60.

[179] SJCA.D98.8 and D98.19. John died a corrodarian in the hospital in 1375, CUL. EDR. Consistory court Arundel, fol. 31r.

[180] SJCA.D17.69 and D20.33.   [181] Raban, *Mortmain legislation*, pp. 98–9.

under the licence of 1362 was seized by the escheator of Cambridgeshire under suspicion of a breach of the Statute, only to be restored in 1380 following an inquisition which proved that a licence had been granted.[182] When the house contemplated a large purchase, the machinery of licensing was put into motion and feoffees were entrusted with the property during the transitional period, but when a small donation was made to the house it was accepted and the brethren relied on their luck. Lands confiscated for infringements of Mortmain were very often restored in exchange for a fine or bestowed upon other religious houses.[183] In 1380 three tenements escheated in Cambridge were granted to HSJC which may have been properties lost to the escheator by religious houses.[184]

With the relaxation of the Statute's enforcement and the frequent emergence of pardons in the fifteenth century the picture of acquisitions changed. Between 1392 and 1448 there were no new additions, but between 1448 and 1500 new holdings were assimilated into the new estates without royal licence. In 1448, Henry VI granted HSJC properties in Over in exchange for tenements needed for King's College.[185] A general pardon was granted in 1458 for offences committed up to that date, and again in 1484, though the form of acquisition was still by groups of feoffees.[186] The hospital purchased a large estate in Great Bradley, Suffolk, which was held for them throughout the 1460s by the prominent burgess Thomas Jakenett in two portions.[187] In 1466, four Cambridge townsmen, a cleric and three laymen, conveyed lands in Cottenham. The next major acquisition came in a flurry of seven charters in 1483 which covered grants of arable in Great Bradley, Cambridge fields, Horningsea and Newnham.[188] This activity must be connected with the then-pending pardon granted by Richard III in 1484. The expectation of a licence put the formal conveyancing machine into motion and these men must have been actual agents in the acquisition of the estate.[189] Long leases were another means of evasion of the Statute of Mortmain developed in the

---

[182] See *Calendar of fine rolls 1377–1383*, p. 216 (12 September 1380) and *Calendar of close rolls 1377–1381*, pp. 416–17 (8 November 1380).

[183] Raban, *Mortmain legislation*, pp. 82–6.

[184] SJCA.D19.163.   [185] SJCA.D17.192 and D32.1.

[186] SJCA.D3.70 (D3.71) and D98.31. The hospital of St John in Oxford acquired similar pardons in the fifteenth century, *Cartulary of the hospital of St. John* III, no. 940 (1401), p. 411 and no. 944 (1437), p. 413.

[187] In 1461, SJCA. Cartulary of HSJC, fol. 79v and in 1470, SJCA.D51.53 and D51.54.

[188] These are SJCA.D51.77, D51.80, D51.82, D51.83, D51.84, D51.238, D51.239.

[189] Only one donation was granted in the fifteenth century, by Richard Gagge who granted half an acre in Horningsea, SJCA.D25.229.

fifteenth century. In such agreements the hospital leased to Barnwell a plot in St Giles' parish in 1472 for 90 years, and to John Horwood and William Hylle (cleric) a close in Cambridge in 1485, for 99 years.[190]

The hospital's leasing policy remained much as it was in the thirteenth century. Being a small house with a dispersed endowment the hospital leased its holdings to tenants for long periods and collected a steady flow of rent. As in the thirteenth century, leases were usually given for the lifetime of the longer-living member of a married couple. Some of the fourteenth-century agreements state a term of 20 years, approximately a life term. These leases allowed the hospital to renegotiate terms and to evict unsatisfactory tenants, the hospital retaining full seisin and rights to distrain. In the fifteenth century the hospital tended to lease the properties for longer periods, thus waiving its rights of intervention in its property, and even alienating the properties *in perpetuum*.[191] It collected the rents and freed itself of the need to renew and review leases. This would imply a less interested and able management of the estate, a conventional feature in fifteenth-century hospitals.

THE MANAGEMENT OF THE ENDOWMENT AND FISCAL ADMINISTRATION

HSJC as a source of charitable finance

The availability of credit is a basic need of most societies and the days have long passed in which the medieval economy was seen as creditless.[192] The providers of credit were those individuals and institutions which had ready sums of cash at their disposal. The prohibition of usury obliged those engaging in lending and borrowing to disguise their transactions.[193] HSJC was part of the credit system in Cambridge from the very first years of its existence.

In the hospital's cartulary there are some entries in the form of an ordinary grant in which the grantor used the formula *dedi, concessi et confirmavi* ('I have given, granted and confirmed') at the end of which a substantial return was granted by the hospital to the donor. These

---

190 SJCA.D32.168 and D32.220.
191 For a case in the estate of St Giles', Norwich see a lease of land in Bastwick for 300 years, NRO. 25/621.
192 M. M. Postan, 'Credit in medieval trade', [first published in *Economic history review* 1 (1928), pp. 234–61] repr. in *Medieval trade and finance* (Cambridge, 1973), pp. 1–27; esp. pp. 1–5.
193 Gilchrist, *The church and economic activity*, pp. 106–7. See above pp. 66–8 on the theology of usury.

donations can be described as sales. However, some grants clearly state the grantor's need and illustrate the hospital's function as a source for liquid funds. Joan, daughter of Anketill, gave the hospital between 1210 and 1233 a yearly rent of 5s 6d from a tenement in All Saints' parish.[194] The hospital provided her with 4 marks of silver for the expenses of her pilgrimage to Jerusalem, which it was to regain within eight years, and continue to enjoy the rent *in perpetuum*.[195] Loans to pilgrims could not carry interest and this rendered it very difficult to find sources of finance before a journey.[196] The hospital received a donation in free alms and in return forwarded the lump sum which the donors may have found difficult to raise or to save from a small steady income. Any such transactions with the hospital may also have been preferred since they created a pious link with the religious house.[197]

In a similar type of transaction the grantor gave the hospital a tenement or rent, stating a pious intent and using the formula of charitable donation, while the hospital supplied a sum of cash to be used 'in order to acquit me of the Jewry'. Around 1210 × 30 Baldwin Blancgernon gave the hospital rents from four houses in Cambridge to the total of 30s 8d per annum and in return received £15 for the payment of his debt with the Jews.[198] In doing so the hospital not only freed a Christian from indebtedness to the Jews but also invested well, as after eight years it would have been repaid the £15 and would continue to collect the rents forever. Some time before Easter 1230 Baldwin entered a bond with Anthony, master of HSJC, to the effect that he and his heirs would pay 27s 6d to the hospital by that date or else lose 1½ acres in Cambridge fields which were offered as security.[199] Baldwin was a townsman–landowner, who developed knightly aspirations and lived beyond his means. He was a benefactor of the hospital

194 SJCA. Cartulary of HSJC, fol. 2r.
195 Similar transactions financed the pilgrimages of Everard of Toft and of Thomas of the Brewery. The former granted around 1220 × 30 11 acres scattered in the Toft fields for which he received 6½ marks towards his pilgrimage expenses, SJCA. Cartulary of HSJC, fol. 46, while the latter diverted part of the rent paid to him by the nuns of St Radegund to the hospital, in return for two marks for his journey, *Priory of St. Radegund*, ed A. Gray (Cambridge, 1898), no. 87, p. 92. R. V. Lennard, *Rural England 1086–1135: a study of social and agrarian conditions* (Oxford, 1965), pp. 166–7.
196 J. A. Brundage, *Medieval canon law and the crusader* (Madison, Wisc., 1969), pp. 176, 179–80. R. Génestal, *Rôle des monastères comme établissements de crédit* (Paris, 1901), pp. 64–5.
197 It is also true that since many sales in the open market combined rents and lump sums, the hospital could, perhaps, forward a whole price where many individual buyers would have preferred the less pressing combination of a smaller price and a larger rent.
198 SJCA. Cartulary of HSJC, fol. 15r.   199 SJCA.D3.34.

and of Barnwell priory, to which he gave the church of All Saints by the Castle which had been in his patronage. Baldwin had been liquidating assets for several years. In the 1230s he rented his stone house, the celebrated School of Pythagoras, to the rising Dunning family for 12 years. In 1250 he sold the house for £22 and borrowed £11 more from a fellow burgess, Maurice Ruffus.[200] He sold 2 acres to Anthony, chaplain of St Giles' church,[201] and 2½ acres to Anger, son of Edric.[202] He subsequently passed some town rents to Geoffrey of Ely who donated them to the hospital,[203] and sold tenements in the parish of All Saints by the Castle to his son Geoffrey.[204] At the same time Baldwin endowed the hospital with 8 acres in Cambridge fields for the welfare of his soul.[205] HSJC played a double role in Baldwin's life; it was a source of credit and at the same time an object of patronage which would be rewarded with spiritual returns. We cannot recreate the sequence in which the transactions occurred, whether benefaction or borrowing initiated it.[206] Baldwin's son continued the pattern of patronage despite his being a poorer man than his father had been.[207]

The case of Robert, son of Lawrence of Papworth, was even more desperate. Around 1240 he granted the hospital 2 acres in Babraham 'to God and the hospital...and to the brethren serving God there and to the weak awaiting God's grace there', for which he received 23s 'to acquit me of the Jewry'.[208] In a document of 1246 × 9 not entered into the cartulary all his land in Babraham (except for the 2 acres already given in free alms) were relinquished in return for 100 marks.[209] A bond of 1248 survives in which Robert of Madingley acknowledged his debt of 2 marks which he promised to repay the hospital in 4 instalments of ½ a mark.[210] His loan was secured by the oaths of two of his fellow villagers, and he too was indebted to the Jews in 1242 and must have turned to HSJC when the loan was due for payment.[211] Thus, the

---

[200] SJCA.D24.92.

[201] SJCA.D21.81. See E. Miller, 'Baldwin Blancgernun and his family: early benefactors of the hospital of St. John the Evangelist', *Eagle* 53 (1948), pp. 73–9; p. 77. On this family, its plight and the final sale to Merton College see *The west fields of Cambridge*, pp. 61–3. Helen Cam expressed doubts on the economic viability of the squire-burgess existence, Cam, *Liberties and communities*, p. 24.   [202] SJCA.D18.47.

[203] SJCA.D3.50.   [204] SJCA.D3.31.

[205] SJCA. Cartulary of HSJC, fol. 16v.

[206] From the names of witnesses it is clear that the loan of 27s 6d was received by Baldwin roughly at the same period as he gave a donation of an acre by the Binbrook, though the two transactions were not explicitly linked.

[207] SJCA. Cartulary of HSJC, fols. 15v, 16r.

[208] SJCA. Cartulary of HSJC, fol. 76.

[209] SJCA. D25.9.   [210] SJCA.D25.20.

[211] PRO. Exch. accounts. Bundle 249/3.

hospital was supplying credit and buying properties through a variety of legal transactions.

HSJC was not alone as supplier of credit in Cambridge, other individuals and institutions took part in such activity.[212] We find townsmen lending money to each other in the thirteenth century. John le Rus pledged $\frac{1}{2}$ acre in Cambridge field to Ralph, son of Henry in return for 1 mark.[213] Adam Wiriel granted two messuages to John, son of Bartholomew, as payment for his debt of 10 marks to John, clearly a consolidation of a mortgage.[214] A burgess of Cambridge, William de la Marche, sold land to two fellow burgesses for the sum of 4 marks which he used for the payment of his debt to the Jews.[215]

Barnwell priory was involved in such activities as well. In the 1279 land survey several of its holdings were described as pledges lost to the Jews and bought by the priory.[216] Since Jews could not be in seisin of Christian lands they were eager to dispose of those lands lost to them by default of payment.[217] In 1244–5 it paid £8 10s to the Exchequer of the Jews for the redemption of some Cambridge burgesses.[218] Religious houses were thus connected with Jewish moneylenders and their property. Many houses previously belonging to Jews were given to townsmen after their expulsion from Cambridge in 1275, and some were subsequently bequeathed to religious houses.[219] Part of Barnwell's fiscal transactions may have been carried out by the very active chaplain of St Giles' church who appears in several charters attesting loans. In 1228, Geva the widow granted the chaplain Anthony a messuage, curtilage and buildings in the parish of All Saints by the Castle in return for 4$\frac{1}{2}$ marks which were paid to the account of her late husband's heirs in the books of the Jew Isaac Blond.[220] Anthony the chaplain was probably the priory's agent, served the church appropriated to it and

---

[212] On the continent religious houses had functioned as 'rural banks' at least since the tenth century, Génestal, *Rôle des monastères*, p. 18; Patzelt, 'Pauvreté et maladies', pp. 169–70.

[213] SJCA.D17.105.   [214] SJCA.D19.155.

[215] SJCA.D17.44.

[216] *Rotuli hundredorum* II, pp. 357, 358, for example p. 358a: 'Item habent ex dono Galfridi Melt pro xv. marcas quas ei dederunt ad acquietandum se de Iewdiasmo quoddam mesuagium'.

[217] Richardson, *The English jewry*, pp. 84–5. The priory was obliged to plead to the Exchequer of the Jews when grants in alms given to it were found to be pledged lands.

[218] *Liber memorandorum*, pp. 137–8. For another example see, *Calendar of the plea rolls of the Exchequer of the Jews* II, p. 12. Even the small leper house at Stourbridge was forced into litigation when a donor pledged a rent from its land to a Jew and thus encumbered the hospital, *Curia regis rolls* II, p. 62.

[219] *Liber memorandorum*, pp. 285, 297.

[220] SJCA.D19.56.

was favourably situated in the town for participation in business. There is a grant of land in the parish by the prior to Anthony which may have served as accommodation for him.

It was a common practice for religious houses to help Christians free themselves from indebtedness to the Jews. As we have seen, the debtors were often townsmen and men of lower knightly rank. In Oxford, the Hospital of St John of Jerusalem paid £35 in 1276 to acquit Sir Ralph of Chesterton.[221] The Hospital of St John, Oxford, received many tenements in the town which had been escheated through default of payment of debts to the Jews.[222] Due to the restrictions on Jewish land-tenure the price of the forfeited pledges must have been lower than the market price and an astute purchaser could buy at a discount. A religious house engaged in lending would also have enjoyed such beneficial conditions when dealing with an embarrassed debtor.[223] Religious houses could enlarge their endowments and offer both spiritual and financial compensation for debtors obliged to liquidate assets.[224] The activities of Walter of Merton are of special interest as he combined charity, piety and economic vision. In the 1260s he was buying lands from Jews around St John's church which he planned to be the chapel of his new college.[225] Walter extended his property not only by buying forfeited pledged lands but also by offering loans to country squires.[226]

[221] *Ibid.* III, ed. H. Jenkinson (London, 1929), pp. 226–7.
[222] Roth, *The Jews of medieval Oxford*, pp. 108–9.
[223] St Frideswide's priory was a buyer of extensive forfeited pledges, *ibid.*, pp. 85, 97–8; Richardson, *The English Jewry*, p. 98. The settlement of the Brethren of Penitence of Jesus Christ in Cambridge was connected with the debts incurred by John Ruffus which forced him to leave his stone house which subsequently was bought and bequeathed to the Brethren. It was sold in 1268, see Peterhouse muniments. Collegii situs. A9. There were a chapel and two houses on the site, one of which was kept by John for life. He appears in the Exchequer's list of Jewish debts, PRO. Exch. accounts. Bundle 249/3. The property passed on to another charitable community, Peterhouse, when the order was finally dissolved, Peterhouse muniments. Collegium. A4.
[224] Upon its loss by the owner the pledge became a pious gift. On the connection between endowment and moneylending see Génestal, *Rôle des monastères*, pp. 76–7.
[225] On Walter of Merton's dealings with the Jewish land market see Aston and Faith, 'The endowments of the university and colleges', pp. 295–8. He also bought lands and houses from a Cambridge Jew as an alternative site for his college if the need arose (or for another college?), *Calendar of the plea rolls of the Exchequer of the Jews* II, p. 71; *The early rolls of Merton College, Oxford*, ed. J. R. L. Highfield (Oxford, 1964), pp. 34–6. The Merton estate in Cambridge was composed primarily of purchases made from the Dunning family and the Blancgernons who had mortgaged their properties to the hilt, and after having pursued all avenues of credit in Cambridge were obliged to part with their properties. See *The west fields of Cambridge*, pp. 57–64 and J. M. Gray, *The school of Pythagoras (Merton Hall)* (Cambridge, 1932), pp. 11–13.
[226] Roth, *The Jews of medieval Oxford*, pp. 140–1.

In all the cases reviewed above the hospital received *in perpetuum* some tangible asset in return for a large sum of money. A different series of documents, which were not copied into the contemporary cartulary, shows the extent of the hospital's activity as a provider of short-term loans. In nine surviving charters a donor gave the hospital some land for a limited term of years in return for a cash rent payable at the beginning of the term. These agreements occur between 1234 and 1272 and are phrased in the form of a fee-farm in which the grantor leased the land to the hospital. These contracts could not be simple fee-farms, for two reasons. First, the usual practice of the hospital was to alienate or to lease arable for a long term of years.[227] Its policy does not suggest an interest in the collection of short-term leases on small parts of fields for a small rent, as the documents in question would seem to imply. Secondly, when paying rent (as well as when receiving it) the hospital paid in the usual twice-yearly or quarterly payments; advance payments for the whole term are totally unknown in genuine leases. One must conclude that the lands were pledged to secure a loan given at the beginning of the term disguised as the lump sum of advance rent. Thus Martin Edbirth granted 2 acres of arable and a meadow in Babraham in 1257–8 for a term of 8 years for 6s rent paid in cash at the beginning of the term.[228] In 1259, John the Smith of Babraham leased to HSJC 1 acre in the village field for 6 years and received 4s in advance.[229]

Two rather highly placed men entered such agreements with the hospital. Sir Roger Alemer received 5 marks in 1248 and mortgaged his meadow in Newnham for 5 years as security.[230] Sehar de Scalar of the knightly Cambridgeshire Scalars who were benefactors of the hospital similarly granted 12 acres of arable, a croft and some pasture in Babraham for the term of 6 years in return for 32s. In the event of his death in mid-term the properties were to pass to the hospital in free alms.[231] Such accumulation of land through the plight of knightly families was a means of investment and expansion for thirteenth-century religious houses.[232] It is most probable that in view

[227] See above pp. 210–12.
[228] SJCA.D25.121.
[229] SJCA.D2.14. Robert and Isabella Lovel mortgaged their 'longmalthouse' at Horningsea for eight years, collecting $\frac{1}{2}$ mark in cash and promising to keep the house in repair, SJCA.D26.77.
[230] SJCA.D24.84.   [231] SJCA.D25.94.
[232] Raban, *The estates of Thorney and Crowland*, pp. 39–40. Yet, we are reminded that although 'few would dispute that the knightly class suffered an overall loss of property to religious houses...Not every alienation was necessitated by financial weakness or was part of a process which culminated in a family's near or total ruin', in

of the temporary nature of the transactions these documents represent only a fraction of this type of lending activity undertaken by the hospital.

What was the nature of such exchanges? If the lump sum of rent paid by the hospital was the capital of the loan then it is possible that the *actual* sum given to the lessor had been smaller, to provide for interest. However, it is more likely that interest was compounded through the grant of fruits and use, the usufruct, during the term of the loan. Some of the agreements describe the term as 'for six reapings', which probably means that the yield collected during the term was to be enjoyed by the hospital. If the lessee did not subtract the value of the usufruct from the capital, the lease was deemed to be a mortgage and the proceeds usurious: holding a pledged property was not in itself a sin, but the usufruct on top of the capital repayment was considered to be unlawful gain.[233] Retaining usufruct during the term of the loan, without subtraction from the capital, was a usurious practice, and was condemned in twelfth-century church councils, so that by the beginning of the thirteenth century it had become obsolete on the Continent when it was replaced by the sale of perpetual rents for lump sums as a means of raising capital.[234] Glanville held that although receipt of mortgage was a sin it was not prohibited by the law, but it was a perilous exchange since when one of the sides to the agreement died the land might be escheated.[235] Many of these mortgage charters were enacted between the hospital and parishioners of Horningsea, the parish appropriated to HSJC.[236] This may be seen as part of the many faceted relationship which existed between a community and its pastor. Here the hospital was connected in business links, just as the parishioners had become benefactors of the house. In the absence of any other large religious house in the vicinity to act as a rural bank, pastoral care came to include

D. A. Carpenter, 'Was there a crisis of the knightly class in the thirteenth century? The Oxfordshire evidence', *English historical review* 95 (1980), pp. 721–52; p. 724. See the process of acquisition followed by Netley Abbey, Meekings and Hunnisett (ed.), 'The early years of Netley abbey', p. 20.

[233] Pollock and Maitland, *The history of English law* II, pp. 118–19.

[234] Génestal, *Rôle des monastères*, p. 79; on the latter form of credit, see *ibid.*, pp. 120–56.

[235] Glanville, *Tractatus de legibus et consuetudinibus regni Anglie qui Glanvill vocatur*, ed. and trans. G. D. G. Hall (Nelson's Medieval Texts, 1965), x.8, p. 124: 'Cum vero res immobilis ponitur in vadium ita quod inde fuerit facta saisina ipsi creditori et ad terminum, aut ita convenit inter creditorem et debitorem quod exitus et redditus interim se acquietent, aut sic quod in nullo se acquietent. Prima conventio iusta est et tenet. Secunda iniusta est et inhonesta que dicitur mortuum vadium sed per curiam domini regis non prohibetur fieri et tamen reputat eam pro specie usure'.

[236] On leases as credit facilities see Hyams, 'The origins of a peasant land market', pp. 30–1.

relief of needs for credit as part of the general connection with the community's welfare, perhaps partly inspired by the charitable association linked with the hospital. Such activities seem to have continued during the period when HSJC was active in the land market and could dispose of some of its cash in the form of loans.

Of 39 Cambridge townsmen appearing as debtors in the list of the Exchequer of the Jews between 1223 and 1240, 16 were benefactors of HSJC.[237] One would have expected that men in debt to the Jews, even if only temporarily and not necessarily deeply, would not be disposed toward profitless charitable giving. Yet, one finds a donor, Simon de Turri, indebted to the Jews and losing his property in 1219.[238] John of Shelford, the founder of a chantry in St Sepulchre's church through a donation to the hospital, owed some £10 to the Jews in 1244.[239] John de Scalar and Nicholas the Goldsmith were also donors who owed considerable sums to the Jews.[240] It is reasonable to deduce that the charitable and the financial connections between the donors and the hospital were mixed.[241] Many small donations were motivated by piety and the quest for spiritual benefits. Some men active in the land market and in need of occasional credit links with the charitable house may have been motivated not only by piety but by economic expediency.[242] Despite the fact that the hospital could bail one out of financial straits, accept lands as collateral, and at the same time bestow spiritual benefits, most people turned first to the Jews who were the formal moneylenders with greater resources, knowing that they could fall back on the hospital or another religious house in case of inability to pay the Jews. This may mean that the hospital's policy was to act as a lender of last resort.

Freeing Christians from Jewish moneylenders was an act of piety and charity. This understanding of the provision of comfortable loans as an act of charity reached its fullest development in the *monti di pietà* founded in the Italian towns in the late fifteenth century.[243] Although

---

[237] PRO. Exch. accounts. Bundle 249/3.

[238] *Calendar of the plea rolls of the Exchequer of the Jews* I, p. 12; II, pp. 29, 92. Unfortunately, the order of these transactions cannot be established since the dating margin is too wide.

[239] *Ibid.* I, p. 62.   [240] *Ibid.* II, p. 307.

[241] On the types of connections maintained between hospital and patrons see *The cartulary of God's House, Southampton*, I, p. xx.

[242] See the case of a quit of rights in a meadow to the hospital of St John, Bath in return for 1 mark needed for an urgent business transaction (and a relaxation of a small rent and some arrears), 'Deeds of St. John's hospital, Bath', no. 94, pp. 50–1. And SJCA.D26.18 where Alan Det granted all his rights in some land in Horningsea in return for 20s 'ad magnum negocium meum'.

[243] On the *monti* see R. C. Mueller, 'Charitable institutions, the Jewish community and

the traditional view was that usury was totally prohibited, it was also understood that low-interest loans were as much an act of charity as a free grant, and were justified by the principle of *lucrum cessans*. Usury and charity were bound in medieval minds; gilds offered comfortable loans to their members as a form of mutual help.[244] As explained by St Bernardino, charity, the love of one's fellow, was injured by the taking of usury: 'It is evident that impious oppression of the poor is contrary to natural law...and opposes fraternal love'.[245] Usurious loans only made the poor poorer.[246] The hospital's charitable orientation and public image did not suffer from its lending activities, since it supplied a vital service for townsmen and for villagers. It provided short-term loans to peasants who needed help until harvest, until a field became productive, or to pass bad years; it was willing to buy town property which a person wished to liquidate in order to finance a pilgrimage, a marriage or a business venture. It was to the Jews, to religious houses and to a few great burgesses that those in need could turn. The hospital was able to bail out and provide a breathing space to those in debt who needed time to dispose of their property. Over the heads of laymen there hung the sword of usury; religious houses had more leeway and a diversity of sources of income that allowed them to take up cases of greater risk. It is reasonable that, though the terms of transactions differed considerably, past favours to the hospital were not forgotten at the time of need. This ability not only to pray but also to provide assistance no doubt attracted many potential benefactors.

If the hospital can be seen as a sometime moneylender and a redeemer of Christian pledges from Jewish hands, it is interesting to reconsider its location in the town. As we have seen, the Jews of Cambridge lived

Venetian society', *Studi veneziani* 14 (1972), pp. 37–82; pp. 62–76; Scarisbrick, *The Reformation and the English people*, pp. 21–2. The *monti* demanded only 15% interest to cover expenses when the current interest rate was 43.5%; see R. de Roover, *Money, banking and credit in medieval Bruges: bankers, Lombards and money changers* (Cambridge, Mass., 1948), pp. 130, 151. Interest rates rarely fell under 35% in the Middle Ages, Noonan, *The scholastic analysis of usury*, p. 294.

[244] Like the Corpus Christi fraternity of Northampton in the fourteenth century, H. F. Westlake, *The parish gilds of mediaeval England* (London 1919), p. 220.

[245] 'Constat enim quod impia oppressio pauperis legi naturali undique adversatur...sit contra fraternae dilectionis', St Bernardino of Siena, *Opera omnia* IV, 'De contractibus', sermon 38, 1.12, p. 254. On the connection between gift-giving and credit in some peasant societies see L. Baric, 'Some aspects of credit, saving and investment in a "non-monetary" economy (Rossel Island)', in *Capital, saving and credit in peasant societies*, ed. R. Firth and B. S. Yamey (London, 1964), pp. 32–52; pp. 49–50. On usury, see above pp. 66–8 and pp. 88–9.

[246] 'nunc modum de paupere pauperior fit', *Opera omnia* VIII 'de contractibus', sermon 43, 3.1, p. 379.

in the cispontine parishes of All Saints and Holy Sepulchre,[247] between the churchyards of St Clement's and St Michael's. HSJC was situated across the street and part of the tenements granted to the hospital in All Saints' parish were formerly Jewish houses.[248] The significance of the placing of the hospital in proximity to the Jewry is enhanced by the former's moneylending activities. The care of the poor and sick so near the unbelievers was combined with a challenge to the Jewish moneylenders through the provision of charitable loans. Since indebtedness to the Jews was seen as harmful to the Christian community, an act which freed a Christian from it was an act of redemption, brotherly love, faith, charity.[249]

The management of the estate, budget and cash flow

The ability to provide loans to parishioners or to past and future benefactors, presupposes a flow of cash from occasional sales and from gifts and offerings. A study of the hospital's rentals, and the very late evidence of accounts, will reveal the ways in which the hospital manipulated the endowment entrusted to it, and the uses to which it harnessed these charitable funds.

Even after the initial enthusiasm slackened and the flow of small gifts of land dried up, the hospital still functioned as a centre of worship and of religious practice, concentrating on liturgical and pastoral obligations.[250] Offerings were forthcoming from believers who frequented the hospital's chapel, who were encouraged by a series of indulgences to those offering alms and helping the house.[251] The earliest indulgence was granted by Cardinal William of Sta Sabina in 1246–7,[252] while a papal indulgence of 1393 remitted 40 days of enjoined penance of those who visited the hospital on the Feast of St John.[253] Bishop Alcock provided the latest indulgence in 1491 to those

---

[247] See above pp. 108–9.

[248] SJCA.D20.50. In Oxford the site given by Henry III to the Hospital of St John the Baptist had been the Jewish cemetery, see above p. 102. The Dominicans installed themselves in Oxford in the midst of the Jewish quarter, Roth, *The Jews of medieval Oxford*, p. 83.

[249] 'cum omnes iudaei, et maxime faenorantes, sint capitales inimici omnium christianorum'), St Bernardino of Siena, *Opera omnia* IV, 'De contractibus', sermon 43, 3.3, pp. 383–4.

[250] For some trends of donation to hospitals in the late Middle Ages see J. M. Jennings, 'The distribution of landed wealth in the wills of London merchants, 1400–1450', *Mediaeval studies* 39 (1977), pp. 261–80; Thrupp, *The merchant class*, pp. 183, 388.

[251] For a general discussion on the grants of indulgences, see below pp. 264–5.

[252] SJCA.D98.43.

[253] *Calendar of papal letters* IV, p. 455; it was published by the Official of Ely in 1396, SJCA.D98.47.

Table 6.3. *Distribution of rent income[a] between urban and rural properties and in selected parishes in selected years (in %)*

Year	Town all[b]	St Mary's parish	Other Villages	Newnham
1283	69.6		25.4	6.0
1343	66.8	7.6	24.6	8.6
1356	59.8	12.1	28.3	11.9
1371	69.8	22.6	19.6	10.6

(a) Nominal rents. (b) Including St Mary's parish.

visiting the chapel of St John the Baptist near the hospital's gate, who contributed to its fabric or recited there three Pater Nosters and three Ave Marias.[254] The alms and gifts to the chapel were a part of the house's income which cannot be assessed and which is not mentioned in its formal accounts. These additions to the constant income must have helped the house to tide over the small deficit which it seems to have maintained, at least from the mid-fourteenth century.

The 10 surviving rentals from the late thirteenth and fourteenth centuries must be handled cautiously. The later rentals recorded the tenants by parish, starting with the Cambridge parishes from north to south and moving on to the rural areas roughly by the size of hospital holdings in them. The rolls display only part of the reality of rent collection and the extent to which obligations were met by the tenants. The earlier rentals, for the years 1283,[255] 1343, *c.* 1348, *c.* 1349 and *c.* 1351,[256] record the tenant's name with the rent appearing on the right-hand column. In the later rolls for the years 1356, 1365–6, 1366–7, 1369 and 1371, the nominal rent is recorded to left of the name and the actual termly payments to the right. These instalments do not always add up to the nominal rent, but neither do they represent real lower rents (as opposed to the ancient ones) since in many cases, where the nominal and the recorded rents diverge, the latter amounts to the sum of two or three quarterly payments. This could mean that, when the final payment was made, the steward did not record it on the roll,

[254] CUL. EDR. Register Alcock, pp. 72–3 (25 July 1491).
[255] SJCA. Cartulary of HSJC, fols. 8r–9v, 24r. In this rental the urban properties are not separated by parish.
[256] SJCA. Rental roll D2.2.1 (dorse), SJCA.D2.2.2, D2.2.3, D2.2.4. Unfortunately the plague left little impression on the copier of the hospital's rental.

but instead copied the name onto the next year's rental.[257] It is all too tempting to deal with the notes as representing real paid rents, but this would be as misleading as following the nominal sums.

From the rentals in table 6.3 a very static picture of the division of the hospital's income between urban and rural areas emerges. However, the increase in the shares of St Mary's parish and of Newnham shows considerable consolidation in the more lucrative parishes both in town and in rural areas. This is an interesting phenomenon revealed in all five late-fourteenth-century rentals: as population and the number of rent-paying holdings declined, the more expensive, better situated properties retained and increased their share in the rent income. The fall in the number of potential tenants would normally lead to a fall in prices and rents due to diminished demand. However, the rise in the standard of living combined with the fall in prices would have induced some townsmen to seek better housing, even at pre-plague prices, which they would now be able to pay more easily than before. This means that although many properties fell into disuse the central town tenements attracted demand and were able to fetch rents close to the level shown in the earlier rentals.[258] In addition, the hospital seems to have been able to enforce its proprietary rights and collect urban rents fairly regularly which means that the share of the town in total nominal rents in table 6.3 is probably an underestimate of the real proportion of urban properties as sources of income. The degree to which HSJC rentals diverge from the real rent income collected by the hospital is apparent from the arrear lists which coexisted as shown in table 6.4.[259] The comparison between the rental of 1365–6 and the arrears list for that year brings to light the full impact of failure of tenants to pay their rent. Out of 68 entries in the arrears list, in a year when collections were expected of 169, 62 tenants could be identified and the number of years of accumulated unpaid rents calculated and presented in table 6.5.

No religious house, however, ever collected all rents due to it. The smaller the house and the less sophisticated its management, the greater

[257] If rents were frozen by custom this might have been a device for reducing real rents. However, this process is unknown from any other HSJC material. Furthermore, the discrepancy between the two amounts for the same property in adjacent years (where the identity of the holding can be confidently said to be the same) is not constant.

[258] Since suburbs were usually inhabited by a poorer section of the population and offered inferior housing, they would be the first sections to be deserted at a time of decline of population. On this and on suburbs of English towns in general see Keene, 'Suburban growth', pp. 79–81.

[259] When arrears were paid they figured formally in the income section of accounts. See the accounts of St Radegund's priory for 1449–50, *Priory of St. Radegund*, p. 145.

Table 6.4 *Arrears and average debts owed by HSJC's tenants 1361–2 to 1382–3*[a]

Year	No. of tenants	Total sum owed	Average debt
1361–2	99	£36 11s 3½d	7s 4½d
1365–6	68	£40 0s 10½d	11s 11d
1366–7	71	£27 0s 9½d	7s 10d
1371–2	84	£33 0s 1d	7s 10d
1382–3	56	£41 1s 1½d	14s 8d

(a) The arrears rolls SJCA.D2.3.1–D2.3.5.

Table 6.5 *Years owed in arrears (by number of tenants)*

Years owed	under 1	1–2	3–5	6–10	above 10
1365–6	20	13	11	6	12
1366–7	21	18	2	11	11

the loss accrued by decay and fraud. The existence of arrears was a normal feature of the administration of landed property even in the most efficient estates.[260] A letter from the Official of the bishop of Ely of 1395 quoted a papal letter of 1379 which had ordered parish priests to excommunicate detainers and withholders of tithes, rents, legacies and all sources of properties and incomes belonging to HSJC.[261] From the first half of the fourteenth century, and especially after the Black Death, the urban land market was becoming slacker, a fact which rendered almost impossible the collection of all outstanding rents and the maintenance of a full rental roll.[262] Rentiers such as HSJC suffered from this fall in the value of their primary source of income, and many small religious houses fell into bankruptcy in this period.[263] However, after a period of realignment the land market adjusted to the new demand as houses of lower quality were being vacated to create a sustained demand for better housing in the town centre.[264]

[260] *The cartulary of God's House, Southampton*, p. lxi; this hospital had accumulated some £200 in arrears by the reign of Richard II.
[261] SJCA.D98.16.   [262] See above pp. 28–9.
[263] See for example the hospitals of Bury St Edmunds, Gottfried, *Bury St. Edmunds*, pp. 197–201.
[264] Bridbury, 'English provincial towns', p. 14.

A small hospital such as HSJC drew its livelihood from the rents collected from its urban and rural holdings. Soon after the house's foundation it became an important holder of property in Cambridge. This meant that it was obliged to play an active part in the land market, that its properties would be attractive to buyers and tenants, and subsequently, that duties connected with such status and power would be added to the house's religious and charitable functions. The compilation of the cartulary in the 1260s reflects the need to cope with a large volume of documents and to be able to sustain claims in a very active land market. The acres, half-acres, half-houses, closes, shops which were showered on the hospital in its first years were all of importance to a house which had no backbone of large estates to fall back on.[265] Many town properties were almost immediately leased at market prices and turned into paying assets. The holders of these properties were usually burgesses, men of the same class as the hospital's benefactors, who proceeded to sublet and manage these properties.[266] These urban landlords who devoted themselves to the management of their affairs could fully exploit the changes in demand, lease at short terms and profit from the strong demand for housing in the thirteenth century. Their business relations with the hospital cannot be divorced from their patronage. Although we have no rentals for the early thirteenth century, the men to whom the hospital alienated property were usually well-established burgesses, who could buy the rent from the hospital, most usually paying a large *gersumma*. In a fragment of a rental from 1314 × 29 21 out of 27 tenants were taxed for moveables in the 1314 subsidy in the highest tax brackets.[267]

As a religious house, HSJC may have enjoyed a greater degree of favour from its business partners, people wishing to enjoy the spiritual benefits accruing from the relation with a charitable house, but its obligation to donors also entailed duties. In one case, *c.* 1260 × 70, when a benefactor's widow was left a tenant of the hospital lacking a source of livelihood, the house provided her with a tenement for life and with 2 bushels of corn yearly.[268] When improvements were needed in a

---

[265] It did attempt to acquire a high-income holding through the fourteenth-century purchase of foreign estates in Essex and Suffolk; see above p. 216.

[266] *Cartulary of God's House, Southampton*, p. lxv–lxvi. In the late Middle Ages most tenants of the urban hospital of Comines were leading burgesses, J.-M. Duvosquel, 'Les biens de la chapelle de l'hôpital de Comines au moyen-âge. Essai de reconstitution du chassereau de 1420', *Sacris erudiri* 26 (1983), pp. 221–47; p. 233.

[267] For a discussion of this subsidy see above pp. 41–4.

[268] SJCA.D3.37, was HSJC more charitable than other religious houses? A similar example is the reduction of rent granted to Alice widow of Thomas Martin for her lifetime, in 1313, SJCA.D24.191. Richard Ketelby and his wife leased from the hospital

Cambridge messuage the hospital allowed the tenant to execute them; and to compensate him for his investment it reduced the rent from 6s 8d to 1s 8d for seven years, then raised it to 3s 4d for the next seven years, after which the original rent was resumed.[269]

When new religious orders were established in Cambridge, the hospital was often involved in their business either as urban proprietor or as rector of St Peter's church. When in 1249 the newly arrived Carmelites wished to enter their holdings in Newnham, in the hospital's fee, they petitioned the hospital and an agreement was reached under the eye of the bishop which allowed the friars to enter their properties and to use St Peter's church for their services.[270] In 1262 the brethren of Penitence of Jesus Christ were allowed to erect an altar in St Peter's church,[271] and *c.* 1270 were given leave to enlarge their site to two hostels near by.[272]

As a landlord holding properties in the most sought-after urban parishes the hospital was involved in transactions with the new colleges setting up and expanding their sites. One of the university's privileges was the supervision of rents paid by scholars for their lodgings.[273] In the *taxatio* of 1246, the earliest charter of the University, which limited rents demanded by Cambridge landlords, the hospital was exempted from the limitations. Following the intervention of the bishop of Ely on their behalf, the hospital was hence allowed to lease its tenements in Cambridge, whenever and for as high a rent as it wished to demand.[274] Its highest paying properties in Cambridge were some six houses held directly by it in the parishes of All Saints, St Michael and St Peter without Trumpington Gate, which were leased as hospices.[275]

land in All Saints' parish for 12d *per annum*. The rent was raised to 18d after their death, SJCA.D17.8. The hospital was favourably disposed towards the pious couple, but their heirs were obliged to pay a rent closer to the market price. For a reduction of rent see also SJCA.D32.78 (1264–5).

[269] SJCA.D20.58 or CCCA.XXXI, 96 (1397). Robert Campion's rent was reduced in 1395 from 9s to 1s during the period in which he developed the tenement held from the hospital, SJCA.D17.95.

[270] Peterhouse muniments. Collegium. A1 (also SJCA. Cartulary of HSJC, fol. 29r).

[271] Peterhouse muniments. St Peter's Church. A5 (and A6).

[272] For 50s *gersumma*, Peterhouse muniments. Collegii situs. A19; SJCA.D20.58. In 1337 the hospital conferred upon the Austin friars the right to extend their site to three abutting tenements which had been granted to them and for which they had acquired royal licences see SJCA.D17.106 and 107; *Calendar of patent rolls (1334–1338)*, pp. 150, 419, 502; also Stokes, *Outside Trumpington Gates*, pp. 54–6.

[273] For complaints against the exorbitant rents charged in Cambridge and Oxford in the early thirteenth century (here, in 1231) see *Calendar of close rolls 1227–1231*, pp. 586–7.

[274] SJCA.D3.58. The document is transcribed in Hackett, *The original statutes of Cambridge university*, p. 55, n. 2.

[275] SJCA. Cartulary of HSJC, fol. 24r or SJCA.D2.2.1. Two of these hostels, in St Peter's, were given to the scholars of the bishop of Ely, in exchange for a yearly payment of

Besides high rents collected from the hospices in the town (all above £1 *per annum*), the hospital leased out properties in All Saints' and St Michael's parishes to University masters. In the early fourteenth century it leased properties to Masters Thomas of Terrington and Edmund of Walsingham.[276] Michaelhouse was founded in 1325 close to the hospital, and took over some rent-producing tenements in the hospital's fee formerly held by Master Roger of Botecourt. The hospital was collecting some 10% of its income from masters and colleges, and these rarely fell into arrears.[277] Corpus Christi College joined the list of tenants in the first rental after its foundation date, taking over some properties previously belonging to its founders, the gild of St Mary and Corpus Christi. The large property-owners of Cambridge, which by the late fifteenth century were mostly colleges, attempted to rationalise their urban estates in a constant process of exchange and mutual set-off of claims. When the King's Hall, the hospital's neighbour to the south, wished to rebuild the northern wall of its site which stood on hospital land, it was granted leave to do so *causa amicitie* ('in the name of friendship') on condition that the other walls were not affected by the weight and that the new wall be high enough to keep inquisitive eyes away from the hospital's grounds.[278] The hospital relaxed some rents paid by Corpus Christi College in 1448,[279] and was relieved from a rent of 2s by Mary Valence Hall (Pembroke) in 1471.[280]

What is clear is that by 1279, when the hospital's properties were surveyed in the Hundred Rolls, it had acquired most of its property. The Rolls recorded only properties held in chief from the king, but some picture of the composition of the hospital's estate can be gleaned. It was said that HSJC held in chief 179½ acres in the fields of Cambridge, one messuage, one shop and four messuages, and collected some £5 13s 10d in rents from 38 tenants in Cambridge.[281] In the *terrier* of the

---

20s, when they and the properties which were the source of their livelihood were removed from the hospital in 1283. The new college was founded in these hostels.

[276] They appear in all mid-century rentals, SJCA.D2.2.2–D2.2.4.

[277] See arrear rental rolls SJCA.D2.3.1–2.3.4.

[278] This agreement took place in 1393, SJCA.D17.114.

[279] CCCA.XIV, 64. The hospital released St Radegund's priory from 12s of rent as reported in the priory's account for 1449–50, *The priory of St. Radegund*, p. 145.

[280] SJCA. Cartulary of HSJC, fols. 6v–7r. When King's College acquired part of the Merton estate through an exchange in 1446, the hospital purchased from it some of the Merton fisheries near the Binbrook, which it was obliged to relinquish when the estate reverted to Merton College, Merton College charters, M2788, M2789; Gray, *The school of Pythagoras*, p. 37. The hospital and colleges were sustained by similar sources of income and incurred similar types of expenditure, which must have induced some degree of cooperation in joint interests. See the analysis of the endowment of Exeter college in its first century, A. F. Butcher, 'The economy of Exeter college', pp. 38–40 and below pp. 274–5. [281] *Rotuli hundredorum* II, pp. 367, 368, 370–86.

Table 6.6 *Components of receipts, 1283*

Income from town properties	£18 2s 11d
Income from rural properties	£ 6 2s 11½d
Income from Horningsea	£ 1 6s 8d
Total	£25 12s 6½d
	(reported as £26 13s)

Table 6.7 *The balance of income and expenditure of HSJC in 1343*
(Rental roll SJCA.D2.2.2)

Income		Expenditure	
Rents		Rents	£2
Others		Wages	£1 6s 1d
		Food	£17 10s[a]
		Stipends	£6[b]
Total income[c] £25 6s 5d		Total expenditure	£26 16s 1d
	Balance		− £1 9s 8d

(a) This sum is taken from the total of the kitchen accounts for 1343 in SJCA. Cartulary of HSJC, fols. 89–90.

(b) These have been calculated for a master and four brethren receiving stipends at the rates specified in HSJC's rule (appendix 1).

(c) The steward's reported receipts; rentals calculated by addition; 'Others' = residual income.

west fields of Cambridge, *c.* 1340, the hospital was the largest holder, with 16.3 % of the fields' acreage,[282] and enjoyed the right to fold sheep on the fallow, in proportion to the extent of its holdings.[283] It is difficult to assess the multitude of early thirteenth-century donations and purchases in accurate financial terms. Even if it could be confidently said that the medieval charters which have reached us are a complete series it is difficult to assess the flow of income produced by the transactions which they recorded. The rentals report only incomes from

[282] Its 941 roods were split into 139 parcels, 13.6% of the total of parcels, which means that the hospital's holdings were slightly above average in their concentration. *The west fields of Cambridge*, text of the terrier in pp. 88–134; table of ownership in the fields, pp. 156–60.

[283] It had disposed of the few grants in the east fields where at the time reflected by the terrier it held no strips at all (Barnwell priory was the chief holder there).

Table 6.8 *Income in 1490 and expenditure in 1485*

Income (1490)			Expenditure (1485)	
Town rents	£22 8s 9½d	31.3%	Rents	£ 1 14s 6d
Rural rents	£15 6s 11½d	21.4%	Food	£27 18s 2d
Foreign estates	£8	11.1%	Maintenance[a]	£28 0s ½d
Horningsea	£18	25.1%	Stipends	£13 5s 8d
Barns	£8	11.1%		
Total	£71 15s 9d	100.0	Total[b]	£70 18s 4½d
			Steward's reported income	£66 0s 4½d
			Balance	−£5 0s 6d

[a] This includes expenses on repairs, travel, fabric, wax and wine for the chapel, gifts and dues.

[b] The steward's calculation of the total was £71 7s 10½d for expenditure; the discrepancies must arise from arithmetical mistakes and from my erroneous interpretation of some of the figures.

land and tenements, and not other sources of income, and the first full set of accounts with full receipts and expenditures is as late as 1485. The first summary of the receipts is made on the dorse of the rent roll for 1283.[284]

On the dorse of the 1343 rental some of the hospital's expenses for the year were recorded (see tables 6.6 and 6.7). The balance, shown in the last line of table 6.7, is not a bad one, considering that the house enjoyed additional income from offerings and gifts in kind. It must have also spent more than is recorded on various unexpected expenses such as litigation and gifts to episcopal officials and to patrons. The next record of the hospital's finances can be found in the account of 1485, a full report on income and expenditure, which we can compare with the rental of 1490.[285] At the end of the fifteenth century the hospital was maintaining a tight but viable balance of income and expenditure;

[284] SJCA. Rental roll D2.2.1.

[285] Analysis of the accounts for years 1505–11 (SJCA.D106.9) has not been presented here since by then management of HSJC had become rather erratic, in what was a transient stage in the refoundation as a college. One of the recurring items in these accounts was trips to 'her Lady Grace' in connection with the refoundation. Expenses were laid out on purchases of building material for the college, and the operation was supervised by the last master of the hospital as *locum tenens* in 1509–11, SJCA.D17.72. On these years see E. Miller, *Portrait of a college. A history of the college of St. John the Evangelist, Cambridge* (Cambridge, 1961), pp. 1–8.

it was by no means decayed or unable to maintain itself and its obligations, which had long ceased to be the maintenance of poor and sick folk (see table 6.8).[286]

CONCLUSION

As the object of spontaneous largesse and interest on the part of townsmen and substantial peasants, HSJC was showered with donations in the first half of the thirteenth century. It soon became an important local proprietor with holdings in every parish of the town, and in all neighbouring villages. Those properties lying in fragmented portions in distant fields were exchanged or leased out for long periods, for the house attempted to concentrate its properties as much as possible. It also tried to benefit from the buoyant thirteenth-century land market and to alienate lucrative properties to burgess landlords, relinquishing its proprietary rights, and some influence, but receiving in return large sums of capital in *gersumma* payments, and retaining steady income from rents. The capital was subsequently invested in other properties, and in moneylending.

It is also clear that the hospital suffered from the perennial problems of landlords: the failure of tenants to pay, sitting tenants, dilapidation of properties. To this must be added the great fall in land values in the fourteenth century, which forced landlords to renegotiate terms of tenancy, even if their rentals are often loath to reflect this reality. The hospital was often obliged to assert its rights and distrain properties. However, being a small and humble house it could not sustain the expenses of litigation, and lists of arrears were growing in length, incomes were falling and rights were gradually eroded and lost. Judicious acquisition in the fourteenth century greatly helped the house, contributing between 1347 and 1500 £8 from Essex and Suffolk. The rent and the income of the rectory at Horningsea formed an important part of the hospital's resources in the late Middle Ages.

When seeking a business partner, the hospital could offer not only a wide and diverse urban estate, but the promise of intercession and connection with a religious charitable institution. In its dispute with Peterhouse the hospital could rally townsmen, past and current town officials, to its support. It was a house founded by the town and endowed by its benefactions, and was connected with the townsmen's

---

[286] On the relation between receipts and expenditure maintained by a small community such as Exeter college see Butcher, 'The economy of Exeter college', appendix 1, p. 51.

view of their own autonomy and welfare. But, with the assumption of fewer charitable obligations, by the fifteenth century it housed only one or two almsfolk, and with the tendency to function more and more like a chantry or a college, the hospital was brought closer to the University. Thus, throughout the late fourteenth and the fifteenth centuries there were scholars lodging in the hospital, and with the foundation of colleges in that period the house found itself surrounded by academic chantries, and found the milieu in which it acted was becoming progressively more dominated by them.

The changes which took place in the hospital's life and functions were intimately related to shifts in the attitudes harboured by potential benefactors and recipients of its services. While the house was developing the liturgical aspect of its routine – its role as a chantry – its administrators were forced to make do with a stagnant or even declining endowment: it had to respond to a changed attitude towards the religious charitable house. The burgess community, and substantial villagers in whose ranks founders and benefactors were to be found, had lost interest in the maintenance of a religious community offering indiscriminate help to poor and sick folk. These same people were coming together in voluntary religious and social groupings which they controlled to provide mutual help and to procure intercession in a more direct fashion. Inasmuch as the hospital and the many colleges which were founded in late medieval Cambridge could fulfil the role of faithful administrators and executors of charitable initiatives, townsmen chose them too as beneficiaries.

Chapter 7

CORPORATE AND INDIVIDUAL ACTS OF CHARITY

Charitable activity was far more widespread than might be indicated by the study of institutions specifically intended for relief. It was carried out by individuals and by a variety of corporate bodies whose primary function was not relief, but which nonetheless had reason to include it in their activities.[1] The scope of distributions is as difficult to assess as it was broad; one can only identify the *types* of occasions on which help would have been dealt to the needy, without attempting an exact computation of the frequency and scope of such occurrences.[2]

The occasions were determined by several religious, economic and social prescriptions. Parish priests were supposed to use at least a quarter of their income for the relief of poor parishioners. Fraternities offered help to their members and offerings on occasions of intercession for dead brethren. Religious houses, including hospitals, were guided towards works of mercy by their rules and statutes, but also as part of their obligation to distribute alms at obits and on feast days. To these should be added a multifarious charitable network comprising individual acts of relief encouraged by preachers and parish priests. At funerals, when anxieties connected with the after-life were most acute, great largesse was manifested. Such relief, like doorstep charity as well as neighbourly and family support, was ubiquitous yet remains very difficult to assess.

DISTRIBUTION IN PARISHES

Charity was connected to parish organisation in two ways: the parish was the framework in which believers executed their religious obligations; it was also the unit in which tithes were collected and oblations

---

[1] This division is applied in a study of charity in a later period: Fairchilds, *Poverty and Charity in Aix-en-Provence*: chapter 4: 'The Poor of the Charities', pp. 73–99; chapter 5: 'The Poor Outside the Charities', pp. 100–28.

[2] On the importance of 'informal' alms even within the ordered giving of confraternities see R. C. MacKenney, 'Trade guilds and devotional confraternities in the state and society of Venice to 1620' (Ph.D., Cambridge, 1982), pp. 180–2.

received – revenues which were seen, from the earliest times of Christian organisation, as wholly or partially owed to the poor. The parish was a residential, social and sometimes occupational unit; the rural parish embraced the whole community, in a town it embodied a neighbourhood and connected people who were tied by kinship and friendship.[3]

Responsibility for the welfare of poor believers lay *ex officio* upon the bishop of a diocese. Gratian's *Decretum* enshrined the view of the bishop as protector of the weak (widows, orphans) and as provider of food and clothing for the poor.[4] Episcopal revenues were to be divided into four portions, one of which was meant to be used for poor relief.[5] Gratian's sources were fifth- and sixth-century letters of popes Simplicius (468–83), Gelasius (492–6) and Gregory I (590–604), and subsequent application of these letters in sixth-century councils.[6] These views were related to a reality vastly different from the one prevailing in the twelfth century, originating in a period before parochial units had fully emerged.[7] By that period parish organisation had already developed into the primary ecclesiastical unit with which most believers maintained their contacts. The Gelasian quadripartite division of episcopal revenues which allocated one part to poor relief and hospitality was applied to parochial incomes by the eleventh century.[8] However, in England a tripartite division of incomes into portions for the poor, the clergy and the fabric was common and was enforced as late as the eleventh century. This interpretation was closer to the original view of the charitable purpose of tithe payments which was formulated in the fifth- and sixth-century Gallic councils.[9] The

---

[3] Chiffoleau, *La comptabilité de l'au-delà*.

[4] *Decretum magistri Gratiani* D.82 *dictum ante* C.1: 'Generaliter etiam pauperibus et his, qui suis manibus laborare non possunt, episcopus necessaria provideat'; D.84 *d.a.* C.2; D.85 *d.a.* C.1: 'Hospitalitas vero usque adeo episcopis necessaria est, ut, si ab ea inveniatur alieni, iure prohibeantur ordinari'; D.87. *d.a.* C.1: 'Viduis autem et orphanis ecclesie presidum implorantibus episcopi debent adesse'.

[5] The basic work on the canonical concept of poor relief is that of Tierney, *Medieval poor law*. On the development of the priest's duty, see *ibid.*, pp. 67–89.

[6] *Decretum*, C.12. q.1. C.23; C12. q.2. C.23, 26–31.

[7] Tierney, *The medieval poor law*, p. 70.

[8] Constable, *Monastic tithes*, pp. 43–4, 56; in the twelfth century: *Decretum*, C.12. q.2. C.30: 'Quatuor debent fieri portiones, una videlicet episcopo et familiae eius propter hospitalitatem atque susceptionem, alia clero, tertia pauperibus, quarta ecclesiis reparandis'; as applied to parishes C.12. q.2. C.28: 'oblationum et redditum ecclesiarum tres portiones presbitero dispensandae credantur'. Quadripartite division was current in eleventh-century Italy, C. Boyd, *Tithes and parishes in medieval Italy* (Ithaca, N.Y., 1952), p. 119.

[9] Constable, *Monastic tithes*, p. 56. A different tripartite division into portions for the bishop, the clergy and the fabric existed in Spain, *ibid.*, pp. 43–4, n. 3.

Decretists undertook the interpretation and application of the early Christian principles to the reality of the High Middle Ages. Their task was to enforce the episcopal charitable obligation upon parish priests and the development of a system of control which would ensure the fulfilment of this duty. Lateran III demanded that no appropriation of churches take place without episcopal supervision and licence attempting to ensure that parochial performance did not suffer;[10] Lateran IV laid down that an absent rector be represented by a sufficiently endowed vicar.[11] Rectors were obliged not only to relieve but also to provide a sufficiently endowed incumbent in every parish to dispense spiritual and charitable services.

The first English synodal statute dealing with parish relief was Canterbury I (1213 × 14) which stated the principle: 'Let priests be as hospitable to the poor as their resources allow, and not mean'.[12] This was restated almost verbatim in the diocesan statutes of Salisbury I (1217 × 19) as well as in Winchester I (1224) and in Exeter I (1225 × 37).[13] Salisbury I defined the duty of hospitality as lying on 'priests and beneficed clergy'. At Worcester III (1240) the duty was imposed on the secular clergy as well as on the religious; hospitality was to be provided *sine murmuratione* in each house according to the respective demands of ecclesiastical law or the order's rule and its financial ability.[14] The additional statutes of the Council of Norwich (1240 × 66) demanded not only hospitality but a kindly and willing disposition on the part of rectors and vicars.[15] Chichester I (1245 × 52) connected residence with the obligation of hospitality: 'We decree that they be resident in their (parish) churches, tending to hospitality and other works of charity as far as their resources allow, unless they are absent for a while for a necessity and by licence granted by us'.[16] A later canon of the council reinforced the demand for proper vicarages in parishes from which the rector was absent, so as to ensure

---

[10] *Conciliorum oecumenicorum decreta*, cc.5, 8, 13, pp. 214, 215, 218.

[11] *Ibid.*, c.32, pp. 249–50.

[12] 'sacerdotes...sint autem secundum redditus suos hospitales et erga pauperes non avari', *Councils and synods* II, c.11, p. 27.

[13] *Ibid.*, c.14 p. 64, c.15 p. 128, c.12 p. 232. Also in the collection of episcopal statutes borrowing largely from Lateran IV named 'constitutiones cuiusdam episcopi' (1225 × 30), *ibid.*, c.41, p. 188.

[14] *Ibid.*, c.61, p. 311, repeated in Salisbury II, c.57, p. 386.

[15] *Ibid.*, c.82, p. 362: 'hospitalitas singulis debet esse amabilis et acceptabilis, rectores nostros et vicarios residentes...'.

[16] 'decernimus ut in ecclesiis propriis resideant, hospitalitati pro modo facultatum et aliis operibus caritatis intendentes, nisi ipsis ut ad tempus abesse possint ex causa necessaria a nobis licentia concedatur', *ibid.*, c.46, p. 461.

that the charitable duties of a parish priest were fulfilled.[17] The duties of parish priests are further developed in the statutes of Salisbury III (1228 × 56) and their vicars are said to have the same duties.[18]

By the mid-thirteenth century the setting aside of a portion of parish revenues for poor relief was well formulated, but it could be effectively enforced only when a rector or a sufficiently endowed vicar was in residence. Echoing canon 29 of Lateran IV, English councils from the Legatine Council of London (1237) repeated the demand for residence.[19] The portion of parish revenues allocated for poor relief was sometimes lower than the traditional quarter, as in cases of approved absence when part of the revenue was used to maintain a vicar. The additional statutes of Salisbury IV (1257 × 68) provided for a mere twelfth of a church's revenues to be spent during the rector's absence,[20] while those residing owed the customary quarter.[21] When a monastery held a living, the duty to allocate tithe incomes to parish uses clashed with the principle of monastic exemption from tithes. The eleventh-century view, influenced by the Reform, held that tithes must be restored wholly to the parish and opposed the holding of tithes other than those produced by a monastery's own work,[22] but the view which came to prevail both in the *Decretum* and in the later canonist collections justified monastic possession of tithes in parishes where they held the *cura animarum* or where any pastoral duties were fulfilled, subject to episcopal licence.[23] In Winchester III (1262–5) portions equal to an eighth or a tenth were allocated to parish use in case of appropriation to a monastic house.[24] The Legatine Council of London in 1268 decided that a sixth of parish revenues be directed to the poor during the suspension of a priest from

---

[17] *Ibid.*, c.68, p. 465: 'et vicarii pauperibus se exhibere valeant hospitales, habita tamen ratione ad ecclesie facultates'.

[18] 'Provideant etiam persone et vicarii…Et debent esse hospitales et debent esse elemosinarii, prout facultates eorum suppetunt, et sint residentes nec alibi nimis diuturnam moram facientes praeterquam in propriis domicilis', *ibid.*, c.9, p. 513.

[19] *Councils and synods* II, part 1, c.13, p. 251; *Conciliorum oecumenicorum decreta*, c.13, pp. 248–9.

[20] *Councils and synods* II, part 1, c.38, p. 564: 'et non minus quem XIImma portio proventuum ecclesiarum suarum…per ordinarios locorum in pias causas convertanda'.

[21] *Ibid.*, pp. 564–5: 'Ceteri, vero non habentes causas absentie memoratas, in quarta parte proventuum suarum tanquam vagabundi et desertores cogantur erogare'.

[22] Constable, *Monastic tithes*, pp. 136–65.

[23] *Ibid.*, pp. 165–85, esp. pp. 182–5.

[24] *Calender of entries in the papal registers relating to Great Britain and Ireland: papal letters, 1198–1492* I, ed. W. H. Bliss, C. Johnson and W. H. Twemlow (London and Dublin, 1893–1978), p. 375. Alexander IV's letter of 1261 demanded that four to five marks be given as a living and that when a parish church was appropriated to a monastery, that 1/8–1/10 be expended on charity.

his living,[25] and demanded that compositions paid by litigants in ecclesiastical courts be forwarded for poor relief.[26]

The duty of residence and the institution of sufficient vicarages was reiterated in the general council at Lyons in 1274 and received renewed attention in English councils. The extensive canons of the Lambeth council of 1281 dealt with the duties of hospitality, and canon 11 summed up all previous strands of thought; 'we have ordained that rectors who do not physically reside in their churches, nor have vicars in their place, still offer hospitality by their agents, as far as the resources of the church allow; so that poor parishioners will be henceforth relieved of extreme need'.[27] At Exeter II (1287) it was further demanded that all income beyond the priest's needs be used for relief.[28] In his injunctions for the parish clergy of his province Archbishop Peckham (1287) demanded the provision for the poor and sick out of parish revenues, according to the ability of each parish and the guidelines of canon law: 'in physical need let them provide as long as the church's resources suffice...and let them provide hospitality as demanded by canonical sanctions'.[29]

The absence of the chief collector of parish revenues caused a major break in the regular execution of parochial duties, one of which was poor relief.[30] A fourteenth-century case recorded in the register of Bishop Fordham of Ely (1388–1425) illustrates what may have been a common occurrence. The parishioners of Gransden complained to

---

[25] *Councils and synods* II part I, c.5, pp. 753–4.

[26] *Ibid.*, c.27, p. 773.

[27] 'Statuimus ut rectores, qui in ecclesiis suis non faciunt residentiam corporalem nec habent vicarios, per yconomos suos hospitalitatis gratiam exhibeant iuxta quod sufficiunt ecclesie facultates; adeo ut saltem parochianorum pauperum necessitati subveniatur extreme', *ibid.*, c.11, p. 907. Interestingly, the canon also demands that the preachers of God's word be fed, p. 908. In a licence granted by Bishop Quivil of Exeter in 1283, a parish priest was allowed to study Theology at Paris or Oxford and to farm his living on the following terms: 'ita quod det i marcam argenti fratribus predicatoribus et minoribus et pauperioribus de parochia', *The registers of Walter Bronescombe (1257–80) and Peter Quivil (1280–91), bishops of Exeter*, ed. F. C. Hingeston-Randolph (London, 1889), p. 321. See also licence to Geoffrey of Wetemstede of 1286, *ibid.*

[28] 'Quicquam ultra vite sue necessaria eis superfuerit de patrimonio Ihesu Christi in usus pauperum quorum dispensatores existunt', *Councils and synods* II part II, c.18, p. 1014. The canon opposes this ideal with the reality of priests spending parish revenues on their concubines.

[29] 'In corporalibus necessitatibus provideant iuxta quod sufficiunt ecclesie facultates...et hospitalitatem etiam servant prout dictant canonice sanctiones', *ibid.*, p. 1079.

[30] In the licence of 1283 to a future student of Theology by Bishop Quivil permitted the farm of the parish 'salva canonica porcione assignanda per episcopum pauperibus ejusdem parochie prout in ultimo concilio Lambethensi est statutum', *The registers of Bronescombe and Quivil*, p. 321.

the bishop that their rector was absent without licence: due to his absence services did not take place, nor hospitality, to the detriment of the parishioners.[31] In the consistory court of Bishop Arundel of Ely we hear of a case brought by the parishioners of Kingston pleading against their rector John Podyngton who had totally neglected the parish: he failed to supply lights at the altars or to celebrate divine hours and did not visit the sick, allowing babies to die unbaptised and the sick to die unshriven.[32] This is not a case where lack of hospitality is mentioned but it shows that parishioners were aware of parochial and pastoral duties of the incumbents and that they sometimes attempted to enforce them.[33]

Another form of information which shows the gap between demands of ecclesiastical legislation and the reality which it tried to influence appears in accounts of complaints against extraordinary exactions from the clergy. Any new impositions would of course be opposed, but the reasoning brought against such exactions is revealing. A demand made in 1240 for a papal subsidy of what seems to have been a fifth of clerical revenues provoked such reaction. In the surviving reply of the rectors of Berkshire to this demand, the state of need in the parishes and the importance of parish relief in alleviating this need was stressed: 'since the incomes of their churches hardly suffice for most clerics...owing to their own poverty, to recurrent famines in the region...and to the large number of poor'.[34] In 1245 complaints were presented at the Council of Lyons among which loomed the problem of foreign beneficed clergy. Parishes were said to suffer from the holding of benefices by foreigners since 'they have not established hospitality and almsgiving in the church as ordained, but take the revenues and transport them outside the realm to the detriment of those properly deserving the living who can and wish to exercise these works of charity and other deeds of mercy'.[35] As we have seen, Cambridge parish churches were being appropriated to religious houses and to

---

31 CUL.EDR. Register Fordham, fol. 177v. For a case of the eviction of a parish priest who withheld and established parochial distribution, in 1327, see J. G. Bellamy, 'The Coterel gang: an anatomy of a band of fourteenth century criminals', *English historical review* 79 (1964), pp. 698–717; p. 699, n. 3.

32 CUL.EDR. Consistory court Arundel, fols. 106v–107r (1378).

33 Another form of protest against parish clergy was expressed in the preference of personal distribution of tithes directly to the poor, Little, 'Personal tithes', pp. 67–88.

34 'Cum clericis vix sufficiant proventus ecclesiarum suarum...tum propter earum tenuitatem, tum quia nonnunquam fames in regione ingruit..tum quia tanta est multitudo pauperum', *Councils and synods* II part I, p. 289.

35 *Ibid.*, p. 393: this appears in the description of Peterborough Chronicle as part of a list of eight reasons brought against the holding of benefices by foreigners.

academic colleges[36] and by the mid-fourteenth century no church in Cambridge was in full command of its incumbent.[37] The vicarages in these churches were usually small, many of them having been determined in the early thirteenth century. Thus, parish revenues were deflected from the use of parishioners and the fabric of the churches to the support of monks, nuns and scholars at Barnwell, St Radegund, Ely priory, West Dereham priory, Michaelhouse, Peterhouse and Corpus Christi College. The vicarage of All Saints near the hospital was worth 10s, that of St Sepulchre was valued at 1 mark. Thus, although Cambridge had a dense parochial network it is most probable that poor relief was not properly provided. Nonetheless, houses such as Barnwell and St Radegund's could not totally disregard their duties to their parishioners, townsfolk on whose cooperation or at least acceptance their peaceful existence depended.[38] The academic colleges, on the other hand, were more independent of local largesse, and so less sensitive to parishioners' expectations.

The difficult task of assessing the reality of parish relief was attempted by B. Tierney through the records of vicarages reported in episcopal visitations.[39] He saw in the constant attention given to the question of vicarages, pluralism and absenteeism a sign that the requirements of hospitality and relief were widely recognised and that parishioners were aware of their rights and fought for their implementation.[40] One may only speculate whether charitable houses adhered more closely to their pastoral charitable duties. In 1330 the episcopal *corrector* examined a member of the parish of Seething, Norfolk, who had conspired to deflect the parish's tithes. In justification of his act, the man claimed that the hospital of St Giles had neglected to repair the belfry and to feed the poor,[41] the parishioners thought that the house had failed in its charity, and took the matters into their own hands.

[36] See above p. 194; as well as Brooke, 'The churches of medieval Cambridge', pp. 49–76.

[37] The number declined slightly in the fourteenth century, see *Liber memorandorum*, pp. 175–7. On the churches of Cambridge see H. M. Cam's article in *VCH. Cambridgeshire* III, pp. 123–33.

[38] See the involvement of townsmen in the affairs of the nunnery as shown in donations to it, *The priory of St. Radegund*. On the pastoral work performed by monks in the twelfth and thirteenth centuries see M. Chibnall, 'Monks and pastoral work: a problem in Anglo-Norman history', *Journal of ecclesiastical history* 18 (1967), pp. 165–72. Appropriation did not fully replace the functions of parish priests which were growing dramatically in the thirteenth century.

[39] Tierney, *Medieval poor law*, chapter 5, pp. 89–109 and chapter 6, pp. 109–33.

[40] Complaints of parishioners against absent rectors are frequently recorded in late medieval episcopal visitations; see C. Harper-Bill, 'A late medieval visitation – the diocese of Norwich in 1499', *Proceedings of the Suffolk Institute of Archaeology* 34 (1977), pp. 35–47, at pp. 41–2.

[41] NRO. 25/522.

An interesting development of parochial charitable responsibility is to be found in the foundations named 'tables' (*mensae*) which appeared in the towns of Flanders, Northern France and Northern Italy between *c*. 1180 and *c*. 1250. These foundations were usually administered by laymen, often in connection with and under the supervision of municipal authorities.[42] Legacies and donations left to them both in kind and in cash were duly distributed according to lists of deserving recipients.[43]

The nature of distributions by the tables can help us to understand parish charity in general, insofar as the commodities handed to the poor can reveal their needs. These included daily portions of bread and pennies, also of shoes and clothes, of meat, herring, oil, peas and beer either on feast days or on a weekly basis.[44] A cold winter, Lent, and special feasts were the occasions of larger and more varied distributions.[45] England had no such parish tables but its rectors and vicars were obviously engaged in relief of the poor, particularly their parish poor. In 1203 a letter from Archbishop Hubert Walter to the bishop of Coventry exhorted fellow bishops to see that subsidies for the poor and for the king were collected. He demanded the dissemination of a message of mutual help by laity and clergy to alleviate the woes of an exceptionally disastrous famine year.[46]

If most of the parish churches which existed in Cambridge in the eleventh and twelfth centuries were the creation of associations of townsmen for the expression and promotion of community and family piety, one may expect that, at least in the beginning, these were close

---

[42] For similar activities in Provence see Chiffoleau, *La comptabilité de l'au-delà*, pp. 307–22.

[43] M.-J. Tits-Dieuaide, 'Les tables des pauvres dans les anciennes principautés belges au moyen-âge', *Tijdschrift voor geschiedenis* 88 (1975), pp. 562–83; *idem*, 'L'assistance aux pauvres à Louvain aux xve siècle', in *Hommage au Professeur P. Bonenfant* (Brussels, 1965), pp. 421–39. Lists of recipients may have been related with the municipal lists of hearths for the purpose of tax-collection: P. Heupgen, 'La commune Aumône de Mons du xiiie au xviie siècle', *Bulletin de la commission royale d'histoire de Belgique* 90 (1926), pp. 319–72, esp. p.323.

[44] T. Leuridan, *La table des pauvres à Roubaix*, n.p., n.d., pp. 33–4.

[45] Tits-Dieuaide, 'Les tables des pauvres', pp. 562, 578–9 and *idem*, L'assistance', pp. 436–7. In Italy similar foundations appeared somewhat later in the thirteenth and fourteenth centuries, connected with both urban and ecclesiastical authorities. Italian bishops played an important role in the supervision of charitable activity: G. C. Bascapé, 'L'assistenza e la beneficenza a Milano dell'alto medioevo alla fina della dinastia sforzesca', *Storia di Milan* VIII (Milan, 1957), pp. 389–419; pp. 389–401.

[46] 'Providimus ut singuli per diocesim suam tam clericos quam laicos ad subveniendum pauperibus et ad ieiuniis et orationibus aliisque bonis operibus plus solito insistendum diligentius exhortentur', Cheney, 'Levies on the English clergy', p. 583. Residents and absentees were included and the latter were reminded to devote a quarter of the parish income to poor relief.

groupings which showed responsiveness to parishioners' needs.[47] The parish framework remained an important unit for distributions of testamentary bequests.[48] Towards the late fourteenth century and in the fifteenth century the parish gains prominence as a chosen administrator of relief. A testament of this period was not complete without some provision towards the maintenance of the lights, bells, fabric or poor of the parish.[49]

DISTRIBUTIONS ON FEAST DAYS BY RELIGIOUS HOUSES AND HOSPITALS

The many Christian feast days were occasions on which greater generosity was expected of believers.[50] The question of church attendance by parishioners is very complex, but insofar as laymen went to church they did so on Sundays and special feasts.[51] Through sermon and prayer the laity was reminded of its Christian duties to the poor.[52]

It is easier to assess the occasions on which religious houses offered distributions. A glance at the calendar of Barnwell priory shows that an elaborate scheme of minor and major feast days punctuated the liturgical year.[53] In this thirteenth-century calendar 37 of 58 were feasts on which no work was to be done; at Lincoln Cathedral 51 feast days were observed.[54] Clearly, laymen did not observe as many feasts,

---

[47] On parish community relations see Brooke, 'The missionary at home', pp. 78–81. For an example of the organisation of parish relief see C. Battle, 'La ayuda a los pobres en la parroquia de San Justo de Barcelona', in *A pobreza e a assistência aos pobres na península ibérica durante a Idade Média* 1 (Lisbon, 1973), pp. 59–71.

[48] In 1498 John Smith of St Peter's parish, Cambridge, left 'Item to every housholde of the parisshe where nede is 4d', SJCA.D23.234; also SJCA.D23.235.

[49] For an analysis of bequests made by the citizens of Norwich to their parish churches see Tanner, *The church in late medieval Norwich*, pp. 126–40.

[50] For the numerous current thirteenth- and fourteenth-century feasts see, C. R. Cheney, 'Rules for the observance of feast days in medieval England', *Bulletin of the Institute of Historical Research* 34 (1961), pp. 117–47. For early sixteenth-century Sunday collections in the parish of St Mary, Cambridge, 1504–1635 see *Churchwardens' accounts of Great St. Mary's, Cambridge*: 1515 – 6s 7d collected per week, p. 23; 1516 – 6s collected per week, p. 29; 1524 – 4s 9d collected per week, p. 55. For some examples of late medieval alms-boxes see J. C. Cox and A. Harvey, *English church furniture* (London, 1907), pp. 240–1.

[51] Murray, 'Religion among the poor', pp. 300–6.

[52] See as an example of a private act of charity: Geoffrey the Goldsmith and his wife granted to Yvo the merchant land in the market of Cambridge from which a rent of 12d. was owed and was to be used 'hospitando singulis noctibusa aliquis pauper pro amore dei qui karitatem petat', SJCA.D19.144 (*c.* 1210 × 40). On the influence of the rhythm of the liturgical year on occasions of distribution of relief see Blockmans and Prevenier, 'Poverty in Flanders and Brabant', pp. 39–40, 44.

[53] *Liber memorandorum*, pp. 3–15.

[54] *Statutes of Lincoln cathedral* III, ed. H. Bradshaw and C. Wordsworth (Cambridge, 1897), pp. 545–7.

but most churches maintained some form of celebration on the major feasts, vigils and saints' days, as well as regular masses. Hardly a week passed without a special day on which religious sentiment was heightened and the poor benefited.

Maundy Thursday and the feast days of patron saints were occasions for large-scale distributions and acts of charity in religious institutions.[55] The almoner of Worcester priory was to find 12 poor men for each monk on Maundy Thursday and to distribute alms and a dole.[56] Some Maundy Thursday distributions were very large: Merceval (Warwickshire) gave 3,000 herrings, beer, bread and 5s to the poor and in many monasteries this annual distribution absorbed much of their charitable expenditure.[57]

The rules of monastic houses usually imposed some charitable obligations on the community.[58] Monasteries often held daily distributions to the poor at their gates, sometimes to an 'apostolic' group of 12 poor people[59] and alms were given on special occasions such as anniversaries of the deaths of abbots, priors and benefactors.[60] When St Wulfstan's alms were distributed, the bread was blessed by the hospital brethren in these words: 'Omnipotent and eternal God who in the observance of fasts and the giving of alms has placed remedy for our sins...bestow your grace upon these alms'.[61] In Cambridge, St Radegund's nunnery and Barnwell priory observed the charitable

[55] On the days of St Nicholas and St Thomas Barking abbey doled a loaf and a herring to each poor person who approached it, Owen, *Church and society*, p. 71.

[56] *Annals of the hospital of St. Wulfstan, Worcester, c. 1230–1513*, ed. F. T. Marsh (Worcester, 1890), pp. 5–6.

[57] Scarisbrick, *The Reformation and the English people*, p. 51. At Stoneleigh abbey £4 5 4 of £5 7 8 were spent on Maundy Thursday, *ibid.*, p. 52.

[58] R. Grégoire, 'La place de la pauvreté dans la conception et la pratique de la vie monastique médiévale latine', *Il monachesimo e la Riforma ecclesiastica (1049–1122)* (Milan, 1971), pp. 173–92. See the chapters regarding charitable acts and hospitality in the Benedictine rule, *La règle de St. Benoît* I, c.4 'Quae sunt instrumenta bonorum operum', pp. 456–64; c.53 'De hospitibus suscipiendis', pp. 610–16.

[59] W. Witters, 'Pauvres et pauvreté dans les coutumes monastiques du moyen-âge', in Mollat, *Etudes* I, pp. 177–215; pp. 201, 206. See also Bienvenu, 'Pauvreté, misères et charité en Anjou', pp. 5–16; on the effect of the execution of charitable duties on a cloistered community, *ibid.*, p. 15.

[60] See the Salisbury Register for distributions in memory of bishops, 'In die vero anniversarii ipsius, centum poscemus pauperes pro anima ipsius in perpetuam de pane et cervisia et ad minus de uno ferculo carnis et piscis', *Vetus registrum Sarisberiense alias dictum registrum S. Osmundi episcopi. The Register of S. Osmund* I, ed. W. H. Rich Jones (London, 1883), p. 228.

[61] 'Omnipotens sempiterne Deus qui in ieiunii observatione et elemosinarum largitione nostrorum posuisti remedia peccatorum...super elemosinam hanc infunde gratiam', *Annals of the hospital of St Wulfstan*, p. 14. The monks of Malmesbury distributed alms and wheat regularly, *Registrum Malmesburiense: the register of Malmesbury abbey* II, ed. J. S. Brewer and C. T. Martin (London, 1880), p. 368.

stipulations of the Benedictine and Augustinian rules respectively. In the nunnery's accounts for 1450–1 an entry records the Maundy Thursday distributions:[62] 3s 1d were distributed among seven poor men and six poor women, and 10d were given to some poor men who had been wounded in the king's wars.[63] The almoner of Canterbury Cathedral priory spent only an average of 0.5% of his income on external poor relief between 1284 and 1373.[64] However, a concept of internal charity existed in monasteries and expressed itself in the distribution of pittances and attendance to sick monks.[65]

Distributions at the gates of hospitals were a normal feature of a house's charitable obligations. These distributions were common on feast and saints' days.[66] At St Giles', Norwich, 13 poor folk were fed daily, and enjoyed 'sufficient and good bread, a dish of meat or fish and sometimes of eggs and cheese and sufficient drink'.[67] St Mary's Hospital in Chichester distributed food to the begging poor from c. 1232 on the anniversary of an early benefactor.[68] In the Hospital of St John the Baptist, Oxford, corn sent by the royal Almoner was distributed to the poor in 1244.[69] We have no evidence relating to the practice of charity by HSJC until the late-fifteenth century. In 1485

---

62 *The priory of St. Radegund*, p. 228: 'Et datum et distributum inter pauperes die Cene – 2s 6d'.

63 *Ibid.* The gild of Corpus Christi and St Mary in Cambridge devoted to the celebration of the feast of Corpus Christi provided a meal for town dignitaries and townsmen after the procession on the day of the feast, and food may have been distributed to the town poor. Josselin relates this tradition, 'quod quotannis, finita dicta processione, erat hoc in more positum et consuetudine, ut pretor cum quibusdam burgensibus siue municipibus et balliuis oppidi ad prandium a collegio invitarentur', which must have emerged in the days of the gild and been continued by the college, Josselin, *Historia collegii Corporis Christi*, p. 13.

64 R. A. L. Smith, *Canterbury cathedral priory: a study in monastic administration* (Cambridge, 1943, repr. 1969), pp. 47–8. A very small part of monastic income was spent on charity: only 1–1½% of the corn income of Bolton abbey was distributed in the thirteenth and early fourteenth century, Kershaw, *Bolton priory*, see data on pp. 141–4.

65 While very little was spent on external alms, see C. N. L. Brooke's introduction to *The book of William Morton almoner of Peterborough monastery 1448–67*, pp. xxvi–xxviii. See above pp. 165–6 for the pittances distributed in HSJC.

66 At St Katharine's hospital near the Tower daily distribution of a halfpenny to each of 24 poor was made, but on 16 November it was given to 1,000 poor. See the rule given by Henry III and confirmed in 1291/2 by Edward I, C. Jamison, *The history of the royal hospital of St. Katharine by the Tower of London* (London, 1952), p. 180. See also N. Gonthier, 'Les hôpitaux et les pauvres', p. 286.

67 As laid down by its rule of 1254×6: 'habebunt panem sufficientem et bonum et ferculum carnis vel piscis [et] quandoque ovorum et casey et potum competenter', NRO. 24/b/1. Bread was also distributed daily between Annunciation and Assumption: 'et erit quantitas panis ut egenorum famem possit depellere'.

68 A canon of Chichester; 'The cartulary of St. Mary's hospital, Chichester', no. 27, p. 50.   69 *Calendar of liberate rolls* II, p. 217.

distributions of bread to the poor were made on the feast of St John the Evangelist, 27 December, 'Item for loaves for the poor on St John the Evangelist's day – 2s 6d'.[70] In the same year 14 ells of cloth were bought for the preparation of garments for the poor.[71] A later entry reports the expenditure of 2d 'for breads as alms to the poor', which would have sufficed for four half-penny loaves[72] and another entry accounts for the erection of a 'monument' for a poor man,[73] probably a headstone or a cross to mark the place of a poor man's burial undertaken by the hospital.[74] One gains the impression that the house no longer accommodated poor people but merely hired them occasionally, distributed food to them on St John's day, perhaps doled the remains from the house's table, and certainly buried them in its cemetery. By the late fifteenth century the house's function had changed considerably from that originally intended by its thirteenth-century donors, but a notional charitable association lingered. When Creake abbey absorbed a hospital of five men in Gedney Fen, it replaced the previous function with distributions of bread, drink, pottage and tunics.[75]

Intercessory obligations were sometimes grafted onto religious houses coupled with charitable duties. Since intercession by clerics and charitable works mutually enhanced the spiritual objective, patrons tried to create a balanced mixture of both activities. The professional celebrations by a chaplain were often followed by periodical distribution of alms and food to the poor.[76] Chantry foundations were often planted in existing religious houses and so we find the latter participating in charitable activity which was never part of their routine and organisation.

In Spinney priory, an Augustinian house of early thirteenth-century

---

[70] 'Item pro panibus propter pauperes die Sancti Iohannis Evangeliste – 2s 6d', SJCA.D106.9, fol. 9v. An identical entry appears in the accounts of 1505: 'Item for bred to por folk on Saynt Jhon day – 2s 6d', SJCA.D106.10.

[71] 'Item pro xiiij ulnis panni linei pro pauperibus – 4s 4d', *ibid.*, 14 ells of cloth would suffice for some 14 shirts. See the instructions for the obit distributions of Guibert de Roubais who provided in 1344 × 62 14 ells of cloth for the preparation of two shirts for each of seven poor women, Leuridan, *La table des pauvres*, p. 64.

[72] 'Pro panibus in elemosina pro pauperibus', SJCA.D106.9, fol. 10r.

[73] SJCA.D106.9, fol. 10r.

[74] On burial of dead poor as a work of mercy see the 1406 ordinance of the gild of the Holy Cross, Stratford, *The register of the gild of the Holy Cross*, p. 3. Sections in graveyards and parts of churches were dedicated for poor burial, see for example Vale, *Piety, charity and literacy*, p. 26.

[75] Owen, *Church and society*, p. 56.

[76] As we have seen above, pp. 142–6 in the case of Newton College the prayers of priests were often deemed insufficient without the added supplication of poor men.

foundation, which maintained a full liturgical routine and interceded for its benefactors, Mary of Bassingbourn founded a chantry and charity endowment in 1301.[77] In return the priory was to maintain four regular canons who would pray for Mary's soul and for the souls of her two husbands and her parents. In addition, an almshouse was created in a messuage given by her in which seven poor and infirm men were to be lodged. These men were supplied with daily rations of bread, herrings and ale as well as with clothing and shoes yearly. Large-scale distributions were made to 1,000 poor people on three occasions every year. As the number of canons declined in the fourteenth century the house could hardly spare four of its members for private celebrations.[78] The huge distributions weighed financially and the invasion of the priory by hundreds of poor people expecting their dole must have disrupted the house's quiet routine. In 1418 the priory's patron reviewed the terms of the Bassingbourn foundation:[79] the duties were limited to the feeding of seven almsmen and to three yearly distributions of penny coins to poor people of the parishes of Fordham and Soham on Good Friday and on Friday in Whit Week up to a sum of one mark at each distribution.[80]

Thus, for part of the fourteenth century, the Bassingbourn charity distributed food to hundreds of poor people in the neighbourhood of Wicken. One can imagine that poor people knew of these distributions and flocked to them. Although the priory was not a charitable house it was seen as a suitable depository of charitable funds and thus was obliged to undertake tasks for the fulfilment of which it had never been intended. As in the case of other sources of income based on land, the

---

[77] *VCH. Cambridgeshire* II, pp. 249–54. She granted the priory 62 acres of arable, 2 acres of meadow, 14 acres of marshland and 13s 4d rents in Wicken parish. This is an accurate description of the actual grant as appears in the escheator's assessment of year 1336 in connection with the mortmain infringement committed by the priory, *Calendar of patent rolls 1334–1338*, p. 242. A licence was granted in 1301 for a slightly bigger donation, *Calendar of patent rolls 1292–1301*, p. 570. Mary of Bassingbourn was also a benefactor of the hospital of St John, Ely, in which she founded an anniversary celebration with the distribution of bread to 144 poor people, see above pp. 133, 187.

[78] Following a petition by the priory, Pope Boniface IX ordered the prior of Anglesey to look into the possibility of substituting the regular canons celebrating in Wicken church by secular priests, *Calendar of papal letters* I, p. 519 (1395).

[79] Land rents had declined in the course of the fourteenth century to allow fewer distributions from the income of the original endowment.

[80] *Calendar of close rolls 1419–1422*, pp. 39–40 (1419). Anglesey priory was released by Thomas of Chedworth, descendant of the founder, from the sustenance of one of the two chaplains (at 5 marks per annum for each chaplain) due to the disrepair and impoverishment of the lands and houses after the great mortality. CUL.EDR. Register Lisle, fol. 36r (1350).

fourteenth century brought diminished resources and in some cases the decay of hospitals and of endowments. In the case of a religious house such as Spinney obligations were refashioned to fit its smaller financial resources.

There may have been many occasions for distributions to the poor not mentioned above. Royal distributions were made as a manifestation of 'good rule'; town fathers relieved poverty and displayed their benevolence. But most encounters were connected with intercession, the poor were approached as the weakest members of society, and through their misery great prizes were to be won.

CHARITABLE ACTIVITIES OF RELIGIOUS GILDS AND FRATERNITIES

The help and support of one's kin was enshrined in family relationships and generally upheld and expected by lay society and the Church, but help of one's friend and neighbour could be an expression of piety and virtue. The combined wish to extend kinship and to maintain the values of fellowship and charity can be discerned in the emergence of the medieval religious fraternity.[81] This form of voluntary association linked men and women who shared the wish to promote their social lives as well as the welfare of their souls through personal participation in a cooperative effort.[82] Religious and charitable undertakings were adopted in occupational gilds[83] and some religious gilds or fraternities were limited to certain professions,[84] but predominantly religious ones

[81] The subject of confraternities has been at the centre of much research inspired by B. Pullan's study of confraternities as important social and political institutions in Pullan, *Rich and poor*. See again Chiffoleau, *La comptabilité de l'au-delà* as well as MacKenney, 'Trade guilds and devotional confraternities'; J. S. Henderson, 'Piety and charity in late medieval Florence' (Ph.D., University of London, 1983); Weissman, *Ritual brotherhood in Renaissance Florence*. For a discussion of the theoretical foundations for the formation of gilds see A. Black, *Guilds and civil society in European political thought from the twelfth century to the present* (London, 1984), esp. pp. 1–75. On the development of trade gilds see E. Coornaert, 'Les ghildes médiévales (ve–xive siècles)', *Revue historique* 199 (1948), pp. 22–55, 208–43.

[82] O. G. Oexle, 'Die mittelalterlichen Gilden: ihre Selbstdeutung und ihr Beitrag zur Formung sozialer Strukturen', *Soziale Ordnungen im Selbstverständnis des Mittelalters*, ed. A. Zimmermann and G. Vuillemin-Diem (Berlin, 1979), pp. 203–26; esp. pp. 204, 207–8.

[83] The rules of religious fraternities often state so clearly in the introduction, see the statutes of the fraternity of All Saints, Cambridge in 1473, Bodl. Rawlinson c.541.

[84] As in the case of the fraternity of the Annunciation in Cambridge, *Cambridge gild records*, 1298–1389, c.7, p. 66: 'Item ordinamus quod de cetero nullus capellanus, pistor, aut uxor in dicta gilda recipiatur'. See also Owen, *Church and society*, p. 127 and Chiffoleau, *La comptabilité de l'au-delà*, pp. 307–8. The Venetian *scuole dell'arti* were such associations, MacKenney, 'Trade guilds and devotional confraternities', pp. 15–27.

seem to have appeared somewhat later, bearing some relation to the more ancient monastic confraternities.[85] Both types have a pre-history in such bodies as the Cambridge thegn gild devoted to St Etheldreda, which existed in the twelfth century and combined the features of both an occupational and a social–religious gild.[86] Religious fraternities undertook, through group effort, the creation and maintenance of a liturgical system: perpetual prayers and commemoration, funerary observances and canonical hours.

G. Le Bras called the thirteenth century: 'The golden age of small associations of piety geared much less towards the practice of sacraments than towards liturgy and good works'.[87] This century saw the flowering of the third orders of laymen connected with the mendicants as well as the hospital–care orders.[88] In Italy such associations engaged in pious work were connected with and dependent upon monasteries, priories and friaries.[89] English religious fraternities were different: they were usually independent lay associations, and some even prohibited membership of clergymen, or their accession to office.[90] They were connected with chapels and parish churches for assembly and worship

[85] G. Le Bras, 'Les confréries chrétiennes: problèmes et propositions', *Revue historique du droit français et étranger* fourth ser. 19–20 (1940–1), pp. 310–63; pp. 314–18.

[86] *Cambridge gild records*, pp. xi, xii. A group devoted to the Holy Sepulchre was the founder and patron of the Round church in St George's parish around 1114 × 30, and is mentioned in a list of tenants in *Chronicon abbatiae Rameseiensis* I, ed. W. D. Macray (London, 1886), p. 284; they are probably to be regarded as Augustinian canons of the church of Holy Sepulchre, Brooke, 'The churches of medieval Cambridge', pp. 59–70. On the significance of the Round Church see, M. Gervers, 'Rotundae anglicanae', *Actes du XXIIe congrès international d'histoire d l'art. Budapest 15–20 Septembre, 1969* (Budapest, 1972), pp. 359–76; p. 363. On early religious gilds see *Parish fraternity register. Fraternity of the Holy Trinity and SS. Fabian and Sebastian in the parish of St. Botolph without Aldergate*, ed. P. Basing (London, 1982), pp. viii–ix.

[87] 'L'âge d'or des petites sociétés de piété tournées beaucoup moins vers la pratique des sacrements que vers la liturgie et les oeuvres'. This comment was quoted by Marc Bloch in his review article written under an assumed name during the Nazi occupation, M. Bloch (as M. Fougères), 'Entr'aide et piété: les associations urbaines du moyen-âge', *Mélanges d'histoire sociale* 5 (1944), pp. 100–6; p. 106.

[88] On the third orders see J. R. H. Moorman, *A history of the Franciscan order from its origins to the year 1517* (Oxford, 1968), pp. 220–5; and W. A. Hinnebusch, *The history of the Dominican order* I (New York, 1965), pp. 400, 402–8; Pullan, *Rich and poor*, p. 49; Meersseman, *Ordo confraternitatis*, pp. 136–49; J. Paul, 'Les franciscains et la pauvreté aux XIIIe et XIVe siècles', *Revue d'histoire de l'église de France* 52 (1966), pp. 33–7; p. 36. For an example of the passage of a hospital–care order to England see Westlake, *The parish gilds of England*, pp. 92–4.

[89] For an example of a gild connected with a mendicant order see the statutes of the Franciscan confraternity at Brescia, ed. P. Guerrini, 'Gli statuti di un'antica congregazione francescana di Brescia', *Archivum franciscanum historicum* I (1908), pp. 544–68; esp. pp. 547–67.

[90] As above, p. 250, n. 84; see also Owen, *Church and society*, p. 25. Pullan, *Rich and poor*, p. 43. See Mueller, 'Charitable institutions', pp. 41–2.

but regulated their own devotional and social activities.[91] Common funds and collective effort were spent on funerals, exequies, perpetual masses, maintenance of altars, lights and mutual assistance.[92] The fraternity took part in all contemporary forms of religious and charitable activity: it assembled on the days of its patron saint, provided masses, attended funerals of members and anniversary celebrations, distributed ritual funerary alms.[93] Some associations attempted to provide help for members who had fallen on hard times, or organised visits to sick brethren.[94] Charitable obligations were usually confined to mutual help within the group,[95] yet more general relief was offered at funerals and obits, in the form of loaves of bread or half-pennies.[96]

The fraternities, the 'corporate families',[97] became central protagonists in the late medieval cult of purgatory.[98] They emerged in large and small towns and in villages; in England fraternities existed in most towns by 1350.[99] The great attraction of the religious fraternity as a framework for devotion lay in two main areas: first, it was a perpetual autonomous corporation in which members were known intimately and which could undertake the care of their souls after death with

---

91 *Ibid.*, p. 317. In Italy many more were connected to mendicant orders, Henderson, 'Piety and charity', pp. 23–44; esp. pp. 24, 46.

92 As in all Cambridge gilds, tabulated in Westlake, *The parish gilds*, pp. 138–49.

93 Le Bras, 'Les confréries chrétiennes', p. 324. See Owen, *Church and society*, p. 128 and Chiffoleau, *La comptabilité de l'au-delà*, pp. 321–2.

94 See below, pp. 254–7; on visiting see the gild of St Thomas, Perugia, founded in 1445: 'Volemo che quando se fa el priore, se degano fare doi visictatore deglie inferme overo ei chonsoglie o altre che paresse a la chompagnia e prochaciare che glie sia sovenuto, si avesse de bisogno, dei biene de la compagnia', O. Marinelli, *La compagnia di San Tommaso d'Aquino di Perugia* (Rome, 1960), c.13, p. 59.

95 MacKenney, 'Trade guilds and devotional confraternities', pp. 19–21, 91–3; also Henderson, 'Piety and charity', pp. 303–30.

96 The goldsmiths of London elected an almoner to deal with such distributions, T. F. Reddaway, 'The London goldsmiths *circa* 1500', *Transactions of the Royal Historical Society* fifth ser. 12 (1962), pp. 49–62; p. 53.

97 G. Le Bras, *Etudes de sociologie religieuse* II (Paris, 1956), p. 432. For an example of statutes regulating solidarity and mutual help see the statutes of the gild of All Saints, Cambridge, of 1473, limiting litigation between brethren by imposing arbitration by gild officials in cases of disputes, Bodl. Rawlinson C 541, fols. 12v–13v.

98 L. Rothkrug, 'Popular religion and holy shrines. Their influence on the origins of the German Reformation and their role in German cultural development', in *Religion and the people 800–1700*, ed. J. Obelkevich (Chapel Hill, N.C., 1979), pp. 20–86; pp. 33–4. They provided what may be called a poor man's chantry service, Owen, *Church and society*, p. 95.

99 In southern France the chronology is slightly later, with most foundations in the second half of the fourteenth century, Chiffoleau, *La comptabilité de l'au-delà*, pp. 309–312. In Florence there were 33 confraternities by the mid-fourteenth century and 96 a hundred years later, Henderson, 'Piety and charity', p. 32.

brotherly affection at the time most crucial for his salvation, the days near his death, and for long after a man's family and friends had died.[100] The resolution with which statutes were enforced and infringements upon them punished, promised regular attendance at funerals and contribution to expenses incurred on these occasions. In addition, the free association of laymen and the direct control exercised by members over the working of the fraternity satisfied the desire to participate directly and influence their spiritual welfare; the system of supervision by fraternity officers was a familiar adaptation of the collegiate and corporate administration of most medieval towns and occupational gilds.[101] Many fraternities were also charged with the administration of the charitable bequests of dead members.[102]

Our acquaintance with the pious associations of medieval England is based on the study of their statutes, accounts and the few surviving fraternity records,[103] and is greatly facilitated by the availability of hundreds of gild returns from the late fourteenth century. A royal writ of 1 November 1388 instructed the sheriffs to demand of all masters and wardens of gilds and fraternities to submit a report on the foundation, statutes, properties and activities of these associations.[104] The hundreds of surviving returns originate mainly from the eastern counties, Cambridgeshire, Norfolk, Essex, Suffolk, Lincolnshire. It is true that the returns do not reflect the reality of fraternity life but the statutes which they were meant to pursue; however, bearing in mind the heavy fines incurred by those who transgressed fraternity statutes, a careful treatment can yield a better understanding of their activities. Returns were sent by 60 gilds in Cambridgeshire: 35 were rural ones

---

[100] On the nature of the gild as a corporation see J. M. Najemy, 'Guild republicanism in Trecento Florence: the success and ultimate failure of corporate politics', *American historical review* 84 (1979), pp. 53–71; pp. 55–71; A. N. Galpern, *The religions of the people in sixteenth century Champagne* (Cambridge, Mass., 1976), p. 35.

[101] Le Bras, 'Les confréries chrétiennes', p. 340.

[102] In Venice the *procuratori di San Marco* who were part of the city's fiscal and religious administration became the largest providers of testamentary supervision which included the management of charitable bequests, Mueller, 'The procurators of San Marco', pp. 105–220. In France and the Low Countries *charité* was used as a synonym for *çonfraternitas*, Bloch [Fougères], 'Entr'aide et piété', p. 102.

[103] See for example *The register of the gild of the Holy Cross*; *Parish fraternity register*.

[104] Their rules, statutes, customs, chattels, revenues and the circumstances of foundation were to be recorded and returned to the Chancery by the feast of Purification, 1389, *Calendar of close rolls 1385–1389*, p. 624. The inquest was conducted for the purpose of future taxation and control of lands entering Mortmain. On the circumstances for the creation of this inquest at the parliament of Cambridge see J. A. Tuck, 'The Cambridge Parliament, 1388', pp. 225–43 and *Parish fraternity register*, pp. ix–x.

from 16 villages, 25 were urban gilds from three towns: Cambridge, Ely and Wisbech.[105] Of the 60, only 20 fraternities offered help to their members at a time of need (33%). Of these 20, 6 were rural and 14 urban. Thus, 17% of the rural fraternities helped their needy members and 56% of the urban groups. Looking at the towns alone, all eight Cambridge fraternities provided a clause in their statutes regarding relief.[106] There were 14 fraternities which limited eligibility for relief to those in manifest need due to an accident, sickness or some other unexpected event: 'if any of our brothers or sisters falls into poverty by God's grace...';[107] 'if a brother of the said gild be oppressed by poverty...and be not culpable'.[108] Two societies restricted their help to cases of very grave need: 'If any of the said brothers or sisters become so needy that he or she cannot support him or herself the Alderman and keepers will give the needy person 3d per week for his support from the gild's collective funds'.[109] Two others related the need to lack of ability to work due to a loss of eye or limb.[110] St Katherine's fraternity in St Andrew's church in Cambridge helped those who had been loyal members[111] while six fraternities made no condition for the receipt of aid, but one may assume that common sense and discretion guided officials in their decisions.

These qualifications of the members deserving relief were connected to current views on almsgiving and its deserving recipients. The

---

[105] However, the distinction between town and country gilds is not clear cut since in the late Middle Ages small towns, such as Wisbech, were often used as centres of rural piety and fraternal activity; see R. H. Hilton, 'The small town as a part of peasant society', in *The English peasantry in the later Middle Ages* (Oxford, 1975), p. 94. The most popular dedication was to the various feasts of St Mary (16 fraternities), next were St John the Baptist and the Holy Trinity (7 fraternities each), Corpus Christi (5 fraternities), All Saints and the Holy Cross (4 fraternities each).

[106] The statutes of the Ely and Wisbech fraternities contained such clauses as well. For tabulation of all returns see Westlake, *The parish gilds*, pp. 138–49. Statutes of all Cambridge gilds appear in *Cambridge gild records*.

[107] 'si aliquis confratrum vel sororum nostrorum per dei graciam in paupertatem descenderit', gild of the Annunciation of St Mary, *Cambridge gild records*, c.6, p. 66.

[108] 'si quis fratrum dicte gilde paupertate depressus...absque culpa sua', Holy Trinity gild, Cambridge, *ibid.*, c.8, p. 116.

[109] 'si aliquis fratrum vel sororum predictorum ad tantam inopiam devenerint quod se sustinere non poterit idem Aldermannus et custodes de bonis gilde predicte collatis dabunt eidem inopi iii d. per septimana pro sustentacione sua', W. M. Palmer, 'Village gilds of Cambridgeshire', *Transactions of the Cambridgeshire and Huntingdonshire Archaeological Society* 1 (1904), pp. 330–402; c.9, p. 362.

[110] The gild of Stretham-in-the-Isle, Westlake, *The parish gilds*, p. 145. All Saints' gild, Cambridge described the circumstances as 'if any brodyr or sustyr of thys forseyde compeny fall into olde age or into grete poverte', Bodl. Rawlinson c. 541, fol. 10v.

[111] 'Et quilibet pauper frater vel soror istius fraternitatis dumtamen fideles extiterint et bene celantes secreta dicte gilde relevabitur', *Cambridge gild records*, c.7, p. 80.

prevailing view was that when confronted with the need to choose between various recipients of alms, the choice should be made according to the recipient's character, his relation to the giver and his age. The distinctions made in the statutes reflect this scale of preference, echoing the canonists' words: 'In almsgiving there ought to be distinction between people…one should rather give to the just…rather to one's own needy than to strangers…to the sick rather than to the healthy'.[112] The willingly idle were shunned by fraternities as by canonists;[113] these ritual brethren helped each other but extended little relief beyond the ritual families they had created.

Every fraternity in Cambridge made provisions for its impoverished members. Seven gilds provided 7d per week and one gave 6d. The Holy Trinity fraternity helped the widows of members as they would have done in the case of their deceased husbands, as long as the women remained unmarried.[114] However, fraternities were forced to divide their help when several brethren were in need. St Mary's in St Botolph's church gave 7d per week and a new tunic annually to an impoverished member, but reduced the sum to 4d weekly and one tunic yearly, if two members were in need.[115] The fraternity of the Assumption left the problem of dealing with more than one needy member to the discretion of its two rectors.[116] The fraternity of the Annunciation promised help as long as its funds lasted.[117] But these stipulations must be viewed cautiously; an examination of the fourteenth- and fifteenth-century accounts of Holy Trinity gild, Wisbech, shows no expenditure on mutual help.[118]

---

[112] 'In elemosyna danda habendus est delectus personarum…prius detur iusto,…prius suis egentibus quam alienis, prius infirmo quam sano…', Tierney, 'The decretists and the "deserving poor"', pp. 360–73. On categories of deserving poor see above pp. 68–73.

[113] Tierney, 'The decretists and the "deserving poor"', p. 370.

[114] *Cambridge gild records*, c.8, p. 116: 'et eodem modo habeat et quieta sit uxor fratris post mortem mariti sui bene se gesserit et honeste et viro alteri non sit nupta'. In 1310 St Mary's gild, Cambridge, freed the widow of a member from the payment of the interest on a loan: 'et remissum est sibi incrementum pro iii. annis pretextu paupertatis', *ibid.*, p. 10.

[115] *Ibid.*, c.3, p. 93: 'tunc quilibet eorum habebit qualibet ebdomada ad terminum vite sue…quatoro denarios argenti et quolibet anno unam novam tunicam', see also *Ibid.*, c.3, p. 125.

[116] *Ibid.*, c.6, p. 72: 'si fuerint plures…ministretur eis de bonis communibus dicte gilde iuxta quantitatem communium bonorum fratrum magis vel minus secundum arbitrium Rectorum'.

[117] *Ibid.*, c.6, p. 66: 'dum pecunia nostra in dicta pixide sive cista ad hoc sufficere possit'. In its statutes of 1473 All Saints' gild, Cambridge, offered 4d to its poor members every week, 'also longe as the catell ther of is worth xls,', Bodl. Rawlinson C. 541, fol. 10r.

[118] This may be explained by the gild's status as the richest gild, whose members were the most affluent townsmen of Wisbech and their wives. The accounts for 1379 and for 60 years of the fifteenth century have survied. In 1379 the gild spent £14 17s 11¼d

The returns of 1389 also reported the value of cash in the gild's coffers at the time of the inquest. Most returns record no cash in hand, nor rent, nor land-revenues, an understandable reply to a royal inquiry; they maintained their candles and lights from members' contributions of wax. Four Cambridge fraternities had no lands or chattels, while two collected subscription fees, yearly contributions, and fines of wax and money. Small payments and legacies were left to the Holy Trinity fraternity, Wisbech, to cover the expenses of perpetual intercession.[119] Indulgences were an important means of attracting potential members and testamentary bequests. In the registers of the bishops of Ely there are five indulgences of this kind: one for a fraternity in London, another for a confraternity in the Dominican convent at Cambridge, two to Cambridge fraternities and one to a rural gild in Shelford.[120] In small fraternities the absence of a regular income may have undermined the fulfilment of statutory provisions for relief. The fraternity of St Katherine in St Benet's church, Cambridge, helped poor members out of the pockets of the luckier ones, when common funds did not suffice.[121]

An interesting development on the themes of mutual help within fraternities and on parochial assistance is the Poor Men's gild of Norwich, founded in St Augustine's parish in 1380 by 'þe pouere men of þe parisshe...in helpe and amendement of here pouere parish chirche'.[122] These may have been men who could not afford the entrance fees to other fraternities, but who were, nonetheless, sufficiently settled in the parish to be organised into a social and religious society.

on the following items: £5 6s 8d on a picture of the Holy Trinity, £4 6s 8d on the wages for the gild's chaplain, £3 6s 4d on the annual meal and £1 18s 3¼d on maintenance and decoration of the altar. This may be an extraordinary year in which the high expenditure on the picture limited other common expenses, Wisbech Corporation archives. Accounts of the Holy Trinity Gild 1, p 1 (kept in the Wisbech Fenland Museum).

[119] In 1431 5s 2d were left for prayers for twelve departed souls, *ibid.* 1, p. 12 and in 1463 19d were left for six souls, *ibid.* 1, p. 31. A tenement in Wisbech was left to the gild for the maintenance of prayers, *ibid.* 1, p. 58.

[120] CUL. EDR. Register Arundel, fol. 50r (1384) – Holy Trinity gild in Holy Trinity church, Cambridge; Register Gray, fol. 57v (1466) – Holy Trinity gild in Shelford; CUL. Register Alcock, pp. 70–1 (1491) – gild of St Peter of Melano and St Ursula in the Dominican friary, Cambridge; p. 79 (1492) – St Ursula's gild in Holy Trinity church, Cambridge; p. 109 (1496) – the gild of the Name of Jesus in St Paul's, London.

[121] *Cambridge gild records*, c.6, pp. 85–6: '...alioquin omnes et singuli confratres et sorores dicte nostre gilde seu fraternitatis statim post de hoc per custodem et promotores predictos premuniti fuerint, poterit post iuramenta prestita, ad ejus sustentacionem de suis bonis propriis contribuere prout quisquis eorum commode poterit'.

[122] *English gilds*, ed. T. Smith and L. T. Smith (London, 1870), p. 40.

The test of poverty and merit which determined eligibility for help in most fraternities was applied here as well: 'And if any broþer or sister of þis pouere gilde falle in any pouerte or secknesse, or any oþer meschef, be þe sendyng of crist, and he may nougth helpe him-self with his owen godis' to whom 3d were given every week 'til þat he be recured';[123] like others this society provided masses and trentals for dead members. The settled poor of Norwich adhered to the forms of piety and mutual help devised and elaborately maintained by their more comfortable neighbours.[124]

Preoccupation with death and the minute instructions given for the observance of funerary ceremonies show us where the heart of the medieval religious fraternity lay. The commemoration of dead members and of benefactors as well as the provision of prayers and masses for their souls were major undertakings of most religious fraternities.[125] Though burial expenses were usually met by the deceased's family, three Cambridgeshire fraternities paid these expenses for its poor dead members: the rural fraternity at March and two Cambridge fraternities.[126] Distributions were made by eight fraternities (six urban and two rural) at funerals,[127] in an attempt to ease the dead man's passage from this world to the next by inspiring grateful prayers in the poor assembled at funerals.[128] In Cambridge, the fraternity of

123 *Ibid.*

124 A strikingly similar phenomenon is recorded in 1392 in a petition to the Venetian Doge made by some old men too poor to work who applied for a licence to set up a confraternity (*scola*): 'quod multi boni homines veneciarum elimosinaliter subvenient et succurrent eis', Mueller, 'Charitable institutions', p. 50.

125 For a gild chiefly dedicated to universal intercession see N. Orme, 'The guild of Kalendars, Bristol', *Transactions of the Bristol and Gloucestershire Archaeological Society* 96 (1978), pp. 32–52; pp. 32–3, 35–7, 39–40. By 1497 the Goldsmiths' gild of London had undertaken the maintenance of two obits and extensive responsibility for the management of properties connected with them, Reddaway, 'The London goldsmiths', pp. 57–8.

126 *Cambridge gild records*, c.6, pp. 85–6: 'non habeat... unde vivus sustentari vel mortuus sepelliri de proprio poterit... ac post ejus mortem sumptibus predictis corpus suum honestius facient sepeliri'; also Holy Trinity gild in St Mary's church, *ibid.*, c.4, p. 126.

127 The statutes of All Saints' fraternity, Cambridge ordered each member to give a farthing at the Requiem mass of a dead brother or sister, or say a psalm instead, Bodl. Rawlinson c. 541, fol. 15v.

128 Thus, the Holy Trinity fraternity in Cambridge. On funerary practices in medieval fraternities see J. Chiffoleau, 'Pratiques funéraires et images de la mort à Marseille, en Avignon et dans le comtat Venaissin (vers 1280 – vers 1350)', *Cahiers de Fanjeaux*, 11 (1976), pp. 271–303; *idem*, *La comptabilité de l'au-delà*, pp. 136–40, 362–5, as well as Scarisbrick, *The Reformation and the English people*, pp. 19–20. In the accounts of Holy Trinity Gild, Wisbech, regular yearly expenses were entered in connection with exequies. The sums were spent on ale and bread for distribution and the wages of a

All Saints distributed bread and farthings at members's funeral.[129]

Thus, the charity of medieval urban fraternities was connected with two kinds of personal welfare for its members: prayers for the soul, and relief of individuals closely associated with the group's status, public image and prestige. The fraternities could not fully solve their members economic problems, in England they were usually too poor and small for large investment and help, but they eased temporary difficulties.[130]

The fraternities of Cambridge did not offer large-scale relief, and they qualified the group of potential recipients. The notion of 'deserving poor' was mixed with that of group responsibility, the wish to support the fraternity's own members. The union created a group which was *exclusive* in relation to the outsider, and which strove together for social and religious fulfilment. Within the fraternity all were worthy of attention, although not all were equal in power; beyond it, relations and interests were determined by their degree of proximity to fraternity members and their common objectives.[131]

Fraternities are a good example of the organisation of self-help in religious life.[132] These voluntary groupings absorbed modes of behaviour recommended by the church, but reinterpreted and executed them in activities which transcended parochial duties.[133] They did not oppose the Church, nor propose alternatives to sacraments, confession and Mass, but they did offer an additional dimension of involvement and a space in which the interpersonal, social and fraternal sentiments could be more fully integrated into a religious code of behaviour. Such a trend is evident in the widespread participation in para-liturgical activities such as the singing of *laude* in the Florentine confraternities,[134] and finds an interesting parallel in contemporary theological inquiries and debates on free will and the efficacy of good

bell ringer. In 1426 the gild spent £3 16s 11½d as follows: £2 9s 9d on the yearly meal, 16s 3½d on wax and candles and 11d on exequies (i, p. 5).

[129] 'and vj. d for to be gyvyn in brede to pore peple of the same parasch', Bodl. Rawlinson c. 541, fol. 16r. If the gild was maintaining a poor member at the time some of the bread pennies would be given to him.

[130] Mueller estimates that even in Venice relief granted by the *scuole* contributed very little to the alleviation of poverty, Mueller, 'Charitable institutions', p. 76.

[131] For an interesting example of a fraternity's help to a brother in need, see the provision made by the Northampton Corpus Christi gild of up to £5 of help to a needy brother, Westlake, *The parish gilds*, p. 220. Pullan, *Rich and poor*, pp. 63–4.

[132] C.-M. de La Roncière, 'La place des confréries dans l'encadrement religieux du contado florentin: l'exemple de la Val d'Elsa', *Mélanges de l'école française de Rome. Séries moyen-âge – temps modernes* 85 (1973), pp. 31–77; pp. 31–4.

[133] *Ibid.*, pp. 41–2.

[134] Henderson, 'Piety and charity in late medieval Florence', chapter 1; Le Bras, 'Les confréries chrétiennes', pp. 351–2.

works.[135] The questioning of authority in spiritual life promoted an atmosphere in which laymen could be directed into transforming their religious lives into forms which were congruent with their ideas of community. Charity assumed the values pursued in the social, occupational and civic activities which in late medieval towns tended to be more sectional and exclusive than communal and open.

DISTRIBUTIONS AT FUNERALS AND ANNIVERSARIES

The testament was an instrument which could control the allocation of funds in favour of family and friends but also in pursuit of spiritual benefits: by the twelfth century wills appear as a binding expression of the wish to deflect a portion of one's goods from the family to the promotion of spiritual welfare.[136] Customs and common law would regulate the division of immoveables but a testator was free to dispose of his moveable belongings. Canon law strove to enshrine charitable giving in the accepted form of the will, which came to contain a number of basic clauses dealing with restitution of unlawful gains as well as with provision for the departed soul.[137] The will was always concerned with the funeral but increasingly it came to govern future commemoration.[138] It attempted to procure the optimal intercession for the testator's soul,[139] by the creation of multiple series of prayers, to be recited by many people on many occasions.[140] On these occasions

---

[135] D. N. Baker, 'From plowing to penitence. *Piers Plowman* and fourteenth-century theology', *Speculum* 55 (1980), pp. 715–25. W. J. Courtenay, 'Nominalism and late medieval religion', in *The pursuit of holiness*, eds. Trinkaus and Oberman, pp. 26–59.

[136] On the development of the will see M. M. Sheehan, *The will in medieval England* (Toronto, 1963). Female testators were granted the right to dispose of their marriage portions even before the death of their husbands, *ibid.*, pp. 234–9; J. Goody, *The development of the family marriage in Europe* (Cambridge, 1983), pp. 66–8, 99

[137] Trexler, 'Death and testament', pp. 48–54. Rosenthal, *The purchase of paradise*, p. 81.

[138] For the structure of bequests in a typical will see Sheehan, *The will in medieval England*, pp. 258–9; also Trexler, 'Death and testament', pp. 40–51.

[139] Preparation for death became more and more elaborate in the late Middle Ages and is reflected in the development of the genre of death literature such as the *ars moriendi*; N. L. Beaty, *The craft of dying: a study in the literary tradition of the Ars moriendi in England* (New Haven, Conn., 1970).

[140] The most important recent study of testamentary patterns had been conducted by Jean Chiffoleau who analysed the bequests of testators from the area of Avignon in the late Middle Ages: Chiffoleau, *La comptabilité de lau-delà*; on multiplication *ibid.*, pp. 147, 323–7, 339–41, and *idem*, 'Pratiques funéraires et images de la mort à Marseille', pp. 290–1, 293. See also Thrupp, The *merchant class*, p. 178. A minority of testators protested against excesses at their funerals, and demanded that theirs be small and humble, Tanner, *The church in late medieval Norwich*, p. 99 and n. 285; some of these testators may have had Lollard sympathies which in some cases can be discerned from the general tone

the poor played an important role; they were granted a place in the funerary file and were present at the burial. The Corpus Christi fraternity at Walden (Essex) paid 8d to the four poor men who carried four torches at funerals of fraternity members.[141] These were the times when the poor were treated with greatest liberality and honour, but were these distributions or payments for effective performance?[142]

The medieval funeral began in the house of the deceased where prayers, the *De profundis, miserere* and gradual psalms were recited by the clergy.[143] In church, a Requiem mass was celebrated, and from there family, clergy and friends proceeded to the place of burial.[144] The route of this last earthly voyage offered opportunities for charitable acts.[145] Although the question of the 'deserving poor' occupied the minds of canonists and theologians, most testators of the fourteenth and fifteenth centuries did not closely identify the recipients of their bounty at funerals; the Holbeach (Lincolnshire) Corpus Christi fraternity distributed farthings to any poor person who presented himself.[146] It was usually the number of poor which was dictated by the deceased rather than the recipients' character. However, there were groups which were often favoured at funerary distributions: the poor of the dead man's burial parish or his native parish were often preferred to strangers: in 1384 Fulk Gray left to the poor of his village: 'And I leave to each paralitic and blind person of the village of Haddenham 2s 6d'.[147]

of the will, Vale, *Piety, charity and literacy*, pp. 12–14; see also Chiffoleau, *La comptabilité de l'au-delà*, pp. 142–3.

141 Westlake, *The parish gilds*, p. 152; Pullan, *Rich and poor*, p. 80. The poor of Venetian almshouses were expected to appear at funerals, *ibid.*, p. 71, which he sees as a form of employment, *ibid.*, p. 77.

142 Trexler, 'Death and testament', p. 52 and see Galpern, *The religions of the people*, pp. 19, 33, 35.

143 A. G. Martimort, *L'église en prière. Introduction à la liturgie* (Paris, 1965), pp. 641–4. Parishes received regularly payments for forgotten tithes, contributions towards the fabric expenses, small sums for the parish chaplain and clerks for their attendance at the funeral, and burial payments; for examples see CCCA.XXXI, 28, 68, 86, 92.

144 For the offices for the dead current among fourteenth- and fifteenth-century laity see the example in *The prymer or lay folks' prayer book* I, ed. H. Littelhales (London, 1895), pp. 52–78.

145 For the description of liturgy of death see Martimort, *L'église en prière*, pp. 638–48.

146 Westlake, *The parish gilds*, p. 164. On legacies to the poor in wills of the English aristocracy see Rosenthal, *The purchase of paradise*, pp. 102, 104; and on the wills of London merchants see Jennings, 'The distribution of landed wealth in the wills of London merchants', p. 276, 11.8% of the testators left sums for distributions among the poor outside charitable institutions; and those leaving sums left most usually a third of their bequests to the poor, Thrupp, *The merchant class*, p. 177.

147 'Item lego cuilibet paralitico et ceco ville de Hadenham 2s 6d', CUL. EDR. Register Arundel, fol. 50v; another example: 13d were distributed on the obit of Thomas Sygo

In 1496 the widow Katherine Cook of Cambridge, amongst other funerary bequests, left 4s for bread and 15d to be distributed 'among poor people dwelling in the said parish most feable in nature'.[148] In his testament of 1315 Alan Wells, a burgess of Cambridge, left £20 for distribution of bread at his funeral.[149] Money was left to parish clerks and chaplains, no doubt in hope of assuring their presence at the funeral.[150]

Some chose the voluntary poor or wished to be buried among them, leaving large legacies to the friars.[151] Almost all English wills between 1300 and 1450 dispensed sums to all four orders of friars; often the Dominicans and the Franciscans received larger sums than the others.[152] The chronicler of Barnwell priory described the flow of testamentary bequests to the friars of Cambridge as being detrimental to his house.[153] A hospital or a leper house would be seen as suitable recipients, and were often preferred to other religious houses, as they were thought to be particularly efficacious in mustering crowds of poor for distribution. Towards the end of the Middle Ages there is a clear

who composed his will in 1439, to the poor of his village Mildenhall, Trinity College Muniments. Otryngham's book, pp. 136–7. A fellow of Queens' college left bequests to the poor of his native parish (Cherry Hinton) and to the parish to which his college belonged (St Peter without Trumpington Gate).

[148] *Annals of Cambridge* I, p. 246.

[149] CCCA.xxxi, 28. A third of Bury St Edmunds' testators left funeral bequests for distribution to the poor, Gotfried, *Bury St. Edmunds*, p. 184.

[150] See examples: CCCA.xxxi, 28 (1315): 2s to the parish chaplain and 6d to the parish clerk; CCCA.xxxi, 39 (1349): 12d to the parish chaplain and 4d to the sacrist; CCCA.xxxi, 92 (1393): 6d to the parish clerk and 6d to the sacrist. See provisions for the parish clergy in the statutes of All Saints' gild, Cambridge of 1473, Bodl. Rawlinson c. 541, fol. 15v.

[151] Rosenthal, *The purchase of paradise*, pp. 82–90; Vale, *Piety, charity and literacy*, p. 20; P. Heath, 'Urban piety in the later Middle Ages: the evidence of Hull wills', in *Church, politics and patronage in the fifteenth century*, ed. B. Dobson (Gloucester, 1984), pp. 209–34, esp. p. 210.

[152] In CCCA.xxxi, 28 (1315) £3 were left to each major order, 6s 4d to the Augustinian friars and 40d to the Carmelites; CCCA.xxxi, 68 (1365): a quarter of wheat to each of the four friaries of Cambridge; CCCA.xxxi, 92 (1393): 5s to the Franciscans, 5s to the Dominicans, 6s 8d to the Carmelites and 6s 8d to the Augustinian friars. For other examples of such provision in Norwich wills see *The register of Henry Chichele* III, p. 409: 'cuilibet ordini fratrum in Norwico mendicancium 40d' (1415), pp. 412–13 (1415), pp. 418–19 (1416). 60% of Bury testators made bequests to the friars, Gottfried, *Bury St. Edmunds*, p. 183. This pattern persisted in some sixteenth-century wills, see *Abstracts from the wills and testamentary documents of printers, binders and stationers of Cambridge, from 1504–1699*, ed. G. J. Gray and W. M. Palmer (London, 1915), p. 10.

[153] 'Mendicancium quidem ordines ante paucos annos erant in Cantebrigia radicati, et sepulturas divitum, et legata et elemosinas verbis mellitis sibi ipsis, procuraverunt, que ante eorum adventum ecclesie conventuali de Bernewelle non mediocriter profuerunt', *Liber memorandorum*, p. 70.

tendency to prefer direct distribution to the poor, rather than to institutional intermediaries.[154]

Most distributions at funerals were in the form of bread, pennies or clothes.[155] Some fraternities obliged their members to offer 'soul-alms', half-pennies offered at the funerals of dead members.[156] Clothes were an important item given at the funerals of the rich, as they wished the funeral procession to be as grand as possible. Thus, the poor were dressed up for the day. John Harreys, once mayor of Cambridge and MP, ordered in his will of 1418 the purchase of fine Irish cloth for the preparation of garments for the poor at his funeral.[157] The poor were allowed to keep lavish garments; these were no doubt sold in order to buy food, drink or clothes, not before they were displayed in the streets. Some funerals were followed by a meal for those attending and for the poor.[158] However, on the whole, giving at funerals seems to have been aimed at procuring a variety of benefits for the dead, not at alleviating the lot of intercessors.

The attempts to mitigate future suffering in purgatory did not end with the funeral. Those who could afford it instituted the observance of periodic occasions for commemoration when masses and prayers were said. These could vary from an annual mass by a parish chaplain to a perpetual chantry.[159] Chantries would usually spend some of their endowed revenues on distributions connected with the anniversary of the founder. In the Wimpole chantry's statutes of 1459 the twice-

---

[154] Rosenthal, *The purchase of paradise*, p. 127. HSJC received no bequests in the 20 surviving wills. Of 148 wills of the Yorkshire gentry between 1370 and 1480 only 13 gave donations to hospitals, Vale, *Piety, charity and literacy*, p. 28.

[155] Sheehan, *The will in medieval England*, p. 259; Thomas of Cottenham, a Cambridge butcher, left 4d for oblations at his funeral, CCCA.xxxi, 25; CCCA.xxxi, 41 (1349): 2s in oblations at the funeral. On the rising importance of the wake after the funeral, in the thirteenth century, see Sheehan, *The will in medieval England*, p. 258; a meal was provided to all friars of Cambridge after the funeral of John Harreys, *Cambridge borough documents* 1, p. 152.

[156] See above pp. 257–8. In a will of a tenant of Havering, distributions of tunics, hose, shoes, and shirts were stipulated: McIntosh, *Autonomy and community*, p. 239, n. 72. The Notre-Dame fraternity of Fanjeaux (Languedoc) distributed coins for deceased members as well as corn, wine, tunics and shirts to the needy at their funerals, A. Ramière de Fortanier, 'Hospitalité et charité à Fanjeaux et dans sa région: les confréries de Notre-Dame', *Cahiers de Fanjeaux* 13 (1978), pp. 147–67.

[157] *Cambridge borough documents* 1, p. 152. He also left £20 for distribution among the poor. Funeral vestments (*indumenta*) were to be distributed 'inter pauperes consanguineos meos', after the funeral, CCCA.xxxi, 86. On the use of white garments at funerals see Chiffoleau, *La comptabilité de l'au-delà*, p. 140.

[158] Chiffoleau, 'Pratiques funéraires', pp. 278–9. Some offered a meal for the mayor and town officials who were entrusted with the execution of the testator's wishes, *Annals of Cambridge* 1, p. 246.

[159] Wood-Legh, *Perpetual chantries in Britain*, p. 4.

widowed foundress ordered the distribution of 6s 8d on the anniversaries of the deaths of both husbands. Each priest present was to be given 4d, each chaplain, 2d, and the rest was to be dealt to the parish poor.[160] But Cambridge abounded with less institutionalised provisions for the remembrance of the dead in the 15 parish churches and in the colleges; they held celebrations for the souls of benefactors, founders and old members, which were usually followed by some distribution to the poor.[161] However, the fellows of colleges did to a large extent see themselves as worthy poor and distributions on funerals and exequies were usually made to the master and fellows rather than to the poor.

The town corporation, as a perpetual body representing the common will of burgesses, was often chosen as the custodian of funds for the celebration of anniversaries of dead townsmen.[162] The surviving fifteenth-century accounts of the corporation show that expenses were incurred yearly in the observation of such celebrations. Between 1423–4 and 1435–6 sums varying between 3s 10d and 8s 6d were expended on John Harreys' exequies.[163] By 1483–4 the town observed the obits of another prominent burgess, Thomas Jakenett, as appears in the accounts for 1483–4/1490–1.[164] In the last year of the fifteenth century five burgesses were remembered through the services of the *custos exequiarum*.[165]

These entries come to show the variety of arrangements by which intercession was sought, and in which the poor could play a part and expect a reward. These increased throughout the late fourteenth and fifteenth centuries with the individualisation of efforts for intercession.[166] It would be quite reasonable to imagine that whenever and wherever a funeral or an obit took place in and around Cambridge the poor of the town were informed.[167] In larger towns, perhaps his

---

[160] CUL. EDR. Register Gray, fol. 121v (1459). See above the provisions in Newton chantry p. 144.

[161] See above pp. 184–92 on the provisions of chantry services by HSJC.

[162] On the activities of the Venetian department of state as investor and executor of pious bequests see Mueller, 'The procurators of San Marco', *passim*, esp. pp. 185–219.

[163] Cambridge Corporation archives x. 70 (1–10).

[164] Cambridge Corporation archives x. 71 (1–6). Thomas Jakenett was the founder of Jakenett's almshouse in St May's parish see above p. 128. In 1493–4 three anniversaries were celebrated and between 9s and 13s 4d were spent on each occasion, Cambridge Corporation archives. x. 71 (7–8).

[165] Cambridge Corporation archives, x. 71 (9–10).

[166] Communal obits were replaced by meticulously laid down provisions for individual ones, J. Blair, 'Religious gilds as landowners in the thirteenth and fourteenth centuries: the example of Chesterfield', in *The medieval town in Britain*, ed. P. Riden (Cardiff, 1980) pp. 35–49; pp. 40–1.

[167] In Provençal villages a crier summoned the community to funerals and distributions, Chiffoleau, *La comptabilité de l'au-delà*, p. 145.

parish and immediately neighbouring parishes were the limits of a poor person's search for relief. The poor's part in the 'economy of redemption' was such that it focused attention on their powers of intercession but not on their living conditions.[168] As seen through the wills and funeral customs the poor were viewed as a group rather than as individuals in need. Their misery was, paradoxically, exalted through the spiritual powers attributed to them. Funerary rites were so laden with anxiety for the deceased's soul that the contractual element was never forgotten even when great liberality was shown in distributions. Yet the frequent distributions at funerals and obits must have counted for a great deal in the eyes of the needy. The funerals were periods of work for the unemployed and unemployable during which they performed their function and received their pay: *dignes est operarius mercede suo* ('the labourer is worthy of his wages...').

DOORSTEP RELIEF AS REGULATED BY EPISCOPAL INDULGENCES

The recipients of charitable bounty can be divided into two groups: the poor, who moved about the countryside lived in and between towns with no permanent abode, begging for support, and the settled town proletariat: day-labourers, low-wage earners and their dependants, widows, the unemployed and unemployable.[169] These were members of parishes, seen daily in the street and market, they were neighbours and employees of their more comfortable fellows, and the recipients of neighbourly and parochial assistance. Their state of need may have been caused by a sudden blow of fate, but was usually a result of inherited social and economic handicaps.

Episcopal registers bear witness to an aspect of the elusive doorstep relief. Indulgences for the relievers of the needy survive in the registers of the bishops of Ely from the time of Bishop Lisle (1345–61) onwards.[170] The number of indulgences granted and known to us is dependent upon the character of each bishop's register, the length of

---

[168] On the application of a system of calculation to arrangements for intercession see *ibid.*, pp. 344–56.

[169] Settled members of rural society, though usually poor, belonged to close-knit communities which probably sustained the transient poor moving in an area surrounding their place of origin. On the identity of the rural poor see a useful analysis for the thirteenth century and the directions of change, G. Duby, 'Les pauvres', pp. 27–9, 31.

[170] On the development of indulgences see B. Poschmann, *Penance and the anointing of the sick*, trans. F. Courtney (London, 1964), pp. 210–32.

his periods of office and residence, and his personal discretion.[171] Those contributing to the relief (*auxiliantes ad relevamen*) of an individual or institution possessing such an indulgence enjoyed the remittance of penance for sins which had been confessed. The recipients of their help could be religious houses, churches, chapels, hermits on nearby bridges. They could be won for maintenance of bridges and causeways, for redemption of prisoners and in return for prayers in favour of a chosen departed soul.

Granting indulgences was not a major episcopal undertaking; it must have occurred in response to sporadic pleas by petitioners, supported by testimonials or letters of recommendation. Thus a family which had lost its home in a fire would petition the bishop during a visitation, or more probably during his stay at one of his manors. Institutions enjoying indulgences would have been represented by an officer of the house; a proctor would present the request of his house in other dioceses.[172]

As the surviving registers of the bishops of Ely are by no means complete records of their activities one must approach the recorded indulgences not as absolute but as relative indications of charitable priorities. The registers which allow us the most extensive knowledge of these criteria are those of Bishops John Fordham, William Gray and John Alcock.[173] Bishop Fordham's register records indulgences granted in 19 out of the 37 years of his office. In Bishop Gray's register, indulgences appear in 15 of the 24 years of his episcopate and in the case of Bishop Alcock in 9 years out of 14. Since the transactions of some years were more closely recorded than those of others, we cannot look at the frequency of indulgences on an average annual basis; these numbers and their division into categories of recipients are shown in table 7.1.

The identity of those chosen to be beneficiaries of episcopal favour was determined by the initiative of religious houses and of individuals,

---

[171] D. M. Owen, 'Ely diocesan records', *Studies in Church history* 1 (1964), pp. 176–83.

[172] Most religious houses which received indulgences from the bishops of Ely were from the diocese of Lincoln or Norwich (only 5 of 16 houses were not). Licences for begging for alms and for pardoning by indulgences were also recorded in the Consistory court register of Bishop Arundel in which apostolic letters of reference presented by *procuratores* of hospitals were examined; CUL. EDR. Consistory court Arundel, fols. 41r–42v. (St. Mary of Mt. Syon, London – 1375–6), fol. 18r (St Anthony's, Rome – 1377), fol. 84r. (St Mary of Roncesvalles at Charing Cross – 1377), fol. 84r (St John the Baptist, King's Lynn – 1377).

[173] The numbers of indulgences appearing in the registers are CUL. EDR. Register Montacute – none; Register Lisle 1345–61) – 3 indulgences in 16 years; Register Arundel (1373–88) – 4 indulgences in 14 years; Register Bourchier (1444–54) – 5 indulgences in 11 years.

Table 7.1 *Number of indulgences granted to needy individuals by bishops of Ely (by category of misfortune)*

	Fordham (1388–1425) 19 years		Gray (1454–78) 15 years		Alcock (1486–1500) 9 years	
	indul.	no. of recipients[a]	indul.	no. of recipients[a]	indul.	no. of recipients[a]
Poor	9	10			2	2
Fire	20	31	6	9	6	7
Loss	2	2				
Robbery	7	8				
Sick	8	7				
Pilgrim	2	2				
Debts	1	1				
Knights	6	7	2	3		
Total	55	68	8	12	8	9
All indulgences[b]	147		33		55	
% of indulgences granted to needy	37.4		24.2		15.1	

Source: CUL. EDR. Registers G/1/1–6

(a) An indulgence might be granted to more than one person (e.g. a couple); hence the discrepancy between people and number of indulgences.

(b) All indulgences, including to religious houses.

by personal preference from the bishop and his circle, by local and changing conditions favouring help to a certain needy group such as prisoners during and after wars. Inasmuch as we can discern the needs from the attempts to acquire an indulgence for their relief, some trends are noticeable. Bishop Fordham granted more than a third of all his indulgences to needy folk. The numbers of religious institutional recipients such as churches, priories, hospitals, hermits is similar. Bishop Fordham granted most indulgences per annum and paid attention to the petitions of individuals in distress. Bishop Gray, acting in the middle of the fifteenth century, was more preoccupied with the welfare of churches and of regular houses. A third of the indulgences granted by him were given for the benefit of chapels and churches and their fabric: religious establishments received more than half of the indulgences issued during his episcopate.[174] Release of prisoners and public main-

[174] Chapels (11) + hermits (1) + hospitals (5) + priory (1) = 18 out of 33.

tenance works, the repair of bridges, causeways and highways were encouraged by a quarter of the bishop's indulgences, as they were by Bishop Fordham. The redemption of prisoners was one of the Christian acts of mercy and the upkeep of means of communications was an act advancing public welfare. Bishop Alcock granted only some 4% of his indulgences for public works and none for the ransom of prisoners. His favour lay in the relief of religious houses, the institutionalised Christian poor.[175] On the whole from the late fourteenth to the late fifteenth century grants of indulgences in favour of religious institutions grew, and those to individuals declined.[176]

Who were the poor individual recipients of episcopal indulgences? Most recipients in this category had suffered loss by fire: aided by the alms of friends and neighbours they could be expected to rebuild their houses and rehabilitate themselves. A similar category was loss through robbery: two of the recipients of Bishop Fordham's indulgences for robbery were well-to-do merchants who had been robbed and lost great quantities of merchandise. In two cases, robberies left their mark on the person of the victims, leaving them mutilated and their chances of rehabilitation smaller. Most recipients in these two categories would not have been poor before misfortune had hit them; they were householders and some had possessed considerable goods in their lost homes. In contrast, the next group in size is that of poor people who were granted indulgences with no indication of the reason for their predicament. In some cases the recipient was labelled *pauper*, meaning the 'professional' poor inasmuch as this was a recognised social status.[177] These were not merely people who lived in a humble way, since most of rural society lived this way as did most artisan and labourer families in towns; the recipients in this category were those rendered unproductive, unemployable, and thus a liability to their communities of origin and to the communities through which they passed.[178]

---

[175] Chapels (12) + hermits (1) + hospitals (16) + priories (6) = 35 out of 53. This combination of charity to institutions harbouring the poor as well as to deserving poor individuals was also practised by the Flemish almoners of the Duke of Burgundy, W. Prevenier, 'En marge de l'assistance aux pauvres: l'aumônerie des comtes de Flandres et des ducs de Bourgogne (13e-début 16e siècle)', in *Recht en instellingen in de oude Nederlanden tijdens de middeleeuwen en de nieuwe tijd. Liber amicorum Jan Buntinx*, Louvain, 1981, pp. 97–120; pp. 110, 111.

[176] A similar shift in interest was expressed in testamentary bequests, see Chiffoleau, *La comptabilité de l'au-delà*, p. 307.

[177] CUL. EDR. Register Fordham, fol. 178r.

[178] The fortunes of such people were conspicuous, frightening and threatening. For examples see cases of death of hunger and exposure reported in *The assizes held at Cambridge*, pp. 2, 19.

An intermediate category of needy were those poor due to a physical handicap, but sometimes a mere ailment. Of seven such recipients in Bishop Fordham's register one was a blind man who received an indulgence twice, one was a 'very infirm' man, three were 'mutilated', which must have meant some very grave wound or perhaps some physical distortion, one having been wounded in battle and another a tiler who was maimed after falling off a roof. These poor were considered 'wounded' or 'sick' which rendered their situation temporary. This qualification of their state of need was an attempt to enter the recipient into the category of 'deserving' poor.

The poor recipients of indulgences were mainly members of the diocese of Ely. Of 43 cases bearing a place of origin for the beneficiary, 30 originated from places within the diocese and 13 from outside.[179] Thus, people tended to approach their diocesan as a source of relief through indulgence, but might also approach the bishop of another diocese who was nearer their homes: a man from Soham, in Norwich diocese, preferred to approach the See of Ely. Of 51 people enjoying the 29 indulgences granted within the diocese, 11 were from Ely, 2 from Cambridge and 4 from Wisbech. A third, 17 out of 51, were townsfolk, with a high proportion from Ely itself.

A similar orientation arises from the study of poor and poverty in fourteenth-century Florence.[180] From the records of the mid-fourteenth-century distributions made by the confraternity of Or San Michele a collective portrait of indigence can be deduced. A large majority of the beneficiaries of the confraternity's distributions were women, widows and heads of families. Men receiving relief were few and were usually fathers of large families.[181] What of the multitude of labourers who lived on meagre wages and who do not appear in the lists? La Roncière believes that these men did not fall into the categories of deserving poverty in the minds of fourteenth-century Florentines who bestowed their bounty on the classic categories of *pauperes christi*, the orphans, the widows and the pilgrims.[182] The Almoner of the dukes of Burgundy described potential recipients of distribution as 'old and poor folk, prisoners, orphans, young marriageable women, victims of fire (*gens brulés de feu*) and merchants in distress

---

[179] Two from York, one each from Wells, Durham and London, and eight from the Lincoln and Norwich dioceses.

[180] de La Roncière, 'Pauvres et pauvreté à Florence', pp. 661–745.

[181] *Ibid.*, p. 691: 66% of the recipients in some months of 1324, 66% of recipients during some months of 1347 and 83–87% of recipients in 1356–7; on the identity of recipient of relief see Henderson, 'Piety and charity', pp. 185–240.

[182] de La Roncière, 'Pauvres et pauvreté, à Florence', pp. 687–8, 703–6. For a discussion of categories of poor see Gonthier, *Lyon et ses pauvres*, pp. 51–67.

by misfortune (*marchands destruits*)'.[183] Recipients of relief from confraternities in Florence were either registered poor, hospitals or confraternity members.[184] Similar priorities seem to have governed the grant of indulgences: those who did not fit into the sanctified niches of accepted virtuous poverty were not deemed worthy; nor were those who did not fall into the town or village community in a way which commanded solidarity and respect. In very extreme cases of vagabondage and violent indigence a certain degree of interest may be aroused to preserve peace and safety;[185] in such cases poverty is seen as a natural evil afflicting the community, like war, flood and pestilence, whose consequences must be alleviated by the leading citizens of town and the prominent members of rural communities.[186] Bishops could offer help through the workings of episcopal courts and the recognition of the status of *pauper* which exempted one from legal expenses.[187]

Those who remained unaided were people who were permanently poor and yet were not part of the marginal group of itinerant workers and urban poor: the labourers, the seasonally employed, those rendered unemployable by age.[188]

CHARITY AND SCHOLARS IN CAMBRIDGE

The development of centres for high academic study throughout Christendom in the twelfth and thirteenth centuries helped create a new academic context for charity and patronage. Many of the students were

[183] Prevenier, 'En marge de l'assistance aux pauvres', p. 110. This is borne out by the evidence of the Almoners' accounts which record distributions to widows, poor scholars, old ducal servants, large families and shamed poor.
[184] From the analysis of some 250 testaments from Val d'Elsa in the *contado* of Florence between 1285 and 1364 the following distribution emerges. 43 % of the testators left for the poor, 41 % left some for confraternities and 12 % left to hospitals, de La Roncière, 'Pauvres et pauvreté à Florence', p. 708.
[185] Vagrants move about because of needs connected with the labour market. For a profile of this group in the sixteenth century see P. Slack, 'Vagrants and vagrancy in England, 1598–1664', *Economic history review* second ser. 27 (1974), pp. 360–79; p. 366.
[186] On the connection between poverty and crime as expressed by some thirteenth century parish priests see *Councils and synods* II part I, p. 400: '...ad quos si deveniatur, pauperes fame peribunt; alii vero cum fodere non valeant et mendicare erubescant, antequam fame pereant necesse habebunt furtis, rapinis...ex quibis multa sequentur homicidia'. For some insights into the tension between sedentary villagers and the vagrants surrounding their communities in early modern England see Houston, 'Vagrants and society in early modern England', p. 18.
[187] Harper-Bill, 'A late medieval visitation', p. 38.
[188] As in Venice where only settled folk who had contributed to the *arti* were considered for relief, not the abject poor, MacKenney, 'Trade guilds and devotional confraternities', p. 88 and Mueller, 'Charitable institutions', p. 44.

poor: their service to God and His people through sacred learning placed them in a favoured status of poverty.

Students at medieval Cambridge and Oxford were not as fortunate as their modern successors. One must think of thirteenth- and fourteenth-century universities as supplying very little in the way of accommodation, support and social framework to their needy scholars.[189] Distributions for scholars occurred sporadically on feasts and at obits but no permanent basis for their support during their terms of study existed.[190] In the academic colleges it was attempted to provide a sound basis for the maintenance of needy and deserving scholars but the proportion of fellows to hall residents was always very small. A meaningful change in this balance is evident only in the second half of the fifteenth century.[191]

Universities were places where rich and poor met and lived side by side;[192] they enjoyed wide privileges which allowed them to control the prices of lodging and of foodstuff.[193] In some German universities poor scholars were exempted from various fees connected with the receipt of their degrees,[194] and the status of poor scholar could be

[189] We are cautioned against overestimating the collegiate element of the medieval university, in Cobban, 'Origins: Robert Wodelarke and St. Catharine's', pp. 27–8. See also Pantin, 'The halls and schools of medieval Oxford: an attempt at reconstruction', pp. 31, 34 and Aston and Faith, 'The endowments of the university and colleges *circa* 1348', pp. 286–7.

[190] For some examples of such distributions to scholars carried into the late Middle Ages see *The mediaeval archives of the university of Oxford* II, ed. H. E. Salter (Oxford, 1921), pp. 276–7, 311, 315, 341. A living was appropriated to Osney abbey from which distributions for poor scholars were to be sustained see *Rotuli Roberti Grosseteste episcopi Lincolniensis MCCXXXV–MCCLIII*, ed. F. N. Davis (London, 1913), p. 461.

[191] G. F. Lytle, 'Patronage patterns and Oxford colleges *c.* 1300–*c.* 1530', in *The university in society* I, ed. L. Stone (Princeton, N.J., 1975), pp. 111–49; p. 135; Pantin, 'The halls and schools of medieval Oxford', pp. 34–6; See also Aston, Duncan and Evans, 'The medieval alumni of the university of Cambridge', pp. 13–18; on sources of sustenance for scholars see *ibid.*, pp. 40–50.

[192] On the social origins of scholars in fourteenth- and fifteenth-century Oxford and on the connections between estate administration and recruitment of scholars by New College see G. F. Lytle, 'The social origins of Oxford students in the late Middle Ages: New College, *c.* 1380–*c.* 1510', in *Les universités à la fin du moyen-âge*, ed. J. Paquet and J. Ijsewijn (Louvain, 1978), pp. 426–54, at pp. 432–3, 444–6. On the types of expenses incurred by medieval scholars see J. Paquet, 'Coût des études, pauvreté et labeur: fonctions et métiers d'étudiants au moyen-âge', *History of universities* 2 (1982), pp. 15–52; pp. 16–17.

[193] P. Kibre, *Scholarly privileges in the Middle Ages* (Cambridge, Mass., 1961), pp. 269–77. Cf. Hackett, *The original statutes of Cambridge university*, c. VII (ii–iii), p. 205 and XII (iii–iv), pp. 213–15; Paquet, 'Coût des études', pp. 18–19.

[194] J. M. Fletcher, 'Wealth and poverty in the medieval German universities', in *Europe in the late Middle Ages*, ed. J. R. Hale, J. R. L. Highfield and B. Smalley (London, 1965), pp. 410–36; J. H. Overfield, 'Nobles and paupers at German universities to 1600', *Societas* 4 (1974), pp. 175–210; pp. 179, 181. For estimates of the size of the group of poor scholars see E. Mornet, '*Pauperes scolares*. Essai sur la condition matérielle des

formally acknowledged by university authorities.[195] Once received it allowed the holder exemption from university dues and preferable terms of employment.[196] The *nationes* at Paris University acknowledged the poverty of some of their members and granted them special standing; some hospices for the poor scholars of each nation were founded.[197] Many were forced to enter employment during their course of study, most usually as teachers, secretaries or scribes.[198] In England they often entered great households, or served as choristers in churches and colleges.[199] Some were reduced to begging for their livelihood[200] and many must have fallen out of scholarship altogether. In the fifteenth century colleges were exempted from the payment of subsidies on their ecclesiastical holdings. Churches appropriated to Peterhouse, Clare Hall, Pembroke, Gonville Hall, King's Hall, were exempted from diocesan dues along with the churches of the religious houses and hospitals of the diocese, in an attempt to facilitate the maintenance of their scholars.[201]

The academic colleges — Peterhouse and after

It is highly instructive for a better understanding of academic charitable patronage to look at the beginnings of the earliest college of Cambridge. In 1280 Hugh Balsham, bishop of Ely, acquired a charter from King Edward I allowing him to introduce some of his scholars at Cambridge into the Hospital of St John.[202] It may well be that the scholars had

étudiants scandinaves dans les universités aux XIVe et XVe siècles', *Le moyen-âge* 84 (1978), pp. 53–102; pp. 61, 64. Paquet, 'Coût des études', p. 16.

[195] A scholar was to take an oath regarding his financial situation, Mornet, '*Pauperes scolares*', p. 58.   [196] Fletcher, 'Wealth and poverty', p. 425.

[197] G. C. Boyce, *The English–German nation in the University of Paris during the Middle Ages* (Bruges, 1927), pp. 94, 145.

[198] Paquet, 'Coût des études', pp. 21–2; G. F. Lytle, 'A university mentality in the later Middle Ages', in *Genèse et débuts du Grand Schisme d'Occident* (Paris, 1980), pp. 201–30; pp. 209–210; Aston, Duncan and Evans, 'The medieval alumni of the university of Cambridge', p. 42.

[199] On regulation of salaries of scholar-servants by the University authorities see *Statuta antiqua universitatis Oxoniensis*, 182–3; Paquet, 'Coût des études', 24–5. In King's Hall, Cambridge, poor scholars were hired as casual help, Cobban, *King's Hall*, 233, n. 2.

[200] In 1461 two Oxford students received a licence to beg, *The medieval archives of the university of Oxford* II, p. 40. See a licence to beg granted by the Vice-Chancellor of Cambridge university to a poor scholar, CCCA.XVI, 286. In debates on begging in the fifteenth century poor scholars were regularly counted among those who were allowed to beg, Schmitt, *Mort d'une hérésie*, pp. 171–2.

[201] CUL. EDR. Register Alcock, p. 143.

[202] The licence was needed because of the king's *sede vacante* patronage; for similar cases see M. E. Howell, *Regalian right in medieval England* (London, 1962), pp. 180–2. See *Calendar of patent rolls 1272–1281*, pp. 420–1 (24 December 1280).

been there for some time before, since a privilege of Henry III's time renewed by Edward I refers to the hospital as a recipient of confiscated foodstuff as 'the scholars and hospital'.[203]

The existence of scholars in a charitable religious house need not surprise us, as by the late thirteenth century the connection between charity to the poor and maintenance of poor scholars was well established. It is revealed in provisions for scholars to be maintained in charitable institutions[204] and urban hospitals often lodged or fed scholars of grammar or song schools. At St Giles', Norwich, 24 scholars were fed daily during term,[205] while a grammar school was founded at St Leonard's York.[206] Thus, the choice of the Hospital of St John was a rather conservative one when placing a group of scholars. There was special facility in the implementation of such a choice since HSJC was in the patronage of the bishops of Ely. If Hugh Balsham wished his scholars to live in the quasi-regular surroundings of a closed community, the hospital was an understandable choice.[207] The other religious houses in Cambridge would not have suited his aim: St Radegund's was a nunnery, Barnwell was too far from the Schools and was ruled by priors who may not have accepted such intervention in their affairs. But there was also an affinity between the hospital and Balsham's new academic venture: they were both subjects of his charity. Under the hospital's roof sick and poor folk, pious brethren and young scholars were to live together, all deserving recipients of charity.

Hugh Balsham's scheme probably foundered owing to the absence of common interest and charitable feeling within the newly combined

---

[203] *Calendar of patent rolls 1292–1301*, p. 18.

[204] On charitable houses entirely devoted to poor grammarians see J. M. Reitzel, 'The medieval houses of *Bons-enfants*', *Viator* 11 (1980), pp. 179–207, *passim*; many were founded already in the 1240s, *ibid.*, p. 181; on the Dix-huit College in Paris founded in 1180, see A. B. Cobban, *The medieval universities: their development and organization* (London, 1975), p. 126. See also Bonenfant, *Hôpitaux et bienfaisance publiques*, pp. 35–6.

[205] NRO. 24/b/1: 'Septem pauperes scholares dociles eligendi in fide ipsius magistri de scolis Norwicensibus de fideli consilio magistri scolarium singulis diebus dum scole durent unum habebunt ibidem pascum et mutabuntur isti cum in gramatica fuerint convenienter edocti'. See also distribution to 24 poor at St. Katharine's by the Tower ordained by its rule, of whom 6 were to be poor scholars, Jamison, *The history of the royal hospital*, p. 180: 'de quibus viginti quatuor pauperibus predictis, sex sint pauperes scolares qui in ecclesia capellanis assistent in adjutorio divini obsequii'.

[206] By statute there were 30 choir boys and 2 schoolmasters at the hospital, J. H. Moran, *Education and learning*, pp. 9–10. The Holy Trinity hospital in York also maintained poor scholars, *ibid.*, p. 7.

[207] For further examples of hospitals providing accommodation and maintenance for scholars or contributing to their livelihood see N. Orme, *English schools in the Middle Ages* (London, 1973), pp. 179, 182. Hugh Balsham had been a monk at Ely Priory before taking the crozier and would have found the atmosphere of a regular house suitable for his aim, see below n. 211, p. 273.

community. We can only guess that the hubbub of a hospital interfered with study or that the high spirits of young students disturbed the Augustinian brethren.[208] In the foundation charter of Peterhouse the differences leading to the separation are reported to have been *ex variis causis*, to such an extent that the two groups could no longer live side-by-side.[209] The experiment lasted only three years; by 1284, and perhaps as early as 1283, the properties were separated and the scholars moved to two hostels on the west side of Trumpington street, south of St Peter's church, which was appropriated to them.[210]

Hugh Balsham had been inspired by the example of Merton College, Oxford, to found an institution which was both an academic community and a college of clerics. The secular collegiate community had become a popular form of life for groups of priests engaged in liturgical and pastoral activities within secular society. The collegiate community attempted to maintain moral standards and some of the rigours of monastic life, but it allowed its members some freedom of movement and activity. These communities were endowed for the support of their members and were communally engaged in liturgical duties for the salvation of the founder's soul. The academic colleges were an off-shoot of the fashion for founding secular colleges of priests and clerks, the type of community that both Walter of Merton and Hugh Balsham had in mind.[211] Since medieval students were clerics engaged in academic pursuits with a spiritual value, and were to be future bishops, archdeacons, priests, canons, canon lawyers, their prayers could

---

[208] On the life style of medieval scholars see, J. I. Catto, 'Citizens, scholars and masters', in *History of the University of Oxford* I, ed. J. I. Catto (Oxford, 1984), pp. 191–52; pp. 183–5.

[209] For this charter see Peterhouse muniments. Collegium. A3. and in SJCA.D98.3. and D3. 66.

[210] In an *inspeximus* of 1339 by the prior of Ely, copied into the sixteenth-century *Registrum vetus* of Peterhouse, one of the inspected documents is dated 5 October 1283, being an agreement for separation between the scholars and the hospital. It is most similar in tone and in contents to the final documents of 1284, but does not lay down the complete agreements regarding the compensation of the hospital for the loss of income incurred by the loss of St Peter's church and two hostels. This would mean that already at the end of 1283 separation was being at least considered, and that Balsham's experiment lasted a very short while. We are no more illuminated by this document as to the reasons for separation except for 'Cumque inter scolares ipsos et nos multiplex ex causis variis et post facto contencionis materia oriretur', Peterhouse muniments. Registrum vetus, pp. 27–8.

[211] On the importance of this new model see the introduction to *The early rolls of Merton College*, pp. 65–6 as well as Cobban, *The medieval universities*, p. 124 and Aston and Faith, 'The endowments of the university and colleges', p. 265. It has recently been suggested that in the composition of the statutes of Peterhouse the rule of St Benedict alongside the Merton rule provided a source of inspiration, H. Mayr-Harting, 'The foundation of Peterhouse, Cambridge and the rule of St. Benedict' (unpublished paper, kindly shown to me by the author).

be highly valued. If they had not sufficient means to sustain themselves they were worthy of a benefactor's help.[212] The most suitable form for the charitable provision for them appeared to be one which supplied shelter, food, clothes, spiritual services, and harmonious surroundings for a young scholar in a framework of piety and discipline. All these were provided by the new academic colleges.

The rule of Peterhouse was based on that of the House of the Scholars of Merton at Oxford.[213] In 1283 or 1284 Hugh of Balsham would have referred to the latest Merton statutes, those of 1274. Walter of Merton started his scheme for academic patronage in a process of endowment for the maintenance of a group of scholars at Oxford. In 1264 a set of statutes was issued for the regulation of the affairs of 20 scholars who were to live on the proceeds of Maldon and Farleigh manors (Surrey) which were entrusted to Merton priory.[214] Two or three chaplains were to reside in the house at Maldon whence the Warden administered the endowment for the scholars.[215] By 1268 Walter of Merton had acquired tenements in Oxford and the advowson of St John's church attached to one of them;[216] he modified his original scheme and issued a new set of statutes to that effect. By the statutes of 1270, 20 scholars, mostly of the Arts received 50s per annum as commons and lived in the tenements in Oxford.[217] Many regular characteristics were introduced into their lives; scholars were to eat, read and pray together.[218] The properties of the house were invested in the college

---

[212] F. Pegues, 'Philanthropy and the universities of France and England', in *The economic and material framework of the medieval university*, ed. A. L. Gabriel (Notre Dame, Ind., 1977), pp. 69–80. For other forms of assistance and inducement encouraging parish priests to study in universities see Boyle, 'The constitution "cum ex eo"', pp. 263–302.

[213] See *Documents relating to the university and colleges of Cambridge* II, c.2, p. 8. One must remember that the rule of Peterhouse is known only from its copy in bishop Montacute's statutes of 1344 which were based on those provided by the founder. There is no doubt about the connection with the Merton statutes, but this does create some difficulty in the attribution of clauses which are not derived from Merton and which survive only in a source of so much later a date. Many thanks are due to Dr Roger Lovatt who pointed this out to me. The statutes for Merton college are to be found as follows: the rule of 1264 in *Merton muniments*, ed. P. S. Allen and H. W. Garrod (Oxford, 1928), pp. 16–17; the statutes of 1270 in *The early rolls of Merton College*, pp. 378–92 and the statutes of 1274 in *Merton muniments*, pp. 21–6; with an introduction to the Merton Rolls in *The early rolls of Merton College*, pp. 49–78.

[214] *Merton muniments*, p. 15.

[215] *Ibid.*, p. 16 Also J. R. L. Highfield, 'The early colleges', in *The history of the University of Oxford* I, ed. J. I. Catto (Oxford, 1984), pp. 225–63; p. 231.

[216] *The early rolls of Merton College*, p. 52. On the development of the endowment through acquisition of tenements forfeited to the Jews see *ibid.*, pp. 34–6, 40–3 and Aston and Faith, 'The endowments of the university and colleges', pp. 294–6.

[217] *The early rolls of Merton College*, c.4, p. 380.

[218] For an assessment of the collegiate nature see Aston and Faith, 'The endowments of the university and colleges', p. 288.

as a corporate owner. In 1274 the Warden of Maldon was moved to Oxford to serve as the head of the college which until then had been ruled by deans. According to the new statutes of 1274 the number of scholars remained at 20, as long as the college could maintain them. The later statutes described the organisation of the college in great detail displaying serious concern about discipline and hierarchy.

Peterhouse was conceived along similar lines of internal organisation. The early contact with an Augustinian house in both cases (Merton priory and HSJC) was connected with the need to endow the community perpetually for its support. Like Walter of Merton in 1270, Hugh of Balsham in 1284 invested in the community the properties separated from the hospital with the addition of the church of St Peter without Trumpington Gate.[219] The college received further grants and acquired lands in the parish for the creation of a basic plot for the erection of college buildings.[220]

It appears that both early founders were hampered by the absence of a precedent for the endowment of poor scholars who were to live as a community, but who did not remain its members forever.[221] Upon the receipt of a lucrative living, a fellow of Merton College was obliged to resign his fellowship.[222] Walter of Merton was preoccupied not only by the wish to provide for poor scholars, he also created perpetual sources of revenue for his relatives and for members of his circle of patronage.[223] All three sets of statutes contain phrases reserving first preference for men of his kin: 'that the said scholars of our kin, so long as they are honest and able...'.[224] Next in favour were scholars originating from the Winchester diocese where Merton held wide landed interests.[225]

Similarly to other charitable houses the colleges were not only the recipients of charity, but instruments in its distribution. The scholars

[219] The separation of the scholars from the hospital started a proprietary conflict between both houses which continued well into the fourteenth century, see above pp. 196–8.

[220] Stokes, *Outside Trumpington gates*, pp. 16–28.

[221] In practice they remained for longer, Cobban, *King's Hall*, p. 56. Dr R. Lovatt has found this to be true in the careers of fourteenth century Peterhouse fellows and kindly pointed this out to me.

[222] *Merton muniments*, p. 22.

[223] *The early rolls of Merton College*, c.41, p. 389.

[224] 'Ut scolares supradicti de nostra sint parentela quamdiu honesti et habiles...', *Merton muniments* p. 15; *The early rolls of Merton College*, c.3, p. 379.

[225] *Merton muniments*, c.13. The same was repeated in 1270 when the same criteria of admission were laid down, *The early rolls of Merton College*, c.3, p. 379. On patronage of kin and its effect of predisposition towards academic charity colleges see Highfield, 'The early colleges', pp. 246–9; as well as G. D. Squibb. *Founders' kin: privilege and pedigree* (Oxford, 1972), pp. 5–8.

who had become fellows were to undertake charitable obligations from the security, at least for some years, of their fellowships. Less fortunate poor scholars were to be admitted, helped and supported by them. When its resources allowed, Peterhouse was supposed to admit two or three young grammarians to live off what the statutes call *vestra eleemosyna*, though we know of none.[226] These young scholars were to fulfil various tasks in the College: one was a Bible reader at meals, the others assisting the deans at services. If they showed great talent and suitable character they could later become fellows of the College. One of the members of the College was to be elected to the office of Almoner who dispensed alms to the poor scholars.[227] Charity was exercised within Merton College in various ways. The statutes of 1274 clearly demanded that the house maintain and educate orphans of Merton's family as well as poor members of the Merton household after the founder's death.[228] Additionally, College officers and servants were cared for in old age; the statutes of 1270 and 1274 ordered the provision of food and clothing for life to the warden, servants and ministers of the house, so long as these people remained loyal to the College and exerted themselves on its behalf.[229] Incurably sick scholars of Merton were sent to live as corrodarians in the Hospital of St John at Basingstoke, Hampshire, and if they died they were properly buried at the College's expense.[230]

The undertaking of support for scholars was a form of charity which appears in England and France with the rise of medieval universities.[231] Most foundations in England, though not the earliest ones, occurred in a period of crisis in patronage and provision for university graduates.[232] Both form and nature of the charitable academic institutions were linked with other contemporary charitable and religious mores. This laudable cause of learning *ad honorem Dei* could also be a source of spiritual benefit to a founder, just as were the monastery,

---

[226] *Documents relating to the university and colleges of Cambridge* I, c.28, pp. 24–5: 'Si facultates Domus predicte ad hos sufficient in presenti et si non, quod citius ad hoc sufficienter creverint, duo vel tres juvenes indigentes scolares in Grammatica…qui de vestra eleemosyna victitent'.

[227] *Ibid.*, c.18, p. 18.   [228] *Merton muniments*, p. 26.

[229] *The foundation statutes*, cc.27, 33, pp. 386, 388 and *Merton muniments*, pp. 25–6.

[230] Which was in Walter of Merton's patronage, *The foundation statutes*, c.4, p. 17; *The early rolls of Merton College*, c.30, pp. 386–7; *Merton muniments*, p. 16. The statutes of 1270 and 1274 encouraged cooperation between these two charitable houses, college and hospital, *The early rolls of Merton College*, c.42, p. 390; *Merton muniments*, p. 26.

[231] On the philanthropic element in the foundation of colleges see Lytle, 'Patronage patterns and Oxford colleges', pp. 111–49; p. 135.

[232] This is true if either one of the chronologies suggested by G. F. Lytle, *ibid.* and by Swanson in 'Universities, graduates and benefices', pp. 28–61, is adopted.

hospital, chapel or secular college. The academic environment was laden with charitable overtones and with potential objects of relief. Not only were the colleges a form of support for poor scholars, they could be a source of continuous charitable activity through the actions of their members.

The strong element of charitable obligations demanded of members of colleges is clearly reflected in the life of Ave Maria College in Paris, founded in 1339. The young scholars of this college continually undertook works of mercy. They distributed food and shoes to the poor every day, and gave away the remains of their table.[233] The endowed college became a centre for other charitable houses. According to the statutes of 1346 a house for ten less-fortunate poor scholars was dependent upon the college, and its members received a bowl of soup and some bread daily.[234] Ten old women lived in a house nearby and participated in parochial charitable works and in prayers for the souls of the founder of the college and his friends,[235] and a house for poor workers gave lodging to ten men of good character.[236] The college was an autonomous endowed community which was obliged by its statutes to undertake various works. It radiated the founder's intentions and served as a perpetual monument in his memory, for his spiritual benefit through relief of honest and deserving poor.

No such extensive individual charitable undertakings were demanded from the members of English medieval colleges, nor was 'Ave Maria' a typical French academic college.[237] But the fellows of Peterhouse were expected to help less-fortunate scholars. It was as if the founders felt that once a fellowship provided for a poor scholar's maintenance, the lack of immediate need might diminish his spirit of charity and render it empty of meaning.[238] At Balliol, New College and Merton

---

[233] A. L. Gabriel, 'The practice of charity at the University of Paris during the Middle Ages: Ave Maria College', *Traditio* 5 (1947), pp. 335–9; p. 338. The statutes of Ave Maria College were highly ornamented with miniatures depicting the young scholars practicing the works of mercy, Paris. Archives Nationales MS.406. See also A. L. Gabriel *Student life in the Ave Maria College, medieval Paris: history and chartulary of the college* (Notre Dame, Ind., 1955), pp. 110–12.

[234] Gabriel, 'The practice of charity', p. 337.

[235] Gabriel, *Student life*, pp. 113–14.

[236] *Ibid.*, pp. 115–16.

[237] On French charities for the sustenance of boys at schools see Reitzel, 'The medieval houses of *Bons-enfants*', *passim*.

[238] The contents of sermons delivered at Oxford university in the late thirteenth century reflect a conservative world view. Does the provision of comfortable surroundings not dampen a man's zeal, in both religious and social issues? See B. Smalley, 'Oxford university sermons, 1290–1293', in *Medieval learning and literature. Essays presented to R. W. Hunt*, ed. J. J. G. Alexander and M. T. Gibson (Oxford, 1976), pp. 307–27.

scraps from the fellows' table were distributed among the poor scholars since charity was to be seen and continually performed.[239] The holders of fellowships also had a reasonable hope of entering a living and a career through college patronage and traditional connections which the college developed; his poverty was probably merely a passing stage, a fact which might diminish his merit as a humble thankful recipient. To counteract this the colleges were made to help destitute scholars and to maintain some, albeit at a much lower level than fellows. The statutes of Peterhouse (1344) and Clare Hall (1359), stipulated the number of fellows and poor boys who were to be maintained until the age of 20.[240]

Not all colleges took part in the support of poor scholars beyond the admission of their fellows; but all functioned as memorials and chantries for their founders.[241] College statutes contain minute instructions for the celebration of the benefactors' obits, anniversaries and for prayers for their souls. The Peterhouse statutes ordered the creation of a Bede Roll in which the names of benefactors were to be entered and recited thrice a year at mass in the parish church annexed to the college church. There was also to be an annual benefactors' memorial service and indulgences were granted to those attending it.[242] The reason for the elaborate celebration for the souls of helpers of the college was said to be a proper compensation and rendering of thanks for temporal gifts.[243] The University celebrated the memory of its friends as well: Bishop Hugh Northwold is mentioned as one of its worthy benefactors in the oldest university statutes.[244]

---

[239] The chaplains and scholars were to live as parallel but separate groups, *Statutes of the colleges of Oxford* I, (London, 1853), pp. vii, ix, 7, 14 (Balliol); p. 78 (New College); I, pp. 24, 30, 31 (Queen's); *The early rolls of Merton College*, p. 72.

[240] For Peterhouse see *Documents relating to the university and colleges of Cambridge* I, pp. 24–5; for Clare Hall, *ibid.* II, p. 140: '…decem pueri dociles, idonei et honesti quos assumi volumus de pauperioribus qui poterint inveniri, et maxime de parochiis ecclesiarum quarum…sunt Rectores, et quod illud ad secundam mensam dicte domus secundum ordinationem Magistri ejusdem congrue sustententur'. See Merton's provision for the education of poor boys, *The early rolls of Merton College*, pp. 69–73.

[241] On college fellows as intercessors see Highfield, 'The early colleges', pp. 251–2.

[242] *Documents relating to the university and colleges of Cambridge* II, pp. 40–1.

[243] 'cum benefactoribus…subsidia temporanea caritatis intuitu, pia mente vobis conferentibus teneamini, tam juris persuasu quam ratione naturali Missarum et Orationum…pro viribus elargendi, ad vestram requisitionem gratam frequentius nobis factam, statuimus et etiam ordinamus, quod in aliqualem saltem recompensationem…faciatis unam missam…', *ibid.*, c.60, p. 41.

[244] Hackett, *The original statutes of Cambridge university*, pp. 25–6 and c.XIII (i), p. 217 for exequies of the king and Hugh Northwold. These statutes were written between 1236 and 1254 (*ibid.*, pp. 23, 175). The *Statuta antiqua* of the University of Oxford include a long list of benefactors, the days of their anniversaries and the prayers to be said for them in *Documents relating to the university and colleges* I, cc.180, 185, pp. 404, 413–14.

As the preoccupation with death and the elaborate provision for intercession at funerals and obits intensified in the late fourteenth and fifteenth centuries, the endowed colleges and their members were chosen as ideal providers of such services.[245] The university was also chosen as the source for suitable chantry priests. In 1257 the executors of William Kilkenny, the late bishop of Ely, left a sum of £200 with the prior of Barnwell for the maintenance of two scholars, students of Theology, as chantry chaplains for his soul, celebrating in Great St Mary's.[246] The fifteenth-century colleges, King's, Queens' and St Catharine's centred their devotion on extensive celebration and prayer for the souls of founders. The story of King's College has often been told, an extraordinary example of royal self-glorification. But the smaller colleges are also examples of a trend evident outside the academic environment, that of the foundation of chantries and secular colleges for the health of the souls of founders and founders' kin.[247]

When Robert Wodelarke, Provost of King's College, founded St Catharine's College in 1473 it was to be a small foundation for students of theology. The model of the earlier large colleges ruled through cooperation and hierarchy clearly did not apply in, nor characterise the model of such a four-fellow college. The statutes drawn by its founder clearly state that St Catharine's College was conceived as a bastion of Christian orthodoxy,[248] but it was also designed as Wodelarke's private chantry. The fellows were all to be in major orders, at least deacons, preferably priests.[249] The coexistence of these two objectives in the charitable motivation is natural and common. It inspired the patrons of Queens' College which was founded and twice refounded by a local priest, Andrew Dockett, rector of St Botolph's church and principal

---

[245] Lytle, 'Patronage patterns and Oxford colleges', pp. 118, 135.

[246] *Liber memorandorum*, pp. 94–6. Already in 1286 the fund may have been misappropriated, as strife ensued between the University and the Priory concerning the fulfilment of this obligation: *ibid.*, pp. 146–8.

[247] The University itself was commissioned with the intercession for the soul of Henry VII for which it received from 1504–5 £10 annually, *Grace book B*, part 1, ed. M. Bateson (Cambridge, 1903), pp. 202, 211, 215, 229, 238, 246. On chantries see above pp. 184–92.

[248] In opposition, no doubt, to the somewhat heretical Oxford, Cobban, 'Origins: Robert Wodelarke and St. Catharine's', pp. 1–32, esp. pp. 9–16. On unorthodox teaching in Oxford University see G. Leff, *Paris and Oxford universities in the thirteenth and fourteenth centuries. An institutional and intellectual history* (New York, 1968), pp. 95–6, 305–8.

[249] *Ibid.* Cobban, 'Origins', p. 18. At Queen's college, Oxford thirteen chaplains were to be sustained, and they were under no academic obligations. At New College ten chaplains were holders of fellowships and had liturgical duties only. See Wood-Legh, *Perpetual chantries in Britain*, pp. 209–10.

of St Bernard's Hostel, with the help of Henry VI and of successive queens. The College was founded in 1446 for a president (Dockett) and four scholars.[250] Like the late fourteenth-century foundations of Oxford, these mid-fifteenth-century Cambridge colleges reflect a convergence of two needs: the wish to provide for a literate and able clergy which could effectively combat religious and social dissent together with the quest for effective and perpetual intercession. These combined in the minds of those benefactors who could contemplate large-scale patronage in the foundation of academic colleges.

The older colleges received some donations from people outside the academic sphere in the fourteenth and mainly in the fifteenth century, for the undertaking of charitable obligations combined with prayers for the donor.[251] In 1345, John Ilegh, rector of Ickleton, granted all his goods in the village to Michaelhouse, for the support of two scholars and one chaplain in the college.[252] In 1434, Robert Turk, a London merchant, created a fund for the support of two scholars in Michael-house, who were to be 'able and honest and of good reputation and working in the schools'. They lived in the College and were to pray for his and his family's souls, and observe an anniversary maintained in perpetuity by the College.[253] Richard Andrew, a burgess of Cambridge left valuable tenements in St Botolph's and St Peter's parishes, as well as in Madingley, to Queens' College, for the maintenance of an obit and for 'a cleric to read the bible at meals and dinner in the said college forever'.[254] Grants were given in exchange for the celebration of anniversaries in college chapels or in churches of their patronage. Thus, Edith Chamber of Cambridge left a messuage in St Michael's lane in 1497, for perpetual celebration of a daily mass for her soul by a fellow of Michaelhouse who served as the parish chaplain, and for yearly

---

[250] In 1448 Queen Margaret of Anjou gave the college more lands for a new site the creation of which was entered in a charter of 1448. The chapel was dedicated in 1454; and in 1465 the house entered the patronage of Queen Elizabeth, wife of Edward IV. For the early history of Queens' see Searle, *Queens' College* I, pp. 1–56; more succinctly in *VCH. Cambridgeshire* III, pp. 408–13.

[251] Fellows and ex-fellows left books, plate and money to the colleges. In 1349 Master John of Tydd, a former fellow, left £10 to Peterhouse, for common use, in return for prayers for his soul and for the members of his family, Peterhouse muniments. Collegium B1. John Caraway left his books for the use of Queens' College, and gave a devotional book to the master Andrew Dockett, CUL. Queens' College muniments (25 May 1449).

[252] Trinity College muniments. Otryngham book, pp. 121–8, 458.

[253] 'ydoneos et honestos et bone fame scholas exercentes', A. E. Stamp, *Michaelhouse* (Cambridge, 1924), pp. 31–3. The bequest was to pass on to Clare Hall in case of neglect by Michaelhouse.

[254] CUL. Queens' College muniments (30 August 1459).

exequies with distributions to scholars and to the poor.[255] The colleges combined the practice and the study of the Christian faith to a degree that rendered them highly suitable both as objects deserving charitable relief and as perpetual intercessors for the souls of their founders and friends.[256] Fellows relied on their colleges for intercession and left sizeable legacies for their maintenance.[257]

The thirteenth century saw the creation of the new endowed academic college as a mode of charitable giving and provision for one's after-life; a form of religious organisation was adapted to new needs of scholars. In the fourteenth and fifteenth centuries, a period which saw most frequent foundation of chantries by great and middling folk, we witness a change in the life of colleges, the chantry element which had always existed in them was becoming increasingly pronounced.[258] Another channel of charity to scholars was the support of friars in the university towns, which lies outside the scope of this study. As they were university scholars mingling with clerics, their particular sources of support allowed other charitable funds to be open to secular scholars.[259] The Franciscan friary at Cambridge was quite large, housing some 60 friars until 1350.[260] The Dominicans numbered some 90 members in Cambridge in the thirteenth and the beginning of the

---

[255] SJCA.D20.61. This grant contained a clause by which the donation would pass to HSJC in case of failure of the original recipient to abide by the agreement. See also chantries in Peterhouse at the beginning of the sixteenth century in Peterhouse muniments. Collegium. A10, B1.

[256] Thus, Richard of Werplesdon founded an obit at Merton college (before 1270) on which day 20s were to be spent on the master and fellows' pittances and wine, *The early rolls of Merton college*, p. 391.

[257] For example, John Wolpet of Queens' left 1 mark for the fabric of the college and 12d to each fellow; his obit was to be observed by them, CUL. Queens' College muniments (25 December 1434). See also the agreement of King's Hall by which it undertook the maintenance of the anniversaries of Richard Holme, a former fellow, CUL. University archives. Luard 101 and 103 (1424); for similar arguments see Luard 136. On the conservative nature of the spiritual life of fellows see G. F. Lytle, 'A university mentality in the later middle ages: the pragmatism, humanism and orthodoxy of New College, Oxford', in *Genèse et débuts du Grand Schisme d'Occident* (Paris, 1980), pp. 201–30; p. 223.

[258] Lytle, 'Patronage patterns', p. 135; G. H. Cook, *Medieval chantries and chantry chapels* (London, rev edn, 1963), pp. 19–20; Cobban, 'Origins: Robert Wodelarke and St. Catharine's', pp. 7–9.

[259] The alms recorded in the accounts of John Botwright, master of Corpus Christi, Cambridge, were distributed to a monk and two friars, E. C. Pearce, 'College accounts of John Botwright, master of Corpus Christi, 1443–74', *Cambridge Antiquarian Society. Proceeding and communications* 22 (1917–20), pp. 76–90; p. 83.

[260] But a great decline came after the Black Death. For numbers see Moorman, *The Grey Friars*, pp. 77–8. On donations to the friars made in testamentary bequests of townsfolk see above p. 261.

fourteenth centuries.[261] The friars lived off alms and gifts in kind and they received them from great and small testators.[262] The friaries would have special expenses incurred in having to supply the needs of their members as scholars. Edward I established a payment of alms to the Dominicans and Franciscans of the university towns: he ordered the payment of 50 marks yearly to each Oxford friary and 25 marks to each Cambridge house.[263]

Few medieval benefactors founded academic colleges and they were usually kings, queens, bishops and great noblemen and noblewomen.[264] Academic charitable activity usually took the form of endowment of grammar schools, and provision of scholarships for scholars in the universities, but Cambridge and Oxford universities and the colleges in them offered a grander type of academic charity. These forms of charitable activity could not but affect the ideas on charity and patronage harboured by members of the town. The emulation of charitable forms between social groups is in itself an interesting phenomenon, and could explain how the leading citizens of Cambridge came together for the creation of a college in their patronage. After the Black Death when the gild of St Mary and Corpus Christi found itself rich with legacies from its dead members, it sought a way to create a perpetual and effective source of intercession for their souls.[265] The foundation of an academic college was their choice, indicating that in the minds of the brethren and sisters of the gild a Cambridge college and a religious fraternity could fulfil some similar objectives.

Loan-chests for the benefit of scholars: university chests

The provision of loans at low interest was an acceptable form of charitable relief. Scholars were (and still are) notorious seekers of credit; the expectation of greater income after the completion of the course

[261] W. A. Hinnebusch, *The early English friars preachers* (Rome, 1951), pp. 18, 74.

[262] Franciscans, Dominicans, Carmelites and Augustinians. See: CCCA.xxxi, 68 (1336); xxxi, 92 (1393); SJCA.D19.53 (1446); *Cambridge borough documents* 1, p. 152 (1419); W. M. Palmer, *The history of the parish of Borough Green* (Cambridge, 1939), p. 89 (1420). As popular intercessors they received funerary bequests as a group of deserving poor. Thus, all friars of Oxford and Cambridge were fed on the obit day of Queen Isabella's death in 1246 *Calendar of liberate rolls preserved in the Public Records Office 1226–1266* (London, 1916–59), p. 71.

[263] For the beginnings of the benefaction see *Calendar of patent rolls 1461–67*, p. 286 and *Calendar of patent rolls 1301–7*, p. 239. The gifts to the Franciscans at Cambridge were studied in Moorman, *The Grey Friars*, pp. 63–75.

[264] Storey, 'The foundation and the medieval college', pp. 3–4.

[265] See the Bede roll in *Cambridge gild records*, pp. 24–5.

of studies prompted them to take loans to acquire the bare necessities.[266] Great pressure on the sources of credit would have affected interest rates and conditions in university towns where so many people were in constant need of credit. In the absence of other valuables, scholars were often forced to pawn Christian books with Jewish moneylenders in order to obtain a loan.[267] From a very early stage in the university's history, devices for the provision of credit were created, supported by gifts of benefactors. These trusts were called 'chests' (*ciste*) and usually carried the name of their founders.

The creation of loan-chests for scholars was a phenomenon peculiar to England.[268] They appeared in mid-thirteenth-century Oxford and towards the end of the century in Cambridge, in a period in which the universities' endowments were embryonic. The first university chest was founded in Oxford in 1240 by Robert Grosseteste in an attempt to free scholars from the need to take loans from the Jews, and to pawn their books with them.[269] In it were 78s 8d, a fine paid by the burgesses of Oxford as punishment for their assaults on university clerics, a sum which was guarded by the canons of St Frideswide's until 1320. In an amendment to the statutes of St Frideswide's chest from before 1350, an oath was demanded of those receiving a loan to ensure that the money would be used for their relief alone.[270] It provided 1 mark to a master, 8s to a Bachelor and 5s to a sophist,[271] and reimbursed the

---

[266] One must remember that most scholars lived in halls and were not supported by the income of a college. The proportion in late fifteenth century Cambridge would have been 150 members of colleges out of a total academic population of 1500, Aston, Duncan and Evans, 'The medieval alumni', p. 17; for Oxford, Aston and Faith, 'The endowments of the university and colleges', p. 286.

[267] Normal rates permitted by Henry III were around 43.3% per annum. See Roth, *The Jews of medieval Oxford*, p. 128. Aston and Faith, 'The endowments of the university and colleges', pp. 274–5. On moneylending as a form of charity see above pp. 224–6.

[268] On the chests of Cambridge see G. Pollard, 'Medieval loan chests at Cambridge', *Bulletin of the Institute of Historical Research* 17 (1939–40), pp. 113–29; p. 114. For a full tabulation of the Oxford chests see Aston and Faith, 'The endowments of the university and colleges', pp. 276–9. By 1360 there were £1300 in the chests of the university of Oxford. *ibid.*, p. 283. The sum for the Cambridge chests cannot be as accurately calculated since for those founded in the thirteenth century, and some of the fourteenth century chests we have no knowledge of the capital, see Pollard, 'Medieval loan chests', pp. 120–5.

[269] Roth, *The Jews of medieval Oxford*, p. 130. For this chest see *Statuta antiqua universitatis Oxoniensis*, pp. 74–6. For an example of a royal limitation on interest exacted from scholars see *Calender of close rolls 1232–1247*, p. 424.

[270] *Statuta antiqua universitatis Oxoniensis*, pp. 77–8: 'Faciat proprio iuramento quod pro relevatione proprie indigencie et nullius alterius persone pecuniam huiusmodi recipiet'.

[271] Aston and Faith. 'The endowments of the university and colleges', p. 267.

borrower for the *excrescentia*, the excess value of the pawn over the original sum.[272]

The earliest Cambridge loan-chest was founded towards the end of the thirteenth century by Thomas of St Botolph, who was personal chaplain to Archbishop John Le Romeyn of York.[273] He allowed loans up to the sum of 6s 8d to each scholar of the university. Nine chests were founded in the fourteenth and fifteenth centuries. Our first set of surviving statutes is from the Neel and Wythorn chest founded in 1345, in a charter existing in the university archives.[274] Some five to nine years later, William Bateman, bishop of Norwich, founded the Holy Trinity chest, the statutes of which were copied into both the Senior and the Junior Proctor's books and which are very similar to the statutes of the Neel and Wythorn chest.[275] Both chests were founded with a capital of £100 and their loans were to be given against the security of an object that was immediately marked, registered and kept by the chests' custodians. The Neel chest allowed loans to be given up to the sum of 60s to masters, 20s to bachelors and one mark to scholars, while the Holy Trinity chest permitted 80s to a master, 30s to a bachelor and 20s to a scholar or bedel. William Bateman also allowed a privilege to fellows of his new college, Trinity Hall, by permitting the lending of the highest sums (as to a master) even to junior members of this college. Custodians of the chests were elected yearly by the congregation of masters and were to be two regent-masters and one non-regent. Audits were held every year and were conducted under the supervision of a doctor of the University. Bishop Bateman deposited his chest in the Carmelite friary (now part of Queens' College, north of the Old Court and Cloister Court).[276] The borrowers were to return the loan within a year, or else the pledge was sold. When this happened the amount of the loan was subtracted from the sale price and the residue was returned to the debtor. Such interest-free chests

---

[272] *Ibid.*, p. 281.

[273] Commemorated as a university benefactor in the *Statuta antiqua universitatis Oxoniensis* of the University of Cambridge and in *Documents relating to the university and colleges of Cambridge* I, c.180, p. 405, c.181, p. 407.

[274] CUL. University archives. Luard 35. The statutes are transcribed in J. W. Clark, 'On the charitable foundations in the University called chests', *Cambridge Antiquarian Society. Proceedings and communications* 11 (1903–6), pp. 78–101. For another set of statutes see those of St John's chest of 1466, CUL. University archives. Luard 130 (and copy in Luard 130a).

[275] CUL. Univ. Archives. Collect. Admin. 1, fols. 58–62 and Collect. Admin. 2, fols. 66–8.

[276] Other university loan-chests were deposited for safety in churches. Gotham chest was kept in St Michael's church and the Billingford chest in St Benet's. In both cases chests founded by Masters of colleges were deposited in the church appropriated to their respective houses.

were bound to become dilapidated with time, as pledges were lost, spoiled or mistakenly valued and expenses were incurred. In 1489 Elizabeth de Clare gave the University the sum of £200 for the restoration of eight chests still existing of the twelve originally founded. The missing four chests must have been dissipated by then, and were not revived. In 1540 the chests were amalgamated into three by joining Bowser and Billingford, Fen and Neel, Darlington and Exeter.[277]

The founders of Cambridge University chests included an archbishop, a bishop, four clerics in episcopal service, two rectors, three holders of offices in royal administration, one duke and two masters of colleges.[278] The capital placed in the chests was very often around the sum of £100 in the fourteenth and fifteenth centuries; there was one with 100 marks and another with 250 marks.[279] Four founders created chests both at Oxford and Cambridge in which case the statutes were almost identical.[280]

It is interesting to note the relation of loan-chests in the academic world to those in lay society. The need for short-term loans existed within towns for the relief of seasonal workers, of people suffering from a spell of illness, for working capital and so forth. A papal letter to the bishops of Bath and Wells and Salisbury of 1251 ordered the creation of chests in which sums collected from many townsmen would form a source of loans for the poor without interest.[281] In 1459 a spicer of Cambridge bequeathed 80 marks, for the provision of loans to townsmen in need against a pledge up to the sum of 26s 8d each.[282] The recipients were to say *de profundis* or recite the Pater Noster and Ave Maria, according to their degree of literacy.

The charitable act of providing credit was expected to bear spiritual returns to the giver. Indeed, the receivers of loans were obliged by the statutes regulating them to pray for the soul of the founder. During the term of the loan the beneficiaries of the Holy Trinity chest were to say the Pater Noster and the Ave Maria thrice daily for the health of bishop Bateman's soul.[283] The statutes of the Neel chest demanded

---

[277] Clark, 'On the charitable foundations', pp. 99–100.
[278] For Oxford, see Aston and Faith, 'The endowments of the university and colleges', pp. 282–3: churchmen, judges, noblemen and noblewomen.
[279] Billingford and Roubery chests.
[280] Roubery, Neel, Exeter and Bourchier (Bowser) chests.
[281] *Calendar of papal letters* I, 267–8.
[282] CUL. Queens' College muniments. As his will was kept in Queens' we may conclude that the man was aware of the benefits that an academic organisation could offer.
[283] CUL. University archives. Collect. Admin. I, fol. 65v (in the Old Senior Proctor's Book).

that the recipients say the Pater Noster and Ave Maria five times.[284] The beneficiaries of the Billingford chest were to say at the time of receipt *de profundis* and three collects for the soul of the late master.[285] University clerics were deemed to be especially deserving of relief and they could provide ample returns. The preamble to the statutes of the Neel and Wythorn chest states this clearly: 'amongst other works of charity it is known that aiding the needs of scholars by providing useful aid is a pious deed'.[286] The creation of chests attracted benefactors since it offered perpetually renewed and evolving charitable acts at a time when the efficacy of intercession and prayers for benefactors was judged by the quantity and frequency with which they were repeated.[287]

Founders of loan-chests were entered as benefactors of Cambridge University to be remembered and prayed for on their anniversaries and on the general benefactors' day.[288] The University also undertook the routine upkeep of the chests: the proctors' accounts found in the Grace Books beginning in 1454–5 contain many entries recording expenditure on locks, keys, wax and parchment for the copying of statutes and the tagging of pledges.[289] In 1488 the University added £12 to the chests which were *in decasu existentium*,[290] and in 1489 it formulated new statutes for the guidance of the custodians of University chests.[291]

[284] CUL. University archives. Luard 35. Clark's transcript in 'On the charitable foundations', c. 18, p. 94.

[285] Masters, *The history of the college of Corpus Christi*, appendix p. 26.

[286] 'Inter cetera caritatis opera pium esse dinoscitur studentium necessitatibus consulere ipsis de oportuno subsidio providendo', CUL. University archives. Luard 35 (or transcript in Clark, 'On the charitable foundations', p. 83).

[287] For a similar evaluation see Aston and Faith, 'The endowments of the university and colleges', p. 284 and on the aspect of multiplicity in the quest for intercession see above pp. 184–92, 259–64.

[288] The *Statuta antiqua universitatis Oxoniensis* of the University mention in the long list of benefactors (c.180): 'fiat una missa pro anima Magistri Thome de Sancto Botolpho hora congregationis...Item singulis annis...pro anima Magistri Willelmi de Blida, qui decem marcas cuidam ciste contulit pro utilitate scholarium...et...pro anima Gilberti de Roubery qui quondam cistam in universitate ista fundavit'. On 24 and 25 January, Bishop Bateman's memory was celebrated 'qui duas aulas et unam cistam in universitate ista fundavit' and in the Octaves of Trinity Sunday he was remembered 'et hoc pro fundatione ciste Trinitatis'. At the end of the section he appears among those who received 'singulis annis anniversariis pro animabus fundatorum cistarum subscriptarum celebrandis', *Documents relating to the university and colleges of Cambridge* I, p. 407.

[289] Examples: In 1464–5: 'pro ligatione ciste de Neyll 26s 8d' or 'pro emendacione cere et clave ciste de derlyngton 4d'; In 1465–6: 'pro reparacione unius cere et factura unius clavis ciste de Neele 12d'. All in *Grace Book A*, ed. S. M. Leathes (Cambridge, 1897), pp. 48, 54, also pp. 130, 186, 187. In addition, *Grace Book B*, part 1 pp. 11–12; *Grace Book B*, part 2, ed. M. Bateson (Cambridge, 1905), pp. 83, 129.

[290] *Grace Book B*, part 1, p. 11.   [291] CUL. University archives. Luard 132.

Loan-chests for the benefit of scholars: college chests

Although most chests existed in the colleges founded before 1400 (11 out of 12), most were created only in the fifteenth century. Of the 11 chests for which we know the year of foundation, two were founded in the fourteenth century (Barker chest – in 1349; Gotham chest – *c.* 1380) and nine in the fifteenth. This may be explained by the fact that the colleges founded in the fourteenth century had offered sufficient commons to meet the needs of their fellows and that the need for credit was small in these comfortable circumstances. In the course of time, as prices rose relatively to the stipends, a greater need for additional cash may have existed as scholars did not have the same buying power with their allowances that their predecessors had had in the fourteenth century.[292] The capital of the college chests was smaller than that customary in University chests. It usually lay between £10 and £40. Regulations for the keeping of these chests were less formal than for others. Some college chests would forward loans to fellows upon a promise to return it, relying on the discretion of the master.[293] Despite the fact that University chests existed throughout the fourteenth century, college relief developed only later, to answer a new need arising in some of the colleges.

Most college chests were founded by masters or fellows of the house. Of ten identified founders, eight were members of the respective colleges in which they founded the chest. In these cases the founders' motivation was the wish to help friends and colleagues. The inspiration can be found in the intimate knowledge of the needs of scholars which the founders possessed. They were also less demanding in spiritual returns than the founders of University chests. The chests carried the name of their founder, but we also find cases of successive masters adding onto the pre-existing chest without a change in title.[294]

College chests were founded by people intimately connected with these institutions, as an act of friendly succour reminiscent of relief offered within gilds. The founders were apparently not greatly preoccupied with the spiritual return from their charitable act; as they were a living part of the college, individually remembered by its

---

[292] See Pollard, 'Medieval loan chests', pp. 125–6. On the college chest of King's Hall see Cobban, *The King's Hall*, pp. 210–11.

[293] Example: the Aylwarde chest at Caius, Pollard, 'Medieval loan chests', p. 125.

[294] In Peterhouse, the Castrobernardi chest was founded by master Thomas of Castle Bernard. His successor added 10 marks to it in 1426 and 20 marks in 1436, see Peterhouse muniments. Registrum vetus, pp. 79–80. In Michaelhouse the Gotham chest, founded in 1380 was replenished with £20 by a fifteenth-century master.

members, their charity evidently stemmed from a feeling of friendship and mutual responsibility bred in a collegiate society. It also reflects in burgess society a tendency towards mutual-help and an awareness of the utility of perpetual institutions through the observation of the academic sector.

Chapter 8

EPILOGUE

Unusquisque prout destinavit in corde suo
non ex tristitia, aut ex necessitate:
hilarim enim datorem diligit Deus

II Cor. 9,7

Rich gifts wax poor when givers prove unkind

Hamlet III, I, 100

As we have explored the institutions of charity in the late Middle Ages, we have seen some very marked change, into whose nature we must now finally and tentatively inquire.

The medieval doctrine of charity brought people together in a network of reciprocal help in which the individual could be a source of comfort to his fellow. The contents of religious and social instruction offered by the Church sought to internalise external values, so as to create an artificial yet intimate link between members of the Christian community.[1] One product of this line of thought is the concept of service developed in the Christian West, an idea which far transcended the preexisting norms of family and feudal loyalties. Through service to one's fellow men God was served, humility and renunciation of self were achieved.[2] By dispossessing themselves of part of their property, medieval men and women sought their own salvation, contributed to society's solidarity and promoted trust in its piety, virtue and affluence.[3]

In the growing towns of twelfth- and thirteenth-century Europe groups of leading citizens were developing an ethos of duty and cooperation in which the common weal became a cherished value entrusted to their hands. The ability to contribute to the general welfare became a test of status and prosperity as well as a reflection of moral

---

[1] R. C. Trexler, 'Charity and the defense of urban elites in the Italian communes', in *The rich, the well born and the powerful*, ed. F. Jaher (Urbana, Ill., 1973), pp. 63–107; p. 104.

[2] Schreiber, *Gemeinschaft des Mittelalters*, p. 313; for examples of the exaltation of service see the sermons to hospital brethren and sisters in *Beati Umberti sermones* (Venice, 1603), sermons 40 and 41; Guth, 'Spitäler in Bamberg und Nürnberg', pp. 41–2.

[3] These effects have been analysed in the context of sacrifice. See H. Hubert and M. Mauss, *Sacrifice: its nature and function*, trans. W. D. Halls (London, 1964), p. 102.

health and virtue.[4] In this framework alleviation of poverty secured both social and spiritual benefits which rendered it a doubly attractive and effective activity.[5] In their charity burgesses and substantial villagers with links to the town not only expressed but reinforced their values as leaders and members of their communities: the belief in prudent and discriminating fulfilment of religious demands on the one hand, and the duty to promote peace and stability, on the other.[6] This is not to say that the undertaking of works of charity stemmed *only* from the wish to pursue personal or group benefits; rather that the fulfilment of needs of certain *others*, strangers seen as brothers, had increasingly become a matter of personal interest.

The availability of surplus funds in twelfth- and thirteenth-century towns generated the ostentation common among comfortable classes, which has been parodied in Veblen's celebrated phrase 'conspicuous waste'.[7] After the fulfilment of one's personal needs and those of dependants, money and effort were employed in the display of affluence and success. Conspicuous waste is achieved by the use of funds in seemingly reckless and uncalculated ways demonstrating an individual's ability to do away with some of his property for enjoyment rather than for the fulfilment of a pressing need. Such consumption is rich in social and psychological benefits as long as its nature is not obscured or lost on those observing it. In the medieval world the value of charitable largesse as a form of conspicuous consumption was based on a delicate balance, since selfless giving *did* bear recognised spiritual rewards which could limit its display value. However, the return for charitable giving, the promise of salvation, was deferred and ambiguous. Charitable activity thus existed in the convergence of two urges: that towards charity and spiritual rewards and the other towards lavish display and

[4] In gift-exchanges where the form, source and occasion of the reciprocal return are vague, the 'moral' element is greater than in straightforward exchanges in which the counter-gift is reasonably expectable and predictable; see J. Pitt-Rivers, 'The kith and the kin', in *The character of kinship*, ed. J. Goody (Cambridge, 1973), pp. 89–106; p. 100. On the view of charitable activity as an expression of the community's spirit see Christian, *Local religion*, p. 120.

[5] Sahlins, 'The sociology of primitive exchange', p. 172.

[6] The relation between collectivity and the poor is a vital aspect of social cohesion, Simmel, *On individuality and social forms*, p. 170. Assistance is part of the same social system allowing and maintaining the existence of the differences in status which render some people poor and weak and others strong and able to offer relief, *ibid.*, pp. 155, 166, 169. For similar evaluations of the role of burgesses in the foundation of charitable institutions see Maréchal, *De Sociale en politieke gebundenheit*, p. 309.

[7] This term is developed and discussed in Veblen, *The theory of the leisure class*, see pp. 202, 217. On the understanding of obligations towards charity and hospitality among the ruling class of sixteenth and seventeenth century England see F. Heal, 'The idea of hospitality in early modern England', *Past and present* 102 (1984), pp. 66–93.

the distribution of one's bounty through largesse.[8] Although charity was most decidedly beneficial for one's salvation and for Christian society, inherent in it was a sufficient element of deliberate and voluntary self-dispossession. This ambiguity may help to explain the behaviour of some benefactors of HSJC, such as Baldwin Blancgernon and Eustace Dunning, who gave donations when they could have least afforded them.

The circumstances of the thirteenth-century economy which favoured burgesses, landlords and substantial peasants, also created great need among wage-labourers, underemployed folk and their dependants. The urban environment rendered those who are weakest in every society, the old, the sick, widows and orphans – the unemployable – more conspicuous in their need and probably more helpless.[9] It was in this period of greatest need that the indiscriminate charitable giving based in endowed institutions was diminishing, precipitating a change in the financial ability, character, and orientation of these houses. In the later period, in the economy and society of England after the Black Death, the work of labourers in town and countryside was in great demand. Hence, the overt need for charity was becoming less obvious just when the ability to apportion surplus funds to public giving, conspicuous or utilitarian, was declining.

In the depopulated and troubled towns of the late Middle Ages the feeling of security among potential leaders and publicly active citizens was on the wane.[10] Town patriciates were striving to maintain their grip, to protect their exclusive privileges through legislation, and to promote their social and occupational interests through the activities of socio-religious associations, such as gilds. These bodies were citadels

---

[8] This paradox is maintained in the rationale of sacrifice: the sacrificer offers a precious object in a disinterested manner, yet expects to achieve peace, equilibrium, to placate the gods and to reestablish their favour, Hubert and Mauss, *Sacrifice*, p. 100.

[9] 'Le pauvre urbain devient un être anonyme, souvent vagabond, sans autre recours que la communauté d'un destin marginal partagé avec ses congénères', Mollat, 'La notion de la pauvreté', p. 13. On the connection between greater distress (especially urban poverty) and society's sensitivity to it see Tierney, *Medieval poor law*, p. 85 and Geremek, 'La popolazione marginale tra il medioevo e l'era moderna', p. 623, also Probst, 'Das Hospitalwesen im hohen und späten Mittelalter', p. 256. For a later period see the shift in awareness and understanding of categories of poverty at a time of economic crisis and wide unemployment, P. Slack, 'Poverty and politics in Salisbury, 1597–1666', in *Crisis and order in English towns. Essays in urban history*, ed. P. Clark and P. Slack (London, 1972), pp. 164–203; esp. pp. 178–92. On the importance of sharing and on the sanctions against hoarding in societies existing on subsistence level see Sahlins, 'The sociology of primitive exchange', pp. 166–7, 169.

[10] Dobson, 'Urban decline', pp. 14–16; Phythian-Adams, 'Urban decay', pp. 164–8, and a qualified interpretation showing evasion mainly amongst middling burgesses, Kermode, 'Urban decline?', *passim*, esp. pp. 196–8.

in which social distances were respected and where mutual interests could be promoted.[11] Alternatively, some turned to the countryside or developed a stake outside the town to secure their income and bolster their status. Reluctance to undertake public office and posts in gilds and fraternities, detected among the burgesses of some large medieval towns, betrays an attitude of mind similar to that which led men to withdraw from communal charitable giving and draw them towards the hectic accumulation of prayers for their souls.[12] The identification of such short-term causes for shifts in attitudes does not exclude the quest for long-term changes in mentalities and their effect on charitable activity. Quite the contrary, we have seen that between the twelfth and fifteenth centuries a realignment occurred, resetting those 'slowly changing features of life that influence people's sense of community, of boundaries between the self and others, and of the character of social relations'.[13]

Richard Titmuss propounded the view that altruism and charity are positively fostered by customary and formal acts of charity. When a society loses these public manifestations, which provide a model for behaviour, it suffers a decline in its altruistic–charitable orientation.[14] If this is true, in a period when new hospitals were no longer being founded and old ones were falling into decay, when acts of giving were deemed less necessary owing to the rise in wages of most labourers, a loss far beyond what can be gauged as pence per head would occur.

Medieval charitable relief was never intended to create a new social order, still less to eliminate poverty.[15] Theories which exalted and preached the redistribution of wealth and renunciation of goods were eventually pushed to the intellectual and social margins.[16] In all forms

---

[11] On the development of social barriers and status distinctions within late medieval Venetian confraternities see Pullan, *Rich and poor*, pp. 66–7. In fifteenth-century Italian towns charity was transformed by the ruling families to channel funds to needy members and thus to preserve the status of leading families of the communes, see Trexler, 'Charity and the defense of urban elites', pp. 63–107 and Maréchal, *De sociale en politieke gebundenheit*, pp. 310–11.

[12] On these developments see the C. Phythian-Adams, *Desolation of a city: Coventry and the urban crisis of the late Middle Ages* (Cambridge, 1979); see J. I. Kermode, 'Urban decline? The flight from office in late medieval York', *Economic history review* second ser. 35 (1982), pp. 179–98.

[13] In the words of Natalie Davis, 'Some tasks and themes', p. 318.

[14] Titmuss, *The gift relationship*, p. 198.

[15] See J. Toussaert, *Le sentiment religieux en Flandre à la fin du moyen-âge* (Paris, 1963), pp. 470, 476; F. Graus, 'Social utopias in the Middle Ages', *Past and present* 38 (1967), pp. 3–19; Génicot, 'Sur le nombre des pauvres', p. 275.

[16] Manteuffel, *Naissance d'une hérésie*, p. 169; Trexler, 'Charity and the defense of urban elites', pp. 68–70; Thouzellier, 'Hérésie et pauvreté', pp. 371–88; Simmel, *On individuality and social forms*, p. 169.

of relief only temporary help was offered, with little regard for the actual needs of the poor; few charitable foundations ever offered more than short-term alleviation of need. However, in the earlier period houses like the Hospital of St John, living on a stable endowment, were geared primarily towards the poor. One may cautiously assume that HSJC's enthusiastic patrons were also more inclined towards door-step charity than their successors. In the later period such institutions were declining and unsupported, few new hospitals were founded and charity tended to centre in religious associations on occasions connected with death, liturgy and particular devotion.[17] Those deemed worthy of help by the consent of gild members or by episcopal indulgences were the productive members of society experiencing a temporary period of distress, but who were basically respectable, and not radically divergent from the giver's own self-image. With the general rise in the standard of living of labourers in the later Middle Ages, those who owned landed property and urban tenements, rentiers and employers, were witnessing a decline in their own fortunes. When an attempt to indoctrinate labourers with a work ethic which would curtail their freedom and welfare failed to produce change, the perception of the poor developed into a general denunciation of those members of society who were not fully productive, and who were seen to be the reason for economic hardship. Labourers and the poor were judged for what was seen as wilful withdrawal from the economy and slothful reliance on others. As the test of productivity came to rule in determining social acceptance and moral approbation, the poor, be they journeymen, servants, widows or friars, came to acquire a label, to be seen as shirkers or 'wastrels'. In the minds of employers and entrepreneurs struggling with an economy afflicted by acute shortage of labour, poverty came to be seen more as a choice than an affliction. Those hospitals founded and maintained in this period which did not become chantries were usually secular foundations with a pronounced punitive and corrective side, providing a regulated and controlled relief of parish poverty.[18]

The Hospital of St John commemorated its past benefactors in a period when new benefactors were few. After the foundation period

[17] In the words of C. de La Roncière summarising the activities of the confraternities of the Florentine contado. 'Dans leur aumônes, ils étaient sensibles à la fin spirituelle plus qu'à l'effet matériel. Le service des pauvres dépendait d'occasions qui lui étaient parfaitement étrangères et restait désordonné', de La Roncière, 'La place des confréries dans l'encadrement religieux', p. 44.

[18] On these characteristics of hospitals in the early modern period see Gutton, *La société et les pauvres*, pp. 25–44, 87–94, 142–55.

of eager patronage by townsmen and villagers, the hospital proceeded to consolidate its holdings and to adapt its duties to the changing economic circumstances and to the altered disposition of its patrons. When parish churches were being appropriated to religious houses and colleges, the hospital was one of the few foundations which retained a purely local urban flavour and which could supply perpetual spiritual services. The townsmen grasped this fact; they rallied behind the hospital in its dispute with Peterhouse and created chantries and anniversary foundations. Many hospitals fell into decay or were transformed in the late fourteenth and fifteenth centuries;[19] in Cambridge HSJC succeeded in maintaining its income and status by accepting commoners and lodgers, and with the help of the benefits awarded by the university privileges. As it was one of the few religious houses which offered intercession, the hospital, for a while, existed between these two worlds, its brethren collecting income from estates given to procure intercession. Others had interests in the hospital as well: university scholars who lodged in it, the bishops of Ely who chose its chapel as a hall for episcopal audiences, and the many officials who used it as their abode. By the late fifteenth century it maintained few charitable obligations, but perhaps sustained some bedesmen in connection with chantry obligations.[20] Thus, only the bishop of Ely was compensated when the house was transformed, as he seemed to be the main loser from its dissolution. He was allowed to present three of the first fellows of the new college, and one of the fellows forever. In 1509, just before her death, Lady Margaret Beaufort had a draft drawn up for the conveyance of the hospital's properties to the new college. The object of the document was: 'about transforming a religious house of religious brethren commonly known as St John's Cambridge into a college of persons, neither lay nor religious, studying the Arts and Theology'.[21] By the late Middle Ages the Hospital of St John the Evangelist had become so similar in its functions to an academic college its final transformation could be represented as doing no harm to the town. Bishop Alcock had only recently argued in converting St Radegund's into Jesus College, that the house was said to be in a state of decay.[22]

---

19 Butcher, 'The hospital of St Stephen and St Thomas New Romney', pp. 17–26; and for Spain see Martz, *Poverty and welfare in Habsburg Spain*, p. 159.

20 The maintenance of bedesmen was a central part of intercession ceremonies of Venetian *scuole* see Pullan, *Rich and poor*, p. 77; also R. C. Trexler, *Public life in Renaissance Florence* (New York, 1980), p. 266.

21 SJCA.D6.10. For a survey of the documentary evidence connected with the refoundation see M. G. Underwood, 'Records of the foundress', *Eagle* 68 (1979), pp. 8–23.

22 We have only his word for it; HSJC's deficits in the late fifteenth century were maintained at around only 6–7%, see accounts for 1485, SJCA.D106.9 and above pp.

The fact that by 1505 the hospital was fulfilling few of its original tasks, allowed the chancellor of the university to form a powerful alliance with the mother of the Tudors for the removal of a hospital and its replacement by an academic college.[23]

Through the study of the forms of giving in one town and its surroundings a general development has been explained: the shift from communal and cooperative forms of charitable organisation towards a more personal and individual search for religious and social benefits. Stourbridge and HSJC, when founded in the mid-twelfth and early thirteenth centuries, combined the attainment of personal salvation and prestige with works beneficial to one's fellow, one's parish and one's neighbours. Charitable foundations of the late Middle Ages centred more on liturgical than communal merit, and tended to form a meticulously planned scheme of intercession. The foundation of asylums was now left more to the responsibility of town government,[24] or to individuals whose names came to be attached to them, and who often kept them within the secular sphere of management and supervision.[25] A disenchantment with the traditional recipients of charity induced givers to plan their foundations so as to contain numerous intercessors in a controlled and regulated position. At the same time, the clergy's discretion in the allocation of charitable funds was much circumscribed, as town corporations, gilds and individual laymen were entrusted with their administration.[26] In Cambridge, the

232–5 as well as the accounts for 1505–10 when the establishment was already being transformed and its management taken over by the agents of Lady Margaret. A similar transfer of charitable funds occurred at the Reformation. When the hospital of St. Giles, Norwich was dissolved as a religious house in 1547, it was granted to the corporation and was maintained as a hospital but a part of its endowment was given to the Norwich Grammar School.

[23] The College may have still been seen as a likely source of relief. With this hope in mind William Shorley, a prisoner at the castle, wrote to the first master of the College (1508–1537), petitioning him for help, SJCA.D56.13: 'besekyng your moste honorabull good mastershyppe in the honor of Iohn to have compassyon on your seyd bedeman'.

[24] As occurred in Florence in the Late Middle Ages, M. Becker, 'Aspects of lay piety in early Renaissance Florence', in *The pursuit of holiness*, ed. Trinkaus and Oberman, pp. 177–99, esp. pp. 177–81.

[25] Such as Elsing Spital in London, or Dick Whittington's College: see Thrupp, *The merchant class*, pp. 179–388. An increasing number of almshouses retained lay patronage and affiliations in the later Middle Ages. This may be reflected in the dedication of only a half (51.3%) of the 151 new foundations between 1301 and 1500 to saints and the other half carrying either a generic name (almshouse, bedehouse) (18.8%), a toponym (15.7%) or a founder's name (Lyon's) (15.2%); based on numbers from Knowles and Hadcock, *Medieval religious houses*, pp. 313–410.

[26] See such developments in Flemish towns: Toussaert, *Le sentiment religieux*, p. 472 and in the bequests of Provençal testators, Chiffoleau, *La comptabilité de l'au-delà*, pp. 321–2. Relations with the clergy increasingly resembled employment, Scarisbrick, *The*

Hospital of St Anthony and Eligius was supervised by a college, and later managed by a lay couple; the chantry at Newton employed the priests for prayers, but engaged bedesmen for merit. While the early academic colleges of Cambridge usually maintained some obligation to poor boys beyond the provision of the fellowships, the fifteenth-century colleges concentrated more strictly on their academic and liturgical functions, acting as personal chantries of their founders.[27] Christ's College replaced a charitable grammar school, God's House, and retained no further charitable provisions.[28]

This study of charity has produced a picture of a world in which the charitable message was familiar, and constantly measured and re-evaluated by its audience. It is a dynamic picture of a society bound by notions of responsibility and mutuality, yet allowing considerable scope for personal interpretation. The solutions formulated in the minds of individuals responded to the changing circumstances of their environment. Within these constraints they strove to behave charitably, as preachers and parish priests taught, but also adhered to the demands of kin and social groups, and to their own prejudices and aspirations. The terms used in wills and in fraternity statutes show that medieval men and women believed themselves to be charitable even when external evidence shows a marked change in their preferences. The degree of self-dispossession, of involvement with the fortunes of the weaker members of society through whom merit and peace were originally sought, declined dramatically in the fourteenth and fifteenth centuries. From activities favouring charity through the endowment and protection of religious communities which provided lodging and care, charity turned into an effort relying on personal participation through rituals in which the poor played a symbolic secondary part.

A similar shift towards spiritual self-help by layfolk is apparent in other areas of lay religious activity. This implies a changing under-

---

Reformation and the English people, p. 19; testators laid down not only the number but the *type* of clergy employed in their commemorations, Vale, *Piety, charity and literacy*, pp. 18–19; Pullan, *Rich and poor*, pp. 203–9. It is intriguing to find in the early fifteenth century the pious lawyer Ser Matteo Lapo urging his close friend and client Francesco Datini to allocate charitable funds from his vast property and to distribute them directly to those in need, rather than maintain churches and clergy, I. Origo, *The merchant of Prato. Francesco di Marco Datini* (London, 1957), pp. 214–20, esp. 217–19.

27 See above pp. 279–80.

28 See the statutes of God's House and of Christ's College in *Early statutes of Christ's College, Cambridge, with the statutes of the prior foundation of God's House*, ed. H. Rackham (Cambridge, 1927), pp. 2–38, 44–120. For a history of these foundations see the exhaustive study by A. H. Lloyd, *The early history of Christ's college, Cambridge, derived from contemporary documents* (Cambridge, 1934). On the circumstances of the foundation of God's House see also Orme, *English schools in the Middle Ages*, pp. 221–2.

standing of the nature of religious participation now favouring personal actions, promoted in peer and solidarity groups. Thus, merit was not sought in the convergence of the different members of the *societas christiana*, but rather in the rigorous and calculated fulfilment of objectives and employment of resources. In the late Middle Ages, fraternities, gilds and sometimes parishes, linked people of similar outlook and interests who also wished to be conventionally virtuous, thus creating a familiar and trustworthy community of piety.[29] These groups provided a framework for the meticulous provision of intercession, for the celebration of feasts and commemorations, and for the channelling of relief to almshouses and secular hospitals.[30] The general trend of charity was both to the flamboyant excesses of funerary and chantry bequests and to the limited and closely watched parish distributions and almshouses of the late fifteenth century.

What changes occurred in the respective goods and merits exchanged in the charitable act? As long as trust in reciprocation and in the eventual balancing of the exchange persisted, communal charitable forms survived. When doubt replaced such trust, the system was transformed. The pauper eventually became a menace, or an anonymous head among the recipients of doles and funerary pennies. It may be claimed that this change was inspired by a declining piety, by diminished predisposition towards adherence to religious norms; but this is manifestly wrong. From the testimony of the resources invested in intercession, the extent of fraternity membership, of religious pageantry, of the circulation of devotional books, a picture emerges of a laity hard at work in its 'pursuit of holiness'. Most people remained within an orthodox set of norms and demands, which could embrace a conventional if sometimes vehement anti-clericalism.[31] Such feelings had long been a significant element in the thoughts of reformers, but not all criticism amounted to a challenge to the sacramental authority of the clergy, like that of the Lollards. On the contrary, their sacramental and pastoral role was more clearly and exclusively sought in a period when many para-liturgical activities were taken up by the

[29] Gilds were not open to all members of urban society, while even parish gilds excluded those who could not pay the entry fines and dues, see C. Phythian-Adams, 'Ceremony and the citizen: the communal year at Coventry 1450–1550', in *Crisis and order in English towns 1550–1700. Essays in urban history*, ed. P. Clark and P. Slack (London, 1972), pp. 57–85; p. 58 and for sixteenth-century London, S. Brigden, 'Religion and social obligation in early sixteenth-century London', *Past and present* 103 (1984), pp. 67–112; p. 99.

[30] The urban hospitals were more developed in the towns of France and the Low Countries: see Gonthier, *Lyon et ses pauvres*, pp. 212–23 and Bonenfant, *Hôpitaux et bienfaisance publiques*, pp. 39–44.   [31] Chiffoleau, *La comptabilité de l'au-delà*, pp. 87–8.

laity in voluntary lay religious groupings. This involvement in religious self-help is reflected in the contents of vernacular books of instruction for the laity, many of which were owned by the urban laity: devotional vernacular handbooks, primers, and catechisms which come to our knowledge through lists in wills and inventories.[32] J. Chiffoleau has been tempted to talk of sophistication and differentiation in the pursuit of wholeness and holiness in the late Middle Ages, and to identify in religious self-help signs of modernisation.[33]

The changes in charity can reflect an underlying shift in social relations and attitudes.[34] Generalised social exchange, at the basis of which must lie deferral of rewards, can be maintained only in a society enjoying trust and security. In a less harmonious social climate, limited pacts between individuals develop bearing fewer social benefits. The society of twelfth- and thirteenth-century towns was a credit-oriented world which had learned the meaning of cooperation and trust as a basis for general welfare. When security and trust vanished, dyadic, restricted and defined forms of charity replaced the old; far more direct and unequivocal returns were expected by more demanding and less trusting social actors.[35]

Informal help rarely comes to our notice in surviving evidence of the period, and must have been practised in ways we can never assess. There must always be some space in our picture for expressions of compassion, sharing and companionship, for the moments when people acted generously compelled by 'no legal bond, no situation of power...no sense of shame or guilt, no gratitude imperative, no need

---

[32] Vale, *Piety, charity and literacy*, p. 29; Moran, *Education and learning*, esp. pp. 29–38; Heath, 'Urban piety in the later Middle Ages', p. 226. On the prominence of the parish in late medieval testamentary bequests see Tanner, *The church in late medieval Norwich*, pp. 1–18; and on bequests for building and maintenance of fabric see *ibid.*, pp. 128–9 and Heath, 'Urban piety in the later Middle Ages', pp. 216–17, 220.

[33] J. Chiffoleau has integrated his findings into a view of evolution of rationality in the *longue durée*, Chiffoleau, *La comptabilité de l'au-delà*, pp. 344–56, which is a difficult concept, especially in its implications of 'modernisation'. However, the careful arithmetical arrangements of late medieval intercession do fall in with a more discerning wish to comprehend and thus control the environment of religious practice.

[34] For a view of charitable institutions as a touchstone of the values upheld in a given society, see C. Jones 'Hospitals in seventeenth-century France', *Seventeenth-century French studies* 7 (1985), pp. 139–52, at p. 13.

[35] Chiffoleau, *La comptabilité de l'au-delà*, pp. 84–9; 323–56; 429–35. On the theory of social exchange see C. Lévi-Strauss, *The elementary structures of kinship*, trans. J. H. Bell and J. R. von Sturmer, ed. R. Needham (Boston, Mass., 1969), pp. 233–309, also 138–9, 441–8. A survey of these theories can be found in Ekeh, *Social exchange theory, passim*. On the dyadic model, see Foster, 'The dyadic contract', esp. pp. 214–15.

for penitence...no guarantee of or wish for a reward or a return gift'.[36] Yet, with the realignment of ideas, which took place over a long period and in different forms in different social groups, the poor were no longer lodged, fed and cared for but rather, they were appended to funerary and commemorative occasions, almost external to the act, just as the clergy was hired and the bells rung. In the words of the labour ordinances and the laws against beggars, suspicion was cast on those relieving poor folk whose identity and quality of life were unknown. This change in attitude is so meaningful that once it had emerged it touched the relations between haves and have-nots in a fundamental way. Even if late medieval chantries distributed alms frequently, those who needed help owing to the structure of the local economy, their health, intelligence, temperament or burden of responsibilities, were less likely to receive it. This view supported by literary evidence and from comparison with Continental towns; they had become a world where charity was measured carefully, began and often remained at home.

This attempt to understand medieval charity has evoked a varied and complex world. It has shown overwhelmingly that the burden of maintenance and support of the needy and weak cannot be left to the discretion and devices of those who by good fortune, talent and birth, control large portions of a society's resources and capabilities. No amount of indoctrination and persuasion, inducements and honours, all of which were offered abundantly to medieval folk when acting charitably, could alleviate the adversity which sets in when economic and social horizons seem bleak, and when weaker members of society are seen as *others* rather than *brothers*. It is too heavy a burden to be borne willingly at all times; they, like us, fell short from its overwhelming demands.

[36] Titmuss, *The gift relationship*, p. 89.

Appendix 1

The Rule of the Hospital of St John the Evangelist

Regula data a venerabili patre Hugone dei gratia Eliensi episcopo fratribus hospitalis sancti Iohannis Evangeliste Cantebr'.

1 In primis precipimus quod fratres omnes clerici et laici qui modo sunt et qui pro tempore erunt regulariter vivant[a].

2 Item omnes simul comedant in una domo et non alibi et simul dormiant si domus sit capax; alioquin si domus non sit capax omni, presbiteri per se in una domo dormiant et laici in alia domo vicina.

3 Item silencium teneant in capella quamdiu divina celebrentur.

4 Item omnes simul intersint misse et horis divinis et nullus excusetur nisi causa evidentis necessitatis.

5 Item quilibet frater capellanus recipiet in anno pro vestitura et aliis necessariis in Pascha 20s. Et frater laicus 13s 4d. Et magister 40s., et sit duplum in omnibus contra alium alium socium ⟨sic⟩ dicti hospitalis, esculentis et poculentis dumtaxat exceptis, de quibus tamen sibi deserviatur iuxta decenciam sui status, sicut et fieri consuevit.

6 Item omnes panno unius coloris vestiantur et nullus presumat in ecclesia stare sine habitu vel portas exire.

7 Item precipimus quod omnes capellani missam celebrent cunctis diebus nisi infirmitate vel alia causa fuerint prepediti et causam exponent priori suo. Si quis autem horum statutorum salubrium transgressor fuerit inventus, die transgressionis solo pane, cervisia et pulmento communi fratrum reficiatur. Et si die transgressionis, monitus per priorem vel per eum qui loco suo erit, hoc non fecerit, proximo die sequenti pane et aqua dumtaxat reficiatur.

8 Item volumus et precipimus quod omnis humanitas fratribus infirmis exhibeatur ita scilicet quod fratres infirmi habeant domum sibi assignatam ubi carnes quibus uti possunt et quas appetant sibi ministrentur, si inveniri possint et facultates domus permittant.

9 Item omnis occasio proprietatis habende tollatur.

10 Item rixantes et contendentes pari pena puniantur pro quantitate delicti.

11 Precipimus eciam quod non comedant neque bibant in villa extra domum propriam sine licencia prioris sui.

12 Item precipimus quod nullus frater deputetur alicui forinceco ministerio seu officio nisi bene et integre fuerit oppinionis.

13 Item districtissime precipimus et in virtute obedientie iniungimus quod

[a] uncant Ms.

300

infirmi et debiles admittantur benigne et misericorditer, exceptis mulieribus pregnantibus, leprosis, vulneratis, contractis et insanis.

14 Item lecti infirmorum et lecticinia per priorem vel aliquem alium loco sui ipsius, videantur[b] et cibaria eis competencia ministrentur, secundum facultates domus.

15 Insuper precipimus quod omnes tam clerici quam laici obediant priori qui nunc vel pro tempore fuerit in omnibus que spectant ad ipsam domum et ipsius domus utilitatem secundum regulam predictam et ordinis constitucionem.

16 Precipimus eciam quod semel in septimana, quando melius potest fieri ⟨et⟩ plures de fratribus sint presentes, teneatur capitulum et ibi recitentur et corrigantur que fuerunt corrigenda, tam in hiis que spectabunt[c] ad ordinem quam in rebus aliis.

17 Item omnes et singuli fratres priori suo confiteantur nisi ex causa fuerit super hoc indultum.

18 Et ne statuta predicta quemquam lateant, precipimus ea bis in anno vel ter in compotis pupplice in presencia omnium fratrum recitari.

19 Item fratres laici dicant pro matutinis, ubicumque fuerint, viginti orationes dominicas cum totidem salutacionibus beate Virginis, pro horis divinis singulis diebus, septem tam de dominicis orationibus quam de salutacionibus, ante prandium priusquam comedant unum pater noster et unam Ave Maria, similiter post prandium pro benedictione ⟨et⟩ gratiarum accione.

This rule was given by Hugh Northwold, bishop of Ely and is to be found in an *inspeximus* by Bishop Montacute of 1344, SJCA.D4.1[1]

b *sic* Ms. perhaps for *provideantur*.
c spectabit Ms.
[1] I wish to thank Professor C. R. Cheney for reading the text of the rule and for offering his advice on some difficult points.

The Masters of the Hospital of St John the Evangelist, Cambridge (1207–1507)[a]

Name of master		Earliest date		Latest date
Herbert, chaplain	occ.	bef.1230[b]		
Adam	occ.	1233[c]		
Thomas	occ.	c.1230 × 40[d]		
Anthony	occ.	1239–40	occ.	1240[e]
Richard	occ.	1246	occ.	4/6/1256[f]
Ralph	occ.	15/3/1257	occ.	1261[g]
Robert of Huntingdon	occ.	1264–5	occ.	c.1268[h]
Hugh of Stanford	occ.	1271[i]		
Geoffrey of Alderheath	occ.	1272[j]		
Nicholas de la Ware	occ.	1275[k]		
Nicholas Cheverel	occ.	1285–6[l]		
Guy	occ.	1294	occ.	1295[m]
William	occ.	1299[n]		
Adam	occ.	1318[o]		
John of Colonia	occ.	1321[p]		
William of Cosefeld	occ.	1332	res.	1333[q]
Alexander Ixning	adm.	20/2/1333	d.	1349[r]
Robert Sprouston	adm.	May 1349	d.	May 1349[s]
Roger Broom	adm.	May 1349	d.	June 1349[t]
William Beer	adm.	30/6/1349	occ.	15/5/1373[u]
Henry Brown	adm.	11/4/1374	occ.	1379[v]
John Stanton	occ.	28/1/1386	res.	1401[w]
William Killum	adm.	17/1/1401	res.	1403[x]
John Burton	adm.	3/6/1403	occ.	1422[y]
John Dunham Sr	occ.	29/9/1426	d.	1458[z]
John Dunham Jr	adm.	22/2/1458	d.	c. Dec. 1474[aa]
Robert Dunham	adm.	28/12/1474[bb]		d. by Nov. 1498
William Thomlyn	adm.	10/11/1498	rem.	3/2/1507[cc]

adm. = admitted by the bishop; bef. = before; occ. = occurs; rem. = removed; res. = resigned; d. = died.

^a A list of masters is provided in *VCH. Cambridgeshire* II, p. 306 which has been amplified and partly corrected here.

^b Herbert may be a master of the hospital. He occurs in a plea concerning the advowson of St Peter's and was recognised as having it in his gift. The roll continues to say: 'et ideo hospitale habeat illam ecclesiam', which would imply that in the early stage of the hospital's life, the chaplain was the head of the community, before its full organisation by episcopal intervention, *Curia regis rolls* V, p. 39.

^c SJCA.D3.4.

^d CCCA.XVI.17.

^e *Pedes finium or fines relating to the county of Cambridge*, ed. W. Rye (Cambridge, 1891), p. 23; SJCA. Cartulary of HSJC, fol. 43r.

^f *Pedes finium*, pp. 26, 28; Merton College charters, M1547.

^g Merton College charters. M1545; SJCA.D17.82 (also Merton College charters M1549 for evidence of occurrence *c.* May 1261).

^h SJCA.D32.78; D27.11.

ⁱ PRO. Assize Roll 84, M14. This may be the same as Hugh of Stanford, M.A. by 1261, Emden, *A biographical register*.

^j *Calendar of the plea rolls of the Exchequer of the Jews* II, p. 29 and SJCA.D3.65.

^k SJCA.D26.15.

^l SJCA.D17.74.

^m *Cambridge borough documents* I, pp. 3,7.

ⁿ SJCA. Cartulary of HSJC, fol. 37v.

^o Rector of St Michael's, Cambridge, *The Register of Thomas of Cobham*, p. 13.

^p SJCA.D2.16; Peterhouse muniments. Ecc. Cant. A13.

^q Oxford. Bodl. Charters. Cambridge 31; SJCA.D98.34.

^r SJCA.D98.34; CUL. EDR. Register Lisle, fol. 20v.

^s CUL. EDR. Register Lisle, fol. 20v.

^t *ibid.*

^u *ibid.*; SJCA.D34.2.

^v CUL. EDR. Consistory court Arundel, fol. 17; SJCA.25.186, D21.10.

^w SJCA.D19.163; CUL. EDR. Register Fordham, fol. 70r.

^x *ibid.*; *ibid.*, fol. 80r. See also Emden, *A biographical register*.

^y *ibid.*; SJCA.D34.29.

^z SJCA.D35.239: CUL. EDR. Register Gray, fol. 29v.

^{aa} *ibid.*, fols. 20v–30r; *ibid.*, fol. 89v.

^{bb} CUL. EDR. Register Gray, fol. 89v; Register Alcock, p. 121.

^{cc} CUL. EDR. Register Alcock, p. 121; SJCA.D3.75, also Emden, *A biographical register*.

BIBLIOGRAPHY

A. MANUSCRIPTS

CAMBRIDGE
Corporation Archives

Deeds
  30/4(1)
Account Rolls
  X, 70 (1–10)
  X, 71 (1–10)
  X, 72
  X, 92
  XVIII, 8
Patent rolls
  P 27/28 (8)

Colleges

Clare College Muniments
  Charters related to the Hospital of St John, Ely
Corpus Christi College Archives
  Deeds:
    CCCA. X, 3a
    CCCA. XIV, 64
    CCCA. XV, 118
    CCCA. XVI, 17, 286
    CCCA. XXXI, 25, 28, 39, 40, 41, 42, 47, 61, 62, 66, 68, 70, 86, 92, 95, 96
King's College Muniments
  Charters 136/1, 136/2.
Peterhouse Muniments
  Registrum vetus
  Deeds:
Ecclesia Cantebrigie A1, A2, A3, A4, A5, A6, A8, A9, A10, A12, A13, A51
      Cista communis C
      Collegium A1, A3, A4, A5, A10, B1
      Collegii situs A9, A19, B2
      St Peter's Church A5, A6
Queens' College Muniments
  Deposited in Cambridge University Library

Bibliography

Saint John's College Archives

 All medieval charters related to the Hospital of St John and its possessions have been studied and used. The following documents have been cited in the body of the work:

Cartulary of the Hospital of St John the Evangelist, Cambridge (C7.1)

Deeds:

 D2.2, 3, 14, 16, 18
 D3.4, 31, 34, 37, 50, 58, 61, 64, 65, 66, 68, 70, 71, 72, 75
 D4.1
 D6.10
 D14.177
 D15.105
 D17.3, 8, 37, 38, 44, 53, 69, 72, 73, 74, 82, 95, 105, 106, 107, 109, 114, 117, 192, 197
 D18.47
 D19.53, 56, 144, 150, 155, 163, 165
 D20.25, 30, 33, 50, 55, 58, 59, 61
 D21.10, 81
 D23.234, 235
 D24.5, 7, 8, 84, 85, 92, 131, 191, 192
 D25.9, 20, 32, 51, 94, 121, 136, 182, 186, 229, 239
 D26.8, 9, 15, 18, 20, 38, 65, 70, 72, 77, 83, 128, 131, 132, 133, 134, 136
 D27.11
 D31.16
 D32.1, 11, 12, 13, 20, 36, 78, 168, 220, 234, 235
 D34.2, 29
 D37.142
 D39.36
 D47.15, 33, 51
 D51.53, 54, 77, 80, 82, 83, 84, 238, 239
 D56.13
 D57.13, 134
 D61.1, 2, 3
 D98.1, 2, 3, 4, 5, 8, 11, 12, 14, 16, 19, 24, 31, 32, 34, 41, 42, 44, 47, 48, 43, 49
 D106.9, 10

Rental rolls:
 D2.2.1–8
 D2.3.1–5

Trinity College Muniments
 The Otryngham book (calendar)

University library

(a) Manuscripts
 Ms. 3824 (T. Tanner's Transcripts)
 Additional Ms. 6845 (statutes of the hospital
  of St Laurence, Canterbury)

(b) Ely diocesan records (EDR)
 Account roll D.8 (Arundel)

Consistory court register. Bishop Arundel
   (1374–1388)
Episcopal registers (register's span in brackets)
   G/1/1 Register Montacute (1337–1345)
   G/1/1 Register Lisle (1345–1356)
   G/1/2 Register Arundel (1373–1388)
   G/1/3 Register Fordham (1388–1422)
   G/1/4 Register Bourchier (1444–1454)
   G/1/5 Register Gray (1454–1476)
   G/1/6 Register Alcock (1486–1500)
   G/1/7 Register West (1515–1529)
   G/1/8 Register Goodrich (1540–1588)
(c) Microfilm 1837 (see Lambeth Palace Library: Register Whittlesey)
(d) University archives:
   Luard *8, *14, 35, *51, 101, 103, 130, 130a, 132, 136, 150.
   Collect. Admin. 1 – Old Senior Proctor's Book c. 1496
   Collect. Admin. 2 – Old Junior Proctor's Book c. 1494

LONDON
British Library

Add. Ms. 5842
Harl. Ms. 45

Lambeth Palace Library
Archiepiscopal Registers: Register Whittlesey (1368–1374)

Public Record Office
PRO. Ancient Deeds
   E40.7671, 14464, 14469
   E326.3052, 3652, 3733, 3791, 3794, 3796
PRO. DL 29.465.7607
PRO. E 101.249.3; 250.3
PRO. E 136.8/24; 7/108
PRO. E 179.23/1
PRO. E 179.81/5
PRO. E 179.81/18
PRO. Exch. accounts. Bundle 249/3
PRO. Just. 1. Assize Roll 84
PRO. Prob. 11/1–10

NORWICH
Norfolk Record Office

Great Hospital Archive
   Case 24, shelf a, 9
   Case 24, shelf a, 16
   Case 24, shelf b, 1

Case 24, shelf b, 5
Case 24, shelf b, 53
Philipps collection charters
Case 25/253
Case 25/310
Case 25/514
Case 25/522
Case 25/621

OXFORD
Bodleian Library

Bodl. Rawlinson B.352
Bodl. Rawlinson C.541
Bodl. Charters Cambridge 31
Bodl. Dodsworth Ms. 153
Bodl. Gough Cambridge 20
Bodl. Rawlinson B Ms. 278

Merton College

Merton College Charters
MI545, MI547, MI549, MI558, M2788, M2789

WISBECH
Wisbech and Fenland Museum

Wisbech Corporation Archives
Accounts of the Holy Trinity Gild, Wisbech, 2 vols.

PARIS
Archives nationales
MM 406

B. PRINTED SOURCES

Abbreviatio placitorum, Record Commission, London, 1811.
Abstracts from the wills and testamentary documents of printers, binders and stationers of Cambridge, from 1504–1699, ed. G. J. Gray and W. M. Palmer, London, 1915.
Account of the executors of Richard bishop of London 1303 and of the executors of Thomas bishop of Exeter 1310, ed. W. H. Hale and H. T. Ellacombe, Camden Society, new ser. 10, London, 1874.
Accounts of the fabric of Exeter cathedral, 1279–1326 I, ed. and trans. A. M. Erskine, Devon and Cornwall Record Society new ser. 24, Torquay, 1981.
Alan of Lille, *Liber poenitentialis*, ed. J. Longère, Analecta mediaevalia Namuracensia 17, Louvain and Lille, 1965.
    'Summa de arte praedicatoria', *PL* 210, cols 109–98.
    Textes inédits, ed. M. T. d'Alverny (Paris, 1965).
An alphabet of tales, ed. M. M. Banks, 2 vols., EETS 126 and 127, London, 1904–5.
Ancient laws of the fifteenth century for King's College, and for the public school of Eton College, ed. J. Heywood and T. Wright, London, 1850.

Bibliography

Annals of (the borough of) Cambridge, 5 vols., ed. C. H. Cooper (v, ed. J. W. Cooper), Cambridge, 1842–1908.

Annals of the hospital of St Wulfstan, Worcester, c. 1230–1513, ed. F. T. Marsh, Worcester, 1890.

Antichi diplomi degli arcivescovi di Milano e note di diplomatica episcopale, ed. G. C. Bascapé, Florence, 1937.

Archives de l'Hôtel-dieu de Paris (1157–1300), ed. L. Brièle with an intr. by E. Coyecque, Paris, 1894.

Archivio storico dell'ospedale civile de S. Croce in Cuneo, ed. P. Camilla, Bibliotheca della società per gli studi storici archeologici e artistichi della provincia di Cuneo 14.

The assizes held at Cambridge, AD 1260, ed. W. M. Palmer, Linton, 1930.

Bernard of Parma, *Decretales d. Gregorii papae IX*, Turin, 1621.

Bernardino of Siena, *Opera omnia*, 9 vols., ed. College of St Bonaventure, Quaracchi (Florence), 1950–65.

The Blickling homilies of the tenth century, 3 parts, ed. R. Morris, EETS 58, 63, 73, London, 1874–80.

Bolton priory rentals and ministers' accounts, 1473–1539, ed. I. Kershaw, Yorkshire Archaeological Society, Record series 132, 1970.

The book of vices and virtues: a fourteenth-century translations of the 'Somme le Roi' of Lorens d'Orléans, ed. W. N. Francis, EETS 217, London, 1942.

The book of William Morton almoner of Peterborough monastery 1448–1467, ed. W. T. Mellows and P. I. King with introduction by C. N. L. Brooke, Northamptonshire Record Society 16, Oxford 1954.

Calendar of Antrobus deeds before 1625, ed. R. B. Pugh, Wiltshire Archaeological and Natural History Society. Records branch 3, 1947.

Calendar of the charter rolls preserved in the Public Record Office, 6 vols., London, 1903–27.

Calendar of the close rolls preserved in the Public Record Office, 1227–1500, 62 vols., London, 1902–55.

Calendar of entries in the papal registers relating to Great Britain and Ireland: papal letters, 1198–1492, 15 vols., ed. W. H. Bliss, C. Johnson, J. A. Twemlow and M. J. Haren, London and Dublin, 1893–1978.

Calendar of the fine rolls preserved in the Public Record Office 1272–1509, 22 vols., London, 1911–62.

Calendar of inquisitions miscellaneous preserved in the Public Record Office 1219–1422, 7 vols., London, 1916–68.

Calendar of inquisitions post mortem preserved in the Public Record Office, 14 vols., London, 1904–52.

Calendar of the liberate rolls preserved in the Public Record Office, 1226–1260, 4 vols., London, 1916–59.

Calendar of the patent rolls preserved in the Public Record Office, 1216–1509, 54 vols., London, 1891–1916.

Calendar of the plea rolls of the Exchequer of the Jews, 4 vols., I–II, ed. J. M. Rigg; III, ed. H. Jenkinson; IV, ed. H. G. Richardson, London, 1905–10, 1929, 1972.

Calendar of wills proved in the Vice-Chancellor's court 1501–1765, ed. H. Roberts, Cambridge, 1907.

Cambridge borough documents 1, ed. W. M. Palmer, Cambridge, 1931.

Cambridgeshire gaol delivery roll 1332–1334, ed. E. G. Kimball, Cambridge Antiquarian Records Society 4, Cambridge, 1978.

Cambridge gild records (1298–1389), ed. M. Bateson, Cambridge Antiquarian Society 39, Cambridge, 1903.

The Cambridgeshire portion of the chartulary of the priory of St Pancras of Lewes, ed. J. H. Bullock and W. M. Palmer, Cambridge, 1938.

Cambridgeshire subsidy rolls 1250–1695, [(repr. from *East Anglian* 7–10 and 12–13 (1898–1908)], ed. W. M. Palmer, Norwich, 1912.

Carte nativorum: a Peterborough abbey cartulary of the fourteenth century, ed. C. N. L. Brooke and M. M. Postan, Northamptonshire Record Society 20, Oxford, 1960.

Cartulaire général de l'ordre des Hospitaliers de S. Jean de Jérusalem, 4 vols., ed. J. Delaville Le Roulx, Paris, 1894–1906

Cartulaire de l'hôpital St.-Jean de Bruxelles, ed. P. Bonenfant, Brussels, 1953.

A cartulary of the hospital of St John the Baptist, 3 vols., ed. H. E. Salter, Oxford Historical Society 66, 68, 69, Oxford, 1914–20.

The cartulary of God's House, Southampton, 2 vols., ed. J. M. Kaye, Southampton Record Series 19–20, Southampton, 1976.

Cartulary of St. Mark's hospital, Bristol, ed. E. D. Ross, Bristol Record Society 21, Bristol, 1959.

'The cartulary of St Mary's hospital, Chichester', ed. A. Ballard, *Sussex archaeological collections* 51(1908), pp. 37–64.

Catalogue of romances in the department of manuscripts in the British Museum, 3 vols., ed. H. L. D. Ward and J. A. Herbert, London, 1883–1910.

Chapters of the Augustinian canons, ed. H. E. Salter, Oxford Historical Society 74, Oxford, 1920.

The charters of the borough of Cambridge (Henry I–1685), ed. and trans. F. W. Maitland and M. Bateson, Cambridge, 1901.

Chronicon abbatiae Rameseiensis, RS, ed. W. D. Macray, London, 1886.

Churchwardens' accounts of Great St. Mary's, Cambridge, 1504–1635, ed. J. E. Foster, Cambridge Antiquarian Society 35, Cambridge, 1905.

Collection of the statutes for the University and Colleges of Cambridge, ed. J. Heywood, London, 1840.

Conciliorum oecumenicorum decreta, ed. G. Alberigo *et al.*, Bologna, third edn, 1973.

Constitutiones Clementis papae quinti cum una apparatu Iohannis Andree, Nurmberg, 1486.

Constitutiones concilii quarti Lateranensis una cum commentariis glossatorum, ed. A. García y García, Monumenta iuris canonici ser. A: Corpus glossatorum 2, Vatican, 1981.

Corpus iuris canonici, 2 vols., ed. E. Friedberg, Leipzig 1879.

Councils and synods with other documents relating to the English Church I (871–1204), ed. D. Whitelock, M. Brett and C. N. L. Brooke, Oxford, 1982.

Councils and synods with other documents relating to the English Church II (1205–1313), ed. F. M. Powicke and C. R. Cheney, Oxford, 1964.

Curia regis rolls (temp. Ric. I–1242), 16 vols., London, 1922–79.

The dance of death, ed. F. Warren, EETS 181, London, 1931.

Decretum magistri Gratiani, in *Corpus iuris canonici* 1, ed. E. Friedberg, Leipzig, 1879.

'Deeds of St John's hospital, Bath', ed. B. R. Kemp, *Somerset Record Society* 73, 1974.

Dives et pauper 1 in 2 parts, ed. P. H. Barnum, EETS 225, London, 1976–80.

Documents relating to Cambridgeshire villages, 2 vols., ed. W. M. Palmer and H. W. Saunders, Cambridge, 1926.

Documents relating to St Catherine's College (Cambridge) (1473–1860), ed. H. Philpott, Cambridge, 1861.

Documents relating to the University and Colleges of Cambridge, 3 vols., Record commission, London, 1852.

Early English proverbs, ed. W. W. Skeat, Oxford, 1910.

The early rolls of Merton College, Oxford, ed. J. R. L. Highfield, Oxford Historical Society, new ser. 18, Oxford, 1964.

Early statutes of Christ's College, Cambridge, with the statutes of the prior foundation of God's House, ed. H. Rackham, Cambridge, 1927.

Early Yorkshire charters IV, ed. C. T. Clay, Yorkshire Archaeological Society, Record ser., Extra ser. 1(1935).

Early Yorkshire schools I–II, ed. A. F. Leach, Yorkshire Archaeological Society, Record ser. 27, 33, 1898–1903.

Ely chapter ordinances and visitation records 1241–1515, ed. S. J. A. Evans, Camden miscellany 17, London, 1940.

Enactments in Parliament concerning the Universities of Oxford and Cambridge, 4 vols., ed. L. L. Shadwell, Oxford Historical Society 58–61, Oxford, 1911–12.

English gilds, ed. Toulmin Smith, L. T. Smith and L. Brentano, EETS 40, London, 1870.

Fernandus Vasquius, *Controversiarum libri tres*, Venice, 1595.

Feudal Cambridgeshire, ed. W. Farrer, Cambridge, 1920.

The foundation statutes of Merton College Oxford, AD 1270, ed. E. F. Percival, London, 1847.

François Villon, *Oeuvres de François Villon*, ed. J. Dufournet and A. Mary, Paris, 1970.

Glanville, *Tractatus de legibus et consuetudinibus regni Anglie qui Glanvill vocatur*, ed. and trans. G. D. G. Hall, Nelson's Medieval texts, 1965.

Grace book A. Proctors' accounts and other records of the University of Cambridge 1454–1488, ed. S. M. Leathes, Cambridge Antiquarian Society. Luard Memorial Series I, Cambridge, 1897.

Grace book B. Proctors' accounts and other records of the University of Cambridge, part 1 1488–1511, part 2 1511–1544, ed. M. Bateson, Cambridge Antiquarian Society. Luard Memorial Series II–III, Cambridge, 1903–5.

Guy of Chauliac, *The Middle English version of the introduction to Guy de Chauliac's 'Chirurgia Magna'*, ed. B. Wallner, Acta Universitatis Lundensis sectio I. Theologica Juridica Humaniora 12, Lund, 1970.

Hall, C. P., 'William Rysley's catalogue of the Cambridge University muniments, compiled in 1420', *Transactions of the Cambridge Bibliographical Society* 4 (1965), pp. 85–99.

Hefele, C. J., *Histoire des conciles d'après les documents originaux*, 20 vols, ed. and trans. H. Leclercq, Paris, 1907–52.

Bibliography

Henry of Bracton, *De legibus et consuetudinibus Angliae*, 4 vols., ed. G. E. Woodbine and trans. S. E. Thorne, Cambridge, Mass., 1977.

Heresy trials in the diocese of Norwich, 1429–1431, ed. N. P. Tanner, Camden Society 4th ser. 20, London, 1977.

The historical register of the University of Cambridge until 1910, ed. J. R. Tanner, Cambridge, 1917.

The homilies of Aelfric II, 2 vols., ed. B. Thorpe, London, 1844–6.

The homilies of Wulfstan, ed. D. Bethurum, Oxford, 1957.

Honorius Augustodunensis, 'Speculum ecclesiae', *PL* 172, cols. 807–1108.

Hostiensis, *In primum...sextum decretalium librum commentaria*, Venice, 1581.

Humbert of Romans, *Beati Umberti sermones*, Venice, 1603.

  'De eruditione praedicantium', in *Treatise on preaching*, ed. W. M. Conlon, London, 1955.

Jacob's well. An English treatise on the cleansing of man's conscience, ed. A. Brandeis, EETS 115, London, 1900.

Jacques of Vitry, *The exempla or illustrative stories from the 'sermones vulgares' of Jacques de Vitry*, ed. T. F. Crane, London, 1890.

  Die Exempla des Jacob von Vitry, ed. G. Frenken, Quellen and Untersuchungen zur lateinischen Philologie des Mittelalters, Munich, 1914.

  Die Exempla aus den sermones feriales et communes des Jakob von Vitry, ed. J. Greven, Sammlungen mittellateinischer Texte 9, Heidelberg, 1914.

  The 'Historia occidentalis' of Jacques de Vitry: a critical edition, ed. J. F. Hinnebusch, Spicilegium Friburgense 17, Freiburg, 1972.

  Sermones in epistola et evangelia dominicalia totius anni, Antwerp, 1575.

John Bromyard, *Summa praedicantium*, Antwerp, 1614.

John of Lapus de Castellione, *Tractatus hospitalitatis*, 15 vols., Lyons, 1549.

John Mirc, *Instructions for parish priests by John Mirc*, ed. E. Peacock and rev. F. J. Furnivall, EETS 31, London, 1868, rev. 1902.

John Peckham, *Fratris Iohannis Peckham tractatus tres de paupertate*, ed. C. L. Kingford, A. G. Little and F. Tocco, British Society of Franciscan Studies 2, Aberdeen, 1910.

John of Salisbury, *Policraticus*, 2 vols., ed. C. C. J. Webb, Oxford, 1909.

John of Turrecremata, *Repertorium Iohannes de Turrecremata super toto decreto*, 3 vols., Lyons, 1519.

Josselin, J., *Historiale collegii Corporis Christi*, ed. J. W. Clark, Cambridge Antiquarian Society 17, Cambridge, 1880.

Kent chantries, ed. A. Hussey, Kent Archaeological Society, Records Branch, Kent records 12, 1936.

The Knights Hospitallers in England, ed. L. B. Larking, Camden Society old ser. 65, London, 1857.

The lay folks' catechism or the English and Latin versions of archbishop Thoresby's instruction for the people, ed. T. F. Simmons and H. E. Nolloth, EETS 118, London, 1901.

The lay subsidy of 1334, ed. R. E. Glasscock. British Academy. Records of Social and Economic History new ser. 2. London, 1975.

Liber elemosinarii: the almoner's book of the priory of Worcester, ed. J. H. Bloom, Worcestershire Historical Society. Collectanea, Oxford, 1911.

Liber Eliensis, ed. E. O. Blake, Camden 3rd ser. 92, London, 1962.

Liber exemplorum ad usum praedicantium, ed. A. G. Little, British Society of Franciscan Studies 1, Aberdeen, 1908.

Liber feodorum: the Book of Fees commonly called Testa de Nevill, 2 vols. in 3 parts, London, 1920–31.

Liber fundationis: the book of the foundation of St Bartholomew's hospital in London, ed. N. Moore, EETS 163, London, 1923.

Liber memorandorum ecclesie de Bernewelle, ed. J. W. Clark, Cambridge, 1907.

Liber regulae Sancti Spiritus, ed. A. Francesco La Cava, Milan, 1947.

Luard, H. R., 'A list of the documents in the University registry, from the year 1266 to the year 1544', *Cambridge Antiquarian Society. Proceedings and communications* 3 (1864–76), pp. 385–403.

Lull, Raymund, *Opera omnia*, 5 vols., ed. F. Stegmüller, Palma de Majorca, 1959–67.

The making of King's Lynn. A documentary survey, ed. D. M. Owen, British Academy Records of Social and Economic History, new ser. 9, London, 1984.

Mansi, J. D., *Sacrorum conciliorum nova et amplissima collectio*, 53 vols., Florence, Venice and Paris, 1759–98, reiss. Paris, 1901–27.

The mediaeval archives of the University of Oxford, 2 vols., ed. H. E. Salter, Oxford Historical Society 70, 73, Oxford, 1920–1.

Memorials of London and London life, ed. H. T. Riley, London, 1868.

Memorials of St Giles's, Durham, ed. J. Barmby, Surtees Society, Durham, 1896.

Merton muniments, ed. P. S. Allen and H. W. Garrod, Oxford Historical Society 86, Oxford, 1928.

The metropolitan visitations of William Courtenay archbishop of Canterbury 1381–1396, ed. J. H. Dahmus, Illinois studies in the social sciences 31/2, Urbana, Ill., 1950.

Middle English sermons, ed. W. O. Ross, EETS 209, London, 1940.

A Middle English version of the Gesta Romanorum, ed. K. I. Sandred, Acta Universitatis Upsaliensis. Studia Anglistica Upsaliensia 8, Uppsala, 1971.

Monuments primitifs de la règle cistercienne, ed. P. Guignard, Dijon, 1878.

Motif-index of folk literature, 5 vols., ed. S. Thompson, Folklore Fellows Communications 106–9, 116, Helsinki, 1932–5.

Observances in use at the Augustinian priory of St. Giles and St. Andrew at Barnwell, Cambridgeshire, ed. and trans. J. W. Clark, Cambridge, 1897.

Old English homilies and homiletic treatises of the twelfth and thirteenth centuries, ed. R. Morris, EETS 29, 34, London, 1867–8.

Old English homilies of the twelfth century, ed. R. Morris, EETS 53, London, 1873.

Oriel College records, ed. C. L. Shadwell and H. E. Salter, Oxford Historical Society 85, Oxford, 1926.

Oxford formularies, 2 vols., ed. H. E. Salter, W. A. Pantin and H. G. Richardson, Oxford Historical Society, new ser. 4–5, Oxford, 1942.

Panormitanus, *Abbatis Panormitani omnia quae extant commentaria*, Venice, 1588.

Parish fraternity register. Fraternity of the Holy Trinity and SS. Fabian and Sebastian in the parish of St Botolph without Aldersgate, ed. P. Basing, London Record Society 18, London, 1982.

Patrologiae cursus completus. Series latina, 221 vols., ed. J. P. Migne, Paris, 1841–64.

Bibliography

Pedes finium or fines relating to the county of Cambridge, ed. W. Rye, Cambridge Antiquarian Society 87, Cambridge, 1891.

Peter of Poitiers, *Summa de confessione. Compilatio praesens*, ed. J. Longère, Turnhout, 1980.

Philip of Beaumanoir, *Coutumes de Clermont en Beauvaisis*, 2 vols., ed. A. Salmon, Paris, 1970.

Piers the plowman: the B version, ed. G. Kane and E. T. Donaldson, London, 1975.

Piers the plowman: an edition of the C text, ed. D. Pearsall, London, 1978.

Pipe Rolls Henry II–John, Pipe Roll Society 1 – new ser. 37. London, 1844–1961.

The priory of St Radegund, Cambridge, ed. A. Gray, Cambridge Antiquarian Society 31, Cambridge, 1898.

The privileges of the University of Cambridge, 2 vols., ed. G. Dyer, London, 1824.

Proprium sanctorum, ed. C. Horstmann, *Archiv* 81(1888), pp. 83–114, 299–321.

Proverbs, sentences, and proverbial phrases from English writings mainly before 1500, ed. B.J. and H. W. Whiting, Cambridge, Mass., 1968.

The prymer or lay folks' prayer book, 2 vols., ed. H. Littlehales, EETS 105, 109, London, 1895–7.

Raoul Ardent, 'Homiliae', in *PL* 155, cols. 1301–1626, 1664–2118.

The records of the borough of Leicester, 1103–1603, 3 vols. ed. M. Bateson, rev. W. H. Stevenson and J. E. Stocks, Cambridge, 1899–1905.

The register of the guild of the Holy Trinity, St. Mary, St. John the Baptist and St. Katherine of Coventry II, ed. G. Templeman, Dugdale Society 19, Oxford, 1944.

The register of the congregation 1448–1463, ed. W. A. Pantin and W. T. Mitchell, Oxford Historical Society, new ser. 22, Oxford, 1972.

The register of the gild of the Holy Cross, the Blessed Virgin Mary and St. John the Baptist of Stratford-upon-Avon (1406–1535), ed. J. Harvey Bloom, London, 1907.

The register of Henry Chichele, archbishop of Canterbury, 1414–1443, 4 vols., ed. E. F. Jacob, Oxford, 1938–47.

The register of Thomas of Cobham, bishop of Worcester 1317–1327, ed. E. H. Pearce, Worcestershire historical society, 1930.

The registers of Walter Bronescombe (AD 1257–80) and Peter Quivil (1280–91), bishops of Exeter, ed. F. C. Hingeston-Randolph, London and Exeter, 1889.

Registrum Malmesburiense: the register of Malmesbury abbey, 2 vols., ed. J. S. Brewer and C. T. Martin, RS, London, 1879–1880.

La regle de St. Benoît, 6 vols., ed. A. de Vogüé, Sources chrétiennes 181–186, série des textes monastiques d'occident 34–9, Paris, 1971–2.

Religious lyrics of the fifteenth century, ed. C. Brown, Oxford, 1939.

Robert of Flamborough, *Liber poenitentialis of Robert of Flamborough*, ed. J. J. F. Firth, Pontifical Institute of Mediaeval Studies. Studies and texts 18, Toronto, 1971.

  Summa de matrimonio et de usuris, ed. J. F. Schulte, Giessen, 1868.

The Romaunt of the Rose and the Roman de la Rose. A parallel-text edition, ed. R. Sutherland, Oxford, 1967.

Rotuli chartarum in Turri Londinensi asservati, 1199–1216, Record commission, London, 1837.

Bibliography

Rotuli hundredorum tempore Henrici III et Edwardi I, 2 vols., Record commission, London, 1812–18.

Rotuli litterarum clausarum (1204–1227), 2 vols., Record Commission, London, 1833–44.

Rotuli litterarum patentium (1201–1216), Record Commission, London, 1835.

Rotuli parliamentorum (1278–1503), 6 vols., Record Commission, London, n.d.

Rotuli Roberti Grosseteste episcopi Lincolniensis MCCXXXV–MCCLIII, ed. F. N. Davis, London, 1913.

Rufinus, *Die summa decretorum der Magister Rufinus*, ed. H. Singer, Paderborn, 1902.

Sacrist rolls of Ely (1291–1360), 2 vols., ed. F. R. Chapman, Cambridge, 1907.

Secular lyrics in the XIVth and XVth centuries, ed. R. Robbins, Oxford, 1912.

Selected letters of Pope Innocent III concerning England (1198–1216), ed. C. R. Cheney and W. H. Semple, Nelson's Medieval Texts, 1953.

Selected rentals and accounts of medieval Hull, 1293–1528, ed. R. Horrox, Leeds, 1981.

Selections from English Wycliffite writings, ed. A. Hudson, Cambridge, 1978.

Speculum christiani: a Middle English religious treatise of the fourteenth century, ed. G. Holmstedt, EETS 182, London, 1933.

Speculum laicorum, ed. J. T. Welter, Paris, 1914.

Speculum sacerdotale, ed. E. H. Weatherly, EETS 200, London, 1936.

Statuta antiqua universitatis Oxoniensis, ed. S. Gibson, Oxford, 1931.

Statutes of the colleges of Oxford, 3 vols., Record Commission, Oxford and London, 1853.

Statutes of Lincoln cathedral, 3 vols., ed. H. Bradshaw and C. Wordsworth, Cambridge, 1892–1897.

Statutes of the realm, 11 vols., ed. A. Luders, T. E. Tomlins, J. Raithby *et al.*, Record Commission, London, 1810–1828.

Statuts d'hôtels-dieu et de léproseries, ed. L. Le Grand, Paris, 1901.

Les statuts de Paris et le synodal de l'Ouest, ed. O. Pontal, Collection de documents inédits sur l'histoire de France 9, Les statuts synodaux français du XIIIe siècle 1, Paris, 1971.

Summa 'elegantius in iure divino' seu Coloniensis, ed. G. Fransen, Monumenta iuris canonici ser. A: corpus glossatorum 1, Vatican, 1969.

The Summa Parisiensis of the decretum Gratiani, ed. T. P. McLaughlin, Toronto, 1952.

La tabula exemplorum secundum ordinem alphabeti, ed. J. T. Welter, Thesaurus exemplorum 3, Paris, 1926.

Thomas Aquinas, *Summa theologiae. Lagtin text and English translation*, 61 vols., ed. T. Gilby, London, 1964–1980.

    Scriptum in quatuor libros sententiarum P. Lombardi, 2 vols., Venice, 1586.

Thomas Brinton, *The sermons of Thomas Brinton, bishop of Rochester (1373–1389)*, 2 vols., ed. M. A. Devlin, Camden third ser. 85, 86, London, 1954.

Thomas of Chobham, *Summa confessorum*, ed. F. Broomfield, Analecta mediaevalia Namuracensia 25, 1968.

Twelfth century homilies, ed. A. O. Belfour, EETS 137, London, 1909, repr 1963.

Die Urkunden des Heiliggeistspitals in München, 1250–1500, ed. H. Vogel, Quellen und Erörterungen zur bayerischen Geschichte. N. F. 16–1, Munich, 1960.

Bibliography

Valor ecclesiasticus, 6 vols., Record Commission, London, 1825–34.

The valuation of Norwich, ed. W. E. Lunt, Oxford, 1926.

Vetus liber archidiaconi Eliensis, ed. C. L. Feltoe and E. H. Minns, Cambridge Antiquarian Society 48, Cambridge, 1917.

Vetus registrum Sarisberiense alias dictum registrum S. Osmundi episcopi. The register of S. Osmund, 2 vols., ed. W. H. Rich Jones, RS, London, 1883–4.

Vices and virtues being a soul's confession of its sins with reason's description of the virtues, 2 vols., ed. F. Holtausen, EETS 89, 159, London, 1888–1921.

Visio Thurkilli, ed. P. G. Schmidt, Leipzig, 1978.

Visitations of religious houses in the diocese of Lincoln 1420–49, 3 vols., ed. A. Hamilton Thompson, Lincoln Record Society and Canterbury and York Society, 1914–29.

'Vita Sancti Eligii episcopi Noviomensis', *PL* 87, cols. 478–594.

The west fields of Cambridge: terrarium Cantabrigiense, ed. C. P. Hall and J. P. Ravensdale, Cambridge Antiquarian Record Society 3, Cambridge, 1976.

William of Auxerre, *Summa aurea in quattuor libris sententiarum*, Paris, 1500, repr. Frankfurt, 1964.

William Lyndwood, *Provinciale seu constitutiones Angliae*, 2 vols., Oxford, 1679, repr. Farnborough, 1968.

C. SECONDARY WORKS

Abucaya, C., *Le testament lyonnais de la fin du XVe siècle au milieu du XVIIIe siècle*, Paris, 1961.

Addyman, P. V. and M. Biddle, 'Medieval Cambridge: recent finds and excavations', *Cambridge Antiquarian Society. Proceedings and communications* 58(1965), pp. 74–137.

Aers, D., '*Piers Plowman* and problems in the perception of poverty: a culture in transition', *Leeds studies in English* new ser. 14(1983), pp. 5–25.

Allison, K. J., 'The lost villages of Norfolk', *Norfolk archaeology* 31 (1955–7), pp. 116–62.

Amargier, P., 'La situation hospitalière à Marseille', *Cahiers de Fanjeaux* 15 (1978), pp. 239–60.

Amundsen, D. W., 'Medieval canon law on medical and surgical practice by the clergy', *Bulletin of the history of medicine* 52 (1978), pp. 22–44.

Anderson, P., *Passages from antiquity to feudalism*, London, 1974.

Antosiewicz, K., 'L'hôpital du St. Esprit à Cracove', *Roczniki humanistyczne* 26 (1978), pp. 35–79.

Ariès, P., 'Le purgatoire et la cosmologie de l'au-delà. Note critique', *Annales* 38 (1983), pp. 151–7.

    L'homme devant la mort, Paris, 1977.

Ashton, R., 'Review of W. K. Jordan, *The charities of London, 1480–1660*', *History* 46 (1961), pp. 136–9.

Aston, M. E., 'Lollardy and sedition, 1381–1431', *Past and present* 17 (1960), pp. 1–44.

    Thomas Arundel: a study of church life in the reign of Richard II, Oxford, 1967.

    '"Caim's castles": poverty, politics and disendowment', in *The church, politics and patronage in the fifteenth century*, ed. B. Dobson, Gloucester, 1984, pp. 45–81.

Aston, T. H., 'Oxford's medieval alumni', *Past and present* 74 (1977), pp. 3–40. 'The external administration and resources of Merton college to *circa* 1348', in *The history of the University of Oxford* I, ed. J. I. Catto, Oxford, 1984, pp. 311–68.

Aston, T. H., G. D. Duncan and T. A. R. Evans, 'The medieval alumni of the University of Cambridge', *Past and present* 86 (1980), pp. 9–86.

Aston, T. H. and R. Faith, 'The endowments of the university and colleges *circa* 1348', in *The history of the University of Oxford* I, ed. J. I. Catto, Oxford, 1984, pp. 265–309.

Atkinson, A. B., *The economics of inequality*, Oxford, 1975.

d'Avray, D. L., 'Sermons to the upper bourgeoisie by a thirteenth century Franciscan', *Studies in Church history* 16 (1979), pp. 187–99.

The preaching of the friars. Sermons diffused from Paris before 1300, Oxford, 1985.

d'Avray, D. L. and M. Tausche, 'Marriage sermons in *ad status* collections of the central Middle Ages', *Archives d'histoire doctrinale et littéraire du moyen-âge* 47 (1980), pp. 71–119.

Avril, J., 'Recherches sur la politique paroissialle des établissements monastiques et canoniaux (xie–xiiie siècles)', *Revue Mabillon* 59 (1980), pp. 453–517.

'Le iiie concile du Latran et les communautés de lépreux', *Revue Mabillon* 60 (1981), pp. 21–76.

'La pastorale des malades et des mourants aux xiie et xiiie siècles', in *Death in the Middle Ages*, ed. H. Braet and W. Verbeke, Mediaevalia Lovaniensia Series I studia 9, Louvain, 1983, pp. 88–106.

Babington, C. C., 'On some remains of the hospital of St. John the Evangelist at Cambridge', *Cambridge Antiquarian Society. Proceedings and communications*, 2 (1860–4), pp. 351–63.

The history of the infirmary and chapel of the hospital and college of St. John the Evangelist at Cambridge, Cambridge, 1874.

Bachoffner, P., 'Remèdes et soins aux malades dans les monastères alsaciens du moyen-age (viiie au xiie siècle)', *Revue d'histoire de la pharmacie* 22 (1975), pp. 329–39.

Baehrel, R., 'La haine de classe en temps d'épidémie', *Annales* 7 (1952), pp. 351–60.

Baker, A. R. H., 'Evidence in the "Nonarum Inquisitiones" of contracting arable lands in England during the early fourteenth century', *Economic history review* second ser. 19 (1966), pp. 518–32.

Baker, D. N., 'From plowing to penitence. *Piers Plowman* and fourteenth-century theology', *Speculum* 55 (1980), pp. 715–25.

Baker, T., *History of the College of St John the Evangelist, Cambridge*, 2 vols., ed. J. E. B. Mayor, Cambridge, 1869.

Baldwin, F. E., *Sumptuary legislation and personal regulation in England*, Baltimore, Md., 1926.

Baldwin, J. W., *The medieval theories of the just price: Romanists, canonists and theologians in the twelfth Century*, Philadelphia, Pa., 1959.

Bibliography

Masters, princes and merchants. The social views of Peter the Chanter and his circle, 2 vols., Princeton, N.J., 1970.

Banton, M., *Roles. An introduction to the study of social relations*, London, 1965.

Barbu, Z., 'Popular culture. A sociological approach', in *Approaches to popular culture*, ed. C. W. E. Bigsby, London, 1976, pp. 39–64.

Baric, L., 'Some aspects of credit, saving and investment in a "non-monetary" economy (Rossel Island)', in *Capital, saving and credit in peasant societies*, ed. R. Firth and B. S. Yamey, London, 1964, pp. 35–52.

Barley, M. W., 'Farmhouses and cottages, 1550–1725', *Economic history review* second ser. 7 (1954–5), pp. 291–306.

Barlow, F., 'The king's evil', *English historical review* 95 (1980), pp. 3–27.

Barnard, E. A. B., 'John Warkworth (*c.* 1425–1500) and his chapel in St. Mary's-the-Less, Cambridge', *Cambridge Antiquarian Society. Proceedings and communications* 35 (1933–4), pp. 131–5.

Bartlett, J. N., 'The expansion and decline of York in the later Middle Ages', *Economic history review* second ser. 12 (1959–60), pp. 17–33.

Bascapé, G. C., 'L'assistenza e la beneficenza a Milano dell'alto medioevo alla fina della dinastia sforzesca', *Storia di Milano* VIII, Milan, 1957, pp. 389–419.

Batany, J., 'Le vocabulaire des catégories sociales chez quelques moralistes français vers 1200', *Ordres et classes. Colloque d'histoire sociale St Cloud 24–25 Mai 1967*, Congrès et colloques 12, Paris, 1973, pp. 59–72.

Battle, C., 'La ayuda a los pobres en la parroquia de San Justo de Barcelona', in *A pobreza e a assistência aos pobres na Península Ibérica durante a Idade Média* I, Lisbon, 1973, pp. 59–71.

Bauer, P. T., *Dissent on development*, London, 1971.

Bean, J. M. W., 'Plague, population and economic decline in England in the later Middle Ages', *Economic history review*, second ser. 15 (1962–3), pp. 423–37.

Beaty, N. L., *The craft of dying: a study in the literary tradition of the Ars Moriendi in England*, Yale Studies in English, 175, New Haven, Conn. 1970.

Becker, M., 'Aspects of piety in early Renaissance Florence', in *The pursuit of holiness in late medieval and Renaissance religion*, ed. C. Trinkaus and H. Oberman, Leiden, 1974, pp. 177–99.

Beier, A. L., 'The social problems of an Elizabethan country town: Warwick, 1580–90', in *Country towns in pre-industrial England*, ed. P. Clark, Leicester, 1981, pp. 46–85.

Bellamy, J. G., 'The Coterel gang: an anatomy of a band of fourteenth century criminals', *English historical review* 79 (1964), pp. 698–717.

Crime and public order in England in the late Middle Ages, London, 1973.

Bennassar, B. and J. Goy, 'Contribution à l'histoire de la consommation alimentaire du XIVe au XIXe siècle', *Annales* 30 (1975), pp. 402–30.

Bennett, H. S., 'Medieval ordination lists in the English episcopal registers', in *Studies presented to Sir Hilary Jenkinson*, ed. J. Conway Davies, London, 1957, pp. 20–34.

Bentham, J., *The history and antiquities of the conventual and cathedral church of Ely*, Norwich, second edn, 1812.

Beresford, M. W., *The lost villages of England*, London, 1954.

Bibliography

Beresford, M., *New towns of the Middle Ages. Town plantation in England, Wales and Gascony*, London, 1967.

Bernstein, A. E., 'Theology between heresy and folklore: William of Auvergne on punishment after death', *Studies in medieval and Renaissance history* new ser. 5 (1982), pp. 5–44.

'Esoteric theology: William of Auvergne on the fires of hell and purgatory', *Speculum* 57 (1982), pp. 509–31.

Betts, R. R., 'The social revolution in Bohemia and Moravia in the later Middle Ages', *Past and present* 2 (1952), pp. 24–31.

Biddle, M., 'A thirteenth-century architectural sketch from the hospital of St. John the Evangelist, Cambridge', *Cambridge Antiquarian Society. Proceedings and communications* 54 (1960), pp. 99–108.

Bienvenu, J.-M., 'Pauvreté, misères et charité en Anjou aux XIe et XIIe siècles', *Le moyen-âge* 72 (1966), pp. 389–424; 73 (1967), pp. 5–34, 189–216.

'Fondations charitables laïques au XIIe siècle. L'exemple de l'Anjou', in *Etudes sur l'histoire de la pauvreté* I, ed. M. Mollat, Paris, 1974, pp. 563–69.

Billson, C. J., *Medieval Leicester*, Leicester, 1920.

Biraben, J. N., 'Les pauvres et la peste', in *Etudes su l'histoire de la pauvreté* II, ed. M. Mollat, Paris, 1974, pp. 505–18.

Bishop, E., *Liturgica historica*, ed. R. H. Connolly and K. Sisam, Oxford, 1918.

Bittle, W. G. and R. T. Lane, 'Inflation and philanthropy in England: a reassessment of W. K. Jordan's data', *Economic history review* second ser. 29 (1976), pp. 203–10.

'A re-assessment reiterated', *Economic history review* second ser. 31 (1978), pp. 124–8.

Black, A., *Guilds and civil society in European political thought from the twelfth century to the present*, London, 1984.

Blair, J., 'Religious gilds as landowners in the thirteenth and fourteenth centuries: the example of Chesterfield', in *The medieval town in Britain*, ed. P. Riden, Cardiff papers in local history 1, Cardiff, 1980, pp. 35–49.

Blench, J. W., *Preaching in England in the late fifteenth and sixteenth centuries*, Oxford, 1964.

Bloch, M., *Les rois thaumaturges*, Strasbourg, 1924.

Bloch, M. (as M. Fougères), 'Entr'aide et piété: les associations urbaines du moyen-âge', *Mélanges d'histoire sociale* 5 (1944), pp. 100–6.

Blockmans, W. P. and W. Prevenier, 'Poverty in Flanders and Brabant from the fourteenth to the mid-sixteenth century: sources and problems', *Acta historiae Neerlandicae* (1977), pp. 20–57.

Bloomfield, M. W., *The seven deadly sins: an introduction to the history of a religious concept*, East Lansing, Mich., 1952.

'A preliminary list of incipits of Latin works on the virtues and vices, mainly of the thirteenth, fourteenth and fifteenth centuries', *Traditio* 11 (1955), pp. 259–379.

Bois, G., *Crise du féodalisme*, Cahiers de la fondation nationale des sciences politiques 202, Paris, 1976.

Bolkestein, H., *Wohltätigkeit und Armenpflege im vorchristlichen Altertum*, Utrecht, 1939.

Bibliography

Bolton, J. L., *The medieval economy, 1150–1500*, London, 1980.

Bolzinger, R., E. Gilbrin and F. Larrang, 'L'hôpital St. Nicholas de Metz avant la Révolution. Sa fondation laïque, ses singulières prérogatives financières', *Histoire des sciences médicales* 13 (1979), pp. 369–77.

Bond, F., *Fonts and font covers*, London, 1908.

Bonenfant, P., *Hôpitaux et bienfaisance publiques dans les anciens Pays-Bas des origines à la fin du XVIIIe siècle*, Annales de la société belge de l'histoire des hôpitaux, special volume 3 (1965), Brussels, 1965.

Bonenfant-Feytmans, A. M., 'Le tableau des organisations hopitalières tracé par Jacques de Vitry', *Annales de la société belge de l'histoire des hôpitaux* 18 (1980), pp. 17–45.

Bonser, W., *The medical background of Anglo-Saxon England: a study in history, psychology and folklore*, London, 1963.

Bosl, K., '"Potens" und "pauper". Begriffsgeschichtliche Studien zur gesellschaftlichen Differenzierung im frühen Mittelalters und zum "Pauperismus" des Hochmittelalters', in *Alteuropa und die moderne Gesellschaft. Festschrift für Otto Brunner*, Göttingen, 1963, pp. 60–87.

Frühformen des Gesellschafts im mittelalterliche Europa, Munich and Vienna, 1964.

'Armut, Arbeit, Emanzipation. Zu den Hintergrunden der geistigen und literarischen Bewegung vom 11.–13. Jahrhundert', in *Beiträge zur Wirtschafts- und Sozialgeschichte des Mittelalters. Festschrift für Herbert Helbig*, ed. K. Schulz, Cologne, 1976, pp. 128–46.

Bossy, J., 'Holiness and society', *Past and present* 75(1977), pp. 119–37.

Christianity in the West, 1400–1700, Oxford, 1985.

Bourdon, J., 'Psychologie de la famine', *Annales de démographie historique* (1968), pp. 9–27.

Bourgeois, A., *Psychosociologie collective et institutions charitables: lépreux et maladreries de Pas-de-Calais*, Arras, 1972.

Boyce, G. C., *The English–German nation in the University of Paris during the Middle Ages*, Bruges, 1927.

Boyd, C., *Tithes and parishes in medieval Italy*, Ithaca, N.Y., 1952.

Boyle, L. E., 'The constitution "Cum ex eo" of Boniface VIII: education of parochial clergy', *Mediaeval studies* 24 (1962), pp. 263–302.

'The "Summa summarum" and some other English works of canon law', in *Proceedings of the second international congress of medieval canon law*, ed. S. Kuttner and J. J. Ryan, Vatican, 1965, pp. 415–56.

'Three English pastoral *summae* and a "Magister Galienus"', *Studia gratiana* 11 *Collectanea Stephen Kuttner* 1, Bologna, 1967, pp. 135–44.

'The summa for confessors as a genre, and its religious intent', in *The pursuit of holiness in late medieval and Renaissance religion*, ed. C. Trinkaus and H. Oberman, Leiden, 1974, pp. 126–30.

'The *summa confessorum* of John of Freiburg and the popularization of the moral teachings of St. Thomas and some of his contemporaries', in *St. Thomas Aquinas 1274–1974. Commemorative studies*, 2 vols., Toronto, 1974, pp. 245–68.

Bredero, A. H., 'Le moyen-âge et le purgatoire', *Revue d'histoire ecclésiastique* 78 (1983), pp. 429–54.

319

Bibliography

Bremner, R. H., 'Modern attitudes towards charity and relief', *Comparative studies in society and history* 1 (1958–9), pp. 377–82.

Bremond, C., J. Le Goff and J.-C. Schmitt, *L"exemplum'*, Typologie des sources du moyen-âge occidentale 40, Turnhout, 1982.

Brenner, R., 'Agrarian class structure and economic development in pre-industrial Europe', *Past and present* 70(1976), pp. 30–75.

Bridbury, A. R., *Economic growth: England in the later Middle Ages*, London, 1962.
'The black death', *Economic history review* second ser. 26 (1973), pp. 577–92.
'English provincial towns in the later Middle Ages', *Economic history review* second ser. 34 (1981), pp. 1–24.

Brigden, S., 'Religion and social obligation in early sixteenth century London', *Past and present* 103 (1984), pp. 67–112.

Britnell, R. H., 'The proliferation of markets in England 1200–1349', *Economic history review* second ser. 34 (1981), pp. 209–21.

Brody, S. N., *The disease of the soul*, Ithaca, N.Y., 1974.

Brooke, C. N. L., 'The earliest times to 1485', in *A history of St. Paul's cathedral*, ed. W. R. Matthews and W. M. Atkins, London, 1957, pp. 1–99, 361–5.
'The missionary at home: the Church in the towns, 1000–1250', *Studies in Church history* 6 (1970), pp. 59–83.
'Princes and kings as patrons of monasteries, Normandy and England', in *Il monachesimo e la riforma ecclesiastica 1049–1122. La Mendola, 1968*, Miscellanea del centro di studi medioevali 6, Milan, 1971, pp. 125–44.
'The churches of medieval Cambridge', in *History, society and the churches: essays in honour of Owen Chadwick*, ed. D. Beales and G. Best, Cambridge, 1985, pp. 49–76.

Brooke, C. N. L. and G. Keir, *London 800–1216, the shaping of a city*, London, 1975.

Bruck, E. F., *Kirchenväter und soziales Erbrecht*, Berlin, 1956.

Brundage, J. A., *Medieval canon law and the crusader*, Madison, Wisc., 1969.

Bullough, V. L., 'A note on medical care in medieval English hospitals' *Bulletin of the history of medicine* 35(1961), pp. 74–7.
'Medical study at mediaeval Oxford', *Speculum* 36 (1961), pp. 600–12.
'The mediaeval medical school at Cambridge', *Mediaeval studies* 24 (1962), pp. 161–8.

Burgess, C., '"For the increase of divine service": chantries in the parish in late medieval Bristol', *Journal of ecclesiastical history* 36 (1985), pp. 46–65.

Burke, P., 'Oblique approaches to the history of popular culture', in *Approaches to popular culture*, ed. C. W. E. Bigsby, London, 1976, pp. 69–84.

Burns, R. I., 'Los hospitales del reino de Valencia en el siglo XIII', *Anuario de estudios medievales* 2 (1965), pp. 135–54.
'Un monasterio-hospital del siglo XIII: San Vicente de Valencia', *Anuario de estudios medievales* 4 (1967), pp. 75–108.

Burstein, S. R., 'Care of the aged in England', *Bulletin of the history of medicine* 22(1948), pp. 738–46.

Butcher, A. F., 'The origins of Romney freemen, 1433–1523', *Economic history review* second ser. 27 (1974), pp. 16–27.

Bibliography

'Rent, population and economic change in later medieval Newcastle', *Northern history* 14 (1978), pp. 67–77.

'The economy of Exeter College, 1400–1500', *Oxoniensia* 44 (1979). pp. 38–54.

'Rent and the urban economy: Oxford and Canterbury in the later Middle Ages', *Southern history* 1 (1979), pp. 11–43.

'The hospital of St. Stephen and St. Thomas, New Romney – the documentary evidence', *Archaeologia cantiana* 96 (1980), pp. 17–26.

Bynum, C. W., 'The spirituality of regular canons in the twelfth century: a new approach', *Medievalia et humanistica* new ser. 4 (1973), p. 3–24.

Caille, J., *Hôpitaux et charité publique à Narbonne au moyen-âge de la fin du XIe à la fin du XVe siècle*, Toulouse, 1978.

'Hospices et assistance à Narbonne (XIIIe–XIVe siècles)', *Cahiers de Fanjeaux* 13 (1978), pp. 261–80.

Caius, J., *De antiquitate Cantebrigiensis academiae libri duo*, London, Second edn, 1574.

Cam, H. M., *The hundred and the Hundred Rolls*, London, 1930, repr. 1960.

Liberties and communities in medieval England. Collected studies, Cambridge, 1933, repr. 1963.

Campbell, B. M. S., 'Agricultural progress in medieval England: some evidence from eastern Norfolk', *Economic history review* second ser. 36 (1983), pp. 26–46.

Candille, M., 'Bibliographie d'histoire des hôpitaux', *Société française d'histoire des hôpitaux* 33 (1976), pp. 31–44.

Cape, C. T., 'St. Bartholomew's hospital, Newbury', *Newbury District Field Club transactions* 7 (1937), pp. 287–94.

Carlyle, R. W. and A. J., *The history of mediaeval political thought in the West*, 6 vols., Edinburgh, 1903–36.

Carpenter, D. A., 'Was there a crisis of the knightly class in the thirteenth century? The Oxfordshire evidence', *English historical review* 95 (1980), pp. 721–52.

Carpentier, E., 'Autour de la peste noire: famines et épidémies dans l'histoire du XIVe siècle', *Annales* 17(1962), pp. 1062–92.

Une ville devant la peste: Orvieto et la peste noire de 1348, Paris, 1962.

Carter, E. H. ed., 'The constitution of the hospital of St. Paul (Normanspital) in Norwich', *Norfolk archaeology* 25 (1935), pp. 342–52.

Catto, J. I., 'Citizens, scholars and masters', in *History of the University of Oxford* I, ed. J. I. Catto, Oxford, 1984, pp. 151–92.

Champion, B. A., 'The gilds of medieval Beverley', in *The medieval town in Britain*, ed. P. Riden, Cardiff papers in local history 1, Cardiff, 1980, pp. 51–66.

Chaput, B., 'La condition juridique et sociale de l'aliéné mentale', in *Aspects de la marginalité au moyen-âge*, Montreal, 1975, pp. 38–47.

Charland, T.-M., *Artes praedicandi*, Paris, 1936.

Chaunu, P., *La mort à Paris. 16e, 17e, 18e siècles*, Paris, 1978.

Checkland, O., *Philanthropy in Victorian Scotland: social welfare and the voluntary principle*, Edinburgh, 1980.

Bibliography

Chédeville, A., *Chartres et ses campagnes*, Paris, 1973.

Cheney, C. R., *From Becket to Langton: English church government 1170–1213*, Manchester, 1956.

'Rules for the observance of feast days in medieval England', *Bulletin of the Institute of Historical Research* 34 (1961), pp. 117–47.

English synodalia of the thirteenth century, Oxford, 1941, repr., 1968.

'Levies on the English clergy for the poor and for the King, 1203', *English historical review* 96 (1981), pp. 577–84.

Cheney, M. G., 'The council of Westminster 1175: new light on an old source', *Studies in Church history* 11 (1975), pp. 61–8.

Chenu, M.-D., *L'éveil de la conscience dans la civilisation médiévale*, Conférence Albert-le-Grand, 1968, Montreal, 1969.

Chibnall, M., 'Monks and pastoral work: a problem in Anglo-Norman history', *Journal of ecclesiastical history* 18 (1967), pp. 165–72.

Chiffoleau, J., 'Pratiques funéraires et images de la mort à Marseille, en Avignon et dans le comtat de Venaissin (vers 1280–vers 1350)', *Cahiers de Fanjeaux* 11 (1976), pp. 271–303.

La comptabilité de l'au-delà. Les hommes, la mort et la religion dans la région d'Avignon à la fin du moyen-âge (vers 1320–vers 1480), Collection de l'Ecole française de Rome 47, Rome, 1980.

Christian, W. A., *Local religion in sixteenth-century Spain*, Princeton, N.J., 1981.

Cipolla, C. M., *Public health and the medical profession in the Renaissance*, Cambridge, 1976.

'Economic fluctuations, the poor, and public policy (Italy, 16th and 17th century)', in *Aspects of poverty in early Modern Europe*, ed. T. Riis, Stuttgart, 1981, pp. 65–77.

Clanchy, M. T., *From memory to written record: England 1066–1307*, London, 1979.

Clapham, J. H., 'A thirteenth-century market town: Linton, Cambridgeshire', *Cambridge historical journal* 4 (1932–4), pp. 194–202.

Clark, J. W., 'An attempt to trace the architectural history and plan of the church and conventual buildings of Barnwell priory, Cambridge', *Cambridge Antiquarian Society. Proceedings and communications* 7 (1888–91), pp. 222–51.

ed., *Endowments of the University of Cambridge*, Cambridge, 1904.

'On the charitable foundations in the University called chests. A transcript and translation of the deed of foundation and statutes of the earliest, the Neel chest, 1344', *Cambridge Antiquarian Society. Proceedings and communications* 11 (1903–6), pp. 78–101.

Clark, J. W. and A. Gray, *Old plans of Cambridge, 1574 to 1798*, Cambridge, 1921.

Clark-Maxwell, 'Some letters of confraternity', *Archaeologia* 75 (1926), pp. 19–60.

'Some further letters of fraternity', *Archaeologia* 79 (1929), pp. 179–216.

Clay, R. M., *The medieval hospitals of England*, London, 1909.

Clay, W. K., *A history of the parish of Horningsey in the county of Cambridge*, Cambridge Antiquarian society publications 7, Cambridge, 1865.

Cobban, A. B., 'Edward II, pope John XXII and the University of Cambridge', *Bulletin of the John Ryland library* 47 (1964–5), pp. 49–78.

The King's Hall within the University of Cambridge in the later Middle Ages,

Bibliography

Cambridge studies in medieval life and thought. 3rd ser. 1, Cambridge, 1969.

'Origins: Robert Wodelarke and St. Catharine's', in *St. Catharine's College, Cambridge, 1473–1973*, ed. E. E. Rich, Leeds, 1973, pp. 1–32.

The medieval universities: their development and organization, London, 1975.

'The medieval Cambridge college: a quantitative study of higher degrees to c. 1500', *History of education* 9 (1980), pp. 1–12.

Cobbett, L., 'The hospitals of St. John the Baptist and St. Mary Magdalene at Ely', *Cambridge Antiquarian Society. Proceedings and communications* 36 (1935), pp. 58–75.

Coleman, D. C., 'Review of W. K. Jordan, *Philanthropy in England, 1480–1660*', *Economic history review* second ser. 13 (1960–1), pp. 113–15.

The economy of England 1450–1750, Oxford, 1977.

'Philanthropy deflated: a comment', *Economic history review* second ser. 31 (1978), pp. 118–23.

Collard, D., *Altruism and economy. A study in non-selfish economics*, Oxford, 1978.

Collegium divi Iohannis Evangeliste, ed. R. F. Scott, Cambridge, 1911.

Collinson, P., *The religion of Protestants. The church in English society 1559–1625*, Oxford, 1982.

Colvin, H. M., *The white canons in England*, Oxford, 1951.

Comford, B., 'Inventories of the poor in Martham', *Norfolk archaeology* 35 (1970–3), pp. 118–25.

Congar, J. M.-J., 'Aspects ecclésiologiques de la querelle entre mendiants et séculiers dans la seconde moitié du XIIIe siècle et le début du XIVe', *Archives d'histoire doctrinale et littéraire du moyen-âge* 28 (1961), pp. 35–151.

Constable, G., *Monastic tithes from their origins to the twelfth century*, Cambridge studies in medieval life and thought, new ser. 10, Cambridge, 1964.

'Wealth and philanthropy in late medieval England. Review of J. Rosenthal, *The purchase of paradise*', *Journal of interdisciplinary history* 4 (1973–4), pp. 597–602.

Cook, G. H., *Medieval chantries and chantry chapels*, London, rev. edn, 1963.

Coornaert, E., 'Les ghildes médiévales (ve–xive siècles)', *Revue historique* 199 (1948), pp. 22–55, 208–43.

Coppin, C., 'Les statuts de l'hospice gantois à Lille (1467)', *Revue du Nord* 29 (1947), pp. 26–42.

Corbet, L., *Les 'charités' en Normandie*, Dijon, 1959.

Cormack, A. A., *Poor relief in Scotland*, Aberdeen, 1923.

Coss, P. R., 'Sir Geoffrey de Langley and the crisis of the knightly class in thirteenth-century England', *Past and present* 68(1975), pp. 3–37.

Courtenay, W. J., 'Token coinage and the administration of poor relief in the Middle Ages', *Journal of interdisciplinary history* 3 (1972–3), pp. 275–95.

'Nominalism and late medieval religion', in *The pursuit of holiness in late medieval and Renaissance religion*, ed. C. Trinkaus and H. Oberman, Leiden, 1974, pp. 26–59.

'The effect of the Black Death on English higher education', *Speculum* 55 (1980), pp. 696–714.

Courtney, F., *Cardinal Robert Pullen. An English theologian of the twelfth century*, Analecta Gregoriana 64, Rome, 1954.

Bibliography

Couvreur, G., *Les pauvres ont-ils des droits? Recherches sur le vol en cas d'extrême nécessité depuis la Concordia de Gratien (1140) jusqu'à Guillaume d'Auxerre (1231)*, Analecta Gregoriana 111. Series Facultatis Theologicae, Rome, 1961.

Cox, J. C. and A. Harvey, *English church furniture*, London, 1907.

Craemer, U., *Das Hospital als Bautyp des Mittelalters*, Koln, 1963.

Creighton, C., *History of epidemics in Britain*, 2 vols., Cambridge, 1891–4, repr. 1965.

Cule, J., 'The prognosis, care and treatment of leprosy in Wales and the Border in the Middle Ages', *Transactions of the British Society for the History of Pharmacy* 1(1970), pp. 29–58.

'Some early hospitals in Wales and the Border', *National Library of Wales journal* 20 (1977), pp. 97–130.

Cunnington, P. and C. Lucas, *Charity costumes of children, scholars, almsfolk, pensioners*, London, 1978.

Curcio, G., 'L'ospedale di S. Giovanni in Laterano: funzione urbana di una istituzione ospedaliera. I', *Storia dell'arte* 32 (1978), pp. 23–39.

Curschmann, F., *Hungersnöte im Mittelalter. Ein Beitrag zur deutschen Wirtschaftsgeschichte des 8. bis 13. Jahrhunderts*, Leipziger Studien VI (1), Leipzig, 1900.

Dahmus, J., 'Preaching to the laity in fifteenth century Germany: Johannes Nider's "harps"', *Journal of ecclesiastical history* 34 (1983), pp. 55–68.

Dainton, C., *The story of England's hospitals*, London, 1962.

Darby, H. C., ed., *The Cambridge region*, Cambridge, 1938.
The medieval Fenland, Cambridge, 1940.
Medieval Cambridgeshire, Cambridge, 1977.

Darby, H. C., R. E. Glasscock, J. Sheail and G. R. Versey, 'The changing geographical distribution of wealth in England 1086–1334–1525', *Journal of historical geography* 5 (1979), pp. 247–62.

Davis, G. R. C., *Medieval cartularies of Great Britain: a short catalogue*, London, 1958.

Davis, N. Z., 'Some tasks and themes in the study of popular religion', *The pursuit of holiness in late medieval and Renaissance religion*, ed. C. Trinkaus and H. Oberman, Leiden, 1974, pp. 307–36.

Davy, M. M., *Les sermons universitaires parisiens de 1230–1*, Paris, 1931.

Day, R. H., 'Instability in the transition from manorialism: a classical analysis', *Explorations in economic history* 19 (1982), pp. 321–38.

Delaruelle, E., *La piété populaire au moyen-âge*, Turin, 1975.

Delattre, J.-L., 'L'hôpital monastique de Nivelles des origines à 1136', *Annales de la société belge de l'histoire des hôpitaux* 1 (1963), pp. 7–17.

'La fondation des hôpitaux de Saint Nicholas et du Saint Sepulchre au XIIe siècle', in *Hommage au Professeur Paul Bonenfant (1899–1965)*, Brussels, 1965, pp. 595–9.

Delmaire, B., 'L'hôpital Saint-Jean-Baptiste d'Aire-sur-la-Lys dans la première moitié du XVe siècle', *Revue du Nord* 51 (1969), pp. 27–74.

De Maitre, L., 'The description and diagnosis of leprosy by fourteenth-century physicians', *Bulletin of the history of medicine* 59 (1985), pp. 327–44.

Denton, J. H., *English royal free chapels, 1100–1300: a constitutional study*, Manchester, 1970.

Bibliography

Dereine, C., 'Vie commune, règle de St. Augustin et chanoines réguliers au xie siècle', *Revue d'histoire ecclésiastique* 41(1946), pp. 365–406.

Devisse, J., '"Pauperes" et "paupertas" dans le monde carolingien: ce qu'en dit Hincmar de Reims', *Revue du Nord* 48 (1966), pp. 273–87.

Dickinson, J. C., *The origins of the Austin canons and their introduction into England*, London, 1950.

Monastic life in medieval England, London, 1961.

A dictionary of saints, ed. D. Attwater, Harmondsworth, 1965.

Dictionnaire d'archéologie chrétienne et de liturgie, 15 vols., ed. F. Cabrol, H. Leclercq and H. Marrou, 1907–53.

Dictionnaire de droit canonique, 7 vols., ed. R. Naz, Paris, 1935–65.

Dictionnaire de théologie catholique, 25 vols., ed. A. Vacant and E. Mangenot, Paris, 1903–50.

Dobson, R. B., 'The foundation of perpetual chantries by the citizens of medieval York', *Studies in Church history* 4 (1967), pp. 22–38.

'Admissions to the freedom of the city of York in the later Middle Ages', *Economic history review* second ser. 26 (1973), pp. 1–22.

Durham priory 1400–1450, Cambridge studies in medieval life and thought, third ser. 6, Cambridge, 1973.

'Urban decline in late medieval England', *Transactions of the Royal Historical Society*, fifth ser. 27 (1977), pp. 1–22.

The peasants' revolt 1381, London, second edn. 1983.

'Introduction', *The church, politics and patronage in the fifteenth century*, ed. B. Dobson, Gloucester, 1984, pp. 9–22.

Dodwell, B., 'Holdings and inheritance in medieval East Anglia', *Economic history review* second ser. 20 (1967), pp. 53–66.

Dollinger, P., 'L'évolution politique des corporations strassbourgeoises à la fin du moyen-âge', in *Pages d'histoire. France et Allemagne médiévales. Alsace*, Collection de l'institut des hautes études alsaciennes 25, Paris 1977, pp. 229–37.

Dossat, Y., 'Les confréres du Corpus Christi dans le monde rural pendant la première moitié du xive siècle', *Cahiers de Fanjeaux* 11 (1976), pp. 357–85.

Douglas, D. C., *The social structure of medieval East Anglia*, Oxford, 1927.

Drake, G. H., 'The hospital of St. Mary of Ospringe', *Archaeologia Cantiana* 30 (1914), pp. 35–70.

Dubois, J., 'Les moines et la société du moyen-âge', *Revue d'histoire de l'eglise de France* 60 (1974), pp. 5–37.

Du Boulay, F. R. H., 'A rentier economy in the later Middle Ages: the archbishopric of Canterbury', *Economic history review* second ser. 16 (1963–4), pp. 427–38.

'Who were farming the English demesnes at the end of the Middle Ages?', *Economic history review* second ser. 17 (1964–5), pp. 443–55.

An age of ambition: English society in the late Middle Ages, London, 1970.

Duby, G., 'Les pauvres des campagnes dans l'occident médiévale jusqu'au xiiie siècle', *Revue d'histoire de l'église de France* 52 (1966), pp. 25–32.

'Les laïcs et la paix de Dieu', in *I laici nella 'societas christiana' dei secoli XI e XII. Atti della terza settimana di studi. La Mendola 1965*, Miscellanea del centro di studi medioevali 3, Milan, 1968, pp. 448–61 and discussion, pp. 462–9.

Bibliography

Dufermont, J.-C., 'Les pauvres, d'après les sources anglo-saxonnes, du VIIe au XIe siècle', *Revue du Nord* 50 (1968), pp. 189–201.

Dufeuil, M. M., *Guillaume de St. Amour et la polémique universitaire parisienne, 1250–1259*, Paris, 1972.

Duggan, C., *Twelfth-century decretal collections and their importance in English history*, University of London historical studies 12, London, 1963.

Dupont-Danican, J.-F., 'Maladreries en pays de Caux et commanderies de Saint-Lazare de Jérusalem', *Société française d'histoire des hôpitaux* 34 (1977), pp. 49–58.

Durkan, J., 'Care of the poor: pre-Reformation hospitals', *Essays on the Scottish Reformation, 1513–1625*, ed. D. McRoberts, Glasgow, 1962, pp. 116–28.

Durvin, P., 'La maladrerie Saint Lazare de Beauvais', *Bulletin de la société nationale des antiquaires de France* (1975), pp. 199–205.

Duvosquel, J.-M., 'Les biens de la chapelle de l'hôpital de Comines au moyen-âge. Essai de reconstitution du chassereau de 1420', *Sacris erudiri* 26 (1983), pp. 221–47.

Dyer, C. C., 'A redistribution of incomes in fifteenth-century England?', *Past and present* 39 (1968), pp. 11–33.

'English diet in the later Middle Ages', in *Social relations and ideas. Essays in honour of R. H. Hilton*, ed. T. H. Aston, P. R. Coss, C. Dyer and J. Thirsk, Cambridge, 1983, pp. 191–216.

Ekeh, P., *Social exchange theory; the two traditions*, London, 1974.

Ell, S. R., 'Concepts of disease and the physician in the early Middle Ages', *Janus* 65 (1978), pp. 153–65.

'The two medicines: some ecclesiastical concepts of disease and the physician in the high Middle Ages', *Janus* 68 (1981), pp. 15–25.

Elm, K., '*Fratres et sorores sanctissimi sepulchri*. Beiträge zu *fraternitas, familia* und weiblichem Religiosentum im Umkreis des Kapitels vom Hlg. Grab', *Frühmittelalterliche Studien* 9 (1975), pp. 287–333.

Elton, G. R., 'An early Tudor poor law', *Economic history review* second ser. 6 (1953–4), pp. 55–67.

'Review of W. K. Jordan, *Philanthropy in England, 1480–1660*', *Historical journal* 3 (1960), pp. 89–92.

Emden, A. B., *A biographical register of the University of Cambridge to 1500*, Cambridge, 1963.

Emminghaus, A., *Poor relief in different parts of Europe*, London, 1873.

Esposito Alano, A., 'Un inventario di beni in Roma dell'ospedale di S. Spirito in Sassia (*a*. 1312)', *Archivio della società romana di storia patria* 99 (1977), pp. 71–116.

Evennett, H. O., 'The last stages of medieval monasticism in England', *Studia monastica* 2 (1960), pp. 387–419.

Fairchilds, C. C., *Poverty and charity in Aix-en-Provence 1640–1789*, Baltimore, Md, 1976.

Farmer, D. L., 'Some price fluctuations in Angevin England', *Economic history review* second ser. 9 (1956–7), pp. 34–43.

'Some grain price movements in thirteenth century England', *Economic history review* second ser. 10 (1957–8), pp. 207–20.

Bibliography

'Crop yields, prices and wages in medieval England', *Studies in medieval and Renaissance history* new ser. 6 (1983), pp. 115–55.

Finucane, R. C., *Miracles and pilgrims. Popular beliefs in medieval England*, London, 1977.

Fletcher, J. M., 'Wealth and poverty in the medieval German universities', in *Europe in the late Middle Ages*, ed. J. R. Hale, J. R. L. Highfield and B. Smalley, London, 1965, pp. 410–36.

Flood, D., 'Poverty in the Middle Ages', *Collectanea franciscana* 43 (1973), pp. 409–15.

Forbes, M. D., *Clare College 1326–1926. University Hall 1326–1346. Clare Hall 1346–1856*, 2 vols., Cambridge, 1928–30.

Foreville, R., 'Les statuts synodaux et le renouveau pastoral du XIIIe siècle dans le Midi de la France', *Cahiers de Fanjeaux* 6 (1971), pp. 119–50.

Forte, S. L., 'A Cambridge Dominican collector of exempla in the thirteenth century', *Archivum fratrum praedicatorum* 28 (1958), pp. 115–48.

Foster, G. M., 'The dyadic contract: a model for the social structure of a Mexican peasant village' in *Peasant society. A Reader*, ed. J. M. Potter, M. N. Diaz and G. M. Foster, Boston, Mass., 1967, pp. 213–30.

Foucault, M., *Folie et déraison: histoire de la folie à l'âge classique*, Paris, 1961.

Gabriel, A. L., 'The practice of charity at the University of Paris during the Middle Ages: Ave Maria college', *Traditio* 5 (1947), pp. 335–9.

Student life in Ave Maria College, mediaeval Paris: history and chartulary of the College, University of Notre Dame. Publications in mediaeval studies 14, Notre Dame, Ind., 1955.

'The college system in the fourteenth century universities', in *The forward movement of the fourteenth century*, ed. F. L. Utley, Columbus, Ohio, 1961, pp. 79–124.

'Motivation of the founders of medieval colleges', *Beiträge zum Berufsbewusstsein des mittelalterlichen Menschen*, Miscellanea medievalia 3, Berlin, 1964, pp. 61–72.

Foreign students, members of the English–German nation at the university of Paris in the fifteenth century, Modena, 1966.

Galpern, A. N., *The religions of the people in sixteenth century Champagne*, Harvard Historical Studies 92, Cambridge (Mass.), 1976.

Gans, H. J., 'Poverty and culture: some basic questions about methods of studying life-styles of the poor', in *The concept of poverty*, ed. P. Townsend, London, 1970, pp. 146–64.

Gautier, L., *La chevalerie*, Paris, 1884.

Gavitt, P., 'Economy, charity, and community in Florence 1350–1450', in *Aspects of poverty in early modern Europe*, ed. T. Riis, Florence, 1981, pp. 79–118.

Geertz, C., 'Religion as a cultural system', in *Anthropological approaches to the study of religion*, ed. M. Banton, London, 1966, pp. 1–42.

Geertz, H., 'An anthropology of religion and magic. 1', *Journal of interdisciplinary history* 6 (1975–6), pp. 71–89.

de Geest, C., 'Les distributions aux pauvres par la paroisse Sainte-Gudule à Bruxelles au XVe siècle', *Annales de la société belge de l'histoire des hôpitaux* 7 (1965), pp. 41–84.

Bibliography

Génestal (du Chaumeil), R., *Rôle des monastères comme établissements de crédit*, Paris, 1901.

Genet, J.-P., 'Economie et société rurale en Angleterre au xve siècle d'après les comptes de l'hôpital d'Ewelme', *Annales* 27 (1972), pp. 1449–71.

Génicot, L., 'Sur le nombre des pauvres dans les champagnes médiévales', *Revue historique* 522 (1977), pp. 273–88.

Gerald Vesey, F., 'St John's hospital, Huntingdon', *Transactions of the Cambridgeshire and Huntingdon Archaeological Society* 1 (1900–3), pp. 121–5.

Geremek, B., 'La popolazione marginale tra il medioevo e l'era moderna', *Studi storici* 9 (1968), pp. 623–40.

    La salariat dans l'artisanat parisien aux XIIIe-XVe siècles, trans. A. Posner and C. Klapisch-Zuber, Industrie et artisanat 5, Paris and La Haye, 1968.

    'La lutte contre le vagabondage à Paris aux xive et xve siècle', in *Ricerche storiche ed economiche in memoria di Corrado Barbagallo*, Naples, 1970, pp. 213–36.

    'Le renfermement des pauvres en Italie (xive–xviie siècle): remarques préliminaires', in *Mélanges en l'honneur de Fernand Braudel. Histoire économique du monde méditerranéen 1450–1650* ii, Toulouse, 1973, pp. 205–17.

    'Criminalité, vagabondage, paupérisme: la marginalité à l'aube des temps modernes', *Revue d'histoire moderne et contemporaine* 21 (1974), pp. 337–75.

Gervers, M., '*Rotundae anglicanae*', in *Actes du XXIIe congrès international d'histoire de l'art, Budapest 15–20 Septembre, 1969*, Budapest, 1972, pp. 359–76.

Ghinato, A., 'A chi si deve attribuare la rivelazione profetica dei monti di pietà?', *Archivium franciscanum historicum* 50 (1957), pp. 231–6.

    Monti di pietà e monti frumentari di Amelia: origine e antichi statuti, Studi e testi franciscani 9, Rome, 1956.

Giannelli, G., 'Documenti relativi ad una "mansio leprosorum"', *Studi senesi* (1952), p. 462–92.

Gibbs, M. and J. Lang, *Bishops and reforms, 1215–1272, with special reference to the Lateran council of 1215*, Oxford, 1934.

Gilchrist, J. T. I., *The church and economic activity in the Middle Ages*, London, 1969.

Giordanengo, G., 'Les hôpitaux arlésiens du xiie au xive siècle', *Cahiers de Fanjeaux* 13 (1978), pp. 189–212.

Giroud, C., *L'ordre des chanoines réguliers de Saint-Augustin et ses diverses formes de régime interne. Essai de synthèse historico-juridique*, Martigny, 1961.

Godard, J., 'La maladrerie de St. Ladre et la condition des lépreux à Amiens au moyen-âge', *Bulletin de la société des antiquaires de la Picardie* 35 (1933–4), pp. 173–291.

Godfrey, W. H., *The English almshouse*, London 1955.

Goffman, E., *Asylums: essays on the social situation of mental patients and other inmates*, Chicago, 1962.

Goglin, J.-L., *Les misérables dans l'occident médiéval*, Paris, 1976.

Gonthier, N., 'Les hôpitaux et les pauvres à la fin du moyen-âge: l'exemple de Lyon', *Le moyen-âge* 84 (1978), pp. 279–308.

    Lyon et ses pauvres au moyen-âge (1350–1500), Lyons, 1978.

Goody, J., *The development of the family and marriage in Europe*, Cambridge, 1983.

Gottfried, R. S., *Epidemic disease in fifteenth century England*, New Brunswick, N.J., 1978.

Bibliography

Bury St. Edmunds and the urban crisis, 1290–1539. Princeton, N.J., 1982.

Gould, J. D., 'Bittle and Lane on charity: an uncharitable comment', *Economic history review* second ser. 31 (1978), pp. 120–3.

Graham, R., *S. Gilbert of Sempringham and the Gilbertines*, London, 1901.

Gramaglia, B. E., 'Vie di communicazione e centri ospitalieri nella piana di Villanova d'Asti nel medioevo', *Bollettino storico-bibliographico subalpino* 78 (1980), pp. 333–68.

Granata, C., 'I documenti più antichi per la storia dell'ospedale di S. Lazzaro di Como (1192–1483)', *Aevum* 54 (1980), pp. 231–56.

Grandin, J., 'Recherches sur les maladreries dans l'Orne au moyen âge', *Cahiers Léopold Delisle* 23 (1974), pp. 3–20.

Gras, N. S. B., *The evolution of the English corn market from the twelfth to the eighteenth century*, New York, edn of 1967.

Graus, F., *Chudina mestska v dobe predhusitske (Urban poor in the pre-Hussite period)*, Prague, 1949.

'Au bas moyen-âge: pauvres des villes et pauvres des campagnes', *Annales* 16 (1961), pp. 1053–65.

'Social utopias in the Middle Ages', *Past and present* 38 (1967), pp. 3–19.

Gray, A., *Biographical notes on the mayors of Cambridge*, Cambridge, 1921.

'A visitation of the religious houses of the diocese of Ely in AD 1373', *Cambridge Antiquarian Society. Proceedings and communication* 30 (1927–8), pp. 54–9.

The school of Pythagoras (Merton Hall), Cambridge Antiquarian society, Cambridge, 1932.

Green, R. B., 'Virtues and vices in the chapter house vestibule in Salisbury', *Journal of the Warburg and Courtauld Institutes* 31 (1968), pp. 148–58.

Greenfield, K., 'Changing emphases in English vernacular homiletic literature 960–1225', *Journal of medieval history* 7 (1981), pp. 283–97.

Grégoire, R., 'La place de la pauvreté dans la conception et la pratique de la vie monastique médiévale latine', *Il monachesimo e la riforma ecclesiastica (1049–1122). Settimana internazionale di studio, Mendola, 1968*, Miscellanea del centro di studi medioevali 6, Milan, 1971, pp. 173–92.

Gregory, C. A., *Gifts and commodities*, Cambridge, 1982.

Grierson, P., 'Commerce in the Dark Ages: a critique of the evidence', *Transactions of the Royal Historical Society* fifth ser. 9 (1959), p. 123–40 [repr. in *Studies in economic anthropology*, ed. G. Dalton, Washington, D.C., 1971, pp. 74–83].

Griffin, R., 'The leper's loop as Swainestrey', *Archaeologia Cantiana* 34 (1920), pp. 63–78.

Grundmann, H., *Religiöse Bewegungen im Mittelalter*, Berlin, 1935, Hildesheim, rev. edn, 1961.

Guerrini, P., 'Gli statuti di un'antica congregazione francescana in Brescia', *Archivum franciscanum historicum* 1 (1908), pp. 544–68.

Gumbley, W., *The Cambridge Dominicans*, Oxford, 1938.

Gurevich, A. J., 'Popular and scholarly medieval cultural traditions: notes in the margin of Jacques Le Goff's book', *Journal of medieval history* 9 (1983), pp. 71–90.

Gussow, Z. and G. S. Tracy, 'Status, ideology and adaptation to stigmatized illness: a study of leprosy', in *Culture, disease and healing: studies in medical anthropology*, ed. D. Landy, New York, 1977, pp. 394–402.

Guth, K., 'Spitäler in Bamberg und Nürnberg als bürgerliche Sozialeinrichtungen der mittelalterliche Stadt', *Jahrbuch für fränkische Landesforschung* 38 (1978), pp. 39–49.

Gutton, J.-P., 'A l'aube du XVIIᵉ siècle: idées nouvelles sur les pauvres', *Cahiers d'histoire* 10 (1965), pp. 87–97.

La société et les pauvres: l'exemple de la généralité de Lyon, 1534–1789, Bibliothèque de la faculté des lettres et sciences humaines de Lyon 26, Paris, 1971.

L'état et la mendicité dans la première moitié du XVIIIe siècle. Auvergne, Beaujolais, Forez, Lyonnais, Thèses et mémoires 5, Saint-Etienne, 1973.

Guy, J. R., 'Of the writing of hospital histories there is no end', *Bulletin of the history of medicine* 59 (1985), pp. 415–20.

Hackett, M. B., *The original statutes of Cambridge university. The text and its history*, Cambridge, 1970.

Hadwin, J. F., 'Deflating philanthropy', *Economic history review* second ser. 31 (1978), pp. 105–17.

'The medieval lay subsidies and economic history', *Economic history review* second ser. 36 (1983), pp. 200–17.

Haines, R. M., 'The practice and problems of a fifteenth century English bishop: the episcopate of William Gray', *Mediaeval studies* 34 (1972), pp. 435–61.

Halcrow, E. M., 'The decline of demesne farming on the estates of Durham cathedral priory', *Economic history review* second ser. 7 (1954–5), pp. 345–56.

Hallam, H. E., 'Some thirteenth-century censuses', *Economic history review* second ser. 10 (1957–8), p. 340–61.

'Population density in medieval fenland', *Economic history review* second ser. 14 (1961–2), pp. 71–81.

Settlement and society. A. study in the agrarian history of south Lincolnshire, Cambridge, 1965.

Rural England 1066–1348, Brighton, 1981.

Hamilton Thompson, A., 'A corrody from Leicester abbey, AD 1393–4, with some notes on corrodies', *Transactions of the Leicestershire Archaeological Society* 14 (1925–6), pp. 114–34.

The history of the hospital and the new college of the Annunciation of St. Mary in Newarke, Leicester, Leicester, 1937.

'The collegiate churches of the bishopric of Durham', *Durham University journal* 36 (1944), pp. 33–42.

The English clergy and their organisation in the later Middle Ages, Oxford, 1947.

Hammer Jr., C. I., 'Patterns of homicide in a medieval university town: fourteenth century Oxford', *Past and present* 78 (1978), pp. 3–23.

Hammond, E. A., 'Physicians in medieval religious houses', *Bulletin of the history of medicine* 32 (1958), pp. 105–20.

Hampson, E. M., *The treatment of poverty in Cambridgeshire 1597–1834*, Cambridge, 1934.

Hands, A. R., *Charities and social aid in Greece and Rome*, London, 1968.

Hankart, R., 'L'hôpital Saint-Michel dit des communs pauvres-en-île à

Bibliography

Liège. Histoire des origines (XIIe–XVe siècles)', *Bulletin de l'institut archéologique liégeois* 90 (1978), pp. 157–95.

Hannecart, L., 'Les établissements de bienfaisance à Chièvres au XIIe siècle', *Annales de la société belge de l'histoire des hôpitaux* 1 (1963), pp. 20–8.

Hardwick, C., 'Robert Woodlark, founder and first master of St. Catharine's Hall', *Cambridge Antiquarian Society. Proceedings and communications* 1 (1851–9), pp. 329–39.

Harper-Bill, C., 'A late medieval visitation – the diocese of Norwich in 1499', *Proceedings of the Suffolk Institute of Archaeology* 34 (1977), pp. 35–47.

Hartridge, R. A. R., *A history of vicarages in the Middle Ages*, Cambridge studies in medieval life and thought, Cambridge, 1930.

Harvey, B. F., 'The population trend in England between 1300 and 1348', *Transactions of the Royal Historical Society* fifth ser. 16 (1966), pp. 23–42.

Harvey, P. D. A., 'The English inflation of 1180–1220', *Past and present* 61 (1973), pp. 3–30.

Hasquin, H., 'Note sur les origines de l'hôpital Notre Dame à Courtrai (1209–1211)', *Annales de la société belge d'histoire des hôpitaux* 9 (1971), pp. 3–10.

Hatcher, J., 'A diversified economy: later medieval Cornwall', *Economic history review* second ser. 22 (1969), pp. 208–27.

Rural economy and society in the duchy of Cornwall, 1300–1500, Cambridge, 1970.

Plague, population and the English economy 1348–1530, London, 1977.

Hatcher, J. and M. M. Postan, 'Agrarian class structure and economic development in pre-industrial Europe. Population and class relations in feudal society', *Past and present* 78 (1978), pp. 24–37.

Heal, F., 'The idea of hospitality in early modern England', *Past and present* 102 (1984), pp. 66–93.

Heath, P., *The English parish clergy on the eve of the Reformation*, London, 1969.

'Urban piety in the later Middle Ages: the evidence of Hull wills', in *Church, politics and patronage in the fifteenth century*, ed. B. Dobson, Gloucester, 1984, pp. 209–34.

Heers, J., *L'occident aux XIVe et XVe siècles. Aspects économiques et sociaux*, Nouvelle Clio 23, Paris, 1963.

Helmholz, R. H., *Marriage litigation in medieval England*, Cambridge, 1974.

Henderson, J., 'The flagellant movement and flagellant confraternities in central Italy, 1260–1400', *Studies in Church history* 15 (1978), pp. 147–60.

Herlihy, D., 'Population, plague and social change in rural Pistoia, 1201–1430', *Economic history review* second ser. 18 (1965), pp. 225–44.

Pisa in the early Renaissance: a study of urban growth, New Haven, Conn., 1958, reiss. Port Washington, N.Y., 1973.

Herlihy, D. and C. Klapisch-Zuber, *The Tuscans and their families: a study of the Florentine Catasto of 1427*, Yale series in economic history, New Haven, Conn., 1984.

Heupgen, P., 'La commune Aumône de Mons du XIIIe au XVIIe siècle', *Bulletin de la commission royale d'histoire de Belgique* 90 (1926), pp. 319–72.

Hibbert, A. B., 'The origins of the medieval town patriciate', *Past and present* 3 (1953), pp. 15–27.

Bibliography

Highfield, J. R. L., 'The early colleges', in *The history of the University of Oxford* I, ed. J. I. Catto, Oxford, 1984, pp. 225–63.

Hilaire, F., 'Architecture hospitalière du moyen âge au XVIIIe siècle', *Monuments historiques* 114 (1981), pp. 8–15.

Hill, J. W. F., *Medieval Lincoln*, Cambridge, 1948, repr. 1965.

Hill, R., '"A Chaunterie for soules": London chantries in the reign of Richard II', in *The reign of Richard II: essays in honour of May McKisack*, ed. F. R. H. Du Boulay and C. M. Barron, London, 1971, pp. 242–55.

Hilton, R. H., 'A study in the pre-history of English enclosure in the fifteenth century', in *Studi in onore di Armando Sapori* I, ed. G. Sapori, Milan, 1957, pp. 673–85 [repr. in R. H. Hilton, *The English peasantry in the later Middle Ages*, Oxford, 1975].

'Rent and capital formation in feudal society', in *Second international conference of economic history, 1962* II, Paris, 1965, pp. 33–68.

'Some problems of urban real property in the Middle Ages', in *Socialism, capitalism and economic growth: essays presented to Maurice Dobb*, ed. C. H. Feinstein, Cambridge, 1967, pp. 326–37.

The decline of serfdom in medieval England, London, 1969.

'Idéologie et ordre sociale dans l'Angleterre médiévale', *L'Arc* 72 (1978), pp. 32–7.

Bond men made free: medieval peasant movements and the English rising of 1381, London, 1973.

'Rents and capital formation in feudal society', in *The English peasantry in the later Middle Ages*, Oxford, 1975, pp. 174–214.

'The small town as part of peasant society', in *The English peasantry in the later Middle Ages*, Oxford, 1975, pp. 76–94.

'Lords, burgesses and hucksters', *Past and present* 97 (1982), pp. 3–15.

'The small town and urbanisation – Evesham in the Middle Ages', *Midland history* 7 (1982), pp. 1–8.

'Small town society in England before the Black Death', *Past and present* 105 (1984), pp. 53–78.

Hinnebusch, W. A., 'The pre-Reformation sites of the Oxford Blackfriars', *Oxoniensia* 3 (1938), pp. 57–82.

The early English friars preachers, Rome, 1951.

The history of the Dominican order I, New York, 1965.

A history of the county of Cambridge and the Isle of Ely II–III, ed. L. F. Salzman, The Victoria history of the counties of England, London, 1948–59, repr. 1967.

A history of the county of London I, ed. W. Page, The Victoria history of the counties of England, London, 1974.

The history of the county of York. The city of York, ed. P. M. Tillott, The Victoria history of the counties of England, London, 1961.

Hobson, J. M., *Some early and later houses of pity*, London 1926.

Homans, C. G., *English villagers of the thirteenth century*, Cambridge, Mass., 1942.

Honeybourne, M. B., 'The pre-expulsion cemetery of the Jews in London', *Transactions of the Jewish historical society of England* 20 (1959–61), pp. 145–59.

'The leper houses of the London area', *Transactions of the London and Middlesex Archaeological Society* 21 (1963–7), pp. 4–61.

Bibliography

Houston, R., 'Vagrants and society in early modern England', *Cambridge anthropology* 6 (1980), pp. 18–32.

Howell, C., *Land, family and inheritance in transition: Kibworth Harcourt, 1280–1700*, Cambridge, 1983.

Howell, M. E., *Regalian right in medieval England*, University of London historical studies 9, London, 1962.

Hubert, H. and M. Mauss, *Sacrifice: its nature and function*, trans. W. D. Halls, London, 1964.

Hudson, A., 'A Lollard sermon-cycle and its implications', *Medium aevum* 40 (1971), pp. 142–56.

Huyghebaert, N., 'L'origine ecclésiastique des léproseries en Flandre et dans le Nord de la France', *Revue d'histoire ecclésiastique* 58 (1963), pp. 848–57.

Hyams, P. R., 'The origins of a peasant land market in England', *Economic history review* second ser. 23 (1970), pp. 18–31.

Imbert, J., *Les hôpitaux en droit canonique*, Paris, 1947.
   'Le régime juridique des établissements hospitaliers du nord de la France au moyen âge', *Revue de Nord* 29 (1947), pp. 195–204.
   Les hôpitaux en France, Paris, 1974.

An inventory of the historical monuments in the City of Cambridge, 2 parts, Royal Commission on Historical Monuments, London, 1959.

Ives, E. W., 'The genesis of the Statute of Uses', *English historical review* 82 (1967), pp. 673–97.

Jackson, S. W., 'Unusual mental states in medieval Europe: 1. Medical syndromes of mental disorder: 400–1100', *Journal of the history of medicine* 27 (1972), pp. 262–97.

Jacob, E. F., 'Petitions for benefices from English universities during the Great Schism', *Transactions of the Royal Historical Society* 27 (1945), pp. 41–59.
   'English university clerks in the later Middle Ages: the problem of maintenance', *Bulletin of the John Rylands Library* 29 (1945–6), pp. 304–25.
   'On the promotion of English university clerks during the later Middle Ages', *Journal of ecclesiastical history* 1 (1950), pp. 172–86.
   'Founders and foundations in the later Middle Ages', *Bulletin of the Institute of Historical Research* 35 (1962), pp. 29–46.
   'Thomas Brouns, bishop of Norwich, 1436–45', in *Essays in British history presented to Sir Keith Feiling*, ed. H. R. Trevor-Roper, London 1964, pp. 61–83.

James, M. R., *A descriptive catalogue of the manuscripts of the library of*, [*various colleges of the university of Cambridge*], 22 vols., Cambridge, 1895–1925.

Jamison, C., *The history of the royal hospital of St. Katharine by the Tower of London*, London, 1952.

Jarrett, B., *Social theories of the Middle Ages*, London, 1926, repr., 1968.

Jenkinson, H., 'A money-lender's bonds of the twelfth century', in *Essays in history presented to Reginald L. Poole*, ed. H. W. C. Davis, Oxford, 1927, pp. 190–210.

Jennings, J. M., 'The distribution of landed wealth in the wills of London merchants, 1400–1450', *Mediaeval studies* 39 (1977), pp. 261–80.

Jetter, D., *Geschichte des Hospitals*, Wiesbaden, 1966.

Bibliography

'Hospitäler in London. Zur Typologie wohltätiger Einrichtungen im Span-
nungsfeld politischer Kräfte'. *Sudhoffs Archiv* 62 (1978), pp. 250–81.

'Klosterhospitäler, St. Gallen, Cluny, Escorial', *Sudhoffs Archiv* 62 (1978), pp.
313–38.

Johnson, P. D., *Prayer, patronage and power. The abbey of la Trinité, Vendôme,
1032–1187*, New York, 1981.

Johnstone, H., 'Poor relief in the royal households of thirteenth century
England', *Speculum* 4 (1929), pp. 149–67.

Jolliffe, P. S., *A check-list of Middle English prose writings of spiritual guidance*,
Pontifical Institute of Mediaeval Studies. Subsidia medieaevalia 2, Toronto,
1974.

Jones, C., *Charity and 'bienfaisance'. The treatment of the poor in the Montpellier region
1740–1815*, Cambridge, 1982.

'The Hôtel-dieu of Beaune', *History today* 32 (1982), pp. 42–4.

'Hospitals in seventeenth-century France', *Seventeenth-Century French Studies*
(1985), pp. 139–52.

Jones, C. H., 'The chapel of St. Mary Magdalene at Stourbridge, Cambridge',
Cambridge Antiquarian Society. Proceedings and communications 28 (1925–6), pp.
126–50.

Jones, G. S., *Outcast London: a study in the relationship between classes in Victorian
society*, Oxford, 1971.

Jordan, W. K., *Philanthropy in England, 1480–1660*, London, 1959.

The charities of London, 1480–1660, London, 1960.

The charities of rural England, 1480–1660, London, 1961.

Joris, A., 'La notion de *ville*', *Les catégories en histoire*, Brussels, 1969, pp. 87–101.

Kealey, E. J., 'Anglo-Norman policy and public welfare', *Albion* 10 (1978), pp.
341–51.

Medieval medicus: a social history of Anglo-norman medicine, Baltimore, Md,
1981.

Kedar, B. Z., *Merchants in crisis. Genoese and Venetian men of affairs and the
fourteenth-century depression*, New Haven, Conn., 1976.

Keene, D. J., 'Suburban growth', in *The plans and topography of medieval towns*,
ed. M. W. Barley, Council for British archaeological research report 14,
London, 1976, pp. 71–82.

'Medieval Winchester: its spatial organisation', in *Space, hierarchy and society*,
British archaeological reports. International series 59, Oxford, 1979, pp.
149–59.

Kenyon, N., 'Labour conditions in Essex in the reign of Richard II', *Economic
history review* 4 (1934), pp. 429–51.

Kermode, J. I., 'Urban decline? The flight from office in late medieval York',
Economic history review second ser. 35 (1982), pp. 179–98.

Kershaw, I., *Bolton priory. The economy of a northern monastery 1286–1325*, Oxford,
1973.

'The great famine and agrarian crisis in England 1315–1322', *Past and present*
59 (1973), pp. 3–50.

de Keyzer, W., 'La léproserie St.-Lazare de Mons et ses statuts de 1202', *Annales
de la société belge de l'histoire des hôpitaux* 12 (1974), pp. 3–18.

'Une léproserie en mutation. La bonne maison St. Ladre de Mons aux XIIIᵉ et XIVᵉ siècles', *Annales de la société belge de l'histoire des hôpitaux* 14 (1976), pp. 5–25.

Kibre, P., *The nations in medieval universities*, Cambridge, Mass., 1948.

Scholarly privileges in the Middle Ages, Medieval Academy of America publication 72, Cambridge, Mass., 1961.

'Arts and medicine in the universities of the later Middle Ages', *Les universités à la fin du moyen-âge*, ed. J. Paquet and J. Ijsewijn, Louvain, 1978, pp. 213–27.

King, E. J., *The rule, statutes and customs of the Hospitallers 1099–1310*, London, 1934.

Knoop, D. and G. P. Jones, *The mediaeval mason*, Manchester, third edn, 1967.

Knowles, D., *The religious orders in England*, 3 vols., Cambridge, 1948–59.

The monastic orders in England, Cambridge, 1940, second edn, 1963.

Bare ruined choirs: the dissolution of the English monasteries, Cambridge, 1975.

Knowles, D. and R. N. Hadcock, *Medieval religious houses: England and Wales*, London, edn of 1971.

Kosminsky, E. A., *Studies in the agrarian history of England in the thirteenth century*, trans. R. Kisch, Oxford, 1956.

Krause, J., 'The medieval household: large or small?', *Economic history review* second ser. 9 (1956–7), pp. 420–32.

Kreider, A., *English chantries: the road to dissolution*, Cambridge, Mass., 1979.

Kuttner, S. and E. Rathbone, 'Anglo-norman canonists of the twelfth century: an introductory study', *Traditio* 7 (1949–51), pp. 279–358.

La Coste-Messelière, R. de and G. Jugnot, 'L'acceuil des pèlerins à Toulouse', *Cahiers de Fanjeaux* 15 (1980), pp. 117–35.

Lambert, M. D., *Franciscan poverty: the doctrine of the absolute poverty of Christ and the apostles in the Franciscan order, 1210–1323*, London, 1961.

de La Roncière, C.-M., 'Pauvres et pauvreté à Florence au XIVᵉ siècle', *Etudes sur l'histoire de la pauvreté* II, ed. M. Mollat, Paris, 1974, pp. 661–745.

'La place des confréries dans l'encadrement religieux du contado florentin: l'exemple de la Val d'Elsa', *Mélanges de l'école française de Rome. Séries moyen âge – temps modernes* 85 (1973), pp. 31–77.

Lavoie, R., 'Endettement et pauvreté en Provence d'après les listes de la justice comtale XIVᵉ–XVᵉ siècles', *Provence historique* 23 (1973), pp. 201–16.

Le Bras, G., 'Les confréries chrétiennes: problèmes et propositions', *Revue historique du droit français et étranger* fourth ser. 19–20 (1940–1), pp. 310–63.

Etudes de sociologie religieuse, 2 vols., Paris, 1955–6.

Leclère, F., 'Recherches sur la charité des bourgeois envers les pauvres au XIVᵉ siècle à Douai', *Revue du Nord* 48 (1966), pp. 139–54.

Lee, G. E., 'The leper hospitals of the Upper Shannon Area', *Journal of the old Althone society* I (1974–5), pp. 222–9.

Leff, G., *Heresy in the Middle Ages. The relation of heterodoxy to dissent c. 1250–c. 1450*, 2 vols., Manchester, 1967.

Paris and Oxford universities in the thirteenth and fourteenth centuries. An institutional and intellectual history, New York and London, 1968.

Le Goff, J., *Marchands et banquiers du moyen-âge*, Paris, 1956.

'Apostolat mendiant et fait urbain dans la France médiévale: l'implantation des ordres mendiants', *Annales* 23 (1968), pp. 335–52.

'Ordres mendiants et urbanisation dans la France médiévale', *Annales* 25 (1970), pp. 924–46.

'Le vocabulaire des catégories sociales chez St. François d'Assise et ses biographes du XIIIe siècle', *Ordres et classes. Colloque d'histoire sociale de St. Cloud, 24–25 Mai 1967*, Congrès et colloques 12, Paris, 1973, pp. 93–123.

Pour un autre moyen âge. Temps, travail et culture en Occident, Paris, 1977.

'Les marginaux dans l'occident médiéval', in *Les marginaux et les exclus dans l'histoire*, Cahiers Jussieu 5, Paris, 1979, pp. 19–28.

'Les trois fonctions indo-européennes, l'histoire er l'Europe féodale', *Annales* 6 (1979), pp. 1187–1215.

La naissance du purgatoire, Paris, 1981.

Le Grand, L., 'La prière des malades dans les hôpitaux de l'ordre de St.-Jean de Jérusalem', *Bibliothèque de l'Ecole des Chartes* 57 (1896), pp. 325–38.

'Comment composer l'histoire d'un établissement hospitalier. Sources et méthode', *Revue d'histoire de l'église de France* 16 (1930), pp. 161–239.

Leistikow, D. *Ten centuries of European hospital architecture*, Ingelheim, 1967.

Le Jan-Hennebicque, R., '"Pauperes" et "paupertas" dans l'occident carolingien aux IXe et Xe siècles', *Revue du Nord* 50 (1968), pp. 169–87.

Lennard, R. V., *Rural England, 1086–1135: a study of social and agrarian conditions*, Oxford, 1959.

Leuridan, T., *La table des pauvres à Roubaix*, n.p., n.d.

Lévi-Strauss, C., 'The principle of reciprocity', in *Sociological theory: a book of readings*, ed. L. A. Coser and B. Rosenberg, New York, 1957, pp. 84–94.

The elementary structure of kinship, trans. J. H. Bell and J. R. von Sturmer, ed. R. Needham, London, 1969.

Lewis, O., *The children of Sanchez*, Harmondsworth, 1961.

Lewis, W. A., 'Economic development with unlimited supplies of labour', *The Manchester school of economic and social studies* 22 (1954), pp. 139–91.

Libois, A., 'La confrérie de St. Eloy de Bruxelles des origines à 1477', *Annales de la société belge de l'histoire des hôpitaux* 5 (1967), pp. 47–75; 6 (1968), pp. 29–77; 7 (1969), pp. 85–112.

Lis, C. and H. Soly, *Poverty and capitalism in pre-industrial Europe*, trans. J. Coonan, Hassocks, 1979.

Little, A. G., 'The friars v. the University of Cambridge', *English historical review* 50 (1935), pp. 686–96.

'The friars and the foundation of the faculty of theology in the University of Cambridge', in *Franciscan papers, lists and documents*, Manchester, 1943, pp. 122–43.

'Personal tithes', *English historical review* 60 (1945), pp. 67–88.

'Corrodies at the Carmelite friary of Lynn', ed. E. Stone, *Journal of ecclesiastical history* 9 (1958), pp. 8–29.

Little, L. K., 'Pride goes before avarice: social change and the vices in Latin Christendom', *American historical review* 76 (1971), pp. 16–59.

'Evangelical poverty, the new money and violence', in *Actes du symposium 'Poverty in the Middle Ages'*, ed. D. Flood, Franziskanische Forschungen 27, Paderborn, 1975, pp. 11–26.

Bibliography

Religious poverty and the profit economy in medieval Europe, London, 1978.

Lloyd, A. H., *The early history of Christ's college, Cambridge, derived from contemporary documents*, Cambridge, 1934.

'Notes on Cambridge clerks petitioning for benefices, 1370–1399', *Bulletin of the Institute of Historical Research* 20 (1943–5), pp. 75–96, 192–211.

Lobel, M. D. ed., [*The atlas of*] *historic towns*, 2 vols., London, 1969–75.

Logan, F. D., *Excommunication and the secular arm in medieval England. A study in legal procedure from the thirteenth to the sixteenth century*, Pontifical institute of mediaeval studies. Studies and texts 15, Toronto, 1968.

Longère, J., 'Pauvreté et richesse chez quelques prédicateurs durant la seconde moitié du XIIe siècle', in *Etudes sur l'histoire de la pauvreté* 1, ed. M. Mollat, Paris, 1974, pp. 255–73.

Oeuvres oratoires des maîtres parisiens au XIIe siècle, 2 vols., Paris, 1975.

La prédication médiévale, Paris, 1983.

Loriaud, B., 'Les pauvres malades et le personnel de l'aumônerie Auffredi à la Rochelle vers 1470', *Revue de la société d'archéologie et d'histoire de la Charente Maritime* 25 (1973–4), pp. 137–42.

Lovatt, R., 'The early archives of Peterhouse', *Peterhouse record* (1975–6), pp. 26–38.

Luttrell, A. T., 'Los hospitalarios en Aragón y la peste negra', *Anuario de estudios medievales* 3 (1966), pp. 499–514.

Lytle, G. F., 'Patronage patterns and Oxford colleges 1300–1530', *The university in society* 1, ed. L. Stone, Princeton, N. J., 1975, pp. 111–49.

'The social origins of Oxford students in the late Middle Ages: New College, c. 1380–c. 1510', in *Les universités à la fin du moyen-âge*, ed. J. Paquet and J. Ijsewijn, Mediaevalia Lovaniensia 1 Studia 6, Louvain, 1978, pp. 426–54.

'A university mentality in the later Middle Ages: the pragmatism, humanism and orthodoxy of New College, Oxford', in *Genèse et débuts du Grand Schisme d'Occident*, Colloques internationaux du CNRS, Paris, 1980, pp. 201–30.

McCall, A., *The medieval underworld*, London, 1979.

McClure, P., 'Patterns of migration in the late Middle Ages: the evidence of English place-name surnames', *Economic history review* second ser. 32 (1979), pp. 167–82.

McDonnell, E. W., *Beguines and beghards in medieval culture*, New Brunswick, N. J., 1954.

McFarlane, K..B., *The nobility of later medieval England*, Oxford, 1973.

McInnes, E. M., *St. Thomas' hospital*, London, 1963.

McIntosh, M. K., *Autonomy and community: the royal manor of Havering 1200–1500*, Cambridge, 1986.

Mackerell, B., *The history and antiquities of the flourishing corporation of King's Lynn in the county of Norfolk*, London, 1738.

MacKinnon, H., 'William de Montibus: a medieval teacher', in *Essays in medieval history presented to Bertie Wilkinson*, ed. T. A. Sandquist and M. R. Powicke, Toronto, 1969, pp. 32–45.

McNeill, J. T. and H. M. Gamer, *Medieval handbooks of penance*, New York, 1938.

Bibliography

Madan, F. and W. M. Palmer, *Notes on Bodleian Mss. relating to Cambridge. I – Town and university, II – County*, Cambridge Antiquarian Society publications 52, Cambridge, 1931.

van der Made, R., *Le Grand Hôpital de Huy. Organisation et fonctionnement, 1263–1795*, Anciens pays et assemblées d'états 20, Louvain, 1960.

Maitland, F. W., *Township and borough*, Cambridge, 1898.

Majarelli, S. and U. Nicolini, *Il monte dei poveri di Perugia: periodo delle origini (1462–74)*, Perugia, 1962.

Mann, J., *Chaucer and medieval estates satire*, Cambridge, 1973.

Manning, B., *The people's faith in the time of Wyclif*, Cambridge, 1919.

Manselli, R., 'Evangelismo e povertà', in *Povertà e ricchezza nella spiritualità dei secoli XI e XII*, Convegni del centro di studi sulla spiritualità medievale 8, Todi, 1969, pp. 11–41.

'Da Dante à Coluccio Salutati. Discussions sur la pauvreté à Florence au XIVe siècle', *Etudes sur l'histoire de la pauvreté* II, ed. M. Mollat, Paris, 1974, pp. 637–59.

Manteuffel, T., *Naissance d'une hérésie: les adeptes de la pauvreté volontaire au moyen-âge*, trans. A. Posner, Paris, 1970.

Marchal, J., 'La lèpre et les maladreries ardennaises', *Revue historique ardennais* 8 (1973), pp. 49–79.

Maréchal, G., *De sociale en politieke gebundenheid van het Brugse hospitalwezen in de Middeleeuwen*, Anciens pays et assemblés d'etats 73, Heule, 1978.

Marinelli, O., *La compagnia di San Tommaso d'Aquino di Perugia*, Temi e testi 8, Rome, 1960.

Martimort, A. G., *L'église en prière. Introduction à la liturgie*, Tournai, third edn, 1965.

Martínez de San Pedro, R., *Historia de los hospitales en Alicante*, Alicante, 1974.

Martz, L. *Poverty and welfare in Habsburg Spain. The example of Toledo*, Cambridge, 1983.

Marx, W. J., *The development of charity in medieval Louvain*, New York, 1936.

Masters, R., *The history of the college of Corpus Christi, Cambridge*, Cambridge, 1753, repr. London, 1898.

Mate, M., 'High prices in early fourteenth-century England: causes and consequences', *Economic history review* second ser. 28 (1975), pp. 1–16.

'The farming out of manors: a new look at the evidence from Canterbury cathedral priory', *Journal of medieval history* 9 (1983), pp. 331–43.

'Agrarian economy after the Black Death: the manors of Canterbury cathedral priory, 1348–91', *Economic history review* second series 37 (1984), pp. 341–54.

Mathias, P., 'Adam's burden: diagnoses of poverty in post-medieval Europe and the Third World now', *Tijdschrift voor geschiedenis* 89 (1976), pp. 149–60.

Matza, D., 'The disreputable poor', in *Class, status and power: social status in comparative perspective*, ed. R. Bendix and S. M. Lipset, London, 1967, pp. 289–302.

Mauss, M., *The gift: forms and functions of exchange in archaic societies*, trans. I. Cunnison, London, 1966.

May, A. N., 'An index of thirteenth century impoverishment? Manor court fines', *Economic history review* second ser. 26 (1973), pp. 389–402.

Bibliography

Mayhew, N. J., 'Numismatic evidence and falling prices in the fourteenth century', *Economic history review* second ser. 27 (1974), pp. 1–15.

Meade, D. M., 'The hospital of St. Giles at Kepier near Durham, 1112–1545' *Transactions of the Architectural and Archaeological Society of Durham and Northumberland* new ser. 1 (1968), pp. 45–58

Meekings, C. A. F., and R. F. Hunnisett (ed.) 'The early years of Netley abbey', *Journal of ecclesiastical history* 30 (1979), pp. 1–37.

Meersseman, G. G. with G. P. Pacini, *Ordo confraternitatis: confraternite e pietà dei laici nel medioevo*, 3 vols., Italia sacra 24–26, Rome, 1977.

Meiss, M., *Painting in Florence and Siena after the Black Death*, Princeton, N.J., 1951.

Mercier, C., *Leper houses and medieval hospitals*, London, 1915.

Michaud-Quantin, P., *Sommes de casuistique et manuels de confession au moyen-âge (XII–XVI siècles)*, Paris, 1962.

Etudes sur le vocabulaire philosophique du moyen-âge, Rome, 1970.

Universitas: expressions du mouvement communautaire dans le moyen âge latin, Paris, 1970

'Le vocabulaire des catégories sociales chez les canonistes et les moralistes du XIIIe siècle', *Ordres et classes. Colloque d'histoire sociale de St. Cloud, 24–25 Mai 1967*, Congrès et colloques 12, Paris, 1973, pp. 73–86.

Midmer, R., *English medieval monasteries, 1066–1540: a summary*, Oxford, 1980.

Miller, E., 'Baldwin Blancgernun and his family: early benefactors of the hospital of St. John the Evangelist', *Eagle* 53 (1948), pp. 73–9.

The abbey and bishopric of Ely, Cambridge studies in medieval life and thought new ser. 1, Cambridge, 1951.

Portrait of a college. A history of the college of St. John the Evangelist, Cambridge, Cambridge, 1961.

'The English economy in the thirteenth century. Implications of recent research', *Past and present*, second ser. 28 (1964), pp. 21–40.

'England in the twelfth and thirteenth centuries: an economic contrast?', *Economic history review* second ser. 24 (1971), pp. 1–14.

Miller, E. and J. Hatcher, *Medieval England. Rural society and economic change 1086–1348*, London, 1978.

Miller, T. S., 'The knights of St. John and the hospitals of the Latin West', *Speculum* 53 (1978), pp. 709–33.

Miskimin, H. A., 'Monetary movements and market structure: forces for contraction in fourteenth- and fifteenth-century England', *Journal of economic history* 24 (1964), pp. 470–90.

'Legacies of London', in *The medieval city*, ed. H. A. Miskimin, D. Herlihy and A. L. Udovitch, New Haven, Conn., 1977, pp. 209–27.

Moisa, M., 'Fourteenth-century preachers' views of the poor: class or status group?', in *Culture, ideology and politics. Essays for E. Hobsbawm*, ed. R. Samuel and G. S. Jones, London, 1983, pp. 160–75.

Mollat, M., 'La notion de la pauvreté au moyen-age. Position de problèmes', *Revue d'histoire de l'église de France* 52 (1966), pp. 5–23.

'Le problème de la pauvreté au XIIIe siècle', *Cahiers de Fanjeaux* 2 (1967), pp. 23–47.

Bibliography

'Pauvres et assistés au moyen-âge', in *A pobreza e a assistência aos pobres na Península Ibérica durante a Idade Média*, I, Lisbon, 1973, pp. 11–27.

'En guise de préface: les problèmes de la pauvreté', in *Etudes sur l'histoire de la pauvreté* I, ed. M. Mollat, Paris, 1974, pp. 11–30.

'Hospitalité et assistance au début du XIIIe siècle', *Actes du symposium 'Poverty in the Middle Ages'*, ed. D. Flood, Franziskanische Forschungen 27, Paderborn, 1975, pp. 37–51.

Mollat, M. and P. Wolff, *Ongles bleus, Jacques et Ciompi. Les révolutions populaires en Europe aux XIVe et XVe siècles*, Paris, 1970.

Monter, W., *Ritual, myth and magic in early modern Europe*, Brighton, 1983.

Moore, R. I., 'Heresy as a disease', in *The concept of heresy*, eds. W. Lourdaux and D. Verhelst, Mediaevalia Lovaniensia I studia 4, Louvain, 1976, pp. 1–11.

Moorman, J. R. H., *Church life in England in the thirteenth century*, Cambridge, 1945.

The Grey Friars in Cambridge, 1225–1538, Cambridge, 1952.

A history of the Franciscan order from its origins to the year 1517, Oxford, 1968.

Moran, J. H., *Education and learning in the city of York, 1300–1560*, Borthwick papers 55, York, 1979.

Morey, A., *Bartholomew of Exeter, bishop and canonist. A study in the twelfth century*, Cambridge, 1937.

Mornet, E., '*Pauperes scolares*. Essai sur la condition matérielle des étudiants scandinaves dans les universités aux XIVe et XVe siècles', *Le moyen-âge* 84 (1978), pp. 53–102.

Morris, C., 'The plague in Britain', *Historical journal* 14 (1971), pp. 205–15.

Morselli, P., 'Some unknown works of Giuliano da Sangallo and Tommaso di Piero Trombetto for the hospital of the Dolce in Prato', *Art bulletin* 63 (1981), pp. 127–30.

Mortimer, R., 'The prior of Butley and the lepers of West Somerton', *Bulletin of the Institute of Historical Research* 53 (1980), pp. 99–103.

Mortimer, R. C., *The origins of private penance in the western church*, Oxford, 1939.

Mosher, J. A., *The exemplum in the early religious and didactic literature of England*, New York, 1911.

Mueller, R. C., 'The procurators of San Marco in the thirteenth and fourteenth centuries: a study of the office as a financial and trust institution', *Studi veneziani* 13 (1971), pp. 105–220.

'Charitable institutions, the Jewish community and Venetian society', *Studi veneziani* 14 (1972), pp. 37–82.

Mullinger, J. B., *The University of Cambridge to 1535*, Cambridge, 1873.

Mundy, J. H., 'Hospitals and leprosaries in twelfth and early-thirteenth century Toulouse', in *Essays in medieval life and thought presented in honor of A. P. Evans*, New York, 1955, pp. 181–205.

'Charity and social work in Toulouse, 1100–1250', *Traditio* 22 (1966), pp. 203–87.

Murray, A., 'Piety and impiety in thirteenth century Italy', *Studies in Church history* 8 (1972), pp. 83–106.

'Religion among the poor in thirteenth-century France: the testimony of Humbert de Romans', *Traditio* 30 (1974), pp. 285–324.

Reason and society in the Middle Ages, Oxford, 1978.

Najemy, J. M., 'Guild republicanism in Trecento Florence: the success and ultimate failure of corporate politics', *American historical review* 84 (1979), pp. 53–71.

Nasalli Rocca, E., *Il diritto ospedaliero nei suoi lineamenti storici*, Milano, 1956.

Nelson, B., *The idea of usury: from tribal brotherhood to universal otherhood*, Chicago and London, second edn, 1969.

Nelson, P., 'Some British medieval seal-matrices', *Archaeological journal* 93 (1936), pp. 13–44.

Neveux, H., 'La mortalité des pauvres à Cambrai (1377–1473)', *Annales de démographie historique* (1968), pp. 73–97.

'Un établissement d'assistance en milieu rural au XIVe siècle: l'Hôtel-dieu de Villers-Bocage', *Annales de Normandie* 27 (1977), pp. 3–17.

Newman, N. H. A., 'The foundation of the hospital of St. John the Evangelist', *Eagle* 48 (1934), pp. 20–33.

Newton, P. A., 'William Brown's hospital at Stamford. A note on its early history and the date of the buildings', *Antiquaries journal* 46 (1966), pp. 283–6.

Nicholas, D. M., 'Crime and punishment in fourteenth century Ghent', *Revue belge de philologie et d'histoire* 48 (1979), pp. 289–334, 1141–76.

Niederer, F. J., 'Early medieval charity', *Church history* 21 (1952), pp. 285–95.

Noonan, J. T. Jr, *The scholastic analysis of usury*, Cambridge, Mass., 1957.

Ntedika, J., *L'évocation de l'au-delà dans la prière pour les morts. Etudes de patristique et de liturgie latines*, Paris, 1971.

Oexle, O. G., 'Die mittelalterlichen Gilden: ihre Selbstdeutung und ihr Beitrag zur Formung sozialer Strukturen', in *Soziale Ordnungen im Selbstverständnis des Mittelalters*, ed. A. Zimmermann and G. Vuillemin-Diem, Miscellanea medievalia 12(1), Berlin, 1979, pp. 203–26.

'Die Gegenwart der Toten', in *Death in the Middle Ages*, ed. H. Braet and W. Verbeke, Mediaevalia Lovaniensia I studia 9, Louvain, 1983, pp. 19–77.

Ombres, R., 'The doctrine of purgatory according to St. Thomas Aquinas', *Downside review* 99 (1981), pp. 279–87.

Origo, I., *The merchant of Prato. Francesco di Marco Datini (1335–1410)*, London, 1957.

Orme, N., *English schools in the Middle Ages*, London, 1973.

'The Kalendar brethren of the city of Exeter', *Reports and transactions of the Devonshire Association* 109 (1977), pp. 153–69.

'The guild of Kalendars, Bristol', *Transactions of the Bristol and Gloucestershire Archaeological Society* 96 (1978), pp. 32–52.

Overfield, J. H., 'Nobles and paupers at German universities to 1600', *Societas* 4 (1974), pp. 175–210.

van Overstraeten, D., 'Les débuts de l'hôpital de Boussu (XIIe–XIIIe siècles)', *Annales de la société belge de l'histoire des hôpitaux* 6 (1968), pp. 3–28.

Owen, D. M., 'Ely diocesan records', *Studies in Church history* I (1964), pp. 176–83.

Church and society in medieval Lincolnshire, History of Lincolnshire 5, Lincoln, 1971.

Bibliography

Ely records: a handlist of the records of the bishop and archdeacon of Ely, Cambridge, 1971.

Owst, G. R., *Preaching in medieval England*, Cambridge, 1926.

The Oxford dictionary of saints, ed. D. H. Farmer, Oxford, 1978.

Page, F. M., 'The customary poor-law of three Cambridgeshire manors', *Cambridge historical journal* 3 (1929–31), pp. 125–33.

The estates of Crowland abbey, Cambridge, 1934.

Palmer, W. M., 'Records of the villein insurrection in Cambridgeshire', *East anglian* 6 (1896), pp. 81–84, 97–102, 135–139, 167–72, 209–212, 234–237.

'Village gilds of Cambridgeshire', *Transactions of the Cambridgeshire and Huntingdonshire archaeological society* 1 (1904), pp. 330–402.

'Cambridge castle building accounts', *Cambridge Antiquarian Society. Proceedings and communications* 26 (1923–4), pp. 66–89.

John Layer (1586–1640) of Shepreth, Cambridgeshire, A seventeenth century local historian, Cambridge Antiquarian society publications 53, Cambridge, 1935.

'The hospitals of St. John the Baptist and St. Mary Magdalene at Ely', *Cambridge Antiquarian Society. Proceedings and Communications* 36 (1935), pp. 76–108.

A history of the parish of Borough Green, Cambridgshire, Cambridge Antiquarian Society publications 54, Cambridge, 1939.

Pantin, W. A., 'College muniments: a preliminary note', *Oxoniensia* 1 (1936), pp. 140–3.

'The halls and schools of medieval Oxford: an attempt at reconstruction', in *Oxford studies presented to Daniel Callus*, Oxford, 1964, pp. 31–100.

'Instructions for a devout literate layman', in *Medieval learning and literature. Essays presented to Richard William Hunt*, ed. J. J. G. Alexander and M. T. Gibson, Oxford, 1976, pp. 398–422.

Paquet, J., 'Recherches sur l'universitaire "pauvre" au moyen âge', *Revue belge de philologie et d'histoire* 56 (1978), pp. 301–58.

'L'universitaire "pauvre" au moyen âge: problèmes, documentation, question de méthode', in *Les universités à la fin du moyen-âge*, ed. J. Paquet and J. Ijsewijn, Louvain, 1978, pp. 339–425.

'Coût des études, pauvreté et labeur: fonctions et métiers d'étudiants au moyen-âge', *History of universities* 2 (1982), pp. 15–52.

Patlagean, E., *Pauvreté économique et pauvreté sociale à Byzance, 4e–7e siècles*, Paris, 1977.

Patzelt, E., 'Pauvreté et maladies', in *Povertà e ricchezza nella spiritualità dei secoli XIe e XII*, Convegni del centro di studi sulla spiritualità medioevale 8, Todi, 1969, pp. 163–87.

Paul, J., 'Les franciscains et la pauvreté aux xiiie et xive siècles', *Revue d'histoire de l'église de France* 52 (1966), pp. 33–7.

'Narbonne et la querelle de la pauvreté', *Narbonne. Achéologie et histoire* 1, Narbonne, 1973, pp. 157–62.

Pearce, E. C., 'College accounts of John Botwright, master of Corpus Christi, 1443–74', *Cambridge Antiquarian Society. Proceedings and communications* 22 (1917–20), pp. 76–90.

Peek, H. and C. Hall, *The archives of the University of Cambridge: an historical introduction*, Cambridge, 1962.

Pegues, F., 'Royal support of students in the thirteenth century', *Speculum* 31 (1956), pp. 454–62.

  'Ecclesiastical provisions for the support of students in the thirteenth century', *Church history* 26 (1957), pp. 307–18.

  'Philanthropy and the universities in France and England', in *The economic and material framework of the medieval university*, ed. A. L. Gabriel, Texts and studies in the history of mediaeval education xv, Notre Dame, Ind., 1977, pp. 69–80.

Pelling, M., 'Healing the sick poor: social policy and disability in Norwich 1550–1640', *Medical history* 29 (1985), pp. 115–37.

Peresblanques, J., 'Histoire de l'hôpital de Dax: le fondateur de l'hôpital du Saint-Esprit', *Bulletin de la société de Borda* 104 (1979), p. 264.

Perroy, E., 'A l'origine d'une économie contractée: les crises du XIVe siècle', *Annales* 4 (1949), pp. 167–82.

Petouraud, C., 'Les léproseries lyonnaises au moyen-âge et pendant la Renaissance', *Cahiers d'histoire* 7 (1962), 425–64.

Pevsner, N., *The buildings of England. Cambridgeshire*, Harmondsworth, Second edn, 1970.

Pfander, H. G., *The popular sermon of the medieval friar in England*, New York, 1937.

Phelps Brown, E. H. and S. V. Hopkins, 'Seven centuries of the prices of consumables compared with builders' wage-rates', *Economica* 23 (1956), pp. 296–314.

Phythian-Adams, C., 'Ceremony and the citizen: the communal year at Coventry 1450–1550' in *Crisis and order in English towns 1500–1700. Essays in urban history*, ed. P. Clark and P. Slack, London, 1972. pp. 57–85.

  'Urban decay in later medieval England', *Towns in societies. Essays in economic history and historical sociology*, ed. P. Abrams and E. A. Wrigley, Cambridge, 1978, pp. 159–85.

  Desolation of a city: Coventry and the urban crisis of the late Middle Ages, Cambridge, 1979.

Pinker, R., *The idea of welfare*, London, 1979.

Pitt-Rivers, J., 'The kith and the kin', in *The character of kinship*, ed. J. Goody, Cambridge, 1973, pp. 89–106.

Pollard, A. J., 'Estate management in the later Middle Ages: the Talbots and Whitchurch, 1383–1525', *Economic history review* second ser. 25 (1972), pp. 553–66.

Pollard, G., 'Medieval loan chests at Cambridge', *Bulletin of the Institute of Historical Research* 17 (1939–40), pp. 113–29.

Pollock, F. and F. W. Maitland, *A history of English law before the time of Edward I*, 2 vols., Cambridge, Second edn, 1898.

Poos, L. R., 'The social context of the Statute of Labourers enforcement', *Law and history review* 1 (1983), pp. 27–72.

Poschmann, B., *Penance and the anointing of the sick*, trans. F. Courtney, Freiburg and London, 1964.

Postan, M. M., 'The fifteenth century', *Economic history review* 9 (1938–9), pp. 160–7.

Bibliography

'Some economic evidence of declining population in the later Middle Ages', *Economic history review* second ser. 2 (1949–50), pp. 221–46.

The famulus: the estate labourer in the twelfth and thirteenth centuries, Economic history review supplement 2, Cambridge, 1954.

'Investment in medieval agriculture', *Journal of economic history* 27 (1967), pp. 576–87.

Credit in medieval trade', in *Medieval trade and finance*, Cambridge, 1973, pp. 1–27 [first published in *Economic history review* 1 (1928), pp. 234–61].

The medieval economy and society, Harmondsworth, 1975.

Pound, J., *Poverty and vagrancy in Tudor England*, London, 1971.

Pourrière, J., *Les hôpitaux d'Aix-en-Provence au moyen-âge, XIIIe XIVe et XVe siècles*, Aix en Provence, 1969.

Poynter, J. R., *Society and pauperism. English ideas on poor relief, 1795–1834*, Toronto, 1969.

Prevenier, W., 'En marge de l'assistance aux pauvres: l'aumônerie des Comtes de Flandres et des Ducs de Bourgogne (13e-début 16e siècle)', in *Recht en instellingen in de oude Nederlanden tijdens de middeleeuwen en de nieuwe tijd. Liber amicorum Jan Buntinx*, Symbolae ser. A10, Louvain, 1981, pp. 97–120.

Probst, C., 'Das Hospitalwesen im hohen and späten Mittelalter und die geistliche und gesellschaftliche Stellung des Kranken', *Sudhoffs Archiv* 50 (1966), pp. 246–58.

Pugh, R. B., 'The Knights Hospitallers of England as undertakers', *Speculum* 56 (1981), pp. 566–74.

Pullan, B., 'Poverty, charity and the reason of state: some Venetian examples', *Bollettino dell'istituto di storia della società e dello stato* 2 (1960), pp. 17–60.

Rich and poor in Renaissance Venice. The social institutions of a catholic state, to 1620, Oxford, 1971.

'Catholics and the poor in Early Modern Europe', *Transactions of the Royal Historical Society* fifth ser. 25 (1976), pp. 15–34.

Putnam, B., *The enforcement of the Statute of Labourers during the first decade after the Black Death 1349–1359*, New York, 1908.

Early treatises on the practice of the Justices of the Peace in the fifteenth and sixteenth centuries, Oxford studies in social and legal history 7, Oxford, 1924.

Pycke, J., 'Documents relatifs à l'administration de l'hôpital capitulaire de Notre Dame de Tournai du XIIe au XVe siècle', *Annales de la société belge de l'histoire des hôpitaux* 8 (1970), pp. 3–54.

Raban, S., *The estates of Thorney and Crowland: a study in medieval monastic land tenure*, Cambridge, 1977.

Mortmain legislation and the English church 1279–1500, Cambridge studies in medieval life and thought third ser. 17, Cambridge, 1982.

Raftis, J. A., 'Geographical mobility in lay subsidy rolls', *Mediaeval studies* 38 (1976), pp. 385–403.

A small town in late medieval England: Godmanchester 1278–1400, Pontifical Institute of Mediaeval Studies. Studies and texts 53, Toronto, 1982.

Ramière de Fortanier, A., 'Hospitalié et charité à Fanjeaux et dans sa région: les confréries de Notre-Dame', *Cahiers de Fanjeaux* 13 (1978), pp. 147–67.

Rapp, F., 'L'église et les pauvres à la fin du moyen-âge: l'éxémple de Geiler de Kaiserberg', *Revue d'histoire de l'église de France* 52 (1966), pp. 39–46.

L'église et la vie religieuse en Occident à la fin du moyen-âge, Paris, 1971.

Rashdall, H. *The universities of Europe in the Middle Ages*, 3 vols., Oxford, 1895. new edn by F. M. Powicke and A. B. Emden, Oxford, 1936.

Ravensdale, J., *Liable to floods. Village landscape on the edge of the fens*, Cambridge, 1974.

Rawcliffe, C., 'Medicine and medical practice in later medieval London', *Guildhall studies in London history* 3 (1981), pp. 13–25.

Razi, Z., *Life, marriage and death in a medieval parish. Economy, society and demography in Halesowen, 1270–1400*, Cambridge, 1980.

'The struggle between the abbots of Halesowen and their tenants in the thirteenth and fourteenth centuries', in *Social relations and ideas. Essays in honour of R. H. Hilton*, ed. T. H. Aston, P. R. Coss, C. Dyer and J. Thirsk, Cambridge, 1983, pp. 151–67.

Reader, R., 'New evidence for the antiquity of leprosy in early Britain', *Journal of archaeological science* 1 (1974), pp. 205–7.

Reaney, P. H., ed., *The place-names of Cambridgeshire and the Isle of Ely*, English Place-name Society 19, Cambridge, 1943.

Reddaway, T. F., 'The London goldsmiths *circa* 1500', *Transactions of the Royal Historical Society* fifth ser. 12 (1962), pp. 49–62.

Redon, O., 'Un traité médical du XIIIe siècle', *Bollettino senese di storia patria* 88 (1981), pp. 304–8.

Reicke, S., *Das deutsche Spital und sein Recht im Mittelalter*, 2 vols., Stuttgart, 1932.

Rein, M., 'Problems in the definition and measurement of poverty', in *The concept of poverty*, ed. P. Townsend, London, 1970, pp. 46–63.

Reitzel, J. M., 'The medieval houses of *Bons-enfants*', *Viator* 11 (1980), pp. 179–207.

Remnant, G. L. with M. D. Anderson, *A catalogue of misericords in Great Britain*, Oxford, 1969.

Remy, P., 'La lèpre, thème littéraire au moyen-âge. Commentaire d'un passage du roman provençal de Jaufré', *Le moyen-âge* 42 (1946), pp. 195–242.

Reynolds, S., *An introduction to the history of English medieval towns*, Oxford, 1977.

Ricci, G., 'I primi statuti della compagnia bolognese dei poveri vergognosi', *L'archiginnasio* 74 (1979), pp. 131–59.

'La naissance du pauvre honteux: entre l'histoire des idées et l'histoire sociale', *Annales* 38 (1983), pp. 158–77.

Richard, J., 'Hospitals and hospital congregations in the Latin kingdom during the first period of the Frankish conquest', in *Outremer*, ed. B. Z. Kedar, H. E. Mayer and R. C. Smail, Jerusalem, 1982, pp. 89–100.

Richards, P., *The medieval leper and his northern heirs*, Cambridge, Mass., 1977.

Richardson, H. G., *The English Jewry under the Angevin kings*, London, 1960.

Rigg, A. G., 'The lament of the friars of the sack', *Speculum* 55 (1980), pp. 84–90.

Rigold, S. E., 'Two Kentish hospitals re-examined', *Archaeologia Cantiana* 79 (1964), pp. 31–69.

Bibliography

Riis, T., 'Poverty and urban development in early modern Europe (15th–18th centuries): a general view', in *Aspects of poverty in early modern Europe*, ed. T. Riis, Florence, 1981, pp. 1–28.

Riley-Smith, J., *The knights of St. John in Jerusalem and Cyprus, c. 1050–1310*, London, 1967.

Roberts, P. B. *Stephanus de lingua tonante. Studies in the sermons of Stephen Langton*, Pontifical Institute of Mediaeval Studies. Studies and texts 16, Toronto, 1968.

Roberts, S. F., 'Les consulats du Rouergue et l'assistance urbaine au XIIIe et au début du XIVe siècles', *Cahiers de Fanjeaux* 13 (1978), pp. 131–46.

Robertson D. W., Jr, 'Frequency of preaching in thirteenth-century England', *Speculum* 24 (1949), pp. 376–88.

Robinson, W. C., 'Money, population and economic change in late medieval Europe', *Economic history review* second ser. 12 (1959–60), pp. 63–76.

Rocher, D., 'Exclusion, auto-exclusion et réadmission du lépreux dans *Le Pauvre Henri*', in *Exclus et systèmes d'exclusion dans la littérature et la civilisation médiévales*, Aix-en-Provence, 1978, pp. 91–103.

Rogers, A., 'The use of deeds for medieval urban history', in *The medieval town in Britain*, ed. P. Riden, Cardiff papers in local history 1, Cardiff, 1980, pp. 1–14.

de Roover, R., *Money, banking and credit in medieval Bruges: bankers, Lombards and money changers*, Cambridge (Mass.), 1948.

'The concept of the just price: theory and economic policy', *Journal of economic history* 18 (1958), pp. 418–34.

La pensée économique des scolastiques. Doctrines et méthodes, Conference Albert-le-Grand 1970, Montreal, 1970.

Rose, R. K., 'Priests and patrons in the fourteenth century diocese of Carlisle', *Studies in Church history* 16 (1979), pp. 207–18.

Rosen, G., 'The hospital: historical sociology of a community institution', in *The hospital in modern society*, ed. E. Friedson, London, 1963, pp. 1–36.

'The mentally ill and the community in western and central Europe during the late Middle Ages', *Journal of the history of medicine* 19 (1964), pp. 377–88.

Madness in society: chapters in the historical sociology of mental illness, London, 1968.

Rosenthal, J., *The purchase of paradise: gift giving and the aristocracy, 1307–1485*, London, 1972.

Rosenwein, B. H. and L. K. Little, 'Social meaning in the monastic and mendicant spiritualities', *Past and present* 63 (1974), pp. 4–32.

Roth, C., *The Jews of medieval Oxford*, Oxford Historical Society new ser. 9, Oxford, 1951.

Rothkrug, L., 'Popular religion and holy shrines. Their influence on the origins of the German Reformation and their role in German cultural development', in *Religion and the people 800–1700*, ed. J. Obelkevich, Chapel Hill, N.C., 1979, pp. 20–86.

Rouse, R. H. and M. A. Rouse, *Preachers, florilegia and sermons: studies on the Manipulus florum of Thomas of Ireland*, Pontifical Institute of Mediaeval Studies. Studies and Texts 47, Toronto, 1979.

'*Statim invenire*: schools, preachers and new attitudes to the page', in *Renaissance and renewal in the twelfth century*, ed. R. Benson and G. Constable, Oxford, 1983, pp. 201–25.

Rowe, J., 'The medieval hospitals of Bury St. Edmunds', *Medical history* 2 (1958), pp. 253–63.

Rowland Burdon, E., 'St. Saviour's hospital, Bury St. Edmunds', *Proceedings of the Suffolk Institute of Archaeology and Natural History* 19 (1927), pp. 255–85.

Rowley, T., 'Medieval field systems', in *The English medieval countryside*, ed. L. Cantor, London and Canberra, 1982, pp. 25–55.

Rowntree, B. S., *Poverty: a study in town life*, London, 1910.

Rubin, S., *Medieval English medicine*, Newton Abbot, 1974.

Rubio Vella, A., *Pobreza, enfermedad e y assistencia hospitaliaria en la Valencia del siglo XIV*, Valencia, 1984.

Runciman, W. G., *Relative deprivation and social justice*, London, 1966.

Russell, J. C., 'Effects of pestilence and plague 1315–1385', *Comparative studies in society and history* 8 (1965–6), pp. 464–73.

Russell, P. M. G.., *A history of the Exeter hospitals 1170–1948*, Exeter, 1976.

Sahlins, M. D., 'On the sociology of primitive exchange', in *The relevance of models for social anthropology*, ed. M. Banton, London, 1965, pp. 139–236.

St-Denis, A. *L'Hôtel-dieu de Laon, 1150–1300*, Nancy, 1983.

St Jacques, R., 'Les mendicants dans l'épopée anglaise au XIVe siècle, in *Aspects de la marginalité au moyen-âge*, Montreal, 1975, pp. 24–33.

Saltmarsh, J., 'Plague and economic decline in England in the later Middle Ages', *Cambridge historical journal* 7 (1941–3), pp. 23–41.

Sandars, S., *Historical and architectural notes on Great St. Mary's church, Cambridge*, Cambridge Antiquarian society publications 10, Cambridge, 1869.

Saunier, A., 'Les conaissances médicales d'un barbier et chirurgien français en 1455', *Annales de l'université d'Abidjan. Histoire* 8 (1980), pp. 27–46.

Saxer, V., *Le culte de Marie Madeleine en Occident des origines à la fin du moyen-âge*, 2 vols., Auxerre and Paris, 1959.

Sayle, C. E., 'The chapel of the hospital of St. John, Duxford (Whittlesford bridge)', *Cambridge Antiquarian Society. Proceedings and communications* 10 (1898–1903), pp. 375–83.

Scarisbrick, J. J., *The Reformation and the English people*, Oxford, 1984.

Schmitt, J.-C., 'Recueils franciscains d'*exempla* et perfectionnement des techniques intellectuelles du XIIIe au XVe siècle', *Bibliothèque de l'Ecole des Chartes* 135 (1977), pp. 5–22.

Mort d'une hérésie, Civilisations et sociétés 56, Paris, 1978.

Schofield, R. S., 'The geographic distribution of wealth in England, 1334–1649', *Economic history review*, second ser. 18 (1965), pp. 483–510.

Schreiber, G., *Gemeinschaft des Mittelalters: Recht und Verfassung, Kult und Frömmigkeit*, Regensburg and Munster, 1948.

Schreiner, J., 'Wages and prices in England in the later Middle Ages', *Scandinavian economic history review* 2 (1954), pp. 61–73.

Schwartz, B., 'The social psychology of the gift', *American journal of sociology* 73 (1967–8), pp. 1–11.

Scribner, R. W., *For the sake of simple folk. Popular propaganda for the German*

Reformation, Cambridge studies in oral and literate culture 2, Cambridge, 1981.

Searle, W. G., [*The history of the*] *Queens' college*, [*Cambridge (1446–1662)*], Cambridge Antiquarian Society 9, 13, 2 vols., Cambridge, 1867–1871.

Sen, A. K., *On economic inequality*, Oxford, 1973.

Employment, technology and development, Oxford, 1975.

Poverty and famines. An essay on entitlement and deprivation, Oxford, 1981.

Severino Polica, G., 'Storia della povertà e storia dei poveri. A proposito di una iniziativa di Michel Mollat', *Studi medievali* 17 (1976), pp. 363–91.

Shahar, S., 'Des lépreux pas comme les autres. L'Ordre de Saint-Lazare dans le royaume latin de Jérusalem', *Revue historique* 267 (1982), pp. 19–41.

Sharp, B., *In contempt of all authority. Rural artisans and riot in the West of England, 1596–1660*, Berkeley, Los Angeles and London, 1980.

Sheehan, M. M., *The will in medieval England*, Pontifical Institute of Mediaeval Studies. Studies and Texts 6, Toronto, 1963.

'The formation and stability of marriage in fourteenth-century England: evidence of an Ely register', *Mediaeval studies* 33 (1971), pp. 228–63.

'The religious orders 1220–1370', *The history of the university of Oxford* 1, ed. J. I. Catto, Oxford, 1984, pp. 193–223.

Shepherd, G., 'Poverty in *Piers Plowman*', in *Social relations and ideas. Essays in honour of R. H. Hilton*, ed. T. H. Aston, P. R. Coss, C. Dyer and J. Thirsk, Cambridge, 1983, pp. 169–89.

Shrewsbury, J. F. D., *A history of bubonic plague in the British Isles (1348–1670)*, Cambridge, 1970.

Siegrist, H. E. 'The special position of the sick', in *Culture, disease and healing; Studies in medical anthropology*, ed. D. Landy, New York, 1977, pp. 389–94.

Sigal, P.-A., 'Maladie, pèlerinage et guérison au XIIe siècle', *Annales* 24 (1969), pp. 1522–39.

Simmel, G., *On individuality and social forms*, ed. D. N. Levine, Chicago and London, 1971.

Sinclair, K. V., 'The French prayer for the sick in the hospital of the Knights of St. John of Jerusalem in Acre', *Mediaeval studies* 40 (1978), pp. 484–8.

Siraisi, N., 'Some recent work on western European medical learning *ca.* 1200–*ca.* 1500, *History of universities* (1982), pp. 225–38.

Siraut, M., 'Accounts of St. Katherine's guild at Holy Trinity church Cambridge: 1514–1537', *Cambridge Antiquarian Society. Proceedings and communications* 67 (1977), pp. 111–21.

Sivery, G., 'Herchier, un village du Hainaut (1267–1314)', *Revue du Nord* 52 (1970), pp. 309–24.

Skelton, R. A. and P. D. A. Harvey (eds), *Local maps and plans of medieval England*, Oxford, 1982.

Skillington, F. E., 'The Trinity hospital, Leicester', *Leicestershire Archaeological and Historical Society* 49 (1973–4), pp. 1–17.

Slack, P., 'Poverty and politics in Salisbury, 1597–1666', in *Crisis and order in English towns. Essays in urban history*, ed. P. Clark and P. Slack, London, 1972, pp. 164–203.

'Vagrants and vagrancy in England, 1598–1664', *Economic history review* second ser. 27 (1974), pp. 360–79.

'Mortality crises and epidemic disease in England', *Health, medicine and mortality in the sixteenth century*, ed. C. Webster, Cambridge, 1979, pp. 9–59.

Slicher van Bath, B. H., *The agrarian history of western Europe*, trans. O. Ordish, London, 1963.

Smalley, B., *The study of the bible in the Middle Ages*, Oxford, third edn, 1983.

'Oxford university sermons, 1290–1293', in *Medieval learning and literature. Essays presented to R. W. Hunt*, ed. J. J. G. Alexander and M. T. Gibson, Oxford, 1976, pp. 307–27.

Smith, B. H., Jr, *Traditional imagery of charity in 'Piers Plowman'*, The Hague and Paris, 1966.

Smith, G. H., 'The excavation of the hospital of St Mary of Ospringe, commonly called Maison Dieu', *Archaeologia Cantiana* 95 (1979), pp. 81–184.

Smith, R. A. L., *Canterbury cathedral priory: a study in monastic administration*, Cambridge, 1943, repr. 1969.

Snape, R. H., *English monastic finances in the later Middle Ages*, Cambridge, 1926.

Southern, R., 'Between heaven and hell. Review of J. Le Goff, *La naissance du purgatoire*', *Times literary supplement* 18 June 1982, pp. 651–2.

Speakman, E., 'Medieval hospitals', *Dublin review* 133 (1903), pp. 283–96.

Spicciani, A., 'The "poveri vergognosi" in fifteenth-century Florence', in *Aspects of poverty in early modern Europe*, ed. T. Riis, Stuttgart, 1981, pp. 119–82.

de Spiegeler, P., 'La léproserie de Cornillon et la cité de Liège (XIIe–XVe siècle)', *Annales de la société belge de l'historie des hôpitaux* 18 (1980), pp. 3–16.

Squibb, G. D., *Founders' kin: privilege and pedigree*, Oxford, 1972.

Stamp, A. E., *Michaelhouse*, Cambridge, 1924.

Steynitz, J. von, *Mittelalterliche Hospitäler der Orden und Städte als Einrichtungen der sozialen Sicherung*, Sozialpolitische Schriften 26, Berlin, 1970.

Stokes, H. P., *The chaplains and the chapel of the university of Cambridge, 1256–1568*, Cambridge Antiquarian society publications 41, Cambridge, 1906.

Outside the Trumpington Gates before Peterhouse was founded, Cambridge Antiquarian society publications 44, Cambridge, 1908.

'The old mills of Cambridge', *Cambridge Antiquarian Society. Proceedings and communications* 14 (1909–10), pp. 180–233.

Studies in Anglo-Jewish history, Edinburgh, 1913.

Outside the Barnwell gate, Cambridge Antiquarian society publications 47, Cambridge, 1915.

The medieval hostels of the university of Cambridge, Cambridge Antiquarian society publications 49, Cambridge, 1924.

Stokes, H. P., and D. H. S. Cranage, 'The Augustinian friary in Cambridge, and the history of its site. I – Augustinian friars, II – The plans and buildings of the friary', *Cambridge Antiquarian Society. Proceedings and communications* 22 (1917–20), pp. 53–71, 71–5.

Stone, L., 'Review of W. K. Jordan, *Philanthropy in England, 1480–1660*', *History* 44 (1959), pp. 257–60.

Storey, R. L., 'The foundation and the medieval college, 1379–1530', in *New College Oxford, 1379–1979*, ed. J. Buxton and P. Williams, Oxford, 1979, pp. 3–43.

Bibliography

Swanson, R. N., 'Universities, graduates and benefices in later medieval England', *Past and present* 106 (1985), pp. 28–61.

'Titles to orders in medieval English episcopal registers', in *Studies in medieval history presented to R. H. C. Davis*, ed. H. Mayr-Harting and R. I. Moore, London, 1985, pp. 233–45.

Sweet, J., 'Some thirteenth-century sermons and their authors', *Journal of ecclesiastical history* 4 (1953), pp. 27–36.

Szittya, P. R., 'The antifraternal tradition in Middle English literature', *Speculum* 52 (1977), pp. 287–313.

Talbot, C. H., *Medicine in medieval England*, London, 1967.

Talbot, C. H. and E. A. Hammond, *The medical practitioners in medieval England. A biographical register*, London, 1965.

Tanner, N. P., *The church in late medieval Norwich 1370–1532*, Pontifical Institute of Mediaeval Studies. Studies and texts 66, Toronto, 1984.

Tenenti, A., *La vie et la mort à travers l'art du XVe siècle*, Cahiers des Annales 8, Paris, 1952.

Tentler, T. N., 'The summa for confessors as an instrument of social control', in *The Pursuit of holiness in late medieval and Renaissance religion*, ed. C. Trinkaus and H. Oberman, Leiden, 1974, pp. 103–26.

Thérel, M.-L., '"Caritas" et "paupertas" dans l'iconographie médiévale inspirée de la psychomachie', in *Etudes sur l'histoire de la pauvreté* 1, ed. M. Mollat, Paris, 1974, pp. 295–317.

Thibaut, J. and H. H. Kelly, *The social psychology of groups*, New York, 1959.

Thomas, K., *Religion and the decline of magic. Studies in popular beliefs in sixteenth- and seventeenth-century England*, London, 1971.

Thomas, P., *Le droit de propriété des laïques sur les églises et le patronage laïque au moyen-âge*, Paris, 1906.

Thompson, E. P., 'Anthropology and the discipline of historical context', *Midland history* 1 (1972), pp. 41–55.

Thompson, J. D. and G. Goldin, *The hospital: a social and architectual history*, New Haven, Conn., 1975.

Thomson, J. A. F., *The later Lollards, 1414–1520*, Oxford, 1965.

'Piety and charity in late medieval London', *Journal of ecclesiastical history* 16 (1965), pp. 178–95.

Thouzellier, C., 'La place de *De Periculis* de Guillaume de St. Amour dans les polémiques universitaires du XIIIe siècle', *Revue historique* 156 (1927), pp. 67–83.

'Hérésie et pauvreté à la fin du XIIe et au début du XIIIe siècle', in *Etudes sur l'histoire de la pauvreté* 1, ed. M. Mollat, Paris, 1974, pp. 371–88.

Thrupp, S., *The merchant class of medieval London, 1300–1500*, Chicago, 1948.

'Social control in the medieval town', in *Society and history: essays by Sylvia Thrupp*, ed. R. Grew and N. Steneck, Ann Arbor, Mich., 1977, pp. 9–24.

Tierney, B., 'The decretists and the "deserving poor"', *Comparative studies in society and history* 1 (1958–9), pp. 360–73.

The medieval poor law: a sketch of canonical theory and its application in England, Berkeley and Los Angeles, 1959.

Bibliography

'Tuck on rights: some medieval problems', *History of political thought* 4 (1983), pp. 429–41.

Timbal Duclaux de Martin, P., *Le droit d'asile*, Paris, 1939.

Tisseuil, J., 'La Régression de la lèpre ne fut-elle pas aussi fonction de l'évolution économique du xive siècle', *Bulletin de la Société française de pathologie exotique* 68 (1975), pp. 352–5.

Titmuss, R. M., *The gift relationship*, London, 1970.

Titow, J. Z., 'Evidence of weather in the account rolls of the bishopric of Winchester 1209–1350', *Economic history review* second ser. 12 (1959–60), pp. 360–407.

'Some evidence of the thirteenth century population increase', *Economic history review*, second ser. 14 (1961–2), pp. 218–24.

English rural society, 1220–1350, London, 1969.

Tits-Dieuaide, M.-J., 'L'assistance aux pauvres à Louvain au xve siècle', in *Hommage au Professor P. Bonenfant: 1899–1965*, Brussels, 1965, pp. 421–39.

'Les tables des pauvres dans les anciennes principautés belges au moyen-âge', *Tijdschrift voor geschiedenis* 88 (1975), pp. 562–83.

Tocco, F., *La quistione della povertà nel secolo XIV. Nuovi documenti*, Nuova bibliotheca di letteratura, storia ed arte 4, Naples, 1910.

Toussaert, J., *Le sentiment religieux en Flandre à la fin du moyen-âge*, Paris, 1963.

Trexler, R. C., 'Death and testament in episcopal constitutions of Florence (1327)', in *Renaissance studies in honor of Hans Baron*, ed. A. Molho and J. A. Tadeschi, Florence, 1971, pp. 29–74.

'The bishop's portion: generic pious legacies in the late Middle Ages in Italy', *Traditio* 28 (1972), pp. 397–450.

'Charity and the defense of urban elites in the Italian communes', *The rich, the well born and the powerful*, ed. F. Jaher, Urbana, Ill., 1973, pp. 63–107.

Public life in Renaissance Florence, New York, 1980.

Tuck, J. A., 'The Cambridge parliament, 1388', *English historical review* 84 (1969), pp. 225–43.

Tuck, R., *Natural rights theories. Their origin and development*, Cambridge, 1979.

Turner, V., *Dramas, fields and metaphors: symbolic action in human society*, Ithaca, N.Y. and London, 1974.

'Death and the dead in the religious process', in *Religious encounters with death*, ed. F. E. Reynolds and E. H. Waugh, University Park, Pa., 1977, pp. 24–39.

Twigg, G., *The black death: a biological reappraisal*, London, 1984.

Underwood, M. G., 'Records of the foundress', *Eagle* 68 (1979), pp. 8–23.

Urry, W., *Canterbury under the Angevin Kings*, London, 1967.

Uyttebrouck, A., 'Hôpitaux pour lépreux ou couvents de lépreux? Réflexions sur le caractère des premières grandes léproseries de nos régions à leurs origines', *Annales de la société belge de l'histoire des hôpitaux* 9 (1971), pp. 3–29.

Vale, M. G. A., *Piety, charity and literacy among the Yorkshire gentry, 1370–1480*, Borthwick papers 50, York, 1976.

Valentine, C. A., *Culture and poverty. Critique and counter-proposals*, Chicago, 1968.

Van Gennep, A., *The rites of passage*, trans. M. B. Vizedom and G. L. C. Caffee, London, 1960.

Bibliography

Varty, K., *Reynard the fox*, Leicester, 1967.

Vauchez, A., 'La pauvreté volontaire au moyen âge', *Annales* 25 (1970), pp. 1566–73.

'Une enquête sur les "spiritualités populaires". Premier bulletin', *Revue d'histoire de la spiritualité* 49 (1973), pp. 493–504.

Veblen, T. B., *The theory of the leisure class*, New York, 1899, edn of Boston, Mass., 1973 [with intr. by J. K. Galbraith].

Venn, J. *et al.* (eds.), *Biographical history of Gonvill and Caius College*, 7 vols., Cambridge, 1897–1978.

Verheijen, L., *La Règle de Saint Augustin*, 2 vols., Paris, 1967.

Vexliard, A., 'Vagabondage et structures sociales', *Cahiers internationaux de sociologie* 22 (1957), pp. 97–116.

Vicaire, M.-H., 'La place des oeuvres de miséricorde dans la pastorale en Pays d'Oc', *Cahiers de Fanjeaux* 13 (1978), pp. 21–44.

Viner, J., *Religious thought and economic society*, ed. J. Melitz and D. Winch, Durham, N.C. 1978.

Violante, C., 'Riflessioni sulla povertà nel secolo XI', in *Studi sul medioevo cristiano offerti a Raffaello Morghen* II, Rome, 1974, pp. 1061–81.

Vogel, C., *Les 'libri paenitentiales'*, Typologie des sources du moyen-âge occidental fasc. 27, Turnhout, 1978.

Walker, D. A., 'The organisation of material in medieval cartularies', in *Study of medieval records: essays in honour of Kathleen Major*, ed. D. Bullough and R. Storey, Oxford, 1971, pp. 132–50.

Walsh, K., *A fourteenth-century scholar and primate. Richard FitzRalph in Oxford, Avignon and Armagh*, Oxford, 1981.

Walter, J. and K. Wrightson, 'Dearth and the social order in early modern England', *Past and present* 71 (1976), pp. 22–42.

Watt, D. E. R., 'University clerks and rolls of petitions for benefices', *Speculum* 24 (1949), pp. 231–29.

Watts, D. G., 'A model for the early fourteenth century', *Economic history review* second ser. 20 (1967), pp. 543–7.

Way, A., 'Notices of the King's seals for passes given to labourers and servants', *Cambridge Antiquarian Society. Proceedings and communications* I (1851–9), pp. 280–6.

Weber, Max, *The city*, trans. D. Martindale and G. Neuwirth, New York, 1958.

van der Wee, H., 'Les archives hospitalières et l'étude de la pauvreté aux Pays-Bas du XVe au XVIIIe siècle', *Revue du Nord* 48 (1966), pp. 5–16.

Weisser, C., 'Das Krankheitslunar aus medizinhistorischer Sicht', *Sudhoffs Archiv* 65 (1981), pp. 390–400.

Weissman, R. F. E., *Ritual brotherhood in Renaissance Florence*, New York and London, 1982.

Wells, C., 'A leper cemetery at South Acre, Norfolk', *Medieval archaeology* 2 (1967), pp. 242–8.

Welter, J. T., *L'exemplum dans la littérature religieuse du moyen-âge*, Paris, 1927.

Werner, E., *Pauperes christi. Studien zur sozial-religiösen Bewegungen im Zeitalter des Reformpapsttums*, Leipzig, 1956.

Westlake, H. F., *The parish gilds of mediaeval England*, London, 1919.

Bibliography

Wickersheimer, E., 'Médecins et chirugiens dans les hôpitaux du moyen-âge', *Janus* 32 (1928), pp. 1–11.

Willard, J. F., 'Taxation boroughs and parliamentary boroughs, 1294–1336', in *Historical essays in honour of James Tait*, ed. J. G. Edwards, V. H. Galbraith and E. F. Jacob, Manchester, 1933, pp. 417–35.

Parliamentary taxes on personal property 1290 to 1334: a study in medieval English financial administration, Cambridge Mass., 1934.

Williams, E. E., *The chantries of William Canynges in St. Mary Redcliffe, Bristol*, Bristol, 1950.

Willis, R. and J. W. Clark, *An architectural history of the University of Cambridge and the colleges of Cambridge and Eton*, 4 vols., Cambridge, 1886.

Witt, R. G., 'The landlord and the economic revival of the Middle Ages in northern Europe 1000–1250', *American historical review* 76 (1971), pp. 965–88.

Witters, W., 'Pauvres et pauvreté dans les coutumes monastiques du moyen-âge', in *Etudes sur l'histoire de la pauvreté* I, ed. M. Mollat, Paris, 1974, pp. 177–215.

Wood, S. M., *English monasteries and their patrons in the thirteenth century*, London 1955.

Wood-Legh, K. L., *Perpetual chantries in Britain*, Cambridge, 1965.

Woodward, J. and G. Burnett, *A treatise on heraldry, British and foreign*, Edinburgh, 1892.

Wrightson, K. and D. Levine, *Poverty and piety in an English village: Terling, 1525–1700*, New York, 1979.

Young, C. R., 'King John of England: an illustration of the medieval practice of charity', *Church history* 29 (1960), pp. 264–74.

Yunck, J. A., 'Dan denarius: the almighty penny and the fifteenth century poets', *American journal of economics and sociology* 20 (1961), pp. 207–22.

Ziegler, P., *The Black Death*, London, 1969.

D. UNPUBLISHED DISSERTATIONS

I wish to thank the following authors for their permission to cite from their unpublished dissertations.

Henderson, J. S., 'Piety and charity in late medieval Florence' (Ph.D., London, 1983).

MacKenney, R. C., 'Trade guilds and devotional confraternities in the state and society of Venice to 1620' (Ph.D., Cambridge, 1982).

Mesmin, S. C., 'The leper hospital of St. Gilles de Pont-Audemer: an edition of its cartulary and an examination of the problem of leprosy in the twelfth and early thirteenth century', 2 vols. (Ph.D., Reading, 1978).

Poos, L. R., 'Population and resources in two fourteenth-century Essex communities: Great Waltham and High Easter 1327–1389' (Ph.D., Cambridge, 1983).

INDEX

wid. = widow of; s. = son of; medieval names are entered under the christian name, post medieval names, under the surname, bishops under their sees.

Adam, master of HSJC (*c.* 1233), 168, 302
Adam, master of HSJC (*c.* 1318), 302
Adam Botecourt, MA, 109
Adam Boudon, MA, 109
Adam Cam, chantry of, 190
Adam Rypp, 103n
Adam Wiriel, Cambridge, 220
Aelfric, 79
Agnes, wid. John d'Argenten, 141
Agnes Knotte, 177
Alan Det, 177
Alan of Lille, 58–9, 61, 91
Alan Wells, Cambridge, 261
Albert the Great, 63
Alexander Ixning, master of HSJC, 169, 173, 197, 200, 302
Alicante: hospital of St John the Baptist, 124n
Alice, Jewess of Oxford, 108–9
Alice, wid. Thomas Martin, 230n
almoners: of the Dukes of Burgundy, 268–9; of the Goldsmiths of London, 252n; royal, 247; of St Radegund's Cambridge, 194; of Worcester priory, 246
almshouses, 175, 295n; *see also* Anglesey, Cambridge, Fordham, Norwich, Stamford, Stow
altruism, 8, 14–15, 52–3, 292
Ambrose, 60, 69, 73
Amiens: hospital, 163, 167
Amphelisa, 140
Andrew Dockett, rector of St Botolph's, Cambridge, and President of Queens' College, 127, 279–80
Andrew of Giselham, Chancellor of the University of Cambridge, 109
Angers: bishop William of Chemille, 159; hospital, 158–9, 177

Anglesey, Cambs.: hospital of St Mary 137–8, 154, 175n; priory, 109, 138, 249
Anthony, chaplain of St Giles', Cambridge, 219–21
Anthony, master of HSJC, 218
Anthony of the Desert, St, 122–3
Anthony of Padua, St, 122
anthrax, 22
anti-clericalism, 95–7, 295–7
Aubrey of Stow, 135–6
Augustine, 60, 69–70, 73
Augustinian order: chapters, 154; communities, 176–7; rule, 110, 114, 154–6, 162–3, 166–7, 247
Aze *ad oppidum*, Cambridge, 175

Babraham, Cambs., 213, 215, 222
Baldwin Blancgernon, Cambridge, 38, 218–19, 221n, 291
Bamberg: hospital of St Katherine, 110n
barbers, 152, 175,
Bartholomew of Exeter, 57, 64; penitential of, 57
Bartholomew s. Orgar, Cambridge, 211
Barton, Cambs., 127, 207
Basingstoke, Hants.: hospital of St John, 276
Bassingbourn, Cambs., 140
Bath: hospital of St John, 187n, 192n, 202n
Bath and Wells: bishop, 285
beggars, 2, 70–3, 92, 120: attitudes to, 92–3; William of St Amour's, 73; legislation against, 32
Benedictine order: rule, 247
Bernardino of Siena, St, 61, 70n, 225
Bernstein, A., 55–6
Black Death and aftermath, 16–17, 22, 48–51, 136, 139, 141–2, 173–4, 229, 291 .

Index

Innocent III, pope, 184
Innocent IV, 110, 153, 156, 162–3, 167
Innocent VII, 142
insanity and the insane, 120, 157–8
intention, 61, 87–9: Peter Abelard on, 61;
  Peter the Chanter on, 61
intercession, 181, 248–9, 259–64, 279–81:
  Speculum sacerdotale on, 66; Thomas
  Aquinas on, 65, 185n; *see also* chantries,
  purgatory
interest, 283n
Iohannes Andreae, 68
Isabella, queen, obit of, 282n
Isaac Blond, 220
Ivo of Chartres, 67

Jacob's well, 93
Jacques of Vitry, 8, 83–4, 86, 91–2, 154,
  159, 166, 177, 180
Jews and jewries, 109, 218–21, 224, 226,
  283
John, king of England, 100, 112, 140
John XXII, pope, 71
John XXIII, anti-pope, 143
John, maltster at HSJC, 175
John s. Adelard, Cambridge, 164
Joan d. Anketill, Cambridge, 218
John Barnwell, chaplain of St Anne's
  hermitage, Cambridge, 122n
John s. Bartholomew, Cambridge, 220
John Berefot, bailiff of Cambridge, 197n
John Botwright, master of Corpus Christi
  College, Cambridge, 281n
John of Brigham, 50
John Caraway, 280n
John Cheney, 51
John Chrysostom, 68–9
John of Colonia, master of HSJC, 173n,
  197, 302
John Colvylle, constable of Wisbeach
  Castle, 142–4
John Cowryks, 215
John Daniel, Norwich, 128n
John Dunham Sr, master of HSJC, 201,
  302
John Dunham Jr, master of HSJC, 174,
  302
John Ehrlich, 191n
John de Frivil, 51
John Harreys, Cambridge, mayor and
  MP, 124, 191n, obit of, 263, will of, 262
John Hogkyns, fellow of King's College,
  Cambridge, 127–8
John Horwood, 217

John Ilegh, rector of Ickleton, 280
John Ingolf, brother of St John's hospital,
  Ely, 131
John the Ironmonger, Cambridge, 214–15
John of Lavenham, parish priest of
  Wicken, 58
John Lovetoft of Horningsea, Sir, 187
John Mirc, 57–8
John of Norwich, warden of St Nicholas'
  hospital, Royston, 141
John Patrik, brother of St John's hospital,
  Ely, 131n
John Podyngton, rector of Kingston, 242
John Porthors, mayor of Cambridge,
  105n
John Ruffus, Cambridge, 221
John de Scalar, 224
John Seggeville, Cambridge, 172, 215;
  Robert, servant of, 172–3
John of Shelford, brother of HSJC, 197n
John of Shelford, Cambridge: chantry of,
  188, 224
John the Smith, Babraham, 124, 222
John Stanton, master of HSJC, 302
John Voneyer (Boneyer), servant at
  HSJC, 175
John s. Walter, Cambridge, 212
John Wolpet, fellow of Queen's College,
  281n
John Wyclif, 95, 97
Jordan, W. K., 5
Josselin, J., 120, 122
Julian, St, 85

Katherine Cook, Cambridge, 261
King's Lynn: hospitals: of St John the
  Baptist, 105n, 265, of St Mary
  Magdalene, 165, 171n, 178n, 181, 209n
Kingston, Cambs., 242
Kingston-on-Hull, 28n
Kneesworth, Cambs., 140

labourers, 8, 268–9, 291–3
Langley, Essex, 213
La Roncière. C. M. de, 268
Layer, J., 140n
Lay folks' catechism, 93
lay instruction, 74–98: council of
  Coventry on, 78; Durham II on, 75;
  French synods on, 76n, 77n; Lambeth
  council on, 77; Lateran III on, 76;
  Lateran IV on, 75; *see also* preaching
lay subsidies, 41–5
leases, 222–3

Index

Oxford, 28n: church of St John, 221
  colleges: Balliol, 277, Merton, 273–8,
    281n, statutes of, 273–5, New
    College, 277, Oriel, 164, Queen's,
    279n; friars, Dominican, 108, 226n,
    282, Franciscan, 282; hospitals, of St
    Bartholomew, 164, of St John the
    Baptist, 102, 108–9, 135n, 158–9,
    162–7, 173, 176–7, 180, 216n, 221,
    226n, 247; Jewry and Jews, 108, 221,
    274n
  University: loan chests, 283–5,
    Roubery chest, 285n, St Frideswide's,
    283; medicine at, 150; scholars, 270

para-liturgy, 258
Paris: college of *Ave Maria*, 277; hospital,
  Hôtel-dieu, 151
parish and parochial framework, 104–5:
  appropriation of, 192–202, 239–41,
  Lateran III on, 239; duties, 195–6,
  200–1, 258; hospitality, council
  Chichester I on, 239, Norwich on, 239,
  Salisbury II on, 239n, Salisbury III on,
  240; income, council of Lyons on, 242,
  Salisbury IV on, 240, *Decretum* on, 240,
  pope Gelasius on, 238, pope Simplicius
  on, 238; parishoners, complaints of,
  241–3; poor, 260–1; priests, instruction
  of, 57–8, 74–8, books for, 77–8, council
  of Lambeth on, 77; relief, 97, 127–8,
  147, 237–45, council of Canterbury I
  on, 239, Exeter II on, 241, London on,
  240, London, Legatine, on, 240–1,
  Lateran IV on, 240, Salisbury I on, 239,
  Winchester I on, 239, Worcester III on,
  239, injunctions of Archbishop
  Peckham on, 241, Teutonicus on, 69;
  residence, 241–2, council of Lyons on,
  241; rights, 105; 'tables' (*mensae*), 244
paupers verecundi, 72–3
Peasants' Revolt, 50–1
Perugia: fraternity of St Thomas, 252n
Peter the Chanter, 61–2
Peter Abelard, 61
Peter Comestor, 59
Peterborough: abbey, 168; hospitals, of St
  Leonard, 130n, of St Thomas, 130n
physicians, 148–52
Piers plowman, 11n, 32, 87n
pilgrimage, 157, 218, 268
poor and poverty, 6–11, 82–98: François
  Villon on, 93, Iohannes Andrea on, 68;
  absolute, 71–2, John XXII on, 71,

William of St Amour on, 71n, attitudes
  to, 27, 50–3, 68, 71–4, 254–5, 291–3;
  burial, 181, 248; categories of, 68–71,
  267–9, Ambrose on, 69,
  Anglo-Norman *Summa* on, 70, John
  Chrysostom on, 68–9, Rufinus on,
  69–70, Stephen of Tournai on, 70,
  Summa elegantius on, 68–70; Christ in,
  59, 93; debate on, 71–2; deserving, 60,
  68–74, Augustine on, 70, Bernardino of
  Siena on, 70n, Jacques of Vitry on,
  91–2; disruptive, 92–3, 98; rights of,
  Peter the Chanter on, 62, Teutonicus
  on, 62; shamed, 72–3, 267, Ambrose
  on, 73, Augustine on, 73, William of
  St Amour on, 73; voluntary, 71–2,
  92–3
popular culture, 54–5
portio canonica, 106
prayers for the sick, 180
preaching: *ad status*, 82–3, 94; on charity,
  74–98; popular, 54–6; techniques,
  79–82; *see also exempla*
pregnant women, 157–9
prices and wages, 15–33
prisoners, 268, 295n
property, 59–65, Albert the Great on, 63,
  Ambrose on, 60, Bonaventure on, 63n,
  Henry of Bohic on, 60, Ockham on,
  59, Stephen Langton on, 63; of church,
  63, *Summa parisiensis* on, 63–4;
  detrimental influence of, Alan of Lille
  on, 59, 91, Humbert of Romans on, 91,
  Jacques of Vitry on, 59, 91; Peter
  Comestor on, 59
Psychomachia of Prudentius, 81n
purgatory, 11, 55–6, 65–6, 185, 252–3,
  259–60, 262; Robert Pullen on, 65,
  Speculum sacerdotale on, 66, Thomas
  Aquinas on, 65n, William of Auvergne
  on, 55–6, William of Auxerre on, 65–6

Quia contigit, 170

Ralph, master of HSJC, 302
Ralph Chesterton, Sir, 221
Ralph of Coggeshall, 85n
Ralph, Lord Cromwell, 145
Ralph s. Henry, Cambridge, 220
Ralph s. Ralph s. Fulk, 141
Raoul Ardent, 60
Raynald of Lynn, 198
Reginald Ely, Cambridge, 127
rent: arrears, 228–9; rolls, 227–8, 226–35